ABNORMAL PSYCHOLOGY:
An Experimental Clinical Approach

ABNORMAL PSYCHOLOGY:
An Experimental Clinical Approach

Gerald C. Davison
John M. Neale

JOHN WILEY & SONS, INC.
New York   London
Sydney   Toronto

Copyright © 1974, by John Wiley & Sons, Inc.

All rights reserved. Published simultaneously in Canada.

No part of this book may be reproduced by any means, nor transmitted, nor translated into a machine language without the written permission of the publisher.

Library of Congress Cataloging in Publication Data:

Davison, Gerald C
  Abnormal psychology.

  Bibliography: p.
  1. Psychology, Pathological. I. Neale, John M.,
1943–   joint author. II. Title. DNLM: 1. Psychopathology. WM100 D265a 1974
RC454.D3   616.8′9   73-19887
ISBN 0-471-19920-6

Printed in the United States of America

10-9 8 7 6 5 4

TO OUR WIVES,
Carol and Gail

About the Authors

Gerald C. Davison received his B.A. from Harvard College in 1961, studied the following year in Germany on a Fulbright Scholarship, and obtained his Ph.D. from Stanford University in 1965. After a postdoctoral clinical fellowship at the Veterans Administration Hospital in Palo Alto, California, he joined the faculty at the State University of New York at Stony Brook, where he is Professor of Psychology and Psychiatry and Director of the Postdoctoral Program in Behavior Modification. He has published widely in the general area of behavior therapy, particularly on theoretical and philosophical issues. He has been on the editorial board of several professional journals, including the *Journal of Abnormal Psychology* and *Behavior Therapy,* and is President (1973–74) of the Association for Advancement of Behavior Therapy. In addition to his teaching and research, he is a practicing clinical psychologist.

John M. Neale, a Canadian, received his B.A. from the University of Toronto in 1965 and his Ph.D. from Vanderbilt University in 1969. Thereafter he spent a year as Fellow in Medical Psychology at Langley Porter Neuropsychiatric Institute and since then has been at the State University of New York at Stony Brook, where he is Associate Professor. His major research interests are schizophrenia, especially the study of children at high risk for the disorder, and television's effects on children. In addition to being a reviewer and an active contributor to professional journals such as the *Journal of Abnormal Psychology* and *Journal of Consulting and Clinical Psychology,* he has co-authored two previous books, *Science and Behavior: An Introduction to Methods of Research* and *The Early Window: Effects of Television on Children and Youth.* Besides his research and teaching activities, he is involved in clinical supervision and training.

Preface

Contemporary abnormal psychology is a field in which there are few hard and fast answers. Indeed, the very way the field should be conceptualized and the kinds of questions that should be asked are hotly debated issues. In this book we have tried to present what glimpses there are of solutions to puzzles such as what causes deviant behavior and which treatments are most effective in reducing psychological suffering.

It has become commonplace in psychology to recognize the selective nature of perception. Certainly the writing of a textbook is guided by biases on the part of the authors, and our effort is no exception. We share a strong commitment to a scientific approach but at the same time appreciate the often uncontrollable nature of the subject matter and the importance of clinical findings. Rather than pretend that we are unbiased and objective, we have tried to alert the reader to our prejudices. Forewarned in this manner, the reader may consider on his own the merits of our point of view. At the same time, we have tried as best we can to represent fairly and comprehensively the major alternative conceptualizations in contemporary psychopathology.

A recurrent theme in the book is the importance of points of view within psychology, or, to use Kuhn's (1962) phrase, paradigms. Our experience in teaching undergraduates has made us very much aware of the importance of making explicit the unspoken assumptions underlying one's quest for knowledge. In our writing we have tried to make these assumptions clear. Long after specific facts are forgotten, the student should retain a grasp of the basic problems in the field of psychopathology.

Related to this issue is the use of more than one model in studying abnormal psychology. Rather than force an entire field into, for example, a social learning paradigm, we argue, from the available data, that different problems in psychopathology are amenable to analyses within different models. For instance, several of the organic disease models seem unavoidable when dealing with mental retardation, but in discussing therapy we prefer a learning conceptualization.

We also have had to choose among numerous topics for inclusion in the textbook. Some readers may be dismayed, for instance, to find that the names of Wilhelm Reich and Eric Berne appear nowhere in the text. At the same time, more recent and also lesser-known developments such as psychosynthesis are included both for their intrinsic interest and for important questions raised at the paradigm level.

The book itself is divided into six major parts. Part I is introductory, providing information on history, models of madness, research methods, and issues in diagnosis and assessment of abnormal behavior. The next four sections each deal with a major category of abnormal behavior. At several points we have departed from the traditional diagnostic nomenclature. For example, we discuss depression in a single chapter even though the diagnostic manual breaks it down into several distinct categories. And several of the so-called personality disorders — for example, neurasthenic and cyclothymic personalities — are omitted because of lack of data and the diagnostic unreliability of these subcategories. Part II concentrates on anxiety and depression. Part III deals with social deviance — problems of addiction, antisocial behavior, the insanity defense, and unconventional or inadequate human sexual behavior. Part IV discusses the problems of psychosis, adult and childhood schizophrenia, and infantile autism. Part V discusses brain dysfunctions and mental retardation. Part VI, on therapy, describes and evaluates a number of insight therapies, behavior modification, and group, community, and biological treatments. The discussion of therapy was reserved for a separate section of the book so that the various approaches to the modification of abnormal behavior could be discussed and criticized in depth.

Many people helped us in bringing our task to completion. We have been fortunate at Stony Brook to be surrounded by a talented and energetic group of students who read and criticized drafts of various chapters. Particularly helpful and extensive comments were offered by Crysta Casey, Emily Davidson, Glenn Davidson, Marsha Linehan, Thomas Oltmanns, Kenneth Price, and Alan Rosenbaum. We are especially indebted and grateful to Nancy Fenrick, who lent her considerable expertise to Chapter 17, Mental Retardation. Thanks are also extended to a long list of colleagues who reviewed one or more of the chapters: Theodore X. Barber, Vernon T. Devine, Frederick Kanfer, Alan Marlatt, David Martindale, Richard McFall, David Pomeranz, Rita Poulos, Richard H. Price, Bernard Rimland, and John Stamm. We are grateful to Wiley Advisory Editor Brendan Maher, as well as to several other Wiley reviewers who remain anonymous. We hope that all reviewers will notice places where their suggestions improved the quality of the manuscript; the final decisions and the responsibility for the present form of the text, however, are ours. We wish to thank the staff at John Wiley and Sons for their efficiency and understanding: Jack Burton, Roger Holloway, John Balbalis, Stella Kupferberg, Ronald Nelson, Jules Perlmutter, Stanley G. Redfern, and Serje Seminoff. A very special thank you is offered to Priscilla Todd, who was the Wiley depth editor on the project. Mrs. Patricia Carl helped with the typing during the last stages of frenzied activity. Finally, gratitude that is difficult to put into words is extended to Mrs. Betty Hammer, who decoded and then retyped the many drafts of the manuscript. One aspect of the book—order of authorship—was unplanned, being decided by a toss of a coin.

Gerald C. Davison
John M. Neale
STONY BROOK, NEW YORK

Contents

PART II
ANXIETY AND DEPRESSION 101

PART III
SOCIAL DEVIATION 201

9
Sociopathy and Legal
Responsibility 203

10
Drug Addiction and Drug
Dependence 233

ABNORMAL PSYCHOLOGY:
An Experimental Clinical Approach

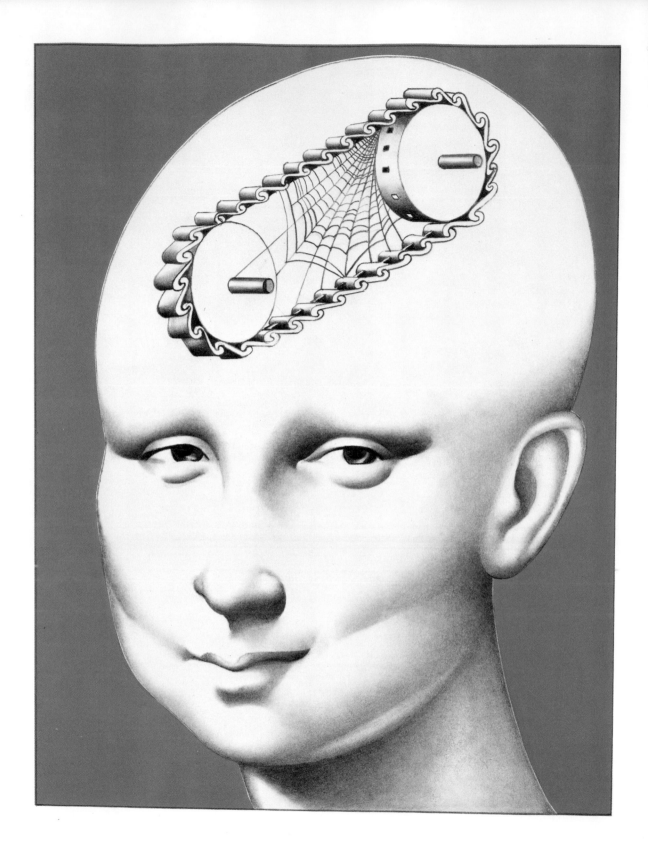

CHAPTER 1
Introduction: Historical and Scientific Considerations

Walking across an emptying campus late one afternoon, you notice several yards to the right of you a girl who is sobbing uncontrollably. Your first impulse is to go to her and see whether you can offer assistance. As she notices your approaching figure, she turns toward you and suddenly begins to scream. Then she dashes away. You could probably catch up with her, but something within you cautions you not to try.

What is that "something" that stops you? Why has the unexpectedly wild look in the girl's eyes so quickly extinguished your intention to offer help? Did you remind her of someone she hates, or loves, or fears? Or had someone else just said something to her that made her flee from you? Perhaps, though, she had been standing there alone and crying for some time. Indeed, as you stand transfixed, watching her flight and asking yourself these questions, is she still crying? Or is she perhaps behaving in an even more unusual fashion?

Every day of our lives we have to deal with people and try to figure out why they conduct themselves as they do. Yet, how difficult it is to understand why another person does or feels something. Indeed, it is sometimes a problem to understand why we ourselves feel and behave the way we do. Acquiring insight into what we consider the normal range of expected behavior is arduous enough, requiring much of our attention and thought, but how far more perplexing is human behavior beyond the normal range, such as that of the sobbing girl.

Our conversational allusions to odd behavior are frequently couched in phrases such as "He's out of his mind," "He's all screwed up," "He's a maniac," "She's an hysteric," or "She's really paranoid." Such terms indicate that as observers we have found a person's behavior inexplicable and can attribute it only to an unbalanced mind. The minds so described are of course very often much sounder than these phrases and adjectives imply. Terrifying instances of unusual behavior, however, although not personally observed by most of us, are very much in the public eye. Hardly a week passes that a violent act, such as an ugly axe murder or multiple slayings, is not reported. The assailant is diagnosed by a policeman or mental health authority as a "mental case" and is found to have had a history of mental instability. Sometimes we learn that the person has previously been confined in a mental hospital. The public attention paid to the case indicates our compelling urge to search out the causes of such violent and seemingly inexplicable behavior.

This book is concerned with the whole range of abnormal behavior and with the various explanations for it, both past and present. There are, however, numerous pitfalls in seeking valid explanations that must be pointed out. To study abnormal psychology, we must have what might be called a "high tolerance for ambiguity," an ability to be comfortable with very tentative, often conflicting pieces of information. Much less is known with certainty about the field than we might hope, presenting problems both for the professional and for the beginning student. Indeed, as already indicated, precious little is known of why human beings behave in a normal fashion, to say nothing of their abnormal behavior. In approaching the study of psychopathology, we do well to keep in mind that the subject offers few hard and fast answers. Although we shall report such findings as there are, many of the facts that will be introduced will undoubtedly be outdated in a matter of years. And yet, as will become evident when we discuss our orientation to scientific inquiry, the study of abnormal behavior is no less worthwhile because of its ambiguities. The kinds of questions asked rather than the specific answers available at any particular time constitute the very essence of the field.

Another problem that professionals share with laymen is the closeness of any human being to the subject matter of behavior. A physicist, for example, would seem better able to detach himself emotionally from his subject matter than a psychologist, particularly one who specializes in the study of abnormal behavior. The pervasiveness and disturbing effects of abnormal behavior intrude on our lives. Who, for example, has not experienced irrational thoughts and feelings? Or who has not known someone, a friend or perhaps a relative, whose behavior was impossible to understand? If you have, you realize how frustrating and frightening it is to find yourself thwarted in trying to understand and help someone else.

Our closeness to the subject matter, of course, adds to its intrinsic fascination; no wonder that undergraduate courses in abnormal psychology are among the most popular in psychology departments and indeed in the entire college curriculum. Although familiarity with the subject matter encourages people to study abnormal psychology, it has one distinct disadvantage. All of us have already developed certain ways of thinking and talking about behavior, certain words and concepts that somehow seem to *fit*. For example, some may assert that the study of fear should concentrate on the immediate *experience* of fear; this is technically known as a *phenomenological* approach and is one formal way of setting about the study of human behavior. But it is not the approach of the authors of this book. We ourselves have had to grapple with the disjunction between what we may *feel* is the appropriate way to talk about human behavior and experience, and what as behavioral scientists we have learned to be more fruitful means of discussing behavior. Where most people might say "feeling of terror," we are more inclined as behaviorally oriented psychopathologists to use a phrase such as "fear-response of high magnitude." In doing so we are not merely playing verbal games. The word "games" does indeed apply in the sense that our procedures have rules, but it does not apply in the sense that we may be engaging in activities that do not mean very much or that might just as well be carried out in any other fashion. The crucial point is that the concepts and verbal labels we use in the serious study of abnormal behavior must be free of the subjec- tive feelings of appropriateness that, as non-specialists, we have come to attach to certain human phenomena. We may be asking you, then, to adopt frames of reference different from those that you are accustomed to, and indeed different from those we ourselves employ when we are not wearing our professional hats.

HISTORY OF PSYCHOPATHOLOGY

Some General Remarks on Historical Analysis

Before we present a brief history of psycho-pathology in order to place contemporary developments in perspective, it may be useful to comment on the manner in which historians go about reconstructing the past. Let us con-sider what archeologists conjecture about *tre-phining,* a crude surgical practice believed to have been prevalent in the Stone Age. They have assumed that people of very early periods chipped holes in the skulls of certain of their confreres to allow the escape of evil spirits which were supposedly causing deviant behav-ior. But on what is this supposition based, since there are no known recorded interviews with people who practiced this primitive surgical art? First of all, skulls with holes in them have been found by archeologists in cer-tain parts of the world (Figure 1.1). The holes in these skulls seem to have been intentionally created by repeated impacts with sharp stones. But why do historians conclude that these holes were made for the purposes just men-tioned rather than, for example, inflicted in the heat of combat?

The currently popular interpretation of tre-phining as a practice to facilitate the exit of evil spirits from a person's mind and body is inextricably related to what historians have been able to learn and conjecture about the na-ture of Stone Age man's social order and pre-scientific beliefs. Even before the trephined skulls were found, historians had anticipated that such practices were in vogue. Finding skulls with holes in them strengthened this supposition, although it is unclear how prehis-toric man determined that the spirits were lo-cated in the head. Conjecture seems a reason-able means for trying to find out what hap-pened in the preliterate past, but we must be mindful of the amount of inference resorted to.

Even when historians can rely on written records, they still have difficulty making gener-alizations. We often hear phrases such as "The Renaissance *began* with the. . . ." What in fact does this mean? Consider a recent event that is likely to be discussed in future history books. When did the so-called drug culture begin? The onset of this important phenome-non might be traced to the visit of Dr. Timothy Leary to Mexico, where he was first exposed to the "magic mushrooms." We could look ear-lier to the publication of a fascinating little book by Aldous Huxley, entitled the *Doors of Perception.* Or perhaps the drug culture

"began" with the expulsion of Leary and his colleague Richard Alpert (who became known as Baba Ram Das) from Harvard in 1962, for up until that time it seems reasonable to assert that only among graduate students at Harvard was psilocybin being used for the deliberate induction of "psychedelic" states. Not until the two men went out into the world could their work have had a more general influence. Consider also the migration of the "flower people" to the Haight-Ashbury district of San Francisco in the 1960s. No doubt any adequate history of this period would have to include all these events and many more. But what brought the phenomenon of taking psychedelic drugs into being? What are the dimensions of the phenomenon? How do we *explain* the initial urge? How far back in time must we go to trace its development? These are difficult questions indeed, and perhaps in the course of this book some light may be shed on these issues; our point here is merely to indicate the difficulties inherent in making generalizations about the sweep of human events.

Historical Overview

As psychopathologists, our interest is in the causes of deviant behavior. The search for these causes has gone on for a considerable period of time, long antedating what we generally regard as the age of scientific inquiry.[1] This search, moreover, has not been a mere scholastic exercise, for the manner in which people have explained deviant behavior has played a vitally important role in how they have attempted to deal with it. For example, if I believe that a man who hears voices from unseen sources is being visited by the devil and I consider the devil an evil force, I am likely to move against that force. If I want to help the man stop hallucinating, I must find some way of getting rid of or exorcising the devil within him. Moreover, my treatment will very likely be tailored to how I anticipate the devil will react to my efforts to cast him out from the person. If I think that the devil will respond to

[1] Much of the following historical review is based on Zilboorg and Henry (1941).

directions from God, I will probably choose prayer as a good treatment. If my theology regards the devil as too strong or evil to respond even to God, I may consider it necessary to deal with the devil at his own level, which might take the form of angry epithets and perhaps even torture of the body possessed by the devil.

Early Demonology

The doctrine that a semiautonomous or completely autonomous evil being, such as the devil, may dwell within a person and control his mind and body is called demonology. We have already presented the current suppositions about trephining, that perphaps half a million years ago Stone Age man, in the belief that abnormal behavior was caused by demons, diligently and probably with good will chipped away parts of the afflicted person's skull so that the evil spirits could escape. Among the ancient Hebrews as well, many thousands of years later, behavior was considered to be controlled by good or bad spirits residing within the person. Christ is reported to have cured a man with an "unclean spirit" by casting out the devil from within him and hurling it onto a herd of swine. The animals were then said to have become possessed and to have run "violently down a steep place into the sea." Similar examples of demonological thinking can be found among the early Chinese, Egyptians, and Greeks. Treatment for such demons typically took the form of elaborate prayer rites, noise making, forcing the afflicted to drink terrible tasting brews, and even more extreme measures such as flogging and starvation. The priests and medicine men practicing exorcism chose treatments they considered most likely to be effective against the particular demon to be removed. In the fifth century B.C. in Greece, Hippocrates received his early training in one of the Greek schools that specialized in treating deviant behavior with exorcism.

Somatogenesis

Hippocrates, often regarded as the father of modern medicine (Figure 1.2), operated outside the *Zeitgeist* or intellectual and emotional orientation of the times. He questioned the prevailing Greek belief that the gods arbitrarily ordained the mental dispositions of men, insisting instead that mental disorders had the same causes as other illnesses and hence should be treated like any other disease. Hippocrates regarded the brain as the organ of intellectual life, and it followed that if someone's thinking and behavior were deviant, there was some kind of brain pathology. He is often considered one of the very earliest proponents of a *somatogenic* hypothesis to explain mental illness — that something wrong with the *soma* or physical body disturbs thought and behavior. He also recognized that environmental and emotional stress can damage the body and mind. Hippocrates classified mental disorders into three categories, mania, melancholia, and phrenitis or brain fever. Through his teachings the phenomenon of abnormal behavior was to become more the province of physicians than of priests.

The treatments suggested by Hippocrates were quite different from the earlier exorcistic tortures. For example, for melancholia he prescribed tranquility, sobriety, careful food intake, and abstinence from sexual activity. Such a regimen was presumed to have a healthful effect on the brain and the body. Because Hippocrates believed in natural rather than supernatural causes, he depended on his own keen observations. Remarkable clinical records de-

FIGURE **1.2**
Hippocrates, pictured at the bedside of a patient in this nineteenth-century engraving.

scribing many of the symptoms now recognized in epilepsy, alcoholic delusion, and paranoia have come down to us from him.

Hippocrates' physiology was rather crude, however, for he conceived of normal brain functioning, and therefore of mental health, as dependent on a delicate balance among four "humors" of the body, namely blood, black bile, yellow bile, and phlegm (Figure 1.3). An imbalance produced disorders. If a person was sluggish and dull, for example, his body supposedly contained a preponderance of phlegm. A preponderance of black bile was the explanation for melancholia, too much yellow bile explained irascibility, and too much blood changeable temperament. Hippocrates' humoral pathology has of course not withstood later scientific scrutiny. His basic premise, however, that man's behavior is directly determined by bodily structures or substances, and that abnormal behavior is produced by some

kind of imbalance or even damage, foreshadowed aspects of contemporary thought. In the few centuries before and after the birth of Christ, Hippocrates' somatogenic premise was generally accepted by other Greeks, such as Plato, Aristotle, and Galen, as well as by the Romans, who adopted the medicine of the Greeks.

The Middle Ages

In a massive generalization, historians have often suggested that the death of Galen in the third century A.D. marked the beginning of the Dark Ages for psychiatry. Galen, a Greek, had practiced in Rome and codified the medicine of antiquity. But after his death there were few medical advances, and many of the later Roman men of medicine again adopted popular superstititions. Then with the advent of the Christian world, Galen's naturalistic approach

INTRODUCTION AND BASIC ISSUES

to abnormal behavior yielded to ancient demonology, modified somewhat by the theology of the new religion. Toward the end of the fifth century A.D. Greek and Roman civilization collapsed. Medical pursuits and the scientific principles of systematic observation that had been established by the Greeks were almost completely abandoned in Europe. Demonological interpretations of abnormal behavior prevailed, and the church prescribed exorcism for the devils that possessed the body and made a person act in strange and disturbing ways.

The second part of the Middle Ages was marked by occasional outbreaks of mass madness. In the thirteenth century a phenomenon known as *tarantism* (Figure 1.4), a kind of possession by alien forces, originated in Italy and spread all through Europe. The bite of a tarantula during the height of the summer heat supposedly caused people to run out of their homes and to jump and dance around in a rather wild fashion. Others who had also been bitten by the spiders soon joined them, and so did those who had been stung during earlier summers. Some of the reports of tarantism contain references to considerable imbibing of alcoholic beverages, which from our twentieth-century point of view might well account for the wild behavior. But tarantism and other outbursts of apparently manic behavior affecting whole groups of people might well have been a reaction to some of the terrible social oppression, famine, and pestilence that was not uncommon in western Europe in the thirteenth through sixteenth centuries.

FIGURE **1.3**
Medieval woodcuts of the four temperaments thought by Hippocrates to result from excesses of the four humors. From left to right: the man with changeable temperament who has plenty of blood; the melancholy man, full of dark bile; the hot-tempered man, who has a surplus of choler or yellow bile; and the sluggish man with too much phlegm.

FIGURE **1.4**
Tarantism, *as illustrated in a 1560 drawing of Pieter Breughel.*

Treatment of mental illness during the Middle Ages was generally in the hands of priests, who would pray and sprinkle the afflicted with holy water. In their zeal and well-intentioned attempts to strike a fatal blow to Satan's pride, however, they often shouted obscene epithets as well. As time went on, terrible tortures took the place of prayers, for the devil within had to be punished and the body harboring him made unhabitable.

Theology recognized two types of possession by the devil, neither of which stood the possessed person in very good social stead. In one form of supposed possession, the victim was unwillingly seized by the devil as God's punishment for sins. These were the mentally ill. In the second form a person became possessed by deliberately entering into a pact with the devil. These were the witches, and they were endowed with supernatural powers because they were doing the devil's work. They could injure their enemies, ruin crops, control the weather, make men impotent, and turn themselves into animals. But by the end of the fifteenth century the distinction between the two forms of demoniacal possession had be-

come blurred (Coleman, 1972). Numerous hapless individuals were labeled as witches or heretics on either of these bases, and they were frequently accused of causing the pestilence and floods that were then rampant throughout western Europe and could not be explained or dealt with in naturalistic ways. Faced with vexing and inexplicable occurrences, people tend to seize on whatever explanation seems available, and in these times events conspired to heap enormous blame on witches. And it was not just evil or stupid people who held that those behaving peculiarly were possessed by or were in league with the devil. To quote from a respected authority of the time, "The greatest punishment God can afflict on the wicked . . . is to deliver them over to Satan who with God's permission kills them or makes them to undergo great calamities. Many devils are in woods or in wildernesses, ready to hurt and prejudice people. . . . I conclude it is merely the work of the devil." The writer of these words was Martin Luther.

Even earlier, in 1484, Pope Innocent VIII had issued a papal bull in which he exhorted the clergy of Europe to leave no stone unturned in the search for witches. The pope based his pronouncement on Exodus 22:18: "Thou shalt not suffer a witch to live." No doubt the pope did not intend to endorse tortures, but the sorry fact remains that this papal decree ushered in one of the most tragic and bizzare periods of all of Western history.

Two Dominican monks who had been appointed by the pope to act as inquisitors in northern Germany compiled a manual, *Malleus Maleficarum,* or *The Witches' Hammer,* which provided some important justifications and procedures for hunting witches. First, it confirmed beyond doubt the existence of witches and asserted that those who did not believe in witches were either stupid or heretical. Then it enunciated various signs by which witches could be detected, for example, red spots or areas of insensitivity on the skin, supposedly made by the claw of the devil when touching the person to seal a pact. Various means of examining and sentencing witches were also detailed. Revered by both Catholics and Protestants, the manual was eventually considered almost divinely inspired. Through such auspices and for more than two hundred years, tens of thousands of mentally ill men, women, and even children were hunted, accused, and tortured to obtain confessions and, if found guilty, were pubicly put to death (Figure 1.5).

During the seventeenth century witch hunting was also quite widespread in the colonies of the New World. Salem, Massachusetts, became the infamous center of the witch hunts of 1692. Within a few months hundreds were arrested, nineteen hanged, and one pressed to death. Recently, during a visit to the State House in Boston, Massachusetts, one of the authors of this textbook came upon a document of some legislative proceedings of the Massachusetts State Legislature. A bill had been passed by the legislature in the 1950s, formally exonerating a woman who had been burned as a witch in seventeenth-century Salem. It is interesting to speculate on what led to the introduction of this bill and on how it was discussed by twentieth-century legislators. Apparently someone in Massachusetts still takes the charge of witchcraft seriously enough to have the stigma removed from a relative by formal state resolution.

The Development of Asylums

Even during the period when throughout Europe persons suspected of witchcraft were being hunted by both clergy and laity, brought to trial, and often put to death, some men expressed more rational views. One of these was a German physician, Johann Weyer. In the sixteenth century he published a book asserting that many if not all "witches" were really sick mentally or bodily and that the barbarous acts perpetrated against these people were terrible wrongs. Weyer was the first physician whose primary interest was mental disorders. His book also contained careful descriptions of mental illnesses, couched in kindly words that implored the reader's understanding. The recorded statement of a priest indicates the typical reaction to Weyer's work: "Recently Satan went to a sabbath [witches' gathering] attired as a great prince, and told the assembled witches that they need not worry since, thanks to Weyer and his followers, the affairs of the devil were brilliantly progressing." In spite of such unfavorable criticism, Weyer's book grew in importance, and he is frequently regarded as the founder of modern psychiatry.

In 1621 the *Anatomy of Melancholy* was first published. This book was to have five subsequent editions by 1651 and to be widely read. Robert Burton, an English scholar, writer,

A

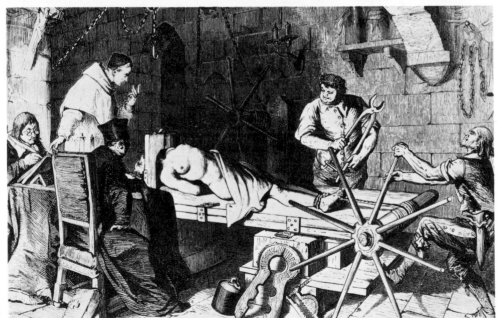

C

12

FIGURE 1.5
(*A*) *This sixteenth-century engraving shows a witch on trial. She was judged guilty if the scales tipped either way. Only if they balanced was she proved innocent. (B) A sixteenth-century engraving illustrates witch burning. (C) The rack—a torture used to extract confessions from accused witches. (D) The water test for witchcraft. The accused was bound and thrown into water; if she floated, she was considered to be in league with the devil. A voluptuous victim is pictured in this nineteenth-century engraving.*

B

D

13

and clergyman, had set himself the task of preparing a medical treatise on melancholy, its causes, symptoms, and cures. This he accomplished with considerable style, common sense, and humanity. For example, various child-rearing practices were viewed as contributors to depression in adult life. "Parents, and such as have the tuition and oversight of children, offend many times in that they are too stern, always threatening, chiding, brawling, whipping, or striking; by means of which, their poor children are so disheartened and cowed, that they never after have any courage, a merry hour in their lives, or take pleasure in any thing" (p. 215).

It should not be assumed, however, that the gradual inclusion of abnormal behavior within the domain of medicine led immediately to more humane and effective treatment. Early asylums left much to be desired. In 1547 Henry VIII handed over to the city of London the Hospital of St. Mary of Bethlehem, henceforth to be used solely for the confinement of the insane. Through the influence of the Moors, several asylums had been established in Spain during the fifteenth century (Figure 1.6), but this was the first to exist elsewhere in Europe. The conditions in Bethlehem were deplorable. Over the years the word "bedlam," a contraction and popular name for this hospi-

FIGURE **1.6**
Conditions in an early asylum are illustrated in this powerful painting by Goya.

INTRODUCTION AND BASIC ISSUES

FIGURE **1.7**

A tour of St. Mary's of Bethlehem (Bedlam) provides amusement for these two upper-class ladies. Hogarth captures the poignancy of the scene in this eighteenth-century painting.

tal, became a descriptive term for a place or scene of wild uproar and confusion. Even in the nineteenth century viewing the violent patients and their antics was considered entertainment, and tickets of admission to the asylum were sold (Figure 1.7). In the so-called Lunatics Tower, constructed in Vienna in 1784, patients were confined in the spaces between inner walls and outer walls. There they could be looked at from below by passersby. The first mental hospital in the United States was founded in Williamsburg, Virginia, in 1773.

A primary figure in the movement for humanitarian treatment was Philippe Pinel. During the French Revolution, in 1793, he was put in charge of a large asylum in Paris known as La Bicêtre. A historian has written of the conditions at this particular hospital.

[*The patients were*] *shackled to the walls of their cells, by iron collars which held them flat*

FIGURE **1.8**
A nineteenth-century painting shows Philippe Pinel ordering the chains to be removed from the patients at La Bicêtre.

against the wall and permitted little movement. . . . They could not lie down at night, as a rule. . . . Oftentimes there was a hoop of iron around the waist of the patient and in addition . . . chains on both the hands and the feet. . . . These chains [were] sufficiently long so that the patient could feed himself out of a bowl, the food usually being a mushy gruel—bread soaked in a weak soup. Since little was known about dietetics, [no attention] was paid to the type of diet given the patients. They were presumed to be animals . . . and not to care whether the food was good or bad (Selling, 1940, p. 54).

Pinel was reluctantly allowed to remove the chains of the people imprisoned in La Bicêtre (Figure 1.8) and to treat them as sick human beings rather than as beasts. Many who had been excited and completely unmanageable became calm and much easier to handle. Formerly considered dangerous, they strolled through the hospital and grounds with no inclination to create disturbances or to harm anyone. Some who had been incarcerated for years were soon restored to health and discharged from the hospital.

Freeing the patients of their restraints was not the only humanitarian reform advocated by Pinel. He believed that the mental patients in his care were essentially normal people who should be approached with compassion and understanding and treated as individual human beings with dignity. Their reason supposedly having left them because of severe personal and social problems, it might be restored to them through comforting counsel and pur-

INTRODUCTION AND BASIC ISSUES

poseful activity. Of course not all asylums adopted these so-called moral practices, but the smaller ones that did achieved remarkable successes. Unfortunately, this personal attention to the patients was no longer possible when the large mental hospitals that are prevalent today began to be built (Bockhoven, 1963).

The Beginning of Contemporary Thought

Earlier Hippocrates was described as the first to enunciate a somatogenic hypothesis of mental illness. His view was revived in the middle of the nineteenth century by a physician named Wilhelm Griesinger. This German doctor insisted that any diagnosis of mental disorder specify a physiological cause. A textbook of psychiatry, written by his well-known follower, Emil Kraepelin, and published in 1883, furnished a classification system to help establish the organic nature of mental illnesses. Kraepelin discerned among mental disorders a tendency for a certain group of symptoms, called a *syndrome,* to appear together regularly enough to be regarded as having an underlying bodily and physical cause, much as a particular medical disease and its syndrome may be attributed to a physiological disorder. He regarded each mental illness as distinct from all others, having its own genesis, symptoms, course, and outcome. Even though cures had not been worked out, at least the course of the disease could be predicted. Kraepelin was able to recognize two major groups of mental diseases, dementia praecox, an early term for schizophrenia, and manic-depressive psychosis. He postulated a chemical imbalance as the cause of schizophrenia and an irregularity in metabolism as the cause of manic-depressive psychosis. Kraepelin's scheme for classifying these and other mental illnesses be-

came the basis for our present psychiatric categories, which will be explained more fully in Chapter 3.

Much was being learned about the nervous system in the second half of the nineteenth century but not enough yet to reveal the potential abnormalities in structure underlying mental disorders. Perhaps the most striking medical success was the discovery of the full nature and origin of syphilis. The venereal disease syphilis had been recognized for several centuries, and since 1798 it had been known that a number of mental patients manifested a similar and steady deterioration of both physical and mental abilities. These patients were observed to suffer delusions of grandeur, insanity, and progressive paralysis. Soon after these symptoms were recognized, it was realized that these patients never recovered. In 1825 this deterioration in mental and physical health was designated a disease, general paresis. Although in 1857 it was established that some patients with paresis had earlier had syphilis, there were many competing theories of the origin of paresis. For example, in attempting to account for the high rate of the disorder among sailors, some supposed that sea water might be the cause. And Griesinger, in trying to account for the higher incidence among men, speculated about the importance of liquor, tobacco, and coffee. Then in the 1860s and 1870s Louis Pasteur established the germ theory of disease; it became possible to demonstrate the relation between syphilis and general paresis. In 1897 Richard von Krafft-Ebing inoculated paretic patients with matter from syphilitic sores. The patients did not develop syphilis, indicating that they had been infected earlier. Then in 1905 the specific microorganism causing syphilis was discovered. Fortunately, measures that can detect the presence of syphilis and prevent its spread were developed soon after the discovery of the spirochete that causes it, and for some time the incidence of general paresis has been far less than it once was.

Psychogenesis

The search for somatogenic causes dominated psychiatry until well into the twentieth century, no doubt partly because of the stunning discoveries made about general paresis. But in other parts of western Europe, in the late eighteenth century and throughout the nineteenth, mental illnesses were considered to have an entirely different genesis. Various so-called *psychogenic* points of view, attributing mental disorders to psychic malfunctions, were fashionable in France and Austria. For reasons that are still not clear to us even today, many people in western Europe were at that time subject to *hysterical states:* they suffered from physical incapacities that made absolutely no anatomical sense. For example, in "glove anesthesia" the person had no feeling in his or her hand, but sensation was present just beyond the wrist and on up into the arm. Since the nerves run continuously from the shoulder down to the fingertips, there is no known physiological explanation for such an anesthesia.

Anton Mesmer, an Austrian physician practicing in the late eighteenth and early nineteenth centuries, believed that hysterical disorders were caused by a particular distribution of a universal magnetic fluid in the body. Moreover, he felt that one person could influence the fluid of another to bring about a change in the person's behavior. Mesmer apparently was very good at changing behavior. He conducted meetings cloaked in mystery and mysticism at which afflicted patients sat around a covered *baquet* or tub. Iron rods protruded from the bottles of various chemicals which were beneath (Figure 1.9). Mesmer would enter a room, clothed in rather outlandish garments, and take various of the rods from the tub and touch afflicted parts of his patients' bodies. He believed that the rods could transmit "animal magnetism" and adjust the distribution of the universal magnetic fluid, thereby removing the hysterical disorder. Whatever we may think of what seems today to be a questionable theoretical explanation and procedure, the fact remains that Mesmer was able to help quite a number of people overcome their hysterical problems. Our discussion of Mesmer's work under the rubric of psychogenic causes is rather arbitrary, since Mesmer regarded the hysterical disorders as strictly physical. Because of the setting in which Mesmer worked with his patients, however, he is generally regarded as one of the earlier practitioners of hypnosis (see Box 1.1). (The familiar word mesmerize is the older term for hypnotize.)

A great Parisian neurologist, Jean Charcot, also studied hysterical states, not only anesthesia but also blindness, deafness, paralysis, convulsive attacks, and gaps in memory brought about by hysteria (Figure 1.10). Practicing in the second half of the nineteenth century, Charcot initially espoused a somatogenic point of view. One day, however, some of his enterprising students hypnotized a normal woman and suggested to her certain hysterical symptoms. Charcot was deceived into believing that she was an actual hysterical patient. When the students showed him how readily they could remove the symptoms by waking the woman, Charcot changed his mind about hysteria and became interested in nonphysical interpretations of these very puzzling phenomena. Further psychological theorizing and research was done by Pierre Janet, one of Charcot's pupils.

In Vienna, toward the end of the century, a physician named Josef Breuer treated a woman who mumbled to herself when in a

A

FIGURE **1.9**
(A) Mesmer's baquet, the device he used to "transmit" animal magnetism. (B) A portrait of Franz Mesmer.

B

BOX **1.1** *Hypnosis*

A discussion of hypnosis could appear in several chapters of this book; inasmuch as it played a central role in the development of psychogenic theories of psychopathology, we include it here.

An initial question to be asked is what exactly is hypnosis. In view of how often psychologists and psychiatrists employ the term, it is sobering to realize how much heated controversy there is about its very nature. Hilgard (1965) suggests the following characteristics.

1. *Increased suggestibility.* Hypnotized subjects seem much more open to suggestions from the hypnotist than they would be in a waking state. Indeed, many hypnotized subjects show annoyance when the hypnotist directs them to do some planning of their own while they are hypnotized. Many theorists believe that hypnosis is nothing more than a state of heightened suggestibility.

2. *Redistribution of attention.* Hypnotized subjects appear extremely attentive to what the hypnotist is saying, thereby becoming less aware of other stimulation, such as noises in an adjacent room. Although the hypnotist often suggests that the subject pay attention only to him, there may be a tendency, even without direct suggestion, for hypnotic subjects to focus on the hypnotist rather than on other things.

3. *Heightened ability to fantasize.* Clinical evidence suggests that visual images are more vivid under hypnosis, although there is a notable lack of controlled experimental data on this point.

4. *Increased tolerance for persistent distortion of reality.* Many hypnotized subjects readily accept all kinds of perceptual distortions that they would not tolerate when awake. Thus hypnotized subjects may accept suggestions that an animal is talking to them or that someone is present

in the room when no one is actually there. The logic that operates during a hypnotic trance, allowing a person to perceive the world in a way remarkably different from how he regards it when awake, has been called "trance logic" (Orne, 1959).

5. *Role behavior.* Subjects have a greater ability to assume a particular role when hypnotized than when awake. Indeed, Sarbin (1950) has constructed an entire theory about the nature of hypnosis in terms of role taking.

These, then, are what many workers regard as characteristics of hypnotized subjects. As in all aspects of human behavior, not all people manifest all these characteristics in the same way, and it is indeed possible for subjects who otherwise appear to be deeply hypnotized not to show all these characteristics at any one time.

Our historical review mentioned Mesmer's therapy for hysterical disabilities and subsequent work by Charcot, Janet, and Breuer. During the same period of time surgeons were "mesmerizing" patients to block pain. For example, in 1842 a British physician, W. S. Ward, amputated the leg of a patient after hypnotizing him, and apparently he felt nothing during what would otherwise have been an excruciatingly painful operation. And in 1849 a mesmeric infirmary was opened in London where hundreds of painless operations were performed while the patients were under hypnotic trances. In the same decade, however, ether was proved to produce insensibility to pain. The term anesthesia had heretofore been applied to the numbness felt in hysterical states and paralysis. Oliver Wendell Holmes is credited with suggesting that it be applied to the effects of this new agent and others like it, and that they be called anesthetics. The availability of these chemicals for surgical operations seems to have fore-stalled the continuing use of hypnosis as an alleviator of pain.

The person who coined the modern term hypnotism is usually considered to be James Braid (1795–1860), a British physician who was also hypnotizing people to reduce pain. Unlike Mesmer, however, Braid did not break with his profession, largely because he described what was happening in terms that were more consistent with the *Zeitgeist*. He described the trance as a "nervous sleep," from which came the name "neurohypnology," later shortened to hypnotism. Braid rejected the mystical orientation of Mesmer and yet continued to experiment with the phenomenon as he saw it. He sought a physiological cause and felt he had found one in his discovery that trances could be readily induced by having people stare at a bright object located somewhat above the line of vision. The object was placed in front of a person in such a way that the levator muscles of the eyelids had to be strained in order to keep it in view. Braid suggested that the muscles were markedly affected by having them remain fixed in this position for a given period of time and that somehow this led to nervous sleep or hypnosis. He therefore placed the cause of the sleep inside the subject rather than external to him, as Mesmer had suggested with his concept of animal magnetism. In this way he was able to perform many public demonstrations without incurring the disapproval of his medical colleagues.

As already indicated, the discovery of drugs for anesthesia discouraged the use of hypnosis in medicine, for drugs are clearly more reliable, although more dangerous as well, than hypnotic inductions. In clinical work many practitioners, have employed hypnotic procedures for psycho-

therapeutic purposes, especially during World War II. To relieve shell shock the frightened soldier was hypnotized and encouraged to relive traumatic events in his imagination.

The scientific study of hypnosis had to await the development of relatively objective measures in the 1950s. Perhaps the principal device is that developed at Stanford University by Weitzenhoffer and Hilgard (1959), the Stanford Hypnotic Susceptibility Scale. In the application of this scale, or, more properly, scales, since there are a number of them, the subject is hypnotized and then asked to engage in a series of tasks. For example, it may be suggested to a subject that his right hand is so heavy that it is doubtful whether it can be raised. Then the hypnotist will ask the subject to try to lift the heavy hand even though he probably will not be able to do so. The hypnotist observes the degree to which the subject can or cannot raise the hand and gives a plus or minus score. After a number of tasks have been presented, the subject can be given a score ranging from zero to twelve, and this score is regarded as a measure of how deeply hypnotized he is.

Most of these scales, however, do not measure the more subjective aspects of hypnosis. For example, many hypnotized subjects, even though they have not been specifically told that it may happen, experience sensations such as floating or spinning. Many hypnotists consider such subjective experiences at least as important as the more observable performances tapped by the various scales. As we might expect, this divergence of interests contributes to the controversy within the field, with the more clinically oriented hypnotists rejecting the validity of such scales as the Stanford. They instead content themselves with what subjects report of their subjective reactions.

FIGURE **1.10**
Charcot, the famous French neurologist, demonstrating hypnosis.

dreamlike state called a fugue. Perhaps not knowing what else to do, Breuer repeated some of her words to her when she was under hypnosis and succeeded in getting her to talk more freely and ultimately with considerable emotion about some very troubling past events. Upon awakening from these hypnotic sessions, she would frequently feel much better. With other hysterical patients Breuer found that the relief and cure of their symptoms seemed to last longer if, under hypnosis, they were able to recall the original precipitating event for the symptom and if, furthermore, their original emotion was expressed. This reliving of an earlier emotional catastrophe and the release of the emotional tension produced by previously forgotten thoughts about the event was called abreaction

or catharsis. Breuer's method became known as the *cathartic method.* In 1895 one of his colleagues joined him in the publication of *Studies in Hysteria,* a book considered to be a milestone in abnormal psychology. Breuer's collaborator was Sigmund Freud, whose thinking we shall examine later.[2]

[2] Anna O., the young woman treated by Breuer with the cathartic method, or "talking cure," has become one of the best-known clinical cases in all psychotherapy literature, and, as stated above, the report of this case in 1895 formed the basis of Freud's important contributions later on. But recent historical investigations by Ellenberger (1972) cast serious doubt on how accurate Breuer's reporting was. Indeed, Anna O.—in reality Bertha Pappenheim, a member of a well-to-do Viennese family—was apparently not helped at all by Breuer's talking cure! Carl Jung, Freud's renowned colleague, is quoted as saying that, during a conference in 1925, Freud told him that

INTRODUCTION AND BASIC ISSUES

SCIENCE: A HUMAN ENTERPRISE

In the dramatic space explorations of recent years highly sophisticated satellites are sent aloft to make observations. Astronauts have also been catapulted to the moon, where they use their human senses as well as man-made machines to make still more observations. It is possible, however, that certain phenomena of important consequence to man are being missed because our instruments do not have sensing devices capable of recording the presence or absence of such phenomena, and because men are not trained to look for them. When Neil Armstrong opened the space capsule and became the first human being to step onto the moon, scientists were filled with awe and even some trepidation, for there was a very definite risk. The dangers against which the life support systems had been constructed could *only* be those of which we had previously had some conception. Although scientists know a great deal about outer space and can make remarkably precise predictions and statements about the movements of heavenly bodies, they accept the perhaps remote but nonetheless real possibility that phenomena exist about which we have not the vaguest inkling.

This discursion on outer space exploration is by way of pointing out that scientific observation is a human endeavor, reflecting both the strengths of man's ingenuity and scholarship as well as his intrinsic incapacity to be fully knowledgeable about the nature of his universe. Scientists are able to design instruments to make only the kinds of observations about which they have some initial idea. They realize that certain observations are not being made because our knowledge about the general nature of the universe is limited. Thomas Kuhn, a well-known philospher of science, has put the problem this way: " . . . the decision to employ a particular piece of apparatus and to use it in a particular way carries an assumption that only certain sorts of circumstances will arise" (1962, p. 59). Thus when we explore together the vagaries of abnormal human behavior, it will be particularly useful to keep in mind that our conceptual framework and methods of study may limit our perspective and our perceptions.

Subjectivity in Science: The Role of Paradigms

We believe that abnormal behavior should be studied according to scientific principles. It should be clear at this point, however, that science is *not* a completely objective enterprise. Rather, as we can infer from the comment by Kuhn, subjective factors *do* enter into the conduct of scientific inquiry. Central to any application of scientific principles, in Kuhn's view, is the concept of *paradigm,* which may be defined as a conceptual framework within which a scientist works. A paradigm, according to Kuhn, is a set of basic assumptions that outline the universe of scientific inquiry, specifying both the kinds of concepts that will be regarded as legitimate as well as the methods that may be used to collect and interpret data. Indeed, every decision about what constitutes a datum, or scientific observation, is made within a particular paradigm. A paradigm has profound implications about how scientists operate at any given time, for "Men whose research is based on shared paradigms

---

Anna O. had never been cured. Hospital records discovered by Ellenberger confirm that she continued to rely on morphine to ease the "hysterical" problems that Breuer is reputed to have removed by catharsis. It is fascinating and ironic to consider that the roots of psychoanalysis may lie in an improperly reported clinical case.

are committed to the same rules and standards for scientific practice" (Kuhn, 1962, p. 11). Paradigms specify what problems scientists will investigate and how they will go about the investigation.

Although made explicit only when scientists address themselves to philosophy, paradigms are nonetheless an intrinsic part of a science, serving the vital function of indicating how the game is to be played. In perceptual terms a paradigm may be likened to a general *set,* a predisposition to see certain factors and not to see others. Within contemporary psychology behaviorism and psychoanalysis may be regarded as two separate paradigms. How difficult it is for people operating within different paradigms even to talk with one another will become evident as we explore the specifics of these two schools of psychology.

In addition to injecting inevitable biases into the definition and collection of data, a paradigm may also affect the interpretation of facts. In other words, the meaning or import attributed to data may depend to a considerable extent on a paradigm. Let us look briefly at the classic example of how for nearly 1400 years a particular paradigm influenced the interpretation of data about the heavens. From the second until the sixteenth century A.D. astronomy was dominated by the Ptolemaic paradigm. The earth was viewed as the center of the universe and the various planets and stars were considered to revolve around it. Although such a point of view seems rather absurd when examined in the light of current scientific data, it was in fact, with some embellishments, able to provide relatively good predictions of the positions of the planets, the sun, and the moon and of such phenomena as eclipses.

Fairly accurate observations and measurements of planetary positions and motions had been made by Hipparchus, 300 years earlier, and Ptolemy had extended this work. The astronomical data to be encompassed by any paradigm interpreting the heavens was therefore considerable. To explain the retrograde, or westward, motion of planets and other orbital eccentricities—changes of position actually reflecting the revolution of the earth about the sun—the Ptolemaic system postulated a number of complicated concepts. A planet was thought to move in a small circle, the epicycle, the center of which was at the same time traveling an orbit, the planet's deferent, around the earth. The earth was not located in the exact center of the diameter of the deferent but a little to the side, at the eccentric (Figure 1.11). The equant was yet another position on the diameter of the deferent, the same distance from the center as the eccentric. Around this point the center of each planet's epicycle appeared to move with uniform speed. To the proponents of the Ptolemaic system, who were certainly no fools, such motions seemed eminently reasonable because they explained a universe of which the earth was the immovable center. Although some minor discrepancies between the predictions and the actual observations of planetary motions remained unexplained, these discrepancies did not lead people to doubt the basic assumption, that the earth was the center of the universe. The task of astronomy for fourteen centuries was the refinement of the Ptolemaic system to improve its predictions.

Kuhn (1959) has labeled such a period "normal science." Astronomers during these centuries shared a common view of the phenomena in which they were interested. Because this shared view, that the earth was the center of the universe, was so strongly held, it was never questioned when contradictory evidence was discovered. Instead, scientists attempted to readjust aspects of the paradigm. To bring the Ptolemaic system more in line with any new observations of the positions and

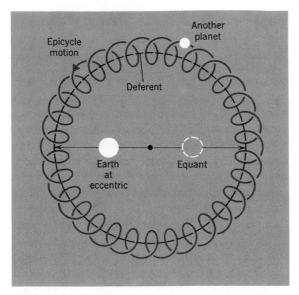

FIGURE **1.11**
*Planetary movements in the Ptolemaic system,
showing the epicycle, deferent, eccentric, and
equant.*

movements of the planets, astronomers elaborated the arrangement of deferents and epicycles.

In 1543 Copernicus proposed a radically different paradigm as a theoretical basis for astronomy. Specifically, he suggested that the sun rather than the earth be considered the center of the universe. Moreover, orbits should be regarded as perfectly circular and uniform and not be subject to complexities such as the equant. *It is important to note that the Copernican revolution was not based on the acquisition of new data.* Rather, the data available to Copernicus were but little different from those available to Ptolemy over 1400 years earlier. What, then, led to the revolution in thought, the paradigm shift?

Two facts seem to have been particularly important to Copernicus in his rejection of the Ptolemaic system. First, he recognized its great complexity and lack of elegance. The Ptolemaic view of the universe had become inordinately flexible and complex—encompassing additional and eccentric epicycles—to avoid being disproved. Second, based on religious-cosmological considerations, Copernicus believed that planetary orbits "ought to be" circular since the circle was the most perfect form in nature. Thus we see that the postulation of a paradigm to interpret observed data can depend heavily on *subjective*, nonscientific views held by the theorist. In fact, when the Copernican system was initially proposed, it provided no increment in predictive efficiency over what could be obtained by adhering to the Ptolemaic system. At least initially, the adoption of the Copernican paradigm was based on factors other than the adequacy with which it could account for the available data.

Subjective factors such as those we have discussed in relation to the Copernican revolution have also greatly affected theorizing about psychopathology. We have already examined several instances of what might be called "paradigm clashes" in the history of thinking about the problems of abnormal behavior. Hippocrates' revolt against demonology, Weyer's denunciation of witch hunting, and the treatment reforms of Pinel can all be considered attempts to change radically the way in which abnormal behavior was viewed. Moreover, at the time these men proposed what we consider more rational approaches to abnormal behavior, they had no definitive proof that their new visions would be better than the old.

An Example of Paradigms in Abnormal Psychology

As implied earlier, there is perhaps no poorer communication within the field of psychology than that between the psychoanalysts and the behaviorists. The chasm that exists between these two camps is made apparent by ex-

BOX **1.2** *Paradigm Clash in the Study of Hypnosis*

Box 1.1 reviewed some of the history of hypnosis and its generally accepted characteristics. There is an interesting paradigm clash about hypnosis, for the very idea that we should talk *at all* about a state called hypnosis has been challenged. Probably the most outspoken critic of "state theories" of hypnosis—conceptions of hypnosis that assume a separate state underlying the phenomena—is an experimental psychologist, Theodore X. Barber. Barber's ideas, presented in scores of theoretical papers and experiments (for example, Barber, 1969), are essentially as follows.

1. "Hypnosis," as a state, is inferred solely on the basis of the presence of behavioral phenomena that it is alleged to cause. A subject's inability to lift his hand when extreme heaviness is suggested is, at the same time, interpreted to be both a sign of hypnosis and a result of hypnosis. To say that the heaviness indicates that the person is hypnotized and then to conclude that the heaviness is caused by hypnosis is to engage in circular reasoning. Nothing has really been explained.

2. Behavior generally regarded as caused by hypnosis can be readily produced in subjects who are not given a hypnotic induction. Barber and Calverley (1964b) found that subjects will report a variety of vivid auditory and visual hallucinations, seeing or hearing something that is not really present, when they are simply urged to try very hard to hallucinate.

3. Therefore it is not scientifically useful nor is it necessary to employ a state concept of "hypnosis."

Not surprisingly, Barber's position has been attacked, sometimes vehemently, by investigators who operate under the assumption that we can talk meaningfully of a state of hypnosis. Spanos (1970), one of Barber's associates, has reviewed and replied to the principal criticisms. State theorists have suggested that the subjects in Barber's experiments, although not given a formal hypnotic induction, nonetheless slip into a hypnotic trance and *therefore* shows signs of hypnosis. Spanos points out that this is a purely *post hoc* argument, an "explanation" offered only after the data are in and therefore impossible to refute. If a nonhypnotized subject does something hypnotic, he can be said to have slipped into a trance; but if, like many subjects, he fails to "look hypnotized," he can always be said *afterward* not to have been in a trance.

Barber's critics (for example, Conn and Conn, 1967) have also proposed that independent evidence of hypnosis can be found in a subject's verbal report of whether he is or is not hypnotized. Spanos replies that scientists do not always believe what subjects tell them and that the tendency to regard a self-report as valid or not is itself affected by one's point of view. For example, suppose a subject tells a hypnotist that he cannot lift his arm because the devil is holding it down. How many present-day scientists would conclude that hypnosis is the devil's doing? Similarly, an investigator must initially believe that there is a separate state of hypnosis *before* attributing validity to the report of a subject that he has been hypnotized.

On the experimental level, some of Barber's research has questioned the very existence of behavioral phenomena that state theorists have accepted on the basis of self-report. For instance, some hypnotized subjects report deafness after it has been suggested to them that they may not be able to hear. Barber and Calverly (1964a) decided to assess deafness in a less obvious fashion, one that would not rely on self-report. Delayed auditory feedback is a procedure whereby a human subject hears through headphones what he is saying, but delayed by a given period of time, for example, one second. Numerous studies have shown that such delayed feedback of speech invariably causes stuttering in otherwise fluent people. Barber and Calverly reasoned that if a person could truly be rendered deaf by hypnotic suggestion, he would not stutter when his words were fed back to him. In a carefully controlled experiment, subjects were, according to objective measures, deeply hypnotized and reported that they could not hear after a suggestion of deafness. Nonetheless, they were markedly affected by delayed auditory feedback of their own speech.

The authors of this book find themselves extremely sympathetic to the arguments of Barber and his colleagues. At the same time, it seems quite reasonable to study phenomena that have been labeled as hypnotic, as indeed Barber himself has done for several years. In our clinical work we occasionally make use of hypnotic inductions to achieve certain specific ends, for example, helping people to relax. It seems possible to do this without affirming allegiance to either state or nonstate theories of hypnosis. The expectations a person has about being hypnotized would seem to be the important factor. Whether a hypnotic induction *really* produces a *state* in which a person imagines more vividly than when awake seems to be secondary in importance to the possibility that a hypnotic induction may make a person *believe* that he can imagine more vividly.

amining a widely quoted and rather controversial report by three behaviorists, Ayllon, Haughton, and Hughes (1965). These investigators were interested in the etiology of psychiatric symptoms, that is, in what factors may account for their development. Being impatient with prevailing psychoanalytic explanations of psychopathologic phenomena, Ayllon and his colleagues set out to demonstrate that "The etiology of many so-called psychotic symptoms exhibited by hospitalized patients or those in need of hospitalization does not have to be sought in the obscure dynamics of a psychiatric disturbance" (p. 5). To prove their point, they chose a female patient hospitalized for chronic schizophrenia and proceeded to encourage her to hold a broom, without sweeping with it, by giving her cigarettes whenever she followed their instructions. They felt that the purposeless behavior they had devised for the woman could be regarded as abnormal. Then to determine how the broom holding would actually be judged, they arranged for unsuspecting psychiatrists to comment on the patient's behavior. One of the doctors described the broom-holding behavior as follows.

Her constant and compulsive pacing, holding a broom in the manner she does, could be seen as a ritualistic procedure, a magical action . . . her broom would be then: (1) a child that gives her love and she gives him in return her devotion, (2) a phallic symbol, (3) a sceptre of an impotent queen . . . (Ayllon et al., 1965, p. 3).

As the investigators point out, the psychiatrist was not aware of the *contrived* origin of this behavior.

What did this demonstration really prove? Ayllon and his colleagues asserted that in per-suading the woman to hold the broom by rewarding her, they had illustrated how psychotic behavior develops in the real world, under nonlaboratory conditions. The fact that the psychiatrists, who were ignorant of the experimental ruse, regarded the behavior as a symptom of the woman's psychosis helped to convince the investigators that they had actually shown how abnormal behavior originates.

If we assume that even bizarre-appearing behavior can be taught in the same way as behavior not designated as abnormal, we must postulate a world of psychopathology far different from that in which deviant phenomena are considered an expression of internal repressed impulses.[3] Although we do not know what the psychiatrists who commented on the broom-holding woman were actually thinking at the time of their observation, it is safe to assume that their psychoanalytic orientation did not allow them even to consider the possibility that she had been taught this behavior. On the other hand, it is significant that Ayllon and his colleagues, in their apparent eagerness to debunk the psychoanalytic approach, committed an error in logic. Because they had shown that under certain contrived circumstances a patient already diagnosed as schizophrenic could easily be encouraged to hold a broom by occasionally giving her cigarettes, they inferred that they had cast light on the manner in which psychotic behavior develops. They committed the error of "affirming the consequent." They assumed that, simply because behavior is generated under one set of circumstances, every time this or similar behavior occurs in nature, it had developed because of the same set of controlling conditions (Davison, 1969; Maher, 1966).

Thus subjective factors pervade psychology

---

[3] Additional details of psychoanalytic thinking are given in Chapters 2, 5, and 18.

and very much affect our conception of the nature of abnormal behavior. Scientists do not resign from the family of man when they formulate hypotheses and conduct controlled research. Perhaps it is especially appropriate for the psychologist-as-scientist to remain aware of this simple, although frequently overlooked, point.

SUMMARY

The study of abnormal behavior is a search for why people behave in unexpected, sometimes bizarre, and typically self-defeating ways. Much less is known than we would like; this book will focus on the ways in which psychopathologists have been trying to learn more about the causes of abnormal behavior.

A brief history of the field was provided, indicating its origins in ancient demonology and crude medical theorizing. Since the beginning of scientific inquiry into abnormal behavior, two major points of view have vied for attention: the somatogenic, which assumes that every mental aberration is caused by a physical malfunction; and the psychogenic, which assumes that the sufferer's body is intact and that difficulties are explained in psychological terms.

Hypnosis was reviewed in some detail, both because it occupies an important position in the historical development of the field and because the controversies about hypnosis provide a good example of how the paradigms of science—the sets of basic assumptions that determine the kinds of scientific questions to be asked and the procedures to be used in collecting data—can vary and affect the conclusions drawn.

CHAPTER 2

Current Models in Abnormal Psychology

This chapter is concerned with the principal paradigms and models that have been used to conceptualize abnormal behavior. Although we shall use these two terms model and paradigm interchangeably, there are subtle differences between them. First, a paradigm is broader in scope than a model, for it applies to an entire field of inquiry rather than only part of one. Second, the term model indicates that an analogy is being made. With a model we attempt to apply concepts from one domain to another, assuming that the new domain is like the familiar one and that it can be better understood by studying it in the same way. For example, the brain can be conceptualized *as if* it were a computer and the eye *as if* it were a camera (Maher, 1966; Price, 1972). This is not to say that the brain *is* a computer, constructed of electronic circuitry, tapedecks, and typewriters. Rather, it is assumed that the *functioning* of the brain can be better understood by likening it to the operation of a computer.

In the field of abnormal psychology the term model is used more frequently than paradigm. In formulating a medical model of mental disorder, for example, certain concepts are taken from medicine and applied, by analogy, to a new domain, abnormal behavior. A model, however, also functions as a paradigm in determining how the subject matter will be approached, what questions will be asked, and what information will be deemed relevant.

We shall discuss three major models that are applied in contemporary abnormal psychology, the *statistical model*, the *medical model,* and the *learning model.* It is important to note that within the field of abnormal psychology models are not as highly developed and formal as are those of some other disciplines and of some areas of psychology. Instead, abnormal psychology models are best considered as rather loose sets of assumptions or points of view. Thus we are unable to list item by item the particular postulates of each model. Instead, we shall try to convey the flavor of three general points of view. Many people go about the study of abnormal psychology without explicitly considering the nature of the model that they have adopted. As we hope to show in this chapter, the choice of a model has some very important consequences for the way in which abnormal behavior is defined and investigated. The assumptions made by the holders of the various paradigmatic positions should be examined.

THE STATISTICAL MODEL

In the statistical approach specific characteristics of people such as personality traits or behavior and the distribution of these characteristics in the population are the subjects dealt with. One type of population distribution, the normal curve (Figure 2.1), depicts the majority of people as being in the middle; that is, very few people fall at either extreme. Within a statistical model an assertion that a person is normal implies that he does not deviate from the average in a particular trait or behavior pattern. For example, if we consider anxiety as one dimension of abnormality, persons who are "average" in anxiety level will be considered normal. In contrast, people who are extremely anxious *or* people who suffer little or no anxiety will be considered abnormal. To use more traditional diagnostic labels (see Chapter 3), a person with considerable anxiety is regarded as neurotic and a person with very little anxiety as sociopathic. Similarly, a person very low in intelligence will be considered abnormal and so will a genius. To make a decision about a person's normality or abnormality, we merely assess the characteristic in question and determine the person's position on the bell-shaped curve. The statistical model, however, does not tell us which traits or behaviors are to be measured. Few of us would seriously make decisions about psychological normality or abnormality on the basis of characteristics such as height, weight, and hair color; rather, a person's tendency to be anxious or to hallucinate would generally be viewed as more appropriate criteria. Since most people do not see visions, the statistical model would indicate that those who hallucinate are abnormal.

As an example of a statistical model, let us consider how Eysenck (1960) categorizes people. He bases his classification on what he believes are the three most pertinent dimensions of personality. The first, neuroticism, refers primarily to emotionality, or the ease with which people can become aroused. The second, introversion-extroversion, refers for the most part to conditionability: extroverts are said to acquire conditioned responses slowly and to lose them rapidly, whereas the

FIGURE **2.1**

The distribution of height among adults, illustrating a normal or bell-shaped curve.

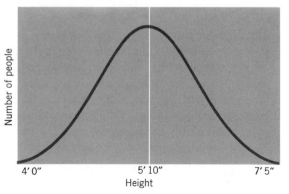

reverse is true of introverts. The third, psychoticism, relates to the person's contact with reality. Each of the three dimensions is assumed to be measurable through various techniques, such as personality questionnaires, laboratory tests, and the like. By determining a person's rating on each of the three dimensions, we can fit him into the more traditional diagnostic scheme. An example of how this can be done for two of the dimensions, neuroticism and introversion-extroversion, is presented in Figure 2.2. Those persons who are deviant, that is, those who are rated either high or low on a particular dimension, are judged abnormal; for example, someone rated high in both neuroticism and extroversion is regarded by Eysenck as psychopathic.[1] The decisions about which dimensions define abnormality are made *outside* the statistical model, according to Eysenck's theory of personality organization.

How may the statistical model of abnormal behavior be evaluated? First, in applying this model the investigator relies on the fact that a low frequency of occurrence is defined as deviant. There is usually a relationship between low frequency and labeling a behavior as abnormal, but there are also instances in which this relationship breaks down. Low IQs may be a proper subject for study by abnormal psychologists, but can the opposite, high IQs, be considered within their province? And just how low does the frequency of occurrence have to be to judge the behavior abnormal? Moreover, the model fails to specify what phenomena we should measure and gives us no hints about what variables may be related to the development of abnormal behavior. Therefore, although providing a partial description of abnormality, the statistical model must be considered rather inadequate.

THE MEDICAL MODEL

As indicated in Chapter 1, the study of abnormal behavior is historically linked to medicine. Many early workers and many contemporaries as well have used the model of physical illness as the basis for defining deviant behavior. Clearly, in current thinking within the field of abnormal behavior the medical model is pervasive. As Maher (1966) has noted, "[deviant] behavior is termed *pathological* and is classified on the basis of *symptoms,* classification being called *diagnosis.* Processes designed to change behavior are called *therapies* and are applied to *patients* in

mental *hospitals.* If the deviant behavior ceases, the patient is described as *cured"* (p. 22).

The Concepts of Disease

The critical assumption of the medical model is that abnormal behavior may be likened to a disease. To determine how a disease model can be applied to abnormal behavior, we must first examine the concept of disease as it is employed in medicine.

First, we may note two rather broad criteria for defining a disease: (1) each disease has a specific cluster of symptoms or a syndrome; (2) a causal agent or etiology is specific to that syndrome. Within this rather general notion of what a disease is, three different kinds may be

---

[1] Eysenck's view of psychopaths as having a high level of neuroticism conflicts with most other theoretical accounts, as will be discussed in Chapter 9.

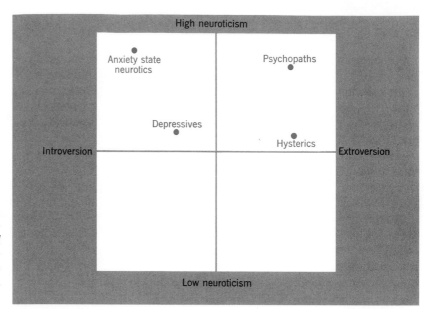

FIGURE 2.2

Eysenck's statistical model, illustrating how various clinical groups can be described according to their positions on the personality dimensions of neuroticism and introversion-extroversion.

distinguished according to their causes (Buss, 1966). In an *infectious disease* a microorganism such as a germ or virus attacks an organ or organ system. The common cold, pneumonia, and hepatitis are three well-known examples. The second kind, a *systemic disease,* represents a malfunction that is *not* produced by an infection. An organ breaks down, perhaps because of an inherited defect. A classic example is diabetes, a malfunction of the cells of the pancreas that usually secrete insulin. The third kind, a *traumatic disease,* is produced by an external, environmental agent. Ingestion of a poisonous substance is a good illustration of this kind of disease. Moreover, a broken arm or leg would also fit within the definition of a traumatic disease, for an external stress applied to the body has elicited a malfunction. Thus we see that to speak only of "*the* medical model" or "*the* disease model" is an oversimplification; there are several such models.

An additional factor characterizes two of these disease models. In infectious and systemic diseases the symptoms, for example a 104-degree temperature or the inability to me-

tabolize sugar, have an *internal cause*. A disease process located within the organism produces the symptoms. The traumatic disease, however, does *not* necessarily involve an internal process. The overt symptom, a broken arm or leg, is the direct result of the application of an *external* agent, for example a severe blow.

Each of the three disease models have been applied to deviant behavior (Table 2.1). The infectious disease model enjoyed great prominence when it was discovered that invading syphilitic spirochetes penetrate the brain, causing neural deterioration which in turn brings on the psychotic state of paresis. Since the symptoms of paresis were judged to be very similar to those of other so-called mental disorders, it was quite naturally assumed that many other such disorders would also be found to be brought on by an infection. No such discoveries were made, however, and today there is little reason to think that infection is the cause of many mental disorders.

In the last few decades the systemic disease model has been widely applied in the field of abnormal psychology. One prominent theory

TABLE 2.1 *Applications of the Medical Model in Abnormal Psychology*

Medical disease	Definition	Applications to abnormal psychology
Infectious—e.g., pneumonia	Invasion by microorganism	Paresis
Systemic—e.g., diabetes	Organ malfunction not caused by external agent	Biochemical theories of schizophrenia Autonomic theories of neuroses
Traumatic—e.g., broken arm	External agent produces malfunction	Psychological stress theories

has attributed schizophrenia to a deficiency in neural transmission. According to this theory, the failure of a bodily system causes schizophrenia. Similarly, neurotic behavior has often been considered to stem from some defect within the autonomic nervous system that allows a person to be too easily aroused. Both of these systemic hypotheses are *somatogenic,* but *psychogenic* systemic disease models, in which psychological processes replace bodily organs as the locus of the disease, are also possible. Thus, in addition to dysfunctions of physical organs such as the brain and nerves, the malfunctionings of psychological processes such as attention, ego strength, and ability to tolerate stress can also be considered systemic diseases. Such theorizing involves metaphor: psychological processes are equated with the functions of bodily organs. But, in fact, psychological processes are quite different from the functions of physical organs. Physical organs are, of course, present in the body and can be observed. In contrast, the psychological processes invoked in psychogenic medical models are *unobservable,* and their existence is only assumed. The usefulness of referring to

such unobserved, inferred processes is discussed in Chapter 4.

Finally, the traumatic disease model has also been widely applied within the field of abnormal behavior. The behavioral abnormality resulting from a severe blow to the head is a somatogenic traumatic disease. Moreover, just as a systemic disease may be the malfunctioning of a psychological process, so may external trauma be psychological rather than physical and assault psychological processes rather than physical organs. Psychogenic traumatic disease models have been adopted by behaviorally oriented psychopathologists. For example, Wolpe (1958) relies heavily on an early experiment by Watson and Rayner (1920), in which an infant was rendered fearful of rats by frightening him with a loud noise whenever such an animal was put in his presence. Wolpe adopts this demonstration as a model for the development of all human neuroses. According to this view, phobias develop when a usually innocuous act, such as standing on heights or in open spaces, in some way becomes a traumatic experience, producing extreme anxiety. Thereafter, whenever the person is confronted with similar circumstances, anxiety is aroused. The person soon learns to avoid such situations any time that he can.

The Psychoanalytic Model

Probably the most widespread psychogenic disease model in psychopathology is the psychodynamic or psychoanalytic model, originally developed by Sigmund Freud.

Topography of the Mind

Freud divided the mind or the psyche into three principal parts, the id, ego, and superego; each of these are metaphors for specific functions or energies. The id is present at birth and is the part of the personality that accounts for all the energy to run the psyche. Freud, trained as a neurologist, regarded all energy of the id as being originally biological and then converted by some means into psychic energy, all of it unconscious and below the level of awareness.

Within the id Freud postulated two basic instincts, Eros and Thanatos. The more important is Eros, which Freud saw as a life-integrating force, principally sexual. The energy of the instinct Eros is called libido. Eros, libido, and sexual energy are sometimes indiscriminately equated, but libido and Eros are also occasionally expanded to include all integrative, life-furthering forces, some of which may not be strictly sexual. At any rate, the life energy of the id is present at birth and is continually being converted from biological energy; this libido, the energy of Eros, is for the most part sexual. Thanatos, the death instinct, plays a relatively small role in Freudian thinking, and indeed its energy never received a name.

The id seeks immediate gratification and operates on what Freud called *the pleasure principle.* When the id is not satisfied, tension is produced and the id strives to eliminate this tension as quickly as possible. For example, the infant feels hunger, an aversive drive, and he is impelled to move about, sucking, in order to reduce the tension arising from the unsatisfied drive. This behavior, called reflex activity, is one means by which the id obtains gratification; it represents the organism's first commerce with the environment. The other means is *primary process,* generating images of what is desired. The infant who wants its mother's milk imagines the mother's breast and thereby obtains some short-term satisfaction of the hunger drive through its wish-fulfilling fantasy. The id, with its need to reduce and eliminate tension, seeks a state of quiescence, which, perhaps ironically, can be achieved only in death.

The second part of the personality, primarily conscious and called the ego, begins to develop out of the id in the second six months of life. The ego must deal with reality and hence often attempts to delay the immediate gratification desired by the id. The ego frowns upon primary process, for fantasy will not keep the organism alive. Through its planning and decision-making functions, called *secondary process,* the ego realizes that operating on the pleasure principle at all times, as the id would like to do, may not always be the most effective way of maintaining life. The ego then operates on the *reality principle* as it mediates between the demands of reality and those of the id.

The ego, however, derives all its energy from the id and may be likened to a horseback rider who receives his energy for riding from the horse beneath him. But a real horseback rider directs the horse with his own energy, not depending on that of the horse for his own thinking, planning, and moving. The ego, on the other hand, derives *all* its energies from the id and yet must direct what it is entirely dependent on for energy.

The superego is the third part of the personality, being essentially the carrier of society's moral standards as interpreted by the child's parents. The superego develops through the resolution of the oedipal conflict, to be discussed shortly, and is generally equivalent to what we call conscience. When the id pressures the ego to satisfy its needs, the ego must cope not only with reality constraints but also with the "right-wrong" moral judgments of the superego. The behavior of the human being, as conceptualized by Freud, is thus a complex interplay of three psychic systems, all vying for the achievement of goals that cannot always be reconciled. This interplay of active forces is referred to as the psychodynamics of the personality.

Freud was drawn into studying the mind by his work with Breuer on hypnosis and hysteria. The apparently powerful role played by factors of which patients seemed unaware led Freud to postulate that much of our behavior is determined by forces that are inaccessible to awareness. Both the id instincts are unconscious, and many of the superego's activities are as well. The ego is primarily conscious, for it is the metaphor for the psychic systems that have to do with thinking and planning. But the ego too has important unconscious aspects, the *defense mechanisms* which protect it from anxiety; these will be discussed in Chapter 5. Basically, Freud considered most of the important aspects of behavior to be unconscious.

Freud saw the human personality as a closed energy system; at any one time there is a fixed amount of energy in the id to run the psychic apparatus. The three parts of the personality therefore conflict for a share in a specific amount of energy. Moreover, Freud regarded the mind as totally deterministic. Natural scientist that he was, Freud saw every behavior, even seemingly trivial slips of the tongue, as having specific unconscious causes.

Stages of Psychosexual Development

Freud conceived of the personality apparatus as developing through a series of five separate psychosexual stages. At each stage a different part of the body is the most sensitive to sexual excitation and therefore the most capable of providing libidinal satisfaction to the id. The first is the *oral* stage, during which the infant derives maximum gratification of id impulses from excitation of the sensory endings around the mouth. Sucking and feeding are his principal pleasures. In the second year of life the child enters the *anal* stage as enjoyment shifts to the anus and the elimination and retention of feces. In the *phallic* stage, which extends from age three to age five or six, maximum gratification comes from stimulation of the genitalia. Between ages six to twelve the child is in a *latency* stage, during which the id impulses presumably play little direct role in motivating behavior. The child behaves asexually, although according to Freud's theoretical schema all behavior is *basically* driven by id impulses. The final and adult stage is the *genital,* during which heterosexual interests predominate.

The manner in which the growing person at each stage resolves the conflicts between what the id wants and what the environment will provide determines basic personality traits that will last throughout the person's life. A person who in his anal stage experiences either excessive or deficient amounts of gratification, depending on his toilet training regimen, and thus does not progress beyond this stage, is called an *anal personality.* One type, the anal retentive, is considered stingy and sometimes obsessively clean. These traits, appearing throughout life but receiving the greatest attention in adulthood, when people typically consult psychoanalysts, are traced back to early events and to the manner in which gratification was provided or denied the child. Freud referred to this "freezing" of development at an earlier psychosexual stage as *fixation*.

Perhaps the most important crisis of development occurs during the phallic stage, around age four, for then, Freud asserted, the child is overcome with sexual desire for the parent of the opposite sex. Through the threat of dire punishment from the parent of the same sex, he may repress the entire conflict, unconsciously pushing it into the unconscious. This desire and repression is referred to as the Oedipus complex for the male and the Electra complex for the female. The dilemma is usually resolved through increased identification with the parent of the same sex and through the adoption of society's mores, which forbid the child to desire its parent. Through this learning of moral values the superego is developed.

Freud's theorizing, presented here in bare outline, changed almost continuously over his lifetime. His students and colleagues have also made important changes in psychoanalytic theory. The *ego analysts* in particular dispute the relatively weak role that Freud assigned to the ego. They have concentrated their attention on the independent decision-making and planning functions of this predominantly conscious part of the personality. Ego analysis will be discussed in greater detail in Chapter 18.

The analytic model of abnormal behavior has aspects that correspond to both traumatic and systemic diseases. Freud viewed psychological traumas in childhood as having an important role in producing neurosis in adulthood. One such trauma is the so-called primal scene, when the young child inadvertently witnesses sexual intercourse by par-

ents. Yet in the psychoanalytic model trauma does not produce neurosis by itself. Drives and needs must be intense. In Freud's theory highly intense id impulses substitute for the malfunctioning organ of a systemic disease. As Freud himself put it,

Quantitative disharmonies are what must be responsible for the inadequacy and suffering of neurotics. The determining cause of all forms taken by human mental life is, indeed, to be sought in the reciprocal action between innate dispositions and accidental experiences. Now a particular instinct may be too strong or too weak innately, or a particular capacity may be stunted or insufficiently developed in life [systemic disease]. On the other hand, external impressions and experiences [traumatic disease] may make demands of differing strength on different people; and what one person's constitution can deal with may prove an unmanageable task for another's (1940, pp. 183–184).

Evaluation

In Box 2.1 several specific criticisms of the psychoanalytic disease model are presented. In this section abnormal disease models in general are evaluated. One common criticism is that in examining the abnormal behavior of an individual, there are no independent means of verifying the existence of a disease. In medicine both the symptoms and the factors producing them, that is the disease process, can often be assessed. It is possible for example, to determine that an individual has a temperature of 104 degrees. Moreover, the particular germ or microorganism that has initiated the processes producing the heightened temperature can also be independently determined, say by taking a throat culture and analyzing it to see what foreign organisms are present. When the disease model is applied to abnormal behavior,

1. There are several difficulties in Freud's methodology that are to be found to some extent in *all* case study work. Although we attach considerable importance to case reporting by clinicians who are "on the front line," clinical reporting by its very nature presents several problems that are extremely difficult to avoid. Freud's theorizing, and to a great extent the thinking of the "neo-Freudians," those who have adapted and changed his basic framework, rest *entirely* on case studies. Like many clinicians, Freud did not take careful notes during his sessions and had to rely very heavily on his recollections. The reliability of his perceptions and recollections is impossible to evaluate. Furthermore, the behavior of a listener has been demonstrated to change what the speaker says. For example, Truax (1966) has shown that during supposedly *nondirective* therapy sessions, Carl Rogers (see Chapter 18) selectively attended to certain kinds of verbal statements from clients and ignored others; the frequency of the statements that were attended to increased. It is possible that Freud's patients were similarly conditioned, at least to some degree, to talk about the childhood events that he was most interested in.

2. The inferential leaps that are made by Freud and other psychoanalysts are difficult to accept unless one has a prior commitment to the point of view. The distinction between observation and interpretation is blurred. Consider an example from the analyst Main (1958). "The little boy who babbles tenderly to himself as he soaps himself in his bath does so because he has taken into himself his tender soaping mother." What, in fact, is readily observed by the average onlooker is the child bathing himself. To *see* an incorporation of his mother embodied in the soapy bath play is to operate at a far higher level of inference. The paradigm problem is once again evident. What we perceive is strongly colored by the models we adopt.

3. There is considerable disagreement whether Freud's theorizing should be considered scientific, for it cannot be disproved. Nearly all the concepts are impossible to measure adequately, and few of the statements are very explicit. Moreover, his theories have little predictive value.

however, it is often not possible to assess independently both the symptoms and the supposed cause of the symptoms. Certain behavior or symptoms are categorized as mental illnesses and given names, but then the name of the illness itself is often cited as an explanation for or cause of these same symptoms. For example, a patient who is withdrawn and hallucinating is diagnosed as schizophrenic; however, when we ask why he is withdrawn

4. Freud's findings do not have general applicability because his sample of patients was very selective and small. Nearly all his patients were from the upper middle class of early twentieth-century Vienna, hardly a representative sampling of human beings. Nonetheless, Freud seemed all too ready to apply his findings to all mankind. In a related vein, after making limited observations, Freud held that a repressed homosexual inclination was the basis for all paranoid disorder. But he never considered, nor for that matter have others who have accepted his point of view, how many paranoids have had homosexual desires in the past and, indeed, how many people with repressed homosexuality do not develop into paranoids.

5. Although Freud insisted that he used concepts like id, ego, superego, and the unconscious as metaphors to describe psychic functions, they seem reified, that is, they are made into independent, behavior-determining agents whose own actions must still be explained. For example, Freud speaks of " . . . immediate and unheeding satisfaction of the instincts, such as the id demands. . . . The id knows no solicitude about ensuring survival . . . " (1937, p. 56). Thus the id "demands" immediate satisfaction and "knows" certain things. In spite of the occasional reminders in psychoanalytic writings that these concepts are meant as metaphors, or as summary statements of functions, they are typically written about as if they had an existence of their own and had a power to push things around, to think, and to act.

It should be obvious by now that the authors of this book view the validity and usefulness of Freud's work with considerable skepticism. On the other hand, it would be a serious mistake to minimize his importance in psychopathology or, for that matter, in the intellectual history of Western civilization. Freud was an astute observer of human nature. His work has also elicited the kind of critical reaction that helps to advance knowledge. He was instrumental in getting people to consider nonphysiological explanations for disordered behavior. Although we may sometimes wish his influence were not so strong, it is nonetheless difficult to acquire a good grasp of the field of abnormal psychology without some familiarity with his writings.

and hallucinating, we are often told that it is because he is schizophrenic. Thus the label schizophrenia is applied to certain behavior and then in addition is specified as a cause of this same behavior, a clear example of circular reasoning.

Although our criticism of the manner in which mental illnesses are assessed is reasonable, it is not always entirely applicable. Someone holding a medical or disease model point of view could take a somewhat more sophisticated position. He could assert that we may make a diagnosis of schizophrenia on the basis of symptoms without claiming that these symptoms are also produced by the presence of schizophrenia. He would propose that although we do not know the cause of the symptoms, such knowledge will eventually be forthcoming. Some deviant chemical may eventually be located within schizophrenics that will reveal the cause of the disorder. In sum, the more sophisticated disease modeler may acknowledge that we currently have little information about causes but that when such information becomes available, it will, in principle, be possible to assess independently both the symptoms and the etiology as is the case in medicine. In a sense he is making his best bet on the likelihood that an aberrant factor will ultimately be discovered and that the pursuit of this factor is facilitated by placing certain individuals into particular diagnostic categories, such as schizophrenia, and then looking for the internal or traumatic causes.

A second common criticism of applying medical models to abnormal behavior involves an alleged difference between the symptoms of physical illness and the symptoms of mental illness. This argument, most often associated with Thomas Szasz (1960), holds that so-called mental symptoms are a patient's communications about himself and others. When we call such statements symptoms, Szasz asserts, we are making a judgment within a particular social and cultural context. For example, a patient's belief that he is Christ might be enough for an observer to make a diagnosis of paranoid schizophrenia. Even in this extreme case, however, the diagnosis depends on the observer's disbelieving the patient's assertion. If the observer gives credence to the patient's assertion, the behavior will clearly not be judged a symptom of mental illness.

In evaluating this criticism, we should consider the allegation by Szasz and his followers that the symptoms of mental illness are *subjective,* whereas those of physical illness are *objective.* This assertion has some merit, but the distinction is not as clear-cut as Szasz would have it (Ausubel, 1961b). For example, a patient who has entered a physician's office may complain that he is suffering pain. But because tolerance of pain differs widely among individuals, how can the physician determine the actual amount of pain the patient in his consulting room is experiencing? Although the importance of subjective factors as they enter into the definition of so-called mental illness should not be minimized, to distinguish between mental and physical illnesses on this basis is questionable. Subjective factors appear to be heavily implicated in judging the presence of physical diseases as well.

Finally, many people have alleged that so-called mental illnesses have neither a specific etiology nor a specific set of symptoms and thus do not qualify as diseases (for example, Milton and Wahler, 1969). Our knowledge of the etiologies of psychopathologies is indeed extremely limited. The fact that these etiologies have not been uncovered as yet, however, does not necessarily mean that we should stop looking for them.

Our failure to define specific sets of symptoms in many categories of deviant behavior may be a more damning criticism. Evidence has accumulated that specific syndromes are simply not to be found for all psychopathologies. Again, however, a person wishing to maintain a medical model for mental illness may counter this criticism with the following line of reasoning. Many medical diseases do *not* have a set of specific symptoms. Paresis is a good example. Before it was discovered to be infectious, there was considerable debate about whether the symptoms had a physical cause or whether paresis should be considered a psychological disturbance. Proponents of the psychological view argued that the symptoms were not entirely consistent from one person to another, for some patients suffer depression rather than delusions of grandeur. Therefore they did not consider paresis a medical disease. Although paresis was indeed found to have a *single* causal agent, the manifestations of its *later* stage may *differ markedly from patient to patient*. Thus even an infectious disease may not necessarily have a homogeneous set of symptoms.

Any judgment made on the basis of the information just presented is a good illustration of how subjective factors may have to be resorted to in science. The medical model is subject to many potential criticisms. For each of these, however, there is a possible rejoinder. Since we do not have the data available to evaluate completely many of these criticisms, the individual scientist is left largely on his own to choose among the various medical models. After you have been exposed to some of the data relating to the clinical categories, you will be in a better position to make your own evaluations.

BEHAVIORISM AND LEARNING MODELS

The Rise of Behaviorism

Before we discuss learning models, it will be helpful to trace briefly the rise of behaviorism within psychology. Early twentieth-century psychology was dominated by the view that the proper subject of study was conscious experience. The goal of psychology was to learn more about what was going on in people's minds. To do this psychologists used what is called the *introspective method*. Trained subjects were asked to report on their conscious experience. What, for example, is the experience "red" like? During this same period a controversy raged about whether thought did or did not always involve images. Such a controversy was, of course, extremely difficult to resolve and, even with the advances that have been made, is still unsolved today. But because introspection provided no means of settling this question at that time, psychologists became discouraged with it as a method and began to question the definition of psychology as the study of conscious experience. This dissatisfaction was brought to a head by John B. Watson (Figure 2.3), who in 1913 revolutionized psychology with statements such as the following.

Psychology as the behaviorist views it is a purely objective branch of natural science. Its theoretical goal is the prediction and control of behavior. Introspection forms no essential part of its methods, nor is the scientific value of its data dependent upon the readiness with which they lend themselves to interpretation in terms of consciousness (p. 158).

To replace introspection, Watson looked to the work of contemporary psychologists who were concerned with learning. In this way learning rather than thinking became the dominant focus of psychology in the post-Watsonian period. The task of psychology was

FIGURE **2.3**
John B. Watson (1878–1958), American psychologist, who was influential in making psychology the study of observable behavior rather than an investigation of subjective experience.

now viewed as an attempt to obtain information about which stimuli would elicit which responses. With such information it was hoped that human behavior could be both predicted and controlled.

With the focus of psychology now on learning, a vast amount of research and theorizing was generated. Two types of learning soon began to attract the research efforts of psychologists. The first type, *classical conditioning,* had initially been discovered by the Russian physiologist Ivan Pavolv at the turn of the century (Figure 2.4). In his studies of the digestive process, he noticed that when a dog is given meat powder, he salivates instinctively, without prior learning. Since the meat powder automatically elicits salivation, the powder was termed an *unconditioned stimulus* (UCS), and the response of salivation was termed an *unconditioned response* (UCR). More importantly, however, Pavlov found that when presentation of the unconditioned stimulus was preceded several times by a neutral stimulus such as the ringing of a bell (Figure 2.5), the tone itself (the *conditioned stimulus,* CS) was able to elicit a salivary response (the

FIGURE **2.4**
Ivan P. Pavlov (1849–1936), Russian physiologist and Nobel Laureate, responsible for extensive research and theory in classical conditioning. His influence is still very strong in Soviet psychology.

INTRODUCTION AND BASIC ISSUES

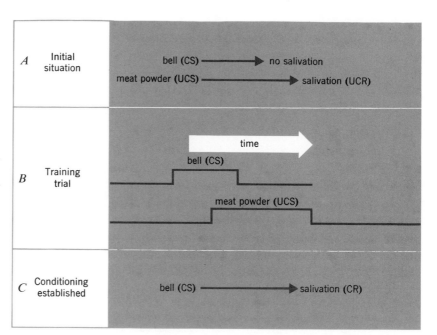

FIGURE 2.5

The process of classical conditioning: (A) before learning the meat powder (UCS) elicits salivation (UCR), but the bell (CS) does not; (B) a training or learning trial consists of presentations of the CS, followed closely by the UCS; (C) classical conditioning has been accomplished when the previously neutral bell elicits salivation (CR).

conditioned response,[2] CR). Figure 2.6A is a typical *learning curve.* As the number of paired presentations of the tone and the meat powder increases, the number of salivations elicited by the bell increases. The *extinction curve* in Figure 2.6B indicates what happens to the established CR when the repeated soundings of the tone are later not followed up by the administration of meat powder. Fewer and fewer salivations are elicited, and the CR is extinguished rather rapidly.

The case of the infant Albert and the white rat (Watson and Rayner, 1920), referred to earlier as an example of a psychogenic traumatic disease model, indicates the possible relation between classical conditioning and the development of certain emotional disorders, in this instance a phobia. Albert, an eleven-month-old boy, was shown a white rat. At first

he indicated no fear of the animal and appeared to want to play with it. But whenever he reached for the rat, the experimenter made a loud noise (the UCS) by striking a steel bar behind Albert's head, causing him great fright (the UCR). After five such experiences Albert became very disturbed by the sight of the white rat, even when the steel bar was not struck. The fear initially associated with the loud noise had come to be elicited by the previously neutral stimulus, the white rat (now the CS).

The second principal type of learning, *instrumental learning,* draws primarily on the work of Edward Thorndike. Rather than investigating the association between stimuli as Pavlov had done, Thorndike was interested in the effect of consequences on behavior. From his early work with cats, he formulated what was to become an extremely important principle, the law of effect: behavior that is followed by consequences satisfying to the organism will be repeated, but behavior that is followed by noxious or unpleasant consequences will be

[2] Recent research (for example, Kimble, 1961) has suggested that the CR is sometimes different from the UCR. Such subtleties, although important for the learning theorist, are relatively unimportant for our purposes and are beyond the scope of this book.

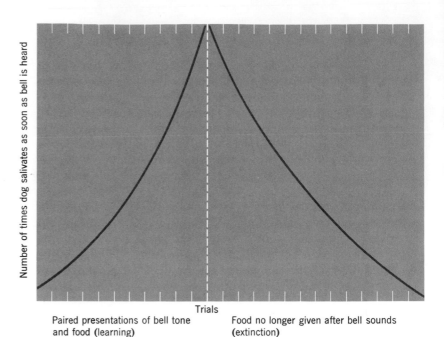

FIGURE **2.6**
Classical conditioning:
(A) typical learning curve;
(B) typical extinction curve.

(Figure labels)
Number of times dog salivates as soon as bell is heard

Trials

Paired presentations of bell tone and food (learning)

A

Food no longer given after bell sounds (extinction)

B

discouraged. Thus the behavior or response that has consequences serves as an instrument, encouraging or discouraging its own repetition. This basic principle has been extensively applied in more recent work by B. F. Skinner (Figure 2.7). The goal of Skinner (1953) and the Skinnerians, like that of Watson, is the prediction and control of behavior. These experimenters hope that by analyzing behavior in terms of stimuli, responses, and consequences, they will be able to determine when certain responses will occur. The information gathered should then help to indicate how behavior develops and how it can be changed. In the Skinnerian approach, often called the operant approach because it studies behavior that operates on the environment, abstract terms are avoided. For example, common words such as need, motivation, and wants are conspicuously absent in Skinnerian writings. To provide an entirely satisfactory account of human behavior, Skinner believes that psychology must restrict its attention to directly observable stimuli, responses, and consequences or reinforcements.

In a prototypical operant conditioning experiment a hungry rat might be placed in a box which has a bar located at one end (the well-known "Skinner box"). Initially the rat will explore his new environment and, by chance, will come close to the bar. At this time the experimenter may drop a food pellet into the receptacle located near the bar. After a few such rewards the animal will come to spend more and more time in the area around the bar. But now the experimenter drops a pellet into the receptacle only when the rat happens to touch the bar. After capitalizing on a few chance touches that are rewarded, the rat begins to touch the bar frequently. With bar touching well established, the experimenter can make the criterion for reward more stringent. The animal must actually press the bar. Thus the desired behavior, bar pressing, is gradually *shaped* by a process of *successive approximations*. The number of bar presses

44

increases as soon as they become the criterion for the release of pellets and decreases as soon as the pellet is no longer dropped into the receptacle after a bar press (Figure 2.8).

In recent years there has been an increased interest in yet a third type of learning, *modeling*. We all realize that we learn by watching and imitating others. Experimental work has proved that witnessing someone perform certain activities can increase or decrease diverse kinds of behavior, such as sharing, aggression, and fear. For example, Bandura and Menlove (1968) used a modeling treatment to reduce fear of dogs in children. After witnessing a fearless model engage in various interactions with a dog, initially fearful children showed a marked increase in their willingness to approach and interact with a dog.

As with the medical model, there is no single learning model. Although some investigators (Ullmann and Krasner, 1969; Bijou and Baer, 1961) equate learning approaches to behavior with a strict Skinnerian behaviorism, by no means do all learning theorists avoid the use of *mediating constructs*, such as drives and beliefs, or limit themselves to the operant approach. These theorists also consider themselves behaviorists and have contributed importantly to the study of internal states and overt behavior within what is often referred to as a mediational framework. In *mediation theory* a stimulus does not initiate a direct response but instead activates an intervening process which in turn initiates the response. The mediating construct is thus a thought or other internal process, an entity inferred as actually existing, although it cannot be observed. In this instance learning theorists work within a paradigm holding that, under certain conditions, it is legitimate to go beyond the observables. In physics and chemistry scientists similarly make ample and effective use of variables that are not directly observ-

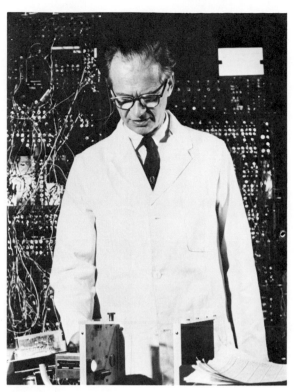

FIGURE **2.7**
B. F. Skinner (1904–   ), perhaps the most influential living psychologist, responsible for the in-depth study of operant behavior and for the extension of experimental findings to American education and society as a whole.

able but whose existence is guessed at or inferred. Considerable attention is paid to this paradigm in Chapter 4.

The Learning Model of Deviant Behavior

We are now ready to examine the implications of applying behavioral principles to the study of deviant behavior. The crucial point of learning approaches is the assumption that abnormal behavior is learned in the same manner as most other human behavior. This view minimizes the importance of biological and genetic

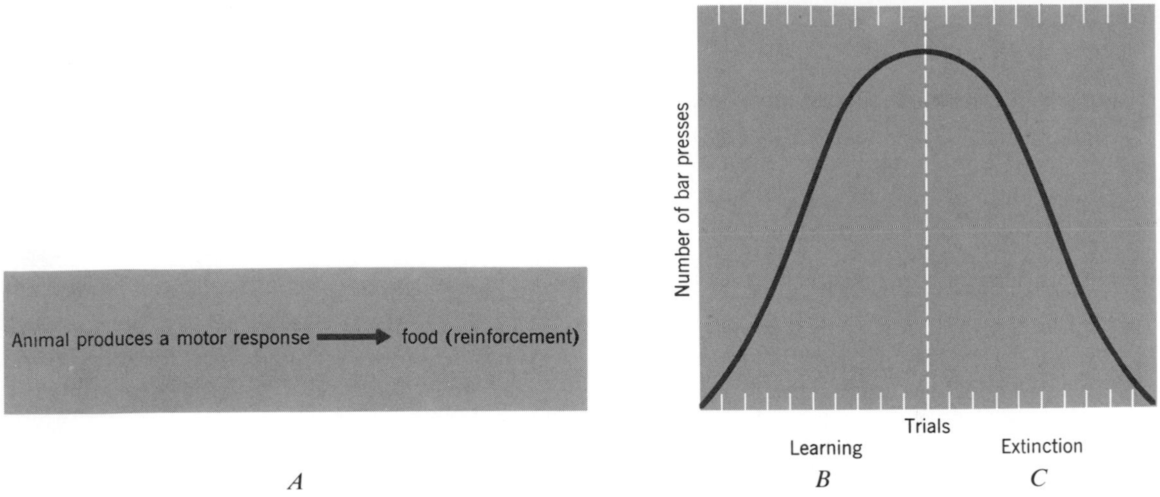

FIGURE **2.8**

(*A*) *Operant conditioning, or instrumental learning, is concerned with the development and maintenance of behavior as a function of its consequences; (B) a typical learning curve, showing increases in responding when the operant behavior is reinforced; (C) a typical extinction curve, showing decreases in responding when the accustomed reward is withheld.*

factors and thus is primarily a psychogenic position. In adopting the learning approach, the focus clearly becomes the elucidation of the learning processes that produced the maladaptive behavior. The gap between normal and abnormal behavior is reduced since both are viewed within the same general framework; thus a bridge is forged between general experimental psychology and the field of abnormal psychology. Moreover, according to many who have adopted the learning model, abnormality is a *relativistic* concept. Labeling someone or some behavior as abnormal is inextricably linked to a particular social or cultural context. For example, hallucinating may be grounds for commitment to a mental institution in the United States. Some African tribes, however, depend on the trances and visions of their witch doctors and shamans to cure the sick and control events affecting their welfare.

One very important advantage of applying the learning view in psychopathology is the increased precision of the observations made.

Stimuli must be carefully measured, responses reliably recorded, and relationships among stimuli, responses, and outcomes carefully noted. Although we judge this and other features of learning models of deviant behavior to be extremely advantageous, it is difficult to persuade those not already committed to the paradigm that the model is adequate. The learning model of abnormal behavior is in much the same position as the medical model. In the medical model of deviant behavior the disease processes have not been uncovered. Similarly, as will be documented in later chapters, in the learning model abnormality has not yet been shown to result from particular learning experiences. Although adopting a learning explanation of abnormal behavior has clearly led to many treatment innovations in the past decade (see Chapter 19), the effectiveness of these treatments does not bear on the adequacy of the learning account of the particular deviant behavior in question. The fact that a treatment based on learning principles is effective in changing behavior does *not* show that the behavior was itself learned in a similar way. For example, if the mood of depressed persons is elevated by providing them with rewards for increased activity, this fact cannot be considered evidence that the depression was initially produced by an absence of rewards (Rimland, 1964). The logical problem may perhaps be made clearer by another example. Because electroconvulsive shock treatment temporarily relieves depression, it does not follow that depression is produced by not receiving electroshock during the formative years.

Finally, the medical and learning approaches may not be as distinct from each other as has been claimed. We have already seen how the classical conditioning of a phobia (Watson and Rayner, 1920) can be regarded as an example of a traumatic mental disease. The unconditioned stimulus functions as a trauma which produces an unrealistic fear of the previously neutral stimulus. If we may venture an observation, the often vehement rejection of the "medical model" by many behaviorists may reflect not so much a dispassionate consideration of the available data as a human desire to create a paradigm sharply differentiated from what has held sway for some time. We do not, however, mean to suggest that there are *no* important differences between medical and learning approaches (Table 2.2), only that the differences are not as clear-cut as generally assumed.

CONSEQUENCES OF ADOPTING A MODEL

The student of abnormal behavior who adopts a particular model necessarily makes a priori decisions concerning what kinds of data he will collect and how he will interpret them. Thus he may very well ignore possibilities and overlook other data in advancing what seems to him the most probable explanation. A behaviorist is prone to attribute the prevalence of schizophrenia in lower-class groups to the paucity of social rewards that these people have received, his assumption being that normal development requires a certain amount and patterning of reinforcement. A systemic disease modeler will be quick to remind the behaviorist of the many deprived people who do *not* become schizophrenic. The behaviorist will undoubtedly counter with the argument that those who do not become schizophrenic had different reinforcement histories. The system disease modeler will reply that such *post hoc* or after the fact statements can always be made. Indeed, data to support the behaviorist position have not been found.

Our systemic disease modeler may suggest that certain biochemical factors which predispose both to schizophrenia and to deficiencies in intellectual skills necessary to maintain occupational status account for the observed correlation between social class and schizophrenia. The learning modeler will be entirely justified in reminding the disease modeler that these alleged factors have yet to be found, to which the disease modeler might rightfully answer, "Yes, but I'm placing my bets that they are there, and if I adopt *your* behavioral model, I may not look for them." To which the learning theorist may with justification reply, "Yes, but *your* assumption regarding biochemical factors makes it less likely that you will look for and uncover the subtle reinforcement factors that in all likelihood account for both the presence and the ab-

TABLE **2.2** *Critical Assumptions of the Disease and Learning Models*

Medical disease model	Learning model
1. Symptoms are produced by disease entities located within the organism, except for those of the traumatic disease model.	"Symptoms" are behaviors; disease entities are irrelevant.
2. The focus is on biological *or* internal dynamic processes as causal agents.	The focus is on environmental eliciting conditions, possible maintaining consequences, and learning as causal agents.
3. Sociological and cultural factors are deemphasized.	Sociological and cultural factors are emphasized.

sence of what you call schizophrenia."

The fact that our two colleagues are in a sense correct and in another sense incorrect is at the same time both exasperating and exciting. They are both correct in asserting that certain data are more likely to be found within a particular paradigm. But they are incorrect to become unduly agitated about the fact that not every social scientist is making the same assumptions about what factors will ultimately be found crucial in the development of mental disorders. Our view is that the field of abnormal behavior is too diverse to be explained adequately by any of our current models. As

we subsequently examine various categories of psychopathology, we will find substantial differences in the extent to which disease or learning models are applicable. And we will often see that the only reasonable way of looking at the data is to assume multiple causation. A particular disorder may very well develop through an interaction of learning and biological factors. As for future discoveries, it is well that psychologists do *not* agree on which paradigm is the *best*. We know far too little to make hard-and-fast decisions on the exclusive superiority of any one paradigm, and there is enough important work to go around.

SUMMARY

This chapter has reviewed the major models used to conceptualize abnormal behavior. The statistical model defines abnormality as a low frequency of occurrence but does not provide us with any means of determining which

behaviors should be assessed. The medical or disease models assume that abnormal behavior can best be viewed as a disease resulting from an internal malfunction (infectious and systemic models) or an external agent (traumatic

INTRODUCTION AND BASIC ISSUES

model). The disorder can be either soma-togenic or psychogenic. Learning models focus on psychopathology as learned behavior. The Skinnerian learning model eschews using terms that refer to internal states. Other learning models, however, have adopted a mediational approach which often brings them closer to a disease model in the way abnormal behavior is construed. The data available at this time do not allow any simple decisions to be made about which model is correct. In fact, it seems unlikely that any one of the current models can adequately account for the great range of behavior considered to be the domain of abnormal psychology. We know too little to adhere solely to any one model.

CHAPTER 3

The Classification of Abnormal Behavior

By the end of the nineteenth century, medicine had progressed far beyond the stage it had been in during the Middle Ages when virtually all physical problems were treated by a common technique, bloodletting. It was gradually recognized that different sorts of problems required different treatments. Diagnostic procedures were improved, diseases subclassified, and applicable treatments administered. Impressed by the successes that new diagnostic procedures had effected in the field of medicine, investigators of abnormal behavior also sought to develop classification schemes by which various symptoms could be grouped into separate categories. Moreover, advances in other sciences such as botany and chemistry had followed the development of classification systems, suggesting that such efforts in the field of abnormal behavior might bring similar progress.

In this chapter we shall first review the diagnostic system of the American Psychiatric Association, which relies much an Kraepelin's groupings of mental disorders and also incorporates many psychoanalytic concepts. Although the system has been revised several times, we shall examine only the most recent one, Diagnostic and Statistical Manual (DSM) II (1968). Then we shall examine some criticisms both of the general concept of classification and of the system itself. Finally, we shall direct our attention to several assessment procedures that provide the data on which diagnostic decisions are based.

THE DIAGNOSTIC SYSTEM OF THE AMERICAN PSYCHIATRIC ASSOCIATION

The current diagnostic system has six major categories and numerous subcategories of abnormal behavior. Table 3.1 outlines only the major classes and subcategories. Subsequent chapters will treat the subcategories in greater detail.

TABLE 3.1 *List of DSM-II Diagnoses*

> I. Mental Retardation
> II. Organic Brain Syndromes
>   A. Psychoses
>   B. Nonpsychotic disorders
> III. Psychoses Not Attributed to Physical Conditions Listed Previously
>   A. Schizophrenia
>   B. Major affective disorders
>   C. Paranoid states
> IV. Neuroses
> V. Personality Disorders and Certain Other Nonpsychotic Mental Disorders
>   A. Personality disorders
>   B. Sexual deviation
>   C. Alcoholism
>   D. Drug dependence
> VI. Psychophysiological Disorders

1. *Mental retardation.* In the diagnostic manual mental retardation is defined as subnormal intellectual functioning associated with impairments in learning, social adjustment, and maturation. The manual specifies that the impairment may be attributed to one of several factors such as infection, gross brain disease, chromosomal abnormality, and environmental deprivation. Within the general category of retardation, various degrees are specified, ranging from borderline to profound.

2. *Organic brain syndromes.* Organic brain disorders are caused by impaired brain functioning that is attributed to tissue or structural lesions. Many human capacities such as intelligence, memory, and the emotions may of course be affected by brain dysfunction. A psychotic organic brain syndrome is defined in the following way. "Patients are described as psychotic when their mental functioning is sufficiently impaired to interfere grossly with their capacity to meet the ordinary demands of life. . . . Deficits in perception, language and memory may be so severe that the patient's capacity for mental grasp of the situation is effectively lost" (American Psychiatric Association, 1968, p. 23). Brain dysfunctions that are not severe enough to produce behavior categorized as psychotic according to the preceding definition constitute nonpsychotic brain syndromes.

3. *Psychoses not attributed to physical conditions.* The definition of this large and important category of deviant behavior is identical to that of psychoses attributable to brain dysfunctions. The important difference is that they are *not* considered to be caused by the physical conditions that produce organic brain syndromes. There are three major distinctions within the general category of psychosis.

   Schizophrenia. A group of disorders characterized by a break down of integrated emotion, thought, and behavior and by withdrawal from human contact and reality.

The major affective disorders. Severely disabling disturbances of mood and feeling.

Paranoid states. Disorders in which the patient either has delusions or mistaken beliefs that he is being persecuted or holds grandiose ideas about himself.

4. *Neuroses.* According to DSM-II the principal characteristic of a neurosis is conscious or unconscious anxiety. There are no gross distortions of reality, nor is the personality significantly disorganized. As with other major categories, several distinctions are made.

Anxiety neurosis. Pervasive or freefloating anxiety, without apparent object or cause.

Hysterical neurosis. An involuntary loss of the function of a part of the body or alterations in consciousness, such as amnesia or sleepwalking.

Phobic neurosis. An intense fear of an object or situation that the patient recognizes as presenting no real danger to himself.

Obsessive-compulsive neurosis. Preoccupation with persistent, unwarranted thoughts, or the compulsion to repeat a certain act again and again.

Depressive neurosis. A deep, prolonged, and excessive sadness caused by some external circumstance such as the loss of a loved one.

5. *Personality disorders and certain other nonpsychotic disorders.* Personality disorders are defined as "deeply ingrained" maladaptive patterns of behavior that are different from those observed in psychoses and neuroses.[1] Included in this category are motivational and social maladjustments such as sexual deviations, drug dependencies, and alcoholism. In addition, many disorders previously noted in the psychotic and neurotic categories are found within this category in what appear to be somewhat less debilitating forms. For example, within this general category are subcategories such as paranoid personality, obsessive-compulsive personality, and hysterical personality.

6. *Psychophysiological disorders.* These disorders are characterized by physical symptoms produced in part by emotional factors. Various organ systems may be implicated. For example, the respiratory system may be debilitated by asthma, the cardiovascular system by high blood pressure, the gastrointestinal system by ulcers, the genitourinary system by impotency, and the skin by hives.

---

[1] The DSM-II does not explain very well how personality disorders are different from neuroses and psychoses. For example, obsessive-compulsive personality is defined as " . . . excessive concern with conformity and adherence to standards of conscience. Consequently, individuals in this group may be rigid, over-inhibited, over-conscientious, over-dutiful, and unable to relax easily. This disorder may lead to an *obsessive compulsive neurosis,* from which it must be distinguished" (p. 43). Exactly *how* to distinguish an obsessive-compulsive personality from an obsessive-compulsive neurosis is not spelled out.

ISSUES IN THE CLASSIFICATION OF ABNORMAL BEHAVIOR

The preceding review of the major categories of abnormal behavior has been brief, for they will be examined in more detail throughout this volume. On the basis of this overview, however, we may scrutinize the usefulness of the system as it exists today. In recent years the diagnosis of mental disorders has been frequently attacked. Two major lines of criticism can be distinguished. One group of critics argue that classification per se is irrelevant to the field of abnormal behavior. These cr[...] hold that there is a *continuum* ranging fr[...] adjustment to maladjustment and consider d[...] crete judgments irrelevant. The second group of critics find specific deficiencies in the current diagnostic system.

Classification Views: Pro and Con

Those opposed to classifying argue that whenever we do so we lose information and hence overlook some of the uniqueness of the subject being studied. To understand this argument better, let us take a simple example of casting dice. Any of the numbers one through six may come up on a given toss of a single die. Let us suppose, however, that we classify each outcome as odd or even. Whenever a one, three, or five comes up on a roll, we call out "odd," and whenever a two, four, or six appears, we say "even." Unless whoever is listening is himself looking at the die, he will not know whether the call "odd" refers to a one, three, or five. Nor will he know whether a two, four, or six has turned up when he hears the call "even." In classification some information must inevitably be lost.

What matters, however, is whether the information lost is relevant, which in turn depends on the *purposes* of the classification system. Any classification system is designed to group together objects having a common property and to ignore differences among the objects that are not relevant to the purposes at hand. If our intention is merely to count odd and even rolls, it is irrelevant whether a die comes up one, three, or five or two, four, or six. In judging abnormal behavior, however, we cannot so easily decide what is wheat and what is chaff, for the relevant and irrelevant dimen-

sio[...] [beha]vior are uncertain. Thus [...] y, we may indeed be [...] her on rather trivial bases [...] remely important differences [...] [al]so be argued that classification, [sinc]e it must consist of entities, does not [allo]w the continuity between normal and abnormal behavior to be taken into consideration. Those who advance this argument hold that abnormal behavior and normal behavior differ only in intensity or degree and not in kind. Therefore the discrete diagnostic categories of DSM-II foster a false impression of discontinuity. Rimland (1969) has summarized this position and, in our opinion, effectively criticized it.

. . . the idea is that if it is difficult to make a distinction between two neighboring points on a hypothetical continuum, no valid distinctions can thereafter be made even at the extremes of the continuum. There are thus persons who would argue that the existence of several variations of gray precludes a distinction between black and white. Hokum. While I will agree that some patients in mental hospitals are saner than nonpatients, and that it is sometimes hard to distinguish between deep unhappiness and psychotic depression, I do not agree that the difficulty sometimes encountered in making the distinction between normal and abnormal necessarily invalidates all such distinctions (pp. 716–717).

In other words, the fact that some distinctions are difficult to make, such as deciding whether sundown is night or day, does not mean that it is impossible to distinguish between noon and midnight.

Another problem of classification lies in its application. Clinicians working within an illness model may tend to see pathology even

A recent study by Rosenhan (1973) illustrates in dramatic fashion the tendency of mental health practitioners to consider patients mentally ill, whatever their behavior. Over a period of three years Rosenhan arranged for eight sane people to be admitted to various psychiatric hospitals across the country. Care was taken to ensure that none of the participants had had psychiatric problems or was otherwise malfunctioning. Each pseudopatient complained at the admissions desk of hearing voices that said "empty," "hollow," and "thud." Otherwise he reported accurately his own life history and, except when his employment was related to mental health, his actual occupation. A pseudonym was also used to prevent the upcoming psychiatric hospitalization from being a handicap to the person in the future.

In no instance did any of the staff detect that this pseudopatient was actually quite sane, even though, immediately after admission was secured, *the pseudopatient stopped talking about the alleged hallucinations and behaved in his usual fashion.* The anxiety of the initial period after admission, which was felt by all the participants, quickly disappeared; if anything, the pseudopatients tended to be somewhat bored. The only instances of detection were those made by the actual hospitalized patients.

Rosenhan comments on the tendency of those who think within an illness model to interpret almost any behavior as a *presumed* illness. What is particularly striking about Rosenhan's study is that the behavior of the pseudopatients was completely unremarkable. The only basis for construing their behavior as abnormal was the fact that they were encountered as patients in a psychiatric ward.

where it does not exist (see Box 3.1). A humorous story, but one with potentially serious consequences, illustrates well how a paradigm can destroy perspective and in this instance even common sense.

A patient hospitalized for anxiety and depression was observed by both the ward psychiatrist and the patient's own therapist. The ward psychiatrist eventually came to feel that the man was hallucinating and reported to the therapist what he considered the significant incident. The previous day, in talking about how depressed he had been feeling, the patient had looked behind him, up toward the ceiling, and declared "It's that little black cloud following me around." On the basis of this comment the ward psychiatrist suggested changing the diag-

INTRODUCTION AND BASIC ISSUES

nosis of the patient's condition from a neurosis to a psychosis.

The therapist, however, had observed no signs of psychosis and decided to investigate further. The next time the therapist visited the patient, he queried him: "Can you tell me a little bit about the black cloud that you mentioned to Dr. X the other day?" The patient looked at him quizzically for a long moment and then asked "You mean that black thing hovering over my left shoulder and my head? Well, what would you like to know about it?" As a more precise description of the cloud was requested, the patient grinned broadly and asked rhetorically, "Haven't you ever heard of a metaphor?"

Many societal decisions are made on the basis of the judgments rendered by mental health professionals. In other circumstances a poorly conceived opinion such as that of the ward psychiatrist might have prevailed, and the patient might have been legally committed to an institution for the insane.

Assuming that differences among various types of abnormal behavior do exist, however, it is essential to classify them, for these differences may constitute keys to the causes and treatments of the various deviant behaviors. For example, one form of mental retardation, phenylketonuria, is attributable to a deficiency in the metabolism of the protein phenylalanine, resulting in the release of incomplete metabolites which injure the brain. One means of treatment is to provide a phenylalanine-free diet. As Mendels (1970) has noted, however,

. . . had we taken 100, or even 1000, people with mental deficiency and placed them all on the phenylalanine-free diet, the response would have been insignificant and the diet would have been discarded as a treatment. It was first necessary to recognize a subtype of mental deficiency, phenylketonuria, and then

subject the value of a phenylalanine-free diet to investigation in this specific population, for whom it has been shown to have value in preventing the development of mental deficiency (p. 35).

Forming classes may thus further knowledge, for once a class is formed, additional information may be ascertained about it. Even though the class is only an asserted and not a proven entity, it may still be heuristically useful in that it facilitates the acquisition of new information. For example, we have just reviewed the definitions proposed in the diagnostic manual of the American Psychiatric Association. Only after a class has been formed can people who fit its definition be studied in hopes of uncovering factors responsible for the development of their problems and treatments to cure them.

Criticisms of the Current Diagnostic System, DSM-II

More specific criticisms are commonly made of the current psychiatric classification scheme. Although the studies to be discussed were done on the previous classification system of the American Psychiatric Association, DSM-I, the two editions are so similar that there is no reason to expect that the findings are not applicable to DSM-II. The principal complaints are that the diagnostic classes are heterogeneous and that they are neither reliable nor valid.

Heterogeneity Within Diagnostic Classes

In a classification scheme each grouping that categorizes a person and his particular pattern of behavior must convey specific and discriminating information about that person. If we know that a given patient is classified as "obsessive-compulsive neurotic," the system is useful only if membership in that category reveals something specific about the patient that differentiates him from nonmembers of the class. One of the defining characteristics of an obsessive-compulsive are the intrusive thoughts which the patient seems unable to control. For example, he may continually worry about the presence of germs. In order for the relation between this symptom and its category to be truly meaningful, people *not* diagnosed as obsessive-compulsive should *not* display this particular kind of behavior. By the same token, intrusive thoughts should be found in any and all persons diagnosed as obsessive-compulsive. To state this point another way, whenever a class is formed, the behavior of all its members should be similar along the dimensions distinguishing the classification. Thus, pursuing the example, if we were to examine a group of people who had been labeled obsessive neurotics, we would expect all of them to have intrusive thoughts. Others not classified as obsessive neurotics should *not* have intrusive thoughts.

Science, alas, is a difficult taskmaster, for recent research indicates that this important criterion of homogeneity is frequently not met. For example, in a well-known study Zigler and Phillips (1961) found that knowing what diagnostic category a patient falls into tells relatively little about the actual behavior of the person. Similarly, they found that certain symptoms appeared in a number of diagnostic categories, thus making it difficult to move reliably from a specific symptom to a specific diagnostic category.

Table 3.2 summarizes the principal findings of the study Zigler and Phillips conducted on 793 patients. After reviewing the hospital records, these investigators categorized the patients into four relatively broad diagnostic groups. The relationship between various symptoms and categories turned out to be so indefinite that membership in a particular category conveyed relatively little information about the symptoms of the patient. As indicated in the second line of the table, for example, each diagnostic category contained a substantial number of patients who were rated as tense: 32 percent of the manic depressives, 46 percent of the psychoneurotics, 33 percent of the character disorders, and 36 percent of the schizophrenics. Thus knowing only that a patient was tense tells us very little about the category to which he was assigned. Similarly, knowing that a person was schizophrenic allows us to make only a rather poor guess whether or not the individual was regarded as tense, for the table shows that only 36 percent of the schizophrenics were considered to have this symptom. Moreover, all the percentages for tenseness are within fourteen points of one another, although many of the other characteristics do show a wider range from category to category.

Although these data raise a serious question about DSM-II, they do not totally negate its usefulness. We would suppose the symptom of depression to characterize many manic-depressives and psychoneurotics, and indeed the figures of 64 percent and 58 percent respectively bear out our expectations. Again, since one of the subcategories of schizophrenia is paranoid schizophrenia, characterized by suspiciousness, it is not surprising that 65 percent of the schizophrenics in this study were regarded as suspicious. This figure is substantially and significantly greater than the percentage figures for suspiciousness in the other three categories.

Furthermore, we must keep in mind that the four diagnostic categories used by Zigler and Phillips were indeed *very broad,* and thus their study cannot be considered a definitive test of

TABLE **3.2** *Percentage of Individuals in Each Diagnostic Category Showing Particular Symptoms*
(*from Zigler and Phillips, 1961*)

Symptom	All patients (N = 793)	Manic-depressive (N = 75)	Psycho-neurotic (N = 152)	Character disorder (N = 279)	Schizo-phrenic (N = 287)
Depressed	38	64	58	31	28
Tense	37	32	46	33	36
Suspiciousness	35	25	16	17	65
Drinking	19	17	14	32	8
Hallucinations	19	11	4	12	35
Suicidal attempt	16	24	19	15	12
Suicidal ideas	15	29	23	15	8
Bodily complaints	15	21	21	5	19
Emotional outburst	14	17	12	18	9
Withdrawn	14	4	12	7	25
Perplexed	14	9	9	8	24
Assaultive	12	5	6	18	5
Self-depreciatory	12	16	16	8	13
Threatens assault	10	4	11	14	7
Sexual preoccupation	10	9	9	6	14
Maniacal outburst	9	11	6	7	12
Bizarre ideas	9	11	1	2	20
Robbery	8	0	3	18	3
Apathetic	8	8	8	4	11
Irresponsible behavior	7	3	7	9	7
Headaches	6	7	10	4	5
Perversions (except homosexuality)	5	0	5	10	2
Euphoria	5	17	2	2	5
Fears own hostile impulses	5	4	9	5	2
Mood swings	5	9	5	4	4
Insomnia	5	11	7	3	5
Psychosomatic disorders	4	7	6	3	5
Does not eat	4	9	4	2	4
Lying	3	0	1	7	0
Homosexuality	3	3	3	8	2
Rape	3	0	3	8	1
Obsessions	3	8	3	1	4
Depersonalization	3	4	1	0	6
Feels perverted	3	0	3	1	5
Phobias	2	4	5	0	2

the point that they were trying to make regarding homogeneity. For example, the general category of schizophrenia is itself made up of several smaller categories; the percentage figures for suspiciousness might be considerably higher for a subcategory such as paranoid schizophrenia.

The Zigler and Phillips study was necessarily limited because it looked only at the presence or absence of specific isolated symptoms. Most psychiatric diagnostic categories are defined by the *joint presence* of a *number* of particular symptoms, rather than simply by the presence or absence of a single one. Psychiatrists and psychologists who find DSM-II useful emphasize the importance of syndromes or clusters of symptoms. For example, schizophrenia is generally defined by a number of symptoms such as delusions, hallucinations, and bizarre motor behavior. But the problem is that the current diagnostic system does not adequately specify how *many* of these various symptoms must be present in order to make a diagnosis, or the degree to which they must be manifest. If psychologists decide to continue working within the current diagnostic scheme, or a revised one, they will need to address themselves to these more quantitative questions.

Lack of Reliability

Whether or not different diagnosticians will agree that a given diagnostic label should be applied to a particular person is the test of its *reliability*. Clearly, for a classification system to be useful, those applying it must be able to agree on what is and what is not an instance of a particular class. Thus reliability becomes the primary requisite for judging any classification system.

Before discussing the evidence, a problem in assessing the reliability of the present diagnostic system should be mentioned. In medicine a diagnosis made by a physician can usually be checked by some sort of laboratory test. That is, an objective measurement is available by which the reliability of a physician's diagnosis can be determined. For diagnosing abnormal behavior no such infallible measurement exists; the only means of assessing reliability is whether or not diagnosticians agree.

The reliability of psychiatric diagnosis has been well researched. One exemplary investigation has been reported by Beck, Ward, Mendelson, Mock, and Erbaugh (1962). Four highly experienced psychiatrists diagnosed 153 patients within one week of their admission to a psychiatric facility. Each patient was interviewed twice in succession by two different psychiatrists. Before beginning their study, the four psychiatrists had met to discuss the current diagnostic manual so that they could agree on its application. No attempt, however, was made to ensure that the various interviewers would employ the same techniques in gathering the necessary information with which to make their diagnoses.

The overall agreement among the psychiatrists, calculated as the number of diagnoses on which they agreed divided by the total number of diagnoses made, was a disappointingly low 54 percent. The amount of diagnostic agreement within the six most frequently applied categories is presented in Table 3.3. The percentage of agreement varied considerably from one category to another, ranging from a low of 38 percent in personality trait disturbance to a high of 63 percent for neurotic depression. Later, the same data were reanalyzed using only three larger categories, psychosis, neurosis, and character disorder. Diagnostic agreement then reached 70 percent, approaching levels that satisfy most clinical researchers.

The percentage of agreement in the Beck

TABLE 3.3

Percentage of Diagnostic Agreement Within Various Diagnostic Categories of the Beck Study (*from Beck et al., 1962*)

Category	Number of diagnoses	Agreement, %
Neurotic depression	92	63
Anxiety reaction	58	55
Sociopath	11	54
Schizophrenic reaction	60	53
Involutional melancholia	10	40
Personality trait disturbance	26	38

study may be atypically low, for studies by Kreitman and others in 1961 and by Sandifer and his colleagues in 1964 had percentages of agreement in the range of 73 to 74 percent for individual, specific diagnostic categories. Other features make the Beck study a noteworthy piece of work, however. In addition to diagnosing the patients, the psychiatrists in this study were also asked to rate the certainty of their diagnosis on a three-point scale. In making diagnostic judgments, there are always "gray areas." Some individuals may be easily classified whereas others fall into larger, indeterminate groups for which diagnosis becomes uncertain. In the Beck study, when both psychiatrists felt sure of their choice, agreement was 81 percent, even in applying the full range of categories. This evidence supports the view that some individuals, the so-called clear-cut

cases, can be reliably classified. Moreover, in one-third of the cases that were seen, the psychiatrists were asked to make a second choice in addition to their primary diagnosis. Presumably, if the diagnostician is presented with a case that is somewhat ambiguous, he will probably be able to narrow the diagnosis down to two categories. According to this line of reasoning, the proportion of cases in which neither the primary nor the alternative diagnoses of the two psychiatrists are in agreement should be very small. This is precisely what the Beck study found, for in only 16 percent of these fifty-one cases was there a total absence of agreement. Thus a substantial number of individuals *can* be reliably classified employing the current psychiatric classification scheme.

As for the patients about whose diagnosis the psychiatrists are less likely to agree, there are several reasons why the diagnostic system is inadequate. First, as others (for example, Maher, 1966) have pointed out, the scheme for categorizing patients is not a taxonomy in the strictest sense of the word, for it is not based on a single, uniform principle. Organic brain syndromes, for instance, are classified according to the causes of the damage to the patient's brain. Disorders such as neuroses are defined largely on the basis of psychoanalytic theory, to wit, that neuroses are characterized by unconscious anxiety. The presence of physiological brain damage and of unconscious anxiety must be determined by vastly different means. Moreover, the usefulness of a psychoanalytic term such as "unconscious anxiety" can and has been questioned, for psychoanalytic theory itself is rather uncertain ground on which to build any part of a classification scheme (see Chapter 2).

The data of the Beck study were later reexamined in an attempt to determine why diagnosticians might disagree (Ward, Beck, Mendelson, Mock, and Erbaugh, 1962). Meeting again after they had completed the interviews and made their diagnoses, the psychiatrists found three major reasons why they had not always reached the same determination. First, accounting for 5 percent of the disagreements, were *inconsistencies on the part of the patient.*

> A young woman was referred for evaluation of a somatic complaint which neither diagnostician could be sure was psychogenic in nature. One of the diagnosticians could therefore make only the diagnosis of "no psychiatric disease." However, to the other examiner, the patient volunteered the history of a previous gastric ulcer . . . information she had previously directly denied to the first examiner. The second physician therefore diagnosed psychophysiological gastrointestinal reaction (p. 200).

The second major group of diagnostic disagreements, 32.5 percent of them, were attributed to *inconsistencies on the part of the diagnostician.* Differences in interview techniques, in judging the importance of particular symptoms, and in interpreting the same pathology constituted most of these inconsistencies.

> Weighing symptoms differently was a sizable factor . . . especially in cases where the diagnostic choice fell between two neuroses. . . . Often what was initially advanced as a chief complaint did not develop to be the predominant area of distress. . . . For example, a patient whose chief complaints were of tension and palpitation was considered by the second examiner to be actually more disturbed by symptoms of mood impairment, fatigue, self-depreciative thought, and loss of interest. When directly asked in the second examination, the patient gave his opinion that the low spirits were more troublesome than the tension. Diagnostic conflict: Anxiety reaction with depressive features vs. neurotic depressive reaction with anxiety features (p. 200).

The third and largest group of disagreements, comprising 62.5 percent of them, were considered to stem from *inadequacies of the diagnostic system.* The diagnosticians found the criteria unclear. Either too fine distinctions were required, or the classification system seemingly forced the diagnostician to choose a major category that was not specific enough.

INTRODUCTION AND BASIC ISSUES

. . . a twenty-one-year-old single white female . . . was seen whose chief complaints were nervous tension and self-consciousness since she was three years old. In recent years, she had been unable to hold down a job, although she had some secretarial training. . . . She had received various forms of psychiatric treatment over the past four years and had seen twelve psychiatrists in all, remaining with only one for a period as long as seven months and leaving all of them with open hostility. . . . It was open knowledge in the family that the patient was supposed to have been a boy; and her parents, especially the somewhat alcoholic father, had told her that she was no good because she was a girl and had approved of her only when she was successfully competitive with boys. The patient finished high school with difficulty, having to leave one school because of her marked discomfort in efforts to make speeches before mixed groups, and also because of much daydreaming, which still continued. She now felt frustrated, bitter, and had long felt that life was not worthwhile. She had never had a serious interpersonal involvement of a positive nature, and to the extent that she let herself react with others, the pattern was that of hostile anticipation, poorly modulated aggression, and suspiciousness. She often wished she were dead and had frequent thoughts of turning on the gas or jumping in front of a car, but at the same time she was aware of an excessively strong fear of death. She was compelled to wash her hands after touching certain articles of furniture; she had phobias of eating with other people. She had many physical symptoms of . . . anxiety and autonomic tension. . . . She had a sleep pattern which was a mixture of anxiety and depression, was not rarely awakened by nightmares in which she saw herself dead or bad things happening to her family. She had on several occasions [experienced] . . . visual images upon awakening from these dreams and had remained anxious and unable to sleep long afterwards. However, she definitely had had no auditory or visual hallucinations in the waking state and had had no clear delusions. There was a peculiar quality to her affect which suggested flatness or a manifestation of depression, though it was hard to distinguish between the two, and neither observer felt that she was making any substantial attempt to be melodramatic or impressive.

Both observers were impressed with the borderline nature of her problem. One was reminded of a previous patient who became "overtly psychotic"; the resemblance was less in specific, recognizable details and more in terms of a vague general feeling of the examiner's. He was also impressed with the chronicity, quantity, and multiplicity of her symptoms. The other examiner volunteered that on another day he might well agree, but as the patient struck him now, after an hour's interview, he felt she had a certain integration and inner consistency; he had seen similar patients who consolidated themselves and improved their adjustment without any clearly psychotic episode. In view of the absence of any clear break with reality, because of the reactive elements in the picture; because the patient was intelligent and did well on routine tests of similarities, differences, and proverb interpretation; because of the potential damage to the patient of being labeled with a psychotic diagnosis; and because of personal antipathy to the poorly conceived phrase "chronic undifferentiated schizophrenic," he gave the patient the benefit of a very sizable doubt as to where schizoid personality left off and schizophrenia began. Diagnostic conflict: chronic undifferentiated schizophrenic reaction vs. chronic anxiety reaction in a severely schizoid personality[2] (pp. 203–204).

[2] Schizoid personality is a personality disorder characterized by seclusiveness, oversensitivity, and eccentricity.

Lack of Validity

Whether or not predictions or valid statements can be made about a class once it has been formed is the test of its validity. We should state at the outset that validity bears a particular relation to reliability: the less reliable a category is, the more difficult it is to make valid statments about the category. Since the reliability of the current diagnostic system is not entirely adequate, we can expect that its validity will not be either.

A psychiatric diagnosis can have three kinds of validity: etiological, concurrent, and predictive. Etiological validity refers to finding that the same historical antecedents have caused the disorder in the patients diagnosed; for a diagnosis to have etiological validity, the same factors must be found to have caused the disorder in all the people who comprise the diagnostic group. Concurrent validity refers to the discovery that symptoms or disordered processes not previously distinguished are characteristic of a particular diagnosis. Finding that most people with paranoid delusions also hallucinate is an example. Predictive validity refers to similar future behavior: for example, members of a diagnostic group are expected to respond in a similar way to a particular treatment. Throughout this volume, as we review the research literature on a particular category of abnormal behavior, we shall also necessarily be reviewing the validity of that diagnostic class.

THE ASSESSMENT OF ABNORMAL BEHAVIOR

The example with which this book began, that of a tearful female student whom you happen to encounter one day on campus, was structured so that we never did find out why she was crying. We were denied the possibility of learning more about her by any one of three

INTRODUCTION AND BASIC ISSUES

principal means commonly available to clinicians: interview, tests, and direct observation of behavior. These three modes of assessment may occasionally be given different, perhaps more impressive-sounding names. An interview may be called "the psychiatric interview," "the diagnostic interview," or "a depth interview"; tests "psychologicals" or "projectives." All three assessment procedures are more or less formal ways of finding out what is wrong with a person, what may have caused his problem or problems in the past, and what steps may be taken to improve his condition.

Clinical Interviews

Most of us have probably been interviewed at one time or another, although the conversation may have been so informal that it was not regarded as an interview. To the layman the word interview connotes a formal, highly structured conversation, but we find it useful to construe the term as any interpersonal encounter, conversational in style, in which one person, the interviewer, uses language as the principal means of finding out about another, the interviewee. Thus a Gallup pollster who asks a housewife whom she will vote for in an upcoming presidential election is interviewing with the restricted goal of learning whom she will vote for. And a clinical psychologist who asks a patient about the circumstances of his most recent hospitalization is similarly conducting an interview.

The model within which an interviewer operates determines the type of information sought and obtained. A psychoanalytically trained clinician can be expected to inquire about the person's childhood history. He is also likely to remain skeptical of the verbal reports because his model tells him that the most significant aspects of a disturbed or normal person's developmental history are repressed into the unconscious. By the same token, the behaviorally oriented clinician is likely to focus on current environmental conditions that can be related to changes in the person's behavior, trying to determine, for example, the circumstances under which the person may become anxious. Our point is that a clinical interview does not follow a prescribed course, rather that it varies with the paradigm adopted by the interviewer. The clinical interviewer in some measure finds only the information he looks for.

Great skill is necessary to carry out good interviews, particularly clinical interviews, for they are, after all, conducted with people who are under considerable personal stress. Vast amounts of information can be obtained by means of the interview; its importance in abnormal psychology is unquestioned. Whether the information gleaned can always be depended on is not so clear, however. In one study, for example (Ward et al., 1962), it was established that patients sometimes gave different interviewers different information in response to the same questions. Often clinicians tend to overlook *situational* factors of the interview that may exert strong influences on what the patient says or does. Consider, for a moment, how a teen-ager is likely to respond to the question "How often have you used illegal drugs?" when it is asked by a young, long-haired psychologist in jeans and again when it is asked by a sixty-year-old, bald psychologist in a three-piece suit.

Interviews may also vary in the degree to which they are structured. In practice, most clinicians operate from only the vaguest outlines, sometimes not even written ones. In our own clinical work with college students, the authors of this textbook undertake an intake (initial) interview in order to answer the questions shown in Table 3.4. Exactly *how* such information is collected is left largely up to the particular interviewer. With years of clinical experience, in both teaching and learning from students and colleagues, each of us has developed ways of asking questions with which we are comfortable and which seem to extract the information that will be of maximum benefit to the client. Thus, to the extent that an interview is unstructured, the interviewer must rely on his intuition and general experience, which may be either good or bad, for obvious reasons.

One system of imposing more structure in interviewing is the Current and Past Psychopathology Scales, developed by Spitzer and Endicott (1969). This instrument consists of an interview guide geared to elicit specific information. During the interview itself the patient's responses to various questions are scored on scales, as indicated in the two examples in Table 3.5. Again, these questions can be understood only within the context of the investigators' *models* of human behavior. Spitzer and Endicott, and anyone else who uses their scales and asks similar questions, as-

TABLE **3.4** *Example of a Form Used To Report the Information Collected During an Interview*

INTAKE REPORT

Name: *Age:*   *Sex:* M F

Class: Fr So Jr Sr Grad   *Date of Interview:*

  I. *Behavior During Interview and Physical Description:*

 II. *Presenting Problem:*
    A. Nature of problem:
    B. Historical determinants:
    C. Current determinants:
    D. Dimensions of problem (duration, pervasiveness, frequency, magnitude, etc.):
    E. Consequences of problem (mood, efficiency, satisfaction, productiveness, interpersonal functioning, etc.):

III. *Other Problems:*

IV. *Personal Assets (physical, aptitudes, abilities, interests, etc.):*

 V. *Target(s) for Modification:*

VI. *Recommended Treatment(s):*

VII. *Motivation for Treatment:* low   medium   high   does not apply

VIII. *Prognosis:* 1. very poor   2. poor   3. fair   4. good
                5. very good   does not apply

IX. *Priority for Treatment:*   none   low   medium   high

INTRODUCTION AND BASIC ISSUES

TABLE 3.5 *Examples of Two Questions and Scales from a Structured Diagnostic Interview, the Current and Past Psychopathology Scales*
(from Spitzer and Endicott, 1969)

Agitation — Excitement Have there been any times recently when you weren't able to sit still . . . or you fidgeted a lot . . . or anything else like that?	1 None	2 Minimal	3 Mild	4 Moderate	5 Severe	6 Extreme
Grandiosity Do you feel that you are a particularly important person or that you have certain special powers or abilities?	1 None	2 Minimal	3 Mild	4 Moderate	5 Severe	6 Extreme

sume that the information collected in their interview bears importantly on a patient's current status and perhaps also on how he will respond to treatment, or, indeed, on whether he even needs treatment.

Psychological Tests

The so-called psychological tests structure still further the process of assessment. The same test can be administered to many people at different times, and the responses collected and analyzed to indicate how certain kinds of people tend to respond. Statistical norms for the test can thereby be established as soon as the data collected are extensive enough. Then the responses of a particular patient can be compared to these statistical norms. In addition, psychological tests may be easier to score, administer, and interpret than a psychiatric interview. Several classes of psychological tests have been developed: projective personality tests, personality inventories, tests for organic damage, and tests of intelligence.

Projective Personality Tests

The Rorschach (Figure 3.1) inkblot test and the Thematic Apperception Test are perhaps the best-known projective techniques. In both of these tests a set of standard stimuli, vague enough not to elicit predictable responses, is presented to an individual. In an inkblot test (Figure 3.2) the subject is shown a series of blots, one at a time, and asked to tell what figures or objects he sees in each of them. Similarly, in the Thematic Apperception Test the examinee is shown a series of pictures one by one and asked to tell a story related to each (Figure 3.3). In both these tests it is assumed that because the stimulus materials are unstructured, the patient's responses will be determined primarily by unconscious processes and reveal his own attitudes, motivations, and modes of behavior. For example, reporting eyes on the Rorschach has been said to indicate paranoia. Those of the psychoanalytic bent tend to favor such tests since they presumably afford an opportunity for the unconscious to express itself. By the same token,

FIGURE 3.1

Hermann Rorschach (1884–1922), Swiss psychiatrist who introduced the famous inkblot test designed to uncover motivations and conflicts that are said to be unavailable to consciousness.

those who use these tests tend to think in psychoanalytic terms.[3]

As might be imagined, the interpretation of the responses to projective tests poses a severe problem, for the examinee is not merely answering yes or no to a series of questions or indicating which of a series of statements are true and which false. Rather, he is providing a complex response to a complex stimulus, which is, by design, open to a fantastic range of interpretations. In many instances the reliability of the scoring of the Rorschach and Thematic Apperception tests is quite low. With extensive training in a particular scoring system, however, examiners can achieve satisfactory levels of agreement (Goldfried, Stricker, and Weiner, 1971). A more serious problem is the often woefully low validities of responses to projective tests. We assume that these responses tell us something important and useful about the person. Generally, the information gathered through a projective technique concerns unconscious conflicts and repressed anxieties. Behavioral psychologists find it difficult to assess the validity of such data, for how can it be known whether the test is in fact measuring unconscious conflicts and repressed anxieties if they are by definition hidden from direct observation?

On the other hand, the inferences drawn from projective test data do sometimes permit attempts at validation. For example, if a patient is asserted to be homosexual on the basis of his Rorschach responses, the validity of this assertion can be determined. But the inferences made about aspects of personality through projective testing do not generally prove accurate. After making an extensive survey of the literature, Nunnally (1967) has written that

. . . most projective techniques do a rather poor job of measuring personality traits. . . . In applied settings, the evidence is clear that projective techniques have, at most, only a low level of validity . . . . they do a poor job of differentiating normal people from people who are diagnosed as neurotic and they do a poor

---

[3] A behaviorist might also make use of projective tests, although for different purposes. The Rorschach and the TAT, being unstructured, may be viewed as examples of ambiguous life demands. Determining the degree of tension evidenced by the respondent when asked to operate in these highly unstructured situations may then be considered a good sampling of his typical reactions to life stresses. For further discussion of the use of tests to secure samples and signs of behavior, see Mischel (1968).

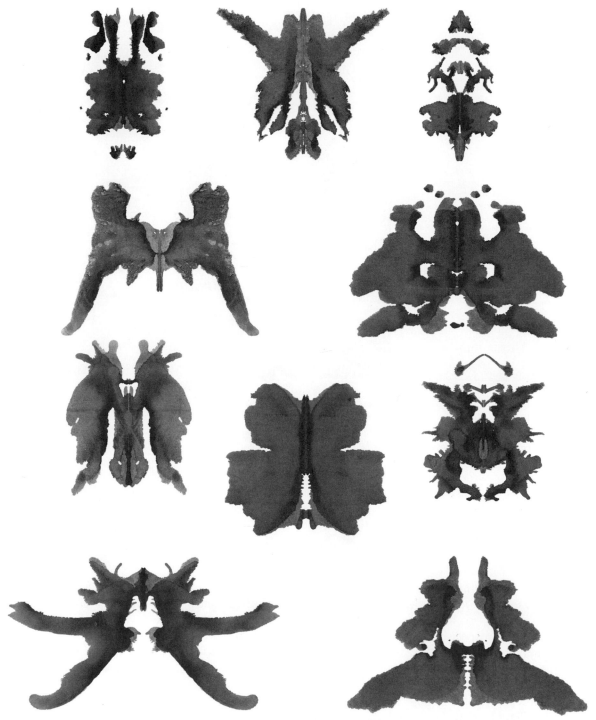

FIGURE **3.2** *Inkblots resembling those used by Rorschach.*

FIGURE **3.3**
Picture from the Thematic Apperception Test, devised in 1935 by Henry Murray and his associates at the Harvard Psychological Clinic. Like the Rorschach, this projective test is designed to reveal unconscious conflicts and concerns.

job of differentiating various types of mentally ill persons (p. 497).

Certain responses to projective tests are sometimes viewed as diagnostic signs, even though the actual association between the response and a particular diagnosis has never been determined. Many clinicians rely to a considerable extent on such signs in making their diagnoses. Moreover, as noted by Chapman and Chapman (1969), clinicians often show considerable consensus in assigning meanings to various signs, even though there is little evidence to back up their interpretations. Let us examine this issue of consensus.

Chapman and Chapman conducted a study which you may participate in right now. Imagine yourself part of a psychological experiment in which you are asked to rate the amount of

INTRODUCTION AND BASIC ISSUES

association between homosexuality and particular Rorschach responses. Specifically, you are to rate the degree to which each of the responses signifies homosexuality, using the following six-point scale: 6, very strong; 5, strong; 4, moderate; 3, slight; 2, very slight; and 1, no tendency at all. The eight Rorschach responses to be rated are presented in Table 3.6.

Now you may compare your ratings to those actually obtained from a sample of undergraduate students. In Table 3.7 the responses are divided into three different classes according to information previously obtained from practicing clinicians. The popular invalid signs are those that clinicians *believe* reflect homosexuality, although they have *not* been validated by research evidence. The unpopular but valid signs are infrequently listed by clinicians, but they do have some modest research support. The filler items are unrelated to homosexuality and to how clinicians assess it. The students in the Chapmans' study gave much higher ratings to the *popular but invalid signs* than to the other responses.

Professional clinicians may rely on particular signs in making a diagnosis because they *assume* such responses are valid indicators of homosexuality. But as Chapman and Chapman themselves noted, "The popular meanings of many test signs, as reported by clinicians, are *illusory correlations* [italics added] based on verbal associative connection of the test sign to the symptom rather than valid observations" (p. 272). They are saying that, in our culture, we all seem to have developed similar ideas of what homosexuals say, think, or do. In this study of how students rated Rorschach responses, the students *assumed,* as clinicians have, that homosexuals would be inclined to see such things as buttocks in the inkblots. But these popular signs are *not* valid. There is no evidence to indicate that they differentiate

TABLE 3.6
Rorschach Responses To Be Rated for Signs of Homosexuality

Response	Rating
Feminine clothing	
Food	
Rectum and buttocks	
Maps	
Figure, part man–part woman	
Sexual organs	
Monsters	
Figure, part animal–part human	

between homosexuals and heterosexuals, yet they continue to be applied to diagnoses.

Personality Inventories

In personality inventories a large number of statements are typically presented to the examinee, and he is asked to indicate whether they do or do not apply to him. Since such tests are standardized, it is possible to establish statistical norms and the responses are easily scored. Furthermore, the investigators who have been involved in the construction of such instruments have often been well schooled in the general principles of test construction. It is therefore rare for a personality inventory to lack reliability. Validity, however, still presents a problem, especially if the personality inventory has been designed to reveal

TABLE **3.7**

*Mean Rated Strength
of Association Between
Particular Rorschach
Responses and
Homosexuality*

(*from Chapman and Chapman 1969*)

	Rated strength
Popular invalid signs	
Rectum and buttocks	4.38
Figure, part man–part woman	3.53
Feminine clothing	3.12
Sexual organs	4.47
Unpopular valid signs	
Figure, part animal–part human	1.93
Monsters	1.68
Filler items	
Food	1.09
Maps	1.09

unconscious conflicts and the like. Some personality inventories have been constructed with more specific purposes in mind. Perhaps the best-known of these is the Minnesota Multiphasic Personality Inventory (MMPI), which was designed as a standardized, inexpensive diagnostic device.

In developing the test, the investigators relied on factual information. First, many clinicians provided large numbers of statements that they considered indicative of various mental problems. Second, these items were rated as self-descriptive or not by people already diagnosed as abnormal according to the DSM. Those items that served to discriminate among the patients were retained; that is, items were selected if one clinical group responded to them more often in the same way

than did other groups. With additional refinements sets of these items were established as scales for determining whether or not a respondent should be diagnosed in a particular way. If he answered a large number of the items in a scale in the same way as had a certain diagnostic group, the more likely was his behavior to resemble that of the particular diagnostic group. The scales of the instrument do, in fact, relate well to psychiatric diagnoses (see Box 3.2). Thus the MMPI has been widely used to screen large groups of people for whom clinical interviews have not been feasible. Samples of the items from the various scales are presented in Table 3.8.[4]

We may well wonder whether answers that would designate the subject as normal might not be easy to fake. A superficial knowledge of contemporary abnormal psychology would alert even a seriously disturbed person to the fact that, if he wants to be regarded as normal, he must not admit to worrying a great deal about germs on doorknobs. In fact, there is evidence that these tests *can,* in the vernacular, be "psyched out." In many testing circumstances, however, the person does not *want* to falsify his responses, for he wants, in fact, to be helped. Moreover, the test designers have included as part of the MMPI several scales designed to detect deliberately faked responses (see Table 3.8). In one of these, the lie scale, a series of statements sets a trap for the person who is trying to "look too good." One such item from the lie scale declares "I read the newspaper editorials every night." The assumption is that few people would be able to

[4] The manner in which the MMPI was constructed is referred to as *empirical,* that is, relying on data or experience rather than speculation. It is also worth noting that the MMPI's diagnostic scheme is based on symptoms listed in DSM. Not surprisingly, those clinicians who dislike DSM are unenthusiastic about the MMPI.

endorse such a statement honestly. Thus persons who do endorse a large number of the statements in the lie scale might well be attempting to present themselves in a particularly good light. Their scores on other scales are usually viewed with more than the usual skepticism.

Tests such as the MMPI are subject to certain other difficulties. One of these is the problem of *response sets*. It has been found that many people tend to answer structured questions on bases other than the specific content of the question. For example, suppose the statement is "I attend a party at least once a

TABLE **3.8** *Typical Clinical Interpretations of Items Like Those on the MMPI* *(adapted from Kleinmuntz, 1967)*

Scale	Sample Item	Interpretation
Cannot say	This is merely the number of items marked in the "cannot say" category.	A high score indicates evasiveness.
Lie	I have never had a bad night's sleep (false).*	Persons trying to look good (e.g., wholesome, honest) obtain high scores.
Frequency	Everything tastes salty (true).	High scores on this scale suggest lack of care or wanting to appear abnormal.
Correction	I am more satisfied with my life than most of my friends (true).	High scores on this scale suggest a guarded test-taking attitude.
Hypochondriasis	I wake up tired most mornings (true).	High scorers have been described as cynical and dissatisfied.
Depression	I rarely see the bright side of things (true).	High scorers are usually withdrawn, sad, and troubled.
Hysteria	My fingers sometimes feel numb (true).	High scorers have multiple bodily complaints.

week." If the individual answers "Yes," or "True," or otherwise indicates that the statement applies to him, can we conclude without reservation that he does attend social gatherings frequently? Research suggests that such answers cannot be accepted as necessarily true, for a certain test-taking or questionnaire "set" may have determined the response.

Several types of *response sets,* as these orientations are called, have been identified. *Response acquiescence,* or "yea saying," is the tendency to agree with statements regardless of their content. *Response deviation* is the tendency to answer items in an uncommon way regardless of their content. A person with a *social desirability* response set will give what he judges to be the most socially accepted answer whether or not it actually applies to

INTRODUCTION AND BASIC ISSUES

TABLE **3.8** *(continued)*

Scale	Sample Item	Interpretation
Psychopathic deviate	I did not like school (true).	High scorers tend to be adventurous and antisocial.
Masculinity-femininity	I do not like sports (true).	Men with high scores tend to be artistic and sensitive. High-scoring women have been described as rebellious and assertive.
Paranoia	I am envied by many people (true).	High scorers on this scale tend to be suspicious and jealous.
Psychasthenia	I have a great deal of self-confidence (false).	High scorers are described as anxious, self-doubting, and rigid.
Schizophrenia	I sometimes smell strange odors (true).	Adjectives such as seclusive and bizarre describe high scorers.
Hypomania	I never have any difficulty making decisions (true).	High scorers tend to be outgoing and impulsive.
Social introversion-extroversion	I avoid getting together with people (true).	High scorers are modest and shy; low scorers are sociable and exhibitionistic.

*The true or false responses in parentheses indicate the answer expected if the respondent is to accumulate a high score on this scale.

him. For instance, in the example just given, an individual who abhors and avoids parties may say that he attends them at least once a week because he wishes to be viewed as typical and feels that such a response is likely to be considered "right" or appropriate.

One obvious means of avoiding this problem is to structure the test-taking situation in such a way that the respondent is motivated to answer honestly. If we are working with an individual in a clinical setting, this is easily accomplished. But what can be done if the test is administered to a group or as part of a research project, where it is difficult to motivate all respondents to answer frankly? The pioneering work of Edwards (1957) illustrates one way of handling the response set of social desirability. He began with an investigation designed to assess the relationship between the social desirability of an item and the likelihood that it would be endorsed. First, a large number of undergraduates were asked to judge 140 different self-descriptions on a nine-point scale in terms of " . . . the degree of desirability or undesirability of these traits in people . . . " (1957). Among the items were the following.

1. To like to punish your enemies.
2. To like to read psychological novels.
3. To like to make excuses for friends.
4. To like to go out with your friends.

In the next phase of the study Edwards presented the same 140 items to a different sample of undergraduates who were asked to respond yes if the particular item was characteristic of their own behavior and no if it was not. The percentage of subjects responding yes to each of the items was computed and then correlated with the judged social desirability of the response. An impressively high correlation was obtained, leading Edwards to conclude that if we know where a statement lies on the social desirability-undesirability dimension, " . . . we can then predict, with a high degree of accuracy, the proportion of individuals who will say, in self-description, that the statement does describe them" (1957, p. 3). Moreover, even when respondents are led to believe that they will remain anonymous, they still ascribe to themselves socially desirable attitudes and activities.[5]

Several methods have been devised for con-

trolling the social desirability response set. In one of these methods, the *forced-choice inventory,* items describing different attitudes and activities are equated in terms of the independently determined social desirability of the behavior and are given in pairs to the respondent. Thus he is forced to choose between two statements describing equally desirable or undesirable alternatives. Edwards himself used this technique in constructing his Personal Preferences Schedule. The manner in which this method forces respondents to make a content-related response is indicated by the following two questions.

Choose A or B for each of the following items:

Item I

> *A:*   *I like to tell amusing stories and jokes at parties.*
>
> *B:*   *I would like to write a great novel or play.*

Item II

> *A:*   *I feel like blaming others when things go wrong for me.*
>
> *B:*   *I feel that I am inferior to others in most respects.*

Like those who have judged these statements before him, the respondent will probably consider the alternatives of each pair equivalent in social desirability. Thus he is more likely to choose the statement that actually describes himself.

The forced-choice inventory is a widely used technique for reducing the likelihood that questionnaire responses will reflect only the degree to which the respondent wishes to appear conventional or likable. By excluding or at least minimizing the role of social desirability factors, those who rely on data from personality inventories can with greater confidence

---

[5] There is more than one possible interpretation of these data. For example, if behavior that is judged the most desirable in a particular culture is also the most common, the probability of endorsing statements describing such behavior would be high, even when subjects were not misrepresenting themselves. But the evidence does not favor this interpretation.

regard the responses as valid indicators of the personality characteristics that the particular test purports to measure.

Tests for Organic Brain Dysfunction

As indicated at the beginning of this chapter, one major section of the DSM-II refers to behavioral problems brought on by organic brain abnormalities. Neurological tests such as checking the patellar reflex, examining the retina for any indication of blood vessel damage, and evaluating motor coordination and perception are useful procedures in diagnosing brain dysfunction. The X-ray is able to detect tumors, and the electroencephalograph (EEG) abnormalities in the brain's electrical activity. We might reasonably assume that neurologists and physicians, with the help of such procedures and technological devices, can make direct observations of the brain and its functions and thus assess brain abnormalities. Most brain abnormalities, however, involve alterations in structure so subtle that they have thus far eluded direct physical measurement. Moreover, we still know very little about how the brain works.

Since how the person functions is the problem—what he does, says, thinks, or feels—a number of tests assessing behavioral disturbances that are caused by organic brain dysfunctions have been developed by psychologists. The literature on these tests is extensive and, as with most areas of psychology, so too is disagreement about them. The weight of the evidence, however, does seem to indicate that psychological tests have some validity in the assessment of brain damage. Reitan (1964), for example, has developed an extensive battery of tests that tap various perceptual, motor, and cognitive functions. Included in the battery are an IQ test, the Trail-Making Test, in which the examinee tries to connect in

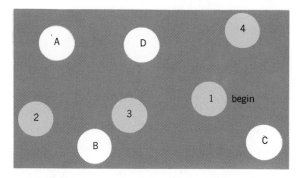

FIGURE **3.4**
Sample item from the Trail-Making Test. The subject is instructed to alternate numbers and letters, for example, 1→A→2→B, and so on.

order a number of circles (Figure 3.4), and tests for tactile, auditory, and visual perception. On the basis of these tests, patients known through medical measurements to have suffered brain injuries can be accurately classified by trained psychologists without prior knowledge of the results of the medical tests. Better assessment of brain dysfunction by both psychological and neurological measurement must, however, wait a better understanding of normal brain function.

Intelligence Tests

Psychological measures of intelligence sometimes enter into certain diagnoses, namely mental retardation. Binet originally constructed mental tests to help the Parisian school board predict which children would profit most from schooling. Intelligence testing has since developed into one of the largest psychological industries. The word aptitude is frequently applied to these widely used standardized procedures. The Scholastic Aptitude Test and the individually administered tests, such as the Wechsler Adult Intelligence Scale and the Stanford-Binet, are all based on the assumption that one sample from an individual's current intellectual functioning can predict how well he will perform in school.

In evaluating such tests, it is important to keep in mind two points that are only infrequently made explicit by those who have a heavy professional commitment to intelligence testing. First, strictly speaking, the tests measure only what a psychologist considers intelligence to be. The tasks and items on an IQ test are, after all, invented by psychologists—they did not come down to us inscribed on stone tablets. Second, the tests are widely used because they do indeed accomplish what they were designed for, that is, predict who will succeed in our educational system. If and when there are major changes in our school systems, we can expect analogous changes in our definition and assessment of intelligence.

Direct Observation of Behavior

Personality tests and inventories use the responses of examinees as *signs* of underlying traits. For example, to assess an individual's aggressiveness, a personality tester might administer the TAT and look for the presence of violent themes in the stories. In contrast, in IQ testing and the more recently developed techniques of assessing behavior through direct observation, the behavior tested is considered a *sample* closely resembling the whole. The more direct, behavior-as-sample approach is favored by those working within a learning paradigm. Their assessment of aggressiveness may involve the direct observation of aggressive behavior in a contrived or real-life setting. A study by O'Leary and Becker (1967) provides an example of this kind of work. In a special classroom setting an attempt was made to reduce the frequency of the children's deviant behavior, defined by the researchers as fighting, crying, and temper tantrums, by rewarding them for good behavior, such as paying attention and remaining in their seats. Observers were carefully trained to count in-

stances of deviant behavior during twenty-second intervals. The curve on the left in Figure 3.5 shows the relative frequency of such behavior during the base line period, that is, before the institution of reinforcement for nondeviant behavior. During reinforcement sessions deviant behavior was also measured, yielding the curve at the right. Clearly, the reinforcements for nondeviant behavior resulted in a marked decrease in deviant behavior. These careful observations of overt behavior enabled the investigators to demonstrate the effectiveness of their remedial program in a fashion more convincing than, for example, giving the children Rorschach tests or asking the teachers how their students were behaving.

The foregoing illustration from the operant literature employs no inferential concepts; the investigators interpreted the observations in a fairly literal way. Behavioral assessment techniques can also be applied within a framework that does make use of mediators (to be discussed in greater detail in Chapter 4). For instance, Paul (1966) was interested in assessing the "anxiety" of public speakers. He decided that a good way to measure the anxiety of the speaker was to count the frequency of behavior that is deemed indicative of this emotional state. One of his principal measures, the Timed Behavioral Checklist for Performance Anxiety, is shown in Table 3.9. Subjects were asked to deliver a speech in front of a group, some members of which were raters trained to consider each subject's behavior every thirty seconds and to record the presence or absence of twenty specific behaviors. By summing the scores, Paul arrived at a behavioral index of anxiety.[6] This study is one example of how observations of overt behavior have been used to measure an internal state.

[6] Additional details of this important experiment are discussed in Chapter 19. Paul used the behavioral index of anxiety in determining the relative efficacy of several forms of therapy devised to reduce anxiety about public speaking.

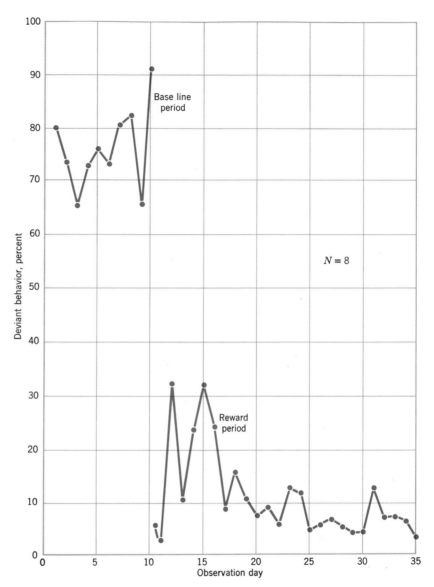

FIGURE **3.5**

Amount of deviant behavior during base line and reward periods. After O'Leary and Becker, 1967.

TABLE **3.9** *Timed Behavioral Checklist for Performance Anxiety* (*from Paul, 1966*)

Behavior observed	Time period								
	1	2	3	4	5	6	7	8	Σ
1. Paces									
2. Sways									
3. Shuffles feet									
4. Knees tremble									
5. Extraneous arm and hand movement (swings, scratches, toys, etc.)									
6. Arms rigid									
7. Hands restrained (in pockets, behind back, clasped)									
8. Hand tremors									
9. No eye contact									
10. Face muscles tense (drawn, tics, grimaces)									
11. Face "deadpan"									
12. Face pale									
13. Face flushed (blushes)									
14. Moistens lips									
15. Swallows									
16. Clears throat									
17. Breathes heavily									
18. Perspires (face, hands, armpits)									
19. Voice quivers									
20. Speech blocks or stammers									

SUMMARY

The six major categories of abnormal behavior—mental retardation, organic brain syndromes, psychoses, neuroses, personality disorders, and psychophysiological disorders—comprising the current diagnostic and statistical manual, DMS-II, were briefly described. Three major criticisms of DSM-II were discussed: heterogeneity of symptoms within diagnostic classes, low reliability, and lack of validity. Although these criticisms are indeed partially deserved, they are not serious enough to justify abandoning all attempts at classification. Some sort of classification or measurement seems essential whenever we wish to learn something new.

The remainder of the chapter dealt with techniques for assessing abnormal behavior. The clinical interview was seen to vary widely in format, for the paradigm of the interviewer inevitably determines the direction of questioning. Psychological tests—projective techniques, personality inventories, tests for brain damage, and intelligence tests—were also reviewed. Projective tests such as the Rorschach were judged to have little value, but the other classes of psychological tests may be useful in some situations. Finally, the distinction was made between behavior as sign and behavior as sample, and several techniques for the direct observation of behavior were discussed.

CHAPTER 4

Research Methods in the Study of Abnormal Behavior

From our discussion of models of abnormal behavior and problems in its classification and assessment, it should be clear that there is less than total agreement on how abnormal behavior ought to be studied. Our approach to the field is based not on the adoption of a particular model but on the belief that more progress will be made through scientific research than armchair speculation. This chapter surveys contemporary research methods in psychopathology.

SCIENCE AND SCIENTIFIC METHODS

In Chapter 1 we emphasized the important role of subjective factors in the collection and interpretation of data, indeed, in the very definition of what constitutes an observation. Thus there is actually no one science or scientific method, although we often read in college textbooks of "*the* scientific method." The phrase *as currently practiced* should really be added.

Let us consider science from the point of view of Baruch Spinoza, a famous Dutch philosopher of the seventeenth century. He believed that the scientists's role was to discover God's law. Today we say that Spinoza did not hold a "constructive" view of science. We do not imply that Spinoza's views were not useful, rather that they can be differentiated from perspectives that emphasize man's role in constructing laws and principles. Contemporary scientists tend to view the laws and theories in existence as constructions or inventions made by scientists. And the rules to be followed in formulating and evaluating these hypotheses and laws are also constructed by man and might very well be changed at any time. Science, as currently practiced, is the pursuit of systematized knowledge through observation. Thus the term refers to a method, the systematic acquisition and evaluation of information, and to a goal, the development of principles that explain the information. Contemporary science strives for explanations that are an outgrowth of, and can be modified by, publicly observed evidence. Observations and explanations must meet certain criteria.

1. *Testability.* A scientific approach requires that all claims be exposed to systematic probes and tests, any one of which could *negate* the scientist's expectations. Statements, theories, and assertions, regardless of how plausible they may seem, must be testable in the public arena. Therefore the attitude of science is an extremely doubting one. It is not enough to assert that particular traumatic experiences during childhood may produce psychological maladjustment in adulthood, or that various stresses in adult life may create problems. These are no more than possibilities or propositions. According to the scientific point of view, such propositions must be amenable to testing.

2. *Reliability.* Closely related to testability is the demand that the observations forming a scientific body of knowledge be reliable. Whatever is observed must occur under prescribed circumstances not once but repeatedly. The event cannot be seen or detected only by a single individual or individuals in a given laboratory, community or country. Instead, it must be reproducible under the circumstances stated, anywhere, anytime, and anyplace. If the event cannot be reproduced, scientists become wary of the legitimacy of the original observation.

3. *The inferences of unobservables.* Even with its emphasis on observables, science often resorts to nonobservable or theoretical concepts in explaining phenomena. Several advantages may thus be gained. First, theoret-ical concepts often bridge spatiotemporal relations. For example, in early physics it was noted that a magnet placed close to some iron filings would cause some of the filings to move toward it. How does one piece of metal influence another over the spatial distance? The inferred concept of magnetic fields proved to be very useful in accounting for this phenomenon. Similarly, in abnormal psychology we may often want to bridge temporal gaps with theoretical concepts. If a child has had a particularly frightening experience and his behavior is changed for a lengthy period of time, we need to explain how the earlier event is able to exert an influence over subsequent behavior. The unobservable and inferred concept of *acquired fear* has been very helpful in this regard.

Theoretical concepts may also account for already observed relationships. For example, we may observe that people who are taking an examination, who expect a momentary electric shock, or who are fighting with a companion all have sweaty palms, trembling hands, and a fast heartbeat. If we ask them how they feel, they report that they are agitated. The relationships can be depicted as shown in Figure 4.1A. Or we can say that all the situations have made these individuals anxious, and that anxiety has in turn caused the reported agitation, the sweaty palms, the faster heartbeat, and the trembling hands. Figure 4.1B shows anxiety as a theoretical concept explaining what has been observed. The first part of the figure is much more complex than the second, where the term anxiety becomes a mediator of the relationships.

With these advantages in mind, we must consider the criteria to be applied in judging the adequacy of a theoretical concept. One earlier school of thought, the *operationist,* proposed that each such concept be directly

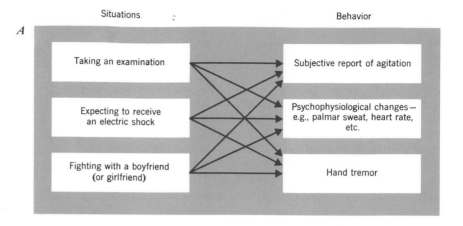

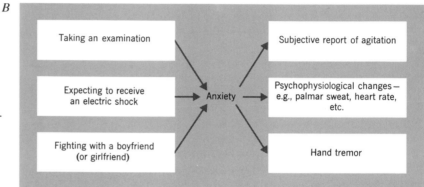

FIGURE **4.1**
An illustration of the advantages of using anxiety as a theoretical concept. The arrows in B *are fewer and more readily understood. After Miller, 1959.*

translated into a single observable operation that can be measured. In this way each theoretical concept would be nothing more than one particular measurable operation. For example, anxiety might be *nothing more* than scoring 50 on an anxiety questionnaire. It was soon realized, however, that this approach would take away from theoretical concepts their greatest advantages. If each theoretical concept is *operationalized* in only one way, its generality is lost. If the theoretical concept of learning, for instance, is defined by a *single* operation that can be measured, such as how often a rat presses a bar, other behavior such as a child performing arithmetic problems or a college student studying this book cannot

also be called learning, and attempts to relate the different phenomena to one another might be discouraged. The early operationist point of view quickly gave way to the more flexible position that a theoretical concept can be defined by *sets* of operations. In this way the concept may be linked to several different measurements each of which taps a different facet of the concept (see Figure 4.1B).[1] Research in different laboratories, carried out with different subjects and experimental arrangements, can then be integrated.

[1] There are also risks when we permit an unobservable concept to be operationalized, or measured, in more than one way. We shall examine some of these when we consider the topic of anxiety in the next chapter.

THE RESEARCH METHODS OF ABNORMAL PSYCHOLOGY

We turn now to a consideration of various research procedures that are currently applied in the study of abnormal behavior. The four most common—the experiment, correlation, mixed design, and single-subject research —vary in the degree to which they allow scientific propositions to be probed and reliable data collected.

The Experiment

The experiment is generally considered to be the most powerful tool for determining causal relationships between events. As an introduction to the basic components of experimental research, let us consider a recently reported study of how violence seen on television influences the aggressive behavior of children (Liebert and Baron, 1972). A group of 136 children participated in the research. Each child was first taken to a room containing a television monitor and was told he could watch it for a few minutes until the experimenter was ready for him. For all the children the first two minutes of film consisted of two commercials. After that, *half* the children viewed a sequence from "The Untouchables" which contained a chase, two fistfights, two shootings, and a knifing. The remaining children saw an exciting sports sequence. For all subjects the last minute of the film was another commercial.

Each child was then escorted to another room and seated in front of a large box which had wires leading to another room. On the box was a white light, below which were a green button labeled HELP and a red button labeled HURT. The experimenter explained that the wires were connected to a game a child in the other room was going to play. The game involved turning a handle, and each time the other child did this the white light would come

on. The experimenter explained that by pushing the buttons the subject could either help the other child by making the handle easier to turn or hurt him by making the handle hot. Each time that the white light came on, the subject had to push one of the buttons, and the longer he pushed it, the more he would help or hurt the other child. After making certain that the instructions were understood, the experimenter left the room. Each subject was given twenty trials; that is, the white light came on twenty times.

Table 4.1 shows the average length of time that the two groups—the children who had seen the violent episodes on television and those who had seen the sports sequence—pushed the HURT button. Those who had viewed the violent television sequences were more aggressive than those who had not.

TABLE 4.1
Effect of Television Viewing on the Aggressiveness of Children (*from Liebert and Baron, 1972*)

Television program viewed	Average duration of aggressive response
Aggressive—"The Untouchables"	9.92
Nonaggressive—sports sequence	7.03

Basic Features of an Experimental Design

The foregoing example illustrates many of the basic features of an experiment. The designer typically begins with an *experimental hypothesis*. Liebert and Baron hypothesized that viewing violence would stimulate aggressive behavior. Second, he chooses an *independent variable* that can be manipulated, that is, some factor that will be under the control of the experimenter. Liebert and Baron exposed some children to an aggressive sequence on television and others to a nonaggressive sequence. Finally, he arranges for the measurement of a *dependent variable,* which is expected to depend on or vary with manipulations of the independent variable. The dependent variable in this study was duration of the HURT response, an operational definition of aggression. When in such an investigation differences between groups are indeed found to be a function of variations in the independent variable, the researcher is said to have produced an *experimental effect.*

Internal Validity

An additional feature of any experimental design is the presence of at least one *control group.* A control group is necessary if the effects in any experiment are to be attributed to the manipulation of the independent variable. In the Liebert and Baron study the control group saw the nonviolent sports sequence. To illustrate this point with another example, consider a study of the effectiveness of a particular therapy in modifying some form of abnormal behavior. Let us assume that persons with initially poor self-concepts have asked for treatment and that they undergo therapy designed to remedy their condition. At the end of six months the patients are reassessed, and it is found that their self-concepts have improved

compared to what they were at the beginning of the study. Unfortunately, such an investigation would not produce valid data. The improvement in self-concept from the beginning of the treatment to the end could have been brought about by several factors in addition to or instead of the particular treatment employed. For example, it may be that certain environmental events occurred within the six months and produced the improvement. Or it may be that people with a poor self-concept acquire better feelings about themselves with the mere passage of time. Variables such as these are often called *confounds;* they make the results impossible to interpret. Studies in which the effect obtained cannot be attributed with confidence to the independent variable are called *internally invalid* studies. The design of *internally valid* research, that is, research in which the effect obtained can be confidently attributed to the manipulation of the independent variable, is a primary goal in social science.

In the example just outlined, internal validity could have been secured by the inclusion of a *control group.* Such a group might have consisted of individuals with poor self-concepts who did *not* receive the therapeutic treatment. Changes in the self-concepts of these control subjects would constitute a base line against which the effects of the independent variable can be assessed. If a change in self-concept is brought about by particular environmental events, quite beyond any therapeutic intervention, the experimental group receiving the treatment and the control group receiving no treatment are equally likely to be affected. On the other hand, if a difference is shown between the self-concepts of the treated group and those of the untreated control group, we can be relatively confident that this difference is, in fact, attributable to the treatment.

The mere inclusion of a control group, however, is not always sufficient to ensure internal validity. As an illustration, let us consider another study of therapy, this time the treatment of two hospital wards of psychiatric patients. An investigator may decide to select one ward in which to apply his experimental treatment and then select another ward as a control. When he later compares the frequencies of deviant behavior in these two groups, he will want to attribute any differences between them to the presence or absence of his treatment. But he cannot legitimately draw this inference, for he will be unable to disprove a competing hypothesis—that even before treatment the ward that happened to receive the treatment might have had a lower level of deviant behavior than the ward that became the control group. The principle of experimental design disregarded in this defective study is that of *random assignment*.

Random assignment is achieved by ensuring that every subject in the research has an equal chance of being assigned to any of the groups. For example, in a two-group experiment a coin can be tossed for each subject. If the coin turns up heads, the subject is assigned to one group; if tails, he is assigned to another. This procedure minimizes the likelihood that differences between or among the groups after treatment will reflect pretreatment differences in the samples rather than true experimental effects.

Even with both a control group and random assignment, the results of the research may still be invalid. An additional source of error is the potential biasing influence of the experimenter or observers. As Rosenthal (1966) has suggested, the expectancies of an investigator about the outcome of a study may conspire to produce results favorable to his initial hypothesis. He may subtly manipulate the subject to give expected and desired responses. Although the pervasiveness of these effects has been questioned (Barber and Silver, 1968),

investigators must remain on guard lest their results be tainted by their own expectations. To avoid biases of this type, many studies apply the so-called *double-blind* procedure. For example, in an investigation comparing the psychological effects of two drugs, the person dispensing the pills is kept ignorant (that is, blind) about their actual content, and the subject is also not informed about the treatment he is receiving. With such controls the behavior observed during the course of the treatment can only under unusual circumstances be attributed to biasing.

Earlier, we briefly defined the term experimental effect, but we have yet to learn how it can be decided that an effect is important. To evaluate this question, researchers employ the concept of *statistical significance*. Essentially, statistical significance refers to the likelihood or probability that the results of an experiment were produced by chance. Thus, in reporting the results of research, the phrase *significant difference* between groups is often employed. Such a difference is one that has little probability of occurring by chance alone and thus can be expected to be duplicated whenever the same experiment is performed again. Traditionally, in psychological research, a difference is considered statistically significant and therefore admissible as evidence if the likelihood is five or less in one hundred that the difference is a chance finding. This level of significance is called the .05 level, commonly written as $p < .05$ and read as "probability less than 5 percent."[2]

[2] Statistical significance should not be confused with the social or real-life significance of research results. An experiment can yield findings that are statistically significant yet devoid of practical importance. Moreover, the level of statistical significance considered acceptable is determined by *social convention,* that is, the rules by which contemporary scientists agree to play the game. Thus if the results of an experiment have a probability of .10 or

External Validity

The extent to which the results of any particular piece of research can be generalized beyond the immediate experiment is the measure of their *external validity*. For example, if an investigator has demonstrated that a particular treatment helps a group of patients he has tried it on, he will undoubtedly want to determine whether this particular treatment will also be effective in ministering to other patients, at other times, and in other places. Liebert and Baron would hope that the findings of their television experiment apply to violence of many kinds, shown on home television sets to children other than those who served as experimental subjects.

The external validity of the results of a psychological experiment is extremely difficult to determine. For example, merely knowing that one is a subject in a psychological experiment often alters behavior, and thus results are produced in the laboratory that may not automatically be produced in the natural environment. In many instances results obtained from investigations with laboratory animals such as rats have been generalized to humans. Such generalizations are hazardous since there are enormous differences between *Homo sapiens* and *Rattus norvegicus*. A researcher must be continually alert to the extent to which he generalizes his findings, for there are, in fact, no entirely adequate ways of dealing with the question of external validity. Some of the ways that have been proposed are discussed by Neale and Liebert (1973).

less that they occurred by chance rather than the probability of .05 or less, it is nowhere mandated that these are chance events and therefore totally worthless. The investigator may decide that, given the kind of experiment run, these results are quite encouraging and should not be thrown out altogether. Then he must convince his colleagues that these findings are indeed valid. In a sense, science is a game of *persuasion*.

Analogue Experiments

Although the experimental method is judged to be the most telling way to determine cause-effect relationships, the method has in fact been little used within the field of abnormal psychology. Who, for example, would attempt to create schizophrenia in a group of individuals as a means of determining the cause of schizophrenia? Thus, as we shall see later in this chapter, most of the research in psychopathology has *not* involved the experimental method.

Instead investigators have attempted to bring a *related* phenomenon, that is, an *analogue,* into the laboratory for more intensive study. In this way internally valid results may be obtained, although the problem of external validity may be accentuated. One type of analogue study involves the production of temporary abnormal behavior by experimental manipulations such as the administration of drugs (LSD), hypnotic suggestions, sensory deprivation, and operant shaping. If "pathology" can be experimentally induced by any one of these manipulations, the same variable, existing in the natural environment, might well be a cause of the disorder. We have already noted the problems involved in this reasoning (see Chapter 1), in the discussion of the broom-holding demonstration of Ayllon and his colleagues (1965). Results of such experiments must be interpreted with great caution.

As another example, in the next chapter we shall have occasion to review experimental work on anxiety. This work has been done almost entirely with white rats, although the results have been generalized to man, including abnormal man. It will be important to keep in mind, therefore, that we are arguing by analogy when we attempt to relate findings on reactions to stress in white rats to anxiety in human beings. At the same time, however, we do not agree with some who regard such analogue

INTRODUCTION AND BASIC ISSUES

data as totally and intrinsically worthless as far as the study of human behavior is concerned. Particularly when we discuss behavior therapy in Chapter 19, we shall have occasion to note that some important advances in the therapeutic modification of abnormal human behavior were originally developed through research with animals. Although man and lower animals differ on many important dimensions, it does not follow that behavioral principles derived from animal research are necessarily irrelevant to human behavior.

Whether a particular experiment is an analogue depends not on the experiment itself but rather on the use to which it is put. We can very readily study avoidance behavior in a white rat by running experiments with rats. The data collected from such studies are not analogue data if we limit our discussion to the behavior of rats. They become analogue data only when we draw implications from them and apply them to other domains, such as anxiety in man.

The Correlational Method

Correlational techniques address questions of the form "Do variable X and variable Y go together or vary together (correlate)?" In other words, questions are asked concerning relationships; for example, "Is schizophrenia related to social class?" or "Is anxiety related to scores obtained on college examinations?" Thus the correlational method establishes whether there is a relationship between or among two or more variables. Numerous examples can be drawn from everyday life. Income correlates positively with the number of luxuries purchased: the higher the income, the more luxuries purchased. Height tends to be positively correlated with weight: taller people are usually heavier. This second relationship, that between

height and weight, is by no means perfect, for many individuals are "overweight" or too fat for their height and "underweight" or too thin for their height. The relationship, however, is a strong one.

The correlational method involves obtaining pairs of observations, such as height and weight, on each member in a group of subjects (Table 4.2). Once such pairs of observations are obtained, we can determine how strong the relationship is between the two sets of observations. The most prevalent means of measuring such a relationship was devised by Karl

TABLE **4.2**
*Data for Determining a Correlation**

Individuals	Height	Weight, pounds
John	5'10"	170
Asher	22"	10
Eve	42"	30
Carol	5' 6"	120
Gail	5' 3"	105
Jerry	5'10"	172
Bob	6' 1"	175
Marv	5' 8"	168
Jim	6' 2"	200
Harry	5' 9"	175
Alan	5' 7"	150

* For these figures $r = +.87$

Pearson and is referred to as the *Pearson product moment correlation coefficient,* often denoted by the symbol r. This statistic may take any value between −1.00 and +1.00 and measures both the *magnitude* and the *direction* of a relationship. The higher the *absolute value* of r, the larger or stronger the relationship between the two variables. An r of either +1.00 or −1.00 indicates a perfect relationship, whereas an r of .00 indicates that the variables are unrelated. If the sign of r is positive, the two variables are said to be *positively related.* As the values for variable X increase, those for variable Y also tend to increase. Conversely, when the sign of r is negative, variables are said to be *negatively related;* in this instance as values for one variable increase, those for the other tend to decrease. The correlation between height and weight, based on the data in Table 4.2, is +.87, indicating a strong positive relationship; as height increases, so does weight.

To have a better feel for a particular relationship, it is often helpful to plot it graphically. Figure 4.2 presents diagrams of several of the correlations just discussed. In the diagrams each entry point corresponds to two values determined for the given subject, the value of variable X and that for variable Y. For perfect relationships all the points fall on a single straight line: if we know the value of only one of the variables for an individual, we can state with certainty the value of the other variable. Similarly, when the correlation is relatively large, there is only a small degree of scatter about the line of perfect correlation. The values tend to scatter increasingly and become dispersed as the correlations become lower. When the correlation reaches .00, knowledge of a person's score on one variable tells us nothing about his score on the other.

The results of any correlational investigation, like those of the experimental method, can be evaluated for their statistical significance. Correlations that could be expected to occur by chance alone fewer than five times in one hundred are conventionally spoken of as being statistically significant. In general, as the size of the correlation coefficient increases, the result is more and more likely to be statistically significant.[3]

Although it is much more widely used in the field of abnormal psychology than the experiment, the correlational method has a serious flaw — it does not allow us to determine cause-effect relationships. But so-called "organismic variables" such as sex, age, social class, and body build are exceedingly difficult or impossible to manipulate in an experiment, for both practical and moral reasons. Moreover, the direct manipulation of certain variables might be acceptable at some levels but not at those found in the natural environment. For example, inflicting mild pain or discomfort might (or might not) be an ethically legitimate experimental procedure, but it would clearly be unethical to induce the extremely painful but psychologically significant experiences to which mankind is only too often subjected. Finally, as we have already indicated, the experimental production of any kind of serious psychopathology would clearly be indefensible. Thus the correlational technique is the major strategy used in psychopathology research.

Many investigators have compared the performances of schizophrenics and normal people on laboratory tasks such as reaction time, proverb interpretation, and size estimation (for

---

[3] Whether a correlation attains statistical significance also depends on the number of observations that were made. The greater the number of observations, the smaller r needs to be in order to reach statistical significance. Thus a correlation of r = .30 is statistically significant when the number of observations is large, for example, 300, although it would not be significant if only 30 observations have been made.

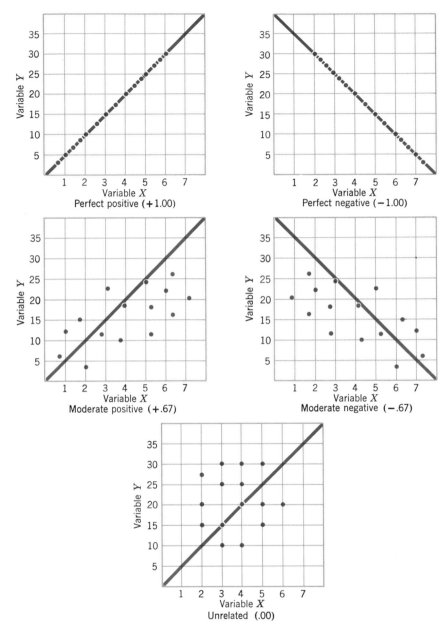

FIGURE **4.2**
Scatter diagrams showing various degrees of relationship.

example, Kopfstein and Neale, 1972). Often these investigations are not recognized as correlational, perhaps because the subjects come to a laboratory for testing. Yet a comparison of a diagnostic group with some control group is not an experiment; no variable has been manipulated since the schizophrenics have already been classified as abnormal before they took the tests.

Directionality and Third-Variable Problems

A correlation cannot be interpreted in causal terms because of two major problems of interpretation, the *directionality problem* and the *third-variable problem*. With respect to directionality, a sizable correlation between two variables tells us only that they are related or tend to covary with one another, but we do not really know whether one is caused by the other, or even if they are at all causally related. For example, correlations have been found between the diagnosis of schizophrenia and social class; lower-class people with emotional problems are more frequently diagnosed as schizophrenic than are middle- and upper-class people. One possible explanation is that the stresses of living in the lower social classes produce the behavior that is subsequently labeled schizophrenic. But a second and perhaps equally plausible hypothesis has been advanced. It may be that the disorganized behavior patterns of schizophrenic individuals cause them to lose their jobs and thus to become impoverished. The problem of directionality is present in many correlational designs; hence the often-cited dictum "Correlation does not imply causation."[4]

As for the third-variable problem, it may be that neither of the two variables studied in the correlation produces the other. Rather, some as yet unspecified variable or process may be responsible for the correlation. Consider the following example.

. . . one regularly finds a high positive correlation between the number of churches in a city and the number of crimes committed in that city. That is, the more churches a city has, the more crimes are committed in it. Does this mean that religion fosters crime or does it mean that crime fosters religion? It means neither. The relationship is due to a particular third variable—population. The higher the population of a particular community the greater . . . the number of churches and . . . the frequency of criminal activity (Neale and Liebert, 1973, p. 86).

Are there any solutions to the directionality and third-variable problems? In general, the answer is yes, although the solutions are only partially satisfactory and do not permit unambiguous causal inferences to be made from correlational data (Neale and Liebert, 1973). In the field of abnormal psychology there are in fact fewer problems with directionality than with third variables. If, for example, we find that schizophrenia is correlated with slow reaction time, few people would argue that slow reaction time causes schizophrenia. The possibility that the relationship is produced by a third variable, such as drug dosage, remains very real, however (see Box 4.1). For this reason we shall examine the technique that is most often used in attempting to control third variables.

---

[4] Although correlation does not imply causation, the determination of whether or not two variables correlate may allow for the *disconfirmation* of certain causal hypotheses. That is, *causation does imply correlation*. For example, if

an investigator has asserted that cigarette smoking causes lung cancer, he implies that lung cancer and cigarette smoking will be positively correlated. His studies of the two variables must show this positive correlation, or his theory will be disproved.

Controlling for Drug Effects in Correlational Research with Institutionalized Patients

Schizophrenics are very likely to be on a heavy regimen of tranquilizing medicine. Comparing them with normal people is complicated by the fact that drugs might well introduce differences between the two groups that have nothing to do with schizophrenia. This problem has been dealt with in several ways. First, if hospital authorities will cooperate, the schizophrenic patients may be withdrawn from their drug regimen for several weeks, the period of time that is required for the drug to leave the body completely. Chapman (1963), however, has noted that the hospital staff may object to the increased pathology manifested by certain patients when medication is withdrawn. Because the greater number of disturbing symptoms of these patients upsets or threatens members of the staff responsible for them, pressure is brought to bear on the investigator to put these patients back on their medicine. The sample of patients remaining off the drug at the end of the "drying out" period is thus a biased one, comprised of individuals with a schizophrenic diagnosis who did not react adversely to the termination of medication.

A second strategy of investigators is to withhold medication from newly admitted patients until a given study has been completed. In addition to the possible ethical considerations raised by such a procedure, a large percentage of newly admitted patients are already taking medication. Moreover, many newly admitted patients are in such a disorganized state that they cannot participate in psychological research. The second strategy has been applied rather infrequently.

Finally, some investigators have tried to assess the potential effects of drugs by correlating level of dosage with the behavior in question. Since only the schizophrenic and not the control group is likely to be medicated, the correlation can only be performed within the schizophrenic group. If a significant relationship emerges—for instance, the higher the dosage, the poorer the performance—it might be argued that schizophrenics perform more poorly than controls because of their medication. Such an argument is flawed, however. The relationship between dosage level and performance may be produced by a third variable, such as severity of pathology, for patients showing the most severe symptoms may also be those who are given the most medication. Thus the practical problem of controlling drug dosage remains unsolved in most investigations of psychiatric patients.

Ex Post Facto Analysis

In ex post facto analysis subjects are matched on a third variable in an effort to simulate experimental procedures. For example, the investigator may be comparing the performance of schizophrenics and hospital aides on a test of cognitive ability. Let us assume that the schizophrenics are found to perform much more poorly than the aides. Clearly, the investigator is interested in attributing the difference between the two groups to the fact that one group is schizophrenic and the other not. Because the variable of interest, schizophrenia, has not been manipulated, however, the presence of a third variable may affect the results. By ex post facto analysis the investigator attempts to match subjects on third variables that seem particularly plausible. In the example we are considering, variables such as social class, intelligence, and years of education are likely candidates for such a matching process. If the effects of these variables can be eliminated, the investigator can with more confidence attribute any differences between the two groups to the presence of schizophrenia in one of them.

The ex post facto technique, however, cannot entirely eliminate the problem of the third variable. First, regardless of the number of variables on which matching occurs, there can be no guarantee that some other unknown variable is not the important controlling factor determining the differences between the two groups. In other words, the phase "third variable" is really a misnomer, for *any* number of variables might account for the observed effects in a way that is masked by the correlational research design.[5]

The ex post facto technique is also subject to other difficulties. For example, matching may drastically reduce the generality or external validity of any conclusions that may be drawn from a study. Let us assume that schizophrenics generally complete less schooling than do hospital aides. Noticing this fact, the investigator decides that he will have to match his subjects on amount of education in order to eliminate the effects of this variable as a potential confound. He may be forced to select for his study only those schizophrenics who have educational levels close to those of the hospital aides. Thus he ends up studying an *unrepresentative subpopulation* of schizophrenics. The results of such an investigation cannot be generalized to the entire population of schizophrenics since the subjects who were studied have, on the average, completed more education that most schizophrenics.

With no viable alternative method available, investigators who study clinical groups must rely on correlational techniques. But they must always keep in mind that certain differences between clinical and control groups may make correlations very difficult to interpret.

Mixed Designs

The experimental and correlational research techniques that we have just discussed can be combined in what is called a *mixed design*. In a mixed design subjects from two or more discrete and typically nonoverlapping populations are each assigned to different experimental conditions. The two different types of populations, for example, schizophrenics and neurotics, constitute correlational variables, the manipulated conditions experimental variables.

To illustrate the primary advantage of a mixed design, we shall consider an investigation of the effectiveness of three types of therapy, the experimental variable, in psychiatric

---

[5] This is but one illustration of why scientists seldom make absolute statements. There always seems to be a qualification that must be added in any scientific generalization or conclusion.

patients who have been divided into two groups on the basis of the severity of their illnesses, the correlational variables. The hypothetical results from such a study are presented in Figure 4.3. Figure 4.3A shows that treatment 3 produced the greatest amount of improvement when the patients were not separated into groups on the basis of the severity of their illness. Hence when no information about differential characteristics of the patients is available, treatment 3 would be preferred. When the severity of the patients' difficulties is considered, however, treatment 3 would no longer be the therapy of choice for *any* of the patients. Rather, as seen in Figure 4.3B, for those with less severe illness treatment 1 would be selected and for patients with more severe illness treatment 2 would be preferred. Thus a mixed design can identify the limitations of particular experimental effects, determining which particular treatment applies best to which group of subjects.

Most mixed designs are analyzed by the same statistical procedures that are employed with pure experimental designs, tempting us to interpret the results as if all the variables were, in fact, manipulated. As we have previously noted, however, one of the variables in a

mixed design is correlational. Therefore the problems we have previously noted in interpreting correlations are to be found in mixed designs as well.

Single-Subject Research

Research does not always have to be conducted on groups of people. In this section we shall consider research designs employing but a single subject. Two major procedures have been developed, the *case study* and the *single-subject experimental design*.

The strategy of relying on a single subject appears to violate many of the principles of research designs that we have discussed. No control group can act as a check on a single subject, and the individual who does serve as our research participant cannot, of course, have been randomly assigned to a particular experimental situation. Moreover, any generalizations made may really relate to a particular or unique aspect of the one individual whose behavior we have explored. Hence the study of a single individual would appear unlikely to yield any findings that could possess the slightest degree of internal or external validity. But, as we shall see, the study of a single sub-

FIGURE **4.3**

Effects of three treatments on patients whose symptoms are severe and less severe. The amount of improvement brought about by each treatment varies, depending on how it is administered. (A) When the severity of the illness is not known, the patients are treated together. (B) When the severity is known, they are divided into groups and treated separately.

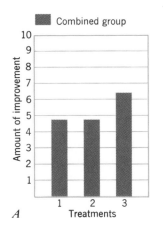

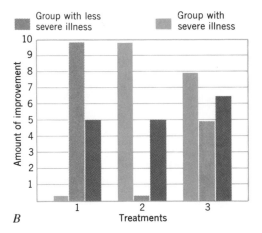

ject *can* be an effective research technique for certain purposes.

The Case Study

In making a case study, the clinician collects historical and biographical information on a single individual. Although case reports from practicing clinicians usually lack the degree of control and objectivity of research done by other methods, these descriptive accounts have played some important roles in the study of abnormal behavior. Specifically, the case history has been used in each of the following ways: (1) to demonstrate important, often novel, methods or procedures of interviewing, diagnosis, and treatment; (2) to provide a detailed account of a rare or unusual phenomenon; (3) to disconfirm allegedly universal aspects of a particular theoretical proposition; and (4) to generate hypotheses for future controlled research.

A famous case history of *multiple personality* reported by Thigpen and Cleckley in 1954 serves several of the foregoing purposes. The investigators described a patient, "Eve White," who displayed at various times three very distinct personalities.

Eve White had been seen in psychotherapy for several months because she was experiencing severe headaches accompanied by blackouts. Her therapist described her as a retiring and gently conventional figure. One day during the course of an interview, however, she changed abruptly and in a surprising way.

As if seized by sudden pain, she put both hands to her head. After a tense moment of silence, both hands dropped. There was a quick, reckless smile, and, in a bright voice that sparkled, she said, "Hi there, Doc!" The demure and constrained posture of Eve White had melted into buoyant repose. . . . This new and apparently carefree girl spoke casually of Eve White and her problems, always using she *or* her *in every reference, always respecting the strict bounds of a separate identity. . . . When asked her name, she immediately replied, "Oh, I'm Eve Black"* (p. 137).

After this rather startling revelation, Eve was observed over a period of fourteen months in a series of interviews that ran to almost a hundred hours. During this time still a third personality, Jane, emerged. At first Jane appeared to be only a composite of the two Eves, but later she became a well-integrated person in her own right.

The case of Eve White, Eve Black, and Jane constitutes a valuable classic in psychiatric literature because it is one of only a few detailed accounts of a rare phenomenon, multiple personality. Moreover, in addition to illustrating the phenomenon itself, the original report of Thigpen and Cleckley provides valuable details about the interview procedures that they followed; and it sheds light on the way in which the behavior may have developed and how this one case of multiple personality was ultimately resolved.

As an example of how the case history can be used effectively to demonstrate various methods of treatment, we include an excerpt from the case of a mute psychotic woman. Through a combination of reinforcement and imitative learning procedures, she was successfully coaxed to speak clearly and loudly enough to be understood (Neale and Liebert, 1969). The excerpt provides reasonably detailed information about novel aspects of the procedure that was developed and thus serves as the basis for its further application by others.

> During these sessions a device was introduced to facilitate the patient's acquisition of more audible responses. From the beginning of treatment Martha's low volume had posed a constant problem. . . . this puts a heavy load on the discriminative capacity of T [the therapist] and thereby lowers the reliability of the reward contingency. The device consisted of a microphone, amplifier, and neon light. T controlled the volume necessary to turn on the light by a rheostat. If one of Martha's responses was insufficient in volume, she was asked to repeat the response. Food was withheld until Martha's volume increased sufficiently to turn on the light.
>
> The effect of this device was dramatic. Martha's volume increased markedly and this change was maintained throughout subsequent sessions. On session 13, when the light was first introduced, Martha produced 47 responses which did not turn on the light. On session 17, however, only 3 responses were produced which were not of sufficient volume (pp. 831–832).

Case histories can provide especially telling instances that negate an assumed universal relationship or law. Freud, for example, initially believed that his female patients' reports of sexual assaults by their fathers or uncles were accurate descriptions of events, and moreover that these events had bearing on the problems being treated. Later, on the basis of a chance finding that the supposed sexual assailant of one of his patients could not have been physically present at the time indicated, he came to recognize that some of these sexual assaults were fantasies. A single case provided a negative instance, and Freud rethought his previously held belief in the truth of his patients' recollections.

The case study plays a unique and important role because it is very often exploratory in nature. Circumstances are permitted to "vary as they will," with the often desirable revelation of new and perhaps important hypotheses that could not have been uncovered in a more controlled investigation.

> . . . it is a serious mistake to discount the importance of clinical experience per se. There is nothing mysterious about the fact that repeated exposure to any given set of conditions makes the recipient aware of subtle cues and contingencies in that setting which elude the scrutiny of those less familiar with the situation. Clinical experience enables a therapist to recognize problems and identify trends that are usually beyond the perception of novices, regardless of their general expertise. It is at this level that new ideas will come to the prac-

titioner and often constitute breakthroughs that could not be derived from animal analogues or tightly controlled investigations. Different kinds of data and different levels of information are obtained in the laboratory and the clinic. Each is necessary, useful, and desirable (Lazarus and Davison, 1971, p. 197).

Thus case studies often provide important hypotheses which experimenters can later subject to more controlled investigation. In the presentation of a case history, however, the controls for confirming one hypothesis and ruling out alternative hypotheses are usually absent. To illustrate this lack of validity, let us consider another case that has received much public attention, the case of "Bridey Murphy."

When hypnotized, a sedate New England woman "regressed," apparently beyond her early childhood and back into an earlier life in which she was Bridey Murphy, an Irish lass. Under hypnosis the woman was able to report, in a distinct Gaelic brogue, many remarkable details of a town in Ireland which she had never visited. Her case history supposedly demonstrated a true instance of reincarnation. Later, however, it was learned that the woman had been reared, in part, by an Irish maid who had described to her most of the accounts later reported under hypnosis. The maid had also provided an excellent model for the brogue that the hypnotized subject used so convincingly. At least in this instance it is apparent that the hypothesis presented by the case history lacked validity.

Single-Subject Experimental Designs.

The experimental method, which we have previously discussed in connection with groups of subjects, may also be applied with a single subject, improving on the internal validity of the case report. A method developed by Tate and Baroff (1966) for reducing the self-injurious behavior of a nine-year-old boy, Sam, serves as an example. The lad, who had been diagnosed as psychotic, engaged in a wide range of self-injurious behavior, such as banging his head against floors and walls, slapping his face with his hands, punching his face and head with his fists, hitting his shoulder with his chin, and kicking himself. Despite his self-injurious behavior, Sam was not entirely antisocial. In fact, he obviously enjoyed contact with other people and would cling to them, wrap his arms around them, and sit in their laps. This affectionate behavior gave the investigators the idea for an experimental treatment.[6]

The study ran for twenty days. For a period of time on each of the first five days, the frequency of Sam's self-injurious actions was observed and recorded. Then on each of the next five days the two adult experimenters accompanied Sam on a short walk around the campus, during which they talked to him and held his hands continuously. The adults responded to each of Sam's self-injurious actions by immediately jerking their hands away from him and not touching him again until three seconds after such activity had ceased. The frequency of the self-injurious acts was again recorded. As part of the experiment, the schedule was then systematically reversed. For the next five days there were no walks, and Sam's self-afflicting behavior was again merely observed. Then for the last five days the experimenters reinstated the punishment

[6] The use of the adjective experimental in this context prompts us to distinguish between two different meanings of the word. As applied to the methods that have been discussed, the adjective refers to the manipulation of a variable that allows conclusions of a cause-effect relationship to be drawn. But here the word refers to a treatment whose effects are unknown or only poorly understood. Thus an "experimental drug" is one about which we know relatively little; however, such a drug *might* well be used in a correlational design.

procedure. The dramatic reduction in undesirable behavior induced by the treatment is indicated in Figure 4.4. Such designs, usually referred to as *reversal* (or ABAB) *designs,* involve the careful measurement of some aspect of the subject's behavior during a given time period, the base line (A), during a period when some treatment is introduced (B), during a reinstatement of the conditions that prevailed in the base line period (A), and finally during a reintroduction of the experimental manipulation (B). If behavior in the experimental period is different from that in the base line period, reverses when the experimentally manipulated conditions are reversed, and "re-reverses" when the treatment is again introduced, there is little doubt that the manipulation, rather than chance or uncontrolled factors, has produced the change.

The reversal technique cannot always be employed, however, for the initial state of a subject may not be recoverable, as when treatment produces an irreversible change. Moreover, in studies of therapeutic procedures, reinstating the original condition of the subject or patient would generally be considered an unethical practice. Most therapists would be extremely unwilling to reinstate the very behavior for which a client has sought help, merely to prove that a particular treatment was indeed the effective agent in changing the behavior.

When the reversal technique does not apply, the *multiple-base-line* procedure, wherein two

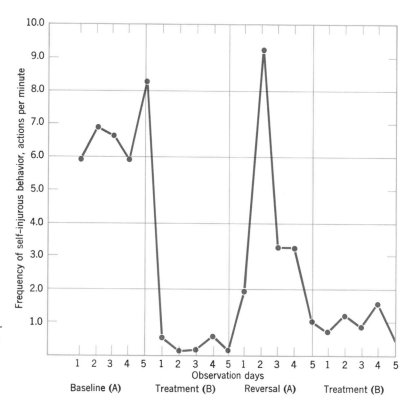

FIGURE **4.4**
Effects of contingent punishment procedure in an ABAB single-subject design. Adapted from Tate and Baroff, 1966.

or more behaviors are chosen for study, is the method of choice. For example, if a child has "learning problems," both mathematical and reading performances might be selected as the two areas for treatment. When observing the child, the investigator may notice that he is inattentive during lessons and proceed to collect base line data on the degree of attentiveness during *both* mathematics *and* reading sessions. Reward is then introduced for attention paid to the mathematics lessons but not for attention paid during reading sessions. Again, the attentiveness of the child during both kinds of lessons is measured. Finally, in a third phase of the experiment, reward is introduced for attention paid during reading as well as mathematics lessons.

A hypothetical pattern of the attentiveness of the child during the course of the experiment is shown in Figure 4.5. If such a pattern were indeed obtained, it would provide convincing evidence that the introduction of reward and not other factors was responsible for modifying the child's behavior. Had some uncontrolled environmental influence improved the child's attention, it presumably would have worked equally well during both mathematics and reading classes. Moreover, if reward were not the agent responsible for change, attentiveness during mathematics lessons would not have markedly improved as compared to attentiveness during reading sessions. Thus, by

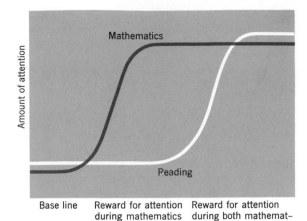

FIGURE **4.5**
Outcome of a multiple-base-line, single-subject experiment.

choosing two base lines of behavior to be modified (hence multiple base lines), the investigator was able to eliminate certain possible sources of invalidity.

As indicated earlier, even though an experimental effect is demonstrated in an experiment with a single subject, no generalization may be possible. The fact that a particular treatment works for a single subject does not necessarily imply that the treatment will be universally effective. If the search for more widely applicable treatment is the major focus of an investigation, the single-subject design has a serious drawback. It may well help investigators to decide whether large-scale research with groups is warranted, however.

SUMMARY

Science represents an agreed-upon problem-solving enterprise, with specific procedures for gathering and interpreting data in order to build a systematic body of knowledge. Scientific statements must have the following characteristics: they must be testable in the public arena, they must entail reliable observations, and although they may infer unobservable processes, the concepts inferred must be operationalized.

It is important to consider the various methods that scientists employ to collect data and arrive at conclusions. The experimental method entails the manipulation of independent variables and the careful measurement of their effects on dependent variables. An experiment usually begins with a hypothesis to be tested. Subjects are generally assigned to at least two groups: an experimental group, which experiences the manipulation of the independent variable, and a control group, which does not. If differences between the experimental and control groups are observed on the dependent variables, we can conclude that the independent variable had an effect. Furthermore, it is important to ensure that experimental and control subjects do not differ from each other before the introduction of the independent variable; thus they are usually assigned randomly to groups. The experimenter must guard against bias by keeping himself unaware of what group a given subject is in, experimental or control. If these conditions are met, the experiment has internal validity. The external validity of the findings, whether they can be generalized to situations not studied within the experiment, can be assessed only by performing experiments in the external domain.

Since most variables in abnormal psychology cannot be experimentally manipulated, correlational methods are the important means of conducting research. Various statistical procedures allow us to determine the extent to which two or more variables correlate or covary. Unlike experimental findings, however, conclusions from nearly all correlational studies cannot legitimately be interpreted in cause-effect terms, although there is great temptation to do so.

Mixed designs are combinations of experimental and correlational methods. For example two kinds of patients may be exposed to various treatments.

Finally, a single individual can be studied in several ways. Clinical case studies serve unique and important functions in psychopathology, such as allowing rare phenomena to be studied intensively in all their complexity. Certain single-subject experimental designs that expose one subject to different treatments over a period of time provide scientifically acceptable information.

A science is only as good as its methodology. Thus students of abnormal psychology must appreciate the rules that social scientists currently abide by if they are to be able to evaluate the research and theories that form the subject matter of the remainder of this book.

PART II

ANXIETY AND DEPRESSION

5

Views on Anxiety

6

Neurotic Syndromes

7

Psychophysiological Disorders

8

Depression

CHAPTER 5
Views on Anxiety

There is, perhaps, no other single topic in abnormal psychology that is as important and controversial as anxiety. This emotional state is considered a symptom of almost all psychopathologies and in particular of the neurotic disorders. Furthermore, anxiety plays an important role in the study of the psychology of normal people as well, for very few of us go through even a week of our lives without experiencing in at least some measure what we would all agree is the emotion anxiety or fear. But the briefer periods of anxiety that beset the normal individual who is not living in trying circumstances are hardly comparable in intensity or duration, nor are they as debilitating, as those suffered by the neurotic. The question of overriding importance to psychopathologists is how we are to conceptualize anxiety.[1] Three methods have been used to assess it: self-report, behavioral, and physiological.

ASPECTS OF ANXIETY

You feel as if you were on the battlefield or had stumbled against a wild animal in the dark, and all the time you are conversing with your fellows in normal peaceful surroundings. . . . With this your head feels vague and immense and stuffed with cottonwool, it is difficult and trying to concentrate; and, most frightening of all, the quality of your sensory appreciation of the universe undergoes an essential change (editors of Lancet, *1952, pp. 83–84).*

---

[1] In the theoretical and research literature the terms anxiety, fear, nervousness, and tension seem to be employed interchangeably. Those of psychoanalytic persuasion prefer to reserve the term anxiety for fear that is experienced in the absence of external danger; most learning theorists, on the other hand, apply the term anxiety to fear learned in the presence of specific harmless stimuli (for example, Maher, 1966). There is much inconsistency. For our purposes we shall employ all these terms interchangeably, specifying only the conditions that seem to elicit a given response. Thus we shall have occasion to speak of unrealistic anxiety or fear and neurotic anxiety or fear, in contrast with realistic anxiety or fear and objective anxiety.

The Assessment of Anxiety

Self-report

The excerpt just given, describing an attack of anxiety, is quoted in *Varieties of Psychopathological Experience* by Landis and Mettler (1964). Their approach, as aptly indicated by the title of their book, is *phenomenological*. In assessing psychopathological symptoms, these authors give overriding importance to the individual's immediate subjective impressions of himself and his world. The very vivid description in this quotation, self-reported by the subject, would be taken by the phenomenologist as the material to work with in trying to understand anxiety.

Allowing a subject to describe the phenomena of his emotions in his own terms, however, makes it difficult to compare his experiences with those of others and, even more important, to quantify what he says. Researchers have therefore devised various self-report questionnaires which attempt to direct the individual's impressions into standardized terms. The following are some sample items from the Taylor Manifest Anxiety Scale (Taylor, 1953), which consists of fifty items drawn from the MMPI.

I work under a great deal of strain.	<u>True</u>	False
I am usually calm and not easily upset.	True	<u>False</u>
I sweat very easily even on cool days.	<u>True</u>	False
I always have enough energy when faced with difficulty.	True	<u>False</u>
My sleep is restless and disturbed.	<u>True</u>	False

An anxious person would underline the true and false responses as indicated. The test is scored by simply summing the number of "anxious" responses made by the subject. This score is then assumed to represent his general level of anxiety.

Overt Behavioral

Another means of assessing anxiety is to observe overt behavior for reactions and movements that are believed to reflect the internal emotional state. A person would be judged anxious when he can be observed to tremble, perspire, bite his nails, or flee from a situation—in short, when he is behaving in ways assumed to reflect anxiety. We have already described in Chapter 3 an experiment that examined and measured anxiety in overt behavioral terms. The observers trained to administer Paul's (1966) Timed Behavioral Checklist for Performance Anxiety (page 78) time-sampled the overt behavior of subjects in a stressful situation, rating them on twenty indices of anxiety.

Physiological

Anxiety is also often defined physiologically, in terms of activities of the autonomic nervous system and the output of certain endocrine glands (see Box 5.1). Some physiological changes that supposedly indicate anxiety can be observed overtly, for example, rapid breathing and sweating, but they may also be monitored with electronic instruments for more precise determinations. Other physiological changes, such as increased heart rate and a greater output of epinephrine by the adrenal glands, can only be determined by monitoring.

Anxiety as a Construct

In the foregoing assessments of anxiety, something important is left out, namely the situation in which measures are being taken. What would be revealed, for example, if recording electrodes were attached to a woman who is about to have sexual relations? Both before and during sexual activity the heartbeat is very likely to be faster, blood pressure higher, perspiration greater, and breathing more rapid, all physiological responses that are generally regarded as indicators of sexual excitement as well as of anxiety. But why would we not conclude that our female subject is, indeed, anxious as she contemplates sexual intercourse? As we shall see in Chapter 11, many people are debilitated by fear in sexual situations. How can an investigator distinguish rapid breathing that reflects sexual excitement from rapid breathing that reflects anxiety? Part of the answer necessarily lies in other observations being made concurrently. If at the time physiological measures are being taken the female subject convincingly reports that she is looking forward to what is to come; and if she ultimately derives great enjoyment from her sexual partner, we would almost certainly choose to interpret her rapid breathing and other physiological responses as indicating sexual arousal. The situation and her self-report of it must be taken into consideration.

Would that things were so simple, that a distinction between two emotional states could always be made on the basis of situational cues and verbal reports. But the many measures of anxiety, besides being indicators of other emotional states, have also been found time and again *not* to correlate well with one another (cf. Martin, 1961; Lang, 1969). In a stressful situation such as being threatened with painful electric shock, many people report being very nervous, but their heart rates may be lower rather than elevated. An individual taking an important examination for which he is ill-prepared may deny feeling anxious and yet be observed trembling. In spite of these low intercorrelations, many workers continue to regard

the concept of anxiety as a useful one for organizing and interrelating data from numerous sources. Maher (1966) and Lang (1969), for example, consider anxiety to be a hypothetical *construct,* a convenient fiction or inferred state that mediates between a threatening situation and the observed behavior of an organism. They also assume that the construct is multifaceted or multidimensional, and that each facet is not necessarily evoked by a given stressful situation or always expressed to the same degree, thus explaining the low intercorrelations of the measures of anxiety.[2]

As a scientific construct, anxiety must be tied to observables, the conditions that produce it and the effects that follow its induction. For this reason Skinner (1953), as we have indicated earlier, argues that mediators are *not* essential in accounting for behavior. Since the construct of anxiety is linked to stimuli and responses, why not dispense with it and talk only of observables? Furthermore, might not the inference of an internal state lead us to believe that an adequate explanation has been found and thereby discourage the continuing search for ways to predict and control behavior?

These are cogent objections, and they have forced workers to exercise great care in their use of the anxiety construct. As noted in

---

[2] It is worth mentioning that similar problems with respect to poor intercorrelations exist in other areas of psychology. For instance, one construct in conditioning is "strength of learning," often operationalized as the number of times a response continues to be evoked after reward has been withdrawn (extinction). Strength of learning, however, is not reflected in a single measurement; rather the concept is measured in a number of different ways by different investigators. For example, they may set up their experiments to measure the force with which a response is made as it is being extinguished, the latency of responses while they are being extinguished, and so forth. Simultaneous measurements of numbers, force, and latency of the responses during extinction do not correlate highly.

BOX **5.1** *The Autonomic Nervous System*

The mammalian nervous system can be considered to be made up of two relatively separate functional divisions: the somatic or voluntary and the autonomic or involuntary. Because the autonomic nervous system is especially important in the study of emotional behavior, it will be useful to review its main characteristics and the ways its activity can be monitored.

Skeletal muscles, such as those that move our limbs, are innervated by the voluntary nervous system. Much of our behavior, however, is dependent on a nervous system that operates generally without our awareness and has traditionally been viewed as beyond voluntary control. Hence the term autonomic. The autonomic nervous system (ANS) innervates the endocrine glands, the heart, and the so-called smooth muscles which are found in the walls of the blood vessels, stomach, intestines, kidneys, and other organs. This nervous system is itself divided into two parts, the sympathetic and parasympathetic nervous systems (Figure 5.1), which sometimes work against each other, sometimes in unison. The sympathetic portion of the ANS, when energized, accelerates the heartbeat, dilates the pupils, inhibits intestinal activity, and initiates other smooth muscle and glandular responses that prepare the organism for sudden activity and stress. Indeed, some physiologists view the sympathetic nervous system as primarily excitatory, whereas the other division, the parasympathetic, is viewed as responsible for maintenance functions and more quiescent behavior, such as deceleration of the heartbeat, constriction of the pupils, and speeding up contractions of the intestines. Division of activities is not quite so clear-cut, however, for the parasympathetic system may be active during conditions of stress. Animals, and humans to their consternation, may urinate and defecate involuntarily when extremely frightened.

The activities of the ANS are frequently assessed by electrical and chemical measurements and analyses in attempts to understand the nature of emotion. Two important measures are heart rate and the galvanic skin response (GSR). Each heartbeat generates spreading changes in electrical potential which can be recorded by an electrocardiograph. Electrodes are placed near the heart and also on a limb and lead to a galvanometer, an instrument for measuring electric currents. The deflections of this instrument may be seen as waves on an oscilloscope, or a pen recorder may register the waves on graph paper. Both types of recordings are called electrocardiograms. Generally, a fast heart rate is taken to indicate increased arousal.

Anxiety, fear, anger, and other emotions elicit greater sweat gland activity. The electrophysiological processes in the cells of the sweat glands in turn change the conductance of the skin, the change referred to as the GSR. Skin conductance may be measured by recording with surface electrodes the very small differences in electrical potential that always exist between any two points on the skin. This voltage shows a pronounced change after stimulation. Or we may record the current that flows through the skin when a small voltage derived from an external source is passed through the subject, usually by means of electrodes pasted to the palm and back of the hand. This voltage also shows a pronounced change after stimulation. The

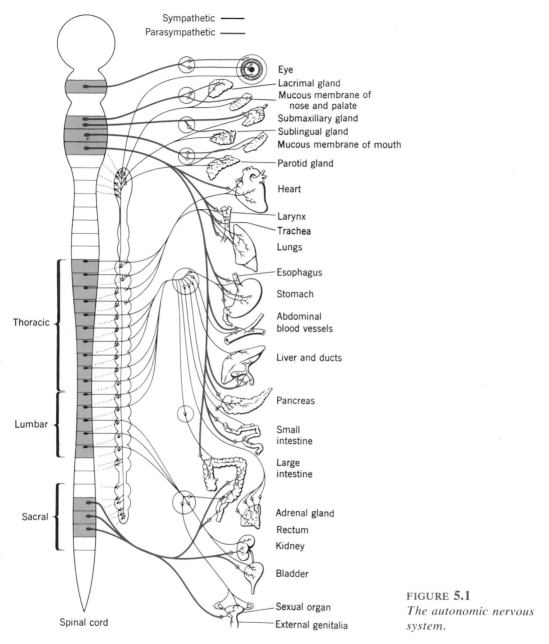

Sympathetic ———
Parasympathetic ———

Eye
Lacrimal gland
Mucous membrane of
    nose and palate
Submaxillary gland
Sublingual gland
Mucous membrane of mouth
Parotid gland
Heart
Larynx
Trachea
Lungs
Esophagus
Stomach
Abdominal
blood vessels
Liver and ducts
Pancreas
Small
intestine
Large
intestine
Adrenal gland
Rectum
Kidney
Bladder
Sexual organ
External genitalia

Thoracic

Lumbar

Sacral

Spinal cord

FIGURE **5.1**
*The autonomic nervous
system.*

percentage of change from the normal or base line conductance is for either
method the measure of reactivity. High conductance, or alternatively low
resistance, is thought to reflect increased autonomic activity. Since the
sweat glands are innervated only by the sympathetic nervous system,
increased sweat gland activity indicates sympathetic autonomic excitation.

Chapter 4, investigators who employ mediators such as anxiety do so in hopes of better organizing their data and of generating hypotheses. We seldom find an experimental psychologist speaking about anxiety without being able at any time to explain how and why he infers that the emotional state exists. Furthermore, it seems that certain experiments would not be undertaken or could not be explained without inferring a mediating state.

To illustrate, let us consider an experiment reviewed by Rescorla and Solomon (1967). Dogs were taught to avoid a stimulus (CS) by pairing it repeatedly with a painful shock (UCS). Then they were totally paralyzed with injections of a curare drug, which prevents movement of the skeletal muscles. One group of animals, while paralyzed, were repeatedly presented with the CS but shock did not accompany it. In Pavlovian, classical conditioning terms, these would be considered attempts to extinguish the conditioned response. Did these animals learn, while paralyzed and unable to move, that the CS was in fact no longer followed by shock? Phrased another way, did the previously-learned fear of the CS undergo any extinction? The answer was obtained on a subsequent day when the dogs in this group had completely recovered from the curare and were confronted with the CS. The unshocked presentations of the CS a day or two earlier had indeed reduced avoidance behavior, even though no overt response could have occurred during the curare paralysis. The control animals, who had been confronted with no stimuli while paralyzed, did not show a reduction in avoidance behavior.

How do we account for such striking findings? Rescorla and Solomon find it necessary, and legitimate, to infer a mediating fear which was lessened when the dogs were presented with unshocked CS while paralyzed with curare. Clearly, something was being unlearned during the time that the dogs could not show overt behavior. By positing a mediating fear, it is possible to make sense of these findings and to relate them to a wealth of other theory and research. The experiment just described does indicate that anxiety, or fear, can be useful as an explanatory device. We turn now to major theories of the development of neurotic or unrealistic anxiety.

THEORIES OF ANXIETY

Psychoanalytic Theory

Freud proposed two different theories of anxiety. In the first formulation, published in 1895, neurotic anxiety was regarded as stemming from the blockage of unconscious id impulses. Such impulses are blocked, for example, under conditions of extreme sexual deprivation. When id impulses are repressed, they can, according to Freud's first theory of anxiety, be transformed into neurotic anxiety. The first theory did not pay much attention to the circumstances surrounding the repression of an id impulse. In his second theory, proposed in 1926, Freud made more explicit the situations that may cause the individual to repress an id impulse, and he reversed the relationship between neurotic anxiety and repression.

Birth was viewed as the prototypic anxiety situation, for the infant is flooded with excitation over which it can exert no control. After the development of the ego in the first year of life (see Chapter 2), anxiety becomes a signal of impending overstimulation. The person is warned that he is in danger of being reduced to an infantile state of helplessness through overstimulation by id impulses and other forces. Anxiety thus plays a functional role, helping the ego to take action before being overwhelmed.

Three kinds of anxiety were differentiated by Freud, depending on their source. *Objective anxiety* refers to the ego's reaction to danger in the external world, as for example the anxiety felt when life is in real jeopardy. This kind of anxiety is the same as realistic fear. *Moral anxiety,* experienced by the ego as guilt or shame, is regarded as the fear of punishment by the superego for failure to adhere to standards of moral conduct.

The form of anxiety that has bearing on this chapter is *neurotic anxiety,* the fear of the disastrous consequences that are expected to follow if a previously punished id impulse is allowed expression. Neurotic anxiety has its roots in reality anxiety. As Hall (1954) has noted,

Neurotic anxiety is based upon reality anxiety in the sense that a person has to associate an instinctual demand with an external danger before he learns to fear his instincts. As long as instinctual discharge does not result in punishment, one has nothing to fear from [the instincts]. . . . However, when impulsive behavior gets the person into trouble, as it usually does, he learns how dangerous the instincts are. Slaps and spankings and other forms of punishment show the child that impulsive instinctual gratification leads to a state of discomfort. The child acquires neurotic anxiety when he is punished for being impulsive (p. 67).

Forms of Neurotic Anxiety

Neurotic anxiety can be expressed in several ways: as free-floating anxiety, as phobia, and as panic reaction. The stimuli triggering all these expressions of neurotic anxiety are actually internal, stemming from previously punished id impulses. In free-floating anxiety the person appears to be apprehensive nearly all the time, in the absence of reasonable danger. The theory assumes that the person is actually afraid of his own id—which, of course, is with him all the time. Phobias are characterized by an intense irrational fear and avoidance of specific objects and situations, such as kittens, open spaces, closed spaces, and nonpoisonous snakes. The feared objects or situations are hypothesized to be symbolic representations of the object or situation chosen earlier for gratification of the id impulse. That choice and thus the impulse were subsequently punished. "Behind every neurotic fear there is a primitive wish of the id for the object of which one is afraid" (Hall, 1954, p. 65). Finally, neurotic anxiety may become manifest as a panic reaction, a sudden and inexplicable outburst of fear, caused by the neurotic denial of id gratification.

Defense Mechanisms

According to Freud, the discomfort experienced by the anxious ego can be reduced by several maneuvers. Objective anxiety, rooted in reality, can often be dealt with by removing or avoiding in a rational way the danger in the external world. Neurotic anxiety, and sometimes moral anxiety, may be handled through an unconscious distortion of reality by means of one of the *defense mechanisms.* A defense mechanism is an ego strategy, unconsciously utilized, which serves to protect the ego from anxiety. Perhaps the most important is *repres-*

sion, whereby impulses and thoughts unacceptable to the ego are pushed into the unconscious. Another defense mechanism, important in paranoid disorders (see Chapter 14), is *projection,* or the attribution to external agents of characteristics or desires possessed by an individual and yet unacceptable to his conscious awareness. For example, a hostile person may *unconsciously* find it aversive to regard himself as angry at others and may project his angry feelings onto them. Other defense mechanisms are *displacement,* redirecting emotional responses from a perhaps dangerous object to a substitute, for instance, kicking the cat instead of the boss; *reaction formation,* converting one feeling such as hate into its opposite, love; and *regression,* retreating to the behavioral patterns of an earlier age. All these defense mechanisms allow the ego to discharge some id energy while at the same time not facing frankly the true nature of the motivation. Because defense mechanisms are more readily observed than other symptoms of a disordered personality, they are very often the reasons offered in persuading a person to consult a therapist.

Evaluation

Since Freud's theorizing on anxiety is inseparable from other aspects of his system, as described in Chapter 2, the criticisms voiced in that chapter also relate to his first and second theories of neurotic anxiety. How, for example, can the theory be adequately tested? How can we determine whether the id and ego are actually in conflict? It is difficult to make predictions based on Freud's theory of anxiety since it is stated in such general terms. When direct tests have been attempted, results have been discouraging. (for example, Sears, Maccoby, and Levin, 1957). Similarly, attempts to find differences in the childhood experiences of normal and neurotic adults have not been successful (Frank, 1965). Finally, efforts to alleviate anxiety using methods suggested by psychoanalytic theory have not proved successful in controlled evaluations (see Chapter 18).

A Stimulus-Response Analysis of Anxiety: Mowrer and Miller

Until the 1930s, American learning theorists, working mostly with rats, were little concerned with behavior commonly thought to reflect anxiety. The study of anxiety was at the time more actively pursued by clinicians, particularly Freudians. Mowrer (1939) is credited with bringing the study of anxiety into the mainstream of experimental psychology. Instead of construing anxiety in Freudian terms as the threat of or the flooding of the ego by excessive stimulation, he suggested that we conceptualize anxiety as an internal response which can be learned by means of classical conditioning.

In a typical experiment rats were shocked repeatedly in the presence of a neutral stimulus such as a tone. The shock (UCS) produced a UCR of pain, fear, and flight. After several pairings the fear that was naturally produced by the shock came to be produced by the tone, fear being assumed the learnable component of the pain-fear response. It was observed that shock could eventually be omitted, and yet the animal would continue to react fearfully to the previously neutral stimulus (CS). In addition, it was shown (for example, Miller, 1948) that the animal could learn new responses to avoid the CS. The question became how to conceptualize the finding that animals would learn to *avoid* a harmless event. Mowrer and others suggested that, in a typical *avoidance learning* experiment, two bits of learning were taking place (Figure 5.2): (1) the animal, by means of *classical* conditioning, learned to fear the CS,

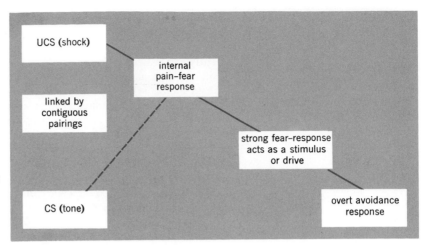

FIGURE 5.2

*Schematic representation of
Mowrer's account of avoidance learning. The dotted
line indicates that the subject
is learning to fear the tone,
the solid line that the subject
is learning to avoid the
shock.*

that is he acquired a fear-drive; and (2) the animal, by means of *instrumental* conditioning, learned an overt behavior to remove himself from the CS and thus to reduce his fear-drive.

Fear as Response, Stimulus, and Drive

The foregoing makes sense only in the context of an unfortunately complicated conceptual scheme. We have called fear a drive, but at the same time it is viewed as an internal response that can be classically conditioned. How can fear be both a response and a drive?

Additional assumptions are necessary. First, according to Mowrer and Miller, every response, whether overt or covert, produces its own stimulus. One way to understand this is to close one's eyes and bend a finger; in spite of the absence of visual cues, one can *feel* that the finger is bent. In Mowrer-Miller terms, the response of finger bending generates its own perceptible stimuli. The sensations of bending the finger act as stimuli to the brain, telling it what has happened. Conceived in this way, a response such as fear can also be said to function as a stimulus.

Second, drives are said to be strong stimuli. Strong responses, like fear, generate their own stimuli which are strong and thus can be con-

sidered as drives. In this fashion fear as a strong internal response is said to function as a drive. Thus fear can be spoken of in three ways, as a response, as a stimulus, and as a drive.

Finally, as a drive, fear functions in the Mowrer-Miller learning model to impel the rat to run away from the tone. As the rat increases his distance from the tone, the fear-drive is reduced, which reinforces the avoidance behavior.

The essential features of this admittedly complicated theorizing are that fear or anxiety can be conceived of both as an internal response, which can be learned as other observable responses are learned, and as a drive which can mediate avoidance behavior. The study of anxiety, then, becomes amenable to the same kind of experimental analysis employed in the investigation of observable behavior. Mowrer and Miller have *assumed* that a useful way to talk about the internal life of organisms is to liken it to overt behavior. They speak of "mediating fear-responses" to make clear the assumption that such responses, although inferred, act in the same way as overt responses. Hopefully, the knowledge that has been gleaned about overt behavior can be transferred to the study of mental and emotional life (see Box 5.2). For instance,

An early experiment by Miller (1935) was designed to assess the usefulness of construing mental life in mediational stimulus-response terms. Imagine that as a subject in his experiment you have shock electrodes attached to your left hand. The experimenter then repeatedly presents to you the letter T and the number 4; you are shocked every time the T is presented but never when the number 4 is presented. Careful electrophysiological recordings are made of your sweat gland activity when the letter T and the number 4 appear. Results show that you perspire more when T is presented than when 4 is presented. The most interesting part of the experiment then follows: you are instructed on a particular signal to *think* of either the letter T or the number 4. What happens?

Thinking about the letter T, which had previously been paired with shock, elicits more sweat gland activity than thinking about the number 4. This outcome is consistent with the assumption that the image or thought of the letter T functions in the same way as the actual physical presentation of the letter. Thought, like fear, is thus construed as a response, which in turn, functioning as a stimulus, can elicit the sweat gland activity.

if we know that repetition of an overt response without reinforcement leads to the extinction of the response, we can predict, as Rescorla and Solomon have indeed shown, that repeated evocation of a fear-response while withholding the expected pain or punishment will reduce the fear. This is no trivial possibility, and indeed, as will be indicated in Chapter 19 when behavior modification is discussed, treatments based on such reasoning have helped people become less fearful of objects or situations that do not merit such reactions.

Building on his own earlier work and that of Mowrer, Miller together with Dollard (1950) translated Freud's theorizing into mediational stimulus-response terms. In this fashion, the anxiety that according to psychoanalytic theory is generated by excessive stimulation of the ego, was conceptualized as an intense response which is learned as are other responses and which functions as a drive. Moreover, Dollard and Miller proposed that thinking could be similarly construed in mediational terms and spoken of as a "thinking-res-

ANXIETY AND DEPRESSION

ponse" or "planning-response." The various defense mechanisms were similarly transformed into covert or unobservable avoidance responses, acquired and maintained because they reduced anxiety or fear.

Many scientifically oriented workers in psychopathology have regarded Dollard and Miller's book as virtually useless, for what are the advantages of translating the problematical theory of Freud into other terms? Our own assessment is much more positive, for the work of Dollard and Miller offered the possibility of studying internal mental life by means that had proved useful in the study of overt behavior. Thus it is their *mode of analysis* that has been of enduring value, contributing to the intensive study of anxiety and its relationships to learning. Moreover, Dollard and Miller's book was an early application of the methods and principles of general psychology to a domain of human behavior historically considered the province of medicine.

Evaluation

As useful as this learning model of the development of anxiety neurosis appears, it cannot be accepted uncritically. Mowrer and Miller assume that an association, or pairing, between a previously neutral stimulus and some sort of strong anxiety-provoking event will endow that stimulus with aversive properties. There are several problems with this classical conditioning formulation. In the first place, there is very little evidence to support the contention that human beings can be classically conditioned to fear neutral stimuli even when such stimuli are paired repeatedly with primary aversive stimuli, such as electric shock (for example, Davison, 1968). Ethical considerations have of course restrained most researchers from employing highly aversive stimuli with human beings, but considerable evidence in-

dicates that fear is extinguished rather quickly when the CS is presented a few times without the reinforcement of moderate levels of shock (Bridger and Mandel, 1965; Wickens, Allen, and Hill, 1963). Moreover, only a few isolated studies have, in fact, shown that a human being can be conditioned to fear something that does not warrant being feared (for example, Watson and Rayner, 1920; Campbell, Sanderson, and Laverty, 1964), and there have been unsuccessful attempts to replicate the Watson and Rayner experiment in which Little Albert was made fearful of a rat (English, 1929). In the face of such weak and even contradictory evidence, it is surprising that classical conditioning continues to be viewed by some behaviorists as the sole explanation and source of neurotic fear and avoidance.

Moreover, although we can find in the past histories of many anxious people what appear to be classical conditioning experiences—for example, a woman may fear to leave her home after being terrified in the street—such experiences are just as often, perhaps more often, *not* found in the histories of those who are unrealistically or neurotically fearful. Grinker and Spiegel (1945) documented many examples of soldiers who suffered shell shock from the strains of modern warfare, but in the same war many men experienced the same horrors *without* developing neurotic symptoms. *Why?*

It has often been suggested that different experiences with stress in childhood account for different reactions to stress in adulthood. Soldiers who were not incapacitated in combat by extreme fear may have had a childhood that somehow prepared them well for emotional turmoil in adulthood. Unfortunately, the same data cited earlier in criticising Freud's views on anxiety (Frank, 1965) are relevant here as well: it has not yet been shown that the development of neurotic anxiety in adulthood relates to particular childhood experiences.

Biologically oriented researchers have sought explanations in the autonomic nervous system. Inasmuch as anxiety is generally assumed to involve the ANS, it is reasonable to propose that the development of neurotic anxiety may depend importantly on the arousability of this system, that is, the ease with which a given amount of stimulation triggers it. Soldiers who cannot cope with the ordeal of combat may have an autonomic nervous system that is especially sensitive to stress. Although this line of reasoning is plausible, there is as yet little direct supporting evidence.

In sum, satisfactory answers to why only some people become chronically anxious remain to be found, and the learning model, although adequate in accounting for much animal behavior, is as inadequate as the psychoanalytic model in completely explaining why human beings sometimes fear what is harmless.

Control and Helplessness

Mandler (1966) suggests that the feeling of not being in control is a central characteristic of all views of neurotic anxiety. According to the psychoanalytic theory, the ego is anxious because it is threatened with overstimulation that it cannot control. Learning theory sees the individual as confronted with a painful stimulus over which it has no control until he learns to avoid it. This concept of helplessness had earlier been examined by workers in several disciplines.

Richter (1957), in an article entitled "On the Phenomenon of Sudden Death in Animals and Man," quoted the following anthropological observation from an earlier source.

A Brazilian Indian condemned and sentenced by a so-called medicine man is helpless against his own emotional response to this pronouncement—and dies within hours. In Africa a young Negro knowingly eats the inviolably banned wild hen. On discovery of his "crime" he trembles, is overcome by fear and dies in 24 hours. In New Zealand a Maori woman eats fruit that she only later learns has come from a taboo place. Her chief has been profaned. By noon of the next day she is dead. In Australia a witch doctor points a bone at a man. Believing that nothing can save him, the man rapidly sinks in spirits and prepares to die. He is saved only at the last moment when the witch doctor is forced to remove the charm (Basedow, 1925, cited in Richter, 1957, p. 191).

That such seemingly supernatural events actually occur in primitive societies is difficult for us to believe. Walter Cannon, a well-known American physiologist of the early twentieth century, studied reports of such "voodoo" deaths and concluded that they do take place and are worthy of serious scientific study (Cannon, 1942). He drew on his own experimental work involving the emotions of rage and fear in cats to propose that a person whose autonomic nervous system is maintained in a highly aroused state with little opportunity for effective action to reduce the tension may indeed die. The doomed individual has no means of controlling his fear of what he regards as all-powerful forces ordaining his death. Under such tension, Cannon suggested, certain vital bodily organs can be irreparably harmed, and death is actually brought about by severe fright.

Bettelheim's (1960) descriptions of the reactions of certain prisoners to conditions in the Nazi concentration camps indicate another way in which the feeling of having lost control may affect people.

*Prisoners who came to believe the repeated statement of the guards—that there was no hope for them, and that they would never leave the camp except as a corpse—*who came to feel that their environment was one over which they could exercise no influence whatever [*emphasis added*], *these prisoners were in a literal sense, walking corpses. . . . They were people who were so deprived of affect, self esteem, and every form of stimulation, so totally exhausted, physically and emotionally, that they had given the environment total power over them (pp. 151–152).*

These Western men, typically well educated, reacted in a helpless and self-defeating manner because they believed that they had no control over their lives.

Experimental psychologists have also been interested in related phenomena. Maier (1949) conducted a series of studies in which he presented insoluble problems to laboratory rats. The behavior of the rats usually became rigid and stereotyped. They would jump in only one direction, even though this movement solved the problem only part of the time. Indeed, after the problem was made soluble, the animals frequently did not recognize the solution and continued instead to jump in only one direction.

Research done by Liddell (1956) demonstrated what has been called "experimental neurosis." He shocked sheep repeatedly with very mild, unavoidable, and inescapable electric current. The animals screamed, defecated, and jumped about wildly when they were placed in the experimental situation in which they received shock and also in other quite harmless situations, for example, when they were about to be fed. Since such fearful behavior was quite out of proportion to the amount of shock received, Liddell regarded it as similar to neurotic behavior in man. Lack of control over environmental stimulation appeared to have been responsible for this breakdown in behavior.

The two studies just mentioned have an important drawback, however; another group of animals was not allowed control over the same aversive stimulation. For example, it is not known for certain whether Liddell's lambs were rendered neurotically fearful by their lack of control over shock or by their extended exposure to the discomfort. The earliest experiment designed to allow one group of animals control and another group none was performed by Mowrer and Viek (1948). Rats were trained to obtain food by performing a particular instrumental action. Then they were all shocked at the feeding place. One group was able to terminate the shock by jumping. Each member of the second group was yoked to, that is, paired with, a member of the first so that the amount and duration of shock received by the pair were identical. But the members of the second group were unable to jump in a way that would give them control. The group of rats who had control over shock exhibited less fear than did those animals who were yoked helplessly to a partner.

Thus far we have examined anecdotal accounts of human behavior and experiments with animals. But rats and lambs are not people, and uncontrolled variables make it impossible to know what may really cause voodoo deaths and extreme apathy in prisoners. Fortunately, some experimental work has been done with human beings. Haggard (1943) showed that human subjects who administered electric shocks to themselves were less anxious about the situation than those who received the same amount and intensity of shock but who had no control over them. Furthermore, Pervin (1953) found that electric shocks that could be con-

BOX **5.3** *Trait versus Situation Anxiety:*
Two Paradigms

A comparison of different self-report anxiety questionnaires provides an opportunity to examine two contrasting paradigmatic positions in anxiety research, and, indeed, in psychology as a whole. The aim of the Taylor Manifest Anxiety Scale, mentioned earlier, is to place a person on a continuum with respect to anxiety *in general.* A person scoring as highly anxious on the MAS is assumed to carry this trait around with him at all times. This ongoing level of tension then interacts with specific environmental situations and helps to determine how that individual will behave as compared, for example, with someone with a low MAS score.

Taylor's notion that each person operates at a certain level of anxiety is referred to as a *trait* approach. The individual supposedly possesses specific enduring traits or predispositions to respond in particular ways in a variety of situations. A clinical example would be the predisposition or trait of a person whose personality is assumed to derive from earlier experiences in one of the Freudian psychosexual developmental stages. An "anal personality," for instance, is described by the trait stingy.

Contrasted with the trait approach is one that emphasizes situations as determinants of behavior (Mischel, 1968). According to this paradigm, consistency in behavior is explained not in terms of an underlying trait but in terms of learned reactions to classes of situations. Research taking this approach has concentrated on measuring the anxiety experienced by persons in various situations. For example, Mandler and Sarason (1952) developed a scale to assess individual differences in anxiety during examinations. Like the MAS, the Text Anxiety Scale has contributed to our understanding of the relationship between anxiety and behavior. Individuals scoring high on test anxiety perform more poorly on exams than do those who have a low score on this dimension.

What are the relative contributions of trait and situation to individual differences in anxiousness? One questionnaire directed toward this issue, the S-R Inventory of Anxiousness, asks subjects to indicate how they respond to a number of situations (Endler, Hunt, and Rosenstein, 1962). The questionnaire presents situations such as "You are going to meet a new date," and "You are entering a competitive contest before spectators." Subjects indicate their degree of reaction to each of these situations on variables such as "Heart beats faster," "Perspire," and "Experience nausea." A complete sample item appears in Table 5.1.

This scale therefore provides separate scores on how anxious an individual rates himself in a variety of settings. He may, for example, consider himself highly anxious about taking a test but not very anxious about situations involving interpersonal relations. Research with this scale has demonstrated that behavior is best predicted by knowing both the individual's general level of tension and the specific situations he is confronting.

ANXIETY AND DEPRESSION

TABLE 5.1 *Sample Item from the S-R Inventory of Anxiousness*

"You are just starting off on a long automobile trip."

1. Heart beats faster	1 2 3 4 5 Not at all Much faster
2. Get an uneasy feeling	1 2 3 4 5 None Very strongly
3. Emotions disrupt action	1 2 3 4 5 Not at all Very disruptive
4. Feel exhilarated and thrilled	1 2 3 4 5 Not at all Very strongly
5. Want to avoid situation	1 2 3 4 5 Not at all Very strongly
6. Perspire	1 2 3 4 5 Not at all Perspire much
7. Need to urinate frequently	1 2 3 4 5 No Very frequently
8. Enjoy the challenge	1 2 3 4 5 Not at all Very much
9. Mouth gets dry	1 2 3 4 5 Not at all Very dry
10. Become immobilized	1 2 3 4 5 Not at all Very immobilized
11. Stomach feels full	1 2 3 4 5 Not at all Very full
12. Seek such experiences	1 2 3 4 5 Not at all Very much
13. Have loose bowels	1 2 3 4 5 Not at all Very loose
14. Experience nausea	1 2 3 4 5 Not at all Very nauseous

trolled were preferred to those that could not be controlled. Another study has indicated that intellectual performance is superior when the individual believes that he has control over the order in which he takes a series of tests (Neale and Katahn, 1968). In all this experimental work with human beings, stressful events that the subjects could exert some control over were less anxiety-provoking than those over which no control could be exercised.

The work done with both animals and human beings led Geer, Davison, and Gatchel (1970) to ask whether a relevant variable might be the subject's *perception* of control rather than actual control. The possibility existed that stress may be reduced because the experimental arrangements induce in the subject a *belief* that he can control the amount of stress to which he is subjected. This hypothesis seemed testable, at least for human beings, if a situation could be devised that would make an individual believe he has control over aversive stimulation, although in actuality he has none. If such subjects are less upset by aversive stimulation than are subjects who share the same actual lack of control, but not the false belief that they have control, it may be assumed that an important variable for human beings is their perception of the situation rather than its objective reality.

In a base line test to establish the amount of arousal by uncontrolled aversive stimulation, subjects were presented with a series of ten painful electric shocks. The subjects were instructed to press a switch as each shock was administered so that their reaction time could be determined. Each shock lasted six seconds and was always preceded by a ready signal. The amount of arousal, as measured by sweat gland activity, was recorded for each shock (Figure 5.3). In the next part of the study, half of the subjects, those who were to perceive themselves in control, were told that the duration of each of the next ten shocks would be cut in half if their reaction time achieved a certain speed. Thus these subjects were led to believe that they could exert control over the next ten shocks. The remaining subjects were simply told that the next ten shocks would be of shorter duration. In actuality, the experimenter arranged for *all* subjects to receive three-second shocks in the second part of the experiment rather than six-second shocks, thus holding constant the actual amount of aversive stimulation.

As expected, during the second part of the experiment, the subjects who assumed that they could control the duration of shocks evidenced significantly less arousal, as measured by sweat gland activity. Believing that they could control the amount of shock—even though they really were not able to do so—made the shocks easier to tolerate. These findings are all the more striking when we consider that the subjects who considered themselves in control might well have been *more* on edge because they were performing work—trying to reduce their reaction time—in order to achieve a goal. Other research indicates that such situations typically lead to an *increase* in the kind of arousal that was measured in this experiment. As Geer and his colleagues state at the end of their report, "Man creates his own gods to fill in gaps in his knowledge about a sometimes terrifying environment, creating at least an illusion of control which is presumably comforting. Perhaps the next best thing to being master of one's fate is being deluded into thinking that he is" (pp. 737–738).

The research and theory on control and helplessness offer a promising way to view anxiety. Not only does this theory have direct support from adequately controlled experiments, but it can also be applied to the views of Freud and the learning theorists. We will also find the model very useful when examining neuroses, psychophysiological disorders, and depression.

ANXIETY AND DEPRESSION

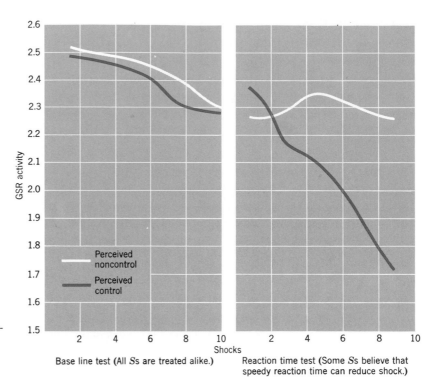

GSR activity

Perceived
noncontrol

Perceived
control

Shocks

Base line test (All Ss are treated alike.)

Reaction time test (Some Ss believe that
speedy reaction time can reduce shock.)

FIGURE 5.3

Anxiety as a function of perceived control. Adapted from Geer, Davison, and Gatchel, 1970.

SUMMARY

Anxiety is regarded as a construct, an unobservable state, which is considered useful in explaining and integrating data and in generating hypotheses regarding the way people deal with stress. An inferred state must be tied to observables; anxiety has been defined in terms of self-report, overt behavior, and physiological changes. Two major views of anxiety were examined. Freud considered anxiety to be a signal of the ego's incapacity to deal with stimulation from id impulses, external danger, and the prohibitions of the superego. Many learning theorists construe anxiety as an internal response that initiates behavior which will remove the individual from the situation that distresses him. Finally, the individual's ability to minimize his feeling of helplessness in the face of threat is regarded as an important factor in determining the extent of his anxiety. In fact, it may be the most important variable in explaining the high levels of anxiety found in neurotic disorders.

CHAPTER 6

Neurotic Syndromes

By the late nineteenth century the fascination with hysteria and hypnosis was nearly a century old and had fostered considerable psychogenic theorizing on the etiology of certain emotional disorders. It had first been recognized that the paralysis and anesthesia of hysteria had no organic cause and could be removed and even induced by hypnosis. Thus hysteria came to be regarded as some form of self-hypnosis. If one mental disorder had a psychological cause, there could be others. Neurotic anxiety, phobias, fugue, and somnambulism were among those investigated. Our historical review in Chapter 1 ended with Freud's collaboration with Breuer on *Studies in Hysteria,* a book important for the impetus it gave to the systematic study of psychological factors in mental disorders.

The prevailing conceptualizations of neurosis, as elaborated in DSM-II and accepted by the greater part of the professional community, did indeed develop out of Freud's work with hysterics and other neurotics and are thus inextricably bound up with psychoanalytic theory. According to DSM-II,

Anxiety is the chief characteristic of the neuroses. It may be felt and expressed directly, or it may be controlled unconsciously and automatically by conversion, displacement and various other psychological mechanisms. Generally, these mechanisms produce symptoms experienced as subjective distress from which the patient desires relief (p. 39).

As we review the more important types of neurosis, it will become clear how thoroughly Freudian theory permeates our very conceptions of them. And as we attempt to compare this prevailing psychiatric view of neurosis with more recent learning views, we will once again witness how a clash of paradigms has played an accustomed and important role in a developing science.

"I need reassurance, Miss Kimball. Send someone in on his hands and knees."

In addition to anxiety, several other symptoms are common to the neurotic syndromes as they are described in DSM-II. The neurotic individual feels inadequate and inferior and tends to avoid challenge rather than face it. He lacks insight into the motives for his behavior and is rigid rather than flexible in handling different problems. He is unable to adopt alternative courses of action more appropriate to varying circumstances. The neurotic has difficulty maintaining satisfying interpersonal relationships and suffers considerable guilt and unhappiness about the way he leads his life (Coleman, 1972).

Both learning theorists and psychoanalysts regard the symptoms just described as *derivatives* of neurotic anxiety. For example, Wolpe (1969), influenced heavily by the work on experimental neurosis reviewed in the preceding chapter, considers the most important aspect of neurotic behavior to be fear of previously harmless stimuli, acquired through classical conditioning. The need to avoid this fear is the principal consequence of acquiring it. From this core of fear and avoidance, Wolpe would *derive* the remaining clinical symptoms of neurosis. Thus someone who is neurotically fearful of leaving the home, an agoraphobic, may well feel inferior, avoid challenge, be unaware of the reasons for his behavior, respond in the same stereotyped way when confronted with different problems, have few friends, suffer great unhappiness and guilt, and be anxious a great deal of the time. Psychoanalytic theory would hold that these same symptoms are derived from what they consider to be the core of neurosis, the repression of childhood conflicts. The major neurotic syndromes are summarized in Table 6.1.[1]

[1] Omitted from the following discussion are the infrequently seen neurasthenic neurosis, hypochondriacal neurosis, and depersonalization neurosis. Depressive neurosis will be treated in Chapter 8.

TABLE **6.1** *Neurotic Disorders*

Type	Major symptom patterns
Phobic neurosis	Extreme fear and avoidance of an object or situation which the person himself is able to recognize as harmless
Anxiety neurosis	Anxiety felt in so many situations that it appears to be "free-floating," without specific cause
Hysterical neurosis, conversion type	Paralysis, lack of sensation, or sensory disturbances without organic pathology
Hysterical neurosis, dissociative type	Alterations in consciousness, manifested as amnesia, fugue, somnambulism, and multiple personality
Obsessive-compulsive neurosis	Flooding of the mind with persistent and uncontrollable thoughts, or the compulsion to repeat a certain act again and again
Existential neurosis	Alienation; the feeling that life is meaningless
Neurasthenic neurosis	Chronic fatigue and weakness
Depersonalization neurosis	Feelings of unreality and estrangement from the self and the environment
Depressive neurosis	Extreme sadness in reaction to a specific event
Hypochondriacal neurosis	Preoccupation with bodily functions and with imagined illnesses

ANXIETY AND DEPRESSION

PHOBIAS

Psychopathologists agree that a phobia is a fear-mediated avoidance, out of proportion to the danger posed by a particular object or situation. For example, when a person is extremely fearful of heights, closed spaces, snakes, or spiders, provided there is no objective danger, the label phobia is likely to be applied to his avoidance and fear.

Over the years complex terms have been formulated as names for such unwarranted avoidance patterns. In each instance the suffix -phobia is preceded by a Greek word for the feared object or situation. Some of the more familiar terms are claustrophobia, fear of closed spaces (Figure 6.1); agoraphobia, fear of open spaces and of leaving the house; acrophobia, fear of heights; and hematophobia, fear of the sight of blood. More exotic fears have also been given Greek-derived names, for example, ergasiophobia, fear of writing; pnigophobia, fear of choking; and taphephobia, fear of being buried alive. All too often the impression is conveyed that we understand how a particular problem originated or even how to treat it merely because we have an authoritative-sounding name for it. Nothing could be further from the truth, however. As with so much else in the field of abnormal psychology, far more theories and jargon have been advanced in connection with phobias than there are firm findings.

In comparison to other diagnostic categories, phobias are relatively common in the general population. For example, Agras, Sylvester, and Oliveau (1969) found a rate of 77 per 1000 in a population study done in New England. This same investigation, however, revealed that most of the phobias were relatively mild, only 2.2 per 1000 being rated as severely disabling. Indeed, many specific fears do not cause enough hardship to compel an individual to seek treatment. If a person with an intense fear or phobia of nonpoisonous snakes, ophidiophobia, lives in a metropolitan area, he will probably have little direct contact with the feared object and may therefore not consider himself to be suffering from anything!

The Psychoanalytic Theory of Phobias

As is true of many of the neuroses, Freud was the first to attempt to account systematically for the development of phobic behavior. A classic case, reported by Freud in 1909, was that of a five-year-old boy, Little Hans, who was afraid of horses and thus would not venture out of his home. The importance of this case is attested to by many psychoanalytic scholars. Jones, Freud's famous biographer, calls it "the brilliant success of child analysis" (1955, p. 289); and Glover, a respected scholar, terms it "a remarkable achievement . . . [constituting] one of the most valued records in psychoanalytic archives" (1956, p. 76).

Freud's analysis of Little Hans was based on information reported in letters written to Freud by the boy's father; Freud actually saw the child only once. Before the development of his phobia, when he was three, Hans was reported to have "a quite peculiarly lively interest in the part of his body which he used to describe as his widdler." When he was three and a half his mother caught him with his hand on his penis and threatened to arrange for his penis to be cut off if he continued "doing that." At age four and a half, while on summer vacation, Hans is described as having tried to "seduce" his mother. As his mother was pow-

dering around his penis one day, taking care not to touch it. Hans said, "Why don't you put your finger there?" His mother answered "Because that would be piggish." Hans replied "What's that? Piggish? Why?" Mother: "Because it's not proper." Hans, laughing: "But it's great fun." These events were taken by Freud as proof that Hans had strong sexual urges, that they were directed toward his mother, and that they were repressed for fear of castration. According to the first theory of anxiety (see page 108), this sexual privation would ultimately be transformed into neurotic anxiety.

The first signs of the phobia appeared about

FIGURE **6.1**
An artist's rendering of three phobias:
acrophobia, fear of heights;
mysophobia, fear of dirt and
contamination; and claustrophobia,
fear of enclosed spaces.
(COURTESY JOHN VASSOS, FROM JOHN
VASSOS, *Phobia*, NEW YORK: COVICI,
FRIEDE, 1931.)

six months later while Hans was out for a walk with his nursemaid. After a horse-drawn van had tipped over, he began crying, saying that he wanted to return home to "coax" (caress) with his mother. Later he indicated that he was afraid to go out because a horse might bite him, and he soon elaborated on his fears by referring to "black things around horses' mouths and the things in front of their eyes."

Freud considered this series of events to reflect Hans's oedipal desires to have his father out of the way so that he could possess his mother. His sexual excitement for his mother was converted into anxiety because he feared that he would be punished. Hans's father was considered the initial source of his son's fear, but the fear was then transposed to a symbol for his father—horses. The black muzzles and blinders on horses were viewed as symbolic representations of the father's eyeglasses and moustache. Thus, by fearing horses, Hans was said to have succeeded unconsciously in avoiding the fear of castration by his father—even though it was the *mother* who had threatened this punishment—while at the same time arranging to spend more time at home with his principal love-object, his mother.

There are many other details in the case study, which occupies 140 pages in Freud's

"Why can't you be more like Oedipus?"
(DRAWING BY CHAS. ADDAMS; © 1972 THE NEW YORKER MAGAZINE, INC.)

Collected Papers. In our brief account we have attempted to convey the flavor of the theorizing. We agree with Wolpe and Rachman (1961) that the data on which Freud's theoretical account was based are very questionable. First, the evidence for Hans's wanting sexual contact with his mother is minimal, making it debatable that Hans wanted to possess his mother sexually and replace his father. Second, there is little evidence that Hans hated or feared his father, and in the original case report it is stated that Hans denied any symbolic connection between horses and his father. This denial was interpreted as evidence *for* the connection, however. Third, there is no evidence, or any reason to believe, that intense sexual excitement was somehow translated into anxiety. Indeed, the fact that Hans became afraid of horses after being frightened by an accident involving a horse is more parsimoniously explained by the classical conditioning model, which we shall now discuss.

Behavioral Theories of Phobias

As in psychoanalytic theory, the primary assumption of all behavioral accounts of phobias is that such reactions are learned. But the exact learning mechanisms and what is actually learned in the development of a phobia are specified differently in the various behavioral theories.

The Classical Conditioning Model

Historically, Watson and Rayner's (1920) demonstration of the apparent conditioning of a fear or phobia in Little Albert (see page 43) is considered the model of how a phobia may be acquired. A major problem exists in the application of this model, however. The fact that fear was acquired by Little Albert in this particular study can *not* be taken as evidence that *all* fears and phobias are acquired through conditioning. Rather, the study demonstrates only the *possibility* that some fears *may* be acquired in this particular way.

As mentioned in Chapter 5, other attempts to demonstrate the acquisition of fear via classical conditioning have *not* been successful. For example, English (1929) attempted to condition fear in a fourteen-month-old girl by pairing the presentation of a duck with a loud noise. Despite fifty trials, no conditioned response to the duck was established. In a more extensive investigation, Bregman (see Thorndike, 1935) tried to condition fear in fifteen infants of about the same age as Little Albert, using various CSs and a loud bell as the UCS. Again, relatively few fears were acquired by the subjects.[2]

In spite of these failures to replicate the Watson and Rayner demonstration, many learning theorists still construe phobias as acquired through classical conditioning. They have elaborated on the case of Little Albert by asserting that the classically conditioned fear of an objectively harmless stimulus forms the basis of an instrumental avoidance response. This formulation, based on a two-factor theory originally proposed by Mowrer (1947), holds that phobias develop from two related sets of learning. (1) Via classical conditioning, a person can learn to fear a neutral stimulus (the CS) if it is paired with an intrinsically painful or frightening event (the UCS). (2) Then like the rat in the Miller experiment (Chapter 5) the person can learn to reduce this conditioned fear by escaping from or avoiding the CS. It is assumed that this second kind of learning is instrumental conditioning; the response is acquired and maintained by its reinforcing consequences.[3]

Certain clinically reported phobias seem to fit such a model rather well. For example, a phobia of a specific object has frequently been reported to have developed after a particularly noxious experience with that object. Many people become intensely afraid of driving an automobile after a serious accident. Other phobias apparently originate in similar fashion.

[2] From an ethical point of view, it is fortunate that these workers failed to produce phobias in their young subjects.
[3] This behavioral model has also of course been construed as a psychogenic traumatic disease model (Chapter 2).

A young boy would often pass a grocery store on errands and when passing would steal a handful of peanuts from the stand in front. One day the owner saw him coming and hid behind a barrel. Just as the boy put his hand in the pile of peanuts the owner jumped out and grabbed him from behind. The boy screamed and fell fainting on the sidewalk.

> The boy developed a phobia of being grasped from behind. In social gatherings he arranged to have his chair against the wall. It was impossible for him to enter crowded places or to attend the theater. When walking on the street he would have to look back over his shoulder at intervals to see if he was closely followed (Bagby, 1922).

Clinical reports suggest that phobias may also develop *without* prior frightening experiences, however. Many individuals with severe fears of snakes, germs, airplanes, and heights report to clinicians that they have had no particularly unpleasant experiences with any of these objects or situations.[4] Similarly, many people who have had an unpleasant automobile accident or bad fall do *not* become phobic to these situations. Thus the classical conditioning model does not appear to account for the acquisition of all phobias.

Questions have also been raised whether laboratory avoidance behavior and phobic reactions are really analogous. On the one hand, conditioned avoidance responses do resemble phobic reactions in that both appear to be particularly resistant to extinction. Once an avoidance response has been established in an animal, these responses tend to be repeated for long periods of time even though the animal is never again shocked by or directly encounters whatever else served as the UCS. The avoidance behavior is maintained in the absence of any direct traumatic experience. Similarly, clinical phobias also appear to persist for long periods of time, even though nothing bad ever happens to the person when he does find himself in the feared situation. Most of the work

on which the accounts of avoidance learning are based was done with dogs and rats, however. The resistance to extinction of avoidance responses appears to be somewhat species-specific. Other animals show wide differences in both the facility with which they acquire specific avoidance responses and their resistance to extinction of these responses (Bolles, 1970). Human beings, in particular, extinguish their laboratory fears very quickly once the UCS is omitted (see Chapter 5). Thus it may be hazardous to generalize about man's behavior on the basis of that of infrahuman species, especially when the relevant behavior varies widely in the lower animals.

Another point of dissimilarity was noted by Costello (1970).

Responses learned in the usual avoidance procedure are adaptive [*emphasis ours*] *because they enable the animal simply to avoid a noxious stimulus. If this were true also . . . of phobic behaviors, they could not be considered maladaptive and would not come to the attention of clinicians. But phobias are maladaptive because they prevent the occurrence of behaviors desired by the individual (e.g., the claustrophobic person cannot sit in a lecture theater or a cinema) and/or desired by society (as in the case of the child with school phobia)* (*p. 250*).

In sum, the data we have reviewed suggest that not all phobias are learned through classical conditioning. Such a process *may* be involved in the etiology of some phobias, but other processes must also be implicated (see Box 6.1).

---

[4] Such accounts are called *retrospective* reports, that is, reports made by people looking back into their past, sometimes for many, many years. Since memory of long-ago events is often distorted, such reports must be viewed with some skepticism. The fact that many phobics cannot recall traumatic experiences with their now-feared objects may indeed be distortions of memory. Accounts of traumatic episodes may be questioned on the same grounds. Retrospective reports are discussed again on page 209.

Modeling

Phobic responses may also be learned through the imitation of others. As we have previously noted (see page 45), a wide range of behavior, including emotional responses, may be learned by witnessing a model. The learning of phobic reactions through modeling is generally referred to as vicarious conditioning. In one study Bandura and Rosenthal (1966) arranged for subjects to watch another person, the model, in an aversive conditioning situation. The model was hooked up to an impressive-looking array of electrical apparatus. Upon hearing a buzzer, the model withdrew his hand rapidly from the arm of the chair and feigned pain. The physiological responses of the subject witnessing this behavior were recorded. After the subject had watched the model "suffer" a number of times, he showed an increased frequency of emotional responses when the buzzer sounded. The subject began to react emotionally to a harmless stimulus even though he had had no direct contact with a noxious event.

Vicarious conditioning may also be extended to include the direct verbal instruction of phobic behavior. That is, phobic reactions can be learned through another's description of what might happen as well as by observing another's fear. As an example from everyday life, a mother may repeatedly warn her child not to engage in some activity lest dire consequences ensue. Vicarious examples can apparently be provided through words.

As with the classical conditioning formulation, however, vicarious learning experiments fail to provide an adequate model for all phobias. In the first place, the vicarious fear extinguishes quickly. Secondly, phobics who seek treatment do not often report that they became frightened after witnessing someone else's distress. Finally, many people have been exposed to the bad experiences of others but have not themselves developed phobias.

Operant Conditioning

Finally, we may consider the possibility that phobic reactions are learned by virtue of the consequences they produce. Avoidance responses may be directly rewarded and thereby learned. For example, a child who wants to stay close to his mother may invent various excuses so that he does not have to attend school. If the mother gives in to his excuses, he is directly rewarded by the positive consequence of being allowed to stay home with her. Within this model fear is not mentioned as a mediator. The child avoids school simply because it produces the results he is seeking.

Although some phobias may develop because of the payoff provided by the environment, the limits of plausibility are strained when we consider the extreme hardships suffered by many phobics because they are compelled to avoid harmless situations. Furthermore, data collected on animals (for example, Solomon, Kamin, and Wynne, 1953) and clinical observations strongly indicate that when the avoidance response is prevented, the animal and the phobic alike become markedly agitated and fearful. Perhaps the control[5] available to the phobic in his well-learned avoidance tactics saves him from experiencing the anxiety that underlies the phobic behavior.

Biological Factors Predisposing to the Development of Phobias

Both the psychoanalytic and learning theories look to the environment for the cause and maintenance of phobias. Indeed, as already indicated, the primary assumption of both theories is that phobias—and in fact all neurotic disorders—are learned. But what is the best way to conceptualize this learning and,

---

[5] The discussion on control and helplessness in Chapter 5 should be recalled.

Classical Conditioning and Preparedness

Perhaps the classical conditioning view of phobias would be more valid if modified slightly to take into account the fact that certain neutral stimuli may be more likely to become conditioned stimuli than others. Pavlov (1928) did not address this question, stating that " . . . every imaginable phenomenon of the outer world affecting a specific receptive surface of the body may be converted into a CS" (p. 88).

Seligman (1971) has recently suggested that phobias may well reflect classical conditioning to stimuli that an organism is biologically predisposed to be sensitive to. Accordingly, classical conditioning experiments that show quick extinction of fear may have employed CSs that the organism is not well "prepared" to learn to associate with UCSs.

An example from the research that has given rise to this preparedness notion may make this hypothesis clearer. Garcia and his associates (Garcia, McGowan, and Green, 1972) found that rats could learn to avoid the taste of a given food if made nauseous following its ingestion—even if the nausea did not begin for many hours. In contrast, they could not be negatively conditioned to the sight of food if they were merely made nauseous in its presence but had not actually tasted the food. Similarly, rats could readily learn to avoid a light paired with shock (a common experimental finding), but they could not learn to avoid taste paired with shock. Thus, as seen in Figure 6.2, visual and tactile modalities are readily associated (light-shock) as are gustatory sensations and illness (taste-nausea). But gustatory and tactile sensations (taste-shock) and visual stimuli and illness (sight of food-nausea) are not.

This and related research prompted Seligman to hypothesize that some associations, and thereby phobias, are easily learned by human beings and

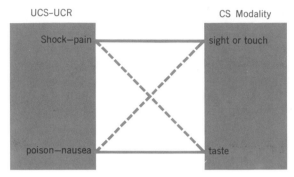

FIGURE **6.2**

Associations that the organism is prepared or unprepared to learn. Solid lines indicate easily made associations; dotted lines connect classes of stimuli that are difficult to associate.

thus are not readily extinguished. Marks (1970), in a related observation, points to the *nonarbitrary* objects and events that human beings tend to be afraid of. People may have phobias of dogs, cats, and snakes—but few lamb phobics have been encountered. It is even more striking to consider how few people phobically avoid electrical outlets, even though they present certain dangers under specified circumstances.

Speculating still further, Seligman proposes that the kind of symbolism mentioned in psychoanalytic theory may one day be found to have a basis in the sensitivities of people and what they are prepared to associate and to learn. Hans, after all, came to fear a horse, not any of the other stimuli present when he saw the animal fall down in the street. Although the symbolic connection with the father is still unclear unless Freud's hypothesis is accepted, it does seem significant that as the aftermath of the incident mentioned in the case report, Hans came to be afraid of horses.

most importantly, why do some people acquire unrealistic fears whereas others do not, given similar opportunities for learning? Perhaps those who are adversely affected by stress have particular characteristics or dispositions that somehow predispose them to develop psychopathology following a particular stressful event. The constitutional predisposition toward disease is called a diathesis, and the position that takes diathesis into account a *diathesis-stress* theory.

Autonomic Nervous System

What characteristics may be important in determining the susceptibility of individuals to particular environmental experiences? One way in which people may react differently to certain environmental situations is the degree to which their autonomic nervous systems become aroused. Lacey (1967) has referred to a dimension of autonomic activity that he calls stability-lability. So-called labile or "jumpy" individuals are those whose autonomic systems are easily aroused by a wide range of stimuli. Clearly, to the extent that the autonomic nervous system is involved in fear and hence in phobic behavior, a dimension such as autonomic lability would assume considerable importance. Since there is reason to believe that autonomic lability is to some extent genetically determined (Eysenck, 1957; Lacey. 1967), researchers have examined the possibility that genetically transmitted characteristics (see Box 6.2) play a role in the development of neurotic disorders.

Behavior Genetics

Several studies have questioned whether a genetic factor is involved in neurosis or anxiety, although none has been directly concerned with whether such a factor is implicated in the

formation of phobias per se. Brown (1942) investigated the incidence of neuroses in relatives of people who had already been diagnosed as neurotic. Consistent with the view that the predisposition for a disorder can be genetically transmitted, he found the incidence of neurosis in first-degree relatives—siblings, mothers, and fathers—to be 16.8 percent. In contrast, for a control group made up of non-neurotic individuals, the incidence of neurosis in first-degree relatives was only 1.1 percent. Rosenthal (1970) has summarized the available studies of pairs of twins. In these studies the incidence of neurosis in the co-twins of the probands, individuals originally diagnosed as neurotic, had been determined. Again, consistent with the theory of genetic transmission, among monozygotic or identical pairs of twins there was a 53 percent concordance or similarity in diagnosis. Among dizygotic or fraternal pairs of twins there was only a 40 percent concordance.

These data do not unequivocably implicate genetics, however. Although close relatives share genes, they also have considerable opportunity to observe one another. The fact that a son and his father are both afraid of heights may indicate not a genetic component but rather direct modeling of the son's behavior after that of his father. In sum, although there is some reason to believe that genetic or innate factors are involved in the etiology of phobias, there has as yet been no clear-cut demonstration of the extent to which they may be important.

Subclassification of Phobias

Up to now we have been discussing phobias as though they are alike in every respect except the object or situation that is fearfully avoided. Behaviorists have been remiss in not considering whether the differences between

BOX **6.2** *Behavior Genetics*

Behavior genetics is the study of individual differences in behavior that are attributable in part to differences in genetic makeup. The biological inheritance of every individual consists of genes, and the total genetic makeup of an individual is referred to as his *genotype*. An individual's genotype is his unobservable, physiological genetic constitution, in contrast to the totality of observable characteristics which is referred to as his *phenotype*. The genotype is fixed at birth, whereas the phenotype changes and is generally viewed as the product of an interaction between the genotype and experience. For example, an individual may be born with the capacity for high intellectual achievement. Whether he develops this genetically given potential depends on such environmental factors as his rearing and education. Any measure of intelligence (IQ) is therefore best viewed as an index of the phenotype.

On the basis of the distinction made between phenotype and genotype, we realize that various clinical syndromes are disorders of the phenotype. Thus it is not proper to speak of the direct inheritance of schizophrenia or neuroses. At most, only the genotypes of these disorders can be inherited. Whether these genotypes will eventually engender the phenotypic behavioral disorder will depend on environment and experience; a predisposition may be inherited but not the disorder itself.

The two major methods of study in behavior genetics are to compare members of a family and pairs of twins. Members of a family are compared because we can determine, on the average, how many genes are shared by two blood relatives. For example, children receive half of their genes from one parent and half from the other. Siblings will, on the average, be identical in 50 percent of their genetic background. In contrast, relatives not as closely related share fewer genes. For example, an uncle shares 25 percent of the genetic makeup of his nephews or nieces. If a predisposition for a mental disorder can be inherited, a study of the family should reveal a correlation between the number of shared genes and the presence of a disorder in relatives. The starting point in such investigations is to collect a sample of individuals who bear the diagnosis in question; these are referred to as *index cases* or *probands*. Then relatives are

fearing a small animal and fearing the prospect of leaving a person's house are important. This neglect of the content of the phobia seems consistent with the fact that behaviorists take a functional stance rather than a topographical one (Wilson and Davison, 1969). Topography is the specification of the actual appearance of behavior. Thus avoidance of a snake is topographically different from avoidance of heights, for the simple reason that a snake is not a studied to determine the frequency with which the same diagnosis might be applied to them.

In the twin method dizygotic (DZ) and monozygotic (MZ) pairs of twins are compared. MZ twins develop from a single fertilized egg and are genetically identical. DZ pairs develop from separate eggs and on the average are only 50 percent alike genetically, actually no more alike than two siblings. MZ twins are always the same sex, but DZs or fraternal twins can be either the same sex or opposite in sex. Again, such studies begin with diagnosed cases and then search for the presence of the disorder in the other twin. When the pair of twins are similar diagnostically, they are said to be *concordant*. To the extent that a predisposition for a mental disorder can be inherited, concordance for this disorder should be greater in MZ pairs than in DZ pairs.

Although the methodology of the family and twin studies is clear, the data they yield are not always easy to interpret. Let us assume that neurotic parents have been found to produce more than the average number of neurotic offspring. Does this mean that neurosis is genetically transmitted? Not necessarily. The increased frequency of neurosis could as well reflect child-rearing practices and exposure of the children to adult neurotic models. Consider also a finding of greater concordance for schizophrenia among MZ than among DZ twins. Again, such data do not necessarily implicate genetics since MZ twins, perhaps because they look so much alike, may be raised in a more similar fashion than are DZs, thus accounting for the greater concordance for schizophrenia among them. There are, however, special but infrequent cases that are not subject to the aforementioned problems: children reared completely apart from their abnormal parents and MZ twins reared separately from very early infancy. A high frequency of neurosis in children reared apart from their neurotic parents would offer convincing support for the theory that genetic factors figure in neurosis. Similarly, greater concordance among separately reared MZ twins than among DZ twins would offer compelling evidence that a predisposition for a disorder can be inherited.

height. According to the functional approach adopted by most behaviorists, however, the two responses may be treated as equivalent because both perform the same function, removing the individual from a fear-eliciting situation. Within a functional framework fear of snakes and fear of heights are viewed as equivalent in the means by which they are acquired, in how they might be changed, and so on.

If behaviorists underplay the content of

phobias, analysts go to the other extreme, seeing great significance in the phobic object as a symbol of important unconscious motivation. Little Hans, it will be recalled, was afraid of encountering horses if he went outside. Freud paid particular attention to Hans's reference to the "black things around horses' mouths and the things in front of their eyes." The horse was regarded as "standing for the father," who wore eyeglasses and had a moustache. Freud theorized that fear of the father had become transformed into fear of horses, which were then avoided by Hans. Countless other such examples might be cited; the principal point is that the content of phobias has important symbolic value to the psychoanalyst.

Marks (1969) has recently presented an extensive scheme for subclassifying various phobias. He has noted many potentially important differences which behaviorists have paid little if any attention to, and which analytically oriented workers have also ignored, but for different reasons. Within each of his categories Marks establishes several subtypes, basing his differentiations on variables such as frequency, sex distribution, age of onset, whether or not additional symptoms are present, the course of the problem, and psychophysiologic responses.

Animal Phobias

Although easy to define, phobias of animals are the rarest seen in clinical practice. Only 3 percent of all phobics have them. The majority of animal phobias occur in women, and they begin very often in early childhood (Marks and Gelder, 1966). It is likely that among boys and girls animal phobias are quite common, but that boys extinguish their phobias because of social pressures. Thus in adulthood the problems are much more common in women. Recordings of autonomic activity while the subject is at rest indicate that arousal levels are within the normal range.

Agoraphobia

A complicated syndrome, agoraphobia is a cluster of fears centering around open spaces. Fears of other situations such as shopping, encountering crowds, and traveling are often a part of agoraphobia. From a patient's point of view, agoraphobia is surely very distressing. Consider how limiting it must be to be afraid of leaving the house. Perhaps for this reason agoraphobia is the most common phobia seen in the clinic, constituting roughly 60 percent of all phobias examined. The restrictive nature of the syndrome forces the agoraphobic to seek help. Most agoraphobics are women, and the majority develop their problems in adolescence and early adulthood. Numerous other neurotic symptoms are also evident, including panic attacks, tension, dizziness, depression, depersonalization, and obsessions. Psychophysiologic responses confirm the clinical impression that agoraphobics are also subject to a rather diffuse, nonspecific anxiety. That is, when recordings are taken of autonomic activity, agoraphobic patients typically show high levels of arousal, even when they are supposedly relaxing.

Social Phobias

A social phobia is a collection of fears generally linked to the presence of other people. Eating, speaking, or virtually any other activity that might be carried out in the presence of others can elicit extreme anxiety. Although this phobia is not uncommon, social phobics seek help much less frequently than do agoraphobics. Women are seen in therapy for these difficulties slightly more often than are men. As might be expected, onset is generally during adolescence when social awareness and interaction with others are assuming much more importance in the person's life. Few additional symptoms are generally present,

WOMEN AND MICE

The reason why a woman is afraid of a mouse is a profound mystery—indeed, it has never been very closely proved that she is. But some women are constantly in such a nervous irritable condition, that the slightest thing annoys and startles them. The cause of this unfortunate state of affairs is usually some functional derangement, some distressing or painful irregularity, some derangement or peculiar weakness incident to her sex; or it may be due to inflammation, ulceration, or displacement of some of the pelvic viscera or to other organic lesions peculiar to her sex. From whichever cause it may arise, Dr. Pierce's Favorite Prescription is a *positive remedy*, so certain in its curative results that its manufacturers sell it, through druggists, under a *guarantee* of its giving satisfaction in every case, or money paid for it will be *promptly refunded*. As a soothing and strengthening nervine, "Favorite Prescription" is unequaled, and is invaluable in allaying and subduing nervous excitability, irritability, exhaustion, prostration, hysteria, spasms, and other distressing nervous symptoms commonly attendant upon functional and organic disease of the womb. It induces refreshing sleep and relieves mental anxiety and despondency.

Dr. Pierce's Pellets,
Anti-Billious Granules, are Laxative or
Cathartic, according to size of dose.　　By Druggists.

although recordings of psychophysiologic responses indicate rather high levels of anxiety.

Miscellaneous Specific Phobias

Included in this catch-all category are phobias of heights, thunder, darkness, travel, closed spaces, driving, infections, running water, and the like. Few other symptoms are generally present. Further evaluation of this category is not possible because few data have been collected.

Phobias of Childhood

Most children have many fears that are apparently "outgrown" in the normal course of development. For example, Jersild, Markey, and Jersild (1933) interviewed 398 children of ages five to twelve. Fears of the following were expressed by substantial numbers: supernatural events, for example, ghosts and witches, 19.2 percent; being alone, in the dark, or in a strange place, being lost, 14.6 percent; attack or danger of attack by animals, 13.7 percent; bodily injury, falling, illness, operations, hurt and pains, 12.8 percent. The results of a similar study of generally younger children appear in Figure 6.3.

Should these fears be regarded as phobias? For the most part, the answer would appear to be no. The childhood fears reported in various studies are transitory, and little information is given to indicate that the feared situation is actively avoided. It is generally agreed that to be classified as a phobia, a fear should be of substantial duration and should entail definite avoidance. One situation, however, attending school, does appear to generate a fear in children that warrants the name phobia. Waldfogel (1959) offers the following definition of school phobia.

School phobia refers to a reluctance to go to school because of acute fear associated with it. Usually this dread is accompanied by somatic symptoms with the gastrointestinal tract the most commonly affected. . . . The somatic complaints come to be used as an auxiliary device to justify staying at home and often disappear when the child is reassured that he will not have to attend school. The characteristic picture is of a child nauseated or complaining of abdominal pain at breakfast and desperately resisting all attempts at reassurance, reasoning, or coercion to get him to school. In its milder forms, school phobia may be only a transient symptom; but when it becomes established, it can be one of the most disabling disorders of childhood, lasting even for years (pp. 35–36).

The frequency of school phobias has been estimated at 17 per 1000 children per year (Kennedy, 1965), and they are more common in girls than in boys. The most prevalent view of the etiology of school phobia may be termed a *separation anxiety* theory. From one investigation involving an intensive study of several cases, the following account emerged (Johnson, Falstein, Szurek, and Svendson, 1941).

First, some environmental event, which may be related to the school setting itself, elicits increased anxiety in the child. At the same time the mother becomes increasingly anxious about her own problems. A dependent relationship between mother and child may then conspire to increase further the anxiety that occurs naturally when mother and child are separated by the child's going to school. Thus the child starts to avoid school and the mother allows him to stay home. The mother may even unwittingly reward the child's nonattendance for her own purposes. Given that the dependent relationship works both ways, the child being dependent on the mother and

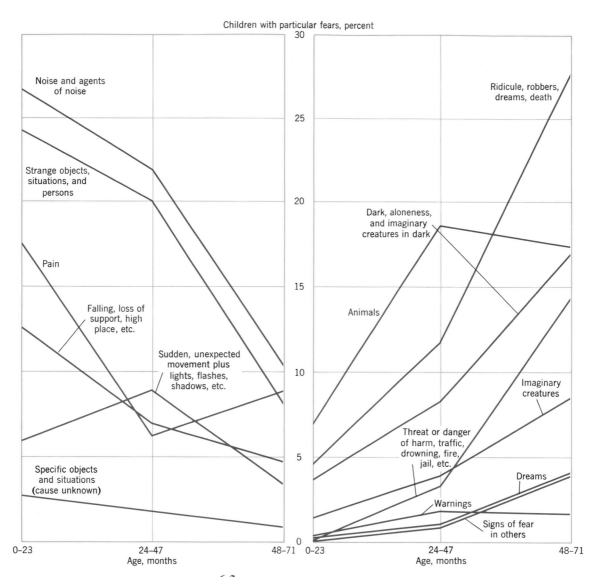

Children with particular fears, percent

Noise and agents of noise

Strange objects, situations, and persons

Pain

Falling, loss of support, high place, etc.

Sudden, unexpected movement plus lights, flashes, shadows, etc.

Specific objects and situations (cause unknown)

Ridicule, robbers, dreams, death

Dark, aloneness, and imaginary creatures in dark

Animals

Imaginary creatures

Threat or danger of harm, traffic, drowning, fire, jail, etc.

Dreams

Warnings

Signs of fear in others

Age, months

FIGURE **6.3**

Relative frequency of fears of various kinds shown by children of different ages who were observed by parents or teachers in the Jersild and Holmes (1935) study. After Gray, 1971.

the mother being dependent on the child, the mother may not wish to lose her child to the school each day. A similar view has also been suggested by behaviorally oriented psychologists (Lazarus, Davison, and Polefka, 1965), who regard the avoidance of school as com-

prising two separable although interrelated elements: intense fear of going to school and reinforcement of avoidance by the mother.

The foregoing illustrates important differences among various clinical phobias (Table

TABLE **6.2**
Summary of Subclassification of Phobias

	Animal phobias	Agoraphobia	Social phobias	Miscellaneous	School phobia
Frequency	Rare	Common	Not uncommon	Not uncommon	Not uncommon
Sex incidence	95% women	75% women	60% women	50% women	More common in girls
Onset age	Childhood	After puberty	After puberty	Anytime	Childhood
Associated symptoms	Few	Multiple — general anxiety, depression, panic	Few	Not determined	Nausea, vomiting, diarrhea
Psychophysiology	Normal	High arousal	High arousal	Not determined	Not determined

6.2). Some, like agoraphobia and social phobias, are associated with high arousal levels indicating that the autonomic nervous system may be especially important in their etiology. Therapy procedures aimed at reducing such fears may have to take this high level of autonomic arousal into account. Similarly, any attempt to deal with school phobia should probably include a change in the mother's behavior. Therefore the topographical features of a phobia have important implications for both etiology and treatment.

ANXIETY NEUROSIS

Anxiety neurosis is characterized by anxious overconcern which may amplify to become panic. Somatic symptoms are frequently associated with this anxiety, which may occur in any circumstance and is not restricted to specific situations or objects. This syndrome is sometimes referred to as "free-floating anxiety." The person is anxious in so many different situations and so much of the time that many psychopathologists have regarded as fruitless any systematic search for specific eliciting causes. Individuals diagnosed as having anxiety reactions are likely to be tense, irritable, and subject to episodes of acute panic. Patients report apprehension, feelings of being out of control, premonitions of impending disaster, and the like. They are also overly sensitive to criticism and easily discouraged. Generally, there are many physiological concomitants such as rapid heart rate, irregular breathing, excessive sweating, and dizziness. Insomnia, restlessness, fatigue, muscular tension, and difficulty in concentrating and making decisions are other symptoms often reported.

ANXIETY AND DEPRESSION

The patient, a thirty-one year old mechanic, had been referred for psychotherapy by his physician, whom he had consulted because of dizziness and difficulties in falling asleep. He was quite visibly distressed during the entire initial interview, gulping before he spoke, sweating and continually fidgeting in his chair. His repeated requests for water to slake a seemingly unquenchable thirst were another indication of this extreme nervousness. Although he first related his physical concerns, a more general picture of pervasive anxiety soon emerged. He reported that he nearly always felt tense and that "If anything can go wrong, it will." He was apprehensive of possible disasters that could befall him as he worked and interacted with others. He reported a long history of difficulties in interpersonal relationships which had led to his being fired from several jobs. As he put it: "I really like people and try to get along with them, but it seems like I fly off the handle too easily. Little things they do upset me too much. I just can't cope unless everything is going exactly right."[6]

Psychoanalytic theory regards the source of anxiety neurosis as a conflict between the ego and id impulses, which are usually sexual or aggressive. The ego cannot allow the impulses to be expressed because it fears that punishment will follow. Since the source of the anxiety is unconscious, the person experiences apprehension and distress without knowing why. The individual suffering from anxiety neurosis carries around with him at all times the true source of his anxiety, namely previously punished id impulses which are striving for expression. In a sense there is no way to evade anxiety; if the person escapes his id, he is no longer alive. Anxiety is felt nearly all the time.

Learning theorists (for example, Wolpe, 1958) attempting to account for anxiety neurosis would, by the very nature of their paradigm, reject a concept of "free-floating anxiety." Instead, they look with greater persistence for external causes. For example, a person anxious most of his waking hours might well be fearful of social contacts, and if that individual spends a good deal of time with other people, it may be more useful to regard his anxiety as tied to these circumstances rather than to any internal factors. This behavioral model of anxiety neurosis, then, is identical to the learning view of phobias. Anxiety is viewed as having been classically conditioned to external stimuli, although the range of conditioned stimuli is considerably broader.

Another learning model focuses on control and helplessness. Consider an individual who has not learned effective responses to cope with a variety of challenges. Since we have already indicated that a lack of control engenders anxiety (Chapter 5), we would expect such a person to exhibit pervasive anxiety.

Genetic researchers have also examined anxiety neurosis. A recent study (Slater and Shields, 1969) showed anxiety neurosis to have a pattern of incidence consistent with genetic transmission. Comparisons were made of seventeen identical pairs of twins and

[6] Case reports such as this one, when not referenced, have been drawn from our own clinical files. Identifying features are changed to protect the confidentiality of the individual.

twenty-eight fraternal pairs of twins; one twin of each pair had been diagnosed as having anxiety neurosis. Of the identical co-twins, 49 percent were also diagnosed as having anxiety neurosis. In contrast, only 4 percent of the fraternal co-twins were so diagnosed.

HYSTERICAL NEUROSES

The third major category of neurotic disorders is hysteria, or to use its more contemporary name, hysterical neurosis. According to DSM-II, hysterical neuroses are divided into two major types, dissociative and conversion reactions. Partial paralysis, anesthesias, disturbances of vision, and the like, all of them occurring in the absence of physical damage of any kind, are examples of conversion reactions. Dissociative reactions are defined as departures from normal states of consciousness.

Dissociative Reaction

Four types of dissociative neuroses are distinguished. *Amnesia* involves loss of memory for a period of time, during which the amnesiac cannot remember his name, where he lives, or anything about his previous life. He will not recognize his relatives or friends but he retains his ability to talk, read, and reason, and perhaps his talents and the knowledge that he has acquired of the world and how to function in it. The length of time that the amnesic state lasts varies, ranging from several hours to several years. *Fugue* also involves loss of memory, but in addition the person flees from his usual surroundings, frequently moving to a new geographic location and starting an entirely new life. *Somnambulism,* commonly referred to as sleepwalking, is also considered a dissociative reaction. *Multiple personality,* the presence of separate and different personalities within the same individual, is perhaps the most dramatic type of dissociative reaction and has already been illustrated in Chapter 4 with excerpts from the case history of Eve.[7]

According to the **psychoanalytic view** of each of the four types of dissociative reaction, one part of the mind or consciousness splits off or becomes dissociated from another part. The individual engages in activities of which he later claims to be unaware. The types of dissociative reaction are tied together conceptually by psychoanalytic theory, being viewed as instances of a massive repression, usually relating back to the unacceptable infantile sexual wishes of the oedipal stage. In adulthood these oedipal yearnings increase in strength until they are finally expressed, usually as an impulsive sexual act. The ordinary form of repression is obviously no longer sufficient; the whole event must be obliterated from consciousness. The person succeeds in this by splitting off an entire part of the personality from awareness (Buss, 1966) and by acquiring a new identity.

[7] Cases of multiple personality are frequently mislabeled in the popular press as schizophrenic reactions. This diagnostic category, discussed in greater detail in Chapters 13 and 14, derives its name from the Greek root *schizo,* which means "splitting away from." Hence the confusion. A split in the personality, wherein two or more fairly separate and coherent systems of being exist alternately in the same person, is different from the split between cognition and affect that is said to produce the schizophrenic's inappropriate behavior.

Learning theorists have generally construed these rare phenomena as avoidance responses that serve to protect the individual from highly stressful events. Although not employing the concept of repression and not emphasizing the overriding importance of infantile sexual conflicts, the behavioral view of dissociative reactions is not dissimilar to psychoanalytic speculations about these disorders.

Some of the aspects of an amnesic dissociative reaction can be seen in the following case history described by Leahy and Martin (1967).

Their patient, after returning from World War II, had been prone to amnesia. During these episodes he would not recognize his wife, talked to her as though she were French, and generally behaved in a way that seemed similar to the patterns of behavior he may have exhibited while in France during the war. At the end of each episode he had no memory of his behavior. The patient eventually sought psychotherapy. While hypnotized he related an important incident that had occurred during the war. He and a fellow soldier found themselves separated from their regular unit, the two of them in charge of four German prisoners. When they stopped to rest in a small hut, his compatriot, an officer of higher rank than he, ordered him to shoot the unarmed prisoners. He refused to do this and in the following argument threw his rifle to the officer, telling him to do the shooting. He then became afraid that the officer might shoot him and in panic crashed through the flimsy wall of the hut and ran back to his unit. While telling this story the patient became very emotional and seemed to relive the experience, even throwing himself against the wall of the interviewing room with such force that he had to be restrained. After hypnotic reexperiencing of this particular incident had been repeated several times,[8] the patient showed considerable improvement. He remained free of his amnesia attacks for only a short period of time, however, and was later readmitted to the hospital.

On this readmission, and again under hypnosis, another important detail of the earlier incident emerged. Specifically, it was now learned that the patient had not really run back to his unit after breaking through the wall of the hut. Rather, concerned about the fate of the unarmed prisoners, he decided to return to them. He encountered the officer outside the hut and stabbed him to death with his bayonet. As might be expected, this incident was recounted with great emotion. This time the reliving of the initial experience seemed to have a longer-lasting effect, and the patient remained relatively free of amnesic episodes.

[8] Breuer and Freud's cathartic method should be recalled (page 22).

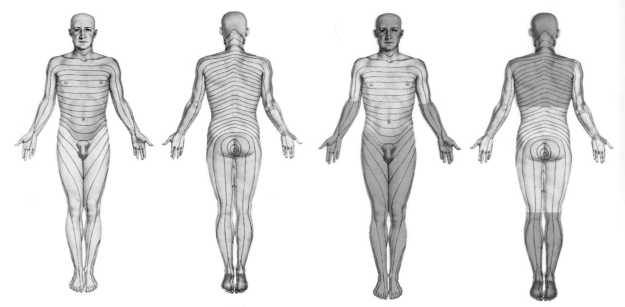

FIGURE **6.4**

Hysterical anesthesias can be distinguished from neurological dysfunctions. On the left are shown the patterns of neural innervation of the skin. On the right are typical areas of anesthesias in hysterical patients. The hysterical anesthesias do not make anatomical sense.

As informative as this kind of case material is, we are unfortunately able to go little beyond descriptive accounts since there are so few concrete data available on this type of problem. Information is scant mainly because of the rarity of the disorder. Abse (1966), for example, reviewed the literature and was able to find only 200 documented cases of various dissociative reactions. Most of these were descriptive clinical accounts such as the one we have just presented. Dissociative reactions remain among the most poorly understood clinical syndromes.

Conversion Reaction

In conversion reactions the operations of the musculature or sensory functions are impaired, although the bodily organs themselves

are sound. We find reports of partial or complete paralyses of arms or legs; anesthesias (Figure 6.4), the loss or impairment of sensations; and analgesias or insensitivity to pain, all occurring in physiologically normal people. Vision may be seriously disturbed: the person may become partially or completely blind or have "tunnel vision" whereby the visual field is constricted as it would be were the observer peering through a tunnel. Hysteria, the earlier term for such disorders, has of course a long history dating back to the earliest writings on abnormal behavior. Hippocrates considered it an affliction limited solely to women that was brought on by the wandering of the uterus through the body. The Greek word *hystera* means womb. Presumably the wandering uterus symbolized the longing of the body for the production of a child.

ANXIETY AND DEPRESSION

On the basis of an extensive survey, Guze and Perley (1963) suggest the following factors as definitive of the conversion syndrome.

The hysterical reactions start early in life.
The problems are limited primarily to women.
Symptoms are often recurrent and difficult to treat effectively.[9]
The patient usually describes the symptoms in dramatic terms.
The complaints, many and varied, are of pain, menstrual disorders, sexual maladjustment, headache, anxiety, and so on.
The patients are often hospitalized an excessive number of times for treatment of their physical complaints.

The consensus among writers is that conversion reactions are found primarily in females. During both world wars, however, a large number of males also developed conversion-like difficulties in combat (Zigler, Imboden, and Meyer, 1960).

People manifesting conversion-like problems have often been suspected of *malingering,* that is, faking an incapacity in order to avoid work. In trying to discriminate conversion reactions

from malingering, clinicians may try to decide whether the so-called symptoms have been consciously or unconsciously adopted. This means of resolving the issue is at best a dubious one, for it is difficult if not impossible to know with any degree of certainty whether behavior is consciously or unconsciously motivated. One aspect of behavior is revealing, however, *la belle indifférence* of hysterics. Hysterics often do not seem upset by their problems, adopting a blasé attitude toward their symptoms. But they also appear willing and eager to talk endlessly and dramatically about them. In contrast, the malingerer is likely to be more guarded and cautious, perhaps because he considers interviews a challenge or threat to the success of his lie.

Psychological versus Organic Cause

Whether the symptoms of conversion reactions are truly psychological or are organically produced is another important issue. Hysterias such as glove anesthesia are not difficult to diagnose because there are no neurological explanations for such a pattern of symptoms. On the other hand, plausible organic accounts of the symptom patterns of various paralyses, analgesias, and sensory problems can be proposed. The findings of authors such as Slater and Glithero (1965) indicate the importance of this possibility. Their study was a follow-up of patients who nine years earlier had been diagnosed as suffering from conversion reaction. An unexpected number, in fact 60 percent, of these individuals had either died in the meantime or developed symptoms of physical disease! A high proportion had diseases of the central nervous system. Similarly, Whitlock (1957) compared the incidence of organic disorders in patients earlier diagnosed as having conversion reactions and in patients earlier diagnosed as having depressive reactions, anxi-

---

[9] Resistance to change is not infrequently mentioned as a criterion or characteristic of a particular syndrome, in the present case conversion reaction. There is a thorny problem here, namely the effectiveness of various therapeutic approaches. As will become clear in the last part of the book, the treatment of mental disorders is truly in its infancy, and we can only hope that better techniques will be developed soon. In the meantime the student would do well to bear in mind that the ease with which a disorder can be cured or ameliorated is necessarily a joint function both of the intrinsic nature of the problem and of the procedures available for trying to change it. That man cannot flap his arms and fly is evident; moreover, it is highly doubtful that he will *ever* be able to do so. But the fact that conversion reactions are persistent over time is probably in part a function of our inability to help those with the problem.

ety reactions, or both. Organic disorders were found in 62.5 percent of the patients earlier diagnosed as having conversion reactions and in only 5.3 percent of the other groups. The most common organic problem was head injury, generally found to have occurred about six months before the onset of the conversion symptoms. Other common organic problems were stroke, encephalitis, and brain tumor. From these data we can see that some symptoms labeled as conversion reactions and thought to have psychological causes may, in fact, be physical disorders. We have already learned that the assessment of organic problems is still rather crude. Therefore it is hazardous to attempt to distinguish between psychologically and organically produced symptoms. It may be that the diagnosis of conversion reaction is applied too frequently; many individuals diagnosed in this way may have an organic problem that has gone undetected. The damage that such inappropriate diagnoses can do is sobering to contemplate.

Theories of Conversion Reaction

According to **psychoanalytic theory,** conversion reactions, like dissociative reactions, are rooted in an early unresolved Oedipus complex. The young female child becomes incestuously attached to her father, but these early impulses are repressed, producing both a preoccupation with sex and, at the same time, an avoidance of it. At a later period of her life, sexual excitement or some other environmental event reawakens these repressed impulses, at which time they are expressed or *converted* into physical symptoms that represent in distorted form the repressed libidinal urges.

Sociocultural theories are based on the supposed decrease in conversion reactions over the last century. Although Charcot and Freud seemed to have had an abundance of female

patients with this sort of difficulty, contemporary clinicians rarely see anyone with such problems. For this reason conversion reaction has been linked to the society and culture of the nineteenth century. In that century most people were not sophisticated enough to realize the relation between psychological factors and symptoms. It may have been easier then for patients and physicians to accept symptoms as true indicators of physical illness. An individual could with relative ease, and without arousing the suspicions of others, develop "physical" symptoms that would remove him from stressful situations and that would bring sympathy, attention, and the like from people concerned about the patient's health. Furthermore, those of a psychoanalytic bent point out that in the second half of the nineteenth century, when the incidence of conversion reactions was apparently high in France and Austria, sexual attitudes were quite repressive and may have contributed to the increased incidence of the disorder. The decline of the conversion reaction, then, is attributed to the greater sophistication of twentieth-century culture and a general relaxing of sexual mores.

A study by Proctor (1958) provides some evidence for this theory. The incidence of conversion reaction was found to be particularly high among children who were patients at the University of North Carolina Medical School Psychiatric Clinic. In interpreting this very high incidence, the author noted that most of the children came from rural areas where the socioeconomic status of the inhabitants was low and little education was provided for them. Moreover, the religious background of these people was generally strong and fundamentalist. The conditions in this area of North Carolina may very well have approximated in some respects those prevailing in nineteenth-century France and Austria.

Weighing against the preceding analysis,

however, is *the fact that there is actually little data to indicate a decreasing incidence of conversion reactions!* For example, Stephens and Kamp (1962) compared the outpatient diagnoses of two periods, the first from 1913 to 1919 and the second from 1945 to 1960. In both they found the incidence of conversion reaction to be 2 percent. We can also find reasons that explain away the seemingly high incidence of conversion disorders found in the nineteenth century. The large numbers seen by clinicians such as Charcot and Freud may have reflected a selective process. Patients with these particular difficulties may have come to these clinicians because they were known to be successful in treating hysterias. Similarly, the high incidence of conversion reactions reported by Proctor may reflect not a "true" high incidence but rather differences in diagnostic practices. In view of the difficulties in assessing incidence at different periods of time, it would seem ill-advised to claim validation for an etiological theory of a disorder on the basis of alleged changes in frequency of occurrence.

A **behavioral account** of the development of conversion reactions has been proposed by Ullmann and Krasner (1969). In their opinion the person with a conversion reaction attempts to behave according to his own conception of how a person with a disease affecting his motor or sensory abilities would act. This theory raises two questions: Are people capable of such behavior? Under what conditions might such behavior be most likely to occur?

Considerable evidence supports an affirmative answer to the first question, that people can adopt patterns of behavior that match many of the classic conversion reaction symptoms. For example, paralyses and analgesias can be induced in people under hypnosis. Similarly, chemically inert drugs called placebos have reduced the pain of patients who had been considered truly ill. As a partial answer to the second question, Ullmann and Krasner specify two conditions that increase the likelihood that motor and sensory disabilities can be aped. First, the individual must have some experience with the role he is to adopt. He may have had similar physical problems himself, or he may have observed them in others. Second, Ullmann and Krasner note that the enactment of a role must be rewarded. An individual will feign a disability only if it can be expected either to reduce stress or to reap other positive consequences.

Ullmann and Krasner describe the case of a veteran originally reported by Brady and Lind (1961). Two of the patient's aunts had been totally blind during their last years. While in the army the patient had developed a problem in one of his eyes that had greatly reduced visual acuity. Thereafter he was given a medical discharge from the army and a small pension. During the twelve years following his discharge, he held a series of semiskilled jobs, remaining at none more than a year and often returning to the hospital with recurrences of his visual problem. Each time after returning to the hospital he applied for a larger pension but was refused because there had been no additional loss of vision.

Twelve years after his discharge, while shopping with his wife and mother-in-law, he suddenly "became blind" in both eyes. At this time, the authors state, "His wife and mother-in-law were being more demanding than usual, requiring him to work nights and weekends at various chores under their foremanship. One immediate consequence of his blindness was, then, partial escape from this situation." During the next two years the patient received various treatments and was enrolled in a course of training for the blind. In addition, he was awarded a special pension for his total disability and received financial assistance from the community for his children and some money from his relatives. Ullmann and Krasner's contention that conversion reactions may develop when the role that is to be adopted is known and rewards are to be expected is plausible; yet, except for case studies like this one reported by Brady and Lind, their theory has not been substantiated.

Genetic and biological factors have been suggested as playing some role in the development of conversion reactions. Slater (1961) investigated concordance rates in twelve monozygotic and twelve dizygotic pairs of twins. Probands of each pair had been diagnosed as having the disorder, but none of the co-twins of either type manifested a clear conversion reaction. Similarly, Gottesman (1962) found the reactions of monozygotic twins to statements on the hysteria scale of the MMPI to be no more similar than those of dizygotic twins. Genetic factors, then, from the studies done so far, seem to be of no importance.

An intriguing case study of a conversion hysteric provides some suggestive information about the possible neurophysiological mechanisms by which a conversion reaction involving a sensory system is produced (Hernández-Peón, Chávez-Ibarra, and Aguilar-Figueroa, 1963). The patient was a fif-

teen-year-old girl with an analgesia in the left arm. To determine the basis of her affliction, these investigators recorded electrical activity of the brain while her arms were pricked by a pin. The cortical responses to pin pricks in the normal right arm were compared to responses obtained from the left arm. The usual pattern of cortical responses was found for the right arm, but no brain response was detected when the left analgesic arm was pricked. These data, consistent with clinical reports, suggest that sensory input was being inhibited. Other research has demonstrated that neural pathways descending from the cortex can exert an inhibitory influence on incoming sensory pathways. That is, certain messages from the brain can block out or inhibit the impulses traveling along incoming sensory nerves. An increase in the activity of these descending inhibitory pathways, then, may be a mechanism by which sensations are altered in conversion reactions. But the possibility that neural pathways are implicated in conversion reactions need not mean that the explanation for these disorders is somatogenic rather than psychogenic, for the increased activity of these descending pathways would still have to be accounted for in some manner.

OBSESSIVE-COMPULSIVE NEUROSIS

Obsessive-compulsive neurosis is the least common of any of the neurotic disorders (Ingram, 1961) and is found to have an onset in early adulthood. Obsessions are intrusive and recurring thoughts which appear irrational and uncontrollable to the individual experiencing them. Two types are distinguished. Obsessive doubting, perpetual indecision, and uncertainty are examples of the first type. The doubting and uncertainty may concern future choices in an individual's life (Shall I do X or not?) or past behavior (Did I turn off the gas?).

Whereas many of us may have similar fleeting thoughts, the obsessive experiences them with such force and frequency that functioning is interfered with. The other kind of obsessive thoughts, which typically generate considerable anxiety, are intrusive fears that the individual may engage in prohibited activities. The individual may become obsessed with the idea that he will swear, make obscene gestures, or even commit murder. Cameron (1963) gives an example illustrating the onset of an obsessive thought in a forty-two-year-old mother:

"Hi, I'm Herb Armstrong. Uncertainty is my thing."
(DRAWING BY WEBER; © 1972 THE NEW YORKER MAGAZINE, INC.)

She was serving the family dinner one evening when she dropped a dish on the table and smashed it. The accident appalled her. While clearing up the fragments she was seized with an unreasonable fear that bits of glass might get into her husband's food and kill him. She would not allow the meal to proceed until she had removed everything and reset the table with fresh linen and clean dishes. After this her fears, instead of subsiding, reached out to include intense anxiety over the possibility that she herself and the children might be killed by bits of glass (p. 384).

A compulsion is the irresistible impulse to repeat some ritualistic act over and over again. Lady Macbeth washed her hands continually after the murder of King Duncan. Virtually any behavior can be viewed as a compulsion if the individual reports an irresistible urge to perform it and experiences considerable distress if prevented from doing so. Often an individual who continually repeats some action fears dire consequences if the act is not performed. The sheer frequency with which an act is repeated may often be staggering. One woman treated by the authors of this book washed her hands over 500 times per day in spite of the painful sores that resulted. She reported that she had a very strong fear of con-

tamination by germs and could temporarily alleviate this concern only by washing her hands.

In **psychoanalytic theory** obsessions and compulsions are viewed as similar, resulting from instinctual forces, primarily aggressive. The symptoms observed represent the outcome of the struggle between the id and the defense mechanisms; sometimes the id predominates, sometimes the defense mechanisms. For example, when obsessive thoughts of killing intrude, the forces of the id are dominant. More often, however, the observed symptoms reflect the partially successful operation of one of the defense mechanisms. An individual fixated at the anal stage may by *reaction formation* resist his urge to soil and become compulsively neat, clean, and orderly. Similarly, in *undoing,* the individual engages in a ritualistic behavior which represents a magical attempt to cancel out the forbidden impulse. Or he does penance for misdeeds in order to erase guilt.

Behavioral accounts of obsessions and compulsions (Meyer and Chesser, 1970) consider them learned behaviors reinforced by their consequences. One set of consequences concerns the reduction of fear. For example, compulsive hand washing is viewed as an instrumental escape-response which reduces an obsessional preoccupation with contamination by dirt or germs. A related view is illustrated by Skinner's famous demonstration of the acquisition of so-called superstitious behavior in pigeons. The birds were reduced to 75 percent of their normal body weight and then presented with food at regular intervals, whatever their behavior happened to be. In this way and quite by chance, as Skinner described it,

One bird was conditioned to turn counterclockwise about the cage. . . . Another repeatedly thrust its head into one of the upper corners of the cage. A third developed a "tossing" response, as if placing its head beneath an invisible bar and lifting it repeatedly (1948, p. 168).

The implication is that obsessive behavior in human beings is similarly learned through chance reinforcement. As plausible as these formulations appear, "The aetiology of obsessional neurosis remains obscure" (Meyer and Chesser, 1970, p. 63).

EXISTENTIAL NEUROSIS

At least implicit in Freud's theorizing is the idea that normal personality development entails a balance or compromise between the biologically based urges of the id and the reality (ego) and moral (superego) considerations imposed upon the individual by his external world and his society. From a behavioral point of view, to grow up without experiencing an appreciable amount of unrealistic anxiety, the individual must not be subjected to too many stressful traumatic situations, and he must acquire social skills to enable him to operate effectively in society. These two views of personality development have a great deal in common—if for no other reason than that both neglect an aspect of man, his freedom, which is given particular emphasis in the writings of existential philosophers and psychologists.

In recent years clinicians have remarked on the emergence of what seems to be a completely different kind of neurotic disorder, *existential neurosis.* Although not recognized as a syndrome by DSM-II, it is somewhat similar to depersonalization neurosis. Even though little research has been done on this disorder, our account of neuroses would be incomplete without at least a description.

The cognitive component of the existential neurosis is meaninglessness, or chronic inability to believe in the truth, importance, usefulness, or interest value of any of the things one is engaged in or can imagine doing. The most characteristic [emotional] features . . . are blandness and boredom, punctuated by periods of depression which become less frequent as the disorder is prolonged. As to the realm of action, activity level may be low to moderate, but more important than the amount of activity is the introspective and ob-

"*Today I'm going to be un-aware, uninvolved, uncommitted, and self-centered.*"

(DRAWING BY DEDINI; © 1972 THE NEW YORKER MAGAZINE, INC.)

jectively observable fact that activities are not chosen. There is little selectivity, it being immaterial to the person what if any activities he pursues. If there is any selectivity shown, it is in the direction of insuring minimal expenditures of effort and decision making (Maddi, 1967, p. 313).

Basing his views on the philosophical and often extremely subjective writings of existentialists, Maddi suggests that even before the in-dividual suffers from existential neurosis, he has developed a *premorbid personality*. Such a person plays social roles, perhaps very well indeed, and satisfies quite adequately his biological needs. These talents are indeed important, as Maddi hastens to point out. If a person's life consists *only* of these acquired skills, however, he is a candidate for existential neurosis, for he has merely "gone along with" society instead of creating his own destiny. He will feel a great sense of emptiness and lack of fulfillment, *in spite of the fact that he may be extremely effective in satisfying society's demands in every possible way.* Then conditions of stress—for example, the imminence of death, a gross disruption in the social order, such as war or an economic depression, or the repeated failure to experience other people and one's own feelings at what Maddi regards as a "deep and comprehensive level"—can easily trigger the onset of the neurosis itself.

Central to any existential theory is the conception of man as capable of making free and independent choices among alternatives. According to this view, man is an initiator in his world, rather than the passive and purely reactive organism implied by both psychoanalytic and behavioral theories. Maddi does not feel,

however, that existential man exists outside the realm of scientific discourse, for his moment-by-moment ability to make choices among alternatives is a link in the causal chain of all phenomena. Maddi is indeed very serious in suggesting that children can be taught to become premorbid existential neurotics if they are valued and rewarded only for their performance of society's social roles and for their increasing ability to satisfy their biological needs. For a more healthy development they should be encouraged to make independent decisions based on some system of values, which may be shared by other people, and to have an active internal life, which they can maintain whatever happens in the external world.

SUMMARY

Anxiety is central to all neurotic disorders. Phobias are fear-mediated escape or avoidance reactions that are out of proportion to the dangers presented by objects or situations. Anxiety neurosis is a more pervasive fear, not clearly elicited by particular objects or situations. In a hysterical dissociative neurosis consciousness is altered. Paralyses, loss of sensation, and sensory disturbances that occur without known organic damage are called hysterical conversion reactions. A person with an obsessive-compulsive neurosis has intrusive thoughts or performs the same act again and again. Existential neurosis, a recently suggested type of neurotic disorder, is the feeling that life is meaningless.

According to psychoanalytic views, neuroses result from repressed conflicts blocking the expression of id impulses. The maladaptive behaviors exhibited by all neurotics are attempts to reduce the overstimulation with which the ego is threatened. For example, in phobias the fear of an actual object is displaced to a symbol. Little Hans's fear of his father was displaced onto horses, which could then be avoided.

Learning theorists view neurotic behavior as responses reinforced either because they reduce fear or because the consequences that they produce are positive. The development of the original fear has been viewed in both classical conditioning and modeling terms.

All theories rest on little direct evidence. None can account well for the fact that among individuals who have experienced stress only *some* become neurotically anxious. It may be that a few people are more predisposed than others to develop neurotic anxiety, and that lability of the autonomic nervous system is the important diathesis or predisposing factor.

CHAPTER 7
Psychophysiological Disorders

In Chapter 5 we discussed voodoo death, a seemingly supernatural phenomenon whereby a curse from a witch doctor dooms his victim to extreme physical suffering and death. To explain such events Cannon (1942) proposed that vital bodily organs are irreparably harmed if the autonomic nervous system is maintained in a highly aroused state through prolonged psychological stress without the opportunity for effective action. Inasmuch as the arousal of the autonomic nervous system is also regarded as one of the bodily indications of anxiety, it is not surprising that psychopathologists have concerned themselves with physical diseases involving this system, in the belief that psychological factors may be implicated. In anxiety the bodily changes of autonomic arousal are viewed as transient; in psychophysiological disorders the usually reversible autonomic and hormonal responses to stress cause irreversible tissue damage (Meyer and Chesser, 1970).

Psychophysiological disorders " . . . are characterized by physical symptoms that are caused by emotional factors and involve a single organ system, usually under the control of the autonomic nervous system" (DSM-II, 1968, p. 46). At the outset, two important points must be firmly established. First, a psychophysiologic disorder is a real disease involving damage to the body. The fact that such disorders are viewed as being caused by emotional factors does not make the affliction imaginary. People can just as readily die from "psychologically produced" asthma or ulcers as from similar diseases produced by infection or physical injury. Second, psychophysiologic disorders should be distinguished from the hysterical reactions that were discussed in Chapter 6. Hysterical disorders do not involve actual organic damage to the body and they are generally considered to affect the function of the voluntary musculature. In contrast, psychophysiologic disorders *do* involve actual damage to bodily tissues.

Nine different types of psychophysiologic disorders are listed in DSM-II. All are attributed in part to the emotional state of the patient; the most obvious difference among them is the part of the body affected.

1. Psychophysiologic skin disorders. Skin reactions such as neurodermatitis (inflammation), pruritis (itching), and hyperhydrosis (dry skin).
2. Psychophysiologic respiratory disorders. Bronchial asthma, hyperventilation (breathing very rapidly), sighing, and hiccups.
3. Psychophysiologic cardiovascular disorders. Tachycardia (heart racing), hypertension (high blood pressure), and migraine headache.
4. Psychophysiologic hemic and lymphatic disorders. Disturbances of the blood and lymphatic systems.
5. Psychophysiologic gastrointestinal disorders. Peptic ulcers, chronic gastritis, ulcerative or mucous colitis, constipation, hyperacidity, and heartburn.
6. Psychophysiologic genital-urinary disorders. Disturbances in menstruation and urination, dyspareunia (painful sexual intercourse), and impotence (difficulty obtaining or maintaining an erection, or both).
7. Psychophysiologic endocrine disorders. Malfunctions of the various endocrine glands.
8. Psychophysiologic disorders of a sense organ. Any disturbance in one of the sensory organs in which emotional factors play a causative role.
9. Psychophysiologic musculoskeletal disorders. Backache, muscle cramps, and tension headaches.

In addition to the list of psychophysiologic disorders proposed by the current diagnostic nomenclature, many other diseases are viewed as being partially caused by emotional or psychological factors. The list, a long one, includes multiple sclerosis, pneumonia, cancer, tuberculosis, and the common cold. In fact, the emotional state of the patient is now recognized as playing an important role in the precipitation or exacerbation of many illnesses. One recent study, for example, examined the frequency of illnesses among the crew of a naval ship (Rubin, Gunderson, and Doll, 1969). The frequency of illness was found to be strongly related to the type of duty: both the overall illness rate and the rates for most individual categories—respiratory, gastrointestinal, and so on—were higher during combat than during in-port periods. Additionally, illness was more frequent among sailors performing dangerous tasks or working in stressful environments.

The present term, psychophysiologic disorders, is now preferred to one that is perhaps better known, psychosomatic disorders. Psychosomatic connotes quite well the principal aspect of these disorders, that the psyche or mind is having an untoward effect on the soma or body. The structure of both these terms, in fact, implies that mind and body are separate and independent, although they may, at times, influence each other (see Box 7.1). Dualism is a deeply ingrained paradigm of human thought. And yet the hope was that these terms would foster a monistic rather than dualistic view of the human being, since " . . . all functioning and all diseases are both mental and physical, because both mental and physiological processes are going on continuously" (Sternbach, 1966, p. 139). Instead of speaking of the emotions as causing body dysfunctions, we could instead, as Graham (1967) has noted, regard the psyche and soma as one and the same. Psychological and physical explanations of dis-

ANXIETY AND DEPRESSION

ease are then simply two different ways of describing the same events. We shall accept the modern concept of a unitary organism, but at the same time allow that psychological and physical aspects can be distinguished one from the other for purposes of separate study.

THEORIES OF PSYCHOPHYSIOLOGICAL DISORDERS

We have known for some time that various *physical* stresses can produce physiological damage (Selye, 1956). In studying psycho-physiologic disorders we are concerned with *psychological* stressors such as emotional tension, conflict, and bereavement. Can they also elicit physiological changes and thus cause a psychophysiologic disorder? In considering this issue we are confronted with three questions: (1) Why does stress produce difficulties in only *some* people who are exposed to it? (2) Why does stress sometimes cause a psycho-physiologic disorder and not another disorder such as a neurosis? (3) Given that stress produces a psychophysiologic disorder, what determines which one of the many possible disorders it will be? We have already discussed the concept of stress as it is related to various neurotic syndromes, and we shall discuss it further in the chapters on schizophrenia. How is it, then, that this general concept can be used to "account for" such a wide range of disorders?

The answers to these questions have been sought by both biologically and psychologically oriented theorists. Biological approaches attribute particular psychophysiologic disorders to specific bodily weaknesses of an individual's organ systems in responding to stress. Psychological theories account for specificity by positing particular stresses for particular disorders.

Biological Theories of Psychophysiological Disorders

Somatic-Weakness Theory

Genetic factors, earlier illnesses, diet, and the like may selectively disrupt a particular organ system, which may then become weak and vulnerable to stress. According to the somatic-weakness theory, the connection between stress and a particular psychophysiologic disorder is the weakness in a particular bodily organ. By way of analogy, a tire blows out at its weakest or thinnest portion. For example, a congenitally weak respiratory system might predispose the individual to asthma.

Specific-Reaction Theory

Some investigators argue that there are differences, probably genetically determined, in the ways in which individuals respond to stress. People have been found to have their own particular patterns of autonomic response to stress. The heart rate of one individual may increase, whereas another may react with increased respiration rate but no change in frequency of heartbeats (Lacey, 1967). Thus individuals seem to respond to stress in their own idiosyncratic way, and the particular body system that is the most affected may be a likely candidate for the locus of a subsequent psychophysiologic disorder. Someone reacting to

Descartes and the Mind-Body Problem

One of the most influential statements about the "mind-body" problem is found in the writings of the brilliant French philosopher of the seventeenth century, René Descartes (Figure 7.1). Being a deeply religious Catholic, he assumed that man differed from other animals by virtue of having a soul and thus being partly divine. But like the other animals, man had a body as well. Although the body was said to work on mechanical principles—Descartes was fascinated by the mechanical models of the body's workings that were prevalent at the time—these mechanics were seen in man to be under the control of the soul, or mind. But how could the body, operating like a machine, be affected by the soul, which is spiritual and nonphysical? How could two such basically different substances, in fact, "touch" each other? If the mind was to affect the body, there must be some point of *contact*. The pineal gland, located in the midbrain, was postulated by Descartes as the locus of this critical interaction, the point at which man's mind could direct the mechanics of his body. By dualizing man in this way, with this vital connection between the mind and the body, Descartes felt that he could retain his religious view of man as being partly divine and yet an integral part of the rest of the animal world.

FIGURE **7.1**
René Descartes (1596–1650), *the French philosopher who proposed a dualistic view of mind and body.*

stress with secretion of stomach acid may be more vulnerable to ulcers, and someone reacting to stress with blood pressure elevation may be more susceptible to essential hypertension. Later in this chapter, when we consider particular psychophysiologic disorders, substantial evidence in support of both the somatic-weakness and specific-reaction theories will be given.

Evolution Theory

What are now considered psychophysiologic disorders may have become so through evolutionary advances. Simeons (1961) and Wolf and Goodell (1968) have emphasized the initially adaptive function of psychophysiologic disorders and consider them to be formerly useful protective reactions. For example, the increased rate of arterial blood flow now known as hypertension may have once been the body's protection against threatened loss of blood. The increased secretion of digestive juices that now produces duodenal ulcer may have originally prepared the body to devour food under trying circumstances. Simeons has speculated that the forebrain, the region of the brain most closely associated with visceral functions, primarily prepared primitive man to flee or fight in an emergency, although modern man does not generally find such measures necessary.

The diencephalon knows nothing of the cortical artifacts which have rendered physical escape unnecessary, and so it keeps on trying to make the body run. . . . Modern man's behavior is like that of an inexperienced driver who does not realize that the engine is running by itself. He keeps his finger pressed down on the self-starter and then wonders what is producing all the unpleasant noise (p. 150).

Psychological Theories of Psychophysiological Disorders

Psychoanalytic Theory

Franz Alexander (1950) has perhaps been the most prominent of the psychoanalytic theorists who have concerned themselves with psychophysiologic reactions. In his view the various psychophysiologic disorders are products of unconscious emotional conflicts specific to each disorder. For example, " . . . it would appear that the crucial factor in the pathogenesis of ulcer is the frustration of the dependent, help-seeking and love-demanding

desires. When these desires cannot find gratification in human relationships, a chronic emotional stimulus is created which has a specific effect on the functions of the stomach" (p. 103). Alexander assumed that ulcer patients have repressed their longing for parental love in childhood, and that this repressed impulse causes the overactivity of the parasympathetic nervous system and of the stomach, leading to ulcers. Physiologically, the stomach is continuously preparing to receive food, which the person has symbolically equated with parental love.

Undischarged hostile impulses are viewed as creating the chronic emotional state responsible for essential hypertension.

The damming up of his hostile impulses will continue and will consequently increase in intensity. This will induce the development of stronger defensive measures in order to keep pent-up aggressions in check. . . . Because of the marked degree of their inhibitions, these patients are less effective in their occupational activities and for that reason tend to fail in competition with others, . . . envy is stimulated and . . . hostile feelings toward more successful, less inhibited competitors are further intensified (p. 150).

Alexander formulated his theory on the basis of his observations of patients undergoing psychoanalysis. Attempts to provide corroborative evidence have not been successful, although some similarity between the available data and Alexander's theory will be noted later when we examine hypertension in some detail.

Graham's Specific-Attitudes Theory

Graham has proposed another psychological theory to account for the specificity of psychophysiologic disorders. According to him, particular attitudes, rather than chronic emotional states, are associated with particular patterns of psychophysiologic changes and hence specific psychophysiologic disorders (Grace and Graham, 1952). A number of patients having psychophysiologic disorders were interviewed to determine their characteristic attitudes. A partial list of psychophysiologic disturbances and the attitudes that were found to be related to them follows.

1. Urticaria (hives). The person sees himself as being mistreated and is preoccupied with what is happening to him, not with retaliation.
2. Eczema. The individual feels that he is being interfered with or prevented from doing something and cannot overcome the frustration. He is more concerned with the interference or the obstacle than with remedying his situation.
3. Raynaud's disease (cold, moist hands). The individual wants to undertake hostile physical action but may not have any idea what the actual activity should be.
4. Asthma. The individual is facing a situation that he would rather avoid or escape. The most important part of his attitude is his desire to have nothing to do with the situation at all and to deal with it by simply excluding it.
5. Hypertension. The individual feels that he must be constantly on guard and prepared to ward off the ever-present threat of danger.
6. Duodenal ulcer. The individual is seeking revenge and wishes to injure the person or thing that has injured him.

The seeming remoteness of connection between such attitudes and these psychophysiologic disorders makes Graham's findings quite striking. But the connections are, of course, correlational in nature and hence subject to the problems of interpretation discussed in Chapter 4. An experimental analogue study was undertaken to test these suggested correlations. Graham and his colleagues (1958) gave normal subjects hypnotic or nonhypnotic suggestions designed to produce the attitudes specific either to hives or to Raynaud's disease. These two disorders were selected for comparison because the skin temperature responses associated with them are different. The skin temperature of the person suffering from hives is higher than normal, that of the person with Raynaud's disease lower than normal. After the particular attitude had been induced in the subject, the temperature of his skin was measured. The actual instructions given to the subjects were as follows.

Hives. *Dr. X is now going to burn your hand with a match. When he does so you will feel very much mistreated, but you will be unable to do anything about it. You can't even think of anything you want to do about it. You are thinking only of what happened to you.*
Raynaud's disease. *Dr. X is now going to burn your hand with a match. You feel mistreated and you want to hit Dr. X. You want to hit him as hard as you can, you want to hit him and choke him and strangle him. That's all you are thinking about, how much you want to hit him.*

Each subject was tested twice, receiving first one set of instructions and then the other. The results, presented in Figure 7.2, show that the "hives attitude" produced a small rise in skin temperature and that the "Raynaud's disease attitude" produced a decrease. In another study the hypertension attitude was induced and produced an increase in blood pressure (Graham, Kabler, and Graham, 1962). These demonstrations support Graham's theory to some extent, although it must be remembered that hives, Raynaud's disease, and hypertension were not actually produced.

A recent study, however, provided data

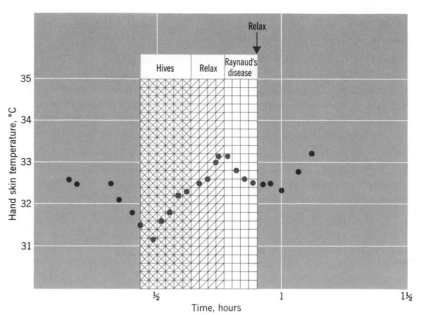

FIGURE **7.2**

Changes in hand temperature during the course of an experimental session. When the hives attitude was induced, there was a sustained rise after a small initial drop. With the induction of the Raynaud's disease attitude, there was a steady drop in temperature. After Graham, Stern, and Winokur, 1958.

much less supportive of Graham's theory. Peters and Stern (1971) selected for study a group of subjects high in hypnotic susceptibility. Each subject participated in several sessions during which the Raynaud's disease or hives attitude was induced, either hypnotically or without hypnosis. Skin temperature was recorded continuously during each session. When hypnotized the subjects showed a *decline* in skin temperature, whichever disease attitude was suggested. When not hypnotized the subjects showed skin temperature *increases* as either attitude was induced. Given these contradictory findings, Graham's theory should be viewed with skepticism.

Conditioning Theories

Both classical and instrumental conditioning may play a role in psychophysiologic disorders, although conditioning is probably best viewed as a factor that can exacerbate an already existing illness rather than cause it. Consider a person who is allergic to pollen and

thus subject to asthma attacks. By classical conditioning, neutral stimuli paired with pollen could also come to elicit asthma, thus broadening the range of stimuli that can bring on an attack (Bandura, 1969). The asthmatic attacks might also be viewed as instrumental responses producing rewards. For example, a child could "use" his asthma as an excuse for not participating in unpleasant activities. Neither of these accounts excludes the importance of biological factors in psychophysiologic disorders, for the original occurrence of the illness must still be accounted for. Both classical and instrumental conditioning hypotheses assume that the physical symptoms already exist. Thus any learning model of a psychophysiologic disorder requires a biological predisposition of some kind.

Our overview of theories of psychophysiologic disorders is complete. We turn now to a detailed review of the disorders that have attracted most attention from researchers—ulcer, hypertension, and asthma. We will see that a combination of a biological predisposition and stress—the diathesis-stress model introduced in Chapter 6—seems to fit most of the clinical and experimental data.

ULCER

A peptic ulcer is a lesion or hole in the lining of the stomach or duodenum (Figure 7.3) that is produced by excessive secretion of hydrochloric acid (HCl). In the digestive process HCl and various enzymes act on ingested food to break it down into components that the body can use. The inner wall of the stomach is protected from the destructive effects of HCl by a layer of mucus. Production of excess amounts of acid for long periods of time erodes the mucous layer, and the acid may digest the stomach wall. Ulcer patients suffer periodic attacks of pain and have to alter their diets to include only bland foods. The following case history illustrates the development of an ulcer.

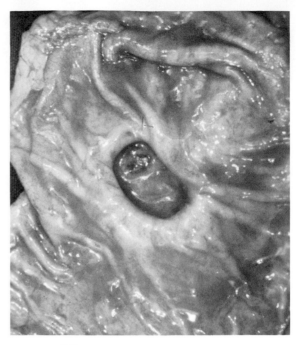

FIGURE 7.3
Pictured here is a stomach ulcer, a lesion in the wall of the stomach produced by excess secretion of hydrochloric acid.

Background. As a child, Mr. A was quiet and obedient, whereas his brother who was three years older was aggressive and independent. Socially, Mr. A was very close to his brother and his brother's companions and was always under the protection of his brother. Mr. A also spent much time with his parents, who provided him with much attention.

Emotion-Arousing Situations. When Mr. A was thirteen his brother died; about two years later his father also died. Both of those events were of major significance in Mr. A's young life. Following the death of his father, his mother became psychologically dependent on him, consulting him about important problems and requiring him generally to substitute for both his older brother and his father, a situation for which Mr. A was completely unprepared intellectually and otherwise. While maintaining a secure outer appearance, Mr. A was aroused emotionally, and his emotional reactions were repeatedly intensified by the excessive expectations of his mother. . . . At age eighteen, Mr. A experienced a short period of stomach discomfort that was followed by the initial hemorrhaging of a duodenal ulcer. When psychotherapy began about five years later, X-ray findings and general symptoms indicated an active ulcer.

Follow-Up. Follow-up study during a three-year period after conclusion of this initial psychotherapy disclosed the following facts. Mr. A had a mild relapse shortly after his marriage when he accepted a very strenuous assignment abroad and had an unsuitable diet; a second mild relapse occurred immediately prior to the birth of his first child, which corresponded in time with his mother's considering remarriage. A few psychotherapeutic consultations at that time involved examination of the existing emotion-provoking problems and apparently resulted in the resumption of more stable functioning. At the end of the three-year period (following conclusion of initial psychotherapy), Mr. A. was on a normal diet with minimal daily medication (Lachman, 1972, pp. 1–2).

Psychological Stress

Although many stressors bring about an increase in the secretion of HCl, the approach-avoidance conflict is the one that has been the most extensively researched. Sawrey devised several illustrative experiments with rats to investigate whether prolonged approach-avoidance conflicts produce ulcers. The animals lived in an environment in which shock was administered whenever they approached food or water. Thus they were in conflict over whether to approach the food or avoid the shock. At the end of approximately two weeks many had developed ulcers, and some had even died from hemorrhages (Sawrey and Weisz, 1956; Conger, Sawrey, and Turrell, 1958).

In elaborating his psychoanalytic theory of psychophysiologic disorders, Franz Alexander attributed the development of ulcers to a conflict between the need for comfort and affection and the antagonistic pressures, especially upon men, to be strong, independent, and aggressive. One deduction from Alexander's theory was tested by Mittelman and Wolff (1942) in their study of the male-to-female ratio of ulcer cases at New York Hospital during the period from 1901 to 1939. As they noted,

[*At the beginning of the twentieth century*] *a man was expected to be "master" in his household,* [*but*] *within this pattern of male domi-*

nance men were permitted emotional dependence upon their women. . . . However, emotional dependence for a man has become more and more difficult, his freedom limited and his privileges curtailed. . . . Coupled with this change, women now compete with men at work . . . but they do not wish their financial contributions to be "counted upon" since there is social justification for the feeling that in giving themselves in marriage and in "running the household," they have already made an adequate contribution. A woman may become the important financial contributor in the home, in which case she often unwittingly creates in her partner a conviction of inadequacy. If she fails in an occupational venture she is justified by society in retiring and being provided for by her husband, brother or father, while such security for a man has no social approval. If a man fails to "provide" he may be denied the feeling of security which his wife's emotional support could give him. Her humiliation of him under these circumstances is endorsed by cultural sanctions. Thus, while society's requirements of the male are essentially as before, the emotional support accorded him in return is less (p. 18).

On the basis of this line of reasoning and Alexander's theory, Mittelman and Wolff deduced that the ratio of male-to-female ulcer cases should have increased dramatically during the period from 1901 to 1939. They found that this is exactly what had happened. From 1901 to 1906 the male-female ratio of ulcer cases was 2.5:1 at New York Hospital, but in the period 1932 to 1939 the male-female ratio was 12:1. Although these data corroborate the deduction, it must be remembered that such correlational findings are difficult to interpret. Another event could have produced the relationships. Nonetheless, if Mittelman and Wolff are correct, it will be interesting to see what effect the women's liberation movement will have in the 1970s.

Biological Predisposition

Although most men living in New York during the first half of the twentieth century were exposed to the same general cultural conditions as the ulcer patients described by Mittleman and Wolff, only a small number eventually developed a peptic ulcer. Similarly, in animal research such as Sawrey's only *some* of the animals exposed to the approach-avoidance conflict developed ulcers. Thus stress can be only part of the story in the development of ulcers. We need also to locate a factor that can interact with stress and greatly increase the probability that an individual having this particular characteristic will develop an ulcer.

Biological predispositions may function in this way. A prime candidate is the amount of pepsinogen secreted by the peptic cells of the gastric glands in the stomach. Pepsinogen is converted into pepsin, the stomach enzyme which digests proteins and which in combination with HCl is the principal active agent in gastric juice. Pepsinogen levels are therefore measures of gastric activity, and hence we might expect them to be implicated in the formation of ulcers. By taking measurements through the umbilical cord, Mirsky (1958) has been able to detect marked individual differences in pepsinogen levels in neonates. Fur-

thermore, young infants with high levels of pepsinogen were found to be members of families with a high incidence of excessive pepsinogen levels. That only some people secrete large amounts of pepsinogen, depending on their genetic inheritance, does demonstrate that this variable has a possible causal role in the development of ulcers. But demonstrating that individuals who do not yet have ulcers but do have high levels of pepsinogen secretion are more likely to develop ulcers than another group, also without ulcers but with lower pepsinogen levels, would provide much stronger evidence.

Such an investigation has in fact been conducted (Weiner, Thaler, Reiser, and Mirsky, 1957). These researchers measured the level of pepsinogen in 2073 newly inducted draftees. From this large number two smaller groups were selected, the 63 with the highest levels of pepsinogen and the 57 with the lowest levels. A complete gastrointestinal examination, given before basic training, showed that none had ulcers at that time. The majority of these men were then reexamined during the eighth and sixteenth weeks of their basic training. Nine cases of ulcers had developed, all of them in the group with high pepsinogen levels. Another study (Mirsky, 1958) of a population of children and civilian adults who had earlier been classified as high and low pepsinogen secreters revealed a similar tendency for ulcers to develop among those with high levels of pepsinogen.

In sum, the data available on peptic ulcers are clearly consistent with a theory implicating in their development both stress and a biological predisposition to secrete excessive amounts of pepsinogen. Consistent with the specific-reaction theory, individuals who develop ulcers appear to be predisposed to react to stress with excessive gastric secretions, which then produce lesions.

ESSENTIAL HYPERTENSION

The pressure produced in the arteries as the heart pumps blood through them is referred to as blood pressure. Blood pressure may be elevated by acceleration of the heartbeat, by increased resistance to the passage of blood through the arteries, that is, by vasoconstriction, or by both. Essential hypertension is a disorder characterized by chronic high blood pressure that cannot be traced to an organic cause. Acceleration of the heartbeat is of some importance in the development of essential hypertension, but constriction of the walls of the arteries is much more important. Cochrane (1971) has speculated that increased sympathetic nervous system activity produced by stress causes greater secretions of norepinephrine which ultimately results in the retention of sodium in the muscles of the arteries. This higher level of sodium sensitizes the arterial walls so that they overrespond to normal neural firings, producing greater vasoconstriction and hence hypertension. Lyght (1966) has offered the following description of the course of hypertension and the symptoms associated with the disorder.

. . . hypertension frequently is present for many years without symptoms or signs other than an elevated blood pressure. In the majority of cases, increased blood pressure first appears during early adult life (mean age of onset, the early thirties). These patients may complain of fatigue, nervousness, dizziness, palpitation, insomnia, weakness and headaches at the same time in the course of the disorder. . . . The mean age of death for untreated patients is in the fifties, and their average life expectancy probably is close to twenty years from the onset, with extremes of from several years to many decades (pp. 218 ff).

Control over Stress and Blood Pressure Increase

Short-Term Effects

Various stressful conditions have been examined to determine their role in the etiology of essential hypertension. Stressful interviews, natural disasters, anger, and anxiety have been found to produce elevations in blood pressure (Innes, Millar, and Valentine, 1959; Ruskin, Board, and Schaffer, 1948; Ax, 1953). More recently, Kasl and Cobb (1970) have examined the effects of the loss of employment on blood pressure. They studied a group of workers beginning two months before their jobs were to be terminated and for two years subsequent to loss of employment. A control group, consisting of men in similar occupations who did not lose their jobs, was examined for the same twenty-six-month period. Each participant in the study was visited at home by a nurse about every two weeks so that blood pressure could be measured. For the control subjects there were no overall changes in blood pressure. In the experimental subjects, however, elevated blood pressure was found both in anticipation of job loss and after termination of employment.

In another group of studies (Hokanson and Burgess, 1962; Hokanson, Burgess, and Cohen, 1963; Hokanson, Willers, and Koropsak, 1968; Stone and Hokanson, 1969), based in part on psychoanalytic theory, researchers have attempted to determine whether blood pressure elevation is associated with the inhibition of aggression. The subjects are placed in two experimental predicaments in the course of these investigations. In the first the subject is given a task to perform, counting backward from 99 by two's, and is then harassed by a confederate of the experimenter.

The subject, however, believes that this confederate is a fellow subject in the investigation. During the harassment it is found that blood pressure tends to rise. Later half the subjects are given the opportunity to aggress against the confederate and half are not, and blood pressure is then remeasured. In the second predicament the subject and the experimenter's confederate are together in a chamber. In front of each is a panel with three buttons labeled shock, reward, and no response. On a signal from the experimenter, the confederate is allowed to press whichever button he "wishes," depending on how he feels at the moment. The confederate consistently shocks the subject, which produces an increase in his blood pressure. The dependent variable is the time it takes for the subject's blood pressure to return to normal as a function of which of the buttons he in turn chooses to press. In the control group the subjects are never given the opportunity to shock the confederate because the experimenter always signals that it is the confederate's turn to respond.

The results of this extensive series of investigations indicate that, for males, aggressing against a source of frustration helps blood pressure to decrease. Similarly, with no opportunity to aggress against the frustrator, blood pressure is significantly slower to decrease after frustration. Only aggression directed at a low-status frustrator (college student) proved helpful in decreasing blood pressure, however, not that directed toward a high-status frustrator (visiting professor). Blood pressure declined rapidly when the frustrator was of high status, whether or not the subject aggressed against him. These findings did not hold for female subjects. Rather, for them making a *positive response*—pressing the reward button—decreased blood pressure.

Alexander has postulated that individuals who develop hypertension handle their aggression poorly and tend to repress aggressive impulses. Because of this repression, they are supposedly unable to find outlets for their aggression; their hostile impulses accumulate and grow in intensity to produce hypertension. The results of Hokanson's investigations may at first appear to offer corroborative evidence for Alexander's theory concerning the etiology of hypertension. Alexander's theory, however, deals with repressed hostility, and in Hokanson's work there is no demonstration of a repression process operating unconsciously. Moreover, other studies performed by Hokanson and his colleagues demonstrate that aggression against a frustrator in itself may not be the key factor in increasing and decreasing blood pressure. Hokanson himself favors the following interpretation of his data: ". . . *any* social response can be viewed as having arousal-reducing concomitants, if that response has been previously instrumental in terminating or avoiding aggression in others" (Stone and Hokanson, 1969, p. 72).

Hokanson's interpretation explains why aggression directed toward a high-status frustrator was not effective. Presumably, subjects have learned that it does not pay to retaliate against a high-status aggressor. Thus an aggressive response will *not* help to reduce arousal since such responses have not previously been rewarding. Similarly, Hokanson's position accounts for the fact that aggressive responses do not seem to reduce arousal for females. Social and cultural conditions prevailing for them when these studies were conducted dictated that the response to frustration not be aggression.

The results of these studies seem to indicate that any response which gives *control* to the subject can decrease blood pressure. This possibility was directly examined in a study (Hokanson, DeGood, Forrest, and Brittain, 1971) in which subjects performed a symbol-

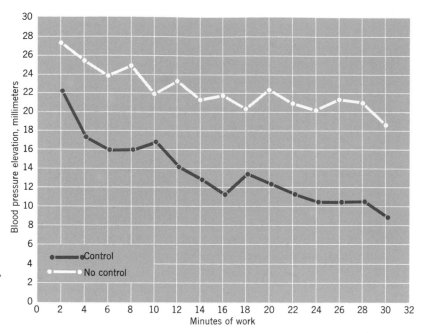

FIGURE 7·4
Differences in blood pressure of "control" and "no control" subjects in the Hokanson et al. (1971) study.

matching task with shocks being delivered for poor performance. The task was set up so that subjects would receive, on the average, one shock every forty-five seconds. Subjects were to spend twenty minutes working at the task but were allowed to take one-minute rest breaks so they would not "become overly fatigued." Subjects who had "control" could take as many breaks as they wanted whenever they wanted. "No control" subjects were matched to the "control" subjects so that the number and timing of their rest periods were determined for them. The results, presented in Figure 7.4, indicate clearly that control, not actual amount of rest, produced lower levels of blood pressure. Not having control, then, is an elicitor of increased blood pressure and perhaps of essential hypertension.

Long-Term Effects

Thus far we have discussed stressors that can produce a temporary increase in blood pressure in normal individuals. But can such short-

term increases develop into sustained, long-term hypertension? The mechanism inducing long-term hypertension would necessarily involve some structural changes in the organism. What might they be? One possibility is that repeated stress causes the heart to be overactive. The arteries would then have to thicken to handle the increased blood flow. Then, because the arteries have become thicker, blood pressure increases and the heart has to "work" even harder to pump the blood throughout the body. This still greater activity of the heart may lead to even more constriction, and so on until blood pressure remains chronically elevated. No direct work has been done with humans to determine whether short-term increases in blood pressure will develop into prolonged hypertension, but some research has been done on animals. Maher (1966) cites a study by Schunk in which cats were exposed to the barking of dogs for a number of months, presumably a stress for them. About half of these cats developed hypertension. Similarly, crowded living conditions and prolonged exposure to avoidance conditioning through experimental procedures have been shown to elicit long-lasting elevations in blood pressure (Henry, Stephens, Axelrod, and Mueller, 1971; Forsyth, 1969).

Predisposing Factors

The research reviewed thus far suggests that lack of control over stress may be an important factor in producing hypertension. But we must also attempt to account for the fact that only some individuals exposed to particular stresses develop hypertension. Again, it is very likely that some organismic characteristic interacts with stress. Unfortunately, the data on biological predispositions for hypertension are not as extensive or clear as those on the biological predispositions for ulcers. Several studies have, however, demonstrated that hypertensives show greater blood pressure reactivity, reacting to stress with blood pressure increases

that are higher than those of normal people (Engel and Bickford, 1961; Shapiro, 1961). In the Engel and Bickford study twenty female hypertensive patients and twenty control subjects were exposed to various stressors. Fifteen of the twenty hypertensives showed an increase in blood pressure, but only five of the controls did. The research cannot be regarded as conclusive, however, for individuals in the experimental group were *already* hypertensive. Their increase in blood pressure might have been a *result* rather than a *cause* of their hypertension.

Clearly, to establish the importance of a biological predisposition, studies must begin with individuals who have the predisposition but who have not yet developed essential hypertension. At this point the most promising theory concerning the etiology of hypertension implicates both stress *and* some biological predisposition affecting a portion of the circulatory system.

ASTHMA

A Characterization of the Disease

Purcell and Weiss (1970) have described asthma in the following way.

Asthma is a symptom complex characterized by an increased responsiveness of the trachea, major bronchi, and peripheral bronchioles to various stimuli, and is manifested by extensive narrowing of the airways which causes impairment of air exchange, primarily in expiration, [thus inducing] wheezing. [The airways may be narrowed] because of edema [an accumulation of excess watery fluid in the tissues] of the

walls, increased mucus secretion, spasm of the bronchial muscles, or the collapse of the posterior walls of the trachea and bronchi during certain types of forced expiration (p. 597).

The major structures of the respiratory system are shown in Figure 7.5.

Emotional states help to induce asthmatic attacks by a variety of mechanisms.

1. The increased autonomic activity associated with emotionality may initiate airway obstruction by stimulating mucus secretion or bronchiole constriction.

ANXIETY AND DEPRESSION

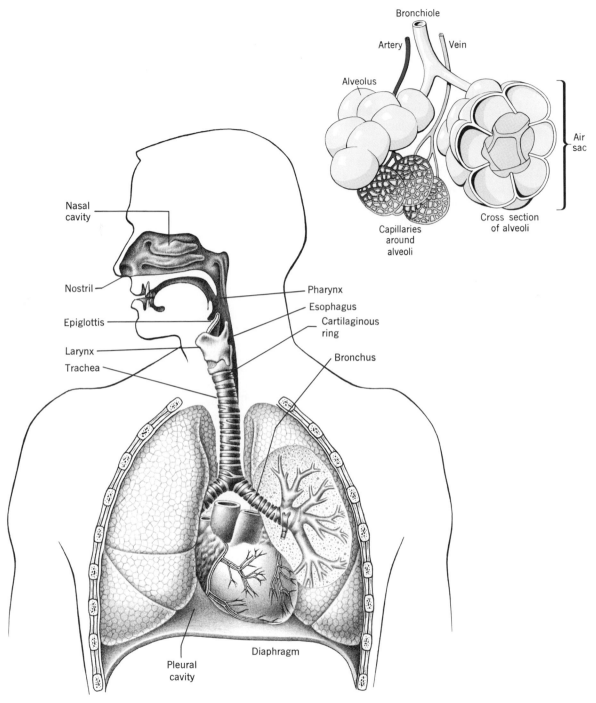

FIGURE 7.5
Major structures of the respiratory stem—trachea, lungs, bronchi, and bronchioles—and the ancillary organs.

2. Emotionality may bring on crying, coughing, and hyperventilation, which disturb respiratory patterns.
3. Emotional stimulation may alter the output of steroid hormones which are known to affect the respiratory system.

Most often, asthmatic attacks begin suddenly. The patient has a sense of tightness in the chest, wheezes, coughes, and expectorates sputum. A doctor will notice that the asthma sufferer takes a longer time than normal to expire air and that whistling sounds can be detected throughout the chest. These sounds are referred to as rales. Symptoms may last an hour or less or may continue for several hours or sometimes even days. Between attacks no abnormal signs may be detected when the individual is breathing normally, but forced, heavy expiration will often allow the doctor to hear the rales.

One patient, to be described, had his first attack at age nine. His condition worsened until he was thirteen, after which he was symptom-free for ten years. From that time on, however, his condition deteriorated to an unusual degree, and the patient eventually died of respiratory complications.

Abundant data from this patient's life suggest the importance of emotional factors in precipitating exacerbations of his asthma. He gives a graphic description of developing wheezing and shortness of breath upon separation from his mother. Once, while away on a trip with either her or his grandmother (it is not clear which), in a strange hotel, separated from his companion by a wall, he suffered through the night, having the feeling that his wheezes might be loud enough to be heard and bring her in to rescue him.

He described clearly the relationship of his symptoms to odors. His response to the scent of flowers may have had an allergic basis. That seems less likely in the case of the scent of "lovely ladies," which he stated also gave him asthma. So did certain "bad" smells, of asparagus and cigar smoke. . . . He had many conflicts around weeping, frequently described being dissolved in tears, but always with the implication that he never really was exhausting the reservoir of "sobbing." . . .

At the time of his brother's marriage, the patient was jealous; he managed to forget to mail the 150 invitations to the ceremony that had been entrusted to him. In the church he was almost more prominent than the bride, walking down the aisle just before the ceremony, gasping for breath, and wearing a fur coat, although the month was July (Knapp, 1969, p. 135).

Asthma is certainly one of the most fascinating of the psychophysiologic disorders. There has been much debate about whether or not psychological factors may be implicated in its etiology. Somewhere between 2 and 5 percent of the population is estimated to have asthma, and it is more common in males than females (Graham, Rutter, Yule, and Pless, 1967).

Williams and McNicol (1969) studied 30,000

TABLE 7.1 *Relative Importance of Psychological, Allergic, and Infective Factors in the Etiology of Asthma According to Rees's (1964) Study*

Factors	Relative importance		
	Dominant, %	Subsidiary, %	Unimportant, %
Psychological	37	33	30
Infective	38	30	32
Allergic	23	13	64

seven-year-old Australian school children. They found a high correlation between the age of onset of the symptoms and the length of time the disorder lasted. If the age of onset was less than one, 80 percent were found to be still wheezing five years later. With ages of onset from three to four, 40 percent were still wheezing five years later, and with an onset age of five or six, only 20 percent were still wheezing five years later. Thus the earlier the disorder begins, the longer it is likely to last.

The Etiology of Asthma

Much of the debate concerning the importance of psychological factors in the development of asthma relates to whether or not emotionality is always implicated. To investigate the etiology of asthma, Rees (1964) divided the various possible causes into three categories, allergic, infective, and psychological. The cells in the respiratory tract may be especially sensitive to one or more substances or allergens such as pollen or dust, bringing on asthma. Respiratory infections, most often acute bronchitis, can also make the respiratory system vulnerable to asthma. Anxiety, tension produced by frustration, anger, depression, and anticipated pleasurable excitement are all examples of psychological factors that may, through induced emotionality, disturb the respiratory system and thus cause asthma.

The part played by allergic factors was assessed through the case histories that were taken and by making cutaneous and inhalation reaction tests with suspected allergens. Patients were also exposed to suspected allergens and inert substances without their knowing which was which. The importance of infective factors was determined through the case histories and X-rays, by examining sputum, and by searching for pus or other evidence of infection in the nose, sinuses, and chest. The potential importance of psychological factors was assessed through the case histories and by direct behavioral observations. The principal results of Rees's study, presented in Table 7.1, demonstrate the importance of conceptualizing asthma as a disease with multiple causes. As can be seen from the table, psychological factors were considered a dominant cause in only 37 percent of the cases. And in 30 percent of the cases psychological variables were regarded as totally unimportant—a conclusion at odds with the popular notion that asthma is always psychosomatic.

Rees's data showed also that the different causes of asthma varied in importance depending on the age of the individual. For those asthmatic individuals less than five years of age, the infective factors predominated. From ages six to sixteen the infective factors still predominated, but psychological variables increased in importance. In the range from ages sixteen to sixty-five, psychological factors decreased in importance until about the thirty-fifth year, thereafter becoming more consequential again.

Psychological Factors Producing Asthma

Rees's studies have demonstrated that some, but by no means all, cases of asthma have psychological factors as a primary cause. Yet even when asthma is originally induced by an infection or allergy, psychological stress can precipitate attacks. Eysenck (1965), for example, has related a case study originally described by Katsch, who had

> . . . arrived at the hypothesis that the patient's mother-in-law, with whom he had many conflicts, constituted the source of the emotional trouble producing the asthmatic attacks and that a very large picture of her which hung in the bedroom of the patient was a . . . stimulus for these attacks. . . . [This hypothesis was] tested [as follows]. . . . Katsch turned the mother-in-law's face to the wall, as it were, and immediately the asthmatic attacks ceased. They could be brought back at will, by turning the picture round again, and they could again be terminated by turning it to the wall once more; in other words, Katsch had achieved complete control over the asthmatic attacks of his patient (p. 207).

In another study exploring somewhat the same ground, Kleeman (1967) interviewed twenty-six patients over an eighteen-month period. According to the reports of these patients, 69 percent of their attacks began with an emotional disturbance.

Dekker and Groen (1956) were able to produce asthma attacks in the laboratory using the following procedure. Before the actual investigation twelve asthmatic patients had described what environmental situations precipitated attacks. When these situations were reproduced in actual or pictorial form in the laboratory, three of the twelve patients developed full-blown asthma attacks, and three others showed less severe respiratory symptoms. The stimuli to which the subjects ascribed their asthma included the national anthem, perfume, the sight of dust, horses, and waterfalls.

Finally, a recent study indicates the "power of suggestion" in inducing asthma attacks even among individuals whose allergic reactions are regarded as the primary cause of their disorder (Luparello, McFadden, Lyons, and Bleecker, 1971). Forty asthmatics and a control group of another forty persons were told that they were participating in a study of air pollution. The investigator explained to each subject that he wanted to determine what concentrations of various substances would induce wheezing. The asthmatics were told that they would inhale five different concentrations of an irritant or allergen that had previously been established as a contributing cause of their asthma attacks. They were led to believe that each successive sample would have a higher concentration of the allergen, but in fact they were given only five nonallergenic saline solutions to inhale. The control subjects were told that they were inhaling pollutants which could irritate the bronchial tubes and make it difficult for them to breathe. Fourteen out of the forty asthmatic patients reacted with significant airway obstruction, and twelve went on to develop full-blown asthma attacks. None of the controls exhibited pathological respiratory reactions. Later the twelve subjects who had developed asthma attacks were given the same saline solution to inhale but were told that the solution was a bronchodilator. The condition of all twelve improved.

Classical Conditioning

The two investigations just described suggest the possibility that asthma may be induced in a variety of situations as a result of conditioning. One conditioning experiment done with human beings as subjects had almost completely negative results, however. Dekker, Pelse, and Groen (1957) paired a known allergen with a neutral solvent. The classical conditioning hypothesis would argue that through repeated pairings of the CS and UCS, the CS should acquire the ability to elicit the asthmatic reaction. In this study, after repeated pairings, only two of a hundred subjects were found to have been successfully conditioned. Moreover, "In a personal communication dated October, 1961, Dekker reported that he was unable to replicate even these results" (Purcell and Weiss, 1970, p. 607). At this time there is no support for a classical conditioning account of asthma.

The Role of the Family

Several researchers have considered parent-child interactions to be important in the etiology of asthma. The investigators at the Children's Asthma Research Institute and Hospital in Denver routinely categorize their patients into those for whom psychological factors are considered the primary cause and those whose respiratory tracts are more greatly disturbed by other factors. In one investigation Purcell and his colleagues (1969) chose a group of twenty-two children. For thirteen children psychological factors were considered the principal precipitants of their asthma. For the other nine allergic or infective factors were considered more significant. These twenty-two children were studied over a considerable length of time which was subdivided into four periods. The first was an initial base line period. In the second period the children lived with their families, in the third they lived in their own homes but with substitute parents, and in the fourth they were reunited with their parents. If the psychological factor disturbing one subgroup was the parent-child relationship, these children should improve when their parents lived apart from them. The children whose asthma was considered induced principally by allergic or infective factors would show no such improvement. The data supported the predictions remarkably well. Daily measurements and observations were made of the following variables: peak expiratory air flow, amount of medication required, wheezing, and frequency of asthma attacks. Seventy percent of the group who were predicted to do well without their parents improved during the separation phase (Figure 7.6). Of the children who were not predicted to do well without their parents, only one of the nine benefited from being separated.

Another study by Rees (1963) supports the theory that disturbed parent-child relationships may be a cause of asthma. He classified the attitudes of the parents of asthmatic children as either satisfactory—the parents promote feelings of security and are affectionate and accepting—or unsatisfactory—parents are rejecting, perfectionistic, and overprotective.

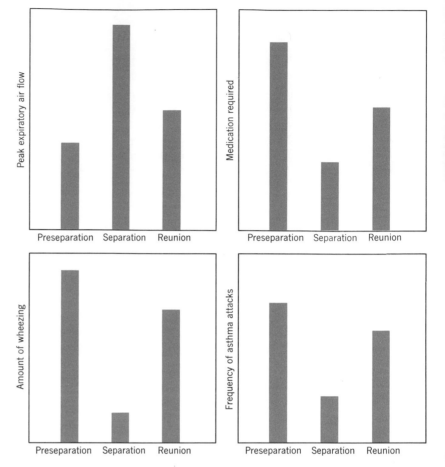

FIGURE **7.6**

*Improvement in measure-
ments of asthma when children were separated from
their parents. After Purcell
et al., 1969.*

Only 44 percent of the parents of asthmatics were rated as having satisfactory attitudes, whereas 82 percent of the parents of control children (accident cases) were rated in this way.

The research that we have discussed reveals the importance of the home life of asthmatics. It should be noted, however, that we cannot tell whether various familial variables are causal agents or maintaining agents. Although certain emotional factors in the home may be important in eliciting early asthmatic attacks in children, the illness may originally develop for nonfamilial reasons, and then the children's parents may unwittingly reward various symptoms of the syndrome. For example, the

parents may cater to the child and treat him specially because of his asthma. Current recommendations for the treatment of asthmatic children supply indirect support for this thesis. Doctors prescribe no special treatment and no overprotection. Instead, asthmatic children are urged to lead as normal a life as possible, even to the extent of participating in athletic events. An attempt is made, then, to keep the children from considering their sickness as the dominating factors in their lives. This attitude is well illustrated in the following interaction presented by Kluger (1969).

PATIENT: I can't go to school today because my asthma is worse.

170   ANXIETY AND DEPRESSION

DOCTOR: I know, but since it's not contagious why can't you be in school?

PATIENT (irritated): Because I'm having trouble breathing!

DOCTOR: I can see that, but you'll have trouble breathing whether you go to school or not. Remaining in bed won't help your breathing.

PATIENT (disgustedly): Boy, they don't even let you be sick in this hospital! (p. 361).

Personality and Asthma

It has often been suggested that asthmatic individuals display particular constellations of personality traits. Several investigators have found that asthmatic individuals have a great many so-called neurotic symptoms: dependency and maladjustment (Herbert, 1965), meekness, sensitivity, anxiety, meticulousness, perfectionism, and obsessions (Rees, 1964). But most of this work consisted of comparing asthmatics to a normal control population. Neuhaus (1958) compared the personality test scores of asthmatic children to those of both a normal group of children and a group of children with cardiac conditions. As in other studies, the asthmatics were found to be more neurotic than those who were normal. But, and this is the important point, *the cardiac children were also more neurotic than normal children.* Thus the increased neuroticism of asthmatic children may reflect only reactions to a chronic illness; neuroticism scores on personality tests are always higher the longer the patient has been sick (Kelly and Zeller, 1967).

Biological Predisposition

Now that the importance of various stresses in eliciting asthmatic attacks has been documented, we must attempt to account for the fact that not all individuals exposed to such stressors develop asthma. Once again the answer appears to lie in a predisposing biological factor. For example, Rees (1964) found that 86 percent of the asthmatics examined had a respiratory infection before asthma developed. Only 30 percent of his control subjects had been so afflicted. This study can be regarded as evidence that inheriting a weak organ, a reaction pattern, or both may figure in the etiology of asthma.

In conclusion, a diathesis-stress model once again seems to fit the data on a psychophysiologic disorder. Once the respiratory system is predisposed to asthma, any number of psychological stressors can interact with the diathesis to produce asthma.

SUMMARY

Psychophysiological disorders are physical diseases produced by psychological factors, primarily stress. Such disorders usually affect organs innervated by the autonomic nervous system, such as those of the respiratory, cardiovascular, gastrointestinal, and endocrine systems. Research has focused on the question of how psychological stress produces a particular psychophysiologic disorder. Some workers have proposed that the answer lies in the specifics of the stressor. They say, for example, that aggressive impulses may create conflicts for an individual that give him an ulcer. The evidence does not generally favor this view. A more viable hypothesis is that stress interacts with a biological diathesis. Ulcer may be induced by stress and a tendency of the stomach to secrete too much acid, hypertension by stress to a labile circulatory system, and asthma by stress affecting a respiratory system that overresponds or has been weakened by prior infection. Although we have spoken of psychological stress affecting the body, it must be remembered that the *mind* and the *body* are best viewed as two different ways of talking about the same organism.

CHAPTER 8
Depression

Just as most people experience at least moments of anxiety every week of their existence, so will each of us probably have more than an ample amount of sadness during the course of our lives, although perhaps not to the degree or with the frequency that the label depression is warranted. A person describing himself in the following manner would probably be regarded as suffering from maladaptive, abnormal depression.

I was seized with an unspeakable physical weariness. There was a tired feeling in the muscles unlike anything I had ever experienced. A peculiar sensation appeared to travel up my spine to my brain. I had an indescribable nervous feeling. My nerves seemed like live wires charged with electricity. My nights were sleepless. I lay with dry, staring eyes gazing into space. I had a fear that some terrible calamity was about to happen. I grew afraid to be left alone. The most trivial duty became a formidable task. Finally mental and physical exercises became impossible; the tired muscles refused to respond, my "thinking apparatus" refused to work, ambition was gone. My general feeling might be summed up in the familiar saying "What's the use." I had tried so hard to make something of myself, but the struggle seemed useless. Life seemed utterly futile (Reid, 1910, pp. 612–613).

Depression has been studied from several perspectives in addition to such phenomenological accounts. The observer of overt behavior considers the patient's movements and his level of activity; cognitive theories focus on what the depressed person's thought processes are; psychoanalytic views emphasize the unconscious conflicts producing depression; and physiological theorists concentrate on what the body is doing at the neural-chemical level. The several theoretical positions to be discussed in this chapter tend to concentrate on one or two of these dimensions, often to the exclusion of the others.

There is general agreement on what the most common symptoms of depression are. Beck (1967) enumerates five.

1. Sad, apathetic mood.
2. Negative self-concept (self-reproach, self-blame).
3. Desire to hide, to stay away from others.
4. Loss of sleep, appetite, and sexual desire.
5. Change in activity level, becoming either lethargic or agitated.

A depressed person may also neglect personal hygiene and appearance and make numerous hypochondriacal complaints of aches and pains that apparently have no physical basis. He feels dejected and worthless and may be apprehensive, anxious, and despondent much of the time. He may even reach such a state of hopelessness that he thinks about and sometimes attempts suicide.

As we might expect, a single individual seldom has all these symptoms of depression at the same time; the diagnosis is typically made if at least a few of them are evident, particularly a mood of profound sadness that is out of proportion to the person's life situation. Fortunately, most depression, although recurrent, tends to dissipate with time. The following case description gives a common clinical picture of depression.

Mr. J was a fifty-one-year old industrial engineer who, since the death of his wife five years earlier, had been suffering from continuing episodes of depression marked by extreme social withdrawal and occasional thoughts of suicide. His wife had died in an automobile accident during a shopping trip which he himself was to have made but was unable to because professional responsibilities changed his plans. His self-blame for her death, which was present immediately after the funeral and regarded by his friends and relatives as transitory, deepened as the months, and then years, passed by. He began to drink, sometimes heavily, and when thoroughly intoxicated would plead to his deceased wife for forgiveness. He lost all capacity for joy — his friends could not recall when they had last seen him smile. His gait was typically slow and labored, his voice usually tearful, his posture stooped. Once a gourmet, he had lost all interest in food and good wine, and on those increasingly rare occasions when friends invited him for dinner, this previously witty, urbane man could barely manage to engage in small talk. As might be expected, his work record deteriorated markedly, along with his psychological condition. Appointments were missed and projects haphazardly started and then left unfinished. When referred by his physician for psychotherapy, he had just been released from a hospital following a near-fatal and intentional overdose of sleeping pills. Not long afterward, he seemed to emerge from his despair and began to feel like his old self again.

FORMAL CATEGORIES OF DEPRESSION

The DSM-II lists depression in three major diagnostic categories—major affective disorders, psychotic depressive reaction, and depressive neurosis. Rather than treating each of these categories in separate chapters, we consider it more useful to discuss various aspects of depression in one chapter, commenting wherever necessary on how it varies with the psychiatric diagnosis.

Major Affective Disorders

Listed under this heading are the manic-depressive illnesses and involuntional melancholia. The concept of *manic-depressive illness* was developed by Kraepelin (1904) to cover all cases of "affective excess." Thus the category is *not* meant to identify only those individuals who show a continuous alternation between mania and depression. It is also applied both to people who are exclusively depressed and to those who are exclusively manic.

The symptoms of mania include disturbances in

1. *Mood.* The patient may be elated and overconfident, yet easily angered and irritable.
2. *Thought.* The patient will generally speak rapidly, often talking about grandiose plans for the future, and may change topics frequently—the so-called flight of ideas.
3. *Motor activity.* There is a marked increase in motor activity, sometimes to the point that some of it is apparently purposeless.

The following description of a manic episode comes from our files.

THERAPIST: Well, you seem pretty happy today.

CLIENT: Happy! Happy! You certainly are a master of understatement, you rogue! (Shouting, literally jumping out of seat.) Why I'm ecstatic. I'm leaving for the West coast today, on my daughter's bicycle. Only 3100 miles. That's nothing, you know. I could probably walk, but I want to get there by next week. And along the way I plan to follow up on my inventions of the past month, you know, stopping at the big plants along the way having lunch with the executives, maybe getting to know them a bit—you know, Doc, "know" in the biblical sense (leering at therapist seductively). Oh, God, how good it feels. It's almost like a nonstop orgasm.

Manic-depression, technically one of the psychoses, has long been a problematical diagnosis since it has been applied to many people after they have experienced only one manic—that is, wildly euphoric, expansive, and too happy—episode. Moreover, depressed people who experience no mood swings to mania have also been diagnosed as manic-depressives (manic-depressive illness, depressed type). According to DSM-II, a depressed person who has no obvious reason for his extreme sadness would be diagnosed in this way. At the present time this diagnostic category is used more often in Great Britain than in the United States, indicating once again the extent to which psychiatric labeling is affected by society and culture.

The other affective disorder, *involutional melancholia,* is said to occur at the "change of life," when both men and women go through physiological changes that make it less likely that they will still be able to reproduce. It used to be thought that these changes were the physical cause of this kind of depression, and some laymen still believe that they are. But we must bear in mind that in addition to somatic changes the individual in his forties and fifties faces considerable other difficulties: doubts about his sexual attractiveness, realization that certain life goals may never actually be achieved, and loss of contact with his children. At the same time, most people go through the climacteric, the cessation of menstruation in the female and a reduction of sexual activity in the male, and sometimes of his competence, without bouts of depression — indeed sometimes with great improvements in their psychological state. Once again, as with other disorders, reality is too complex to make a unicausal explanation of involuntional melancholia a likely one.

Neurotic versus Psychotic Depression

Of the current psychiatric categories of depression, the two most important are neurotic and psychotic depressions. These two categories of depression are distinguished, in part, from manic depression, depressed type, by the fact that some environmental event is assumed to have elicited the reactions. What are the differences between neurotic and psychotic depressions? Beck (1967), in his classic book on depression, concludes that the delusions of psychotic depressives — mistaken, unverifiable beliefs, unjustified feelings of unworthiness, and apprehensions that the body is being physically altered — constitute the principal *qualitative* differences.

The patient, a thirty-six-year old woman, had just been readmitted to a psychiatric hospital. Her husband reported that during the past few weeks she had virtually stopped behaving, seeming to lose interest in all activities, both household chores and hobbies. During the intake interview, the woman's sadness was very apparent; her speech was slow, her posture stooped, and her facial expression was almost frozen in a look of extreme grief. When asked when she had begun to feel depressed and why, she reported that "About a month ago, everything just seemed to start to go wrong. My husband lost his job and two of my children became very ill. There just wasn't anything I could do about it." Later, in response to further questions, she described herself in a way that indicated that the diagnosis of psychotic depression would be appropriate. "When I first noticed myself getting depressed I knew that I couldn't do anything about it. No one would help because of my wickedness. I'm being punished for my past sins and have been given over to the devil."

In addition, there is evidence that the common indications of depression (Figure 8.1) are present in psychotic depressives to a significantly greater degree, making *quantitative* differentiation between neurotic and psychotic depressions possible. Beck compared the records of fifty patients diagnosed as psychotic depressives and fifty diagnosed as neurotic depressives for the severity of various manifestations of depression — sad faces, hopelessness, guilt, and so on. As indicated in Table 8.1, most of these symptoms were found to be more severe in the psychotic patients. Two symptoms, daily mood variations and

TABLE **8.1** *Frequency of Clinical Symptoms in Neurotic Depressive Reaction (NDR) and Psychotic Depressive Reaction (PDR)* (*from Beck, 1967, p. 85*)

Clinical symptom	Symptom present		Symptom present to severe degree	
	NDR, % (N = 50)	PDR, % (N = 50)	NDR, % (N = 50)	PDR, % (N = 50)
Sad faces	86	94	4	24
Stooped posture	58	76	4	20
Speech: slow, etc.	66	70	8	22
Low mood	84	80	8	44
Diurnal variation of mood	22	48	2	10
Hopelessness	78	68	6	34
Conscious guilt	64	44	6	12
Feelings of inadequacy	68	70	10	42
Somatic preoccupation	58	66	6	24
Suicidal wishes	58	76	14	40
Indecisiveness	56	70	6	28
Loss of motivation	70	82	8	48
Loss of interest	64	78	10	44
Fatigability	80	74	8	48
Loss of appetite	48	76	2	40
Sleep disturbance	66	80	12	52
Constipation	28	56	2	16

constipation, were found to be markedly more evident in the psychotic depressives. Thus the more severe the symptoms, the more likely the diagnosis of psychotic depression rather than neurotic.

Endogenous versus Exogenous Depression

As implied by the distinction made between manic-depression, depressed type, and neurotic or psychotic depression, extreme unhappiness may be regarded as either *endogenous,* that is, internally caused, or *exogenous,* externally caused. Endogenous means "originating within the body" and is an adjective applied to a disorder assumed to have an *internal physical cause.* In other words, a physiological malfunctioning is believed to bring on endogenous depression. Exogenous, "originating outside the body," is applied to sadness with an *environmental cause;* sometimes the word reactive identifies this type of depression.

The labeler's judgment of how reasonable the person's unhappiness is at a given moment in time probably determines to a great extent whether the depression will be considered endogenous or not and even whether a diagnosis of depression will be made at all. If an individual has just suffered a terrible personal loss,

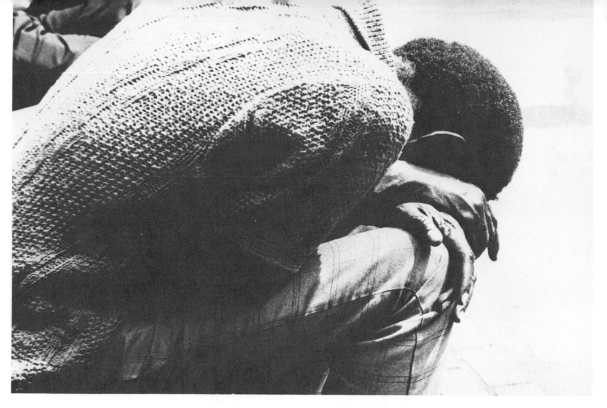

178

TABLE 8.2 *Summary of Classification of Depression*

Severity	Precipitating environmental stress	
	Yes	No
Mild	Neurotic depression Exogenous depression	
Severe	Psychotic depression	Manic-depressive, depressed type Endogenous depression Involutional melancholia

In sum, the behavior of depressed people varies both qualitatively and quantitatively. Psychotic depressives exhibit delusions and, in general, have more severe symptoms than neurotic depressives. The endogenous-exogenous distinction, when made on the basis of behavior and not on the cause, also appears to be a promising way of subclassifying depressed people. As we subsequently review research and theory on depression, we shall, wherever possible, indicate when the data apply to one particular group of depressives (Table 8.2).

Laboratory Findings

Thus far we have considered the clinical and descriptive characteristics of depressive disorders. Before examining major theoretical explanations of depression, it will be useful to review a few controlled studies in order to give a more complete picture. Then we will have a better idea of the various aspects of depression that any given theory must seek to explain.

Although the clinical lore tells us that depressed patients complain of decreased ability to think and to solve problems, some recent data suggest that these complaints are unfounded. Granick (1963), for example, determined that psychotic depressives and normal individuals did not differ on certain intelligence

tests. Similar findings have been reported in numerous other studies. Thus there is no support for the contention that depressives, as a group, suffer from intellectual impairment. On the other hand, depressives seem to *believe* that they suffer such impairment. This contrast between what they can apparently do and how they evaluate what they do is probably an important aspect of their problem.

A related finding has to do with the passage of time. Depressed patients frequently complain that time drags by, almost interminably. And yet, if they are asked to estimate time intervals ranging from a second to thirty minutes, during periods of depression and later when they are not depressed, their estimates are equally accurate for both. Although they may have claimed that time stopped dragging by after they felt better, they nonetheless estimate time as well when depressed as after recovery (Mézey and Cohen, 1961).

Other studies have examined the effects of success and failure on subsequent expectations and actual performance. Loeb and his colleagues (1966) found that the moods of depressed patients are more easily changed than are those of normal individuals. After success depressives feel much better and after failure they feel much worse; that is, they appear to be more affected by the evaluation of their performance than are normal people. In addition, their actual performance on various problem-solving tasks improves more after an earlier successful performance, whereas the functioning of nondepressed patients improves more after an earlier failure.

THEORIES OF DEPRESSION

As is true in the study of other abnormal syndromes, theories of depression point to both psychological and physiological factors. It will be seen that each theoretical position emphasizes one or another aspect of depression at the expense of others.

Psychological Theories of Depression

Psychoanalytic Theory

As we have already seen, there are difficulties in distinguishing between sadness, which is normal, and depression, which is not. The contrast between normal grief and abnormal depression is the focal point of Freud's (1917) celebrated paper, "Mourning and Melancholia," which will serve to illustrate the kind of thinking engaged in by psychodynamically oriented theorists. There are several variations on Freud's thesis, well summarized by Mendels (1970); our own expository purposes are served by restricting critical attention to Freud's original work.

Predictably, Freud saw the potential for depression being created early in childhood. He theorized that during the oral period the child's oral needs may be insufficiently or oversufficiently gratified. The person therefore remains "stuck" in this stage and dependent on the instinctual gratifications particular to it. With this arrest in psychosexual maturation, referred to as a *fixation*, he may develop a ten-dency to be excessively dependent on other people for the maintenance of his self-esteem (Fenichel, 1945).

From this happenstance of his rearing, how can the adult come to suffer from depression? The reasoning is complex, assuming as it does that several unconscious processes are a part of mourning. Freud hypothesized that after the loss of a loved one the mourner first introjects or incorporates the lost person into himself. The grieving person identifies himself rather completely with the lost one, perhaps in a fruitless attempt to undo the loss. Because, as Freud asserted, we unconsciously harbor negative feelings against those we love, the mourner himself now becomes the object of his own hate and anger. In addition, the mourner also resents being deserted and feels guilt for real or imagined sins against the lost person. The period of introjection is followed by the period of *mourning work,* during which the mourner recalls memories of the lost one and thereby separates himself from the person who has died and loosens the bonds that introjection has imposed.

The grief work can go astray in overly dependent individuals and develop into an ongoing process of self-abuse, self-blame, and depression. Such an individual does not loosen his emotional bonds with the person who has died, continuing to castigate himself for the faults and shortcomings perceived in the loved one who has been introjected into himself. The mourner's anger toward the lost one continues to be directed inward upon himself. This hypothesis is the basis for the widespread psychodynamic view of depression as anger turned against oneself.

One further point must be made. Since many people can become depressed and remain so *without* having recently suffered the loss of a loved one, it became necessary to invoke the concept of "symbolic loss" in order to keep the theoretical formulation intact. For example, a person may unconsciously interpret a rejection as a total withdrawal of love.

We see numerous problems in this formulation. First, since the person presumably both hates and loves the individual he has lost, why is it that only the hate and anger are turned inward and not the love that is also there? Since the depressed person is said to have introjected the loved one, thus directing to himself the feelings previously directed to the loved one, why do anger and resentment predominate? If the mourner directed his positive feelings about the lost one to himself, he would be a happy rather than a depressed person. Psychoanalytic theorists have tried to resolve this inconsistency by postulating that the loss of a loved one is viewed as another instance of rejection or withdrawal of affection. Interpreted in this way, a negative emotional state is more likely to predominate. The crucial point, though, is the absence of direct evidence that depressives do interpret death as a rejection by the deceased.

A second difficulty is common to all Freud's hypotheses that involve the concept of fixation at an earlier psychosexual stage of development. Freud states that fixation at the oral stage can come about *through either too little or too much gratification.* How much, it could be asked, is *enough* to prevent fixation? Freud's theory, being nonquantitative, does not deal adequately with this question.

The term "symbolic loss" presents a third problem. From our critical perspective, this concept is introduced only after the fact to account for depression when no actual object loss can be specified. The concept would not be invoked for people who are not depressed. If it is inferred only *after* a diagnosis of depression and only *after* no actual object loss can be discerned, the diagnostician is engaging in the kind of confused reasoning referred to as *post hoc, ergo propter hoc,* after this, therefore because of this.

Little research has been generated by psychoanalytic points of view, neither Freud's nor those of others that are not discussed here. Our assessment is in agreement with that of Mendels (1970), who finds nothing to support these views other than the often-repeated assertions by adherents that things are as they conceive them to be. The conceptual system itself is elastic enough to explain any finding, *after the fact.*

Cognitive Theories

At the end of Chapter 5 we discussed the fact that certain writers have attached great importance to the role of a person's cognitive or thought processes in his emotional behavior. In some theories of depression as in some of anxiety, thoughts and beliefs are regarded as causing the emotional state. In a way Freud is a cognitive theorist too, for he viewed depression as resulting from a person's *belief* that loss is a withdrawal of affection.

Perhaps the most important theory of depression to regard thought processes as causative factors is Beck's (1967). His central thesis is that depressed individuals feel as they do because they commit characteristic logical errors. From an examination of his therapy notes he found that his depressed patients tended to distort whatever happened to them in the direction of self-blame, catastrophes, and the like. Thus an event interpreted by a normal person as irritating and inconvenient, for example, the malfunctioning of an automobile, would be interpreted by the depressed patient as yet another example of the utter hopelessness of life. Beck's position is not that the depressive thinks poorly or illogically in general, for his cognitive capacities have been revealed as equal to those of normal individuals in numerous problem-solving tasks. Rather the depressive draws illogical conclusions as far as his evaluation of himself is concerned.

These errors in thinking constitute what Beck calls "schemata" or characteristic sets which color how the person actually perceives the world. The depressed person is seen as operating within a schema of self-deprecation and self-blame. This set disposes him to interpret or label events in a way that justifies his saying "What a jerk I am," "How hopeless this is," and so on.

Beck describes several logical errors committed by depressed people in interpreting reality.

1. *Arbitrary inference.* A conclusion drawn in the absence of sufficient evidence or of any evidence at all. For example, a person concludes that he is worthless because it is raining the day that he is hosting an outdoor cocktail party.
2. *Selective abstraction.* A conclusion drawn on the basis of but one of many elements in a situation. A worker blames himself entirely for the failure of a product to function, even though he is only one of many people who have produced it.
3. *Overgeneralization.* An overall, sweeping conclusion drawn on the basis of a single, perhaps trivial, event. A student regards his poor performance in a single class on one

particular day as final proof of his worthlessness and stupidity.
4. *Magnification and minimization.* Gross errors in evaluating performance. A person believes that he has completely ruined his car (magnification) when he sees that there is a slight scratch on the rear fender; or a person still believes himself worthless (minimization) in spite of a succession of praiseworthy achievements.

It is important to appreciate the thrust of Beck's position. Whereas many theorists have seen man as a victim of his passions, a creature whose intellectual capacities can exert little if any control over feelings—which is Freud's basic position—in the theory just outlined the cause-effect relationship operates in the opposite direction. Our emotional reactions are considered to be a function of how we construe our world, and indeed the interpretations of depressives are found not to mesh very well with objectively defined reality. Beck sees the depressive as the victim of his illogical thought processes.

In evaluating Beck's theory, at least two points need to be demonstrated. First, depressed patients, in contrast to nondepressed individuals, must actually think in the illogical ways that Beck has enumerated. This first point has been tentatively confirmed by Beck's clinical observations, which show that depressed patients do, in fact, manifest at least some of the errors in logic listed by him (Beck, 1967).

Second, it should be demonstrated that this cognitive distortion is not a function of a primary emotional disturbance, that it does in fact cause the depressed mood. Many studies in experimental psychology have in a general way shown that a person's feelings can be influenced by how he construes events. The

Geer, Davison, and Gatchel study (1970), for example, indicated that people are less aroused when they believe that they have control over a painful stimulation, even when that belief is false. No study that we know of, however, directly demonstrates that the various noncognitive aspects of depression are truly secondary to or a function of the distorted cognitive schemata that Beck believes operate in this disorder. Beck has found that depression and cognitive distortions are *correlated,* but a specific causal relationship cannot be determined from such data; depression could cause illogical thoughts or illogical thoughts could cause depression. Or the relationship could reflect some third variable such as a biochemical disturbance.

In spite of these difficulties, an important advantage of Beck's theory is that it is testable and has encouraged considerable research on depression. Even more important, it has encouraged therapists to work directly on depressed patients' thinking in order to change and alleviate their feelings.

Learning Theories

Current learning conceptualizations of depression bear some resemblance to Freud's theory, although, of course, the metaphors differ. Freud proposed as a causative factor the loss of a loved one by a person whose oral dependencies retained from childhood make him particularly vulnerable to a lessening of external supports. It seems but a short step to regard depression as a reduction in activity that occurs when accustomed reinforcement is withdrawn. When a loved one dies, an important source of positive reinforcement is certainly lost.

For social learning theorists the concept of reduction in reinforcement is primary; uncon-scious mourning processes such as introjection and the like play no part in their explanation of depression. Once the person stops behaving as he used to when reinforcement was plentiful (Ferster, 1965; Lazarus, 1968b), the new lower level of activity may itself be reinforced (Ullmann and Krasner, 1969). For example, the depressed person may receive sympathy or special dispensations from others, who expect less of him than they did before his loss. The outlook for improvement is all the more bleak for those who lack social skills for acquiring in new or different ways the rewards that used to be available. Social learning theory explains, more directly than did Freud, the depression that is not preceded by the loss of a loved one; accustomed reinforcements may be cut off for a number of reasons, for example, changes in occupational status or of locale.

The learning conceptualization of depression as a reduction in activity because reinforcement is lacking has been elaborated on and researched by Lewinsohn and his colleagues (for example, Lewinsohn, in press). Figure 8.2 is a schematic representation of Lewinsohn's model of depression. The following assumptions are made.

1. The feeling of depression and other symptoms of the clinical syndrome, such as fatigue, can be elicited when behavior receives little reinforcement.
2. This "thin" schedule of positive reinforcement, in turn, tends to reduce activity even more, and then reinforcements are even fewer.
3. The amount of positive reinforcement is a function of three sets of variables: (*a*) the number of potential reinforcers available to an individual as a function of his personal characteristics, such as age, sex, and attractiveness to others; (*b*) the number of potential reinforcers available as a function of the

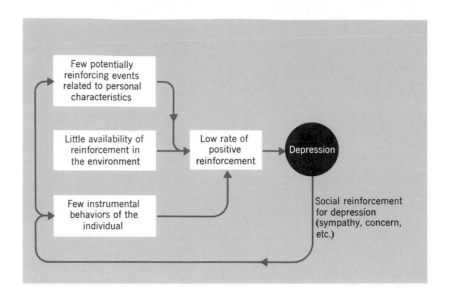

FIGURE **8.2**
Schematic of Lewinsohn's model of depression. After Lewinsohn, in press.

environment that the person is in, such as being at home rather than in prison; and (*c*) the person's repertoire of behavior that can gain reinforcement, for example, his vocational and social skills.

As Figure 8.2 indicates, a low rate of positive reinforcement reduces still further the activities and expression of qualities that might be rewarded. Both activities and rewards decrease in a vicious circle. A little reflection will reveal how difficult it would be to collect data that confirm this model. Careful, yet unobtrusive trained raters, such as those who conducted the Paul study (page 78), would have to count the number of reinforcements individuals receive in their everyday lives. Only after such a study could we state that depressed people receive fewer reinforcements than nondepressed individuals. We would also have to demonstrate that the activity of the individual is indeed less because of the reduced rates of positive reinforcement rather than other factors. Many studies from Lewinsohn's group confirm to some degree the central hypothesis, that depression may be caused by low rates of positively reinforced behavior

(Libet and Lewinsohn, 1973; Lewinsohn and Libet, 1972), but considerable research is still needed to establish specific causal relationships between reinforcement and mood. At this point the theory appears promising.

A learning model of *depression as learned helplessness* has been proposed by Seligman (in press), who suggests that anxiety is the *initial* response to a stressful situation. But if the person comes to believe that control is unattainable, anxiety is replaced by depression. To examine Seligman's theory we will first describe a typical learned-helplessness experiment with animals. Dogs receive painful electric shock in two different situations. In the first part of the experiment some dogs are subjected to numerous painful electric shocks from which they cannot escape. In the second part these animals, as well as dogs who did not have this prior experience with inescapable shock, are placed in an avoidance apparatus. Painful shock can be avoided if the dogs learn to run to another compartment of the box as soon as they hear a warning tone or see a light come on. The behavior of the dogs is markedly affected by whether they were earlier exposed to inescapable shock. Animals who have not

ANXIETY AND DEPRESSION

had the earlier experience become quite upset when they receive the first few electric shocks, but fairly soon thereafter they learn to run quite effectively when they hear or see the conditioned stimulus and thereby avoid further painful shock. The animals who have had the earlier experience with inescapable shock behave quite differently. Soon after receiving the first shocks they stop running around in a distressed manner; instead they seem to give up and passively accept the painful stimulation. Not surprisingly, they do not acquire the avoidance response as efficiently and effectively as the control animals do. Such experiments imply that animals can acquire what might be called a "sense of helplessness" when confronted with uncontrollable aversive stimulation. This helplessness later tends seriously and deleteriously to affect their performance in stressful situations that *can* be controlled. They are deprived of the ability to learn to respond in an effective way to painful stimulation.

On the basis of this and other work on the effects of uncontrollable stress, Seligman (in press) has proposed that learned helplessness in animals can provide a model for depression in man. Table 8.3 shows the principal details of his analysis. To establish the usefulness of his model of depression, Seligman had to document similarities between the manifestations of helplessness observed in animal laboratory studies and at least some of the symptoms of depressed people. These similarities are remarkable. Like depressed people, the animals appear passive in the face of stress, failing to initiate action that might allow them to cope. They develop anorexia, having difficulty in eating or retaining what is eaten, and lose weight. On a biological level, one of the neurotransmitter chemicals, norepinephrine, was found to be depleted in Seligman's animals. Drugs that are known to increase levels of

norepinephrine in man have been shown to alleviate depression. Although effectiveness of treatment does not, as we have often indicated, prove etiology, the fact that depression is reduced by a drug that increases the level of norepinephrine is consistent with the finding that learned helplessness in animals is associated with lower levels of the chemical.

Building on these behavioral and biological parallels, Seligman then examines possible commonalities in the causes of helplessness and depression. What makes the dogs behave in a helpless manner is known, for the carefully controlled experiments *create* the condition. The causes of human depression are much less clear, for the information available consists primarily of clinical observations. It is striking, however, how often those of diverse theoretical persuasions remark on the inability to control events, such as the loss of loved ones, physical disease, aging, and failure. As the model would seem to indicate, an important precursor to at least certain kinds of human depression may well be the belief that one cannot act to reduce suffering or to gain gratifications.

Seligman is well aware of the limitations of his model. He does not purport to explain all forms of depression but limits himself to depression that seems a reaction to environmental stress and that is also marked more by lethargy and inertia than by agitation. He has also noted differences between learned helplessness in animals and depression in man; for example, animals are not known to commit suicide, as many depressed people attempt to do.

A recent experiment by Miller and Seligman (1973) provides corroborative evidence for Seligman's model. College students were classified as either depressed or nondepressed on the basis of the Beck Depression Inventory, a self-report measure containing items such as

TABLE **8.3** *Seligman's Learned Helplessness Model of Reactive Depression*

	Learned helplessness in animals	Reactive depression in humans
Manifestations	Passivity in face of stress	Passivity, "paralysis of the will" (Beck, 1970)
	Retardation in learning to deal with stress	Negative expectations in dealing with stress or challenge, even when performance is adequate; feelings of hopelessness
	Dissipation of effect with time	Dissipation with time, although the length of time is very indefinite, ranging from days to years
	Anorexia	Anorexia
	Weight loss	Weight loss
	Brain norepinephrine depletion	Improvement when norepinephrine increases
Etiology	Uncontrollable stress—not stress per se but learning that no response reliably reduces aversive stimulation	Inability to control events in life, such as loss of a loved one, physical disease, and failure to act either to relieve suffering or to gain gratification

those listed in Table 8.4. Then they were given several trials on each of two kinds of problems. One task consisted of guessing which of two slides would appear on a given occasion, the order being randomized. Success was a purely chance event. The second task required them to move a platform upward in such a way that a steel ball was kept from rolling off it; success apparently required skill. After each trial the subjects were asked whether they expected to be successful on the next. How was each subject's expectation of success on the next trial affected by success or failure on a given trial? According to the helplessness formulation, depressed people do not readily perceive that any activity they engage in will bring them re-

wards. The depressed person's expectancy for success when performing a task requiring skill should be less affected by previous success than would be the case for a nondepressed person. In the task for which success depends on chance, the expectancies of success of both depressed and nondepressed subjects should be similar. According to Seligman's theory, depressives are not supposed to have a distorted view of situations whose outcomes do not depend on their behavior.

As can be seen in Figure 8.3, the results of the experiment strongly confirmed the hypothesis. Keeping the steel ball on the platform during one trial made the nondepressed subjects feel rather confident of success on the

TABLE 8.4 *Sample Items from the Beck Depression Inventory*

		Depression inventory
Sadness*	0	I do not feel sad.
	1	I feel blue or sad.
	2a	I am blue or sad all the time and I can't snap out of it.
	2b	I am so sad or unhappy that it is quite painful.
	3	I am so sad or unhappy that I can't stand it.
Pessimism	0	I am not particularly pessimistic or discouraged about the future.
	1a	I feel discouraged about the future.
	2a	I feel I have nothing to look forward to.
	2b	I feel that I won't ever get over my troubles.
	3	I feel that the future is hopeless and that things cannot improve.
Guilt	0	I don't feel particularly guilty.
	1	I feel bad or unworthy a good part of the time.
	2a	I feel quite guilty.
	2b	I feel bad or unworthy practically all the time now.
	3	I feel as though I am very bad or worthless.
Self-dislike	0	I don't feel disappointed in myself.
	1a	I am disappointed in myself.
	1b	I don't like myself.
	2	I am disgusted with myself.
	3	I hate myself.
Self-accusations	0	I don't feel I am any worse than anybody else.
	2	I am critical of myself for my weaknesses or mistakes.
	2	I blame myself for my faults.
	3	I blame myself for everything bad that happens.
Suicidal ideas	0	I don't have any thoughts of harming myself.
	1	I have thoughts of harming myself but I would not carry them out.
	2a	I feel I would be better off dead.
	2b	I feel my family would be better off if I were dead.
	3a	I have definite plans about committing suicide.
	3b	I would kill myself if I could.

* The words to the left do not appear in the actual inventory but are given here to indicate what attitudes each group of items is meant to measure.

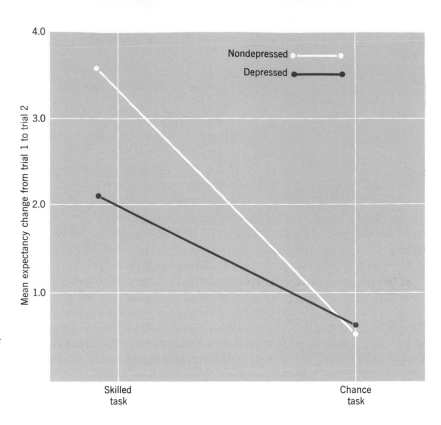

FIGURE **8.3**
Average changes in expectancy on skilled tasks versus chance tasks for depressed and nondepressed subjects. Adapted from Miller and Seligman, 1973.

next trial, the depressed subjects less so. No differences were found in the expectancies of the two kinds of subjects as they performed the chance task.

What is noteworthy — and what points up the cognitive nature of Seligman's formulation — is that success on *both tasks* was controlled by the experimenter in order to make reinforcements of all subjects the same. A hidden electrical switch enabled the experimenter to decide whether, on a given trial, a subject would perform the skilled task successfully or not. The behavior of the subjects was not really effective or for that matter ineffective; it was simply irrelevant. The experimenter created the mistaken belief of success or failure on a given trial. The fact that the task was a ruse is significant, for it demonstrates the overriding importance of the individual's beliefs about himself in relation to the environment. The

depressed subject was sometimes successful in performing the skilled task, but this favorable outcome did not increase his expectancy of succeeding on the next trial. A person may be profoundly depressed in the midst of environmental gratification that he has earned. If he does not believe that he has earned the rewards, Seligman's model predicts his depression.

One final note on this experiment. Table 8.4 contains some items from the Beck Depression Inventory, which was the basis for dividing the students into Miller and Seligman's depressed and nondepressed subject groups. None of the items seems to predict in any precise way the results of the Miller-Seligman experiment. We would suppose, of course, that highly depressed subjects are *generally* more pessimistic about their ability to solve problems. But the learned-helplessness model makes a

ANXIETY AND DEPRESSION

more specific prediction, namely that only on tasks that require skill—when a person might possibly view his behavior as leading to success or failure—will we find differences between the expectations of depressed and nondepressed subjects. The fact that this non-obvious hypothesis, derived from the helplessness model, was so strongly confirmed is impressive evidence of the usefulness of Seligman's model and should encourage further research, which may ultimately generate more effective preventive and curative procedures for certain kinds of depression.

These findings point up an important difference between the reduced-behavior–low-reinforcement view of depression and the learned-helplessness one. The first view, as enunciated by Ferster (1965) and Lewinsohn (in press), is basically noncognitive, assuming that overt behavior is a direct function of how it is rewarded. Alterations in mood and in thinking are viewed as a function of the overt behavior. Seligman, on the other hand, influenced by Beck's (1967) cognitive formulation, emphasizes the individual's *perception of control,* allowing for the possibility that a person's beliefs about how well he controls events need not be in line with his actual control. Similarly, his behavior may well be effective in achieving control, but he may not interpret it as such.

Physiological Theories of Depression

Since physiological processes are known to have considerable effect on moods, it is not surprising that investigators have sought physiological causes for depression. At the outset we should indicate that disturbed physiological processes must be important in the causal chain if a predisposition for depression can be genetically transmitted. Evidence indicating that depression is, in part, inherited would, then, provide some support for the theory that depression has a physiological basis.

Rosenthal (1970) has reviewed studies of manic-depressive psychoses diagnosed among the first-degree relatives of an index case. The data indicate that first-degree relatives are about ten times more likely than members of the general population to be diagnosed as manic-depressive. The incidences of manic-depressive psychosis found among monozygotic and dizygotic twins whose co-twins had originally been diagnosed as having the psychosis are also revealing. Price (1968) reviewed all the existing genetic studies and found the following: 66 of 97 monozygotic pairs of twins were concordant for manic-depressive psychosis, and only 27 of 119 dizygotic pairs were concordant. In sum, the data suggest, although they do not conclusively prove, that genetic factors, and thus physiological processes, are important in the etiology of manic-depressive psychosis. Unfortunately, studies on the genetic factors in depression have been limited almost exclusively to the manic-depressive syndrome; it may be hazardous to generalize about neurotic and psychotic depressions.

There are two major theories of what physiological processes may be disrupted to bring on depression, and both implicate biochemical factors. The first is concerned primarily with electrolyte metabolism and the second with the chemicals involved in neural transmission.

Electrolyte Metabolism in Depression

Electrolytes dissolve and dissociate into electrically charged particles which move and thus carry an electric current. Electrolytes play an important role in the functioning of the nervous system. Two of the most important of these are sodium and potassium chlorides. The positively charged sodium and potassium particles are distributed differently on either side of the membrane of a nerve cell. There is a higher concentration of sodium outside the neuron and a higher concentration of potassium within it. This difference is important in maintaining what is referred to as the resting potential of the cell. Alterations in the distribution of sodium and potassium produce changes in the resting potential, which in turn affects the excitability of the neuron, that is, whether it is readily fired by the impulse that is transmitted from another neuron.

Several workers have discovered disturbances in the distribution of sodium and potassium in depressed patients (Coppen, 1967; Shaw, 1966). The level of intracellular sodium has been found to be elevated in psychotic depressive patients. A corresponding decrement in the level of extracellular sodium has also been determined. Furthermore, measurements taken after patients have recovered from depression reveal that the level of intracellular sodium has decreased and become more nearly normal.

The effect of increased concentrations of sodium within the neuron is to *lower* its resting potential, making it excitable. Neural transmission in the nervous system is known to be an electrochemical phenomenon. An electrical impulse travels down the neuron and stimulates the release of a chemical substance, a neurotransmitter, which then crosses the synapse, the small gap between two neurons, and elicits a nerve impulse in the next neuron. If the neuron is hyperexcitable, it will readily transmit the impulse as soon as the neurotransmitter reaches it. Data in addition to those on intracellular sodium levels indicate that the depressive's nervous system is hyperexcitable,

even though his behavior patterns might make us expect it to be *less* excitable than that of the normal individual. For example, the responses evoked in the cerebral cortex by sensory stimuli are of greater magnitude in psychotic depressive patients than in normal individuals (Shagass and Schwartz, 1962). Similarly, Paulson and Gottlieb (1961) found that an arousal pattern recorded in the electroencephalograms of depressives tended to persist for a longer period of time than was the case after these individuals had recovered. It is not clear whether the apparent hyperexcitability of the depressive's nervous system is a paradox, contradicting the sadness and retarded motor activity typically observed. It may be that once we learn more about the specific relationships between the nervous system and behavior, the seeming inconsistency will be explained.

Levels of Norepinephrine

A second theory, almost directly opposite to the preceding proposal, suggests that depression results from an inhibition of neural transmission, that is, a retardation of the transmission of impulses from one neural fiber to another. But this theory applies only to the sympathetic nervous system and its neurotransmitter norepinephrine. Several pieces of evidence support this theory indirectly. As indicated earlier, Seligman has found that "depressed" dogs have low levels of the neurotransmitter norepinephrine. Second, the drugs that have been demonstrated to be effective in the treatment of depression are known to facilitate neural transmission in the sympathetic nervous system. For example, the so-called monoamine oxidase inhibitors act to increase the availability of norepinephrine. Similarly, the tricyclic drugs, which also alleviate depression, allow more free norepinephrine to be present and increase the likelihood of neural transmission in this part of the nervous system. Thus it is conceivable that depression is caused by diminished levels of norepinephrine (Davis, 1965; Cole, 1964b).

These biochemical data lend some support to theories that depression has physiological causes. Does this mean that psychological theories are irrelevant or useless? Not in the least. To assert that behavioral disorders have a basis in somatic processes is to state the obvious. No psychogenic theorist would deny that behavior is mediated by some kinds of bodily changes. The question rather is how do psychological and physiological factors interact. We have already grappled with this philosophical issue in Chapter 7. It may well be, for example, that depletion of norepinephrine does cause certain kinds of depression, but that an earlier link in the causal chain is "the sense of helplessness" or "paralysis of will" that psychological theorists have proposed as important.

SUICIDE

In some religions suicide is considered a mortal sin. As late as 1823 a citizen of London who took his own life was buried with a stake pounded through his heart (Shneidman, 1973). Moreover, until 1961, suicide in England was a criminal offense. Sanctions, then, have been quite strong in many societies. And yet it is fair to say that the idea of killing oneself comes to most people at one time or another. To "explain" the thought, or the deed, by asserting that it is caused by depression or insanity is more likely to hinder the search for answers than to facilitate it. The fact that many depressives have suicidal thoughts and often make genuine attempts to take their own lives is the rationale for including a discussion of suicide in a chapter on depression. A significant number of people who are not depressed, however, make suicidal attempts and commit the act. An adequate understanding of suicide cannot come by concentrating only on the tendency of the majority of depressed people to think about suicide.

Facts about Suicide

No single theory is likely to take into account all the available information about suicide. The diversity of facts that are known about the act may help us appreciate how complex and multifaceted self-intentioned death is (Resnick, 1968; Gibbs, 1968; Douglas, 1967; Shneidman, 1973):

1. Every thirty minutes someone in the United States kills himself, and this rate is probably a gross underestimate.
2. Three times as many men kill themselves as women.
3. Three times as many women as men attempt to kill themselves but do not die.
4. Suicide is found in both the very old and the very young—above ninety years and even below ten years.
5. Suicide is found almost equally at all social and economic levels.
6. No other kind of death leaves in friends and relatives such long-lasting feelings of distress, shame, guilt, puzzlement, and general disturbance.
7. Guns are the most common means of suicide in the United States. Men in particular usually choose to shoot themselves. Women are more likely to use sleeping pills. Elsewhere in the world methods vary

by country; for example, coal gas is chosen most often in England, gas and hanging in Austria, pills and poisons in the Scandinavian countries.

8. The national suicide rates, as collected by the World Heath Organization (1972), were in 1969 highest for Hungary, Czechoslovakia,[1] Finland, and Austria. Among the lowest reported rates are those of Greece and Ireland.

9. Suicide ranks tenth as a leading cause of death among adults and third among college students.

10. Most of the people who kill themselves in the United States are native-born Caucasian males between forty-five and sixty years of age.

11. Suicide rates go up during depression years, remain stable during years of prosperity, and decrease during war years.

12. There are close to 500 self-inflicted deaths of adolescents and children each year in the United States.

Theories of Suicide

Mintz (1968) has summarized the numerous motivations for suicide mentioned in the literature: aggression turned inward; retaliation by inducing guilt in others; efforts to force love from others; efforts to make amends for "perceived" past wrongs; efforts to rid oneself of unacceptable feelings, such as sexual attraction to members of one's own sex; the desire for reincarnation; the desire to rejoin a dead loved one; and the desire or need to escape from stress, deformity, pain, or emotional vacuum. Two major theoretical positions are currently popular among suicidologists, the psychoanalytic and Durkheim's sociological theory.

[1] The figures given for Czechoslovakia in the *World Health Statistics Annual, 1969* are, unlike the others, for the year 1968.

Psychoanalytic Theories of Suicide

Freud proposed two major hypotheses to account for suicide. One is an extension of his theory of depression. When a person loses someone whom he has ambivalently loved and hated, and introjects that person into himself, his aggression is directed toward himself. If these murderous feelings are strong enough, the person will commit suicide. The second theory postulates that the death instinct, Thanatos, can turn inward and make the person take his life.

Freud's views on suicide are subject to many of the problems raised earlier in this text about psychoanalytic theorizing. Moreover, a careful analysis of suicide notes by Tuckman and his colleagues (1959) has provided information that is in marked disagreement with the psychoanalytic position. They found that only a very small minority of the notes expressed hostility. A possible rebuttal—which we find unsatisfactory—might be that a suicide note, written at the conscious level, could not be expected to reflect repressed hostility.

Durkheim's Sociological Theory of Suicide

Durkheim (1897), after analyzing the records of suicide for various countries and during different historical periods, distinguished three different kinds of self-annihilative behavior. *Egoistic suicide* is committed, according to Durkheim, when a person has too few ties to his society and community. These people feel alienated from others, cut off from the social supports that are important to keep them functioning adaptively as social beings. *Altruistic suicides,* in contrast, are viewed by Durkheim as responses to societal demands. Some people who commit suicide feel very much a part of a group and sacrifice themselves for the good of society. The self-immolations of Buddhist monks during the Vietnam war would fit into this category. Finally, *anomic suicide* may be triggered by a sudden change in a person's relations to society. A successful businessman who suffers severe financial reverses may experience *anomie,* a sense of disorientation, because what he believed to be his normal way of living is no longer possible for him.

As with all sociological theorizing, Durkheim's hypotheses have trouble accounting for the different reactions of individuals in a given society to the same demands and conditions. Not all those who unexpectedly lose their money commit suicide. It appears that Durkheim was aware of this problem, for he suggested that individual temperament would interact with any of the social pressures that he found causative. Perhaps at the most general level a person's suicide may be regarded as what he considered the best means for withdrawing from his particular and apparently insoluble problem in living. Even this suggestion, however, is inadequate, for it does not explain why person A chooses suicide whereas person B withdraws from stress by "going crazy." All explanations remain strictly *post hoc* until and unless a theory better predicts why individuals differ in their reactions to the same set of social conditions. Psychologists have recently attempted to make such predictions based on personality characteristics.

Prediction of Suicide from Personality Tests

It would be of both theoretical and practical importance to be able to predict suicide on the basis of personality tests. Theoretically, knowing what characteristics a potential suicide has would help us understand what makes people consider killing themselves. On practical, social-action grounds, being able to detect who is likely to make an attempt would obviously help those who wish to intervene and save lives.

Many investigators have studied personality characteristics of those who have attempted suicide and of those who have been successful, but the overall results are quite discouraging (Lester, 1970). One principal difficulty stems from the fact that personality tests can seldom be given to numbers of people who may *later* kill themselves. Furthermore, in addition to this problem of obtaining data before a suicide attempt has been made, it is impossible to obtain information, other than biographical data from relatives and a few other sources, after someone has been successful. The literature, then, consists of reports of psychological tests given to people *after* they have made an unsuccessful attempt at suicide. Clearly, the data obtained from such tests reflect the fact that those tested have recently tried and failed to kill themselves. Their state of mind is likely to be quite different from what it had been before the attempt. For example, many who have tried unsuccessfully to take their lives feel extremely guilty and embarrassed. It is impossible to know with any exactness how test scores and interview behavior are affected by such postattempt factors.

What do we discover when we compare questionnaires answered by those who have only thought of suicide and by others who have made an attempt? A few studies have collected such important information. Rosen, Hales, and Simon (1954) compared the MMPI scores of fifty patients who had attempted suicide, a hundred who had thought about suicide, and, as a control, several who had never attempted or thought about suicide. Generally, the results showed that members of the group who had thought of suicide were more deviant than those who had attempted suicide as well as being more deviant than those in the control group. In a later study Simon and Gilberstadt

BOX **8.1** *Some Myths about Suicide*

There are many prevalent misconceptions about suicide (Pokorny, 1968; Shneidman, 1973).

1. *People who discuss suicide will not commit the act.* The fact is that up to three-quarters of those who take their lives have communicated the intent beforehand, perhaps to ask for help, perhaps to taunt.

2. *Suicide may be committed without warning.* The falseness of this belief is readily indicated by the preceding statement. There seem to be many warnings, such as the person's saying that the world would be better off without him, or his making unexpected and inexplicable gifts to others.

3. *Only people of a certain class commit suicide.* Suicide is actually neither the curse of the poor nor the disease of the rich. People in all classes commit suicide.

4. *Membership in a particular religious group is a good predictor of whether or not a person will consider suicide.* It is mistakenly thought that the strong Catholic prohibition against suicide makes the risk that Catholics will take their lives much lower. This is not supported by the data, perhaps because an individual's formal religious identification is not an accurate index of his true beliefs.

5. *The motives for suicide are easily established.* The truth is that we have only the poorest understanding of why certain people commit suicide. For example, the fact that a severe reverse in finances precedes a suicide does not mean that the reversal adequately explains the suicide.

6. *Most of the people who commit suicide are depressed.* This fallacy may account for the tragic fact that signs of impending suicide are over-looked because the person is not depressed. Although reliable data are difficult to collect, some experts believe that the majority of people who take their lives are *not* depressed. As we have indicated, however, a majority of depressed people do at some time think of or attempt suicide.

7. *A person with a terminal physical illness is unlikely to commit suicide.* A person's awareness of impending death does not preclude suicide. Perhaps the wish to end their own suffering or that of their loved ones impels many to choose the time of their death.

8. *To commit suicide is insane.* Although most suicidal persons are very unhappy, most do appear to be completely rational and in touch with reality.

9. *A tendency to commit suicide is inherited.* Since suicides often run in families, the assumption is made that the tendency to think in terms of self-annihilation is inherited. There is no evidence for this.

10. *Suicide is influenced by seasons, latitude, weather fronts, barometric pressure, humidity, precipitation, cloudiness, wind speed, temperature, and days of the week.* There are no good data to substantiate any of these myths.

11. *Suicide is influenced by cosmic factors such as sunspots and phases of the moon.* No evidence confirms this.

12. *Improvement in emotional state means lessened risk of suicide.* The fact is that people often commit the act after their spirits begin to rise; this appears to be especially true of depressed patients.

13. *Suicidal people clearly want to die.* Most people who commit suicide appear to be ambivalent about their own deaths.

(1958) compiled **MMPI** data on successful suicides, the tests obviously having been administered prior to the act. They then compared
these data with the **MMPI** scores of Rosen's
subjects, those who had thought of or attempted suicide. In general, the scores of those
who were to commit successful suicides were
not different from the scores of the control
group. Data from other studies on suicide are
either similarly inconclusive or utterly unin-
terpretable because experimental blunders
were made, such as not testing a nonsuicidal
control group for comparison purposes.

The Prediction of Suicide from Demographic Variables

Rather than employing psychological tests devised for other purposes, many workers advocate the development of assessment procedures specifically designed to predict suicide.
Attention is paid to demographic factors such
as age, sex, marital status, and living arrangements, which turn out to be very useful pre-
dictors—more helpful than the personality
variables just considered.

Suicide prevention centers, such as those in
Los Angeles and in Buffalo, rely on demogra-

phic factors (Shneidman, Farberow, and Litman, 1970). In the Buffalo Suicide Prevention and Crisis Service, for example, workers receiving phone calls from people in suicidal crises have before them a checklist to guide their questioning of each caller (Figure 8.4), for they must immediately assess how great the risk of suicide may be. For example, a caller would be regarded as a lethal risk if he were male, middle-aged, divorced, and living alone and had a history of previous suicide attempts.

Another procedure is the "psychological autopsy," pioneered at the Los Angeles Suicide Prevention Center (Shneidman et al., 1970). In effect, these workers analyze information obtained from crisis phone calls, from interviews with relatives and friends of those who are thinking about suicide or have committed the act, and from notes left behind by those who have ultimately killed themselves. This type of clinical case study has yielded a wealth of provocative and often useful information.

Of particular interest is a study (Shneidman and Farberow, 1970) of notes left by people who subsequently committed suicide. At least in the Los Angeles area, about 15 percent of suicides do leave notes, and the contents of these notes were analyzed by judges trained to rate them on the presence or absence of in-structions and specific themes, such as self-blame, discomfort, death as relief, and the like. Having determined that such ratings could indeed be made reliably by independent judges. Shneidman and Farberow compared these actual suicide notes with simulated notes prepared for them by individuals who were *not* oriented toward killing themselves but who were matched to those who had on such demographic variables as age, sex, and social class. These control subjects were instructed to write *as if* they were about to commit suicide. The genuine notes contained a greater number of instructions, such as explicit orders about how to dispose of the body; there was also evidence of significantly more anguish.

As is the case in nearly all areas of abnormal psychology, not as much is known about suicide as we would like. In this instance the lack of information is all the more worrisome since the very existence of many people is at stake. Fortunately, those who have devoted their professional lives to preventing suicide are not waiting for all the data to come in before attempting to intervene. The absence of a good theory does not preclude action based on working principles such as those derived from statistical studies that determine which individuals are the most likely to make lethal attempts.

SUMMARY

Depression is found in a number of formal psychiatric categories, principally manic-depressive illness, depressive neurosis, and psychotic depression. The distinctions made among these categories have been based on whether precipitating events can be found and on the presence or absence of thought disorder. More recently, workers have distinguished between exogenous and endogenous depression on the basis of different patterns of affect and behavior.

Psychological theories of depression have been couched in psychoanalytic, cognitive, and learning terms. Psychoanalytic formulations stress unconscious identification with a loved one whose desertion of the individual has made him turn his anger inward. Beck's cognitive theory ascribes causal significance to certain kinds of illogical thinking. Learning theorists have focused both on low rates of positive reinforcement and on learned helplessness. Physiological theories suggest that defects in the transmission of neural impulses, possibly genetically determined, underlie the phenomenon of depression.

Finally, the topic of suicide was explored, although self-annihilative tendencies are not restricted to those who are depressed. A review of the facts and myths about suicide suggest that any single theory is unlikely to account for the diverse forms that suicide can take.

PART III
SOCIAL DEVIATION

CHAPTER 9
Sociopathy and Legal Responsibility

Crime is one of contemporary society's most pressing problems. From 1960 to 1968 the crime rate increased by 80 percent while the population increased only 11 percent. Not all criminals, however, can be regarded as abnormal: crime, after all, is a legal concept, and many people who do not otherwise appear to be abnormal, for example, juvenile delinquents and rioters, become identified as criminals. Our attention, then, is restricted to one segment of the criminal population—those who can be diagnosed as having an antisocial personality. Later in the chapter we shall discuss the involvement of the mental health field in decisions concerning legal responsibility for criminal acts, examining in detail the plea of "not guilty by reason of insanity."

ANTISOCIAL PERSONALITY (SOCIOPATHY)

In DSM-II antisocial personalities are described as

. . . individuals who are basically unsocialized and whose behavior pattern brings them repeatedly into conflicts with society. They are incapable of significant loyalty to individuals, groups, or social values. They are grossly selfish, callous, irresponsible, impulsive, and unable to feel guilt or to learn from experience and punishment. Frustration tolerance is low. They tend to blame others or offer plausible rationalizations for their behavior. A mere history of repeated legal or social offenses is not sufficient to justify this diagnosis (p. 43).

In current usage the term sociopath is employed interchangeably with antisocial personality and psychopath. The concept has an interesting history. In the eighteenth century Philippe Pinel conceived of *manie sans delire,* mania without delirium, and Pritchard described the disorder moral insanity in an attempt to account for behavior so far outside the usual ethical and legal codes that it seemed a form of insanity. Pinel's term was first applied to an easily angered aristocrat who whipped a horse, kicked a dog to death, and threw a peasant woman into a well. Since the early concept was used to explain a wide variety of strange behaviors, it is not surprising that it came to function somewhat as a wastebasket diagnosis, encompassing not only violence but unconventional sexual practices as well.

Before considering current views of these problems, we shall examine excerpts from two case histories that reveal the scope of sociopathic reactions. The first case illustrates many of the classic characteristics of the sociopath but is unusual in that the person described was neither a criminal nor in psychiatric treatment at the time that the data for the case study were collected. This is an important point, for the majority of sociopaths who are the subjects of research studies have broken the law and been caught for doing so. Only rarely do we have the opportunity to examine in detail the behavior of an individual who fits the diagnostic definition but yet has managed not to break the law. The second case history presents the more usual picture of the criminal sociopath.

The Case of Dan

This case history was compiled by a psychologist (McNeil, 1967) who happened to be a personal friend of Dan.

Dan was a wealthy actor and disc jockey who lived in an expensive house in an exclusive suburb and generally played his role as a "personality" to the hilt. One evening, when the two men were out for dinner, Dan made a great fuss over the condition of the *shrimp de Johnge* that he had ordered. McNeil thought that the whole scene had been deliberately contrived by Dan for the effect it might produce, and he said to his companion,

"I have a sneaking suspicion this whole scene came about just because you weren't really hungry." Dan laughed loudly in agreement and said, *"What the hell, they'll be on their toes next time." "Was that the only reason for this display?"* . . . *"No,"* he replied, *"I wanted to show you how gutless the rest of the world is. If you shove a little they all jump. Next time I come in, they'll be all over me to make sure everything is exactly as I want it. That's the only way they can tell the difference between class and plain ordinary. When I travel I go first class."*

"Yes, . . . but how do you feel about you as a person—as a fellow human being?"

"Who cares?" he laughed. *"If they were on top they would do the same to me. The more you walk on them, the more they like it. It's*

like royalty in the old days. It makes them nervous if everyone is equal to everyone else. Watch. When we leave I'll put my arm around that waitress, ask her if she still loves me, pat her on the fanny, and she'll be ready to roll over any time I wiggle my little finger" (p. 85).

Another incident occurred when a friend of Dan's committed suicide. Most of the other friends whom Dan and McNeil had in common called the psychologist to see if he could provide any information about why the man had taken his life. Dan did not. Later, when McNeil mentioned the suicide to Dan, all he could say was "That's the way the ball bounces." In his public behavior, however, Dan's attitude toward the incident appeared quite different. He was the one who collected money for the deceased and presented it personally to the new widow. In keeping with his character, however, Dan remarked that the widow had a sexy body which really interested him.

These two incidents convey the flavor of Dan's behavior. McNeil had witnessed a long succession of similar events which led him to conclude that

[The incidents] painted a grisly picture of life-long abuse of people for Dan's amusement and profit. He was adept at office politics and told me casually of an unbelievable set of deceptive ways to deal with the opposition. Character assassination, rumor mongoring, modest blackmail, seduction, and barefaced lying were the least of his talents. He was a jackal in the entertainment jungle, a jackal who feasted on the bodies of those he had slaughtered professionally (p. 91).

In his conversations with Dan, McNeil was also able to inquire into Dan's life history. One early and potentially important event was uncovered.

I can remember the first time in my life when I began to suspect I was a little different from most people. When I was in high school my best friend got leukemia and died and I went to his funeral. Everybody else was crying and feeling sorry for themselves and as they were praying to get him into heaven I suddenly realized that I wasn't feeling anything at all. He was a nice guy but what the hell. That night I thought about it some more and found out that I wouldn't miss my mother and father if they died and that I wasn't too nuts about my brothers and sisters for that matter. I figured there wasn't anybody I really cared for but, then, I didn't need any of them anyway so I rolled over and went to sleep (p. 87).

The moral depravity described long ago by Pinel and Pritchard clearly marks Dan's behavior. A person may be otherwise quite rational and show no loss of contact with reality and yet conduct himself in a habitually and exceedingly unethical manner. The final excerpt illustrates Dan's lack of feeling for others, a characteristic that will later be seen to have considerable relevance in explaining sociopathic behavior.

The Case of Jim

Jim, the fourth child in a family of five, grew up in the lower social class of a small Midwestern town. During his childhood the member of his family who made the greatest impression on him was his older brother, whom he described as follows.

He was always a bully, promiscuous, and adventurous. He was always involved with some local girl, before I was even old enough to realize what was going on. He started drinking early, and had several scrapes with the law. He had rough companions, whom I later inherited, who helped me on my way.

He married a tramp, ended up in a stolen car, and was given the choice of jail or the army, as this was the Korean war time. I cannot directly link him to my life of crime, although he introduced me to those who later helped me along. Also, he condoned some of my early petty thievery (Bintz and Wilson, as reprinted in Milton and Wahler, 1969, p. 92).

During early adolescence Jim engaged in many petty antisocial acts. For example, on one occasion he stole some change from his mother's pocketbook. His father reacted by whipping both brothers until Jim confessed. Once Jim had admitted taking the money, however, the punishment ended. This became standard practice for the family, with Jim being able to avoid punishment by confessing as soon as he was accused of misbehavior, regardless of whether he was guilty or not. Moreover, the petty thievery that Jim committed in the community was generally successful, and even when he was caught consequences were minimal.

Jim's first serious trouble with the law occurred when he was charged with raping a girl whom he had picked up at the local skating rink. He was sentenced to five years at a reform school but received an immediate parole on the condition that his sentence would be activated if he violated it. After several parole violations such as sleeping with a girl, being detained for speeding, and petty theft, he was sentenced to one year at the reform school. By the time he returned to his hometown a year later, he had become a young hoodlum. Jim himself stated that the principal consequence of the year in reform school had been the opportunity afforded him to fraternize with more experienced thieves. Shortly thereafter Jim and a friend committed their first major theft, stealing $1700 from a tavern safe. Then the same pair attempted to burglarize a lumberyard but were unable to open the safe. The next day they were arrested, and the burglary tools were found in Jim's car. He served a ninety-day sentence for attempted burglary. Three months after being released, Jim was incarcerated again, this time for statutory rape. As soon as he was free again, he and a friend planned another robbery. They reasoned that a bootlegger would be a good target for a holdup for, being outside the law himself, he would be reluctant to report the incident to the police. They bungled the job badly, however, and both were sentenced to five-year terms. Jim served three of the five years and upon his release met the girl he was soon to marry. He described her as follows.

Diane was a tramp, I could tell from the start. She forced the introduction and the first date. I had sexual relations with her on the first date, she was my third sexual partner on that particular day. She was neat, but not really attractive. The next four and a half months we were intimate almost every night. She wanted to marry, I did not. I could not see myself married to this plain-looking tramp. In fact, toward the last, I was trying to think of a scheme to get rid of her . . . (p. 100).

During this period Jim held a job, but he soon began to get deeper and deeper into debt. Eventually, an opportunity for another theft presented itself. Again the job was spectacularly unsuccessful and Jim was sentenced to ten years in the state penitentiary. While in the county jail, before the trial, he was visited often by Diane and finally married her just before going to prison. As a substitute for a wedding ring, Jim had the words "Love me, Diane" tattooed on his penis.

Cleckley's Concept of Sociopathy

Both of these case histories illustrate many of the symptoms of the sociopathic syndrome as it has been defined by Cleckley (1964). On the basis of his vast clinical experience, he has formulated a set of criteria for the disorder.

1. Average or superior intelligence.
2. Absence of irrationality and other commonly accepted symptoms of psychosis.
3. No sense of responsibility.
4. Disregard for truth.
5. No sense of shame.

6. Antisocial behavior without apparent regret.
7. Inability to learn from experience.
8. General poverty of affect.
9. Lack of genuine insight.
10. Little response to special consideration or kindness.
11. No history of sincere suicide attempts.
12. Unrestrained and unconventional sex life.
13. Onset of sociopathic characteristics no later than early twenties.

These thirteen characteristics are quite similar to the description of antisocial personality found in DSM-II. But some appear to be more central than others. Perhaps the most critical aspect to be considered in making a diagnosis of sociopathy are the reactions of the individual to his antisocial behavior. Thus Cleckley's criteria *no sense of responsibility* and *no sense of shame* are particularly important. The sociopath is viewed as not responding emotionally after committing an act that generally elicits shame and guilt in most people. Presumably, the lack of these affective reactions may also be linked to the sociopath's inability to learn from experience, particularly to avoid punishment. The sociopath continues to engage in the same antisocial activities, even though they prove unsuccessful. Learning to avoid actions that continually fail may be mediated by emotional arousal; because the sociopath does not become emotionally aroused, he is less likely to suffer from and to change his unproductive and antisocial ways.

Before examining the existing research on the sociopathic syndrome, we should emphasize that most of it has been conducted on sociopaths who have already been convicted as criminals. Individuals such as Dan have not been studied in research settings. We must therefore keep in mind that the available research does not allow us to generalize about the behavior of those sociopaths who elude arrest and the subsequent label of criminal. Nor indeed are all criminals sociopaths, as we have already explained. For example, at Sing Sing prison 64 percent of the inmates were diagnosed as having sociopathic personalities. The behavior of the others, although they are socially defined as criminals, could not be described as sociopathic.

THEORY AND RESEARCH ON THE ETIOLOGY OF SOCIOPATHY

The Role of the Family

Since much sociopathic behavior violates social norms, it is not surprising that many investigators have focused on the primary agent of socialization, the family, in their search for the explanation of such behavior. Many sociopaths have apparently experienced the trauma of losing a parent. Greer (1964) found that 60 percent of his sample of sociopaths had lost at least one parent during childhood, whereas only 28 percent of the control sample of neurotics and 27 percent of a control sample of normal subjects had. In a similar vein, McCord and McCord (1964) concluded, on the basis of a review of the literature, that lack of affection and severe parental rejection were the primary causes of sociopathic behavior. Several other studies have related sociopathic behavior to the parents' inconsistencies in disciplining the child and in teaching him his responsibilities to others (Bennet, 1960). Furthermore, the fathers of sociopaths are likely to display antisocial behavior.

But such data on early rearing must be interpreted with extreme caution. They were gathered by means of *retrospective reports*. Information about early family experiences and about how the child was taught to behave socially is obtained either from an adult sociopath or from his parents, relatives, and friends at a time very much later than when events acually occurred. Recent studies of the reliability of the information obtained in this way indicate that such data may be of little use. As Garmezy has noted,

Studies of normal families have revealed the unreliability of the case history, with its exclusive reliance on retrospective reconstruction of an earlier time period . . . investigations conducted with normal mothers of primary school age (and younger) children provide evidence that not only do mothers suffer deficits in recalling events in the early years of their children's lives but that the deficiency is particularly acute [in remembering] emotions and affectively-tinged attitudes . . . (1971, p. 105).

When people are asked to recollect the early events in the life of someone who is now known to be a sociopath, the fact that they have knowledge of his adult status may have some effect on what they remember or report about his childhood. Potentially deviant events are more likely to be recalled, whereas incidents that do not dovetail with the person's current behavior may be overlooked.

One way of avoiding the problems of retrospective data is to follow up in adulthood the lives of a large group of individuals who as children were seen at a child guidance clinic.

In one such study very detailed records had been kept on the children, including the type of problem that had brought them to the clinic and information on numerous variables related to the family (Robbins, 1966). Ninety percent of an initial sample of 584 cases were located thirty years after their referral to the clinic.[1] In addition to the clinic cases, 100 control subjects who had lived in the same geographic area served by the clinic but who had *not* been referred to it were also followed up in adulthood.

By interviewing the now-adult individuals chosen for both the experimental and control samples, the investigators were able to diagnose and describe any maladjustments of these individuals. Then adult problems were related back to the characteristics that these people had displayed as children to find out which childhood characteristics predicted sociopathic behavior in adulthood. Robbins summarized these as follows.

If one wishes to choose the most likely candidate for a later diagnosis of sociopathic personality from among children appearing in a child guidance clinic, the best choice appears to be a boy referred for theft or aggression who has shown a diversity of antisocial behavior in many episodes, at least one of which could be grounds for Juvenile Court appearance, and whose antisocial behavior involves him with strangers and organizations as well as with teachers and parents. . . . more than half of the boys appearing at the clinic [with these characteristics were later] diagnosed sociopathic personality. Such boys had a history of truancy, theft, staying out late, and refusing to obey parents. They lied gratuitously, and showed little guilt over their behavior. They

[1] It should be appreciated that being able to track down this large a percentage of individuals thirty years after their contact with the clinic is an incredible feat.

were generally irresponsible about being where they were supposed to be or taking care of money. They were interested in sexual activities and had experimented with homosexual relationships . . . (p. 157).

In addition to these characteristics, variables related to family life were found to be important. Both inconsistent discipline and no discipline at all predicted sociopathic behavior in adulthood, as did antisocial behavior in the father.

In sum, the data we have reviewed emphasize the importance of child-rearing practices. The fathers of sociopaths appear to provide a model for antisocial behavior. We must caution, however, that poor training in socialization has been implicated in the etiology of a number of clinical syndromes including delinquent, neurotic, and even psychotic behavior (Wiggins, 1968), and that many individuals who come from what appear to be similarly disturbed social backgrounds do *not* become sociopaths or develop any other behavior disorders. This point is important: adults may have no problems whatsoever in spite of the inconsistent and otherwise undesirable manner in which they were reared. Thus family experience may be important in the development of sociopathic behavior, but it can *not* be the whole story.

Genetic Correlates of Sociopathic Behavior

Twin Studies

Most of the studies concerned with the possible genetic basis for sociopathic behavior have focused on criminality rather than on sociopathy per se. Thus these data are difficult to interpret since not all sociopaths are criminals nor are all criminals sociopaths. Lange's research (1929) comparing concordance rates for criminality in identical and fraternal twins showed them to be a great deal higher for identical twins, supporting the theory that genetic factors may be involved. Kranz (1936), in a study that used better sampling procedures, found the following patterns of concordance: identical twins, 66 percent; fraternal twins of the same sex, 54 percent; fraternal twins of the opposite sex, 14 percent. Although at first glance these data also seem to support the notion that genetic factors are important, they in fact give only slight support to this hypothesis. The critical piece of information is the marked *difference* in concordance rates of fraternal twins of the same sex and those of fraternal twins of the opposite sex. Both of these pairs of twins are equally alike genetically, but we can expect the parental rearing practices to which they are exposed to be markedly different. Fraternal twins of the same sex are probably treated more alike than are fraternal twins of the opposite sex. Thus these data point toward the importance of environmental factors.

XYY

One genetic aberration that has received considerable publicity recently is the presence of an extra male chromosome in men who have committed particularly violent crimes.[2] Chromosomes are the carriers of the genes. Human beings have forty-six chromosomes in twenty-three pairs within the nucleus of each and every cell. One pair is of a special kind and determines the sex of the individual and the later development of secondary sexual characteristics. The normal male cells have one X and one Y chromosome; the normal

[2] Again we must caution that such data may be of only limited relevance to sociopathy.

female cell has two X chromosomes. The cells of some men have recently been reported to have one Y chromosome too many, XYY, and thus they may be considered "supermales." But Rosenthal (1970) has noted that of the large number of criminals and delinquents tested to date, only about 1.5 percent have shown this pattern. In the report of the Center for Studies of Crime and Delinquency of the National Institute of Mental Health, which convened a nationwide conference of experts in June 1969, the available evidence was carefully reviewed. Some of the studies showed behavior by men with XYY chromosomes to be *less* aggressive than that of normal men. The report concludes that it is premature to consider this chromosomal abnormality as an important contributor to aggressive or criminal behavior. The conference participants also urged in the strongest possible terms that the XYY aberration not be made a basis of relieving offenders of legal responsibility for their criminal acts.

Central Nervous System Activity and Sociopathy

Many studies have examined patterns of brain wave activity (see Box 9.1) in sociopaths and various groups of control subjects. Ellingson (1954) reviewed these studies and reported that in thirteen out of fourteen of them, investigating a total of about 1500 sociopaths, between 31 and 58 percent showed some form of electroencephalogram (EEG) abnormality. The most frequent form of abnormality was slow-wave activity, which was generally widespread throughout the brain. There is, however, some evidence that among extremely impulsive and aggressive sociopathic individuals the EEG abnormalities are localized in the temporal lobes of the cerebral hemispheres (Hill, 1952). Finally, some individuals who

respond with impulsive, aggressive, and destructive behavior to seemingly trivial stimuli show what are referred to as *positive spikes*. These occur in the temporal area of the brain and consist of bursts of activity with frequencies of 6 to 8 cycles per second (cps) and 14 to 16 cps. Hare (1970) has interpreted these EEG data as follows.

It is quite possible . . . that these EEG abnormalities reflect some sort of dysfunction in the underlying temporal and limbic mechanisms [which] are involved in sensory and memory processes and in the central regulation of emotional and motivational behavior. . . . The limbic mechanisms appear to play a particularly important role in the regulation of fear-motivated behavior, including learning to inhibit a response in order to avoid punishment. . . . The temporal slow-wave activity frequently observed in the EEG records of psychopaths reflects a malfunction of some limbic inhibitory mechanism and this malfunction makes it difficult to learn to inhibit behavior that is likely to lead to punishment (pp. 33–34).

Thus Hare links the various EEG abnormalities of sociopaths to their inability to avoid punishment. It is this subject of punishment and the failure to learn to avoid it that we shall now discuss as a fourth correlate of sociopathy.

Avoidance Learning and Sociopathy

As we have previously noted, one of the criteria formulated by Cleckley in defining the sociopathic syndrome is the inability of these persons to learn from experience. In particular, they seemingly feel no need to avoid the negative consequences of social misbehavior.

BOX **9.1** *The Electroencephalogram*

The electroencephalogram or EEG is a graphic recording of the electrical activity of the brain. The brain is known to be continuously active, chemically and electrically, throughout life, even in sleep. Individual neurons of the central nervous system fire spontaneously at regular or irregular intervals, creating differences in electrical potentials, that is, fluctuations in voltage. The fluctuations in voltage in the cortex, the portion of the brain immediately below the skull, can be picked up by two or more sensitive electrodes pasted to the scalp (Figure 9.1). The recording machine, the electroencephalograph, amplifies the pulsations one to two million times and connects them to a pen recorder (or recorders) which registers them on graph paper as a pattern of oscillations. The spontaneous activity of the brain, known as its waves, varies in different cortical areas and in the other less accessible portions of the brain. In young children the patterns of activity vary with age. Perhaps most importantly, the dominant

brain waves reflect the degree to which the brain has been aroused.

In a normal adult subject, awake but resting quietly with his eyes closed, the dominant rhythm has a frequency of between 8 and 13 pulsations or cycles per second (cps) and an amplitude of from 40 to 50 microvolts. This low-frequency, high-voltage wave is called the *alpha* rhythm. When a stimulus is presented, the alpha rhythm is replaced by a high-frequency (14 to 25 cps), low-voltage rhythm, the *beta* rhythm. If very low-frequency waves are found dominant in the awake adult, they are considered abnormal. These slow waves, which are sometimes found in sociopaths while they are awake, are referred to as the theta (4 to 7 cps) and the delta (less than 4 cps) rhythms. Delta rhythms occur during deep sleep; theta waves are recorded from subcortical parts of the brain. Examples of these various rhythms as well as the positive spikes referred to in the text may be seen in Figure 9.2.

FIGURE **9.1**
Subject being prepared for an electroencephalogram. Electrodes are being pasted to the scalp so that minute amounts of electrical brain activity can be recorded by the sensitive instruments.

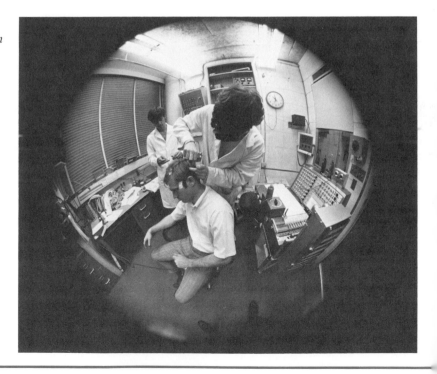

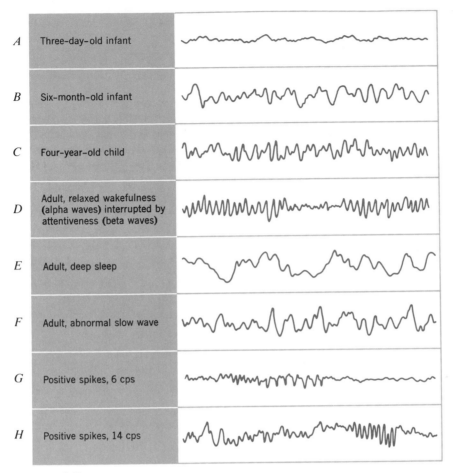

A	Three-day-old infant
B	Six-month-old infant
C	Four-year-old child
D	Adult, relaxed wakefulness (alpha waves) interrupted by attentiveness (beta waves)
E	Adult, deep sleep
F	Adult, abnormal slow wave
G	Positive spikes, 6 cps
H	Positive spikes, 14 cps

FIGURE **9.2**
Patterns of electrical activity in the brain recorded by the electroencephalograph. After Hare, 1970.

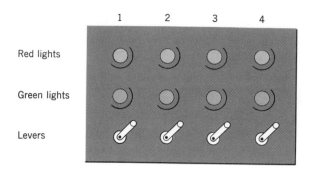

Red lights

Green lights

Levers

1 2 3 4

FIGURE **9.3**
*Schematic of the apparatus used by Lykken (1957)
in his study of avoidance learning in sociopaths.*

*For the first lever press assume that lever 3 is
correct, that is, that pressing it lights the green
bulb; that levers 1 and 4 are incorrect, lighting red
bulbs; and that pressing lever 2 lights a red bulb
and gives the subject a shock. For the second lever
press the meaning of the levers may change
entirely; for example, lever 2 may be correct, levers
3 and 4 incorrect, and lever 1 may give a shock.
The subjects had to learn a series of twenty
correct lever presses.*

Lykken (1957) deduced that the sociopath may have few inhibitions about committing antisocial acts because he suffers little anxiety. He performed several tests to determine whether sociopaths do indeed have low levels of anxiety. One of these tests involved avoidance learning.

A group of sociopaths, judged to be so on the basis of Cleckley's criteria, was selected from among a penitentiary population. Their performance on an avoidance learning task was compared to that of nonsociopathic penitentiary inmates[3] and of college students. It was of course critical that only avoidance learning and not learning mediated by other possible rewards be tested. If a subject perceives that his task is to learn to avoid pain, he may be motivated not only by the desire to avoid the pain but also by a desire to demonstrate his cleverness to the investigator. To ensure that no other motives would become manifest, Lykken made the avoidance learning task *incidental*. He used the following apparatus. On a panel in front of the subject there

were four red lights in a horizontal array, four green lights below each of the red ones, and a lever below each column, as illustrated in Figure 9.3. The subject's task was to learn a sequence of twenty correct lever presses, but for each he first had to determine by trial and error which of the four alternatives was correct. The correct lever turned on a green light. Two of the remaining three incorrect levers turned on red lights, indicating an error. The third incorrect lever delivered an electric shock to the subject. The location of the correct lever was of course not always the same. The subject was told simply to figure out and to learn the series of twenty correct lever presses. He was not informed that avoiding shock was desirable or possible, only that shock was randomly administered as a stimulant to make him do well. Thus the task yielded two measures of learning: the total number of errors made before the subject learned the correct sequence of twenty presses and the number of errors that produced shock. Avoidance learning is measured by this second index.

In terms of the overall number of errors made, there were no significant differences among any of the groups in Lykken's study.

[3] In the literature such people are sometimes referred to as neurotic sociopaths. We have avoided using this confusing term since, by definition, a sociopath is not neurotic.

The college students, however, were apparently best able to remember the sequence of presses that produced shock and thus sharply decreased their proportion of shocked errors. The sociopaths made the most shocked errors, but the differences between their shocked errors and those of the other penitentiary inmates only approached statistical significance. The results of Lykken's investigation therefore tentatively support the hypothesis that sociopaths operate under lower levels of anxiety than do normal individuals.

Lykken also tried to verify his reduced-anxiety hypothesis by giving his subjects standard psychological tests for measuring anxiety, such as the Taylor Manifest Anxiety Scale. On these tests the sociopaths did indeed show lower levels of anxiety. In addition, Lykken devised his own instrument, the Activity Preference Questionnaire, which presents subjects with a series of items, each involving a forced choice between two unpleasant events. One is unpleasant and has social relevance, such as having an accident in a borrowed car or spilling a glass of water in a restaurant. The other is merely distastful or tedious, such as cleaning up a bottle of syrup or draining and cleaning a cesspool. It was thought that, by virtue of their minimal anxiety in social situations, sociopaths would choose relatively more of the unpleasant but socially relevant incidents. Control subjects, on the other hand, were expected to choose more of those that were unpleasant but not socially so. Lykken's hypothesis again received clear support: sociopaths chose more of the socially unpleasant incidents than did the controls, indicating less sensitivity to social mores.

Lykken's pioneering work was subsequently followed up by Schachter and Latané (1964). These investigators reasoned that if sociopaths do not learn to avoid unpleasant stimuli because they have little anxiety, a procedure that increases their anxiety should remove their avoidance learning deficit. Inasmuch as anxiety is viewed as being related to activity of the sympathetic nervous system, they injected adrenalin, an agent whose effects mimic sympathetic activity, in order to increase anxiety.

Sociopathic and nonsociopathic prisoners from a penitentiary were studied with the same task and apparatus that had been devised by Lykken. This time each subject was tested twice. The subjects were led to believe that the effects of a hormone on learning were being investigated. Half received a placebo injection on the first day of testing and half an injection of Adrenalin. On the second day of testing the injections received by the subjects were reversed.

The results of Schachter and Latané's experiment were important in several ways. First, the overall number of errors replicated Lykken's results: no difference was found between the sociopathic and nonsociopathic prisoners in the total number of errors committed in learning the sequence, whether they had been injected with Adrenalin or the placebo. Second, the nonsociopathic prisoners injected with the placebo markedly reduced their proportion of shocked errors after a number or runs, but the sociopaths injected with the placebo showed no such improvement. In this part of the study the difference between the performances of the two groups of prisoners was greater than that revealed in Lykken's experiment and considerably larger than the amount necessary for statistical significance. Third, and most important, when injected with Adrenalin, the sociopaths showed a great reduction in the number of shocked errors, but the prisoners who were not sociopaths were adversely affected by the Adrenalin and did not learn to avoid the shock in their state of high arousal (Figure 9.4). Thus the hypothesis of the anxiety-free and underaroused sociopath

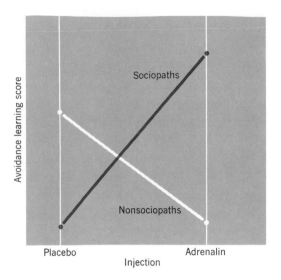

FIGURE **9.4**
Results of Schachter and Latané's (1964) study of the effects of Adrenalin on avoidance learning in sociopathic and nonsociopathic prisoners. Higher scores reflect better avoidance learning.

received considerable support from the work of Schachter and Latané.[4]

An avoidance learning study by Schmauk (1970) qualifies the findings of Lykken as well as those of Schachter and Latané by showing that a particular kind of punishment, losing money, *can* have an effect on sociopaths. His study involved three groups, sociopathic prisoners, nonsociopathic prisoners, and a control group consisting of farmworkers and hospital attendants. As in the previous two studies, an avoidance learning task was devised, but this time three different aversive stimuli could be avoided: a physical punishment — electric shock; a tangible punishment — losing a quarter from an initial pile of forty; and a social punishment — the experimenter's saying "wrong" to the subject. There were again no differences among the groups in the total number of errors made before the task had been mastered. The major finding of this study (Figure 9.5) indicated that the sociopath's performance varies with the nature of punishment. When the punishments confronting them were physical and social, the members of the control group were vastly superior to the sociopaths in learning to

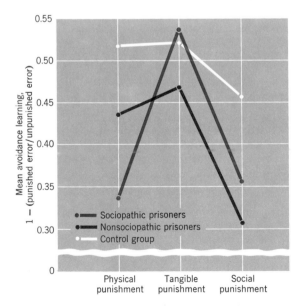

FIGURE **9.5**

Mean avoidance learning scores plotted for three subject groups confronted by three different punishments, physical, tangible, and social. After Schmauk, 1970.

[4] The finding that the Adrenalin injection apparently debilitated the avoidance learning performance of the nonsociopathic prisoners is difficult to interpret. A follow-up test by Schachter and Latané did not reproduce this effect.

avoid punishment. But the sociopaths outdid them in learning to avoid the tangible punishment of losing a quarter. The nonsociopathic prisoners did better than the sociopaths in learning to avoid physical punishment but less well in avoiding social punishment.

Sociopaths *can* learn to avoid punishment. The differences found between sociopaths and nonsociopaths in previous investigations may *not* reflect a general deficit in avoidance learning ability but rather the fact that some punishments have no meaning for the sociopath. Evidently, sociopaths will learn to avoid punishment that is relevant to their system of values, and money may very well be particularly important to them. According to this hypothesis, then, the sociopath differs from nonsociopaths in that he does not view *certain* consequences as negatively as others do.

Underarousal and Sociopathic Behavior

Sociopaths are often described as lacking the ability to respond emotionally when confronted by both familiar and new situations that most people would find either stressful or unpleasant. Cleckley (1964) has written about this aspect of their behavior.

Regularly, we find in him [the sociopath] extraordinary poise rather than jitteriness or worry, a smooth sense of physical well-being instead of uneasy preoccupations with bodily functions. Even under concrete circumstances that would for the ordinary person cause embarrassment, confusion, acute insecurity, or visible agitation, his relative serenity is likely to be noteworthy (p. 267).

This description is remarkably consistent with the Schachter and Latané finding that sociopaths do not ordinarily avoid electric shock but that they do so when their au-

tonomic arousal is increased by injections of Adrenalin. Because of the assumed central role of the autonomic nervous system in states of emotion, several investigators have examined sociopaths both for their resting levels of autonomic activity and for their patterns of autonomic reactivity to various classes of stimuli. Hare (1970) has summarized the results of many of these investigations.

During periods of relative quiescence [sociopathic] subjects tend to be hypoactive [less active than normal] on several indices of autonomic activity, including resting level of skin conductance and autonomic variability [spontaneous fluctuations in GSR and cardiac activity]. Although these findings must be interpreted with caution, they are at least consistent with most clinical statements about the psychopath's general lack of anxiety, guilt, and emotional "tension." The situation with respect to autonomic responsivity is more complex. Nevertheless, it appears that psychopaths may give relatively small electrodermal responses to "lie detection" [tests] and to situations that would ordinarily be considered stressful (p. 57).

The data showing such underarousal in the sociopath have additional implications. Quay (1965) has suggested that the sociopath's impulsiveness, his thirst for excitement, and his inability to tolerate routine and boredom are fostered by his state of lowered arousal. This reasoning is based on the hypothesis that there is an optimal level of arousal for human beings. When arousal is too high an individual will take steps to reduce it, and when it is too low he will take steps to increase it. Much of the sociopath's "thrill seeking" behavior could then be viewed as an attempt to increase his level of arousal enough to approach this optimal state.

If it is true that sociopaths seek excitement

to raise their arousal levels, we might expect their performance on a tedious and monotonous task to be especially poor. Orris (1967) has tested prisoners on such a task. The findings bore out the prediction. Sociopathic prisoners performed less well than did the others. We might also predict that given a choice, sociopaths will prefer novel and complex stimuli. Such stimuli are generally viewed as having high-arousal properties, and thus the sociopath might be expected to show a preference for them. Skrzypek (1969) tested this hypothesis on a sample of sociopathic and other prisoners and found that sociopaths indeed showed a somewhat greater preference for novelty and complexity than did the other prisoners.

The case histories, studies, and the theories that we have reviewed show the sociopath to be an individual who does not experience the same emotions that most of us do. The potential consequences of antisocial behavior do not elicit anxiety and therefore seem to have no deterrent effect. The sociopath seeks thrills without regard for society's rules. Often, of course, such individuals come into contact with the law and the courts. At that time the issue of legal responsibility for their acts is raised. In the following section we shall examine the complex question of legal responsibility and psychiatric disorders, which include but are not restricted to sociopathy.

MENTAL ABNORMALITY AND LEGAL RESPONSIBILITY

For more than a hundred years judges and lawyers have called on psychiatrists and psychologists for assistance in dealing with criminal acts thought to have been committed when the accused was suffering extreme emotional upset or anguish. Are such emotionally disturbed perpetrators less criminally responsible than those who are not distraught but commit the same crimes? Should an individual who fails to appreciate the immorality of his behavior or who, like the sociopath, appears unresponsive to the threat of punishment be prosecuted in court for a transgression against society's laws? Although the efforts made to elicit professional opinions on these issues were undoubtedly well intentioned, injustices are still wreaked on those whose emotional states and mental capacities have created doubts about their legal responsibility for their acts.

It will be recalled from our historical review in Chapter 1 that those whose disordered behavior was explained as possession by the devil were seldom treated humanely. In fact, during the sixteenth and seventeenth centuries people whose behavior threatened society or was difficult to fathom—although they may have committed no crimes—were hunted as witches, tortured, and killed. Some have argued that allegations of possession by the devil were made by those in power to justify sanctions quite outside the existing legal system. Almost as early as the concept of a *mens rea* or guilty mind and the rule "No crime without an evil intent" had begun to be accepted in English common law, insanity had to be taken into consideration, for a disordered mind may be regarded as unable to formulate and carry out a criminal purpose. At first insanity was not a trial defense, but the English crown sometimes granted pardons to people who had been convicted of homicide if they were judged completely and totally mad (Morris, 1968). By the reign of Edward I (1272–1307) the concept of insanity had begun to be argued in court and

SOCIAL DEVIATION

could lessen punishment. During the rest of the fourteenth century it became the rule of law that a person proved to be wholly and continually mad could be defended against a criminal charge. But the unfortunates convicted as witches two and three centuries later could not offer this defense, for according to religious dogma they had made a voluntary and purposeful pact in delivering themselves to the devil.

After the religious dogma about witchcraft had lost its hold, treatment of those regarded as mentally deranged might have been expected to improve as mental illness became the province of medicine and as the insanity plea became better established in the courts. But this did not always happen. We have already seen in Chapter 1 how deplorable were the early asylums. Many of the individuals retained in mental hospitals were placed there for committing antisocial acts. The continuing problems of these hospitals in both the nineteenth and the twentieth centuries (Figure 9.6) can be looked to as evidence that not being held responsible for antisocial behavior has seldom assured the individual of humane treatment by society.

Landmark Decisions on Legal Responsibility

Historically, in modern Anglo-American criminal law, there have been three important court rulings that bear on the problems of legal responsibility and mental illness. The so-called "irresistible impulse" concept was formulated during an Ohio case in 1834, wherein it was decided that an insanity defense was legitimate if a pathological impulse or drive that the person could not control had compelled him to commit the criminal act. The second well-known concept, the McNaghten rule, was announced in the aftermath of a murder trial in England in 1843. Daniel McNaghten had mistaken the secretary of Sir Robert Peel for his employer, the British prime minister, whom McNaghten had been instructed to kill by the "voice of God." The judges of England ruled that " . . . to establish a defence of insanity, it must be clearly proved that, at the time of the committing of the act, the party accused was labouring under such a defect of reason, from disease of the mind, as not to know the nature and quality of the act he was doing; or if he did know it, that he did not know he was doing what was wrong." This "right-wrong" concept has been applied in the United States for many years. It is currently the most prevalent ruling. The third decision, made in the 1954 case of *Durham* v. *United States,* says that the "accused is not criminally responsible if his unlawful act was the product of mental disease or mental defect." David Bazelon, the presiding justice, believed that by referring simply to mental illness the profession of psychiatry would be free to apply its full knowledge, unbound by decisions about impulses or knowledge of right and wrong. The Durham test, as it is known, does not incorporate any particular symptoms of mental disorder that may later become obsolete. The psychiatrist is accorded great liberty to convey to the court his own evaluation of the accused's mental condition. We shall see shortly some of the tremendous difficulties that this renowned Durham ruling has introduced into criminal law.

In 1962 the American Law Institute (ALI) proposed its own guidelines which were intended to be more specific and informative to lay jurors than the "mental disease or mental defect" of the Durham test.

1. A person is not responsible for criminal conduct if at the time of such conduct as a result of mental disease or defect he lacks sub-

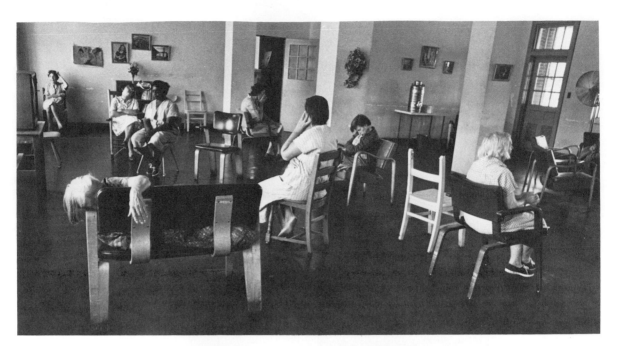

FIGURE **9.6**
Portrayed here are common scenes in mental hospitals. Some of the more progressive institutions offer more stimulating environments, but the grim barrenness pictured in these photographs prevails in far too many of these so-called asylums.

stantial capacity either to appreciate the criminality (wrongfulness) of his conduct or to conform his conduct to the requirements of law.
2. As used in the Article, the terms "mental disease or defect" do not include an abnormality manifested only by repeated criminal or otherwise antisocial conduct (The American Law Institute, 1962, p. 66).

The first of the ALI guidelines combines the McNaghten rule and the irresistible-impulse concept. The second concerns those who are repeatedly in trouble with the law: they are not to be deemed mentally ill only because they keep committing crimes. The American Law Institute had thus countered the vagueness of the Durham decision, which relied solely on psychiatric judgment concerning the presence of mental disease, without specifying the role that the presumed mental disability played in the person's criminal behavior. For an individual can, indeed, be diagnosed as mentally ill and still appreciate the consequences of his behavior and have significant control over himself.

Many issues are raised by the insanity defense as men attempt to apply abstract principles to specific life situations. As in all aspects of the law, terms can be defined in a number of ways—by defendants, defense lawyers, prosecutors, judges, and, of course, jurors—and testimony can be presented in diverse fashion, depending on the skill of the interrogators and the intelligence of the witnesses.

To take but one example, Goldstein (1967), a law professor, has pointed out that in actual practice the McNaghten rule has not always tied the hands of psychiatrists by restricting their expert testimony to the issue of whether the defendant knew right from wrong at the time he committed the crime. Goldstein has cited numerous cases in which psychiatrists and attorneys *interpreted* the McNaghten

ruling in a way that allowed more general statements to be made about mental illness—a practice that most textbooks tell us was permitted only after the Durham decision. For instance, a trial judge in Wisconsin, where the McNaghten right-wrong principle was operative, ruled that expert testimony offered to show that the defendant could not control his behavior was inadmissible as evidence. The judge stated that such evidence was relevant only to proving "irresistible impulse." The supreme court of Wisconsin overturned this ruling, however, arguing that evidence bearing on the defendant's inability to control himself should have been admitted: "Even under the right-wrong test, no evidence should be excluded which reasonably tends to show the mental condition of the defendant at the time of the offense" (Goldstein, 1967, p. 55).

A final point should be stressed. Only the defendant's mental condition *at the time the crime was committed* is in question. Obviously retrospective, often speculative, judgment on the part of psychiatrists, attorneys, judges, and jurors is required.

Case Example

To illustrate the problems that may be raised by an insanity plea, let us consider the case of Charles Rouse, as reported in a *New Republic* article by James Ridgeway (1967). Rouse, a twenty-year old resident of Washington, D.C., was arrested one night while carrying a suitcase containing a .45 Colt automatic pistol, ammunition, two electric drills, and some razor blades. The maximum penalty for carrying such lethal weapons in the District of Columbia is one year, yet Rouse was confined much, much longer. How did this happen?

The Durham decision of 1954 applies in the District of Columbia. During his trial Rouse was examined by court psychiatrists and judged to be suffering from "antisocial reaction," sufficient grounds to be acquitted by reason of insanity according to the Durham test. Rouse received such an acquittal. But this "acquittal" did not lead to freedom. Rather, he was incarcerated in a federal mental hospital, St. Elizabeth's, in Washington, for psychotherapeutic treatment of his personality disorder. As of 1967 Rouse had been there for over four years, three years *longer* than he would have been confined had no issues been raised about his sanity.[5]

Those who favor close liaison between mental health workers and the courts argue that it would have been unjust to Rouse to hold him legally responsible for his misdemeanor, and that the most charitable and effective course of action—both for him and for society at large—was to treat the mental disorder that presumably caused the arrest in the first place. But how therapeutic was Rouse's forced hospitalization? After two years of confinement in St. Elizabeth's, Rouse had his attorney file a writ of habeas corpus, a procedure that an incarcerated person can institute in order to get a court hearing to decide whether continued detainment is justified. At this hearing Dr. E., Rouse's psychiatrist in the hospital, was asked to report on Rouse's behavior. The doctor cited examples of what he regarded to be "poor judgment": Rouse had refused to accept an invitation to leave maximum security and to move to less constricted areas of the prison hospital, preferring instead to seek relief through the litigation that had resulted in the court hearing. He had also left group therapy in a "cavalier manner," evidence, Dr. E. said, of lack of insight and poor judgment and of the continuing mental illness that had been the basis of his acquittal two years earlier.

[5] We might question the advisability of Rouse's opting for an insanity plea, for the maximum penalty for his crime, as stated above, was only one year.

The doctor also mentioned additional examples of what he considered to be diseased behavior, such as Rouse's reluctance to become involved with the other patients. "And because he does not get together with people I conclude that he is antisocial, antisocial since he cannot tolerate the anxiety that comes with having relationships with people" (p. 25). Dr. E. recommended to the judge that Rouse not be released yet, for "In my opinion if Mr. Rouse were placed at liberty at the present time it would be a precipitous thing to do and he would be dangerous to himself and to other people by virtue of his mental illness. I think he needs supervision over the long haul" (p. 25). Indeed Dr. E. stated further that, if released, Mr. Rouse would be likely to obtain guns and ammunition and to shoot someone.

In his defense, Rouse's attorney produced testimony by another psychiatrist who felt that further hospitalization would be *detrimental* and that Rouse should therefore be discharged. The judge, however, agreed with Dr. E., saying that Rouse had not taken advantage of the help available at St. Elizabeth's and that therefore he was not ready for release. The case was carried to various higher courts, with Dr. E. reasserting his earlier testimony and judgment that Rouse was still suffering from an antisocial reaction.

A number of general problems are highlighted by this case.

1. The judgment of psychiatrists plays a crucial role in how long a person remains in a mental hospital for treatment of a problem that is said to have caused a criminal act. But psychiatrists frequently *disagree* about the presence of the problem.
2. The hospital psychiatrist may interpret as evidence of continued mental illness any efforts made by the patient to escape from the hospital environment, even if by legal

means. In fact, *almost anything* the person does *can* be construed as symptomatic of the presumed illness.

3. Unorthodox behavior, particularly if it breaks a law, can be regarded as evidence of a dangerous mental disorder and can thereby remove the individual from the direct jurisdiction of the courts, deprive him of his civil rights, and even cause him to be incarcerated for longer periods of time than he would have served had he been convicted and sentenced for the unlawful act.

Rouse's case is, of course, only one among many that could be discussed, and few others show forensic psychiatry[6] in as unfavorable a light. The record is bad enough, however, that many persons advocate reducing the role played by mental health professionals in the legal process. Before looking into this problem more closely, we should consider the initial judgment confronting the forensic psychiatrist, deciding whether a person accused of a crime is mentally competent to stand trial at all.

Competency To Stand Trial

In addition to testifying in court on the mental state of the accused person at the time the crime was committed, psychiatrists are called upon to help judges decide whether a person is mentally capable of standing trial at all. Neither of the two best-known rulings—Mc-Naghten and Durham—deal with competency to stand trial. Over the years, however, most jurisdictions in this country have shown concern that the accused may be "presently insane or otherwise so mentally incompetent as to be unable to understand the proceedings against him or properly to assist in his own

[6] This term refers to the activities of psychiatrists concerned with legal responsibility and criminal commitment.

defense" (Pfeiffer, Eisenstein, and Dabbs, 1967, p. 322). Another way to state this problem of competency is to say that the courts do not want a person to be brought to trial *in absentia*. Literally, of course, a disturbed person can be physically present; what is referred to here is his mental state. If a person is deemed too mentally ill to participate meaningfully in a trial, the trial is routinely delayed. Indeed, and this is perhaps the most alarming prospect, it is possible for the trial to be delayed indefinitely. The person, who is incarcerated in the meantime with the hope that means of restoring adequate mental functioning can be found, may not for some time be judged by psychologists or psychiatrists to be competent to stand trial. Sometimes the charges are dismissed, but sometimes they are held in abeyance for months, even years, while the court waits for the mental state of the accused to improve. A dramatic example is the case of George Metesky, the "mad-bomber" who terrorized New York City in the mid-1950s. He was accused of manufacturing bombs and placing them in public places such as telephone booths and movie theaters. He was judged insane and incompetent to stand trial and committed to a mental hospital in 1957. As of 1973 he has remained there for fifteen years without a trial (*Newsday*, February 27, 1973).

A person can be judged competent to stand trial and yet be judged mentally ill nonetheless (Pfeiffer et al., 1967) and subsequently acquitted. That is, whether an accused person is "acquitted by reason of insanity" does not depend on whether he has been judged competent to stand trial in the first place. Indeed, how could an acquittal occur without the person's standing trial? Clearly, different criteria are applied in deciding whether a person would be *in absentia* during a trial.

Robey (1965) attempted to enumerate specific guidelines for deciding, on psychiatric grounds, whether an accused person is competent to stand trial. The basic principle, already mentioned—that no one can be tried *in absentia*—is taken from English common law. Robey points out that many psychiatrists, when asked to render a competency judgment, assume that if they judge the person to be mentally disturbed in any way, it follows that he cannot stand trial; thus many people have been deprived of their day in court. Even a psychotic person, however, may sufficiently understand his position in the legal proceedings to be able to talk with his attorney rationally. Robey's guidelines specify that a person may come to trial even though he may behave in bizarre ways before and during the proceedings. To be sure, the accused is at a severe disadvantage if, during the trial, he is confused, deluded, hallucinating, and so on. But even a severe emotional disorder may not prevent him from participating in court proceedings. A somewhat inequitable trial may be preferable to being incarcerated until behavior is judged by prison hospital psychiatrists to be normal once again. It should be kept in mind that many of the people we are talking about are proved, once they are brought to trial, *not* to have committed the crime of which they were accused.

FIGURE **9.7**
Thomas S. Szasz, for years an outspoken critic of involuntary mental hospitalization. He has argued that psychiatrists should stop playing a central role in court proceedings.

Thomas S. Szasz and the Case Against Forensic Psychiatry

"By codifying acts of violence as expressions of mental illness, we neatly rid ourselves of the task of dealing with criminal offenses as more or less rational, goal-directed acts, no different in principle from other forms of conduct" (Szasz, 1963, p. 141).

This quotation from one of Szasz's most widely read books enunciates the basic theme of his polemic against the weighty role that his own profession of psychiatry plays in the legal system. To understand the view of this outspoken and eloquent critic of forensic psychiatry (Figure 9.7), it is important, first of all, to understand the distinction between *descriptive* and *ascriptive* responsibility. As Szasz points out, a person may be judged descriptively responsible in the sense that all agree a particular act was, in fact, performed by him. Ascriptive responsibility, however, is a social judgment about consequences society will inflict upon someone deemed descriptively responsible. The court verdict of "not guilty by reason of insanity" says, first, that John Doe was descriptively responsible for committing a crime, but second, that society will not ascribe legal responsibility to him and punish him for what he did. Killing in wartime is another example of this divergence between descriptive and ascriptive responsibilities. To murder the enemy as a member of a nation's armed forces is to be responsible for another person's death. Yet the soldier is not punished for his action and indeed may win honors for it.

To hold a person criminally responsible is to ascribe or attribute legal responsibility to him. A given social group makes the judgment that the person who is descriptively responsible for a criminal act will receive criminal punishment. As Szasz points out, criminal responsibility is not a trait that is inherent in a person and that society uncovers. Rather society at a given time and for a given criminal act decides that it will hold the perpetrator legally responsible and punish him.

Szasz goes on to suggest that psychiatry's role in the criminal courts began when people acted in a way that was considered particularly irrational and threatening to society. According to Szasz, these exceptional cases all involved violence against people of high social rank. For shooting at a Lord Onslow in 1724, a man named Arnold was believed to have as little understanding of his murderous act as "a wild beast." Another man, James Hadfield, was deemed deranged for attempting to assassinate King George III in 1800 as he sat in a box at the Theatre Royal. And a third, Oxford by name, was regarded as insane for trying to kill Queen Victoria in 1840. The best-known case has already been mentioned, that of Daniel McNaghten (1843), who killed Sir Robert Peel's private secretary after mistaking him for Peel. In all these cases from English law, which form the basis for modern insanity defenses,

people of low social rank openly attacked their superiors. Szasz believes that " . . . the issue of insanity may have been raised in these trials in order to obscure the social problems which the crimes intended to dramatize" (1963, p. 128).

A few recent cases here and abroad, such as the assassinations of John and Robert Kennedy and of the South African prime minister Hendrik Verwoerd, may to a degree reflect the social ills of today. Moreover, court proceedings in the Soviet Union are ominous. In *A Question of Madness*, the well-known Russian biochemist Zhores Medvedev (1972) tells how Soviet psychiatrists collaborated with the state in attempting to muzzle his criticism of his government. They diagnosed him as suffering from paranoid delusions, split personality, and other mental ailments that would make it dangerous for him to be at large in society. But pleas of insanity are made in far more ordinary cases. And of course Szasz does not claim that all the pleas in these many cases involve some sort of silent conspiracy of the establishment to cover up social ills. Szasz sets forth a polemic much broader in scope. His more basic concern is with individual freedom, which includes the right to be *deviant* from prevailing mores. Far from advocating that people be held *less* accountable for antisocial acts, he argues that legal responsibility be extended to *all,* even to those whose actions are so far beyond the limits of convention that some people are inclined to explain their behavior in terms of mental illness.

Szasz's villain is what he calls "psychoauthoritarianism." He traces all contemporary thought on the matter to Alexander and Staub (1929), who argued that the usual legal proceedings may be appropriate for "normal criminals," but that psychoanalysis should form the basis for the handling of "neurotic" criminals. They presented their position in a forthright manner.

We propose a more consistent application of the principle that not the deed but the doer should be punished. . . . The implementation of this principle requires expert diagnostic judgment which can be expected only from specially trained psychiatric experts. Before any sentence is imposed, a medical-legal diagnosis should be required. This would amount to an official recognition of unconscious motivations in all human behavior. The neurotic criminal obviously has a limited sense of responsibility. Primarily he is a sick person, and his delinquency is the outcome of his emotional disturbances. This fact, however, should not exempt him from the consequences of his action. If he is curable, he should be incarcerated for the duration of psychiatric treatment as long as he still represents a menace to society. If he is incurable, he belongs in a hospital for incurables for life (p. xiii).

These are strong statements. Some have criticized Szasz for erecting a straw man, the assumption being that nowadays no one really believes the Alexander and Staub position to be well founded. In all likelihood, however, this view still prevails, both in this country and elsewhere, to an extent that we cannot be complacent about its effects.

Of the many problems presented by the Alexander and Staub argument, Szasz suggests that the following are especially important.

1. Our legal system is based on the premise that deeds are punishable, not doers. People are supposed to be brought to trial for what they are accused of doing, not for the kind of people they are. Certain inequities, such as the generally inadequate legal assistance available to the poor, may make a person's financial means a factor. But clearly the direction of our legal system is not that advocated by Alexander and Staub.

2. Whether "expert diagnostic judgment" can

be reliably executed is something we examined in Chapter 3. Reliabilities of diagnoses were found to be adequate if psychiatrists do not have to make fine distinctions, but even so the degree of accuracy is not reassuring. Disputes in legal proceedings in which insanity is an issue are common; the prosecution and the defense routinely produce "expert" witnesses whose positions are diametrically opposed.

3. In view of the criticisms that have been made of Freud, a proposal for the "official recognition of unconscious motivations in all human behavior" seems an anachronism. To base such important social judgments on a poorly tested theory appears almost foolhardy. It should be mentioned in passing that Freud himself recommended that psychological opinions *not* play a role in court.

4. It is *at least* open to question whether enforced psychotherapy can ever be meaningful and effective. Rouse's case is a good example of the undue power that a prison psychiatrist can have over a criminal entrusted to him for "treatment," and of the trouble that the patient can get into if he refuses or resists psychotherapy.

Judge Bazelon, author of the Durham decision, is another target for Szasz's criticisms. Szasz accuses the judge of being naive about the quality of treatment available in mental hospitals, especially those reserved for criminals. He further castigates Bazelon for the fact that far too much power is placed in the hands of hospital psychiatrists. When the Durham test is applied, hospital psychiatrists are largely responsible for deciding when the individual is ready to be discharged. Finally, Szasz laments the impetus given by the Durham decision to a general denigration of the defendant: "Instead of recognizing the deviant as an individual different from those who would judge him, but nonetheless worthy of their respect, he is first discredited as a self-responsible human being and then subjected to humiliating punishment defined and disguised as treatment" (1963, p. 108).

Szasz's zeal to improve the lot of many patients committed on both civil and criminal grounds[7] led him to make a series of proposals that appear less and less radical as the years go by and as elements of his thinking slowly become policy. His proposals encompass both long-term and short-term goals.

Long-Range Goals

1. **Abolition of involuntary hospitalization.** In 1971 Szasz founded an organization to agitate for the abolition of involuntary detainment in mental hospitals. He acknowledges that psychiatric emergencies do sometimes arise, such as when a person becomes violent or stuporous, but he urges that a patient's stay in an institution be kept as short as possible and that, at any rate, he not be forced to take treatment once the emergency passes.

---

[7] A distinction must be drawn between criminal and civil commitment. We have been examining criminal commitment, whereby people accused of illegal behavior may be hospitalized against their will. It is possible, however, to be in no legal trouble at all and still be incarcerated against one's will. Each state has civil commitment laws, according to which physicians, sometimes at the request of the family, can certify that an individual is mentally ill, perhaps a danger to himself or to others, and hospitalize him for varying periods of time—even if the person insists that he wishes to remain free. There have been widespread abuses in civil commitment, although there seems to be a trend in the direction of *limiting* the power of mental hospitals to detain people against their will. Nonetheless, it is still possible to be forced into the sometime nightmare of a mental hospital stay if a sufficient number, one or two, of society's mental health gatekeepers certify that the person is mentally ill. The problem has been the subject of more than one engrossing piece of fiction, for example, Ken Kesey's *One Flew Over the Cuckoo's Nest.*

2. **Retention of civil rights.** When hospitalized, the patient should not lose his rights as a citizen. In most states committed patients, whether their internment is civil or criminal, lose voting rights, the right to own property, and other civil rights. As others have pointed out (for example, Goffman, 1961), the withdrawal of ordinary responsibilities and rights seems to contribute to and even create additional psychological problems for committed mental patients.

3. **Abolishment of the insanity plea.** Only extreme conditions that can be judged by *lay* people, such as the patient's being a raving maniac, should delay a trial. Psychiatrists should have nothing to do with deciding the ascriptive responsibility for an offense. Convicted criminals should be sentenced whether or not psychiatrists believe them to be insane. Although inequities would clearly develop, Szasz believes that they would be no worse than those that already exist. For example, under any circumstances a highly intelligent person can assist much better in his defense than someone of lesser intelligence. In jail, a convicted person could still be *offered* mental health services, but they would be accepted only voluntarily and would have no bearing on the length of sentence.

Short-Range Goals

The basic aim of Szasz's short-term goals is to improve the bargaining power of mental patients until the long-range goals are achieved.

1. Since involuntary hospitalization does exist, we should at least acknowledge openly that the relationship between committed patients, especially those criminally committed, and their hospital psychiatrists is of necessity an antagonistic one. Szasz asserts

that it is highly unlikely that the psychiatrist can really be on the side of the committed patient. Among other reasons, a psychiatrist cannot guarantee confidentiality since his overriding allegiance is to the state or federal hospital system.

2. Watchdog agencies should be created to protect the rights of mental patients. Such groups have, in fact, been formed in several states. A number of patients are being helped to shorten their involuntary hospitalization by committees of concerned social workers, lawyers, and other civil-rights-minded professionals (see Box 9.2).

3. People should be educated about the dangers of being confined in any kind of mental institution. Although fewer hospitals these days resemble the "snake pits" of the nineteenth century, conditions in many state asylums are still depressing. Moreover, given the stigma that is still unfortunately attached to being a "former mental patient," confinement can be detrimental to the individual's future. The diagnosis each patient receives on admission has an unfortunate way of being applied to him for years afterward.

Evaluation

As might be expected, Szasz has been answered by many whom he has criticized and by others who sincerely believe that psychiatry, because of its expertise, should have an important role in deciding how to deal with people whose criminal acts seem so bizarre that they must be attributable to mental illness. When society acts with great certainty on the basis of "expert scientific opinion," however, particularly when that opinion denies to an individual the rights and respect accorded others in his society, it may be well to let Szasz remind us that Sir Thomas Browne, a distinguished British surgeon, in 1665 testified in a court of law that witches did indeed exist, "as everyone knew."

The abuses documented by Szasz should not blind us to the fact that—for whatever combination of physiological and psychological reasons—some people are, at times, a danger to others and to themselves. Although Szasz and others object to the mental-illness metaphor as an explanatory device, it is difficult to deny that there is, indeed, madness in the world. People *do* occasionally imagine persecutors, whom they sometimes act against with force. Some people *do* hallucinate and on this basis may behave in a dangerous fashion. Our concern for the liberties of one individual has always been tempered with our concern for the rights of others.

But does it help a criminal acquitted by reason of insanity to place him in a prison mental hospital with an indeterminate sentence, pending his rehabilitation? The answer can surely not be an unqualified yes. Should such a person, then, be treated like any other convicted felon and be sent to a penitentiary? Considering the psychic damage that we know may occur in ordinary prisons, a yes to this question cannot be overly enthusiastic. But a prison sentence is a finite term of incarceration. If we cannot demonstrate that enforced rehabilitation in hospitals is effective, perhaps it is just as well to rely on our prisons and on efforts of penologists and behavioral scientists to improve these institutions and to assist the inmates in making changes that can prevent recurrence of their antisocial behavior after release.

The *Wyatt* v. *Stickney* "right-to-treatment" decision made in 1972 by an Alabama federal court concerns the rights of the civilly committed mental patients. The court ruled that the only justification for the civil commitment of patients to a state mental hospital is treat-

BOX **9.2** *Recent Trends*

In addition to the watchdog committees already operating in a few states, other changes that point in the direction advocated by Szasz and others are discernible. The following is a short article reprinted from a 1968 issue of the *New York Times,* documenting a New Jersey Supreme Court ruling that a person accused of a crime cannot be forced to submit to a psychiatric examination. Up to that time in New Jersey, and even now in most states, many defendants, particularly those accused of murder, could be forced into an examination to determine their mental status if the prosecution asked for one.

CURBS ON THE PSYCHIATRIST IN COURT

WASHINGTON — One of the remarkable legal developments of recent years, a growing estrangement between law and psychiatry, produced a new right for defendants last week — the right not to be examined by a psychiatrist.

Until the past five years or so it had been considered a mark of legal enlightenment that the professional judgments of psychiatrists played so crucial a part in the criminal process.

While most issues of fact in criminal trials have been entrusted only to juries, psychiatrists were permitted to give juries their conclusion as to two central questions: whether the defendant was too deranged to stand trial, and whether he was so insane at the time of the crime that he could not be held responsible for it.

All but a handful of the states had laws permitting prosecutors to subject defendants to mental examinations before trial. Furthermore, the Supreme Court ruled in a 1966 case, *Pate* v. *Robinson,* that the Constitution requires judges to order mental examinations whenever a defendant's demeanor indicates he might be incompetent to stand trial.

The motives for these exceptions to criminal responsibility were humanitarian ones. It was felt that such individuals should be treated, not convicted.

In practice, this theory appears to have two flaws. First, some psychiatrists have been too quick to find people insane, since the "treatment" in asylums for the criminally insane has seldom been likely to make them rapidly well. Second, defendants have been known to bare their souls to the state's psychiatrists, only to have the doctors repeat their admissions in court.

The average ward patient in a public asylum sees a doctor for only about 15 minutes each month and defense lawyers have gradually come to realize that their clients may be locked up for much longer in a mental hospital, and under worse conditions, than if they were convicted. One case turned up recently where a defendant had been held 14 years before trial. Another defendant spent 34 years in an asylum before he was considered competent to stand trial.

Last December the Court of Appeals for the District of Columbia issued an order that psychiatrists would no longer be permitted merely to confront juries with their conclusion that defendants suffered from such conditions as "schizoid personality," "psychopathy" and "passive-aggressive personality." Instead, the doctors must relate in detail what the defendants are likely to think and do, and leave to the juries to decide if they are sufficiently deranged to escape conviction.

Last week the Supreme Court of New Jersey took another major step when it ruled that a defendant could not be forced to submit to psychiatric examination unless he wishes to plead insanity.

In the case of a man accused of murder, the lower court judge had followed the usual procedure and ordered a psychiatric examination when the prosecutor asked for one. The defendant, Daniel Obstein of Milburn, protested that he had no intention of pleading insanity. His objection was not that he might be locked up for years as a lunatic but that the psychiatrist would ask him questions about the alleged crime, and might well become the key witness against him in court. The Supreme Court of New Jersey unanimously agreed that a forced psychiatric examination might violate Obstein's privilege against self-incrimination.

Alan M. Dershowitz, a Harvard law professor who has warned that psychiatry has become "a knife that cuts both ways" in the law, applauded the ruling but said even more protection is needed. He asserted that courts must also consider how the privilege against self-incrimination protects defendants from being forced to give evidence that can be used to put them away for years under civil commitments.

Basically, he argued, a defendant should never be required to see a psychiatrist because the prosecutor considers the defendant incompetent to stand trial. No matter how odd the defendant's conduct appears to the prosecutor, the trial should begin, the defendant should not be turned over to the mental doctors unless the trial judge perceives that he is not able to participate in his own defense.

"I don't think prosecutors should act as if they have the best interests of the defendant in mind," Dershowitz said. "They should leave that to the defense attorney."   —*Fred P. Graham* ment. Although the restoration of the patient to mental health has in a theoretical sense always been the goal of commitment, we realize how seldom this objective is achieved. Such organizations as the American Civil Liberties Union, the American Psychological Association, and the American Orthopsychiatric Association used their influence to bring the *Wyatt* v. *Stickney* case to court. Through their efforts it was decided that state mental hospitals in Alabama must ensure the following.

That "No person shall be deemed incompetent to manage his affairs . . . solely by reason of his admission to commitment to the hospital";

That involuntary commitment be more restricted;

That individualized and more extensive treatment programs be instituted;

That staff-patient relations be improved;

That patients not be forced into hazardous treatments like lobotomy and electroconvulsive shock;

That suitable educational opportunities be afforded regardless of psychiatric diagnosis.

The individual and civil rights of those committed to mental hospitals, so long and well pleaded for by Szasz and others, do appear on their way to being both acknowledged and preserved.

SUMMARY

This chapter has dealt with two ways in which psychopathologists have influenced legal conceptions of criminal behavior. The psychiatric diagnosis of the sociopath describes him as an individual who habitually engages in antisocial behavior without showing shame or regret. One mechanism that may underlie such behavior is an inability to learn to avoid punishment. This problem may have both psychological and physiological correlates—exposure to deviant parental models and inconsistent disciplinary practices, and underarousal of the autonomic nervous system.

Sociopaths as well as others who have been diagnosed by psychopathologists as suffering from psychiatric disorders have frequently been freed of legal responsibility for criminal behavior, only to be incarcerated for extended—often indefinite—periods of time in prison hospitals. Questions have been raised about the justice of such practices, particularly when patients have not received effective treatment under such coercive conditions. The right to a speedy trial has also been denied on the grounds that a mental disease precludes adequate comprehension and thus renders the accused incompetent to stand trial. The writings of Thomas Szasz and others have stimulated doubts about the wisdom and justification for removing legal responsibilities from those whose behavior is unconventional or difficult to comprehend.

CHAPTER 10

Drug Addiction and Drug Dependence

From prehistoric times man has used various substances in the hope of reducing physical pain or altering his state of consciousness. Almost all peoples have discovered some intoxicant that affects the central nervous system, relieving physical and mental anguish or producing euphoria. Whatever the aftermath of taking such substances into the body, their effects are usually ameliorating or pleasing, at least initially.

Alcoholic beverages from the fermentation of many fruits and grains, of milk, honey, and molasses, and even of tree sap; opium, the dried milky juice obtained from the immature fruit of the opium poppy; hashish and marihuana from *Cannabis,* the hemp plant; and cocaine, an alkaloid extracted from coca leaves—these are the major natural drugs that have a long history of both use and abuse, and that continue today to present problems for society. In the United States and other Western countries, morphine, an alkaloid extracted from opium, and heroin, derived from morphine, are more prevalent than the raw opium, and dried marihuana is used more often than hashish. Also available are a number of newer synthetic drugs, most importantly the barbiturates, the amphetamines, and LSD. Of all the potentially dangerous drugs, the one craved by the greatest number of people is nicotine, the principal alkaloid of tobacco. Alkaloids are organic substances that are found for the most part in seed plants, usually not singly but as mixtures of similar alkaloids. They are the active agents that give a number of natural drugs their medicinal and also their toxic properties.

The current diagnostic system, DSM-II, classifies drug dependence and addiction with personality disorders and designates them more generally as nonpsychotic mental disorders. This categorization suggests that the excessive use of alcohol and other drugs is a manifestation of underlying personality disturbances. Alcoholism is divided into several subcategories. The individual who becomes intoxicated as frequently as four times per year is considered by DSM-II to be an episodic excessive drinker. Twelve or more intoxications per year constitute habitual excessive drinking. If the individual is unable to go for more than one day without drinking or if he has been drinking heavily and continually for at least three months, he is considered an alcohol addict. Such a definition of alcoholism is very broad; tens of millions would be classified as alcoholics if it were employed.

Drug dependence is defined as the habitual use of a drug, frequently out of a perceived sense of need. The term dependence is sometimes used interchangably with addiction, but there seem to be important distinctions between the two.

Addiction is a physiological process by which the body responds to certain drugs. When addicting drugs are ingested for prolonged periods of time, greater and greater amounts of them are *tolerated*. The bodily systems habituate to the particular chemical so that larger and larger doses are necessary to maintain similar intoxicating effects. Then when the frequency of ingestion or the amount of the drug is suddenly decreased, the bodily systems suffer *withdrawal reactions*. The prolonged use of the drug has so altered the physiological conditions of the body that it is disturbed when the drug is not administered. For example, when an addict suddenly ceases to take morphine, he usually suffers from hypertension and cramps, is restless, and sweats profusely.

But not all drugs, even if they are taken regularly, bring on either tolerance or the later withdrawal reactions when their use is terminated. For this reason the concept of *psychological dependency* was proposed to describe reliance on drugs that are *not* addicting. A drug may be taken because its effects make stressful or anxiety-provoking situations more bearable. But the dosage of the drug does not have to be continually increased to produce these effects, nor is there a withdrawal reaction if the drug is not taken. This is not to say that the individual with a psychological dependence on a drug feels no unpleasant effects when the drug is not available. If a person is deprived of *anything* that he has come to rely on, he is likely to react negatively to its absence by becoming restless, nervous, or otherwise upset. These reactions sometimes resemble the withdrawal symptoms obtained with addictive drugs, but they should not be regarded as such *unless* there is also evidence of tolerance.

ALCOHOLISM

Written reports of the use of wines, beers and other alcoholic beverages date back to 3000 B.C. (Figure 10.1), but not until about 800 B.C. was the distillation process applied to fermented beverages, making possible the manufacture of the highly potent liquors that are available today. It has been estimated that in the United States about 80 million people consume alcohol and about 5 million are judged alcoholic according to some definitions (Chafetz, 1967). Although most of the people who have a drinking problem do not seek professional help, alcoholics do constitute a large proportion of new admissions to mental and general hospitals. Moreover, some estimate that they account for 25,000 highway deaths each year. Alcohol also presents law enforcement problems, for 31 percent of all arrests in

FIGURE **10.1**
Winemaking has been a venerable institution for thousands of years, as illustrated in this Egyptian painting.

the United States are for public drunkeness. Homicide is an alcohol-related crime; and parental child abuse and suicide are also frequently associated with excessive drinking (Brecher, 1972). The World Health Organization has defined alcoholics as

. . . excessive drinkers whose dependence on alcohol has attained such a degree that they show noticeable mental disturbance or an interference with their mental and bodily health, their interpersonal relations and their smooth social and economic functioning; or who show the prodromal [beginning] signs of such developments (Kessel and Walton, 1965, p. 18).

The essential points made by this definition are that *control over the consumption of the beverage is lost* and that *consumption disrupts the individual's life.*

The definition established by the World Health Organization excludes two of the three subcategories mentioned by DSM-II, for it applies only to those people who would by DSM-II be diagnosed as *addicted* to alcohol. In the following discussion we will not con-

sider in any depth those individuals who would be judged excessive or habitual drinkers by DSM-II; rather, our study will be limited to persons who are addicted to alcohol.

Short-Term Effects of Alcohol

After being swallowed, alcohol passes rapidly into the bloodstream. A small part of the alcohol ingested into the body passes immediately into the bloodstream through the stomach walls, but most of it goes into the small intestines and from there is absorbed into the blood. It must then be metabolized by a process referred to as oxidation. In this process alcohol fuses with oxygen and is broken down so that its basic elements leave the body as carbon dioxide and water.[1] The primary site of oxidation is the liver, which can break down about

---

[1] Various types of alcohol differ in the rate at which they can be oxidized. Ethyl alcohol, the type found in alcoholic beverages, oxidizes the most rapidly, whereas methyl or wood alcohol oxidizes much more slowly. Because of slow oxidation, large amounts of methyl alcohol may accumulate in the blood, causing death or blindness. Another type of alcohol, denatured alcohol, is a deadly poison because of the toxic substances added to it.

one ounce of 100 proof (that is, 50 percent alcohol) whiskey per hour. Quantities in excess of this amount remain in the bloodstream, which in turn depends on the amount stimulates the appetite and helps circulation by dilating the peripheral blood vessels. Many of the effects of alcohol vary directly with the level of concentration of the drug in the bloodstream, which in turn depends on the amount ingested in a particular period of time, the presence or absence in the stomach of food to retain the alcohol and reduce its absorption rate, the size of the individual's body, and the efficiency of his liver.

Because the drinking of alcoholic beverages is accepted in most societies, alcohol is rarely regarded as a drug, especially by those who drink. But it is indeed a drug, affecting the central nervous system. Alcohol, acting as a depressant, first numbs the higher brain centers, those that are primarily inhibiting. Thus the initial effect of alcohol is stimulating. Tensions and inhibitions are reduced, and the individual may experience an expansive feeling of sociability and well-being. Larger amounts interfere with complex thought processes, and then motor coordination, balance, speech, and vision are impaired. Alcohol is capable of blunting pain and in larger doses of inducing sedation and sleep. Before modern techniques of anesthesia were discovered, liquors were often administered to a patient about to undergo surgery.

The short-term effects of moderate amounts of alcohol are not harmful to the experienced drinker, except when he engages in activities requiring keen concentration and coordinated muscular movements, such as driving a car (Figure 10.2). For the inexperienced drinker even moderate amounts of liquor can cause unpleasant feelings of nausea, dizziness, and headache.

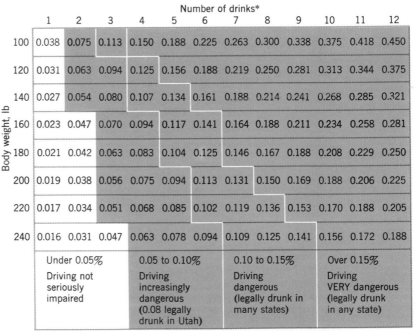

FIGURE 10.2

Increased consumption of alcohol results in higher blood levels of alcohol and greater danger when driving an automobile. Presentation adapted from CRM, Abnormal Psychology. Data from the New Jersey Department of Law and Public Safety, Division of Motor Vehicles, Trenton, New Jersey.

	Number of drinks*											
Body weight, lb	1	2	3	4	5	6	7	8	9	10	11	12
100	0.038	0.075	0.113	0.150	0.188	0.225	0.263	0.300	0.338	0.375	0.418	0.450
120	0.031	0.063	0.094	0.125	0.156	0.188	0.219	0.250	0.281	0.313	0.344	0.375
140	0.027	0.054	0.080	0.107	0.134	0.161	0.188	0.214	0.241	0.268	0.285	0.321
160	0.023	0.047	0.070	0.094	0.117	0.141	0.164	0.188	0.211	0.234	0.258	0.281
180	0.021	0.042	0.063	0.083	0.104	0.125	0.146	0.167	0.188	0.208	0.229	0.250
200	0.019	0.038	0.056	0.075	0.094	0.113	0.131	0.150	0.169	0.188	0.206	0.225
220	0.017	0.034	0.051	0.068	0.085	0.102	0.119	0.136	0.153	0.170	0.188	0.205
240	0.016	0.031	0.047	0.063	0.078	0.094	0.109	0.125	0.141	0.156	0.172	0.188

Under 0.05%	0.05 to 0.10%	0.10 to 0.15%	Over 0.15%
Driving not seriously impaired	Driving increasingly dangerous (0.08 legally drunk in Utah)	Driving dangerous (legally drunk in many states)	Driving VERY dangerous (legally drunk in any state)

*One drink equals 1 ounce of 100 proof liquor or 12 ounces of beer.

Long-Term Effects of Prolonged Alcohol Use

The possible long-term effects of prolonged
drinking (Figure 10.3) are vividly illustrated
in the following case history.

At the time of his first admission to a state hospital at the age of
twenty-four, the patient, an unmarried and unemployed laborer,
already had a long history of antisocial behavior, promiscuity and addiction to alcohol and other drugs. . . . There had been eight brief
admissions to private sanatoria for alcoholics, a number of arrests for
public intoxication and drunken driving, and two jail terms for assault.

The patient had been born into a wealthy and respected family in a
small town. The patient's father, a successful and popular businessman, drank excessively and his death at the age of fifty-seven was
partly due to alcoholism. The mother also drank to excess. The
parents exercised little control over the patient as a child, and he was
cared for by nursemaids. His father taught him to pour drinks for
guests of the family when he was very young and he reported that he
began to drain the glasses at parties in his home before he was six; by
the time he was twelve he drank almost a pint of liquor every weekend and by seventeen was drinking up to three bottles every day. His
father provided him with money to buy liquor and shielded him from
punishment for drunken driving and other consequences of his
drinking.

The patient was expelled from high school in his freshman year for
striking a teacher. He then attended a private school until the
eleventh grade, when he changed the date on his birth certificate and
joined the Army paratroops. After discharge, he was unemployed for
six months; he drank heavily and needed repeated care at a sanator-
ium. When a job was obtained for him he quit within a month. On his
third arrest for drunken driving he was jailed. His father bailed him
out with the warning that no more money would be forthcoming. The
patient left town and worked as an unskilled laborer—he had never
acquired any useful skills—but returned home when his father died.
During the next few years he was jailed for intoxication, for black-
ening his mother's eyes when he found a male friend visiting her, and
for violating probation by getting drunk. He assaulted and badly hurt
a prison guard in an escape attempt and was sentenced to two additional years in prison. When released, he began to use a variety of
stimulant, sedative and narcotic drugs as well as alcohol (Rosen,
Fox, and Gregory, 1972, pp. 312–313).

FIGURE **10.3A**
*The degraded life of the
skid-row alcoholic is the not
too infrequent consequence
of prolonged, heavy drinking.*

The life histories of alcoholics are considered to share a common progression. On the basis of an extensive survey of 2000 alcoholics, Jellenick (1952) described the alcoholic as passing through four stages on the way to his addiction. The first *prealcoholic* phase lasts from several months up to two years. In this stage the individual drinks socially and also on occasion rather heavily to relieve tension and to forget about his problems. At first the heavy drinking is infrequent, but in time the crises and the occasions for seeking the bolstering effects of alcohol recur with greater regularity. In the second *prodromal stage* drinking may become furtive and may also be marked by

SOCIAL DEVIATION

blackouts. The drinker remains conscious, talks coherently, and carries on other activities, without even appearing to be greatly intoxicated, but later he has no recall of the occasion. Alcohol begins to be used more as a drug and less as a beverage. The individual becomes preoccupied with his drinking, feeling guilty about it but at the same time worrying where and when he will have his next drink.

Jellinick terms the third phase *crucial,* choosing this adjective because he sees the alcoholic in this stage as being in severe danger of losing everything that he values. He has already lost control of his drinking. Once he takes a single drink, he continues to consume alcohol until he is too sick or in too much of a stupor to drink anymore. The individual's social adjustment also begins to deteriorate. He starts to drink during the day, and this becomes evident to his employer, family, and friends. He neglects his diet, has his first bender, a several-day period of excessive drinking, and may experience hallucinations and delirium when he stops drinking. At this stage the individual still has the ability to abstain. He can give up alcohol for several weeks or even months at a time, but if he has just one drink the whole pattern will begin again. The alcoholic even comes to feel that he needs a drink to steady himself for the day, and he starts to drink in the morning.

In the final *chronic stage* drinking is continual, and benders are frequent. The individual lives only to drink. His bodily systems have become so accustomed to alcohol that they must be supplied with it or he suffers withdrawal reactions. If liquor is not available to him, he will consume any liquid he can find that contains alcohol—shaving lotion, hair tonic, various medicinal preparations, whatever. He suffers from malnutrition and other physiological changes. He neglects his personal appearance and, having lost his self-esteem, feels little remorse about any aspect of his behavior. Finally, he cares nothing for family, friends, occupation, or social status.

Jellenick's description has been widely cited, but the available evidence is not always corroborative. One study found that blackouts do *not* occur in conjunction with modest drinking and that many alcoholics have never experienced a blackout (Goodwin, Crane, and Guze, 1969). More recent evidence questions the commonly accepted notion that a single drink stimulates an irresistible impulse to continue drinking (see Box 10.1).

In addition to the psychological deterioration brought on by alcoholism, severe physiological damage is also a serious consequence of chronic drinking. Almost every tissue and organ of the body is affected by the prolonged consumption of alcohol. The malnutrition suffered may be severe. Because alcohol provides calories, the alcoholic greatly reduces his food intake. But alcohol, although it furnishes energy, does *not* supply any of the nutrients essential for health. In the older chronic alcoholic a vitamin B deficiency is believed to cause severe memory loss (Korsakoff's psychosis, page 416). A drastic reduction in the intake of protein causes cirrhosis of the liver, a disease in which an excessive amount of fibrous connective tissue is formed, replacing active liver cells and thus impeding blood circulation. Other common physiological changes include damage to the endocrine glands, heart failure, hypertension, and capillary hemorrhages, which are responsible for the swelling and the redness in the face, and especially of the nose, of chronic alcoholics.

The effects of the abrupt withdrawal of alcohol from a chronic alcoholic may be rather dramatic, for his body has become profoundly accustomed to the drug. Subjectively, the patient is often frightened, depressed, weak, restless, and unable to sleep. Tremors of the muscles, especially of the small musculature of the fingers, face, lips, and tongue, may be marked, and there is an elevation of pulse and blood pressure. An alcoholic who has been drinking for a number of years may also suffer from *delirium tremens* (DTs) when the level of alcohol in his blood drops suddenly. He sweats profusely, and the pupils of his eyes react slowly to changes in light. He becomes delirious as well as tremulous. His hallucinations are primarily visual but they may be tactile as well. Unpleasant and very active creatures — snakes, cockroaches, spiders, and the like — may appear to be crawling up the wall or all over the alcoholic's body, or they may fill the room. Feverish, disoriented, and terrified, the alcoholic may claw frantically at his skin to rid himself of the vermin, or he may cower in the corner to escape an army of fantastic animals (Figure 10.4).

Delirium tremens would certainly seem to constitute a physiological withdrawal reaction, one of the criteria for considering a drug addictive. Increased tolerance is also evident. Mello and Mendelson (1970) found that alcoholics could drink a quart of bourbon a day without showing signs of drunkenness. Moreover, levels of alcohol in the blood were unexpectedly low after what would usually be viewed as excessive drinking.

In short, *the psychological, physiological, and social effects of prolonged consumption of alcohol are extremely serious.* Because the alcoholic's own functioning is so severely disrupted, the people he interacts with are also deeply affected and hurt by his conduct. Society too suffers, for the alcoholic is unlikely to be able to hold a job. The combined cost — the money spent in maintaining the necessary supply of liquor, the time lost in work efficiency, the damage of traffic accidents caused by impaired coordination, the expense of physicians and psychologists — runs to millions of dollars each year. The human tragedy, even more serious, is virtually incalculable.

BOX **10.1** *The One-Drink Myth*

The widespread assumption that once an alcoholic takes a single drink he will not be able to stop drinking has been challenged in an ingenious investigation by Marlatt, Demming, and Reid (1973).

Alcoholics and social drinkers were recruited for a study of taste preferences. Half the subjects in each group were told that the study involved a comparison of three types of vodka, the remainder that three kinds of tonic water were being evaluated. Actually, only half the subjects in each group were to be allowed to taste what they expected; thus the participants actually formed four groups: expect alcohol–taste alcohol, expect alcohol–taste tonic, expect tonic–taste tonic, expect tonic–taste alcohol.

Twenty minutes before the actual taste testing was to begin, subjects who were later to compare vodkas were given a vodka and tonic and those scheduled to taste tonic were given a glass of tonic water. In all instances subjects believed that the beverage was nonalcoholic. The vodka and tonic was the "primer" of the experiment. If the loss-of-control hypothesis is correct, it should have stimulated the alcoholics to excessive drinking. During the period of waiting the drinks for the taste test were prepared for two of the groups. For each of those who expected alcohol and were to taste alcohol, four ounces from three vodka bottles (Smirnoff's, Petruska, and Brand X) were poured into three decanters and twenty ounces of Schweppes tonic were added to each decanter. The three decanters for each expect tonic–taste tonic subject were filled with different kinds of tonic water. The bottles for the subjects who were not to taste the expected liquids had been filled earlier. The decanters that were supposed to contain some vodka held only tonic, and the tonic bottles had some vodka in them.

The subjects were asked to taste as much as they wanted from each decanter, rating each one on adjectives such as bitter, strong, watery, and sweet. During the tasting the experimenter excused himself to "set up another study."

The principal measure was the amount of fluid consumed. If the loss-of-control hypothesis had proved correct, of the alcoholics who had received a "primer" of vodka, those given vodka to taste should have consumed more liquid than those given tonic to taste. The alcoholics primed with and tasting vodka should also have consumed more than the social drinkers in their group. They did not. Surprisingly, the actual beverage served during the waiting and testing periods did not influence drinking. Instead, expectancy was the relevant variable: subjects who expected alcohol—whether they actually received it or not—drank more than those who expected tonic. No evidence was found for the loss-of-control hypothesis.

FIGURE **10.4A**
*Scene from a
nineteenth-century play
depicting the hallucinations
often experienced during
delirium tremens.*

THEORIES OF ALCOHOLISM

In trying to understand alcoholism, we must draw a distinction between conditions that induce a person to start drinking and those that play the central role in maintaining the behavior. Chronic drinking is an addiction; hence an alcoholic eventually continues drinking because his body demands alcohol. But the later physical need does not explain why an individual starts drinking in the first place. Those who attempt to explain the origins of habitual drinking refer to either psychological or physiological factors. Within each of these two broad categories there are several theories.

FIGURE **10.4B**
The evils of alcohol as illustrated by a nineteenth-century woodcut.

Psychological Theories

The Psychoanalytic View

Most analytic accounts of alcoholism point to fixation at the oral stage of development as the precipitating cause. Early mother-child interactions supposedly frustrate dependency needs during this stage of maturation. The various psychoanalytic theories differ in the function attributed to excessive drinking. For example, Knight (1937) proposed that the alcoholic's experience with an overprotective mother has developed in him a strong need to remain dependent. When this need is frustrated, he becomes angry and aggressive and feels guilty about his impulses. He drinks heavily to reduce these impulses and also to punish those who withhold affection from him. In a related vein, Fenichel (1945) stated that being frustrated by the mother turns the young male child toward his father, which in turn produces unconscious homosexual impulses. These repressed impulses compel him to drink in bars with other men, an activity that supposedly allows the alcoholic to obtain some of the emotional satisfaction he has not received from women. (It is not clear what the psychodynamic significance of solitary drinking would be.) Bergler (1946), emphasizing the self-destructive nature of alcoholism, hypothesized that alcohol addiction is a means of attempting to destroy a bad mother with whom the individual has identified. Little evidence is available to support these notions.

Other analytic accounts of alcoholism describe excessive drinking as a defense mechanism adopted to reduce emotional conflicts or eliminate guilt (see Box 10.2). A common analytic quip defines the superego as the part of the personality that is soluble in alcohol. The notion that the consumption of alcohol can reduce distress is also advanced in learning-based accounts of alcoholism.

BOX **10.2** *Alcoholism and the Need for Power*

David McClelland has recently advanced a rather novel psychodynamic theory of the origins of both social and excessive drinking, linking them to a personality trait, the need for power (McClelland, Davis, Kalin, and Wanner, 1972). He proposes that men drink to increase their sense of power. Ingesting alcohol in small doses supposedly brings to mind a greater number of thoughts about social power—being able to affect others for their own good—and larger doses increase thoughts of personal power, and in particular of sexual and aggressive conquests.

In one experiment lending support to the theory, men were recruited to participate in a study of the effects of social atmosphere on imaginativeness. On arriving at the laboratory, each member of the group responded to a series of four TAT-like pictures (see Chapter 3). Twenty-five minutes of social interaction followed, during which the experimental manipulation took place. Half the men were allowed to drink alcohol but the others consumed only soft drinks. Then the subjects responded to four more TAT cards. In support of the theory, only those who drank alcohol told in the second testing a greater number of power-related TAT stories—stories that involved prestige, dramatic settings, and positive feelings aroused in others—than they had related in the first testing.

According to McClelland's theory, the need for personal power that makes the alcoholic drink heavily is intense and excessive. Moreover, instead of fostering instrumental behavior that might indeed earn increased power, this excessive need impels the alcoholic to choose drinking as an alternate path to his goal. Two studies did indeed show that the experimental induction of concerns about power led to increased drinking. What remains unclear is how an excessive need for power develops, and why some individuals with this need attempt to fulfill it by drink rather than action.

Learning Accounts

An early experiment by Conger (1951) demonstrated that alcohol can serve to relieve fear. First, animals were trained in a classic approach-avoidance situation: after having been trained to feed in a particular place, the animals were subjected to shock when they approached their food. Half of the animals were then injected with alcohol. These animals were found to approach the food more readily than did the controls. The fear previously associated with the goal was apparently decreased by the alcohol in the bloodstream of the animals. Some recent investigations have replicated this finding and also shown that conflict increases alcohol consumption (Freed, 1971; Von Wright, Pekanmaki, and Malin, 1971).

Generalizing from these studies, we might argue that drinking alcohol is a learned response that is acquired and maintained because it reduces distress. Alcohol, however, has other effects besides the immediate allaying of tension, as our review of the long-term deleterious effects of continual drinking has revealed. Should not these extremely serious long-term negative effects outweigh the transient relief from stress felt when alcohol is first consumed? Dollard and Miller (1950) offered as a solution to this seeming paradox their concept of a *delay of reward gradient*. According to this formulation, the effectiveness of both rewards and punishments, in terms of their impact on a particular behavior, tends to decrease as they become farther and farther removed in time from the response. Thus a small but immediate reward can often exert a more powerful effect than can a larger one that does not immediately follow the response. Similarly, an immediate punishment is a much more effective agent of change than a punishment imposed several days, weeks, or even months later. In this sense the short-term reduction of distress offered by alcohol is seen as a rather large and immediately reinforcing benefit. Conversely, the longer-term effects of alcohol are

"Double Scotches for me and my super-ego, and a glass of water for my id, which is driving."

(DRAWING BY HANDELSMAN; © 1972 THE NEW YORKER MAGAZINE, INC.)

relatively ineffective in discouraging its consumption because they are suffered so long after the actual drinking.

The theory that the alcoholic drinks because alcohol reduces tension must be viewed as an incomplete explanation, however. It may explain why many people *begin* drinking, but it does not appear to account for the continuation of drinking over long periods of time. For example, Nathan and his colleagues have recently reported a study in which chronic alcoholics were carefully observed while residing in a specially designed hospital ward (Nathan, Titler, Lowenstein, Solomon, and Ross, 1970). The patients were allowed to work to obtain points which could later be exchanged for alcohol. Although the patients themselves reported that they drank to relieve anxiety and depression, an assessment of their moods by means of a self-report adjective checklist indicated that they were actually *more* anxious and depressed after drinking. Similar results were reported by Mendelson (1964).

We might well ask why it has so long been assumed that drinking is initially maintained because it reduces anxiety. Perhaps the theorists have failed to distinguish between addictive alcohol consumption and social drinking. Those who have theorized about alcoholism are, after all, unlikely to be chronic, addicted alcoholics. They are more likely to be social drinkers who enjoy an occasional cocktail in the company of others, especially after a trying day. It may be, then, that our closeness to the subject matter has prevented until recently a critical examination of the view that prolonged drinking reduces tension.

Personality and Alcoholism

In the 1930s a long-term research project was begun in Oakland, California. Called the Oakland Growth Study, a large sample of children were studied in great detail and followed up at periodic intervals. In the mid-1960s many of these middle-aged individuals were contacted again and interviewed (Jones, 1968, 1971) concerning their current alcohol consumption patterns, their reasons for drinking, their attitudes toward drinking, and the like. Based on their answers to these questions, the individuals were classified into five categories: (1) problem drinkers, (2) heavy drinkers (two or three drinks every day), (3) moderate drinkers, (4) light drinkers, and (5) nondrinkers and abstainers. The information that had been collected on the members of the population sample during their junior and senior high school years was extensive. Parents had contributed details about background and homelife, teachers had reported on classroom behavior, classroom peers had rated one another, and the individuals in the sample had rated themselves on personality tests and in interviews. All these data collected in adolescence were then correlated with adult drinking patterns.

Jones found that the adult male problem drinkers still had some of the same traits that had characterized them in adolescence: impulsiveness which was never controlled, extroverted behavior, and a tendency to overemphasize their masculinity. Moreover, as compared to high school contemporaries who did not later become excessive drinkers, adult male problem drinkers had been described in adolescence as less aware of impressions made on others, less productive, less calm, more sensitive to criticism, and less socially perceptive. The traits of the future problem drinker had apparently caused him social difficulties even in high school. Later these difficulties may have served as the source of stress that induced him to begin drinking.

Among the women, the picture was much less clear, for Jones found marked similarities in adolescence between those who later became problem drinkers and those who abstained altogether from alcohol in adulthood. Both groups had been characterized in high school as vulnerable, withdrawn, dependent, irritable, and sensitive to criticism. The pattern of apparently poor social adaptation—which correlated with heavy drinking in men—was in women associated with *either* problem drinking *or* total abstinence.

The Sociocultural View

It has been argued that ethnic groups such as the Jews, Italians, and Chinese, who clearly specify appropriate ceremonial, nutritional, or festive uses of alcohol, have lower rates of alcoholism. Although these people condone the drinking of alcohol under specified circumstances, they frown on overindulgence. For other national groups, such as the Irish and the English, the circumstances in which the consumption of alcohol is deemed appropriate are less clear.

A study carried out by McCord, McCord, and Gudeman (1959, 1960) reveals the importance of ethnic and cultural backgrounds in the etiology of alcoholism of males in the United States. Young men who had been intensively studied several years earlier as adolescents were followed up. In examining the earlier histories of those who had become alcoholics, the investigators found no support for theories relating the habit to oral fixation, parental pampering, or self-destructive tendencies, but they did find the relation of alcoholism and ethnic background to be significant. More young men with American Indian, western and eastern European, and Irish backgrounds were alcoholic than were those of Italian and other Latin extractions. The investigators also found a relation between alcoholism and social class: more of the alcoholics were from the middle class than from the lower class. Although social and cultural factors are clearly important,

they obviously cannot be the only ones. The relationship between ethnic background and alcoholism is not one to one; some Jews are of course alcoholics, and not every Irishman is addicted to the beverage. Furthermore, comparisons among various countries reveal a pattern of alcoholism not entirely consistent with this view. The rate of alcoholism in Ireland, for example, is in the bottom third of the list given in Table 10.1. Italians, who are said to drink primarily at mealtime, have the second highest rate.

The psychosocial theories that we have just reviewed attempt to account for the origins of heavy drinking. None of the views enjoys great support from the available data. Perhaps this should come as no surprise, inasmuch as chronic alcoholism is known to be a physiological addiction. Other theorists point to physiological factors in attempting to explain why some people begin a drinking pattern that eventuates in addiction.

Physiological Theories

Food Addiction Theory

Roueche (1962) has proposed that some people are sensitized to certain foods which act in some way to decrease unpleasant feelings. But since the relief that is produced is only short-lived, the person must soon again consume the food to gain further relief from the offensive feelings. The grains that are the prime sources of alcoholic beverages, wheat, corn, and rye, are hypothesized to be the foods that diminish these unpleasant sensations. There is little evidence to support this theoretical position.

Genotrophic Theory

Williams (1959) has proposed that alcoholism develops from a nutritional deficiency. He has

TABLE 10.1

*Annual Drinker Consumption,
Estimated Rates of Alcoholism,
and Rates of Death from Cirrhosis
of the Liver* (*from de Lint and Schmidt, 1971*)

Country	Liters of absolute alcohol consumed by each drinker, 1966 or 1967*	Estimated rates of alcoholism per 100,000 population aged 15 and older†	Rate of death from cirrhosis of the liver per 100,000 population aged 15 and older, 1963, 1964, or 1965‡
France	25.9	9405	45.3
Italy	20.0	5877	27.3
Portugal	19.5	5652	42.7
Spain	17.1	4635	24.3
Austria	16.0	4212	35.0
West Germany and West Berlin	16.0	3978	26.7
Switzerland	15.8	3901	19.7
Luxembourg	12.5	2988	34.2
Hungary	12.4	2952	12.9
United States	12.0	2198	18.4
Czechoslovakia	11.4	2655	13.1
Canada	11.1	2272	10.0
England and Wales	10.9	1946	3.7
Republic of Ireland	10.9	1946	4.5
Denmark	9.4	1848	10.2
Belgium	9.3	2052	12.9
Poland	9.0	1752	8.6
Sweden	8.4	1515	7.9
Netherlands	7.7	1456	4.9
Finland	5.9	945	4.6
Norway	5.9	945	4.7

* Alcohol consumption data were taken from the 1968 Annual Report of the Dutch Distillers' Association.
† Alcoholics are defined as drinkers of daily averages in excess of 150 ml of absolute alcohol. Their numbers were tabulated on the basis of data provided in J. Hyland and S. Scott, Alcohol consumption tables: An application of the Ledermann equation to a wide range of consumption averages, 1969.
‡ Figures were taken from United Nations, *Demographic Yearbook, 1966*, New York: 1967.

suggested that alcoholics have an inherited inability to produce certain enzymes and thus cannot digest certain nutrients. The excessive consumption of alcohol somehow assuages the physiological need for the missing substances. In formulating his theory, Williams relied heavily on an early study in which vitamin-deprived rats were found to prefer alcohol to water. It appeared that their consumption of liquor might be in response to a nutritional deficiency.

Other research, however, has offered little support for Williams's theory. Lester and Greenberg (1952) studied the effects of nutritional deficiencies on alcohol consumption in a situation somewhat similar to that set up by Williams for his study. In addition to allowing rats to choose between alcohol and water, however, they also provided a sucrose solution. In their study sucrose was greatly preferred to alcohol. Thus a vitamin deficiency may give the animal a nonspecific hunger for *any* nutrient. When water is the only alternative, alcohol is preferred but it will not be if another nutrient is available.

The evidence collected so far does not indicate that a physiological predisposition for alcoholism is transmitted genetically. Although the relatives of alcoholics and the children of alcoholic parents have a greater incidence of alcoholism than is found in the general population, their habits have very likely been acquired through exposure to drinking within the family. Living with a person who drinks excessively may provide a model and increase the likelihood of acquiring the same behavior. Roe, Burks, and Mittelman (1945) studied children who had been separated from their alcoholic parents and reared in foster homes. These children would have inherited a predisposition for alcoholism if such a thing exists, but they were not exposed to alcoholic models. In this important study the children of the alcoholic parents were found in later life no more likely to become alcoholic than were the children of nonalcoholic parents. Thus there is no evidence that a physiological defect triggers alcoholism initially even though, in its extreme forms, it must be regarded as a physiological addiction maintained by a physical need.

HARD DRUGS

Until 1914 addiction to drugs was disapproved in the United States, but it was tolerated. The 1914 Harrison Narcotics Act changed this, making the unauthorized use of various drugs illegal and those addicted to them criminals. The drugs to be discussed, not all of which are illegal, may be divided into two general categories. The major *sedatives,* called "downs," slow the activities of the body and reduce its responsiveness. In this group of drugs are the organic narcotics—opium and its derivatives morphine, heroin, and codeine—and the synthesized barbiturates. The second group,

the stimulants or "ups," act on the brain and the sympathetic nervous system to increase alertness and motor activity. The amphetamines are synthesized stimulants; cocaine is a natural stimulant extracted from the coca leaf.

Sedatives

Narcotics

Opium, the principal drug of illegal international traffic, was known to the people of the

Sumerian civilization dating back to 7000 B.C. They gave the poppy that supplied this narcotic the name by which it is still known and which means "the plant of joy" (Figure 10.5). Opium is a mixture of about eighteen alkaloids, but until 1806 people had no knowledge of these substances to which so many natural drugs owe their potency. In that year the alkaloid morphine, a bitter-tasting powder, was separated out from raw opium. It proved to be a powerful sedative and pain reliever. Before its addictive properties were noted, it was commonly used in patent medicines. In the middle of the century, when the hypodermic needle was introduced in the United States, morphine began to be injected directly into the veins to relieve pain. Many soldiers wounded in battle and suffering from dysentery during the Civil War were treated with morphine and returned home addicted to the drug. After that its social misuse increased considerably. Concerned about administering a drug that could so disturb the later lives of patients, scientists began studying morphine. They thought that part of its molecule might be responsible for relieving pain and another part for its addictiveness. In 1874 they found that morphine could be converted into another powerful pain-

FIGURE **10.5**
Opium den of the nineteenth century. As a means of escape, opium addicts regularly spent several hours a day smoking themselves into a pleasant oblivion.

SOCIAL DEVIATION

relieving drug which they named heroin. It was used initially as a cure for the withdrawal symptoms of morphine and was substituted for morphine in cough syrups and other patent medicines (Figure 10.6). Heroin proved to be even more dangerous than morphine, however, acting more quickly and with greater intensity. By 1909 President Theodore Roosevelt was calling for an international investigation of opium and the opiates.

Opium and its derivatives heroin and morphine produce states of euphoria, drowziness, reverie, and sometimes a lack of coordination. These drugs are central nervous system depressants and can relieve pain. Although there are some differences in the action of these drugs, all three are clearly addicting in the physiological sense, for users show both increased tolerance of the drugs and withdrawal reactions when they are unable to obtain another dose.

It has been estimated that the frequency of narcotics addiction (Figure 10.7) in the general population is about one person per 3000 (Richards and Carroll, 1970). Among certain subgroups, however, the rate is much higher. One in every hundred physicians is reported to be addicted, for example, and there are a greater number of addicts in large cities. Moreover, there is also a sex difference: male addicts outnumber female addicts by about eight to one.

Deaths, often attributed to overdoses, are also frequent, but the actual cause remains in doubt (see Box 10.3). Among the effects of prolonged narcotic addiction are malnutrition from poor eating habits, loss of sexual interest, and respiratory difficulties. In addition, there is an ever-present danger of abscesses and of contracting bloodstream infections, tetanus, and hepatitis from the use of unsterile needles.

Reactions to the abrupt withdrawal of narcotics can be severe, at least after high tolerance has built up. Within the first twelve hours

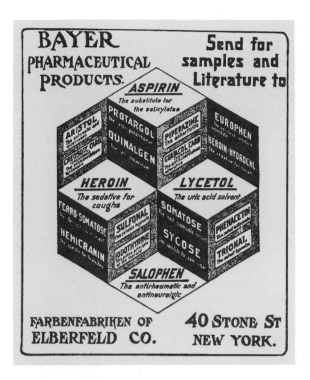

FIGURE **10.6**
Early ad from the Bayer Company illustrating the legal sale of heroin as a medicant for coughing.

the individual will typically have muscle pain, will sneeze, sweat, become tearful, and yawn a great deal. Within about thirty-six hours the withdrawal symptoms become more severe. There may be uncontrollable muscle twitching, cramps, restlessness, and a rise in heart rate and blood pressure. The addict is unable to sleep, vomits, and has diarrhea. These symptoms typically persist for about seventy-two hours and then diminish gradually over a five- to ten-day period.

In addition to the potentially serious bodily harm to the user, narcotics addiction has serious social effects. Since narcotics are illegal, the addict must deal with the underworld in order to maintain his habit. The high cost of the drugs—the addict must often spend $100 per day to feed his habit—means that he must either have great wealth or acquire money

through illegal activities. Thus the correlation between addiction and criminal activities is striking, undoubtedly contributing to the popular notion that drug addiction per se causes violence. A comparison of the ways in which addicts are treated in America and in Great Britain belies this conclusion, however, and indicates that the correlation need not exist. In England drugs are administered to addicted

SOCIAL DEVIATION

FIGURE **10.7**

individuals under the care of a physician, and there is no compulsory treatment for addicts. In an earlier report Schur (1965) compared the American and British systems and concluded

This entire approach [the British one] has worked remarkably well. . . . All the evidence indicates that there are very few addicts other than those receiving their supplies through

BOX **10.3** *The Heroin Overdose Mystery*

The rate of deaths attributed to heroin overdose has risen dramatically — by 50 percent in the 1950s, by 70 percent by 1969, and by 80 percent in 1970. But the deaths do *not* appear to be a result of injecting a particularly powerful dose. The estimates of what constitutes a lethal dose range from 120 to 350 milligrams, but the average dose contained in a New York City "bag" is only 10 mg. Furthermore, when packets of heroin are found near the bodies of dead addicts, they do not differ from the usual dose. After the coroner has ruled out death by suicide, violence, or "natural causes," the evidence that he relies on to substantiate his verdict of heroin overdose is, in fact, nothing more than the knowledge that the deceased had been an addict. Contrary to widespread belief, there is no real evidence that these deaths are caused by heroin (Brecher, 1972).

But if not heroin, what? The fact that the frequency of such deaths has recently increased must be regarded as significant. Is there another factor or variable that has increased during this same period? One hypothesis proposes that the quinine used to "cut" heroin is the culprit. Quinine was introduced in 1939 when New York City addicts were hit by an epidemic of malaria spread by contaminated needles. Since then the use of quinine as a cutting agent has gradually become widespread. Quinine can cause a rapid flooding of the lungs with fluid, a condition found in many of the so-called overdose deaths.

Another hypothesis suggests an interaction between alcohol and heroin. Evidence does indicate that alcohol can dramatically reduce the amount of narcotic that need be taken for it to be a lethal dose. Many early studies found that heroin addicts disliked alcohol, using it only as a substitute during withdrawal. Recently, however, addicts seem to alternate between alcohol and heroin because the price of heroin is so high. Thus deaths such as the following may be caused by an interaction between alcohol and heroin.

The quart bottle of Southern Comfort that she held aloft onstage was at once a symbol of her load and a way of lightening it. . . . Last week, Janis Joplin died on the lowest and saddest of notes. Returning to her Hollywood motel room after a late-night recording session and some hard drinking [*emphasis added*] *with friends at a nearby bar, she apparently filled a hypodermic needle with heroin and shot it into her left arm* (Time, *October 19, 1970*).

legal channels. No sizable underworld drug traffic exists. The addict furnishes no economic incentive for contraband peddling and needn't become a thief or prostitute to pay for drugs. . . . It would seem that by refusing to treat the addict as a criminal, Britain has kept him from becoming one (p. 153).

Since this assessment was offered, however, there has been an increase of drug use in England. As of 1969, there were 1530 addicts, and the number of teen-age addicts had increased from none in 1959 to 764 in 1968. Although these figures are small indeed compared to those for the United States, the British have moved toward tighter controls. The import of this information is that making narcotics freely available, thus removing the profit of trafficking them, may still not keep the population of addicts from growing. Italy has a drug policy similar to that of the United States, yet the number of addicts has remained very small (Markham, 1972).

Barbiturates

Barbiturates were synthesized as aids for sleeping and relaxation. The first was produced in 1903 and since then over fifty derivatives of barbituric acid have been made. Two types are usually distinguished—long-acting barbiturates for prolonged sedation and short-acting barbiturates for prompt sedation and sleep. The short-acting drugs are usually viewed as addicting. Initially, the drugs were considered highly desirable and were prescribed very frequently. In the 1940s, however, a campaign

was mounted against them because they were discovered to be addicting, and doctors prescribed barbiturates less frequently. Today in the United States they are manufactured in vast quantities, enough, it is estimated, to supply each man, woman, and child with thirty pills per year. Many are shipped legally to Mexico and then brought back into the country and trafficked illegally (*U.S. News and World Report,* December 27, 1971, p. 44).

Barbiturates are depressants,[2] relaxing the muscles and in small doses producing a mildly euphoric state. Excessive doses, however, may make the person irritable and cause him to lose weight. The impairments of cognitive functioning may be extreme. Very large doses can be fatal because the diaphragm muscles relax to such an extent that the individual suffocates. As we have indicated in Chapter 8, barbiturates are frequently chosen as a means of suicide.

Barbiturates are the second most common class of drugs to which people become addicted. Increased tolerance follows prolonged use, and the withdrawal reactions after abrupt termination are particularly severe and long lasting. The following is a description of one stage of the withdrawal reaction of a middle-aged woman who had been taking barbiturates for many years.

[2] Methaqualone, a sedative sold under the trade names Quaalude and Sopor, is similar in effect to barbiturates and has recently become a popular "street" drug. Besides being addictive, its other dangers are internal bleeding, coma, and even death from overdose.

She had a marked tremor and was unsteady on her feet. She hallucinated, thought she heard the voice of her husband telling her that he was coming to get her in a taxi and she cried out to him. Soon she began seeing people climbing trees and looking through the window at her. She became violent and abusive to the staff. Even after receiving sedative medication she remained restless, muttering to herself incoherently. Her tremor increased, her face became flushed and she began to perspire excessively. At times she twitched convulsively. A little later she began picking up imaginary objects and muttering "thank you" as if someone were handing them to her. Later she was observed reaching for an imaginary glass and drinking from it. She ate imaginary food and picked imaginary cigarettes out of the air; she heard nonexistent doorbells and an ambulance siren (Rosen, Fox, and Gregory, 1972, pp. 317–318).

Stimulants

Amphetamines

The first amphetamine, Benzedrine, was synthesized in 1927. Almost as soon as it became available in the early 1930s as an inhalant to relieve stuffy noses, the public discovered its stimulating effects. Doctors thereafter prescribed it and the other amphetamines soon synthesized to control mild depression and the appetite. During World War II soldiers on both sides were supplied with the drugs to ward off fatigue.

Amphetamines such as Benzedrine, Dexedrine, and Methedrine produce effects similar to those of norepinephrine in the sympathetic nervous system. Wakefulness is heightened, intestinal functions are inhibited, and appetite is reduced — hence their use in dieting. The heart rate is increased, and blood vessels in the skin and mucous membranes dilate. The individual becomes euphoric, more outgoing, and possessed with seemingly boundless energy. Larger doses can make the person nervous, agitated, and confused, subjecting him to palpitations, headaches, dizziness, and sleeplessness. There are some reports of extremely large doses inducing paranoid delusions of persecution.

Although not considered to be physiologically addictive, increased tolerance does develop rapidly, so that mouthfuls of pills are required to produce the stimulating effect. As his tolerance increases, the user may stop taking pills and inject Methedrine, the strongest of the amphetamines, directly into the veins. The so-called speed freak gives himself repeated injections of the drug and maintains intense and euphoric activity for a few days, without eating or sleeping, after which he is exhausted and sleeps or "crashes" for several days. Then the cycle starts again. After several repetitions of this pattern the physical and social functioning of the individual will have deteriorated considerably. His reactions will be quite erratic, and he may become a danger to himself and to others.

Cocaine

The Spanish conquistadors introduced *coca* leaves to Europe. The Indians of the Andean uplands, to which the coca shrubs are native, chew the leaves, but the Europeans chose to brew them instead in beverages. The alkaloid cocaine was extracted from the leaves of the coca plant in 1844 and has been used since then as a local anesthetic. In 1884, while still a young neurologist in Vienna, Sigmund Freud began using cocaine to combat his depression. Convinced of its wondrous effects, he prescribed it to a friend with a painful disease and published one of the first papers on the drug, "Song of Praise," which was an enthusiastic endorsement of the exhilarating effects he had experienced. One of the early products using coca leaves in its manufacture was Coca-Cola, first marketed in the United States in 1896. For the next ten years Coke was the real thing, but by 1906 the manufacturer had switched to coca leaves from which the cocaine had been removed.

In addition to its pain-reducing effects, cocaine acts on the cortex of the brain, increasing mental powers and inducing a state of euphoria. Sexual desire is accentuated, and feelings of self-confidence and well-being suffuse the user's consciousness. An overdose may produce psychotic symptoms and hallucinations, which tend to be terrifying.

THEORIES OF THE ORIGINS OF ADDICTION TO HARD DRUGS

Physiological Theories

Many have regarded the physiological changes in the body effected by drugs as the most important factor bringing on drug addiction. Because the physiology of the body has been changed by the drug, it reacts when the substance to which it has become accustomed is no longer administered. To avoid withdrawal reactions, the addict continues taking the drug into his system. Physiological alterations are, in turn, viewed as having been established through accident or curiosity. A person takes the drug by chance or because he wants to experience its effects. He is then ensnared by the changes in his bodily chemistry and the concomitant severity of withdrawal reactions. The addict is regarded as an unwitting victim of his physiological reactions, continuing to use the drug to ward off the distress of withdrawal.

Ausubel (1961a) has challenged this interpretation by alleging that the effects of withdrawal are in reality no more severe than a bad case of influenza. Anecdotal evidence exists to support Ausubel's claim that the effects of withdrawal are not as severe as is often imagined. Synanon (Yablonsky, 1967), a self-governing corporation which offers a community-living treatment for drug addiction, does not "allow" a severe withdrawal reaction among the participants in its program. Rather, the addict is told that the effects of withdrawal will not be severe and that he will be able to continue his daily life. In fact, strong social pressures are applied to make him meet responsibilities during withdrawal. Apparently, the method has some success, and severe withdrawal reactions are not often reported among people who live at the various Synanon centers.

Even though the real effects of withdrawal may not be severe, we must consider what the average addict, one who is not being helped by organizations such as Synanon, *believes* withdrawal to be. If the addict believes that severe cramps, retching, sweating, chills, and loss of control are inevitable consequences of abstaining, it may matter little what the actual withdrawal reaction is like. As we learned in Chapter 5, even a nonveridical belief can strongly affect behavior. This is not to say that drug addiction is entirely unrelated to physiological processes, rather that psychological variables may play an important role in the maintenance of the habit as well as in the initial taking of the drug.

Psychological Theories

Psychological theories of the origin of drug addiction usually emphasize reduction of distress and the pleasant feeling and euphoric state that the drugs produce. These theories also attempt to give reasons why particular kinds of people seem to "need" these effects. An association has often been noted between criminality, drug abuse, and the sociopathic personality. In this context drug abuse may be considered as part of the thrill-seeking behavior of the sociopath discussed in Chapter 9. We might also expect narcotics to be used by anxious individuals in order to reduce the distress that they often experience. Drug addicts have often been found to be deviant on various personality questionnaire measures. But we must question whether these personality characteristics antedated the addiction. For example, we might find that drug addicts tend to be more suspicious than nonusers, but of course correlation does not imply causation. To conclude that suspiciousness contributes to the use of drugs would not be justified, for it might well be the addict's *reaction to* his illegal status as a drug user. Data on personality variables such as those that were collected by Jones on alcoholism (page 246) are not available on narcotics addiction.

Some similarities in family background have been identified in the life histories of drug addicts (Chein, Gerard, Lee, and Rosenfeld, 1964). In many cases the father is absent from the home of the future addict. If the father is present, he tends to be a shadowy figure or to be overtly hostile and distant. If present he may also serve as a model for criminal behavior, and the relations between the mother and father are likely to be stormy. Chein and his colleagues therefore proposed that the personality defects of the drug addict, whatever they are, were developed by his family background. Initial experiences with addicting drugs were also shown to be nonaccidental. Most addicts were found to have been introduced knowingly to the drugs, not by an adult but rather by a member of their peer group, suggesting the importance of peer pressure and other sociocultural factors. In ghettoes where narcotics are readily available, and the culture of the streets prevails, the incidence of drug use is especially high.

In sum, there is little evidence available concerning the origins of drug addiction. Personality characteristics, peer pressure, family background, the ease with which the drug can be acquired, and the frequency with which it is used in a particular culture are all possible factors, but as yet the role of any of them has been only vaguely specified.

NICOTINE AND SMOKING

The history of tobacco smoking bears much similarity to the use of other addictive drugs (Brecher, 1972). For a variety of reasons —peer pressure, imitation of high-status models in advertisements—people begin smoking and gradually become addicted to the drug, in this case nicotine. The use of tobacco spread through the world from Columbus's commerce with the native American Indians. It did not take long for sailors and merchants to imitate the Indians' smoking of rolled leaves of tobacco—and to experience, as the Indians did, the increasing craving for the stuff. When not smoked, tobacco was chewed or else ground into small pieces and inhaled as snuff.

Some idea of the addictive qualities of tobacco can be appreciated by considering how much people would sacrifice to maintain their supplies. In sixteenth-century England, for example, tobacco was exchanged for silver *ounce for ounce*. Poor people squandered their meager resources for their several daily pipefuls. Even the public tortures and executions engineered by the Sultan Murad IV of Turkey during the seventeenth century could not dissuade those of his subjects who were addicted to the weed. Today the threat of ill health, documented convincingly by the United States Surgeon General (1964), is similarly failing to force smokers to reduce their tobacco consumption, even though the overwhelming majority of them believe the dire predictions of the Surgeon General. Perhaps one of the most tortured addicts was Sigmund Freud, who continued smoking up to twenty cigars a day in the full knowledge that the nicotine was taxing his heart and causing cancerous growths in his mouth. With his jaw later entirely removed, Freud suffered great difficulty swallowing and endured excruciating pain, but he was still unable to bear the anguish of abstaining. Although many heavy smokers do succeed in stopping, Freud's tragic case was certainly not the exception.

In the literature on smoking there is, however, considerable controversy whether nicotine is an addictive drug. Part of the confusion may stem from a failure to distinguish among different kinds of smokers. Those smoking more than two packs a day may well be addicted to nicotine, whereas those who limit their smoking, for example, to social situations and consume less than a pack a day do indeed smoke from habit, but they may not be addicted. The evidence, at any rate, is somewhat equivocal; workers interpret the same results in different ways. Consider a well-controlled experiment that attempted to determine whether nicotine is the "culprit."

On the assumption that "nicotine hunger" plays an important role in maintaining smoking, Lucchesi, Schuster, and Emley (1967) recruited cigarette smokers and required them to sit in a laboratory and smoke as much as they wanted while various chemical solutions were steadily dripped into a vein via a catheter. Periods during which a saline (salt) solution was injected were alternated with periods during which varying amounts of nicotine solution were injected directly into the vein. The subjects were expected to smoke significantly fewer cigarettes when the injected solution contained nicotine if, in fact, the body does crave the substance. While 4 mg of nicotine per hour was being injected—an amount equivalent to the nicotine obtained by smoking two average cigarettes per hour—smoking was 60 percent less than during the period that the subjects were receiving the saline solution. Thus injecting nicotine directly into the blood did reduce the number of cigarettes smoked. The findings can be interpreted in several ways, however. The authors themselves concluded that "The results obtained suggest that nicotine plays a small but significant role in the smoking habit and that part of the craving for a cigarette can be satisfied by the intravenous administration of the alkaloid . . . [but] if the pleasure of smoking or craving for tobacco were due to the general effects of the alkaloid we should have observed a much greater reduction in the smoking frequency" (p. 795). In his well-known review of the role of nicotine in cigarette smoking, Jarvik (1970) seems to vacillate between regarding this study as strong evidence that smoking is a hunger for nicotine and considering it evidence that nonnicotine factors, such as habit, are important.

Although it is unrealistic to expect total agreement among investigators—Bernstein (1969), for example, disagrees with the addiction view—it is probably fair to say that *some* smokers are addicted. No doubt each of us knows someone who has tried numerous times

BOX **10.4** *Smoking — Arousing, Relaxing, or Both?*

Most cigarette smokers report that their habit is relaxing (Ikard, Green, and Horn, 1968), yet smoking a cigarette typically increases the heart rate from fifteen to twenty-five beats per minute, as well as elevating blood pressure (United States Department of Health, Education, and Welfare, 1964). A recent experiment was designed to demonstrate these two paradoxical effects.

Nesbitt (1973) arranged for both smokers and nonsmokers to undergo a series of increasingly uncomfortable electric shocks under three conditions: when not smoking, when smoking a high-nicotine cigarette, and when smoking a low-nicotine cigarette. He reasoned that if smoking is at the same time physiologically arousing yet psychologically relaxing *to regular smokers,* they would endure greater levels of painful shock when smoking and would also endure even more shock when smoking a high-nicotine cigarette than when smoking one low in nicotine. Inasmuch as nonsmokers should not be expected to experience a cigarette as relaxing, he did not believe that he would find this improvement in ability to endure shock among the subjects of the nonsmoker control group.

First, by monitoring the heartbeats of his subjects with the electrocardiograph, he was able to demonstrate that smoking a cigarette does indeed increase heart rate, especially when the cigarette contains a high concentration of nicotine. More interesting was the ability of a regular smoker to endure shock as a function of whether he was smoking while taking more and more uncomfortable electric shocks. As Figure 10.8 indicates, regular smokers took more shock when smoking, especially when smoking a high-nicotine cigarette. Smoking did not alter the shock-taking behavior of the nonsmokers.

Assuming that increased endurance of shock is a valid measure of the reduction of anxiety, Nesbitt concluded that smoking is relaxing to those who are accustomed to smoking, even while physiological arousal is increasing. Nonsmokers, unfamiliar with the effects of smoking — indeed, even feeling somewhat queasy — do not relax psychologically while physiologically aroused by cigarettes. The paradox was thus confirmed: smoking psychologically relaxes those accustomed to it while it arouses them physiologically. Why this happens is by no means clear.

to stop smoking. Indeed, even members of organizations that engage in antismoking campaigns are sometimes unable to overcome their habit. Brecher (1972) makes the case for addiction rather convincingly. First, cessation of smoking does seem to produce fairly consistent withdrawal symptoms — nervousness, drowsiness, and headaches. Second, people do seem to develop a tolerance to nicotine, although there is of course an upper limit on how much nicotine can be taken into the body, for people can smoke just so much during their waking hours.

SOCIAL DEVIATION

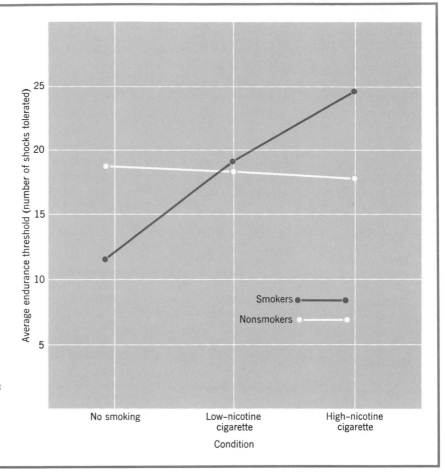

MARIHUANA

Marihuana consists of the dried and ground leaves and stems of the female hemp plant, *Cannabis sativa*. It is most often smoked, but it may be chewed, prepared as a tea, or eaten in baked goods. Hashish, much stronger than marihuana, is produced by drying the resin of the marihuana plant. Both marihuana and hashish have been known to man for thousands of years, and their poor reputation among the general public is not entirely new. For example, the English word assassin comes from the Arabic word hashshāshīn, meaning those addicted to hashish and the name of an order of Muslims who took hashish and murdered Christians at the time of the Crusades. In early American history the plant was extensively cultivated, not for smoking but for its fibers, which were used in the manufacture of cloth and rope. By the nineteenth century the medicinal properties of *Cannabis* resin were noted, and it was a recommended treatment for rheumatism, gout, depression, cholera, and neuralgia, as well as being smoked for pleasure (Figure 10.9). Until 1920 marihuana was little seen in the United States, but with the passage of the Eighteenth Amendment, which prohibited the sale of alcohol, marihuana began to be brought across the border from Mexico and smoked for intoxication by members of the lower classes. Unfavorable reports in the press attributing crimes to marihuana use led to the enactment of a federal law against the sale of marihuana in 1937.

FIGURE **10.9**
Early recreational use of hashish in a fashionable apartment in New York City. An 1876 issue of the Illustrated Police News *carried this picture with the title "Secret Dissipation of New York Belles: Interior of a Hasheesh Hell on Fifth Avenue."*

SOCIAL DEVIATION

TABLE **10.2** *Frequency*
with Which Marihuana Users
Try Other Drugs

(from National Commission on Marihuana and Drug Abuse, 1972)

Substance	Percent who take			
	Once to several times a year	Several times a month	Several times a week	Daily
Hashish	31	21	5	0
LSD	4	0	0	0
Mescaline	19	0	0	2
Psilocybin	4	0	0	0
Heroin	2	0	0	0
Codeine	11	0	0	2
Amphetamines	7	0	4	0
Barbiturates	10	4	0	0
Cocaine	19	2	4	0
Glue	0	0	0	0

Again in the 1960s there was another dramatic increase in the smoking of marihuana, and the drug became very much a part of the public scene. As of 1972, a total of 24 million Americans—15 percent of the adults eighteen years and older and 14 percent of those from twelve to seventeen—are estimated to have used marihuana at least once.

Much of the current public concern about the use of marihuana stems from a number of allegations made against the drug. The Official Report of the National Commission on Marihuana and Drug Abuse (1972) has refuted some of them. First, it has been claimed that marihuana smoking leads to antisocial and criminal behavior. It is true that early studies had demonstrated heavier use of marihuana among criminals. But that association was more pronounced before the rapid upswing in marihuana smoking in the 1960s. The National Commission noted on the basis of their studies

that "if anything, marihuana generally seems to inhibit [violent and aggressive] behavior" (p. 91). Second, it has been claimed that smoking marihuana is a steppingstone to addiction to heroin and other more harmful drugs, for it is known that among heroin addicts there are a large number of former marihuana users. The National Commission has undertaken research to determine the association between marihuana smoking and the use of other drugs. As can be seen in Table 10.2, only 2 percent of all who habitually use marihuana now also take heroin, and then only several times a year. Nineteen percent of marihuana smokers have tried mescaline and cocaine, but few are daily users. Thus, although most heroin addicts have used marihuana, it is also true that most marihuana users do not go on to heroin. The widely known "steppingstone" theory has no support. Third, it has often been claimed that marihuana smoking can cause psychotic behavior.

Evidence to support this assertion is not convincing. In cases in which marihuana apparently did precipitate some sort of disturbed behavior, the individual had an earlier history of psychiatric problems. Fourth, marihuana has been thought to produce genetic damage. Again, there is no definitive evidence to support this assertion. Finally, even though marihuana is not physiologically addictive, it has been asserted that heavy long-term use may lead to an undesirable psychological dependence on the drug, the so-called *amotivational syndrome;* the individual is said to lose interest in virtually all activities, become lethargic, and show moral, social, and personal deterioration. Although there appears to be some correlation between chronic, heavy use of marihuana and the amotivational syndrome, it can be neither causal nor absolute, for not all heavy users become apathetic. In fact, according to the National Commission report,

Intensive studies of the Greek and Jamaican population of heavy long-term cannabis users appear to dispute the sole causality of cannabis in the [amotivational] syndrome. The heavy ganja [a stronger form of marihuana] and hashish using individuals were from lower socioeconomic groups, and possessed average intelligence but had little education and small chance of vocational advancement. Most were married and maintained families and households. They were all employed, most often as laborers and small businessmen, at a level which corresponded with their education and opportunity (p. 79).

Since evidence is minimal that marihuana smoking is potentially dangerous, why are there such strong societal reactions against the use of the drug? Perhaps it is because marihuana smoking increased dramatically during the period of the hippie movement and the development of the radical youth counterculture. In the minds of many people, unconventional life styles, diminished interest in vocational achievement, and dropping out of society probably became associated with the dramatic increase in the smoking of marihuana. Thus marihuana has perhaps been viewed as abetting the destruction of the current social order. There are few threats societies react more strongly against than that of their own destruction.

Short-Term Effects of Marihuana

We shall now examine marihuana as an intoxicant. As with most drugs, its effects depend in part on potency and size of the dose. Users report that smoking marihuana makes them feel relaxed and sociable. The effects of the dried leaves contained in the typical American marihuana cigarettes are mild. In fact, it is often said that the smoker has to *learn* to get a "high" from a marihuana cigarette, which he often shares with others (Becker, 1963). Nonetheless, like any intoxicant, marihuana can impair visual and motor functions; activities such as driving a car are dangerous after using marihuana.

The major active chemical in marihuana has recently been isolated and named tetrahydrocannabinol (THC). Although there are wide ranges in potency,[3] the marihuana available in the States typically contains less than 1 percent of THC. Hashish is much stronger and often contains between 5 percent and 12 percent THC. Large doses of marihuana have been reported to produce rapid emotional changes, a dulling of attention, fragmented

[3] The potency of the leaves is thought to vary with the region in which the hemp plant is cultivated. The leaves of plants grown in hot, relatively dry climates contain larger amounts of THC.

thought, impaired memory, and in some cases a feeling of enhanced insight. Extremely heavy doses have sometimes been found to induce hallucinations and other effects similar to those of LSD. Occasionally, marihuana elicits intense anxiety, but usually only among novices who may fear that the changes taking place are not produced by the drug or that they are irreversible.

In one of the studies reported by the National Commission on Marihuana and Drug Abuse, the following description of the short-term effects of marihuana was offered.

. . . no harmful effects were observed on general bodily functions, motor functions, mental functions, personal or social behavior, or work performance. Total sleep time and periods of sleep were increased. Weight gain was uniformly noted.

No evidence of physical dependence [i.e. addiction] or signs of withdrawal were noted. In the heaviest smokers, moderate psychological dependence was suggested by an increased negative mood after cessation of smoking . . . Neither immediate nor short-term (twenty-one-day) high-dose marihuana intoxication decreased motivation to engage in a variety of social and goal-directed behavior . . . Marihuana smoking appeared to affect patterns of social interaction. Although use of the drug was found to be a group . . . social activity around which conversation and other types of social behavior were centered, it was not uncommon for some or all of the smokers to withdraw from social interaction and concentrate on the subjective drug experience. During the first part of the smoking period, both intermittent and daily users demonstrated a marked decrement in total interaction. Total interaction continued to diminish among intermittent users but increased. . . among the daily users during the later part of the smoking period. The quality of the interaction was more convivial and less task-oriented when marihuana was available to the group. Additionally, an assessment of the effect of marihuana on risk-taking behavior revealed that daily users tended to become more conservative when engaging in decision-making under conditions of risk (p. 74).

Reasons for Use

The National Commission found that the motivations for smoking marihuana varied, depending on how often it was smoked. Those who smoked the drug less that once a month reported that they did so primarily out of curiosity and the desire to share a social experience with their peers. Intermittent users, those smoking the drug from two to ten times per month, started for the same reason but continued because they enjoyed the socializing and recreational aspects of the drug and found that it contributed to the formation of close social relationships. Moderate and heavy users, those smoking marihuana from eleven times per month up to several times per day, mentioned the "kicks" of the drug more often than did other groups. They also reported relying on the drug to relieve anxiety and boredom. There is also some indication of an association between personality traits and the use of marihuana. In a study reported by the National Commission, 148 undergraduates filled out the California Psychological Inventory anonymously. Marihuana users were found to have greater social presence, flexibility, empathy, and inclinations for independent achievement. In contrast, adamant nonusers were found to have greater responsibility and self-control and to be conformists in their outlook.

Why is marihuana the favorite drug of so many? There are several plausible explanations. One, which we have already noted, concerns the development of the youth culture. Youth seems to have become a separate force in today's society and the smoking of marihuana an accepted activity in their counterculture.[4] Moreover, it has been suggested (Marin and Cohen, 1971) that a strong desire for new and interesting phenomenological experiences plays a central role in the use of drugs such as marihuana. It is perhaps no accident that many of those who enjoy marihuana also show an interest in meditation. We must also remember that the United States, even before the upswing in the use of marihuana, was already a drug-taking culture. Sleeping preparations, tranquilizers, diet pills, pep pills, and alcohol were all widely ingested by a great many Americans. Therefore it is hardly surprising

[4] The authors of this book feel uncomfortable making this generalization, that youth has become a separate cultural force. Recent years have seen changes which, viewed from close proximity, appear phenomenal. But it is extraordinarily difficult to gauge the significance of social changes, and it may well be that what seems important from our present vantage point will years from now be considered a rather trivial or transient development.

that youth found and adopted its own drug.

Because the cultivation, sale, and possession of marihuana are illegal, the great increase in its use makes it a serious social problem. For example, in Louisiana as of 1970, the punishment for possession of marihuana, first offense, was a mandatory minimum sentence of five years at hard labor. In Utah a person may receive a life sentence for a first offense involving the sale of the drug. These and other harsh penalties are frequently more severe than sanctions imposed on those who commit crimes of physical violence. In spite of these laws, the frequency of arrest for these offenses has jumped over 300 percent from 1965 to 1970, a statistic which questions the efficacy of the currently severe laws. In the National Commission Survey only a small percentage of those who smoke marihuana reported being deterred because of the legal penalties for its use. Thus we are left with a disjunction between the law and the behavior of many people. The pressure for changes is beginning to be felt. If this trend continues, the penalties for possession of marihuana are likely to be lessened.

LSD AND RELATED DRUGS

In 1943 a Swiss chemist, Albert Hoffmann, recorded a description of an illness he had seemingly contracted.

Last Friday . . . I had to interrupt my laboratory work . . . I was seized with a feeling of great restlessness and mild dizziness. At home, I lay down and sank into a not unpleasant delirium, which was characterized by extremely exciting fantasies. In a semiconscious state with my eyes closed . . . fantastic visions of extraordinary realness and

with an intense kaleidoscopic play of colors assaulted me (cited by Cashman, 1966, p. 31).

Earlier in the day Dr. Hoffmann had manufactured a few milligrams of *d*-lysergic acid diethylamide, a drug which he had first synthesized in 1938. Reasoning that he might have unknowingly ingested some and that this was the cause of his unusual experience, he deliberately took a small dose and confirmed his hypothesis.

After Hoffman's experiences with LSD in

1943, the drug was referred to as psychotomimetic because it was thought to produce effects similar to the symptoms of a psychosis. More recently, the term psychedelic has been applied to emphasize the subjectively experienced expansion of consciousness reported by users of LSD and two other drugs, *mescaline* and *psilocybin*. In 1896 mescaline, an alkaloid and the active ingredient of peyote, was isolated. Peyote is obtained from small, disc-like growths of the top of the peyote cactus, most of which extends below ground. The drug has been used for centuries in the religious rites of Indian peoples living in the Southwest and northern Mexico. Psilocybin is a crystalline powder which was isolated from the mushroom *Psilocybe mexicana*.

During the 1950s these drugs were dispensed by physicians and scientists in research settings and used to produce what were thought to be psychotic experiences. In 1960 Timothy Leary and Richard Alpert of Harvard University began an investigation of the effects of psilocybin on institutionalized prisoners. The early results, although subject to several confounds, were encouraging: released prisoners who had had a psilocybin trip proved less likely to be rearrested. At the same time the investigators started taking trips themselves and soon had gathered around them a group of people interested in experimenting with psychedelic drugs. By 1962 their activities had attracted the attention of law enforcement agencies. As the investigation continued, it became a scandal, culminating in Leary and Alpert's departure from Harvard. The scandal seemed to give tremendous impetus to the use of the psychedelic drugs, particularly since the manufacture of LSD and the extraction of mescaline and psilocybin were found to be relatively easy and inexpensive. After their expulsion from Harvard, Leary and Alpert founded the International Foundation for Internal Freedom, an organization which emphatically espoused the desirability of properly guided psychedelic trips. It can probably be said that the proselytizing efforts of Leary and Alpert shifted attention from the supposedly psychotic experiences induced by the drugs to their mind-expanding effects. The user's state of consciousness and intensification of sensory perceptions were considered extremely positive and beautiful.

The typical dose of LSD is from about 100 to 350 micrograms, administered as a liquid absorbed in sugar cubes or as capsules or tablets; for psilocybin the usual dose is about 30,000 micrograms; and for mescaline the usual dose is between 350,000 and 500,000 micrograms. The effects of LSD and mescaline usually last about twelve hours, those of psilocybin about six.

The effects of varying doses of LSD were studied by Klee, Bertino, Weintraub, and Callaway (1961). Neither the subjects nor the observers knew the amounts of the drug that had been administered. Nonetheless, experienced observers could readily judge the dose levels ingested by a particular subject from his reports of visual effects and from his somatic or bodily reactions, particularly of the sympathetic nervous system; intellectual impairment and also confusion increased with higher doses.

Perhaps more than with any other kind of drug, the effects of the psychedelics depend on a number of psychological variables in addition to the dose itself. A subject's set, that is, his attitudes, expectancies, and motivations about taking drugs, are widely held to be important determinants of his reactions to psychedelics. In an excellent review of the literature, Barber (1970) specified the effects of psychedelic drugs and related them to variables such as dose, personality, set, and situation. Table 10.3 summarizes these relationships.

Variables	Reactions	Aftereffects
A. Drug: chemical structure and dose B. Situation: where the drug is administered, the way subject is treated by experimenter and by others, the emotional atmosphere, whether subject is alone or in a group C. Set: subject's attitudes, expectancies, and motivation D. Subject's personality characteristics	1. Somatic-sympathetic effects: pupillary dilation; increased blood pressure; increased body temperature; occasional nausea; subjective reports of weakness and giddiness (variable A) 2. Changes in body image: strange and distorted feelings about body or limbs (variable A) 3. Dreamy, detached feelings: light-headedness and detachment from reality; unusually rapid flow of ideas (variable A) 4. Reduced intellectual proficiency: impaired performance on tests measuring memory, mathematical skills, and	1. Chromosomal damage: reported in some early studies, but *not* replicated and currently believed not to be a danger 2. Positive psychological effects: self-reports of improved functioning, but little adequately controlled documentation (variables A, B, C, D) 3. Negative psychological effects: rare instances of psychotic-like reactions, most often in people with a past history of psychopathology; occasional "flashbacks," vivid reexperiencing of some portion of an earlier drug experience (variables A, B, C, D)

Some of the individual studies on psychological variables have been relatively simple, others complex. Expectancies were examined by Metzner, Litwin, and Weil (1965). Before receiving 25,000 to 30,000 micrograms of psilocybin, subjects were asked, "How apprehensive are you about taking the drug?" and "How good do you feel about taking the drug today?" Reports of greater apprehensions

TABLE **10.3** (*continued*)

Variables	Reactions	Aftereffects
	ability to accomplish other tasks requiring focused attention (variable A)	
	5. Changes in time perception: marked slowing of the passage of time (variable A)	
	6. Changes in sensory experience: increased richness of colors; heightened sensitivity to touch and smell; changes in depth and size perception; occasional synesthesias, for example, "smelling a sound" or "feeling a color" (variable A)	
	7. Changes in moods and emotions: highly variable, ranging from ecstasy and transcendental experience to great anxiety, depression, and despair (variables A, B, C, D)	

about taking the drug correlated significantly with increased anxiety, headache, and nausea during the drug experience itself. Similarly, Linton and Langs (1964) administered a battery of personality tests before giving the subjects a dose of 100 micrograms of LSD. Those who were judged to be guarded and overdependent on the basis of the personality tests had the greatest number of bodily reactions, particularly of the sympathetic nervous system, and experienced the greatest anxiety during the LSD session. Persons who had shown themselves to be mistrustful, complaining, and fearful had paranoiac reactions from taking LSD (Klee and Weintraub, 1959; Von Felsinger, Lasagna, and Beecher, 1956).

Pahnke (1963) performed a considerably more remarkable and original piece of research. He attempted to maximize all the situational variables that might contribute to a religious or mystical experience. Subjects in his investigation were theological students who first had to attend meetings at which the possibilities of having religious experiences after taking psilocybin were stressed. Twenty students were given psilocybin and twenty an active placebo by a double-blind procedure. Nicotinic acid was chosen as the placebo because it does produce some effects, such as a tingling sensation in the skin. After receiving the drug or the placebo, each subject participated in a two-and-a-half-hour-long religious service which included meditation, prayers, and the like. To heighten the significance of the occasion, the experiment was conducted on Good Friday. After the session each subject wrote a description of his experience and answered an extensive questionnaire. The mystical and transcendental experiences of the group who took psilocybin were found to be significantly greater than those of the group who took the placebo.

SUMMARY

The habitual use of drugs is regarded by DSM-II as a symptom of an underlying personality disorder. The assumption seems to be that only a mentally disordered person would continue using a drug that is not only harmful but sometimes illegal as well. Little evidence was found to support this view. Therefore attention was focused on the variables that appear to play a role both in the person's initial taking of a drug and in his continuing use of it, even though he may want to stop.

A number of psychological and social factors figure in the initial use of many legal and illegal drugs; these variables include peer pressure, a need to relieve tension, irritation, curiosity, boredom, cultural approval of drug use, and perhaps even a desire of most people to alter their state of consciousness.

Once an individual is using a drug with some regularity, his body may become addicted to it, thereby making it extraordinarily difficult to abstain. Taking drugs such as alcohol, nicotine, heroin, and the barbiturates for prolonged periods appears to develop true physiological addictions: increasing dosages are required to achieve the same effect, and the withdrawal pattern when the particular drug is no longer taken is fairly predictable.

In recent years dispassionate observers have questioned both the sense and morality of the harsh punishments legislated for the use of nonaddicting drugs like marihuana when at the same time the promotion and sale of harmful drugs such as alcohol and nicotine are allowed.

HEROIN

Heroin, synthesized from morphine, is from two to ten times as potent as this alkaloid, depending on measuring techniques. Shown (upper left) are some of the earliest samples of heroin, which was first prepared in 1874 but not produced commercially until 1898, and the various present-day forms and packages of heroin now available only illegally.

OPIUM POPPY, GUM OPIUM, AND MORPHINE

Opium is obtained as a milky secretion from the unripened opium poppy (foreground) and prepared as gum opium (right). The most active constituent is morphine (background), a bitter crystalline base processed here as a small block.

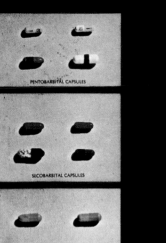

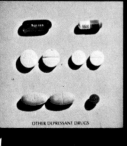

PENTOBARBITAL CAPSULES

SECOBARBITAL CAPSULES

AMOBARBITAL CAPSULES

AMOBARBITAL WITH SECOBARBITAL

PHENOBARBITAL TABLETS

MISCELLANEOUS BARBITURATE TABLETS

OTHER DEPRESSANT DRUGS

 Yellows
Yellow Jackets

 Purple Hearts

Blue Devils
Bluebirds

Double Trouble
Rainbows

Red Devils
Seccy

B

DEPRESSANTS (A) Alcohol, bromides, chloral hydrate, and paraldehyde are all depressants, or sedatives. The most potent and most commonly abused of the sedatives, however, are the barbiturates. There are many different barbiturates on the market, and most of them have been given brand names by the manufacturers. They are medically prescribed in the form of tablets, capsules, syrups, and injectables. (B) The different barbiturates (slang term, "downers") are known by a variety of street terms in the illicit traffic. Secobarbital is known as "seccy" to abusers and as "reds," "red birds," and "red devils," pentobarbital as "yellows," "yellow jackets," or "nimbies." Amobarbital is called "blue heavens," "blue-birds," or "blue devils," and a product combining amobarbital and secobarbital is nicknamed "double trouble" or "rainbows."

MARIHUANA JOINTS. The popular method of using marihuana is by smoking it in cigarettes, called "joints" or "reefers." But marihuana is also taken orally in various drinks such as marihuana tea and in cookies and candy. Small gummy lumps of hashish are smoked in pipes, very often water pipes called hookahs.

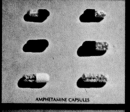

AMPHETAMINE CAPSULES

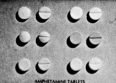

AMPHETAMINE TABLETS

AMPHETAMINE TABLETS

AMPHETAMINE TABLETS

AMPHETAMINE-BARBITURATE COMBINATIONS

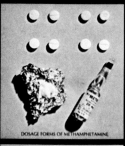

DOSAGE FORMS OF METHAMPHETAMINE

PHENMETRAZINE TABLETS

STIMULANTS
A very common natural stimulant is the alkaloid caffeine, but the most powerful stimulants to the central nervous system are the synthesized amphetamines.

COCAINE
Cocaine, obtained from the leaves of **Erythroxylon coca,** *began to be prescribed a stimulant in 1878. It is known by such street terms as "C," "heaven dust," and "gold dust."*

GLUE SNIFFER KIT
This "glue sniffer kit" was found on a dead boy in New York City. Death from inhaling such preparations usually occurs by suffocation. When aerosols containing the propellant Freon are sniffed, anoxia or the toxic effects of the Freon itself may cause death.

PEYOTE CACTUS

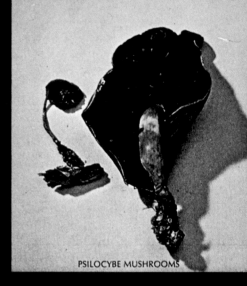

PSILOCYBE MUSHROOMS

PEYOTE BUTTONS AND GROUND PEYOTE BUTTONS

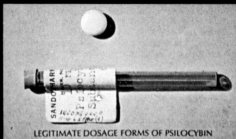

LEGITIMATE DOSAGE FORMS OF PSILOCYBIN

PEYOTE

The "mescal buttons" of the peyote cactus were chewed by the ancient Aztecs to enter into a visionary state. These buttons, which contain the hallucinogen mescaline, can be ground or the alkaloid can be synthesized.

PSILOCYBIN

The Mexican mushroom from which psilocybin is extracted has been eaten for centuries by Indians seeking direct communion with supernatural powers. Another compound psilocin is also extracted from the mushroom, and both are similar in effect to mescaline.

ILLICIT LSD

LSD is one of the most potent drugs known, producing effects in microgram quantities. Illicit LSD is available in capsule and tablet forms and as a solution absorbed in sugar cubes.

CHAPTER 11

Unconventional Sexual Behavior and Human Sexual Inadequacy

Of all the aspects of human functioning that receive the attention of psychopathologists, perhaps none has been the object of as much bad counsel as sexual activity. Most people recall from their own development some concerns about sexuality. All too often their worries originated with, or were at least exacerbated by, some piece of explicit misinformation from authorities. The Boy Scout Manual used to counsel maturing young men against masturbation, falsely inculcating in them the fear that self-stimulation might weaken their minds. Some psychiatrists and psychologists have been known to admonish an individual who is sexually attracted to members of his or her own sex that giving in to homosexual ways will lead to psychical ruination. A substantial proportion of the average psychotherapist's time is, or should be, devoted to undoing the harm caused by such misinformation. It has indeed been estimated (Masters and Johnson, 1970) that more than half of all marriages in the United States are marked at some time by sexual difficulties, sometimes of such severity that tenderness itself is lost, let alone the more intense pleasure of sexual activity.

CATEGORIES OF UNCONVENTIONAL SEXUAL BEHAVIOR

We have already commented several times on the relativistic, subjective nature of psychiatric labeling. The psychiatrist's judgment of the appropriateness and intensity of sadness, for example, seems to determine whether or not it will be considered depression. In deciding what sexual behavior is unconventional, the arbitrariness of psychiatric diagnosis reaches an extreme. Let us examine first how problems are listed in DSM-II. Two disorders typically regarded as sexual in nature and already alluded to in Chapter 7, namely impotence in

271

the male and dyspareunia or painful intercourse in both sexes, are not considered sexual deviations but rather psychophysiologic disorders. These and other relatively widespread sexual inadequacies are discussed in the second part of this chapter. Our attention in this section is directed to the so-called sexual deviations which, like addiction, are classified with personality disorders, all of them being given in DSM-II the more general designation nonpsychotic mental disorders. The subcategory sexual deviation is applied to

. . . individuals whose sexual interests are directed primarily toward objects other than people of the opposite sex, toward sexual acts not usually associated with coitus, or toward coitus performed under bizarre circumstances as in necrophilia [sexual relations with dead bodies], pedophilia [sexual contacts with children], sexual sadism and fetishism. Even though many find their practices distasteful, they remain unable to substitute normal sexual behavior for them. This diagnosis is not appropriate for individuals who perform deviant sexual acts because normal sexual objects are not available to them (DSM-II, p. 44).

This definition is problematic for several reasons.

1. It is assumed, from the general definition of personality disorders, that sexual deviations are "deeply ingrained . . . lifelong patterns," as contrasted with behavior that might originate in adulthood and not be a "core" part of the individual.
2. To feel sexually toward a member of the same sex is regarded *ipso facto* as abnormal.
3. It is asserted that sexual activity is abnormal unless it is "associated with coitus."

According to this definition, someone who prefers an orgasm produced by manual stimulation to one produced by intercourse may be considered abnormal.
4. To decide whether intercourse is performed "under bizarre circumstances" clearly demands a definition of what is bizarre.

Unconventional sexual behavior may be categorized in terms of *object chosen* and *activity engaged in.* Thus, when the individual chooses someone of the same sex, the behavior is homosexuality; an inanimate object or part of the body, fetishism; a close relative, incest; a child, pedophilia. The second category, unconventional activity, may have some connection with the first, choice of an unconventional object. In addition to or instead of engaging in sexual intercourse, the individual may prefer to watch others undress or engage in sexual behavior, which is voyeurism; expose his genitals to some audience, which is exhibitionism; obtain sexual gratification forcibly, which is rape; inflict pain, which is sadism; or endure pain, which is masochism. Two other forms of unconventional behavior are more difficult to fit into these two major categories: transvestism, dressing in the clothing of the opposite sex; and transsexualism, believing that one is actually a member of the opposite sex and merely "trapped" in the wrong body. Transvestism does, however, somewhat resemble fetishism, except that the person carries the behavior one step further and dons the inanimate object.

A number of other sexual activities are regarded as deviations, probably falling into the open categories of "other" or "unspecified" sexual deviations. They are defined briefly in the following list (McCary, 1967).

Troilism. Having sexual relations with or in the presence of more than one person.

Sexual oralism. Exclusive reliance on oral-genital contact for sexual gratification.

Sexual analism. Exclusive reliance on the anus instead of the vagina for penile insertion.

Zoophilia (bestiality). Sexual contact with animals, for either intercourse or masturbation.

Frottage. Obtaining sexual satisfaction by rubbing or pressing against another person, typically without engaging in sexual intercourse.

Saliromania. Obtaining sexual gratification from soiling or mutilating female bodies or clothing.

Gerontosexuality. Preference for older people as sexual partners.

Mate swapping. Exchange of marital partners.

Coprophilia. Obtaining sexual gratification from handling feces.

Little is known about how patterns of sexual behavior develop or are maintained. In psychoanalytic theories each of the sexual deviations is viewed as some kind of defensive maneuver against intolerable levels of neurotic anxiety aroused by the threat of engaging in "normal" sexual activity, that is, having intercourse with a person of the opposite sex. Thus the exhibitionist who is sexually excited by showing his genitalia to others under inappropriate social circumstances is considered fearful of coitus because he connects it with castration. Male homosexuality is viewed as having a similar etiology. Learning accounts of the various problems are more varied, but neither they nor the psychodynamic theories are supported by reliable data.

Homosexuality, a significant social and personal problem, will not be discussed as unconventional sexual behavior. This subject will receive separate and extended consideration in Chapter 12.

Unconventional Choices of Sexual Object

Fetishism

Many men take particular pleasure in observing and fondling certain parts of women's bodies, referring to themselves in the vernacular as "leg-men" or "breast-men." A woman may place great importance on the size of a man's penis or be sexually excited by the shape and texture of his hands. Through cultural and personal preferences certain physical attributes come to be regarded as sexually arousing. But interest in a particular part of the body is not considered a fetishism unless it is so strong that the rest of the person is disregarded. For a fetishist a particular inanimate object or part of the body is the center of all or nearly all sexual interest. Subjectively, the attraction felt by the person toward the object or part of the body is involuntary and irresistible. The fetishism may be a dominant force in the person's life. For example, a man may be so enthralled with women's ankles that he takes a job as a shoe salesman, even though he could qualify for a better-paying position, preferring instead to titillate himself with frequent and close contacts with female ankles.

The inanimate objects that are common sources of arousal for fetishists, who are usually men, are underwear, shoes, stockings, gloves, toilet articles, and the like. Or a man may be uncontrollably aroused by the sight of and contact with furs or even a baby carriage, a fetish which seems to be far more prevalent in Great Britain than in the States. Often fetishistic objects are used in masturbation, although they may also serve as the arousing factor for conventional heterosexual intercourse—as when a husband demands that his wife wear black net stockings and leather gloves during lovemaking.

As already indicated, psychoanalytic theorists generally consider fetishisms, like other deviations, to serve some sort of defensive function, warding off anxiety about normal sexual contacts. Learning theorists usually invoke some kind of classical conditioning in the person's social-sexual history. For example, a young boy may, early in his sexual experiences, masturbate to pictures of women in black leather. Indeed, one experiment (Rachman, 1966) lends some mild support to learning propositions. Male subjects were shown slides of nude and alluring females repeatedly interspersed with slides of women's boots. The subjects were eventually aroused by the slides of the boots alone. The "fetishistic attraction" induced, however, was weak and transient.

Transvestism and Transsexualism

When a person is sexually aroused by dressing in the clothing of the opposite sex while still regarding himself as a member of his own sex, the term *transvestism* is applied to his behavior. Transvestites, male or female, also enjoy appearing socially as a member of the opposite sex (Figure 11.1). Arousal appears to be the primary motivation of most transvestites, who typically masturbate when cross-dressed. Transvestism should not be confused with homosexuality; many transvestites are heterosexual and not all homosexuals "go in drag."

If a man dresses as a woman because he truly believes that he is of that sex and that nature had played an unfair trick on him by giving him the wrong body, he is called a *transsexual*. These individuals, almost always men, maintain their belief despite firm evidence that their bodies are, in fact, biologically male in every respect (Benjamin, 1953).[1] When they are dressed in clothing of the opposite sex,

[1] Hermaphrodites actually have both male and female sexual organs, but this physical disorder is rare.

they regard themselves as properly clothed. Indeed, more and more often transsexuals are taking the drastic step of undergoing sex-change surgery (Figure 11.2) which removes their male genitalia and substitutes an artificial vagina. Appropriate female hormones are also given to reduce hair growth and stimulate development of the breasts (Money, 1968). Transsexuals do not become particularly aroused when dressing in the clothes of the opposite sex.

Although transsexualism is regarded as a nonpsychotic mental disorder, subcategorized as a sexual deviation, the research literature now available, as well as clinical experience, indicates that transsexuals may well be suffering from a thought disorder, a classic symptom of psychosis. They do not think logically, insisting vehemently that they are *really* women in spite of the fact that they appear to be normal males. Of course, it may well be that contemporary science has not progressed far enough to detect that transsexuals do differ physiologically from men.

Both psychoanalysts and learning theorists seem to agree that transvestism and transsexualism develop under circumstances in which the person is confused about which sex he or she belongs to—*gender identity* is not well established or is even reversed. In the literature on both disorders, case histories in which the male child is praised for dressing up in his mother's clothing are cited. What this kind of anecdotal evidence fails to explain, however, is why one child who is allowed to cross-dress develops into a transvestite, another into someone who truly believes that he is a she, and still others into conventional adults.

Nonsexual factors have been implicated in transvestism. Some clinicians have treated transvestites who regard cross-dressing as a refuge from the responsibilities that they have to bear as men in our society. The clothing,

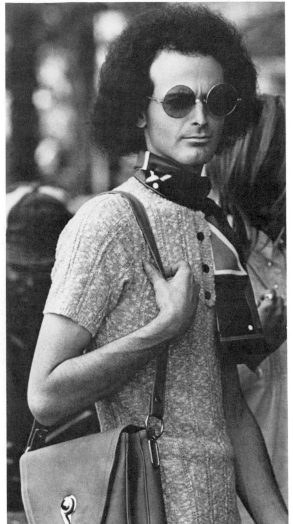

FIGURE **11.1**
On the left is a transvestite who not only dresses in female attire but also wears a wig, makeup, and lipstick. The young man on the right, in contrast, makes no attempt to conceal the fact that he is a male.

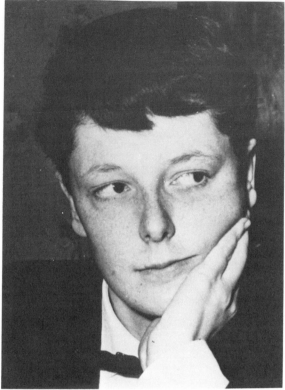

FIGURE **11.2**

On the left is Annie M., a transsexual, on her sixteenth birthday. Four years later, as shown on the right, she has undergone a sex-change operation and begun to lead the life of a man. Most transsexuals, however, are men who believe that they are women.

then, has a particular *meaning* for them that is more complex than sheer sexual arousal and role playing. In other words, conceptualizing transvestism solely in sexual terms may be an oversimplification.

Some survey research has been done on transvestism. Through the cooperation of a national transvestite organization, Bentler (Bentler and Prince, 1969, 1970; Bentler, Shearman, and Prince, 1970) was able to send a standard personality test to a nationwide sample of transvestites. The replies of the subjects were compared to those of control groups matched for age. His results generally support clinical impressions that transvestites are not necessarily grossly disturbed individuals, for they were not that different from the normal controls on neurotic and psychotic scales. The transvestites did indicate a preference for routine and a disinclination to act on impulse. They revealed themselves as rather socially withdrawn, as less sympathetic to others, less concerned with what others think of them, less dominant over others, and more self-reliant and rebellious. Unfortunately, the personality characteristics revealed by Bentler's research provide little insight into the etiology of transvestism.

Incest

The taboo against incest seems virtually universal in human societies. A notable exception were the marriages of Egyptian pharoahs to their sisters or other females of their immediate families. In Egypt it was believed that the royal blood should not be contaminated by that of outsiders. Some anthropologists consider the prohibition against incest to have served the important function of forcing larger and wider social ties than would have been likely had family members chosen their mates only from among their own.

Incest, which includes all varieties of sexual relations that culminate in at least one orgasm, seems most common between father and daughter, and between brother and sister—especially in lower-income homes where siblings tend to share the same beds. Gebhard, Gagnon, Pomeroy, and Christenson (1965) found, in their well-known study on sex offenders, that most fathers who had relations with physically mature daughters tended to be very devout, moralistic, and fundamentalistic in their religious beliefs.

Statistics on the incidence of incest are notoriously difficult to collect since, by definition, this behavior occurs within the family; other members are very reluctant to report the incest offenders to authorities. Explanations of incest run the gamut from sexual deprivation to the Freudian notion that human beings have basic human desires for such relationships.

Pedophilia

Pedophiles are adults, usually men at least as far as police records indicate, who derive sexual gratification through physical and often sexual contact with children. Although violence is seldom a part of the molestation, society's reaction to pedophiles is far more punitive than it is toward rapists, who employ physical force. Often the pedophile is content to stroke the child's hair, but he may also manipulate the child's genitalia, encourage the child to manipulate his, and less often, attempt intromission. The molestations may be repeated over a period of weeks, months, or years if they are not discovered by other adults or protested by the child. There are both heterosexual and homosexual pedophiles, but it is of interest that most homosexuals restrict their sexual attentions to other adults and regard with disdain those who do not.

Pedophiles tend to be rigidly religious and moralistic. As with most of the aberrant sexual behaviors that have been described, there is a strong subjective feeling of compulsion in the attraction that draws the pedophile to the child. According to Gebhard and his colleagues (1965), pedophiles typically know the children they molest, being a next-door-neighbor, uncle, or grandfather. Most older heterosexual pedophiles are or have been married at some times in their lives.

The question of how seriously disturbed pedophiles are was investigated by Mohr, Turner, and Jerry (1964). The pedophiles in their sample were found to cluster into three age groups, adolescence, mid-to-late thirties, and mid-to-late fifties, with the mid-thirties group the largest. Adolescent pedophiles were found to be sexually inexperienced with people of their own age. Those in their mid-thirties had developed serious mental and social maladjustments, including alcoholism, which was frequently associated with the act. The older pedophiles were better adjusted but usually suffered from loneliness and isolation. These differences indicate that etiological factors vary with the age of the offender.

It has been suggested that the drive to approach a child sexually sometimes reflects a sense of having failed in the adult world, both socially and professionally as well as sexually.

Occasionally, though, an adult predisposed toward pedophilia may be seduced by a child's innocent, uninhibited show of affection. The child, however, does not infuse his behavior with the sexual overtones that the pedophile perceives and responds to. If we accept the Gebhard (1965) finding that the pedophile approaches children as old as twelve, some of the youngsters may well be incipiently mature physically and, given recent similar styles of clothing for both children and adults, appear older than their chronological age. In defining pedophilia, state laws prescribe an upper age limit for those who are to be considered children, making it a crime to approach sexually any younger person. The age varies in different states.

When a child tells a parent that an adult has fondled him or her, the parents face the dilemma of how to react. Many experts feel that the child tends not to interpret the interaction in the same sexual terms that adults do. Even if the molester has an orgasm, it is not always clear to the child what has happened, and to react with adult alarm can lend needless negative meaning to an unfortunate incident. But at the same time the young child must be protected from a prolonged and harmful sexual relationship with an adult.

Unconventional Choices of Sexual Activity

Unconventional sexual acts with adult members of the opposite sex are generally considered abnormal and are labeled as disordered behavior if they are preferred to conventional, heterosexual relations between consenting adults. When the acts are performed *in addition to* conventional activities or under conditions of involuntary deprivation of these activities, the diagnostic label is not usually applied.

Voyeurism ("Peeping")

Now and then a man may by chance happen to observe a nude woman without her knowing he is watching her. If his sex life is primarily conventional, his act would be voyeuristic, but he would not generally be considered a voyeur.

Strictly speaking, voyeurism is viewed as a deviation when it is preferred to coitus or indulged in at serious risk. It is socially unacceptable when the person is observed without her knowledge and would be offended if she became aware of it.

The typical voyeur is not interested in ogling his own wife or girl friend. In 95 percent of incidents he observes strangers. What draws him to peep through windows is in large measure the danger and excitement entailed. . . . [He typically masturbates] while watching or immediately thereafter (Katchadourian and Lunde, 1972, pp. 288–289).

A true voyeur, who is almost always a man, will not find it particularly exciting to watch a woman who is undressing for his special benefit (Figure 11.3). The element of risk seems important, for he is excited by his anticipation of how the woman may react if she finds out he is watching. Some voyeurs derive special pleasure from secretly observing couples having sexual relations. As with all categories of behavior that are against the law, frequencies of occurrence are difficult to assess, since the majority of *all* illegal activities go unnoticed by the police. We might suppose that those few women who are voyeurs would not be reported as often to the police as male voyeurs are.

From what we know, voyeurs tend to be fearful of more direct sexual encounters with others, their peeping serving as substitute gratification and possibly giving them a sense of power over those watched. They do not

FIGURE **11.3**

These photographers, delighted with their pastime of viewing a partially nude woman, would not *be considered voyeurs. A voyeur must obtain most of his sexual enjoyment from peeping and do so in a socially disapproved fashion. Could the woman be regarded as an exhibitionist?*

seem to be otherwise disturbed, however. After all restrictions against the sale of pornographic materials to adults had been lifted in Denmark, one of the few observed effects of this liberalization was a significant reduction in peeping, at least as reported to the police (Kut-chinsky, 1970). It may be that the increased availability of completely frank pictorial and literary material, which is typically used in masturbation, satisfies the needs that had earlier made some men without other outlets voyeurs.

Exhibitionism

Voyeurism and exhibitionism together account for close to a majority of all sexual offenses that come to the attention of police. Again, the frequency of exhibitionism is much greater among men. A common quip holds that a man surreptitiously looking at a nude woman is a voyeur, but that a woman looking at a naked man is watching an exhibitionist.

Exhibitionism is a deviation when an adult male obtains sexual gratification from exposing his genitals to women or children who are involuntary observers, usually complete strangers. In a typical sequence the exhibitionist drives or walks in front of a passing woman with his genitals exposed. He usually, but not always, has an erection. Usually, as soon as she has seen him, he flees. Sometimes he wears a coat and exposes himself periodically while riding on a subway or bus. . . .

The exhibitionist, in common with the voyeur, does not usually attack or molest his "victim." His gratification comes from observing her reaction, which is predictably surprise, fear, disgust, and so on. . . . Some men ejaculate at the scene of exposure; others merely enjoy the psychic release. Others become highly aroused and masturbate right afterward (Katchadourian and Lunde, 1972, pp. 289–290).

The urge to expose seems overwhelming and virtually uncontrollable to the exhibitionist and is triggered by feelings of anxiety and restlessness as well as by sexual arousal. Because of the compulsive nature of the urge, the exposures may be repeated rather frequently and even in the same place and at the same time of day. Generally the exhibitionist is immature in his approaches to the opposite sex and otherwise unsuccessful in all interpersonal relationships, although these characteristics cannot

be said to cause exhibitionism, at least by themselves. Over half of all exhibitionists are married, but their sexual relationships with their wives are unsatisfactory (Mohr, Turner, and Jerry, 1964).

Younger exhibitionists may not manifest other kinds of psychopathology, but some of those who expose themselves come from the ranks of the mentally retarded and the senile. Some who exhibit do so while having a temporal lobe epileptic seizure (see page 430). Because the behavior of these people may be without deliberation and intent, it is problematic whether they should be considered exhibitionists. In applying the label of exhibitionism, not only overt behavior but also intent should be established, which may be difficult.

The fact that the exhibited penis is sometimes flaccid raises interesting questions about the *sexual* aspects of the act. How sexually arousing can it be for a man to expose himself if his penis is not erect when doing so? It may be that his arousal is diminished by guilt over what he is doing or fear that he will be apprehended by the police. Or the exhibitionist, deficient as he seems to be in more conventional social skills, may regard his act of exposure as the best social interaction that he can manage. The fact that a nonchalant reaction on the part of the observer is not satisfying to the exhibitionist suggests that he is seeking a certain reaction from those to whom he exposes himself. These are only a few of the aspects of exhibitionism about which we have no certain knowledge at present.

The search to determine how exhibitionism develops has turned up very little. An intriguing learning hypothesis emphasizes the reinforcing aspects of masturbation. McGuire, Carlisle, and Young (1965) reported on the development of exhibitionism in two young men who were surprised during urination by an attractive woman. After the embarrassment had passed and when they were in private, the thought of being discovered in this way aroused them and they masturbated while fantasizing the earlier experience. After repeated masturbating to such fantasies, they began to exhibit.

Rape

Few other kinds of antisocial behavior are viewed with more disgust and anger than the obtaining of sexual gratification forcibly and often violently through rape. A special category, statutory rape, refers to sexual intercourse between a male and any female who is a minor. The typical age of consent, as decided by state statutes, is eighteen years. It is assumed that a younger girl should not be held responsible for her sexual activity. A charge of statutory rape can be made even if it can be proved that the girl entered into the situation knowingly and willingly. Thus statutory rape need not involve force, being simply a consummated intercourse with a minor that was reported to the police.

Definitions of rape vary greatly in different police jurisdictions, making it extremely difficult to draw meaningful comparisons between the incidences in various cities and locales. For example, in Los Angeles the police classify as forcible rape any encounter between a man and a woman in which the man seeks sexual gratification from her against her will. This broad definition includes instances in which no sexual intercourse takes place. In Boston the fondling of immature girls by physically immature boys has been considered rape; not only may no intercourse take place, but the offenders may not be adults (Chappell, Geis, Schafer, and Siegel, 1971). In other jurisdictions such episodes would be categorized as delinquent behavior, not rape.

Forcible rape elicits great attention from law enforcers and can create terror in women who, in general, are significantly weaker in physical strength than men. Rapists often inflict serious bodily injury in forcing themselves sexually upon their victims, and some may, after the sex act, murder and mutilate the women they have attacked. Because rape is a mixture of both sex and aggression, the motivation is difficult to determine. The rapist may have a sadistic streak, but unlike the sadist he often does not know the victim beforehand and attacks someone who is unwilling. The sadist usually has an established, ongoing relationship with a masochist. In many cases a pattern of repeated rape is part of a sociopathic life style (see page 206).

Rape victims are sometimes traumatized by the experience both mentally and physically. Masters and Johnson (1970) have provided several case histories indicating how the experience of rape can leave a mark on a woman for many years afterward, giving her a negative attitude toward her sexual relationship with her husband. Ligaments in the pelvic area can be torn during a woman's struggles against her attacker. Fortunately, rape victims are often able, in a reasonable amount of time, to dismiss from their minds the potentially traumatic effects of the experience.

Some reports of rape are made by women who have some prior acquaintance with their attacker. A man may pick up a woman in a bar, take her home to her apartment, and then misread the signals, realizing only after he has become sexually aroused that the woman is not really interested in intercourse. When the desires of the woman are either unclear or contrary to what the man has assumed them to be, the male may force intercourse (Gagnon, in press). Certain girls have "bad" reputations with the police of their communities. Under these circumstances a truly forceful and even violent rape may not be categorized as such in the stationhouse, especially when the status in the community of the boy or man involved is higher than that of the girl. In this way a biased incidence of rape, as well as of other unconventional sexual behavior, may be obtained if attention is restricted to police records. Overriding these considerations, however, is the unfortunate fact that the woman may feel that great shame is attached to her involuntary role in rape. Three times as many rapes are estimated to occur as are reported to the police.

Sadism and Masochism

The majority of sadists, as indicated earlier, establish relationships with masochists to derive mutual sexual gratification. The sadist may derive full orgastic pleasure by inflicting pain on his partner, and the masochist may be completely gratified by being subjected to pain (Figure 11.4). For other partners the sadistic and masochistic practices are a prelude to sexual intercourse. A married couple seen for behavior therapy had practiced the following ritual.

As a prelude to sexual intercourse, the young man would draw blood by cutting a small incision on the palm of his wife's right hand. She would then stimulate his penis, using the blood of her right palm as a lubricant. Normal intercourse would then ensue, and the moment the wife felt her husband ejaculating, she was required to dig her nails deep into the small of his back or buttocks (Lazarus and Davison, 1971, pp. 202–203).

Some sadists murder and mutilate; fortunately, however, most of the time sadism and masochism are restricted to fantasies. The increasing number of "sex shops" in large cities do a lucrative business in providing pictorial and literary materials to those who need at least the vicarious experience of pain in

FIGURE **11.4**
Window of a New York City shop that caters to the sexual needs of sadists and masochists.

order to satisfy themselves sexually. One young man who sought help (Davison, 1968a) found it sexually stimulating to imagine an attractive woman tied to stakes on the ground and tearfully trying to extricate herself. His sexual life was restricted to masturbation and thinking of this and similar images of women in pain or extreme discomfort.

How can it happen that a person, often quite normal in other respects, must inflict or experience suffering, directly or vicariously, in order to become sexually aroused? If it is assumed, as some psychoanalysts do, that pain provides sexual pleasure, the answer is readily available, but of course this "explanation" really explains nothing. Another psychoanalytic theory holds that the sadist has a castration complex and inflicts pain to assure himself of his power and masculinity. It may also be that in childhood or adolescence sadomasochistic elements are present while orgasms are experienced. Although it is plausible to suggest that classical conditioning may have occurred, there are as yet no data to support this theory.

A related hypothesis suggests that the physiological arousal from inflicting and experiencing pain is not, in fact, dissimilar to sexual excitement. In the early stages of being sexualized, discriminations may be more difficult to make, especially if the pain-inducing act also includes sexual elements. In this way the individual may learn to label pain-produced arousal as sexual. Interesting as it may be, this hypothesis is also purely speculative at this point.

HUMAN SEXUAL INADEQUACY: THE WORK OF MASTERS AND JOHNSON

Thus far in this chapter the unconventional patterns of sexual behavior of a small minority of the population have been described. But many "ordinary" people are likely to have problems that interfere with conventional sexual enjoyment, at least to some extent during their lives. In examining these problems, we shall be drawing extensively on the clinical and research data on dysfunctional human sexual behavior collected by Masters and Johnson (1966, 1970) in the context of their extensive research and therapy programs in St. Louis, Missouri.

Masters and Johnson separate the sexual response system into two interacting subsystems, the *biophysical* and the *psychosocial.* Severe physiological damage or deficit, such as low levels of hormones, may hinder sexual responses, but such impairments are very rare. Most human beings will respond sexually to appropriate sensory stimulation if their acquired psychosocial system does not interfere. In other words, assuming adequate biological endowment and given sensory stimulation such as stroking of the genitalia, it is inevitable that a person will respond sexually when their reactions are unhindered by fear or disgust.

Background of the Masters and Johnson Work

Inquiry into human sexual behavior has not always been a common and acceptable field of scientific activity as it is today. While still a medical student at the University of Rochester, William H. Masters decided to undertake a scientific and clinical investigation of human sexual response for the principal reason that very little was known about the physiology of human sexual functioning. Like other sex researchers before him, Masters chose obstetrics and gynecology as his specialty; during his residency he worked on hormone problems of the aging. The medical profession has seldom been known as particularly innovative in a social and political sense. Masters was repeatedly rebuffed and discouraged by his older colleagues before he was able to begin his pioneering research on sexual response. Fortunately, his earlier very reputable and conservative work in hormone replacement therapy encouraged Washington University to sponsor him. He obtained permission to set up a laboratory in 1953 and started the actual work in July 1954.

Masters realized that he was risking his professional reputation by working in this area.

If you do cancer research for ten years and don't come up with anything noteworthy, nobody is going to question you professionally. I went into sex research with full knowledge that I had to win. I had to come up with something or I would have been destroyed professionally. Even with results, sex research invites criticism (Belliveau and Richter, 1970, pp. 19–20).

For about ten years Masters's work was supported by Washington University, some private grant money, and some funding from the National Institutes of Health. These sources of funds were eventually exhausted, however, and in 1963 and 1964 he moved to private quarters, setting up his own clinic, the Reproductive Biology Research Foundation, entirely separate from the university. He had been joined in 1957 by Virginia Johnson, in what has become an extremely fruitful collaboration (Figure 11.5).

The initial work was not directed toward developing therapy techniques but proposed to measure in the laboratory the physiological responses of normal human subjects to sexual stimulation. One of the first problems was to set up the instruments necessary for observation and measurements. For example, an artificial penis was constructed out of clear plastic through which filmed observations could be made of the vagina during sexual excitement. Finding suitable volunteer subjects was also a challenge. For over a year only female prostitutes were studied, but because prostitutes frequently do not have orgasms, other subjects were eventually sought. Masters and Johnson let it be known in the university community that volunteer subjects were needed; in this liberal setting they came forth without too much hesitation. Extensive interviewing and history taking established that the subjects included in the study were not emotionally disturbed and were capable of normal sexual functioning, that is, able to have an orgasm with sufficient physical and psychological stimulation. The persons tested were in no sense a random sample of the population, nor did Masters and Johnson ever claim that they were. All potential subjects knew that they would be observed during acts of intercourse or masturbation, and that their physiological responses would be recorded. Of course, confidentiality was absolutely assured.

Sexual Response in Men and Women

After eleven years of study the principal findings of the laboratory research on normal volunteers were reported in the first Masters and Johnson book, *Human Sexual Response* (1966). The responses of men and women had been found to be unexpectedly similar; Masters and Johnson were able to delineate a four-stage cycle of sexual arousal for both sexes (Figure 11.6).

The excitement phase *is initiated by whatever is sexually stimulating to a particular individual. If stimulation is strong enough, excitement builds quickly, but if it is interrupted or if it becomes objectionable, this phase becomes extended or the cycle may be stopped. If effective sexual stimulation is continued, it produces increased levels of sexual tension. . . . This increased tension is called the* plateau phase. *If the individual's drive for sexual release in this phase is not strong enough, or if stimulation ceases to be effective or is withdrawn, the man or woman will not experience orgasm, but will enter a long period of gradually decreased sexual tension. The climactic or* orgasmic phase, *a totally involuntary*

FIGURE **11.6**
*Graphic portrayal of A, male, and B, female sexual response cycles. The
blue lines indicate the most common patterns of response, the white lines
variations. The female cycle does not always climb to orgasm, but when it
does there is not the inevitable refractory period found in the male cycle.
After Masters and Johnson, 1966, p. 5.*

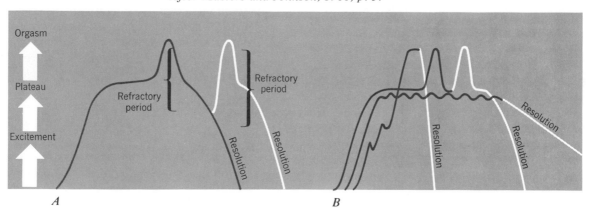

BOX **11.1** *A Technique for Assessing Sexual Arousal*

An important device developed to further research on human sexual behavior is the penile plethysmograph (Freund, 1963; Bancroft, Jones, and Pullan, 1966). A plethysmograph is a device that measures blood flow. The most widely used plethysmograph for measuring blood flow in the penis, and therefore erection, consists of a strain gauge, a very thin rubber tube filled with mercury. Placed just behind the head of the penis, this tube stretches with even the slightest increase in penile circumference. As the mercury becomes thinner, its electrical resistance is changed. With appropriate wiring this increase in resistance can be transformed into a record on a polygraph. Since increase in length of the penis correlates highly with increase in circumference, this simple device can provide a very satisfactory measure of penile erection, which is commonly regarded as a good indicant of male sexual arousal. Like all technical innovations, the availability of this device has spurred a remarkable volume of research on male sexual behavior. A promising means of measuring female sexual arousal has recently been developed. (Geer, personal communication, 1973).

As valuable as physiological measures appear to be in assessing sexual arousal, it may be unwise to equate them with sexual inclination. The interest that a particular picture, image, or idea holds for a male may not be translated into an increase in penile blood volume. Not all sexuality can be measured by genital urges.

response, consists of those few seconds when the body changes resulting from stimulation reach their maximum intensity. During the resolution phase, *after orgasm, there is a lessening of sexual tensions as the person returns to the unstimulated state. Women are capable of having another orgasm if there is effective stimulation during this phase. The resolution period in the male includes a time, which varies among individuals, when restimulation is impossible. This is called the refractory period. In both sexes, the basic responses of the body to sexual stimulation are myotonia (increased muscle tension) and vasocongestion (filling of the blood vessels with fluid), especially in the genital organs, causing swelling. Of course these basic physiologic responses take on a different appearance in a man than they do in a woman. Interestingly enough, the basic physiologic sexual responses remain the same regardless of the stimulation—coital, manipulative, mechanical, or fantasy. However, intensity and duration of responses vary with the method of stimulation used. Masturbation produced the most intense experiences observed in the laboratory, partner manipulation the next, and intercourse the least (Belliveau and Richter, 1970, pp. 33–34).*[2]

The impact of the first book by Masters and Johnson has been very great, contributing immensely to our knowledge of the physiology of human sexuality. Even before the book was published, however, the information obtained through research was put to use in the treatment phase of the project. By knowing how the body works to achieve maximum sexual response, Masters and Johnson were able to elaborate methods of treating sexual dysfunction. Some of the treatments that they have developed are discussed in Chapter 19. They were also able to provide firm data on certain controversial points and to dispel a few myths.

1. Although the clitoris (Figure 11.7) is quite important in transmitting sexual stimulation in the female, it has been a mistake to advise men to try to stimulate it continually during intercourse. During the plateau phase the clitoris retracts, making access to it extremely difficult and indeed sometimes painful for the woman. In point of fact, it is very difficult to have intercourse without stimulating the clitoris *indirectly,* which is the type of stimulation that most women prefer.

[2] Belliveau and Richter have written a lucid and highly readable summary of the background and principal findings of Masters and Johnson.

2. Others stated the opinion before, but Masters and Johnson were able to prove with hard data that orgasms in women obtained from stimulation of the clitoris, without entrance into the vagina, are as intense as and indeed objectively indistinguishable from orgasms obtained by having an erect penis in the vagina.

Probably few pieces of misinformation have caused more consternation than Freud's insistence that the vaginal orgasm is superior to the clitoral orgasm. He asserted, and practitioners have parroted to hundreds of thousands of people for years since, that a woman who can have an orgasm only by stimulation of her clitoris is settling for second best; further, that failure to have an orgasm via stimulation of the vagina by the man's penis is a sign of psychosexual fixation and immaturity. Even before the work of Masters and Johnson, some sexologists had been trying to disabuse people of this notion (for example, Ellis, 1961), pointing out that the walls of the vaginal barrel are poorly supplied with sensory nerve endings, whereas the clitoris, like the glans of the penis, is amply supplied. The fact that orgasms achieved by masturbation and manual manipulation by the partner, both of which typically concentrate on the clitoris, were found to create *greater* sexual excitation than intercourse pretty much puts to rest the bugaboo about vaginal orgasms. Of course, this finding in no way implies that conventional intercourse (penile-vaginal containment) cannot be extremely enjoyable; it merely indicates that the clitoris is largely responsible for female orgasm.

3. The goal of having simultaneous orgasms, held up to young married people in numerous marriage manuals as a sign of true love and compatibility, was shown to be hardly a mark of superior sexual achievement. Instead, it can often distract each of the partners from his or her own sexual pleasure.

4. It was also found that not only do most women *not* object to intercourse during menstruation, but they even tend to enjoy it more, particularly during the second half of the period.

5. During the second three months of pregnancy, women seem to desire intercourse at least as much as when not pregnant. Although there is some danger of spontaneous abortion in the early stages, particularly for women who have a history of spontaneous miscarriage, most women continue to desire sexual stimulation, sometimes until they go into labor. At any rate, little harm seems to come to the woman and to the baby in the uterus through intercourse, at least during the first six months of the pregnancy.

6. Various facts about the male's penis were also confirmed. The size of a man's erect penis was not found to be a factor in the enjoyment he can derive himself and impart to his sexual partner. The vagina is a potential not an actual space; that is, it distends just enough to accommodate the penis. Hence a very large penis will not create more friction for the man or the woman than a smaller one. Furthermore, small penises when flaccid may double in size when erect, whereas penises that are large in the limp state increase less proportionately. In other words, there does not seem to be as much variation in the size of the *erect* penis as had been assumed. The idea that the size of a man's penis is an index of his virility was completely dispelled.[3]

[3] Some women have voiced disagreement with Masters and Johnson's conclusion about the merits of a large penis. No doubt psychological variables, as well as the purely physiological ones that Masters and Johnson have dealt with, play a part in determining how an individual woman reacts.

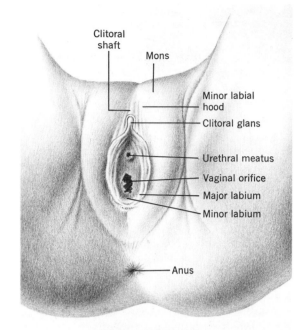

Female pelvic anatomy

A

Types of Human Sexual Inadequacy

Masters and Johnson define and discuss the following types of sexual inadequacy, all of which would be classified by DSM-II as psychophysiological disorders.

1. *Primary impotence.* The man has never been able to achieve an erection sufficient for successful intercourse, either heterosexual or homosexual.

2. *Secondary impotence.* The man is at present unable to achieve an erection sufficient for successful intercourse, either heterosexual or homosexual, but he has in his history at least one intromission.

3. *Premature ejaculation.* The man is unable to inhibit ejaculation long enough for his female partner to have orgasm in 50 percent

FIGURE **11.7**

A, exterior view of female genitalia. B, cross section of male genitalia.

(FROM ALVIN NASON AND ROBERT DEHAAN, *The Biological World,* NEW YORK: WILEY, 1973.)

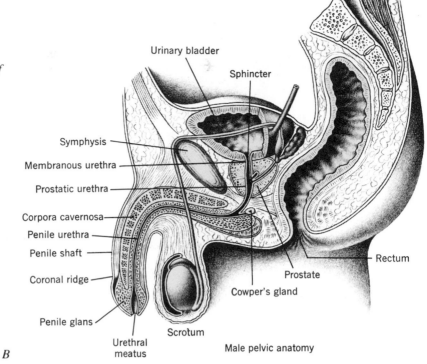

Urinary bladder

Sphincter

Symphysis

Membranous urethra

Prostatic urethra

Corpora cavernosa

Penile urethra

Penile shaft

Coronal ridge

Penile glans

Urethral meatus

Scrotum

Prostate

Cowper's gland

Rectum

Male pelvic anatomy

B

of their contacts. Masters and Johnson were keenly aware that this definition raises problems, for women vary widely in the amount of stimulation required for orgasm. In some cases ejaculation occurs without an erection.

4. ***Ejaculatory incompetence.*** A man with this rare disability cannot ejaculate intravaginally, although erections and intromissions are not problematic.

5. ***Dyspareunia.*** Intercourse is painful in some way for the man or woman.

6. ***Primary orgasmic dysfunction.*** The woman has never had an orgasm either from masturbation or intercourse.

7. ***Situational orgasmic dysfunction.*** The woman is unable to have orgasms in particular situations. She may, for example, climax easily when on vacations but never at home.

8. ***Vaginismus.*** The outer third of the vaginal barrel is subject to involuntary spastic contractions, often making the insertion of the penis or a finger impossible.

Etiology of Human Sexual Inadequacy

Masters and Johnson found in the backgrounds of the individuals they examined a number of untoward attitudes and events that they consider responsible for the development of sexual problems. The two researchers distinguish between *historically* relevant factors and two *currently* relevant variables that they believe underlie the *maintenance* of all human sexual inadequacies (Figure 11.8). Sexual disorders are maintained because during intercourse one or both of the participants either adopt a *spectator role* or have crippling *fears about*

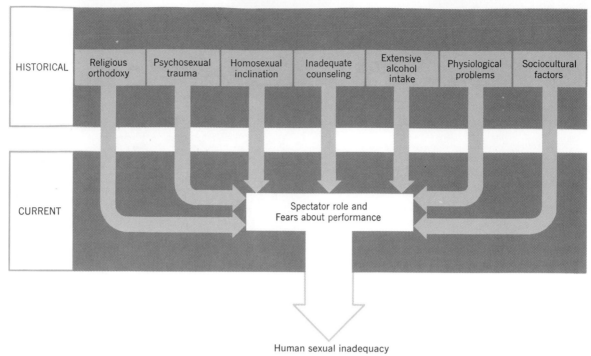

| HISTORICAL | Religious orthodoxy | Psychosexual trauma | Homosexual inclination | Inadequate counseling | Extensive alcohol intake | Physiological problems | Sociocultural factors |

CURRENT — Spectator role and Fears about performance

Human sexual inadequacy

FIGURE **11.8**
Historical and current causes of human sexual inadequacies. After Masters and Johnson, 1970.

performance. These two attitudes focus a great amount of attention on performance rather than allowing a relatively passive and uncritical acceptance of sexual stimulation, which if unimpeded leads naturally to sexual enjoyment, including orgasm. As Masters and Johnson have stated, "fear of inadequacy is the greatest known deterrent to effective sexual functioning, simply because it so completely distracts the fearful individual from his or her natural responsivity by blocking reception of sexual stimuli. . . ." (1970, pp. 12–13). The individual adopts the spectator role and is fearful about performance because of the unfortunate attitudes instilled by his upbringing and the difficult experiences of his earlier years. It should be noted, however, that a great many individuals have unfortunate attitudes

and experiences *without* developing sexual dysfunctions.

Historical Factors

Religious Orthodoxy. One or both partners may have negative attitudes toward sex because they have been brought up with strict religious beliefs which denigrate sexual enjoyment. For example, a woman with vaginismus who was interviewed by Masters and Johnson had been

. . . taught that almost any form of physical expression might be suspect of objectionable sexual connotation. . . . she was prohibited when bathing from looking at her own breasts either directly or from reflection in the mirror

290   SOCIAL DEVIATION

for fear that unhealthy sexual thoughts might be stimulated by visual examination of her own body. Discussion with a sibling of such subjects as menstruation, conception, contraception, or sexual functioning were taboo. . . . Mrs. A. entered marriage without a single word of advice, warning, or even good cheer from her family relative to marital sexual expression. The only direction offered by her religious advisor relative to sexual behavior was that coital connection was only to be endured if conception was desired (p. 254).

Psychosexual Trauma. Some patients trace their fears of sexual contact to particularly frightening or degrading experiences during initial sexual exposures. One young man had been assured by a prostitute that "He would never be able to get the job done for any woman—if he couldn't get it done here and now with a pro." One woman could date her vaginismus to a gang rape from which she suffered severe physical and psychological damage.

Homosexual Inclinations. Impotent men and inorgasmic women may be unable to enjoy heterosexual relations because they have homosexual inclinations.

Inadequate Counseling. Bad advice from professional workers may create or exacerbate sexual inadequacies. Some men were told by physicians that secondary impotence is incurable, others that it is a natural part of the aging process. A few had been warned by clergymen that their impotence was God's punishment for sins.

Excessive Intake of Alcohol. Secondary impotence sometimes begins with unfortunate concern about a normal reduction in sexual responsiveness brought on by excessive drinking. In the typical pattern suggested by Masters and Johnson, a man who works very hard may develop a habit of drinking a good

deal. Alcohol is known to suppress sexual feeling and appetite in the male, while at the same time, ironically, lowering his inhibitions. Having drunk too much, the man may find that no erection develops. Instead of attributing his lack of sexual arousal to his drinking, however, he begins to ruminate. Fear accumulates, and after a number of failures he may become secondarily impotent. The wife often attempts to be understanding and supportive of the husband. He, for any number of reasons, interprets this solicitude as further questioning of his dominance and masculinity. Or the wife, concerned that she may no longer be sexually attractive to her husband, pushes for sexual encounters, aggravating the situation. Soon she may withdraw from any physical contact whatsoever, even affectionate hugs and kisses, for fear that the husband will interpret this as a demand or invitation for intercourse. The communication between the couple worsens, aggravating the man's anxiety and setting a pattern difficult to reverse without professional assistance.

Vaginismus. As yet another example of the intimate relation between the sexual reactions of the two partners, Masters and Johnson found that some men develop secondary impotence because of the partner's vaginismus.

Physiological Causes. Several of the disorders are attributable to physical damage. Clitoral or vaginal infections, torn ligaments in the pelvic region, scarred tissue at the vaginal opening from incisions made during childbirth (episiotomies), and—especially in older, postmenopausal women—insufficient lubrication of the vagina may make intercourse painful for women. Infection of the glans of the penis, which usually develops because it is not kept clean, may make intercourse painful for men. A minority of men with secondary impotence are found to suffer from metabolic problems of diabetes, and in some cases sexual arousal is dulled by addiction to certain tranquilizers.

Sociocultural Factors. Especially in female dysfunctions, cultural biases play a role. "Sociocultural influence more often than not places woman in a position in which she must adapt, sublimate, inhibit, or even distort her natural capacity to function sexually in order to fulfill her genetically assigned role. Herein lies a major source of woman's sexual dysfunction" (p. 218). The man has the blessing of society to develop his sexual expressiveness, but the woman at least until recently has not had this freedom, and her needs have often been ignored. Compounding her difficulties is the fact that she does not require sexual arousal in order to function adequately as a partner during sexual intercourse. Vaginal lubricants are available to substitute for the natural secretions that accompany sexual excite-

ment. According to the laboratory studies in *Human Sexual Response,* women seem capable of more sustained and more frequent sexual arousal than men, which makes the neglect of their sexuality particularly ironic.

Evaluation

As Masters and Johnson caution, these factors are *hypothesized* to be the reasons that during intercourse individuals assume a spectator role and have crippling fears about performance. The data are based entirely on the retrospective reporting of the couples who were treated at the foundation between 1959 and 1969. As indicated in Chapter 4, such data are notoriously open to bias and distortion. At the same time there are no better sources of information.

SUMMARY

This chapter has dealt with unconventional sexual behavior and human sexual inadequacy. The first category includes "sexual deviations" characterized either by unusual choice of object — fetishism, transvestism, incest, and pedophilia — or by statistically infrequent activities — voyeurism, exhibitionism, rape, sadism, and masochism. Psychoanalytic theories tend to explain virtually all this behavior as a defense against anxiety aroused by the idea of engaging in conventional heterosexual intercourse. Learning theorists have considered sexual arousal to be conditioned to stimuli that happen to be present during early erotic experiences. Few hard data support either of these hypotheses. Moreover, the fact that what is

considered unacceptable or unconventional behavior depends on cultural definitions raises the question whether some of these activities should be categorized as abnormal.

The clinical research of Masters and Johnson has dealt with problems that interfere with the full enjoyment of conventional sexual relations. Their basic hypothesis holds that virtually all disorders such as impotence and frigidity are maintained because the individual assumes a spectator role and has fears about his performance. The etiology of these inadequacies was sought in excessively puritanical religious beliefs, earlier unpleasant sexual experiences, misinformation, and other factors in the individual's background.

CHAPTER 12
Homosexuality

The decision to include in an abnormal psychology textbook a discussion of homosexuality was a difficult one, for the authors of this book are not in favor of continuing to regard such behavior as psychopathological. We opted to include the topic because we believe that students of abnormal psychology should be provided the opportunity to reflect on the history and nature of an aspect of human sexuality that has generally been viewed as a sign of emotional disturbance.

Imagine for a moment that you are an anxious person and that being anxious is against the law. You must try to hide your fears from others. Your own home may be a safe place to feel anxious, but a public display of apprehension can lead to arrest or at least to social ostracism. At work one day an associate looks at you suspiciously and says, "That's funny. For a crazy moment there I thought you were anxious." "Heck, no," you exclaim a bit too loudly, "*not me!*" You begin to wonder if your fellow worker will report his suspicions to your boss. If he does, your boss may inform the police, or will at least change your job to one that requires less contact with customers, especially with those who have children.

There are many parallels between the way an anxious person is treated in this seemingly improbable fantasy and the current plight of homosexuals. In the United States alone it is estimated that at least four million people are predominantly homosexual. If each such individual makes an average of two contacts per week, a quarter of a billion homosexual acts are engaged in each year in this country. Millions of other people who are bisexual are involved in homosexual activity from time to time (Gebhard, 1972). In this chapter we shall examine the extent and nature of homosexual behavior, its legal status, and some of the consequences of the attitudes that most citizens harbor toward homosexuality.

Sexual attraction among members of the same sex has been amply documented throughout recorded history as well as in many different cultures. In many societies homosexual practices have been suppressed by harsh laws, and indeed in most states of contemporary America laws exist by which homosexuals can be arrested and imprisoned, although not all these statutes are rigidly enforced. Never have societal sanctions eliminated homosexuality, nor does it seem likely that they ever will. The widespread prevalence of homosexuality, even though such practices are often threatened by punishment, has led some workers to believe that this aspect of sexuality is, in some important way, part of man's very nature.

Ford and Beach's (1951) survey of the anthropological literature suggests that forty-nine out of seventy-six primitive societies on which fairly reliable data were available considered some form of homosexual activity quite normal and acceptable, although seldom sanctioning such sexual behavior as desirable for large numbers of the community. One North African tribe considered it odd for a man not to have sexual affairs with both women and other men. Other tribes have believed that sodomy, so named for its prevalence in the "sinful" biblical city of Sodom, makes young men strong. Some North American Indians recognized and tolerated groups of exclusively homosexual men and women within their predominantly heterosexual cultures.

Ancient Greece is justifiably cited as a civilization in which homosexual love flourished and was celebrated. It is believed that the Greeks regarded such love as especially noble and beautiful. The bodies of young male athletes were particularly admired. An older man was often a mentor to a younger one, providing advice, tutelage, and a substantial measure of sexual gratification. Those who have read Plato's *Symposium* will remember that it contains an endorsement of homosexual love by Greece's leading philosophers.

In contrast, in early imperial Rome homosexuality was common and fashionable but was not held in such esteem. In fact, homosexual acts took their place among the debaucheries and tortures that were practiced.

Nero's disgusting and cruel orgies, in which men and women suffered equally, reached the depths of squalor. He had Sporus, his favourite, castrated, after which he went through all the ceremonies of marriage and made the unfortunate youth his "wife" (West, 1967, p. 25).

Thus this widespread desire of some human beings to engage in sexual acts with members of their own sex has been vilified or dignified, depending on the particular cultural mores.

On the assumption that there are meaningful continuities between human beings and subhuman species, it is of interest that same-sexed contacts are prevalent among other mammals.

All wild male and female mammals except the higher primates are ready for breeding only once, yearly or periodically, the male usually having a prolonged season of rut during which the females have shorter estrous periods. Male domestic mammals, however, have no season of rut, being capable of copulation throughout the year. Male cows, dogs, and other male domestics often mount members of their own sex. Attributing feelings of sexual attraction to such mountings is of course problematic, for the females of these species are periodically unresponsive. Among monkeys and apes, as well as man, the female ovulates periodically but is receptive to copulation at any time, whether or not pregnancy is possible. Even so, some male primates have been known to have homosexual contacts when their females are available.

All and all, there is nothing new or rare about homosexuality (see Box 12.1).

BOX **12.1** *Homophobia and Exclusive Homosexuality*

In arguing that heterosexuality is normal and homosexuality abnormal, the statement is often made that exclusive homosexuality is unknown in the animal kingdom when members of the opposite sex are available. It is also proposed that heterosexual contacts are maximized in all species so that adequate reproduction can take place. Moreover, it is apparently the case that no human cultures in which exclusive homosexuality is encouraged for sizable numbers of people have been found.

These arguments are cogent, but they overlook one essential characteristic of human sexuality, namely that bisexuality is more prevalent than exclusive homosexuality. Churchill (1967) has made the provocative suggestion that exclusive homosexuality may well be encouraged by anti-homosexual societies such as our own. Because sexual contacts between members of the same sex are so severely condemned, some bisexuals may be forced into making a choice and *thereby* become committed to contacts only with members of their own sex rather than continuing to find sexual relationships with members of both sexes meaningful. What some call "homophobia" (Weinberg, 1972) may actually help create exclusive homosexuality.

SURVEY DATA ON HOMOSEXUALITY

The Kinsey Surveys

The fact that homosexuality can be mentioned in most social settings without anyone's becoming apoplectic reflects a considerable and recent liberalization in at least the discussion of this aspect of sexuality. Without question the pioneering, brave work of Alfred Kinsey (Figure 12.1) and his co-workers in the 1940s and 1950s under the auspices of the Institute of Sex Research contributed importantly to lifting the taboos on sex research

A biologist by training, Kinsey was appalled at the lack of even minimally reliable information on American sexual practices. He trained

FIGURE **12.1**
Alfred C. Kinsey, renowned Indiana University biologist. His courageous explorations of sexual practices in the United States helped establish the respectability of scientific sex research in this country.

sensitive people to elicit self-reports on present and past sexual practices by means of a comprehensive interview and then sent them out to see as many members of a given social group as would agree to talk to them. The groups were chosen to achieve a wide geographic, economic, and socioreligious distribution. For example, a Kinsey interview team would arrange to speak to an Elk Lodge, explaining the

scientific purposes of the project and the careful safeguards that would be taken to ensure confidentiality. Interviews were then scheduled with those present who agreed to donate their time and reveal to total strangers intimate information about themselves. Indeed, it seems likely, since the interviews were conducted in the 1940s, that many who participated had never openly discussed with another human being such topics as masturbation, premarital intercourse, and homosexual acts.

As we noted in Chapter 4, self-reporting is open to many sources of bias, such as a desire to appear normal and to avoid disapproval. And all self-reports are subject to the distortions that time may impose on memory. But the Kinsey data have remained the most comprehensive information on American sexual customs, and the skills of the interviewers, who were reassuringly matter-of-fact when asking about intimate details of the participants' lives, argue in favor of taking the statistical findings seriously until better data are collected. Results of other surveys of sexual behavior, both here and abroad, have not been dissimilar to Kinsey's (Gebhard, 1972).

The Kinsey Study on Men

Homosexual experiences are separable into two major categories. People may have orgasms through physical contact with another person of the same sex, or they may be sexually aroused by some homosexual stimulus without necessarily having physical contact or an orgasm. The first is an overt behavioral experience, the second a covert attitudinal one. *Both* kinds are considered to be homosexual in nature (Kinsey, Pomeroy, and Martin, 1948).

Since most of the men in the sample were neither exclusively homosexual nor heterosexual, Kinsey deemed it fruitless to speak in terms of "the homosexual" or "the heterosexual." Rather, it seemed more sensible to speak in terms of relative frequencies of each kind of sexual response. Figure 12.2 shows graphically the heterosexual-homosexual rating scale devised by the Kinsey group. The legend briefly describes each of the seven points along the continuum.

Kinsey's findings on homosexuality in men, based on interviews with 5300 white males, can be summarized as follows.

1. Thirty-seven percent of men have experienced homosexual orgasm at some time since the onset of adolescence.
2. An additional 13 percent have felt homosexual urges without overt contact leading to orgasm.
3. Of the males who remain bachelors until thirty-five, 50 percent have had homosexual

experience to the point of orgasm since the onset of adolescence.
4. Twenty-five percent of men have more than incidental homosexual experiences between the ages of sixteen and fifty-five (these men would rate between 2 and 6 on the Kinsey scale).
5. Eighteen percent of men have at least as much of the homosexual as the heterosexual in their histories (ratings 3, 4, 5, and 6) for at least three years between the ages of sixteen and fifty-five.
6. Ten percent are almost exclusively homosexual (ratings 5 and 6) for at least three years between the ages of sixteen and fifty-five.
7. Four percent are exclusively homosexual throughout their lives, after the onset of adolescence.
8. Homosexuality is found among all social and occupational groups.

Overall, then, Kinsey and his colleagues found a *considerable* level of homosexual behavior and feelings among the men they interviewed in the 1940s. Considering the widespread public revulsion against homosexuality, at least at that time, the estimates probably err in the conservative direction.

The Kinsey Study on Women

While collecting and writing up the data on male sexual behavior, Kinsey, Pomeroy, Martin, and Gebhard (1953) were also working on a similar report on female sexuality. Some improvements in conception and design were made, one being to add to the interview questions about the emotions aroused by overt sexual acts and the woman's attitude toward her behavior. In writing the second book the investigators were also able to include numerous comparisons of the sexual activities of

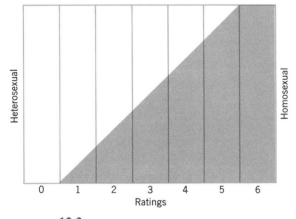

FIGURE **12.2**
Kinsey rating scale on homosexuality-heterosexuality. Definitions of the ratings are as follows: 0, entirely heterosexual; 1, largely heterosexual, but with incidental homosexual history; 2, largely heterosexual, but with a distinct homosexual history; 3, equally heterosexual and homosexual; 4, largely homosexual, but with distinct heterosexual history; 5, largely homosexual, but with incidental heterosexual history; 6, entirely homosexual.

men and women. Unfortunately, because of the length of both studies and the fact that they were conducted over much the same period of time, Kinsey was unable to meet in the second volume all the criticisms made of the first.

The interviews of 5940 white women indicated a much lower incidence of homosexuality than that found among the men surveyed in the 1948 report. Whereas 37 percent of men had experienced homosexual orgasm after the onset of adolescence, the figure for women was 13 percent. Furthermore, only about 3 percent of the women had been primarily or exclusively homosexual at any given age period, compared with a figure of 10 percent for men. The pattern was also different; whereas men were often highly promiscuous, 71 percent of the women who made homosexual contacts restricted them to a single partner or two.

Kinsey and his colleagues were aware that this finding of significantly less homosexuality among women than among men went against the idea then widely held by men that females in American society engage in a greater number of sexual acts with women than men do with men. The researchers suggested that because American women are freer to touch and kiss one another in ordinary social encounters, men may have inferred that such contacts were likely to arouse sexual feelings. On the basis of the data collected by the Kinsey interviewers, this male assumption appears to have been incorrect.

Methodological Problems in the Kinsey Data

Because of their controversial nature, the Kinsey reports have received searching and critical evaluations. It should be stated at the outset, however, that Kinsey himself was very much surprised by the high incidence of homosexuality, especially among men. It seems unlikely that the investigators found the amount of sexual contact among members of the same sex that they did because they were looking for it.

Problems in the Interview. Terman (1948) pointed out that the exact wording of each question of the standard interview was not published, and we know that each interviewer was free to rephrase and probe at his own discretion, depending on what he perceived the requirements at the moment to be. We know from numerous other sources that interviewers may not produce comparable data when such innovation is allowed. For example, two of the key interviewers of men, in addition to Kinsey, were Pomeroy and Martin, each of whom obtained results quite different from Kinsey's. Kinsey's figure for men who had had premarital coitus was much higher than either Pomeroy's or Martin's. The self-reports of homosexual contacts elicited by Martin were less than one-fourth those elicited by Kinsey and Pomeroy. Since each interviewer was assigned cases covering the whole range of demographic variables (age, social background, and so on), it appears that differences in the behavior of the interviewers produced significantly different answers. Moreover, all interviewers for both studies were male. We know from other sources that the sex of the interviewer is an important variable in what the respondent reports, especially if the interview pertains to sex. More sexual experiences are reported when interviewer and respondent are of the same gender (Walters, Shurley, and Parsons, 1962).

Some subjects may have been gently coerced into falsely admitting to certain activities. Terman points out, for instance, that the interviewer was instructed to convey the assumption that a given practice had been engaged in unless the respondent strongly denied it. In one method employed, "proving

SOCIAL DEVIATION

the answer" (Kinsey et al., 1948, p. 55), the interviewer pretends that he has misunderstood a negative reply and asks additional questions as though the original answer had been in the affirmative, for example, "Yes, I know you have never done that, but how old were you the *first time* you did it?"

Another possibility is that some respondents might have simply lied. Kinsey was clearly aware of this problem and believed that he had overcome it through the anonymity of the interview and the generally trusting atmosphere that the highly skilled and sensitive interviewers are said to have created. But a lower-class male respondent might find it easier to admit to premarital coitus than to frequent masturbation. Sociological studies reveal that classes differ in their opinions of what is acceptable sexual behavior. The fact that lower-class males reported less masturbation than college-educated men may therefore not be a completely reliable indication of the actual frequencies.

Some of the questions required considerable retrospection back to the events of early adolescence. Determining the onset of puberty provides a good example, for chronological age was seldom referred to. Instead, criteria such as first ejaculation and growth of pubic hair were employed. Recollection of such details poses problems.

Sampling Problems. Through lectures and other public relations efforts, various groups throughout the country were asked to participate, and efforts were made to persuade everyone at a given meeting to sign up. Not every member of a given group was in attendance at that recruitment meeting, however. The purpose of the meeting had been announced in advance, and we cannot know anything about people who did not attend even this session. We do know that in the male sample, for instance, sixty-two groups yielded 100 percent

samples, and that the members of forty-two of these groups had generally attended college. This statistic strongly suggests greater willingness among men who have attended college to participate in a study involving potential embarrassment. But the manner in which the data were reported precludes an assessment of the effects of this greater willingness to participate found among better-educated groups. Perhaps the most glaring sampling deficiency was the intentional exclusion of nonwhites. Properly speaking, then, both reports refer to white Americans.

The Generality of the Data. Terman (1948) also examined several of Kinsey's tables very carefully to determine the numbers of respondents on which some of the sweeping conclusions about men were based. Thus the generalization already mentioned, that among men who remain unmarried until age thirty-five, 50 percent have had homosexual orgasm, is in fact based on the responses of fewer than 200 individuals. Terman points out that Kinsey made numerous highly complex interpretations and evaluations, some of them very prescriptive in tone and few of them really supported by data. For example, of the 179 males who engaged in the least amount of sexual activity, Kinsey asserted that 52.5 percent were ". . . timid or inhibited individuals—afraid of their own self condemnation if they were to engage in almost any sort of sexual activity . . . [and that] some of these individuals become paranoid in their fear of moral transgression, or its outcome" (Kinsey et al., 1948, p. 211). Terman points out that such pronouncements might well frighten sexually inactive young men into greater sexual activity lest they become paranoids or worse.

One important characteristic of the report on men, although the methodology was changed for that on women, is the emphasis on objective descriptions. The *meaning* that various sexual activities had for the respondents was almost completely ignored. As a biologist Kinsey was not used to concerning himself with how the objects of a study *felt* about what they were doing. Thus the information collected is restricted to whether the male had performed a particular sexual act. He was not asked whether he enjoyed it or was ashamed of it.

Scientific and Social Implications

Kinsey was interested in removing the taboos about the scientific study of sexuality and in instigating dispassionate research into its bases and very nature. He rightly pointed out that it is difficult to understand the nature or significance of any aspect of human behavior until we have some firm idea of its prevalence and patterning.

In view of the past and continuing intolerance of American society toward anything homosexual, Kinsey's findings on the social realities of this form of sexuality are of special interest. Since half of the male sample had had at least one homosexual experience (orgasm or arousal) by the age of fifty-five, and many had had several, with 4 percent being rated as exclusive, lifelong homosexuals, this form of sexuality is obviously not rare. Unless we wish to regard half of American men as abnormal, and of course some do, it is difficult to entertain the notion that homosexuality is, by itself, evidence of psychopathology. Some homosexuals may be disturbed, but disturbances are found in the lives of those who have never had a homosexual experience. In view of the pressures society imposes on those who have had even a very small number of homosexual experiences, it seems possible that homosexuals with emotional problems have them because of society's reactions rather than that the emotional disturbance preceded or caused the homosexuality.

Kinsey suggested that the incidence of homosexuality might very well be higher if societal penalties were abolished. His figures, as we have already mentioned, *might* be underestimates. Kinsey believed also that the prevalence of homosexuality in ancient Greek civilization, coupled with the wide diversity of Americans who his investigation determined have had homosexual experiences and continue to seek them out, argues in favor of a conception of the human being as eminently conditionable to respond to erotic stimulation from the same sex, the opposite sex, or both. According to this theory, the human being is neither inherently homosexual nor inherently heterosexual. Rather he is inherently sexual, with the direction of his attraction being determined importantly or entirely by the circumstances of his environment. If there is one aspect to being human that psychologists have established without doubt, it is our fantastic capacity to change as a function of experience. Whatever else we may be, we are certainly organisms who can learn a wide variety of things. Different people may, through learning, find a tremendous variety of human characteristics sexually arousing.

At the end of the book on women, Kinsey and his colleagues speculate on the learning variables involved in the acquisition of sexual inclinations, placing particular emphasis on the normality of homosexual behavior.

The data indicate that the factors leading to homosexual behavior are (1) the basic physiological capacity of every mammal to respond to any sufficient stimulus; (2) the accident which leads an individual into his or her first sexual experience with a person of the same sex; (3) the conditioning effects of such experience; and (4) the indirect but powerful conditioning which the opinions of other persons and the social codes may have on an individu-

al's decision to accept or reject this type of sexual contact. . . .

Exclusive preferences and patterns of behavior, heterosexual or homosexual, come only with experience, or as a result of social pressures which tend to force an individual into an exclusive pattern of one or the other sort. Psychologists and psychiatrists, reflecting the mores of the culture in which they have been raised, have spent a good deal of time trying to explain the origins of homosexual activity; but considering the physiology of sexual response and the mammalian background of human behavior, it is not so difficult to explain why a human animal does a particular thing sexually. It is more difficult to explain why each and every individual is not involved in every type of sexual activity (Kinsey et al., 1953, pp. 447–451).

A Survey of Gay Groups

Since publication of the two Kinsey volumes, several other investigations have been done on homosexual behavior. Saghir and his colleagues (Saghir and Robins, 1969; Saghir, Robins, and Walbran, 1969) conducted interviews with male and female members of gay groups. To be included in the samples people had to be experienced homosexually and could never have been hospitalized in a psychiatric setting or arrested for a sexual offense. Both samples, then, were admittedly not truly representative of homosexuals in general—for all the men and women had "come out of the closet" at least to the extent of joining a homosexual organization. They tended also to be of relatively high socioeconomic class.

Information was gathered on a number of variables, including frequency of masturbation, degree of sexual arousal, extent and nature of sexual behavior, and nature of personal relationships. The major findings can be summarized as follows.

1. The male homosexuals began masturbating much earlier than the females and continued to do so much more often, even when involved in an active homosexual relationship.
2. Both groups reported definite sexual arousal to people of the same gender at a very early age, usually before adolescence.
3. The male homosexuals, by the end of adolescence (defined as age nineteen), were engaging in overt homosexual behavior to a significantly greater extent than the females.
4. A given male or female tended to alternate between "active" and "passive" roles in homosexual relationships.
5. The frequency of homosexual contacts in adulthood was much higher for the men.
6. The men were much more "promiscuous" than the women, having fewer long-term relationships with a single lover and, even when involved in an ongoing relationship, caring little about fidelity.
7. The males engaged in much more oral-genital contact (fellatio) than the females, who tended to favor manual stimulation of the clitoris.
8. Both groups engaged in periodic sexual activity with members of the opposite sex during adolescence, but in adulthood they lost interest in heterosexual encounters.

These findings are revealing in a number of ways. First, a very early onset of homosexual interests, typically before physical maturity, was reported. Second, the men seemed much more "genital" and explicitly sexual in their homosexuality. Third, the men enjoyed many "one-night stands," whereas the women tended to opt for long-term relationships, which, moreover, were not as explicitly sexual as the men's.

Perhaps the most significant conclusion to be drawn by Saghir and his colleagues was that ". . . when it comes to sexual behavior homosexual men are more like heterosexual men (or the stereotype) and homosexual women are more like heterosexual women (or the stereotype)" (Saghir, Robins, and Walbran, 1969, p. 228). A study of pathological factors underlying the choice of a same-sexed person as a sexual partner will, by implication, tell us less about homosexuality than will a consideration of how people of both sexes are sexualized and socialized in our society.

With these survey data as background, we turn now to an examination of several theories on homosexuality—psychoanalytic, learning, biological, and sociological.

THEORIES OF HOMOSEXUALITY

The search for factors that contribute to the development of all unconventional patterns of human behavior is exceedingly difficult. Some writers, especially sociologists, take the position that variables important in the life history of the person, such as how he was reared, do not contribute much to our understanding of *current* behavior. The way a person's parents treated him may be of little help in explaining why the individual's behavior follows a certain pattern today. In the study of homosexuality the decision to attribute more importance to one set of factors than to another is especially evident. The most prevalent theoretical point of view, the psychoanalytic, directs attention almost exclusively to what happened in the first few years of life, whereas other theories emphasize factors playing a role in the homosexual's current life. As the various theories are reviewed, it must be kept in mind that each of them is highly speculative.

Psychoanalytic Theory

A review of the psychoanalytic literature to find the theories explaining any form of behavior reveals divergent points of view. The psychoanalytic theories of homosexuality are no different. Klein, Heimann, Isaacs, and Riviere (1952) and Bergler (1957) suggest that another man's penis is desirable because it represents the breast to the orally fixated homosexual. The basic premise of most psychoanalytic interpretations of homosexuality, however, can be summed up in one word, *heterophobia,* which means fear of sexual contact with the opposite sex (Bieber et al., 1962; Rado, 1949). This fear is of course traced back to events in early life. Although Freud suggested that human beings have genetically determined predispositions toward activity, or masculinity, and passivity, or femininity, he did not clarify the importance of these predispositions. In most of his theorizing on homosexuality, he treated it as learned behavior.

We have already indicated the importance that Freud and most of his followers attached to the oedipal conflict; how this dilemma of each person's life is resolved is regarded as crucial for the direction that sexual preference takes. In his first years the child is bisexual, responding libidinally to any human contact regardless of that person's gender. Around the age of four, however, the male child begins to note striking differences between his mother and father. Incestuous wishes come to the fore, the boy child wishing to replace the father in the mother's affections. The gratification of these sexual desires is thwarted, however, by the threat of punishment from the father-rival, the paramount threat being that of castration. The conflict is sometimes increased by seductive behavior on the part of the mother, especially when the marriage is not a happy one. Moreover, the father sometimes withdraws from the mother and child and fails thereby to provide a good model for the son to identify with. If the boy cannot resolve the conflict by repressing his desire for his mother and identifying with his father, he may try to escape from his oedipal conflict by avoiding all sexual contact with women. They come to represent to the maturing young man's unconscious his unresolved incestuous feelings toward his mother. The mother may also contribute to the heterophobia by discouraging masculine assertiveness and heterosexual approaches to girls his own age, thereby keeping her son close to her. As he reaches adulthood the unresolved conflict may make the young man fantasize that his penis will be injured by insertion into a woman's vagina. The sight of a woman's genitalia, because she is without a penis, can trigger castration anxieties, making his thoughts dwell on the possibility of losing his own penis. The young man can then have sexual relations only with another male who, because he does have a penis, will not remind him of the threat of castration. Presumably in less severe cases heterophobia renders the man impotent only when he is with women who in some way remind him of his mother. But intercourse may be possible with prostitutes, whom the man sharply differentiates from his mother.

The Bieber Study

This psychoanaltyic theory was examined in a well-known study by Bieber et al. (1962). The case records of 106 homosexual patients and 100 heterosexual control patients who were being seen by 77 New York psychoanalysts in their private practices were made available for the study. In addition to their qualitative, clinical observations, all the analysts were asked to collect specific bits of information from their interviews with their patients. Some of the questions asked concerned the following.

Was the patient the mother's favorite?
Did the mother express affection for the patient? In physical acts such as hugging and kissing?
Does the analyst consider that the mother was seductive in her activities with the patient? Did the patient sleep with the mother? Was there dressing or undressing with the patient?
Did the mother encourage masculine attitudes and activities?
Did the patient consider the father sexually potent?
Did the father encourage masculine attitudes and activities?
Did the patient feel "babied" by the mother?
Did the mother give the patient frequent enemas?

On the basis of the information gathered from these and other questions, Bieber concluded that his study had provided strong support for the psychoanalytic interpretation of homosexuality.

A considerable amount of data . . . has been presented as evidence that fear of heterosexuality underlies homosexuality, for example, the frequent fear of disease or injury to the genitals, significantly associated with fear and aversion to female genitalia. . . . The capacity to adapt homosexually is, in a sense, a tribute to man's biosocial resources in the face of thwarted heterosexual goal achievement. Sexual gratification is not renounced; instead, fears and inhibitions associated with het-

erosexuality are circumvented and sexual responsivity with pleasure and excitement to a member of the same sex develops as a pathologic alternative (1962, p. 303).

Particular importance was placed on the "close-binding intimate" mother, who "exerted an unhealthy influence on her son through preferential treatment and seductiveness on the one hand, and inhibiting, over-controlling attitudes on the other. In many instances, the son was the most significant individual in her life and the husband was usually replaced by the son as her love object" (p. 47). The most common behavioral pattern among the fathers of homosexual patients was detachment and hostility. Although not all the homosexual patients had such parents, "We are led to believe that . . . maternal close-binding intimacy and paternal detachment-hostility is the 'classic' pattern and most conducive to promoting homosexuality . . . in the son" (p. 144). ". . . the chances appear to be high that any son exposed to this parental combination will become homosexual or develop severe homosexual problems" (p. 172).

Bieber's study is widely cited as proof of the validity of psychoanalytic theory in explaining male homosexuality. (As is typical in Freud's writing, short shrift is given to female sexuality.) But the way in which the investigation was conducted presents a few problems.

1. Those who collected the data were psychoanalysts, already biased in favor of the psychoanalytic theory. "We assumed that the dominant sexual pattern of the adult is the adaptive consequence of life experiences interpenetrating with a basic biological tendency toward heterosexuality" (p. 28).
2. To answer the questions, a high degree of inference was necessary on the part of the analyst.

3. Many of the questions required the patient to think back over a number of years for answers.
4. All the homosexuals had sought psychoanalytic treatment. They are therefore representative neither of homosexuals who undergo other forms of psychotherapy nor of homosexuals en masse, most of whom are not in therapy of any kind.

Perhaps because of these obvious difficulties, the behavioral patterns noted by Bieber in the family backgrounds of homosexual patients are often ignored by those who find psychoanalytic theorizing problematic. But with a replication of the Bieber study—especially a study done with homosexuals who were not in therapy—important information on the etiology of male homosexuality might be obtained. Such a study has been reported.

A Replication of Bieber's Study

Evans (1969) adapted the scales used by the psychoanalysts in the Bieber study to construct a twenty-seven item questionnaire. Instead of having therapists rate their patients, he recruited male subjects from a nonpatient population of homosexuals and heterosexuals, and, in the context of a study on cardiovascular disease, had 43 homosexuals (all members of a Los Angeles homosexual organization) and 142 heterosexuals report on their recollections of childhood. In addition to answering the twenty-seven questions, the homosexual subjects rated themselves on the Kinsey scale and completed a short "sexual identification" questionnaire designed to determine the extent to which they regarded themselves as masculine or feminine.

The results were fascinating. Of the twenty-seven items on the questionnaire, twenty-four discriminated very strongly between the male homosexuals and heterosexuals. And in every instance Bieber's findings were confirmed.

Specifically, in retrospect, the homosexuals more often described themselves as frail or clumsy as children and less often as athletic. More of them were fearful of physical injury, avoided physical fights, played with girls and were loners who seldom played baseball and other competitive games. Their mothers more often were considered puritanical, cold toward men, insisted on being the center of the son's attention, made him her confidant, were "seductive" toward him, allied with him against the father, openly preferred him to the father, interfered with his heterosexual activities during adolescence, discouraged masculine attitudes, and encouraged feminine ones. The fathers of the homosexuals were retrospectively considered as less likely to encourage masculine attitudes and activities. . . . [The subjects] spent little time with their fathers, were more often aware of hating him and afraid he might physically harm them, less often were the father's favorite, felt less accepted by him, and in turn less frequently accepted or respected the father. Unlike Bieber's patients, these homosexuals were no different from the heterosexuals in amount of time they estimated their parents spent together or in the interests shared by their parents (Evans, 1969, pp. 130, 133).

Another outcome is of interest: 95 percent of the subjects considered themselves as moderately or strongly *masculine*, consistent with the opinions of the Bieber analysts, who rated only 2 percent of their homosexual patients markedly effeminate.

Evans cautions against assigning the various child-rearing factors etiological significance. A father may reject a son who does not enjoy competitive sports for reasons that have nothing to do with effeminacy. Because Evans's study was a retrospective one, it no doubt also reflects the usual problems of recalling past happenings and attitudes.[1] Evans calls attention to this point and urges that prospective studies be done.

And yet the differences between heterosexuals and homosexuals are strikingly similar to those revealed by the Bieber study, done several years earlier in an entirely different part of the country and with men who were in psychoanalytic therapy. Although the retrospective correlational data cannot be regarded as strong proof that homosexuality is pathological heterophobia stemming from repressed incestuous desires for the mother, the serious scientist cannot dismiss the findings of the Bieber and the Evans studies.

Learning Theory

Interestingly enough, one of the most widely known learning accounts of homosexual behavior comes not from experimental psychologists but from the Kinsey group, whose speculations on the role of conditioning in the development of sexual preferences have already been detailed. They see the human organism as neither intrinsically heterosexual nor intrinsically homosexual, but responsive to stimuli from both sexes. The sexual preference is said to be entirely a function of conditioning experiences, and neither kind of behavior is regarded as normal or abnormal.

More recently, Feldman and MacCulloch (1971) have proposed a theory that incorporates both biological and learning elements. They distinguish between primary and secondary homosexuals, the first group having no history of heterosexual arousal or behavior. On the basis of animal data indicating that repro-

---

[1] The reports of homosexuals might also have been biased by their readings of the popular and scientific literature on the topic.

is very cautious in the conclusions he has drawn. Moreover, others have failed to replicate his unusually high concordance rates (for example, Parker, 1964), finding numerous monozygotic twin pairs in which only one member is homosexual. The necessary adoptee studies to determine the concordance rates of homosexuality for monozygote twins who have been separated from their natural parents at an early age and raised by others have yet to be done.

Hormonal Bases of Homosexuality. Probably because homosexual feelings and behavior appear to be so resistant to change—either through therapy or through threat of legal prosecution—many have suggested that homosexuality is caused by some kind of imbalance of sex-related homones. Testosterone is regarded as crucial to the proper development of all secondary sex characteristics typical of mature men, such as growth of facial hair, deepening of the voice, and, in particular, the enlargement of the testes for production of sperm. Estrogen serves the important function of making a woman what she is physically. It is well to keep in mind that the biologically oriented researchers who have investigated whether homosexuals have less of the sex hormone appropriate for their sex assume that for a man to love a man, he must somehow be less of a man. They have expected the homosexual man to have lower levels of testosterone, the homosexual woman to have lower levels of estrogen.

In a recent study Loraine, Adamopoulos, Kirkham, Ismail, and Dove (1971) determined what amounts of several sex-related hormones were present in the urine of homosexual men and women and compared these figures with those for heterosexual men and women. The findings showed that the urine of homosexual men contained less testosterone than that of heterosexual men. The urine of lesbians contained higher levels of testosterone and lower levels of estrogen than did the urine of heterosexual women. Loraine and his colleagues cautioned against interpreting these preliminary findings as proof that homosexuality is attributable to certain levels of the sex hormones, for it is conceivable that homosexual behavior causes the hormonal differences.

Findings consistent with those of Loraine and his colleagues have been reported by Kolodny, Masters, Hendryx, and Toro (1971). They determined the levels of testosterone in the blood and the nature and quantity of sperm in young, physically healthy male homosexuals, comparing them with those of male heterosexuals. Exclusive and near-exclusive homosexuals had lower levels of plasma testosterone as well as markedly lower sperm counts and more misshaped sperm than did the controls.

Taken together, the two studies indicate that in males strongly committed to homosexuality, levels of the male hormone testosterone are lower and sperms fewer, with some abnormalities in the sperm. But both teams of workers caution against considering the findings proof that these hormonal differences cause homosexual behavior, for the studies are correlational in nature. Kolodny and his colleagues point out that ". . . the depressed plasma testosterone levels could be the secondary result of a primary homosexual psychosocial orientation" (p. 1173).

Sociological Views on Homosexuality

The theoretical accounts considered thus far, although different in major respects, have all emphasized what happens early in life. The guiding assumption has been that an understanding of homosexuality will come from an examination of prenatal events and of the experiences of childhood and adolescence. Sociologists have instead tended to concentrate on variables operating in adult life. In addition to preferring members of the same sex as sexual partners, homosexuals also hold jobs, have their likes and dislikes, own things, live somewhere—in short, engage in the common activities of adulthood. Furthermore, homosexuals can be men *or* women, and the psychological literature is barren of discussion of female homosexuality and its similarities to and differences from male homosexuality. Some ideas and observations from the sociological literature, hypotheses as well as data, may provide a much broader perspective that can aid in understanding homosexual behavior.

Gagnon and Simon (1973), two sociologists formerly affiliated with the Kinsey group, suggest that we have allowed

. . . the homosexual's sexual object choice to dominate and control our imagery of him [or her]. We have let this single aspect of his [or her] total life experience appear to determine all his products, concerns and activities. This prepossessing concern on the part of nonhomosexuals with a purely sexual aspect of the homosexual's life is something we would not allow to occur if we were interested in the heterosexual. . . . the mere presence of unconventional sexuality seems to give the sexual content of life an overwhelming significance. [But] homosexuals . . . vary profoundly in the degree to which their homosexual commitment and its facilitation becomes the organizing principle of their lives (p. 137).

Gagnon and Simon believe that we tend to regard the sexual preferences of homosexuals as all important in understanding their lives as a whole. Thus a person who is homosexual and an artist tends to have his artistic inclinations explained or defined in terms of his sexual commitment, but a heterosexual's choice of a particular field of study is not attributed to his love of members of the opposite sex. A full understanding of homosexuality, then, is not possible without an appreciation of how homosexuals handle the kinds of problems that all people face in society and with themselves.

Most social scientists rely heavily on the Kinsey data. The manner in which these data is interpreted is quite intriguing, especially when they are integrated with other information collected in recent years both through interviews and through the participant observations of those who have entered into homosexual settings as unobtrusively as possible in order to observe, as well as an outsider is able, the various homosexual life styles.

Male Homosexuality

Life Styles. Sociological studies reveal that our concept of homosexuality may be deceptively unitary. We have a tendency to speak of *the* homosexual and to construct theories to explain his sexual development. The actual situation seems far more complex. What effects does a homosexual commitment have on a man? How do homosexuals find partners? Are some homosexuals married? As in the heterosexual world, those desiring homosexual contacts have many options for meeting men socially and sexually. There are similarities between how homosexual and heterosexual men make contacts, or would like to. Homosexual men can meet other men in certain movie houses, at beaches, in bars and gyms, at particular highway rest areas, behind or inside trucks, and in public toilets, referred to as "tearooms." These are the locations where men look for "impersonal sex" (Humphreys, 1970). After appropriate signaling, an arrangement is made for a contact that is purely sexual in nature—words are often never spoken.

Performing fellatio in a men's toilet can be easy, but it can also lead to an arrest by a plainsclothesman. If the homosexual is older, or unattractive, he may have to pay a male prostitute for gratification (see Box 12.3). The

BOX **12.3** *Male Homosexual Prostitution*

The appeal of youth and the general search for desirable partners make homosexual prostitution an established and flourishing sexual institution, but it varies from heterosexual prostitution in a number of ways. A female prostitute is paid by a male heterosexual so that the male can have an orgasm, but in homosexual prostitution the male prostitute is usually paid for *his* having an orgasm. Thus, unlike the female prostitute, the male prostitute must become sexually aroused and have an orgasm. In the heterosexual world the female prostitute is regarded as degraded, but in the male prostitute world the homosexual who pays for sex is degraded (Gagnon and Simon, 1973).

In addition to the older confirmed homosexuals who seek new and youthful partners, clients include married men who are especially vulnerable to disclosure of their homosexuality. By going to the homosexual prostitute and paying for sex, the risk of discovery is less. But fee-paying customers are sometimes beaten up and robbed by delinquent adolescents who act as prostitutes but may also prey on their customers. Or an inexperienced prostitute may panic when he feels pleasure, fearing that he too may be "queer," and resort to violence to reassert his sense of masculinity (Reiss, 1961).

With male prostitutes who are predominantly or entirely heterosexual, a rather regimented set of procedures minimizes the homosexual nature of the contact. No reciprocity is expected. The male prostitute maintains his erection and has an orgasm without apparently compromising his conception of himself as a heterosexual. Some of these young men, of course, are homosexually inclined themselves or may become so through repeated orgastic pleasure. They may then engage reciprocally in these paid encounters, which makes them less attractive to the homosexual who wants to fellate a heterosexual male to reduce his own sense of deviancy by confirming his belief that all men have a streak of homosexuality.

degree to which a man is "out of the closet" also affects how openly he goes about satisfying his desires. Men may enter into homosexual marriages, complete with household. The sexual activities engaged in by male homosexuals are similar to those of heterosexuals. There may be kissing and general fondling, especially when the partners know and love each other. The practices leading to orgasm include fellatio, manipulation of the penis, and insertion of the penis or fingers in the anus.

Many, perhaps most, male homosexuals can be said not to "look" it. The stereotype is the "swishy" effeminate man who identifies with women not only through his sexuality but also by avoiding "masculine" pursuits. Male hairdressers are often considered to be homosexual, even though many are not, and football players may be regarded as surely not, even though some are. Some homosexuals dress in female attire, called "going in drag," perhaps even passing themselves off to heterosexual men as female prostitutes; this may account for the frequent confusion of homosexuality with transvestism (see Chapter 11).

Male Homosexuals in Heterosexual Marriages. Kinsey (1948) determined that 10 percent of married American men between the ages of sixteen and twenty-five have had homosexual experiences. Since married men would probably wish to hide such activity, even from a professional interviewer, this figure is likely to be a gross underestimate of homosexual inclinations and behavior among married men. Moreover, as Humphreys (1970) has shown in his study of homosexual behavior in toilets, substantial numbers of married males have impersonal sexual encounters with men.

The fact that a man can be homosexual to some degree and have a conventional heterosexual marriage may strike people as contradictory, but it does happen. Few studies have been made of the married homosexual. One preliminary investigation was done by Ross (1971) in Belgium. He interviewed eleven couples in which one partner, usually the man, was a homosexual. Obviously, these were marital situations in which the nonhomosexual partner knew of the spouse's homosexuality. The findings, although very tentative and in need of replication under better-controlled conditions, are of interest.

Why did the homosexuals get married in the first place? Several reasons were offered. Some of the men reported not realizing that they were attracted to other men until after the mar-riage. Some were aware of their sexual feelings toward men but hoped that being married to a woman would change these feelings. (Homosexuals are not infrequently advised to marry for this very reason, with discouraging results.) Others wanted companionship and the stability of having children and a home. Fear that social and professional advancement would be hindered by the lack of a conventional homelife was another motive.

Ross found considerable conflict within the eleven marriages examined. The frequency of marital sexual relations often declined, sometimes to zero. A number of the homosexual partners had outside relationships, usually of a one-time nature. The resolution of these marriage difficulties took several forms. Some couples separated. Some had nonsexual marriages and somehow adjusted to them, perhaps with outside means of sexual gratification. One of the marriages was described as "innovative"; the man's lover lived with the married couple, a so-called *ménage à trois*.

The Aging Homosexual. It is widely assumed by both homosexuals and heterosexuals that growing old occasions for homosexuals considerable distress and loneliness, more extensive than that experienced by heterosexuals. The pun "Nobody loves you when you're old and gay . . ." (Stearns, 1961 p. 202) is believed to be a sad statement of fact.

To test whether this generalization is really valid, Weinberg (1970) enlisted the help of the Mattachine Society of New York. An extensive questionnaire, to be filled out anonymously, was mailed to over 3000 male homosexual members. Weinberg was also able to obtain data from a sample of homosexuals in Chicago who were not members of any homosexual society. Unfortunately, only 30 percent of the questionnaires were returned. Weinberg himself was aware of problems in generalizing from such a restricted sample. Nonetheless, the findings are of considerable interest.

The data confirmed the widely held belief that male homosexuals who are forty-five or older have fewer sociosexual contacts with other homosexuals. Whereas homosexual bars and clubs were visited at least once a month by more than half the homosexuals under age twenty-six, only a quarter of those who were forty-six or older visited bars and clubs that often. Older homosexuals were also more likely to be living alone and to be having far less homosexual sex than they had had as younger men.

The loneliness and psychological distress of older gays, however, appeared to be no greater than that of younger homosexuals. Indeed, the older gays appeared to be less worried about their homosexuality and more accepting of themselves.

Weinberg addressed himself to the question why people generally believe that growing old is a particularly terrible experience for homosexuals. He suggests that this myth is perpetuated by younger homosexuals and by straight journalists and social scientists who first imagine how they would feel if they were old gays and, concluding that they would be companionless, believe that older gays are lonely. Perhaps both homosexuals and heterosexuals lower their aspirations as they age, settling for less in many areas of life. By the time the homosexual is middle-aged, he has probably come to terms with himself, including his sexuality. Younger homosexuals are more likely to be torn by conflict and guilt.

Female Homosexuality

Our review of the Kinsey data has indicated that the incidence of lesbianism is apparently much, much lower in America than the incidence of male homosexuality. Moreover, the amount of research and writing done on female homosexuality has been much less than that on male homosexuality.

The Nature of the Lesbian Relationship. It has been proposed that female homosexuals follow the same developmental patterns as female heterosexuals, and that their attitudes are in ways similar to those of female heterosexuals (Gagnon and Simon, 1973; Martin and Lyon, 1972). Gagnon and Simon speculate that during puberty sexual development for boys is primarily genital, with nearly all young males having experienced orgasm, usually from masturbation, within two years of the onset of biological maturation. In contrast, girls are introduced to sexuality through social learning organized around romance and marriage, not through orgastic arousal. Not until they have reached their late twenties do women generally experience the number of orgasms that seventeen-year-old males do.

To pursue this line of reasoning further, Gagnon and Simon point out that masturbation, engaged in by an overwhelming majority of teen-age boys but not of girls, is "detached sex activity—activity whose only sustaining motive is sexual" (Simon and Gagnon, 1970, p. 32). Moreover, during masturbation, which is usually intensely satisfying, especially in adolescence, young men generally fantasize a great deal. They therefore have

a tendency to see large parts of the environment in an erotic light, as well as the ability to respond, sexually and perhaps poetically, to many visual and auditory stimuli. . . . [On the other hand] girls appear to be well-trained precisely in that area in which boys are poorly trained—that is, a belief in and a capacity for intense, emotionally-charged relationships and the language of romantic love. When girls during this [adolescent] period describe themselves as having been aroused sexually, they more often report it as a response to romantic, rather than erotic, words and actions (pp. 33–36).

In maturity, according to Gagnon and Simon, the separation of sexual gratification from emotional and romantic involvement is not appealing to most women, whether heterosexual or homosexual. The Kinsey data, for example, showed that only 29 percent of those interviewed who were exclusively lesbians had had sexual relations with three or more partners. This figure is very similar to the number of male partners female heterosexuals have and is much, much lower than that for men. Furthermore, female homosexuals and heterosexuals both appear to be less aroused by fantasy and visual stimuli than men, and more aroused by touch and by romantic involvement. Sexual arousal tends to be restricted to "legitimizing emotional circumstances," not detachable from some kind of meaningful relationship with another person. A female homosexual relationship, then, is said to be built more on caring than on sexual need, whereas male homosexuals tend to define their relationships in terms of the orgasm. And lesbian relationships tend to last longer than those of male homosexuals. The image of the lesbian as a counterfeit man does not appear accurate.

What we have stated so far are massive generalizations, which, even if generally accurate, may well change as sexual mores in the society at large change. The women's liberation movement may have a decided impact. As female heterosexual relationships become freer and more orgastic, which seems to be happening, at least among some groups, it will be fascinating to see whether lesbian relationships will follow suit.

Life Styles and Adjustment. The female homosexual, like the male homosexual, must organize her life to handle and legitimize her sexual interests. Gagnon and Simon (1973) conducted extensive interviews with about two dozen lesbians. The lesbians could not generally be considered heterosexual rejects, that is, too ugly or otherwise undesirable to interest men, but some did fit the "butch" or "dyke" stereotype. Gagnon and Simon do not view this occasional "masculine" behavior pattern as confirming the psychoanalytic notion that homosexuality is some failure in appropriate gender identification. Rather, they relate this behavior to the fact that lesbians must be more aggressive than female heterosexuals in making sexual contacts. Inasmuch as a lesbian is more likely than a heterosexual woman to assume responsibilities largely defined as masculine—for example, repairing household appliances—the masculinity of some "butch" lesbians may reflect the necessary assumption of certain aspects of the male role.

Like any member of society, lesbians have to make decisions on how to deal with family, how to earn a living, what kind of friends to seek, how to find a partner, and how to achieve some degree of self-acceptance. Obviously these problems in living are made all the more difficult by societal sanctions.

I work very hard at not letting people in the office know. But I don't think I would get fired or anything. It's just the nervousness I know it would start. The other girls look at you curiously. Any touching, even accidental, is taken for a pass. I've had it happen before, when I got careless and let someone know who talked. I got so I'd wait for the john to be empty before I'd go in. I don't want to go through that again (Simon and Gagnon, 1967, pp. 271–272).

Regardless of the many obstacles societal sanctions create for lesbians, their general mental well-being has been attested to. From interviews that were conducted with sixty-five females who were exclusively homosexual, Hedblom (1972) found little support for the contention that homosexuality is a sign of psychopathology. More than three-fourths of the respondents felt strongly that homosexuality was as normal as heterosexuality. Such a statement may or not be a rationalization, but then practically *any* statement made by anybody can be so regarded. The lesbians also felt that homosexuals are highly creative and sensitive individuals. In this nonpsychiatric sample, 91 percent said that they had never sought help for their homosexuality, although 26 percent had sought professional advice on nonsexual problems.

Finally, Hedblom and others have reported that the initial sexual encounters between women already inclined sexually toward each other are overwhelmingly positive, apparently because of the greater understanding one woman has of another's physiological and psychological needs. Kinsey and his workers (1953) commented in a similar vein that arousal techniques used by two women with each other are virtually identical to those used in heterosexual petting or foreplay and at least as effective. Percentages of female orgasm reported in heterosexual intercourse during the first five years of marriage were significantly lower than those reported for women with five years of homosexual experience.

It would be rash and inaccurate to state, however, that a greater degree of familiarity can by itself account for female, or male, homosexuality. Intimate physical contact, as physicians and their patients are well aware, is readily desexualized if the setting is not construed as sexual. Even the most sensitive bodily stimulation by another person will be reacted to with sexual arousal only if that person is accepted as a legitimate partner beforehand.

Conclusion

Theories about the development and maintenance of homosexual behavior are as diverse as those explaining other behavioral phenomena. It seems to us unlikely that any single theory will ever encompass the entire range of what is termed homosexuality. People appear to become involved in same-sexed erotic pursuits for a multitude of reasons, and perhaps also for different reasons at different times. It is also possible that some homosexuals are preset by the hormonal balance in the uterus of the mother (Money, 1970) to acquire later same-sexed preferences. The failure thus far to demonstrate convincingly that homosexuality is genetically determined may be an indication of the heterogeneous origins and maintenance of homosexuality. It is possible that, in any given sample of homosexuals, at least some individuals differ from one another with respect to the causes of their sexual behavior. By lumping them all together in one group—homosexuals—we may be assuming homogeneity where there is none.

LEGAL AND SOCIAL IMPLICATIONS OF HOMOSEXUALITY

Earlier in this chapter the reader was invited to reflect on how he or she might react if anxiety were against the law, even if the emotion were felt only in private. In this section we shall examine more closely the legal status of homosexual behavior, its consequences for homosexuals and other citizens, and how the laws affecting homosexuality may be changed in the future.

When we look at the legal aspects of homo-

BOX **12.4** *A Reinterpretation of Sodom?*

There is considerable controversy among theologians (for example, Bailey, 1955) regarding the true meaning of the story of Lot. The belief that the Sodomites desired homosexual relations with the male guests, and that God destroyed Sodom and Gomorrah out of His abhorrence of homosexuality has been based on the words used by the male citizens of Sodom, who are said to have surrounded Lot's house and demanded that he usher the male visitors outside "that we may know them" (Genesis 19:5). The controversy centers around the meaning of the Hebrew "yadah," to know, which was occasionally used in the old Testament to refer to sexual intercourse. As Bailey has pointed out, the verb "yadah" is used 943 times in the Old Testament, only a few times clearly referring to sexual relations. More progressive theologians (for example, Treese, 1966), eager to change the position of organized religion on homosexuality, have attempted to reinterpret passages which, like the story of Lot, have typically been used to demonstrate the sinful nature of homosexuality in the eyes of God. Although others who are also trying to remove the stigma of homosexuality must surely wish these theologians well, an important aspect of the story works against their argument. Why did Lot offer the Sodomites his daughters instead of the angels if indeed sexual relations were not intended? "I pray you, brethren, do not so wickedly. Behold now, I have two daughters which have not known man; let me, I pray you, bring them out unto you, and do ye to them as is good in your eyes; only unto these men do nothing. . . ." (Genesis 19:7, 8).

sexuality, we find that some Western societies have been extremely punitive. The Jews of the Old Testament were very intolerant of homosexual behavior, and this attitude was clearly reflected in the laws under which they lived. In Leviticus 20:13, it is stated, "If a man also lies with mankind, as he lieth with a woman, both of them have committed an abomination; they shall surely be put to death; their blood shall be upon them." The story of Lot reveals the attitude of Judaism toward homosexuality. Lot, who lived near the gate of Sodom, gave lodging for the night to two men, actually the Lord's angels. Male citizens of Sodom who wanted to have homosexual relations with the guests came to Lot's house and asked to be given the travelers. So abhorrent was this request, and so degraded were women in those days, that Lot offered the Sodomites his virgin daughters rather than hand over the two male visitors. When the Sodomites tried to break down Lot's door, the angels smote them with blindness. The next day the angels led Lot and his family from the city. "Then the Lord rained upon Sodom and upon Gomorrah brimstone and fire from the Lord out of heaven; and He overthrew those cities, and all the plain, and all the inhabitants of the cities, and that which grew upon the ground" (Genesis 19:24, 25).

The Laws Affecting Homosexuality

The Jewish prohibition against homosexuality (see Box 12.4) was introduced into Christianity by St. Paul and has come down to us through both Roman law and English church and civil law. In medieval England sodomists were tried in the ecclesiastical courts and could, according to the church laws, be buried alive, burned alive, or put to death by other means. During the reign of Henry VIII an act was passed that absorbed the church laws into English civil law. The death penalty for anal intercourse was not reduced to a maximum of life imprisonment until 1861. Mutual masturbation, however, although referred to by a law passed in 1885 as "an act of grossly indecent nature between male persons," was at the time judged a misdemeanor punishable with two years of imprisonment.

In the United States the prohibition against homosexuality has taken an interesting turn, for there is no specific law against homosexuality. Rather, the laws specify sexual acts that are not permitted, and all these are performed in both homosexual and heterosexual relationships, for example, oral-genital contact and anal intercourse (Hoffman, 1968).

Some states, for example, prohibit "the crime against nature with man or beast" or "sodomy with man or beast." Traditionally, sodomy referred only to anal intercourse, whether heterosexual or between two male homosexuals. Thus a heterosexual married couple who engaged in anal intercourse were considered to break the law, whereas a homosexual couple who performed mutual fellatio were not. To make the sodomy laws more inclusive, some courts redefined them to include fellatio or cunnilingus. In 1897 the statement by a California court that the sodomy statute did not apply to fellatio or cunnilingus led to the enactment of a separate statute outlawing oral copulation. Hoffman emphasizes that this California statute prohibits heterosexual as well as homosexual oral-genital relations. Similar legislation has been enacted in a number of other states. Statutes prohibiting sexual acts other than penile-vaginal intercourse are thus employed to legislate against homosexuality.

These laws are not the only ones that are used against homosexuals, however. A variety of vaguely worded misdemeanor statutes have been employed by the police. In California three categories of public behavior are regarded as misdemeanors: outrageous conduct, lewd and lascivious behavior, and vagrancy. At one time or another homosexuals have been charged with all of them. A study done by the UCLA Law Review in March 1966 and reviewed by Hoffman (1968) showed that in California homosexuals were generally punished under the disorderly conduct statute, Section 647 of the California penal code, according to which "Every person who commits any of the following acts shall be guilty of disorderly conduct, a misdemeanor: Who solicits anyone to engage in or who in any public place or in any place open to the public or exposed to public view engages in lewd or dissolute conduct . . . who loiters in or about any toilet open to the public for purpose of engaging in or soliciting any lewd, lascivious or any unlawful act."

About 95 percent of all homosexual arrests in California are for violations of this section of the penal code. Police sometimes act as decoys to attract homosexuals. Officers, usually young and handsome, are accompanied by a fellow policeman who keeps out of sight and witnesses what happens. Oral testimony from the arresting officer alleging that the defendant asked to engage in a "lewd act" with the decoy is usually sufficient to convict. The law distinguishes between "entrapment," which is not proper, and "enticement," the distinction being "whether the intent to commit the crime originated in the mind of the defendant or in the mind of the officer." In practice it is the word of the arresting officer against the word of the defendant that must be judged in drawing this very fine line. The UCLA Law Review study strongly recommends that police manpower not be used for this kind of enforcement of law. It points out that homosexuals have their own sets of signals and would not likely commit public outrages by confronting a heterosexual man.

The laws against certain sexual acts are applied in an absolute way; a person can be defined as a homosexual because of a single arrest for a single homosexual act. Whether the individual would rate as a 2 or 6 on the Kinsey scale is not considered. Indeed, according to the old Kinsey data reviewed earlier, one-third of the white American population qualify for arrest as sex offenders. Nor are the circumstances in which the act was performed considered; being inebriated, depressed, or curious has no bearing. Furthermore, the acts for which homosexuals are arrested are the very same ones performed frequently by heterosexuals, who only rarely are arrested for

them. Indeed, numerous sex manuals available in the soberest of bookstores advise heterosexuals to engage in such practices on occasion. If these heterosexual practices are also taken into account, it is likely that about 96 percent of American men could be arrested for violation of sodomy laws (Churchill, 1967).

Hoffman believes that society views the male homosexual as a violent threat to heterosexuals, especially boys. But most sex that involves violence is in fact heterosexual in nature; moreover, the adult homosexual who does have relations with a boy usually masturbates or fellates him but does not have anal intercourse, which might be more injurious. The men who molest children, however, are not generally homosexuals.

Szasz (1970), whose work on criminal behavior and the law was reviewed in Chapter 9, is predictably outspoken about the discrimination against homosexuality. In a historical review of the topic, he remarks that the Roman Catholic Church's stand against homosexuality rests not only on the presumed unnaturalness of the act but also on its being separated from the human function of procreation. Sex without the possibility of conception has generally been viewed askance by the Catholic hierarchy, although less and less so by the laity.

In Kinsey's report on females (1953) an interesting statistic underlining the scant attention paid to female homosexual offenses is cited.

Our search through the several hundred sodomy opinions which have been reported in this country between 1696 and 1952 has failed to reveal a single case sustaining the conviction of a female for homosexual activity. . . . Even in such a large city as New York, the records covering the years 1930 to 1939 show only one case of a woman con-

victed of homosexual sodomy, while there were over 700 convictions of males on homosexual charges and several thousand cases of males prosecuted for public indecency, or for solicitation, or for other activity which was homosexual (p. 485).

The markedly lower incidence of legal prosecution of lesbians does not, however, necessarily mean that there is tolerance for female homosexuality. Martin and Lyon (1972) document considerable persecution of suspected lesbians in the federal civil service as well as in the women's armed forces.

Gay Liberation

The Beginnings of the Movement

As a reaction against the downtrodden legal status of homosexuals and the prevailing view of some mental health professionals who continue to accept the psychoanalytic notion of homosexuality as a pathological fear of the opposite sex, there has developed in this country a militant and radical sociopolitical movement to achieve recognition of the normality of homosexuality (Figure 12.3). The slogan of this group proclaims that "Gay is good."

In June of 1969, outside a gay bar called the Stonewall in Greenwich Village, New York City, homosexuals rioted openly in the streets, objecting to what they regarded as police harrassment. Many view this as the explosive beginning of gay liberation, although forces had already been developing to make such a public revolt inevitable. The originally social Mattachine societies in various large cities had during the early 1960s become outspoken in their efforts to establish rights for homosexuals. One of the most articulate gay liberation people, Franklin Kameny, has proclaimed on behalf of the movement,

We have been shoved around for some 3,000 years. We're fed up with it and we're starting to shove back. If we don't get our rights and decent treatment as full human beings which we deserve, and get them now, there is going to be a lot more shoving back (1971, p. 19).

The gay liberation movement forms alliances with other oppressed groups and supports humanitarian and political causes. The principal concern is with the rights of individuals to conduct their lives as they see fit, provided they not infringe on the rights of others. Kameny has attacked the "psychiatric establishment" in angry tones reminiscent of Szasz's rhetoric. He rejects totally the authority of contemporary psychiatry, and, at least by implication, clinical psychology, to deem any sexual relations sick, regarding such an attitude as social prejudice rather than a dispassionately formulated scientific opinion. At the end of his polemic he offers to help in a psychiatrists' liberation movement: "In a spirit of forgiveness, charity, and humanity, we will be pleased to assist in the administration of therapy to a profession badly in need of it, in order to achieve its liberation" (p. 27).

In "Refugees from Amerika: A Gay Manifesto" Wittman (1970) offers indirect criticisms of Bieber, as well as support for the Kinsey position.

Nature leaves undefined the object of sexual desire. The gender of that object has been imposed socially. . . . [homosexuality] is not a makeshift in the absence of the opposite sex; it is not hatred or rejection of the opposite sex; it is not genetic; it is not the result of broken homes. . . . Homosexuality is the capacity to love someone of the same sex. . . . [And het-

erosexuality] *is a fear of people of the same sex.*

Homosexuality in DSM-II

The Gay Liberation movement has begun a drive to have homosexuality dropped from DSM-II and thereby be formally recognized by the mental health profession as a "normal variant" of sexual behavior rather than as a disorder or illness. A hearing was held in New York City on February 8, 1973, before the Nomenclature Committee of the American Psychiatric Association. Statements were made by several gay activists in an effort to persuade the psychiatrists. Charles Silverstein, a gay psychologist, reminded the committee that earlier psychiatric manuals had contained such obsolete and now-humorous categories as "Vagabondage," "Pathologic mendacity," and "Cruel." The current DSM-II, he argued, is little justified in labeling homosexuality a disorder since no evidence indicates greater emotional disturbance among male and female homosexuals than among heterosexuals. Letters from recognized authorities—including Wardell Pomeroy, one of the original Kinsey researchers, and the American Psychological Association—strongly supported the stand of gay groups against continuing to retain an illness label for homosexual behavior. At its annual meeting in May 1973, the American Psychiatric Association discussed the issue in greater depth; the association has been asked to modify the listing of homosexuality to include only those homosexuals who wish to change their sexual orientation. The suggested new listing would be "sexual orientation disturbance."

Reform of Our Sex Laws

The increasing weight of scientific evidence indicates that homosexual behavior is not intrin-sically harmful to those who engage in it whether exclusively or only occasionally. Moreover, citizens generally object to the legal regulation of sexual behavior. For these reasons reforms are underway to remove from public scrutiny the private sexual activities of consenting adults.

In 1954 the House of Lords in England commissioned a study of homosexuality, chaired by Sir John Wolfenden. The well-known Wolfenden report of 1957 came out strongly in favor of repealing England's prohibitions against homosexual acts, arguing that sexual behavior in private between consenting adults is not the law's business. Not until ten years later, in 1967, were the recommendations implemented by parliamentary repeal of the century-old statutes.

Similar events have been taking place in the United States, although they do not yet affect the whole country. In 1955 the American Law Institute made recommendations similar to those of the Wolfenden report. And in 1961 Illinois became the first state to drop the laws against private sexual acts between consenting adults. Connecticut and Oregon in 1971, Colorado in 1972 and Hawaii, Delaware, and Ohio in 1973 have followed suit.

Hoffman (1968) makes the disturbing observation that the change in law in Illinois has not really improved the situation for homosexuals, for the constitutional protections against improper search of the home had, in fact, already made it possible for people to do in private what they wanted. What have *not* been changed, and what still allow police to harass homosexuals, are the laws against public conduct; making contacts and arrangements for later private relations is still illegal. Ironically, the police in Chicago *increased* their arrests of homosexuals in the five years following the change in the sodomy laws. Perhaps the strongest impetus for social and legal change

FIGURE **12.3**
Portrayed here is the open—sometimes bla-
tant—declaration of homosexual life styles. The
photograph on the opposite page in particular in-
dicates the militancy with which many of the out-of-
the-closet homosexuals refuse to endure any longer
the prejudice and persecution of "straight society."

321

will come from the recommendations of a blue-ribbon task force of experts working under the auspices of the National Institute of Mental Health. They concluded with these words:

We believe that most professionals working in this area—on the basis of their collective research and clinical experience and the present overall knowledge of the subject—are strongly convinced that the extreme opprobrium our society has attached to homosexual behavior, by way of criminal statutes and restrictive employment practices, has done more social harm than good and goes beyond what is necessary for the maintenance of public order and human decency (Livingood, 1972, pp. 5–6).

SUMMARY

This chapter has reviewed data and speculation on the nature, origins, and extent of homosexuality. The most extensive sources of data are the two Kinsey reports, which indicate a considerable amount of homosexual behavior and interests among American men and women. Kinsey regarded the choice of a partner of the opposite or of the same sex for sexual activity as determined by chance, being dependent on early sexual experiences. Psychoanalysts have tended to favor a heterophobic conception, according to which the male homosexual, having mishandled his oedipal dilemma, develops a neurotic fear of castration which often turns into a fear of the vagina. Some learning theorists also propose a heterophobic interpretation of homosexuality. There is no evidence for a genetic factor, but suggestive correlational data indicate that homosexuals and lesbians have lower levels of appropriate sex hormones. Sociological studies have tended to concentrate on how a homosexual organizes his or her life and how sociosexual contacts are made. Of considerable interest is the finding that the socialization and sexualization of female homosexuals is apparently more nearly like that of female heterosexuals than that of male homosexuals. Thus trying to understand a homosexual's life by concentrating on the sexual aspects of it may impede scientific understanding. The legal problems of homosexuals were also reviewed, as well as the significant movements for the recognition of their rights. Many experts agree that a serious reexamination of our attitudes is in order.

PART IV
THE SCHIZOPHRENIAS

CHAPTER 13

Schizophrenia: Description

Schizophrenia is the most prevalent and incapacitating of the psychological disorders. At the present time 20 percent of all first admissions to mental hospitals are diagnosed as schizophrenics; and because of their poor prognoses and relatively long periods of hospitalization, they constitute roughly half of all patients in these institutions. Thus, understandably, schizophrenia has been one of the most thoroughly investigated disorders in the field of abnormal psychology. In this chapter and the following we shall review the literature on schizophrenia. In this first chapter we examine the various forms of the disorder, its symptoms, and other descriptive aspects. In Chapter 14 we shall consider the different theories of the etiology of schizophrenia and the data that support them.

In various editions (1896) of his famous nineteenth-century textbook of psychiatry, Emil Kraepelin (Figure 13.1) applied the term dementia praecox to a syndrome that consisted of such symptoms as hallucinations, delusions, inappropriate emotional responses, stereotyped motor behavior, and deficient attention. He viewed dementia praecox as one of the two major groups of endogenous or organically caused psychoses, differentiating it from manic-depressive illness. Kraepelin supposed that the sex glands malfunctioned, producing a chemical imbalance which in turn affected the nervous system. The Latin adjective *praecox,* meaning premature, was applied to the disorder because it was believed to begin in adolescence, the noun *dementia* because a mental deterioration from which there could be no recovery was considered the inevitable progression. Kraepelin's early conception of the symptoms of the disorder is remarkably similar to the current descriptions of schizophrenia.

In 1911 Eugen Bleuler (Figure 13.2) wrote a monograph on what he termed "the group of schizophrenias" and in which he modified some of Kraepelin's early notions. Bleuler suggested the term *schizophrenia* because he viewed the essential feature of these discloser to investigate. As she approached, the noises became more distinct and she interpreted them to be the voices of a man and woman who were having intercourse. After listening for a while, she thought she recognized the man's voice to be that of a former boyfriend who she claimed was a homosexual. When she realized who the man was, she became frightened and ran into her house.

On subsequent days when she returned home, she again heard sexual goings-on in the house next door. In addition, she reported that she overheard conversations in which her former boyfriend extolled the sexual virtues of his current partner and labeled Jane as frigid. A few days later Jane began to see the couple as they departed the house after their sexual contact. She became increasingly upset and on three successive days called the police to report the intruders. Each day the police came, and each day they found no one there.

Motor Symptoms

Disturbances in motor activity are obvious and bizarre. The schizophrenic may grimace or adopt strange facial expressions. He may gesture repeatedly, using peculiar and sometimes complex sequences of finger, hand, and arm movements—which often seem to be purposeful, odd as they may be. Some schizophrenics manifest an unusual increase in the overall level of activity. There may be much excitement, wild flailing of the limbs, and great expenditure of energy similar to that seen in mania. At the other end of the spectrum is *catatonic immobility:* unusual postures are adopted and maintained for very long periods of time (Figure 13.3). A patient may stand on one leg, with the other tucked up toward his buttocks, and remain in this position virtually all day. The limbs of catatonic patients may have what is referred to as *waxy flexibility.* Another person can move them about and put them into strange positions that will then be maintained.

Affective Symptoms

Three affective abnormalities are often found in schizophrenic patients. In some affect is said to be *flat;* virtually no stimulus can elicit an emotional response. This shallowness or complete blunting of emotions renders the schizophrenic apathetic. The patient may stare vacantly, the muscles of his face flaccid, his eyes lifeless. When spoken to he answers in a flat and toneless voice. Other patients display *inappropriate affect.* The emotional responses of these individuals are out of context—the patient may laugh on hearing that his mother has just died or become enraged when asked a simple question about how a new garment fits. These schizophrenics are likely to shift rapidly from one emotional state to another for no discernible reason. Finally, the affective responses of some schizophrenic patients can be *ambivalent.* A single person or object may simultaneously arouse both positive and negative emotions. A patient may express strong hatred and strong love toward another person at about the same time.

Withdrawal and Autism

Autism is a withdrawal from contact with the world and a consequent overemphasis on one's own thoughts and fantasies. The schizophrenic becomes unable to distinguish be-

FIGURE **13.3**
This patient, diagnosed as a catatonic schizophrenic, spends nearly all his waking hours in this crouching position.

tween his own imagining and reality and is often spoken of as "being out of contact." Because schizophrenics are often buried in their own private and inner world, they lack interest in what is happening around them, being particularly withdrawn from any sort of social interaction. They frequently have few friends, little interest in the opposite sex, and a history of actively avoiding close social contacts with others.

SUBCATEGORIES OF SCHIZOPHRENIA

The Kraepelinian Subtypes

Three of the subtypes of schizophrenic reaction that are now included in the current diagnostic and statistical manual—hebephrenic, catatonic, and paranoid—were initially proposed by Kraepelin many years ago. Later, after Bleuler had written about the disorders, Kraepelin added a fourth, the simple type. DSM-II has added several others more recently, the one most frequently applied being chronic undifferentiated. The diagnostic reliability for all these subtypes is low (see

Chapter 3), and many patients who are diagnosed schizophrenic do not fit easily into any one of them. The descriptions, however, do provide further information on what schizophrenia is like and on the great diversity of behavior that relates to the diagnosis.

The *simple* form of schizophrenia begins at an early age. The individual progressively withdraws from social interaction, becomes listless and apathetic, and spends a great deal of time daydreaming. Typically, these patients do *not* have delusions or hallucinations and are often difficult to distinguish from retardates, who are also uncommunicative and seemingly unresponsive to the environment. The conversation of this schizophrenic becomes meager as he withdraws from his family and friends. He has little interest in work, being content to lead a simple existence alone in his room. If he leaves his family, he chooses to live in the least demanding manner possible. Often social ne'er-do-wells such as tramps and hobos could be diagnosed as simple schizophrenics.

A case history follows.

> Lotte is a forty-year-old woman who was examined and admitted to the hospital at the request of her mother. Shortly before this, the father had died and left her mother and Lotte with no financial support. Lotte had "sat around the house" for the previous twelve years, having lost her temporary employment in the office of a government agency because of inefficiency. She had no friends, interests, or hobbies. According to her own account, she did not read or watch television but did occasionally perform a few simple household tasks when pressured by her mother. Her one job had been secured during the manpower shortage during World War II and consisted of simple filing and sorting of documents. She found this work "too fast" and was ultimately discharged for incompetence. From her high school days on, Lotte seemed to have no relationship of even a casual kind with men. She did not finish high school; her parents took her out of it "because it made her nervous."
>
> On admission, she was quiet and almost completely passive about the prospect of her hospitalization. She was neat and clean and obedient to the instructions of her mother regarding such matters as where to sit, when to remove her hat and coat, etc. This pattern of behavior was repeated on the admission ward during the subsequent weeks (Maher, 1966, p. 304).

The most obvious symptoms of the *catatonic* type of schizophrenia are the motor disturbances discussed earlier. Such individuals typically alternate between catatonic immobility and wild excitement, but one or the other type of motor symptoms may predominate. The onset of catatonic reactions may be more sudden than other forms of schizophrenia, although the person has probably already shown some apathy and withdrawal from reality. The limbs of the immobile catatonic may become stiff and swollen; in spite of his apparent obliviousness, he may later relate all that has happened around him during his stupor. In the excited state the catatonic may shout and talk continuously and incoherently, all the while pacing with great agitation. There are some indications that this form of schizophrenia is becoming relatively rare, perhaps because drug therapy is now so frequently administered (Arieti, 1955). The following description is taken from our files.

Bob, a twenty-two-year-old, was admitted to the hospital after a brief period of bizarre behavior at home. His parents reported that for several days he had stayed in his room, coming out only for meals. Then, at dinner one evening, he suddenly "became rigid." Alarmed, the parents called the family physician, but by the time he arrived Bob had entered a period of intense activity. He ran through the house, rolled on the floor, and strenuously resisted efforts to restrain him. Finally, he was sedated and taken to the hospital.

In the hospital Bob continued to alternate between periods of catatonic immobility and wild excitement. He refused to speak or eat and often did the exact opposite of what was requested of him, going to bed when asked to get up and remaining up when asked to go to bed.

Initially, Bob was placed on a drug therapy regimen which lasted for several months. Little improvement was shown. Then a course of electroconvulsive therapy was begun, but again there was little improvement. The periods of excitement abated, but Bob remained mute, withdrawn, and frequently adopted catatonic postures.

A more common subdiagnosis is *paranoid* schizophrenia. The key to this diagnosis is the presence of numerous and systematized delusions, usually of persecution but sometimes of grandeur or of being controlled by an alien force. Vivid auditory and visual hallucinations may also accompany the delusions. These patients often develop what are referred to as *ideas of reference:* they incorporate unimportant events within a delusional framework, reading personal significance into the seemingly trivial activities of others. They think that phrases of overheard conversations apply to them, and the continual appearance of a person on a street where they customarily walk means that they are being watched. What they see on television or read in the newspapers also somehow refers to them. But the paranoid schizophrenic is more alert and verbal than other schizophrenics, and his thought processes, although deluded, have not fragmented.

Another case from our records illustrates these symptoms.

Roger was initially seen as an outpatient. He had come for treatment because he had been rejected by the army for psychiatric reasons and "wanted to do whatever was necessary to get into the army and go to Vietnam." He thought that he was a "born soldier" and related several incidents to support this assertion. In one of them he had been registering at a hotel desk, and the clerk had asked him how long his "leave" was going to be. Roger was unable to see that his short hair, marching gait, and the fact that he wore an army jacket were the likely cues the clerk was responding to.

Over the course of several weeks of outpatient therapy little happened. Roger remained very guarded and maintained that there really wasn't anything wrong. He showed almost no affective responses and claimed that his ideal was Mr. Spock, the intellectual, unemotional Vulcan of a science fiction television program. One week, as he was leaving, he announced that he had "figured out what was going on and knew what to do."

Three days later he was hospitalized. He had threatened to blow up an army recruiting post, claiming that aliens from another planet had taken over. He now believed that he was one of the last "true" earthmen. The aliens had already infiltrated the bodies of most human beings, beginning first with those of army men and then moving into the bodies of the rest of the human race as well.

The *hebephrenic* form of schizophrenia is characterized by a variety of rather diffuse and regressive symptoms. Hallucinations and delusions—sexual, hypochondriacal, religious, and persecutory—are profuse and less organized than those of the paranoid schizophrenic. The patient may be subject to bizarre ideas, often involving deterioration of the body. Much of his behavior is marked by a pattern of silliness and absurdity. He may grimace or have a meaningless smile on his face. He giggles childishly and speaks incoherently, stringing together similar-sounding words and inventing neologisms. He frequently deteriorates to the point that he becomes incontinent, voiding anywhere and anytime. He completely neglects his appearance, never bathing, brushing his teeth, or combing his hair.

The patient was a twenty-four-year-old single woman. After graduation from college she worked for two years with an advertising agency. During both her college days and later she was very seclusive and had few friends. She had never had any sexual experience, either homosexual or heterosexual. In the few weeks before hospitalization she had stopped going to work, remaining in her apartment and becoming inattentive to personal hygiene and grooming.

When she was admitted to the hospital, she was unkempt, disheveled, and dirty. Meaningful conversation with her seemed impossible. She maintained a silly grin and occasionally would spontaneously burst into wild fits of laughter, even though she might be describing how her bones were melting. Her verbal behavior was nonsensical. Asked whether she wanted to go on a ward outing, she replied, "Outing, inning, being out is in and in is out" (*laughter*).

Finally, the most prevalent of the schizophrenic subtypes is *chronic undifferentiated*.[1] This diagnosis seems to be frequently applied because, as previously noted, many patients do not exhibit a pattern of symptoms consistent enough to fit one of the other subtypes. For example, a patient may have delusions or motor disorders, but not to the extent that he is considered either a paranoid or a catatonic schizophrenic. This particular category is quite unsatisfactory, for it has become somewhat of a wastebasket diagnosis applied to patients who are difficult to categorize.

Evaluation

The Kraepelinian subtypes still form the basis of the current diagnostic system, yet many have questioned their usefulness. Making subtype diagnoses such as these is extremely difficult, which often means that diagnostic reliability is dramatically reduced. Furthermore, the subtypes have little validity: knowing that a patient has been diagnosed as having one or another form of schizophrenia does not give us information that will be helpful in treatment or in predicting the course of the problems. Finally, there is considerable overlap among the subtypes. For example, patients with all forms of schizophrenia may frequently have delusions. Thus the Kraepelinian system of subtyping has not proved to be an optimal way of trying to deal with the variability in schizophrenic behavior.

Some differentiations among schizophrenics may be useful, however. We have already noted the great diversity of symptoms shown by these individuals. There may be more worthwhile ways in which they can be grouped than by the subtype syndromes initially proposed by Kraepelin.

Dimensions of Schizophrenia

Researchers have found several variables or dimensions that appear to be useful to them in the subclassification and study of adult schizophrenics—paranoid-nonparanoid, acute-chronic, and good-poor premorbid adjustment. The paranoid-nonparanoid distinction is based primarily on the Kraepelinian subtype and is the only one of his categories that has proved helpful in contemporary research. Schizophrenics distinguished according to this dimension are classified in two groups, those who do and do not have delusions.

Acute-Chronic

The acute-chronic dimension has been defined in two ways. In DSM-II we find diagnostic types referred to as acute and chronic schizophrenics. The difference between them lies in the symptomatology being exhibited and in the suddeness with which the symptoms begin. Acute patients show a rapid onset and more obvious and florid symptomatology. Very often the disorder appears to have developed just after an emotionally painful experience. The chronic patient has more gradually withdrawn from others. The onset of symptoms has been insidious and apparently related to no particular incident.

In actual research practice, however, this distinction has referred primarily to length of hospitalization. Patients who have been hospitalized for only a short period are designated acutes, and those who have lived longer terms in an institution are called chronics.

[1] It might be supposed that this diagnosis is applied only to patients who have been hospitalized for long periods of time. This is not the case, for the label chronic undifferentiated is often applied on a patient's first admission.

Although the exact cutoff points have varied, many workers have accepted two years after first admission as the upper limit of time for continuing to regard patients as acute (Neale and Cromwell, 1970). This cutoff point was chosen because after the patient has remained in a hospital two years, it is unlikely that he will be subsequently discharged (Brown, 1960).

The research definitions of the acute-chronic dimension very likely relate to two aspects of schizophrenia. First, schizophrenics with shorter periods of hospitalization will be more likely to show the clear-cut, often bizarre and intense symptomatology of the acute patient as he is described in the psychiatric literature. Schizophrenics with longer periods of hospitalization are likely to be apathetic and withdrawn. Second, the research definition is also relevant in attempting to determine the effects of prolonged institutionalization. There is reason to believe that institutionalization itself can profoundly and adversely influence behavior (Goffman, 1961). Thus the research definition divides patients according to the extent that they may have been affected by hospitalization (Figure 13.4).

Premorbid Adjustment

A person's social and sexual adjustment before the onset of his symptoms is referred to as his premorbid adjustment. Several means of assessing premorbid adjustment have been devised, the most prominent being the Phillips Scale (1953), shown in Table 13.1, which was initially developed as a method of predicting the success of electroconvulsive therapy. Although it was somewhat useful in determining whether this therapy should be tried, the Phillips Scale proved better at predicting prognosis among schizophrenics, regardless of treatment modality, on the basis of what it revealed about their earlier adjustment. The scale is filled out by the researcher from case history material that has been collected on the patient's social and sexual functioning during adolescence and early adulthood. On the basis of earlier behavior as rated by the scale, patients can be divided into those who showed good premorbid adjustment and those who showed poor premorbid adjustment. Patients with good premorbid adjustment had adequate interpersonal and sexual relations before the onset of their problems, but those with poor premorbid adjustment were socially and sexually incompetent.

Actually, the total amount of information collected on the Phillips Scale reveals no more about the premorbid adjustment of a male schizophrenic than asking a single question. Has he been married? The behavior that designates a male schizophrenic as having good premorbid adjustment—having friends, dating, and the like—may also have eventuated in his marriage. In contrast, such traits as having few interests, not dating, and avoiding others are likely to lead to a solitary life, at least for men. In women similar attributes may be interpreted as shyness or demureness, traits that have not generally been considered socially undesirable for them. Therefore a relatively "schizoid" adolescent female may be more likely to become married than her male counterpart would. The traditional social role of women conspires to weaken marriage as a measure of the premorbid adjustment of a female schizophrenic. What will the changing roles of men and women do in the future to marriage as a measure of premorbid adjustment? Perhaps the growing equality between the sexes will eventually make marriage as valid a measure of the premorbid adjustment of female schizophrenics as it is now for males.

Later in this chapter we shall examine the bearing that premorbid adjustment has on the laboratory performances of schizophrenic patients. Here its connections with nonlaboratory aspects of schizophrenia will be explored. Most important perhaps are onset, symptomatology, and prognosis. A patient who has had a good premorbid adjustment has a more rapid onset of more severe symptoms and improves more rapidly than do those who have had a poor premorbid adjustment (Phillips, 1953). Until the rapid onset of his difficulties, most people considered the good premorbid to be a relatively normal individual. Then in response to some stress, such as a divorce or the loss of a loved one, his behavior suddenly became bizarre and psychotic. Almost overnight the patient has found the world changed, and he is perplexed and depressed. Other people believe that he has lost his mind. His thinking and speech are disorganized, and he may have delusions and be in a great panic because he does not understand what is happening to him. He is confused and terrified by the loss of control over his thoughts and feelings, but he is also likely to be quite verbal and intensely excited.

In contrast, the patient with poor premorbid adjustment appears to have been a relatively deviant individual for a long period of time. He probably had difficulties at school and did not date much or have many friends. Gradually, he has become more seclusive and more withdrawn, until finally his deterioration could not be ignored and he is hospitalized. Rather than manifesting particularly severe and bizarre symptomatology, however, he is uncommunicative, apathetic, and inactive and seems to accept the way he is. Having suffered insidious yet massive depletion of thought, emotions, interests, and activity, and having functioned poorly for so long, the poor premorbid schiz-

ophrenic is unresponsive to treatment and has a poor prognosis.

Interdependence of the Dimensions

Not only can patients be subclassified on the basis of each of the dimensions just discussed, but they may also be subclassified on the basis of *combinations* of them. In fact, it is perhaps more appropriate to subdivide on the basis of combinations than on the basis of any of them singly. The dimensions described are *not* independent or unrelated; rather they are interdependent. We have noted that patients with poor premorbid adjustment have a poor prognosis. They are more likely to remain in the hospital and thus to become chronic according to the research definition of that term. Therefore, even though we know that one group of schizophrenic patients had good earlier adjustment and the other poor, we cannot be certain that the differences between the two groups stem from the varying earlier adjustments or from the longer hospitalizations of the members of one of the groups.

Premorbid adjustment is also related to whether or not the patient has paranoid delusions (Goldstein, Held, and Cromwell, 1968; Neale, Kopfstein, and Levine, 1972). Patients with good premorbid adjustment have been found to be about equally divided between those who do and those who do not exhibit symptoms of paranoia, but almost all patients with poor premorbid adjustment have been found to have no paranoid delusions. Again, although we know that one group of schizophrenic patients had good premorbid adjustment and another poor, we cannot be sure that the differences between them reflect their varying earlier adjustments or the fact that the members of one group may not be subject to delusions.

FIGURE **13.4**
*The photograph to the right
is of a man diagnosed
as a hebephrenic schiz-
ophrenic, largely because of
his inappropriate mirth. That
at the top of the opposite
page portrays the isolation
in which a great many pa-
tients in a mental hospital
ward live. Their confinement
together is not enough to foster social interaction. In the
bottom photograph a number
of mental hospital patients,
some of them mentally re-
tarded, engage in a game as
part of a "play therapy."*

TABLE **13.1** *Phillips Scale of Premorbid Status in Schizophrenia* (*from Phillips, 1953*)

	Numerical weight
A. Recent sexual adjustment	
1. Stable heterosexual relation and marriage	0
2. Continued heterosexual relation and marriage, but unable to establish home	1
3. Continued heterosexual relation and marriage broken by permanent separation	2
4a. Continued heterosexual relation and marriage but with low sex drive	3
b. Continued heterosexual relation with deep emotional meaning but emotionally unable to develop it into marriage	3
5a. Casual but continued heterosexual relations — "affairs"	4
b. Homosexual contacts with lack of or chronic failure in heterosexual experiences	4
6a. Occasional casual heterosexual relations or homosexual experience with no deep emotional bond	5
b. Solitary masturbation; no attempt at heterosexual or homosexual experiences	5
7. No sexual interest in men or women	6
B. Social aspects of sexual life during adolescence and immediately beyond	
1. Always showed healthy interest in girls, with steady girl friend during adolescence	0
2. Started taking girls out regularly in adolescence	1
3. Always mixed closely with boys and girls	2
4. Consistent deep interest in male attachment, with restricted or no interest in girls	3
5a. Casual male attachments with inadequate attempts at adjustment to going out with girls	4
b. Casual contact with boys and girls	4
6a. Casual contacts with boys with lack of interest in girls	5
b. Occasional contact with girls	5
7. No desire to be with boys and girls; never went out with girls	6

TABLE **13.1** (*continued*)

	Numerical weight
C. Social aspects of recent sexual life: 30 years +	
1. Married and has children, living as a family unit	0
2. Married and has child but unable to establish or maintain a family home	1
3. Has been married and had child, but permanently separated	2
4a. Married, but considerable marital discord	3
b. Single, but has had engagement or deep heterosexual relation—emotionally unable to develop into marriage	3
5. Single, short engagements/relationships with females which do not appear to have emotional depth for both partners, that is, "affairs"	4
6a. Single, has gone out with a few girls, but no indications of a continuous interest in women	5
b. Single, consistent deep interest in male attachments, no interest in women	5
7a. Single, occasional male contacts, no interest in women	6
b. Single, no interest in men or women	6
D. Social aspects of recent sexual life: below 30	
1. Married, living as family unit with or without children	0
2a. Married, with or without children, but unable to establish or maintain a family home	1
b. Single but engaged in a deep heterosexual relationship (presumably leading to marriage)	1
3. Single, has had engagement or deep heterosexual relation; emotionally unable to carry to marriage	2
4. Single, consistent, deep interest in male attachments, with restricted or no interest in women	3
5. Single, casual male relationships with restricted or no interest in women	4
6. Single, has gone out with a few girls casually but without indications of continued interest in women	5

TABLE **13.1** (*continued*)

			Numerical weight
	7a.	Single, never interested in or associated with men or women	6
	b.	Antisocial	6
E.		Personal relations: history	
	1.	Always had a number of close friends but did not habitually play leading role	1
	2.	From adolescence on had a few close friends	2
	3.	From adolescence on had a few casual friends	3
	4.	From adolescence on stopped having friends	4
	5a.	No intimate friends after childhood	5
	b.	Casual but never any deep intimate mutual friendships	5
	6.	Never worried about boys or girls; no desire to be with boys or girls	6
F.		Recent premorbid adjustment in personal relations	
	1.	Habitually mixed with others, but not a leader	1
	2.	Mixed only with a close friend or group of friends	3
	3.	No close friends; only very few friends; had friends but never quite accepted by them	4
	4.	Quiet; aloof; seclusive; preferred to be by self	5
	5.	Antisocial	6

LABORATORY RESEARCH WITH ADULT SCHIZOPHRENICS

In their quest for a better understanding of schizophrenia, researchers have examined innumerable psychological processes, among them motivation, learning, perception, and cognition. The primary goal of this research has been to obtain a more detailed and precise knowledge of processes that may become deviant and are thus relevant to certain important types of schizophrenic behavior (see Box 13.1). Researchers attempt to answer questions such as "Why do schizophrenics exhibit deviant associations?" "What produces hallucinations?" "How is schizophrenic attention deviant?"

In any research on pertinent psychological processes, the performance of a group of adult schizophrenics is compared to that of a non-schizophrenic control group. Generally, schizophrenics are found to do more poorly than the control group, and the poor performance of the patients is termed a *psychological deficit*. The major difficulty of this research, discussed

BOX **13.1** *How Does Laboratory Research Attempt To Increase Our Understanding of Schizophrenia?*

We have already noted that clinicians view disorders of thought and language as crucial signs of schizophrenia. But what exactly is disordered in thought disorder? Chapman and Chapman (in press) report the following answer that a schizophrenic patient gave to the question "Why do you think people believe in God?"

Uh, late, I don't know why, let's see balloon travel. He holds it up for you, the balloon. He don't let you fall out, your little legs sticking out down through the clouds. He's down to the smoke stack, looking through the smoke trying to get the balloon gassed up you know. Way they're flying on top that way, legs sticking out, I don't know, looking down on the ground, heck, that'd make you go dizzy you just stay and sleep you know, hold down and sleep there. The balloon's His home you know up there. I used to sleep outdoors, you know, sleep outdoors instead of going home. He's had a home but His not tell where it's at you know.

The patient's response is clearly disordered, but can we specify the nature of the disorder more precisely? The patient wanders off the topic,

bringing in details, such as sleeping outdoors, that seem irrelevant to the question asked. Chapman and Chapman note that different observers might account for irrelevancy in varying ways.

1. The patient is unable to organize his thoughts coherently. A disordered associative process leads the patient from thinking of God's home, which he believes to be in the sky, to thinking of balloons because they are also in the sky.
2. The patient can only deal with one idea at a time.
3. The question was too abstract for the patient.
4. The patient's own personal feelings of being weak and alone intrude into his answer. He mentions the possibility of "falling out," "little legs," and so on.

These several descriptions of a single bit of schizophrenic dialogue illustrate that clinical data can be explained in a variety of ways. Laboratory research tries to determine which account is best by arranging special tests that pit the competing explanations against one another and allow incorrect ones to be discarded.

previously in Chapter 4, is that it is correlational in nature. The variable of primary interest is schizophrenic-nonschizophrenic, which has *not* been manipulated. Thus differences between schizophrenic and control groups in addition to the diagnosis may be regarded as plausible rival hypotheses to account for the varying performances. And there are many such differences and rival hypotheses. The schizophrenic and control groups are likely to vary on dimensions such as social class and intelligence; moreover, the schizophrenics are likely to be taking a tranquilizing medication and to be institutionalized. We must keep in mind that because this research is correlational, the conclusions drawn can be only tentatively accepted.[2]

We turn now to a selective review of three areas that have attracted the most attention from researchers—effects of punishment, perception, and cognition.

The Effects of Punishment on Schizophrenics

Why does the schizophrenic lose contact with reality? One answer to this question, proposed in 1957 by Rodnick and Garmezy, is that schizophrenics are especially sensitive to failure or censure. In many life situations a person may experience a sense of not measuring up or of having incurred the disapproval of others. He may say the wrong thing when with a group of friends or perform poorly in an academic or vocational setting. If schizophrenics are particularly sensitive to the potential for failure, they might be expected to take steps to reduce this source of distress. One means would be to withdraw into a private world.

Comparing the reactions of schizophrenics and normal people to criticism is one way of testing the theory that schizophrenics are sensitive to failure. Garmezy (1952) compared the performance of schizophrenic and control subjects on a perceptual task after each had been censured or praised. In support of the theory, the schizophrenics were found to make more errors after censure than after praise; the members of the control group improved their performances after being censured. Similar results were found by Webb (1955) on a conceptual task, by Bleke (1953) on a memory task, and by Alverez (1957) on a size judgment task.

[2] Much of the research on the etiology of schizophrenia, which is discussed in the next chapter, is also correlational in design and thus subject to the same problems mentioned here.

These studies had also subdivided their schizophrenics into those who had had good premorbid adjustment and those who had had poor. Schizophrenics with poor premorbid adjustment were found to suffer more from censure.

Not all investigators, however, have found that punishment or censure makes schizophrenic patients perform more poorly. In fact, the results of a number of these investigations have indicated the opposite. As Buss and Lang (1965) noted, "in all studies employing physical punishment there has been a definite reduction, and in a few instances a temporary elimination of psychological deficit . . . both a negative evaluation and specific verbal or physical punishment for errors can lead to a significant improvement in performance rather than further deficit" (pp. 10–11).

Garmezy (1966) has attempted to reconcile these two seemingly conflicting sets of data. He still assumes that schizophrenics are particularly sensitive to censure, but he proposes that the effects of censure depend on the situation in which it occurs. Censure makes schizophrenics perform more poorly when it is irrelevant to the task and cannot be avoided. In contrast, censure makes them perform better when it follows an incorrect response and thus helps them eliminate that response on future occasions. In reanalyzing the data from several earlier studies, Garmezy demonstrated that schizophrenics, especially those with poor premorbid adjustment, avoided censured responses more often than did members of various control groups. Whether this avoidance of the censured response facilitated or debilitated performance depended on the characteristics of the task at hand. In one experiment, performance on a reaction time task (see next page) was *facilitated* by censuring slow responses. In this instance, being sensitive to censure, schizophrenics reacted more quickly in order to avoid censure (Cavanaugh, Cohen, and Lang, 1960). But another task might, for example, require the subject to learn a sequence of lever presses A and B, with incorrect responses being censured. The correct order might be A, B, A, A, A, B. Suppose that a schizophrenic presses A twice; his second press would then be censured because B is the correct response. Since he is sensitive to censure, after an A response proves incorrect, he is likely to avoid the A lever and press B on the third trial. But A is the correct third response. In this task censure would lead to *poor* performance. In an experiment similar to this, Bleke (1953) did find that censure interfered with performance.

This finding that schizophrenics are especially sensitive to censure fits well with certain aspects of their behavior. Their social withdrawal, their lack of friends, and their reluctance to seek work may indicate that they wish to avoid the possible failure and censure that might ensue if they did try to find friends and a job.

Perceptual Research

Attention

Disordered attention has long been viewed as an important aspect of schizophrenia. And schizophrenics themselves report difficulty in attending to the world around them (see page 331). But what does it mean to say that attention is disordered in schizophrenics? Recent research has construed the concept of attention in two different ways, as alertness or readiness to respond and as a selective process. The first interpretation of attention, namely alertness and readiness to respond, has been the focus of numerous studies performed by

Shakow and his colleagues.

Reaction time is the amount of time it takes to make a response to a particular stimulus. A frequently used reaction time task requires a subject to lift his finger from a telegraph key as soon as a light comes on or a tone is sounded (Figure 13.5). Schizophrenics have consistently been shown to have slower reactions on such tests than various other control subjects. This slowness is more marked in chronic and nonparanoid patients than in acute or paranoid patients (Shakow, 1963). The finding that the schizophrenic's reaction time is slow does not, of course, point directly to a deficit in attention, for difficulty in making voluntary motor responses could also be responsible. Other studies on reaction time make lack of attention a plausible interpretation, however.

The preparatory interval in a reaction time task is a highly significant determinant of reaction time performance; this interval is the time between the onset of the warning signal and the showing of the actual stimulus. Chronic patients take much longer to react to the actual stimulus when the preparatory interval is long, eight or more seconds. They do not appear to be able to maintain a readiness to respond to the upcoming stimulus.

The second interpretation of attention, that it is a selective process, points up the fact that there is simply too much information present in our world for us to process, making some selection necessary. The cognitive disorganization shown by many schizophrenic patients may very well reflect a failure to select, and in fact schizophrenics have been found to have difficulties in *selective* attention. Rappaport (1967) investigated the performance of schizophrenic and normal subjects in a competing message task. Several auditory messages were simultaneously presented. The subjects were required to attend to only one of them and

FIGURE **13.5**

*Monitoring equipment for
a reaction time test. A subject
in a separate, darkened room
is presented with stimuli of
varying intensity and duration.
This device measures his
reaction time.*

repeat it back. The number of simultaneously presented messages varied from one to seven. The performance of the schizophrenics was always deficient whenever more than one message was presented. In a similar study Neale, McIntyre, Fox, and Cromwell (1969) investigated the performance of schizophrenics on a task in which alphabetic letters were presented on a screen for a brief period. Subjects were told that each display would contain either a T or an F and that their task was simply to report which of the two letters they had seen. The letters were presented in two ways. In one either a T or an F was flashed on the screen for each trial. In the second either a T or an F was flashed on the screen together with seven irrelevant or "noise" letters.

The results of the investigation, presented in Figure 13.6, indicated that all three groups were virtually equivalent in performance when a T or an F was presented by itself. But whenever either of the target letters was presented on the screen with several irrelevant letters, both schizophrenic groups were significantly poorer in performance than the control subjects.

The most plausible explanation of these findings is that schizophrenics are unable to differentiate between relevant and irrelevant information (Cash, Neale, and Cromwell, 1972). Instead, they try to process everything and thus are inefficient when selection is required. Moreover, as indicated by Rappaport's (1967) work, they are easily distracted by irrelevant information.

The findings on the attention of schizophrenics can be summed up by two statements.

1. Schizophrenics are unable to maintain a readiness to respond.
2. Schizophrenics have difficulty discriminating relevant from irrelevant information.

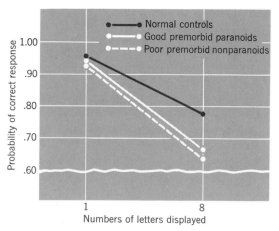

FIGURE **13.6**
Probability of a correct response by the control and schizophrenic groups when one or eight letters are displayed. After Neale, McIntyre, Fox, and Cromwell, 1969.

The two points may be related. Perhaps the schizophrenic fails to maintain a readiness to respond because of the "pull" of distracting, irrelevant information. Both points may help to explain the schizophrenic's thought and speech disorders. Because he does not discriminate between relevant and irrelevant information, "cognitive clutter" is the result. There is too much information for the schizophrenic to process; when he tries to order his thoughts, he becomes incoherent and confused. This confusion plus his inability to maintain attention then become evident in the irrelevancies and loose associations of the schizophrenic's speech.

Hallucinations

Another kind of schizophrenic perceptual disturbance that has been researched is the hallucination. Mintz and Alpert (1972) hypothesized that having an impaired perception of reality and a predisposition for vivid imagery may explain why schizophrenics hallucinate. They administered two tests to three groups of hospitalized psychiatric patients, hallucinating schizophrenics, nonhallucinating schizophrenics, and nonschizophrenic patients. The first test assessed the vividness of the subject's auditory imagery by asking him to close his eyes and imagine hearing a phonograph record playing "White Christmas" with both words and music. After thirty seconds the subject rated the vividness of the image he was able to produce on a scale ranging from "I heard a phonograph record of 'White Christmas' clearly and believed that the record was actually playing" to "I did not hear the record." For a second test earphones were placed on the subject through which he was to hear a set of twenty-four sentences, each with an intelligibility level of about 50 percent. Each time a sentence was presented, the subject tried to repeat exactly what he had heard and rated his confidence in the accuracy of his rendition on a scale ranging from "positive correct" to "positive incorrect."

On the imagination task 85 percent of the hallucinating schizophrenics reported either that they had heard "White Christmas" and believed that it was actually playing or that they had heard the record clearly but knew that a record was not really playing. One of the hallucinating schizophrenics who had not heard "White Christmas" said that his voices were talking too loudly for him to listen to the record. In contrast, only 5 percent of the non-hallucinating schizophrenics reported having heard the record with any vividness. On the sentence detection task accuracy scores and the ratings by which the subject indicated his confidence in his own renditions were compared. The correlation was +.54 for the hallucinating schizophrenics and +.84 for the non-hallucinating schizophrenics. Hallucinating schizophrenics were poorer at judging the accuracy of their performance.

What do these results reveal about hallucinations? How well the subject imagined hearing "White Christmas" was assumed to reflect his vividness of imagery. His capacity to perceive reality was supposedly measured by the correlation between the actual accuracy of his sentence renditions and his confidence in their accuracy—for anyone in contact with reality is assumed able to assess his performance of a task. Hallucinating schizophrenics showed *both* vivid imagery *and* a defective capacity for perceiving reality. Hallucinations may therefore reflect a failure to discriminate between self-produced images and stimulation in the external world. A greater capacity for vivid imagery and loss of contact with reality should increase the likelihood of hallucinations.[3]

In a corroborative study McGuigan (1966) instructed patients to press a key whenever they experienced an auditory hallucination. At the same time recordings were made of electrical activity in the subject's larynx. In this fashion McGuigan could compare the outputs of this organ when the patient was experiencing auditory hallucinations and when he was not. The patient's report that he was hallucinating correlated remarkably with an increase in electrical activity in the larynx. Patients reporting auditory hallucinations may merely be talking to themselves but interpreting the internal speech as coming from the external world.

Cognitive Research

Researchers have also tried to elucidate the deviant cognitive processes that may contribute to the incoherent speech of schizophrenics. Many investigators have attempted to demonstrate qualitative differences between the responses of schizophrenic and normal subjects. Structured word association tests, for example, have been used to determine whether the patient's associations to common words are particularly deviant. In these tests a standard list of words is read to patients after they have been instructed to respond to each with the first word that comes to mind. Schizophrenics, especially chronics, have frequently been found to give more unusual associations than various control groups. For example, instead of responding "dog" to the word "bark," the schizophrenic might say "moon." In one investigation groups of good premorbid and poor premorbid schizophrenics and a control group of hospitalized tuberculosis patients were tested twice on the same word association test (Dokecki, Polidoro, and

---

[3] The correlation between vivid imagery and hallucinations may also indicate that the experience of hallucinating facilitates vivid imaginings.

TABLE 13.2 *Hypothetical Probabilities of Associative Responses to a Stimulus*

Stimulus word	Associative responses	Probability that normal subjects will give response	Probability that schizophrenic will give response
table	chair	.60	.23
	top	.25	.18
	tennis	.11	.16
	car	.02	.13
	run	.01	.14
	shoe	.01	.16

Cromwell, 1965). Poor premorbid patients gave less common responses than did either of the other two groups.

Most theoretical explanations of deviant schizophrenic associations involve the notion of a response hierarchy. Any stimulus can evoke a number of responses, which vary in the likelihood of occurrence. For example, the stimulus word "table" may evoke several responses varying from the very probable "chair" to a less probable "tennis," down to rare responses such as "night." Broen and Storms (1966) have proposed that the response hierarchies of schizophrenics have partially collapsed, and that the probabilities of the dominating and competing responses have become more nearly equal (Table 13.2). The result, of course, would be both more deviant and idiosyncratic responses. But not all evidence favors the view of an idiosyncratic associative repertoire.

Cohen and Camhi (1967) tested schiz-ophrenic and control subjects in a word communication task somewhat similar to the television game "Password." One subject, the speaker, is shown a series of word pairs, one pair at a time. For each word pair, for example, "car-automobile," the experimenter designates one of the words as the target. The speaker is then told to provide a one-word clue so that another person will be able to distinguish the target word from the other one. Effective clues to the word "car," in the car-automobile pair, might be "sports," "hop," or "railroad." The words "crash," "vehicle," and "wheels" would be less effective clues. A second subject, the listener, is given each word pair and the speaker's clue. His task is to guess which member of each word pair is the target.

Four groups of subjects were studied—schizophrenic speakers with schizophrenic listeners, schizophrenic speakers with normal listeners, normal speakers with schizophrenic listeners, and normal speakers with

TABLE **13.3** *Results of the Cohen and Camhi Study Showing Schizophrenics To Be Poor as Speakers but Good as Listeners*

Communication accuracy, percent of
correct choices made by each
speaker-listener group

Speakers	Listeners	
	Schizophrenic	Normal
Schizophrenic	66	67
Normal	72	74

normal listeners. The results (Table 13.3) reveal that schizophrenic speakers were inferior to normal speakers. That is, the clue words chosen by schizophrenics made the listeners perform significantly more poorly whether they were schizophrenic or normal. In contrast, with a normal speaker, schizophrenic listeners were about as accurate as their normal counterparts.

The results are difficult to explain if it is assumed that schizophrenics have deviant associative hierarchies (see also Lisman and Cohen, 1972). Such a deficit should make them perform as poorly as listeners as they do as speakers. The listener must decide which word is the target on the basis of what associations best link the clue word to one of the paired words. To the extent that the listener's associative hierarchies are idiosyncratic, his linking of clue words to the target would supposedly be less accurate. The finding that the schizophrenic's accuracy as listener matches that of the normal control indicates that, at least with regard to word association hierarchies, there may not be a *qualitative* difference between the two populations.

Adopting a somewhat different approach, other investigators have sought *quantitative* abnormalities in schizophrenic cognitive performance. On the basis of the results of several investigations, Loren Chapman and his colleagues have proposed that the types of errors characterizing schizophrenic performance are also committed, although less frequently, by normal subjects. In many instances schizophrenics do not make errors that are *qualitatively different* from those made by normal individuals. Rather they make *more* of the *same* kinds of errors (Chapman, Chapman, and Miller, 1964).

In an early study Chapman (1958) employed a card-sorting task in which single words were printed on cards. The subject was shown an array of three different cards, then handed a fourth card and asked to place it with the card that belonged to the same category. For example, on one trial the subject was given the word "gold." The alternatives with which it could be sorted were "fish," an incorrect response which is related associatively to "gold"; "steel," the correct response, also a metal; and "typewriter," an irrelevant, incorrect response. The inclination to respond to "gold" by selecting "fish" is a normal error. Chapman hypothesized that schizophrenics would produce significantly more errors of this type than normal subjects, but that they would not produce more irrelevant errors ("typewriter"). This was in fact found to be the case, lending support to the assertion that the thought processes of schizophrenics are quantitatively but not qualitatively deviant from those of normal individuals.

In a related series of studies Chapman, Chapman, and Miller (1964) demonstrated that schizophrenics frequently interpret double-meaning words on the basis of the stronger of their two meanings, even when the context indicates that the weaker one is appropriate. They constructed a test composed of items such as the following.

When the farmer bought a herd of cattle, he needed a new pen. This means
A. *He needed a new writing implement. (Incorrect response in this context, but the usual definition of the word.)*
B. *He needed a new fenced enclosure. (Correct response in this context, but a less usual definition of the word.)*

C. *He needed a new pick-up truck. (Irrelevant response.)*

The schizophrenics chose the A alternative more often than did the normal subjects. Neither group made the error of choosing C with any great frequency. On the basis of these and other findings, the investigators concluded that an exaggeration of normal errors explains the frequent misinterpretation of words by schizophrenics.

Although Chapman has thus far tested his quantitative theory only in studies of the schizophrenic's misuse of words, it has potentially much greater implications. In particular, there is a strong similarity between the results of these studies and those, discussed in an earlier section, that revealed the inability of the schizophrenic to differentiate between relevant and irrelevant aspects of a stimulus complex. The cognitive distortions of schizophrenics may reflect their frequent and inappropriate use of contextual cues when they are processing information.

SUMMARY

We have examined how schizophrenics behave in clinical and in laboratory settings. The basic symptoms of schizophrenia are autism and withdrawal as well as disturbances in cognition and thought—thought disorder, loose associations, and delusions; in perception and attention—hallucinations and difficulties in maintaining attention; in motor behavior—grimacing, gesturing, and flailing of the limbs or catatonia and waxy flexibility; and in affect—flat, inappropriate, and ambivalent. A review of the schizophrenic subtypes proposed by Kraepelin and in DSM-II indicated the great variability in the behavior of schizophrenic patients. Although the Kraepelinian system has not proved useful in research, except for the paranoid-nonparanoid dimension, distinguishing schizophrenics by premorbid adjustment and chronicity has facilitated research. The performance of schizophrenics on laboratory tasks has indeed furthered our understanding of some schizophrenic behavior. For example, schizophrenics may withdraw from social relationships because of a heightened sensitivity to censure. Some of the cognitive deficits may reflect a failure to discriminate relevant from irrelevant information. Any theory of the etiology of schizophrenia will have to account for the descriptive and laboratory data presented in this chapter.

CHAPTER 14
Schizophrenia: Theory and Research on Etiology

There are several important theories on the etiology of schizophrenia, and considerable research has been carried out in an effort to establish the factors causing this very prevalent and debilitating disorder. Several major theoretical views — psychoanalytic, social learning, and the experiential theory of R. D. Laing — will be reviewed first. Then the research on etiological factors such as social class, the family, genetic backgrounds, biochemical abnormalities, and the developmental histories of individuals who have later in life become schizophrenic will be examined.

MAJOR THEORETICAL POSITIONS

Psychoanalytic Theory

Because Freud himself dealt primarily with neuroses, he had relatively little to say about schizophrenia. He did occasionally speculate on its origins, though, using some of the psychoanalytic concepts that he applied to all disordered personalities. His basic notion was that the schizophrenic has regressed to a state of "primary narcissism," a phase early in the oral stage before the ego has differentiated from the id. There is thus no separate ego to engage in reality testing — a crucial function whereby the ego takes actions that test the nature of its social and physical environment. By regressing to this stage the schizophrenic has effectively lost contact with the world; he has withdrawn his libido from attachment to any objects external to himself. The cause of the regression is viewed as an increase, during adulthood, in the intensity of id impulses, especially sexual ones. Whether the threats of the intense id impulses provoke schizophrenia or a neurosis depends on the strength of the ego. Neurotics, having developed a more stable ego, will not regress to the first psychosexual stage, as the schizophrenic does, and will not lose contact with reality.

Some of the major symptoms of schizophrenia—lack of interpersonal relationships and passivity—are considered to reflect this regression. Other symptoms such as hallucinations and bizarre speech are regarded as the outcomes of attempts to deal with the id impulses and with reality—attempts to cope with the flood of id impulses demanding discharge and at the same time to reestablish contact with something other than the self. The patient, having withdrawn from reality, creates an inner world of hallucinations.

The psychoanalytic theory of schizophrenia has stimulated little research and, except for the speculative analysis of case history material, there are no data to support it (see Box 14.1).

Social Learning Theory

"The crucial behavior, from which other indications of schizophrenia may be deduced, lies in the extinction of attention to social stimuli to which 'normal' people respond" (p. 383). In these few words Ullmann and Krasner (1969) have summarized their position on the development of schizophrenia. They view the extinction of attentional responses as causing much of the classic schizophrenic behavior discussed in the previous chapter. They argue that a dysfunction in attention in which other than usual cues are heeded can account for the loose associations and irrelevancies of the schizophrenic's speech. At the same time, inattention to the cues that are part of the culture, and that consist very importantly of other people, makes the individual appear aloof and socially isolated.

In addition, Ullmann and Krasner see schizophrenia as a social role, one which the mental health professionals and the psychiatric hospital to a great extent determine. In short, they see the mental health professional as selectively rewarding schizophrenic behavior. This is an important and sensitive issue in the study of schizophrenia and has both scientific and social significance. Many of the descriptions of schizophrenia refer to behavior observed within a mental hospital, making it difficult to know how much of the peculiar behavior is caused by the presumed illness and how much is caused, in part, by the social setting of the mental institution. Ullmann and Krasner hold that the behavior we term schizophrenic must be regarded for the most part as a reaction to the reinforcement it receives within the mental hospital. According to this theory, patients choose to "talk crazy" because hospital staff members attend more to them when their verbalizations are bizarre than when they are quiet and rational.

A series of studies performed by Braginsky and his colleagues is regarded as support for the view that schizophrenia is a learned social role. One investigation (Braginsky, Grosse, and Ring, 1966) was designed to examine whether hospitalized patients can manipulate the impressions they create on others. Acute and chronic patients completed a short form of the MMPI. Some patients were told that the more items answered true, the more severely ill they were, and the more likely they were to remain in the hospital for a long time. Others were told that the more items answered true, the more they knew about themselves, the less severely ill they were, and the more likely they were to remain in the hospital for only a short period.

It was hypothesized that the chronic patients, who had been in the hospital for a long period of time, actually wished to remain there since they had adjusted to the hospital milieu.

BOX **14.1** *Paranoia and Repressed Homosexuality*

According to DSM-II paranoid delusions may occur in both paranoid schizophrenia and in the so-called paranoid state. The paranoid state is a more transitory psychosis characterized principally by delusions. The patient's contact with reality is impaired, but his behavior is not as disordered as that of a schizophrenic. Freud's theory of paranoia, commonly accepted even today, is that delusions result from repressed homosexual impulses which are striving for expression. The anxiety stemming from their threatened expression is handled primarily by the defense mechanism of projection, attributing to others feelings that are unacceptable to one's own ego (Freud, 1915). The basic unconscious thought is "I, a man, love him" (or "I, a woman, love her"). Freud considered the common paranoid delusions of persecution and grandiosity to derive from distortions of this basic homosexual urge.

In *delusions of persecution* the homosexual thought "I, a man, love him," being unacceptable to the ego, is converted into the less threatening statement "I, a man, hate him." Since the emotion expressed by this premise is also less than satisfactory, it is further transformed by projection into "He hates me, so I am justified in hating him." The final formulation may be "I hate him because he persecutes me." Freud asserted that the persecutor of a paranoid is always a person of the same sex who is unconsciously a love object for the individual.

Delusions of grandiosity (*megalomania*) begin with a contradiction of the homosexual impulse. The sentence "I, a man, love him" is changed into "I do not love anyone." But since libido must be invested in or attached to something or someone, the psychic reality becomes "I love only myself."

One of Freud's lesser-known cases of a patient with paranoid delusions is of special interest, for it seems initially to challenge Freud's basic tenet that the persecutor must be a person of the same

sex. The kinds of inferences that constitute the argument of this case study are typical of those made by Freud in his attempts to understand his clinical data and to test his hypotheses.

Freud was consulted by a lawyer in Vienna who had been hired by a woman to sue a male business associate for making indecent allegations about her. She stated that the man had had photographs taken of them while they were making love and was now threatening to bring disgrace upon her. Because of the unusual nature of her allegation, the lawyer had persuaded her to see Freud so that he could offer an opinion.

The woman, about thirty years of age, was an attractive single person who lived quietly with her mother, whom she supported. A handsome man in her firm had recently begun to court her. After much coaxing he had persuaded her to come to his apartment for an afternoon together. They became intimate, at which point she was frightened by a clicking noise coming from the direction of a desk in front of the window. The lover told her that it was probably from a small clock on the desk. As she left the house that afternoon, she encountered two men, one of them carrying a small package. They appeared to whisper something to each other secretively as she passed. By the time she reached home that evening, she had put together the following story. The box was a camera, the men were photographers, and her lover was an untrustworthy person who had arranged for photographs to be taken of them while they were undressed. The following day she began to berate the lover for his untrustworthiness, and he tried equally hard to change her mind about her unfounded suspicions. Freud read one of the letters that the man had written to the girl. It struck him that the lover was indeed sincere and honest in denying any involvement in such a plot.

At this point Freud faced a dilemma common in

scientific inquiry. What should the investigator do when confronted by an instance that negates his hypothesis? The persecutor of the young woman appeared to be a member of the opposite sex. Freud could, of course, have completely abandoned his theory that paranoia originates in homosexual impulses. Instead, he looked more closely into the case to see whether there were subtle factors that would allow him to preserve the integrity of his theory.

During a second meeting with Freud, the woman changed the story somewhat. She admitted that she had visited the man twice in his apartment, not once, and that only on the second occasion had she heard the suspicious noise. After the first and uneventful visit—as far as her paranoia was concerned—she had been disturbed by an incident that she had witnessed at the office. The next day she had seen her new lover speaking in low tones to an older woman who was in charge of the firm. This older person liked the younger woman a great deal, and the younger woman in turn found that her employer reminded her of her own mother. She was therefore very concerned about their conversation and became convinced that her suitor was telling the woman about their lovemaking the previous afternoon.

Then it occurred to her that her lover and her employer had been having a love affair for some time. At the first opportunity she berated her lover for telling their employer of their lovemaking. He naturally protested and after a while succeeded in undoing her suspicions. Then she made her second visit to his apartment and heard the reputed clicking.

Let us examine Freud's comments on this portion of the case history.

These new details remove first of all any doubts as to the pathological nature of her suspicion. It is easy to see that the white haired elderly man-

ageress is a mother-substitute, that in spite of his youth the lover had been put in the place of the father, and that the strength of the mother-complex has driven the patient to suspect a love-relationship between these ill-matched partners, however unlikely such a relation might be. Moreover, this fresh information resolves the apparent contradiction with the view maintained by psychoanalysis, that the development of a delusion of persecution is conditioned by an overpowerful homosexual bond. The original *persecutor—the agency whose influence the patient wishes to escape— is here again not a man but a woman. The manageress knows about the girl's love-affairs, disapproves of them, and shows her disapproval by mysterious allusions. The woman's attachment to her own sex hinders her attempts to adopt a person of the other sex as a love object (1915, p. 155).*

To protect herself from her own homosexual impulses, the girl is presumed to have developed a paranoid delusion about the man and the elderly woman. A crucial aspect of the case, according to Freud, was the click that the girl had heard and interpreted as the sound of a camera shutter. Freud assumed that this click was actually a sensation or beat in her clitoris. Her sexual arousal, then, provided the basis for her paranoid delusion of being photographed.

Freud allowed himself a remarkable amount of unverified inference in this particular case. Because he wanted to hold to a homosexuality-based theory of paranoia, he inferred that the woman regarded her female superior as a substitute for her mother, that she had an undue homosexual attachment to her own mother and by generalization to this older woman, and that the click which she had heard was sexual excitation, construed in a paranoid fashion to be the sound of a camera shutter.

TABLE **14.1** *Average Number of True Responses Made by Chronic and Acute Patients.*

(from Braginsky et al., 1966)

Groups	True means mental illness	True means self-insight
Chronic patients	18.80	9.70
Acute patients	13.00	18.80

In contrast, acute patients were thought to be more desirous of leaving. Assuming that patients can indeed manage the impression that they create on others, the following outcomes were expected. Acute patients would give more true responses when they thought these answers reflected self-insight, fewer when they believed them to reflect mental illness. Chronic patients would give more true responses when they believed them to prove mental illness, fewer when they considered them to prove self-insight. The results, presented in Table 14.1, clearly supported the hypotheses. It indeed appeared that patients could manipulate the impression that they created on others in order to enhance their chances of either staying in the hospital or leaving it.

In addition to problems in replicating these findings (Price, 1972b; Ryan and Neale, 1973), questions should be raised about what can logically be concluded from any study demonstrating that a hospitalized mental patient can create a particular impression in an interview or testing situation. The fact that a person diagnosed as schizophrenic can look "less sick" if told how to do so does not in itself justify the conclusion that schizophrenia is nothing more than the adoption of a social role. If a person with a stomach ache that is caused by a viral infection is told that negative consequences will follow admitting to his discomfort, he may lie to a physician and not report the pain in his stomach. But this does not mean that he does not have a stomach ache or a viral infection. Similarly, the fact that the schizophrenics in the Braginsky study answered true on the MMPI so as to create a particular impression does not demonstrate that schizophrenia is only a social role. It indicates that schizophrenics can, under certain circumstances, be sensitive to social cues. The patients in the Braginsky study, it must be borne in mind, were not discharged on the basis of their faked MMPI responses! It might also be noted that although Ullmann and Krasner use Braginsky's data as support for their position, Braginsky's demonstration is inconsistent with the hypothesis that schizophrenics have withdrawn their attention from social stimuli. The position of Ullmann and Krasner is conceivable, but no data give it direct support.

An Experiential Theory

Ronald Laing (Figure 14.1) has offered a view of schizophrenia that is similar in some respects to Ullmann and Krasner's. For him schizophrenia is not an illness but a label for a certain kind of problematic experience and behavior.

. . . the experience and behavior that gets labelled schizophrenic is a special sort of strategy that a person invents in order to live in an unlivable situation. . . the person has come to be placed in an untenable position. He cannot make a move or make no move without being beset by contradictory pressures both internally, from himself, and externally, from those around him. He is, as it were, in a position of checkmate (1964, p. 186).

Laing considers the family to be the primary culprit producing the behaviors that are labeled

FIGURE **14.1**

Ronald D. Laing, the British existential psychiatrist who believes that schizophrenia is a behavioral strategy adopted as a means of escaping the reality of an unlivable world.

schizophrenia. Rather than trying to remove the patient's symptoms, Laing argues that we should accept his experience as valid, understandable, and potentially meaningful and beneficial. The schizophrenic is on a psychedelic trip, necessitated by untenable environmental demands, and he is in need of guidance—not control— if the destination of that trip is to be a state of enlightenment.

Laing's ideas are popular among those who object to what they consider to be hypocrisies of society and of the mental health establishment. Those who experience the suffering associated with schizophrenia may also take comfort in the belief that they are going through a positive growth process. At this point, however, there is little evidence that experiencing schizophrenia can make a "better person" of the patient. Most poor premorbid schizophrenics, even when released from the hospital, live a marginal existence, isolated from social relationships. Nor, as we shall see later in this chapter, is there much evidence to support Laing's assertion that schizophrenia is caused by familial experiences.

Conclusion

In sum, none of the major theoretical positions discussed has much support. Freud's views on regression to the oral stage, social learning theories that emphasize role taking reinforced by the attitudes of family and mental hospital staff, and Laing's hypothesis that schizophrenia is a trip to improved functioning—all are without substantiating evidence.

Rather than construct elaborate theories, it may prove more fruitful to determine the etiological significance of particular discrete variables. A review of these variables will indicate how very complicated a theory will have to be to account for the problems called schizophrenia.

RESEARCH ON THE ETIOLOGY OF SCHIZOPHRENIA

Social Class and Schizophrenia

Numerous studies have shown a relation between social class and the diagnosis of schizophrenia. The highest rates of schizophrenia are found in central city areas inhabited by the lowest socioeconomic classes (for example, Hollingshead and Redlich, 1958; Srole, Langner, Michael, Opler, and Rennie, 1962). The relationship between social class and schizophrenia does not show a continuous progression of higher rates of schizophrenia as the social class becomes lower. Rather there is a sharp *discontinuity* between the number of schizophrenics in the lowest social class and those in others. In the ten-year Hollingshead and Redlich study of social class and mental illness in New Haven, Connecticut, the rate of schizophrenia was found to be twice as high in the lowest social class as in the next to lowest. In addition, the correlation between schizophrenia and class appeared to be particularly strong among women. The findings of Hollingshead and Redlich have been replicated cross-culturally in countries such as Denmark, Norway, and England (Kohn, 1968).[1]

The correlations between social class and schizophrenia are consistent, but still difficult to interpret in causal terms. Some people, especially sociologists, believe that being in a low social class may in itself cause schizophrenia. The degrading treatment a person receives from others, his low level of education, and the unavailability of rewards and opportunity, taken together, may make membership in the lowest social class such a stressful experience that the individual develops schizophrenia.

Another explanation of the correlation between schizophrenia and low social class has

been suggested. During the course of their developing problems schizophrenics may "drift" into the poverty-ridden areas of the city. The growing cognitive and motivational problems shown by these individuals may so impair their earning abilities that they cannot afford to live elsewhere. Or they may by choice move to areas where little social pressure will be brought to bear on them and where they can escape intense social relationships.

One way of resolving the conflict is to study the social mobility of schizophrenics. Three studies (Schwartz, 1946; Lystad, 1957; Turner and Wagonfeld, 1967) have found that schizophrenics are downwardly mobile in occupational status. But an equal number of studies has shown schizophrenics *not* to be downwardly mobile (Hollingshead and Redlich, 1958; Clausen and Kohn, 1959; Dunham, 1965). Kohn (1968) has suggested another way of examining this question. Are the fathers of schizophrenics also from the lowest social class? If they are, this could be considered evidence in favor of the hypothesis that lower-class status is conducive to schizophrenia, for class would be shown to *precede* schizophrenia. If the fathers are not, the drift hypothesis would be the better explanation.

Goldberg and Morrison (1963) conducted a study in England and Wales. They found that the occupations of male schizophrenic patients admitted to hospitals indicated them to be from a low social class, but that their fathers' occupations were more remunerative or prestigious. Similarly, Turner and Wagonfeld (1967) found that schizophrenics failed to achieve as high an occupational level as would have been expected of them, judging from their family's social class. These data contradict the hypothesis that being brought up as a member of a lower social class may somehow induce schizophrenia.

---

[1] There is perhaps one exception to this finding; the relationship may disappear in nonurban areas (Clausen and Kohn, 1959).

Perhaps the most important decision facing a researcher interested in the relationship between social class and schizophrenia is determining how schizophrenia will be indexed. Many studies use hospital admission rates, especially those of public hospitals. But lower-class individuals are more likely to come to a public hospital than to a private one. Furthermore, many studies have shown that some people who suffer serious mental disorders never enter a mental hospital at all.

Researchers have attempted to make their sampling more complete by trying to sample from all treatment facilities in a given area. But the same kind of problem holds. For example, there are social class differences between people who have been treated for mental illness and severely impaired people who have never had any kind of treatment (Srole, Langner, Michael, Opler, and Rennie, 1962). Thus using treatment as an index of schizophrenia is suspect.

An alternative approach is to go into the community and examine everyone, or a representative sample of everyone. The problem of relying exclusively on treatment is solved, but other difficulties are raised. Operating in the community makes diagnostic reliability and even the definition of abnormal behavior a difficult proposition. The raters employed in the community studies have usually received much less training than those who conduct studies in psychiatric facilities. In addition, community studies settle for what is termed *prevalence* rather than *incidence* data. Incidence refers to the number of new cases found in various population groups during a particular period of time and thus is theoretically the most relevant measure in an investigation of this sort. In the community studies, however, a simple count of the number of abnormal people is made. This prevalence measure is somewhat inappropriate, for it reflects both incidence and duration of illness. Since there is a correlation between duration of illness and social class (Hollingshead and Redlich, 1958), we cannot determine from prevalence data whether the correlation between social class and schizophrenia reflects incidence or duration of the disorder.

All in all, however, workers have continued to find a relation between social class and schizophrenia, whatever the methodologies employed, indicating that their data can be accepted.

Perhaps, though, social class has different effects that depend on the premorbid adjustment dimension. From the description of the poor premorbid schizophrenic offered in Chapter 13, it seems reasonable to predict that such a person would fail to achieve the expected level of social status. In contrast, the good premorbid patient functions adequately but then becomes schizophrenic in response to stress, perhaps the stress associated with the disheartening and disruptive experiences of lower-class existence. A final resolution of the role of social class in schizophrenia awaits data relevant to these questions.

The Role of the Family

Many theorists have regarded family relationships, especially those between a mother and her son, as crucial in the development of schizophrenia. This view has been so prevalent that the term "schizophrenogenic mother" has been coined for the supposedly cold and dominant conflict-inducing parent who is said to produce schizophrenia in her offspring. These mothers have also been characterized as rejecting, overprotective, self-sacrificing, impervious to the feelings of others, rigid and moralistic about sex, and fearful of intimacy.

Methods of Study

Three methods have been employed to assess the potential role of the family. First, when patients are in treatment, their families can be studied by the *clinical observational method.* Although such studies may provide hypotheses, the data collected cannot serve as scientific proof (see Chapter 4). Second, in *retrospective studies of child rearing,* parents and other relatives and friends of the patient being treated are questioned about historical events related to family life. The information collected by this method is also subject to a severe problem, the fallibility of recall over time. Third, in the *family interaction method* structured situations are devised to reveal how family members interact with one another. One of these procedures is the *revealed-differences technique*. Members of a family are given several questions to respond to, such as "What is the appropriate time for teen-agers to begin dating?" and then are asked to resolve any differences in the answers given by the individual members of the family. As they attempt to resolve their differences, their interaction is video-recorded so that the information can be reliably coded (Figure 14.2). The family interaction method has a clear advantage over the other two in the validity of the data that it can provide. It also has limitations, for knowledge that the family conversation is being studied may alter communication patterns. Moreover, since one member of the family is already psychotic, the validity of the information collected rests on the assumption that the currently observed family interaction patterns are the same as those existing *before* one member of the family became schizophrenic. The parents, however, may be *reacting* to the fact that an offspring is schizophrenic rather than acting as they did earlier when they may have been instrumental in causing the development of the disorder. If problems are noticeable in the family of a schizophrenic, the directionality of the correlation is difficult to ascertain. The family problems may have caused schizophrenia in one of its members, or the schizophrenia may be causing family problems that did not exist earlier.

Fontana (1966) has found that the great majority of family studies are inadequate in various ways and has recommended some basic methodological requirements that should be met in setting up these studies. Only families of schizophrenics should constitute the experimental group, the families of male and female patients should be analyzed separately, and all the diagnoses of schizophrenia should be reliable. Moreover, families of patients hospitalized for a physical illness must constitute the control group, for *all* families with a member hospitalized for any reason have been found to have problems.

Of the hundreds of family studies of schizophrenia, Fontana was able to find only five that met these criteria. And on the basis of these five he was able to draw only two conclusions.

1. There is more conflict between the parents of schizophrenics than between those of control parents.

FIGURE **14.2**

Many laboratories and clinics have one-way mirrors which allow the observation of therapy sessions by researchers and clinicians in training. These arrangements are also used to study family interaction patterns which are thought to have some bearing on the etiology of schizophrenia.

2. Communication between the parents of schizophrenics is more inadequate than that between control parents.

When the most stringent controls are applied, conflict and lack of communication between parents assume more significance than any qualities of the supposed schizophrenogenic mother. But whether the difficulties between the parents antedate the development of schizophrenia in an offspring remains to be settled. A noteworthy attempt to resolve this issue is described in Box 14.3.

The Double Bind

Thus far we have examined the role of the family in a rather general way and found the amount of conflict and accuracy of communication to be problems. More specific hypotheses have also been advanced, the most

prominent being the *double bind* proposed by Bateson, Jackson, Haley, and Weakland (1956). These writers believe that an important factor in the development of schizophrenic thought disorder is the constant subjection of an individual to a so-called double-bind situation which has the following aspects.

1. The individual has an intense relationship to another, so intense that it is especially important to him to be able to understand communications from that individual accurately so that he can respond appropriately.
2. The other person expresses two messages when he makes a statement, one of which denies the other.
3. The individual cannot comment on the mutually contradictory messages and cannot withdraw from the situation or ignore the messages.

BOX **14.3** *Trying To Unravel the Direction of Causality in Family Studies of Schizophrenia*

In a detailed and careful study, Mishler and Waxler (1968) attempted to decide among the varying interpretations of the correlation between certain family interaction patterns and schizophrenia. They used the revealed-differences technique with two sessions for each family. In one session the parents participated with their schizophrenic child, and in the other with a nonpsychotic offspring of the same sex and approximately the same age as the patient. The design included in the experimental group both male and female patients and patients with good and poor premorbid adjustment. The control families had pairs of normal siblings of the same sex and nearly the same age. An attempt was made to balance the two groups so that family incomes, father's occupation, parents' education and religion, and parents' and grandparents' birthplaces were not too different.

By having two revealed-differences sessions, the researchers hoped to determine whether the patient's presence or absence affected the parents' behavior. If, for example, the parents expressed less emotion and were uncommunicative only in the session with the patient, their behavior might be interpreted as a *response* to the disturbed child. But if the parents of a schizophrenic child were unexpressive and uncommunicative toward both the disturbed child *and* his normal sibling, their behavior was less likely to be a specific reaction to a schizophrenic child. And if differences could be found between the ways families of schizophrenics and normal families generally treat their children, the theory implicating parental behavior in the development of schizophrenia would be supported.

Strategies of control were one of the variables studied in the two sessions. In normal families there was a coalition between mother and father and a clear status hierarchy. In contrast, in families with a schizophrenic son the father was excluded and a coalition between mother and son was formed. In families with a schizophrenic daughter, she was the excluded one. These patterns were evident only when the patient was present, not

The parent rarely communicates with the child in a simple and direct way. What he says may be contradicted by how he says it, by what he does, or by emotion conveyed in other ways. And the child cannot complain that he does not understand, nor can he ask for clarification. It becomes impossible for him to order his thinking; his responses may eventually become even more confused than the communications he receives. In their original paper Bateson and his colleagues gave the following example.

364

THE SCHIZOPHRENIAS

during the session that the parents had with their normal offspring, suggesting that control strategies were a reaction to the schizophrenic child's behavior.

Another variable observed was speech disruptions—fragments of thought, repetitions, and incomplete sentences. Contrary to expectation, the greatest frequency of speech disruptions occurred in the sessions with families of normal children. They were less noticeable in the conversations of families with a poor premorbid schizophrenic child and even less frequent in the conversations of families with a good premorbid schizophrenic child. Thus disrupted verbal communications could not be implicated as causative factors.

Mishler and Waxler also studied "acknowledgement," that is, responding in an acknowledging manner to a verbalization by someone else. The normal families were found to be more acknowledging than families with a good premorbid schizophrenic offspring, who were, in turn, more acknowledging than families with a poor premorbid schizophrenic child. Mishler and Waxler gave the following interpretation of this finding.

. . . parents who have had to live with a chronic schizophrenic child have learned to ignore, that is, fail to acknowledge, his behavior so as to minimize disruption and disturbance in the family; they would then appear as the least acknowledging. The good premorbid [parents], faced with a more recent problem, would fall between the poors and the normal families (p. 292).

Mishler and Waxler were unable to establish a definite causal relationship between any aspect of parental behavior and the development of schizophrenia, but they did go well beyond a simple and general comparison of the behavior of normal families and that of families with a schizophrenic child.

A young man who had fairly well recovered from an acute schizophrenic episode was visited in the hospital by his mother. He was glad to see her and impulsively put his arm around her shoulders whereupon she stiffened. He withdrew his arm and she asked, "Don't you love me anymore?" He then blushed and she said, "Dear, you must not be so easily embarrassed and afraid of your feelings." The patient was able to stay with her only a few minutes more and following her departure he assaulted an aide. . . .

Obviously, this result could have been avoided if the young man had been able to say, "Mother, it is obvious that you become uncomfortable when I put my arm around you, and you have difficulty accepting a gesture of affection from me." However, the schizophrenic patient doesn't have this possibility open to him. An intense dependency in training prevents him from commenting upon his mother's communicative behavior, though she comments on his and forces him to accept and to attempt to deal with the complicated sequence. . . .

The impossible dilemma thus becomes: "If I am to keep my tie to my mother, I must not show her that I love her, but if I do not show her that I love her then I will lose her" (pp. 258–259).

Although the double bind has been a popular and widely known explanation of how schizophrenia develops, it is not supported as a factor of great etiological significance by any available data. Most of the literature on the double-bind hypothesis is uncontrolled and descriptive, consisting of case histories and transcripts of therapy sessions. In one controlled study Ringuette and Kennedy (1966) had different groups of judges try to identify double binds communicated in letters.[2] Two sets of letters were used, those written by parents to their hospitalized schizophrenic and nonschizophrenic offspring, and letters that had been written by volunteers instructed to compose them as though they were writing to hospitalized offspring. The groups of judges included

three of the people closely involved in originally formulating the double-bind hypothesis, psychiatric residents who had been taught earlier how to recognize a double-bind communication, and experienced clinicians who also knew the double-bind interpretation.

The judges did not generally agree on which letters did and did not contain a double-bind communication. *The correlation among the judgments of the experts was only +.19.* This investigation, then, provided little support indeed for the viability of the double-bind hypothesis, for whether a double-bind communication was or was not present in a given letter could not be reliably determined.

The Genetic Data

Suppose that an individual who will one day be diagnosed as schizophrenic must be selected and that no behavior patterns or other symptoms can be considered. This problem, suggested by Paul Meehl (1962), has only one solution that has an even chance of picking a potential schizophrenic. *Find an individual who has a schizophrenic identical twin.* There now exists a convincing body of literature indicating that a predisposition for schizophrenia is transmitted genetically. The major methods employed in this research, as in other behavior genetics research projects, are the family and twin studies (see Box 6.2). The findings obtained from them will be discussed first and thereafter studies of adopted children.

The Family Studies

Rosenthal (1970) has provided a summary of the available studies using the family method (Table 14.2). The data vary markedly. The morbidity risk for the parents of a schizophrenic index case ranges from 0.2 to 12.0 percent. Twelve of the fourteen studies, how-

---

[2] Although the use of letters in this study may seem strange, many of those who have studied the double bind have paid particular attention to the contents of letters written by parents of schizophrenics, for they believe that written communications are likely to resemble spoken communications.

ever, show a risk estimate higher than the incidence expected in the general population (about 1.0 percent). The risk that siblings of schizophrenic probands will develop the disorder ranges from 3.3 to 14.3 percent, according to the studies examined. These risk estimates are uniformly higher than would be expected for members of the general population.

The statistics in Table 14.2 exclude one possible mode of genetic transmission. If schizophrenia were being passed on by the pairing of single recessive genes or by a dominant gene, the expected risk rates in siblings and parents would be, respectively, 25 and 50 per-

cent. It is more likely that the simultaneous action of a number of genes, each one making a small contribution to the end result, furnishes a predisposition for the disorder. The behavioral expression of these genes is then subject to modification by the environment.

When, in addition to the schizophrenic proband, a parent is also schizophrenic, the morbidity risk for all siblings increases dramatically. Garrone (1962) found a morbidity risk of 33.7 percent among the siblings of schizophrenics if there was also one schizophrenic parent. The offspring of two schizophrenic parents has a likelihood of about 35 percent of becoming schizophrenic (Rosenthal, 1970).

In sum, the data gathered by the family method support the notion that a predisposition for schizophrenia can be transmitted genetically. And yet relatives of a schizophrenic proband share not only genes but also common experiences. The influence of a schizophrenic parent's behavior on a developing child is likely to be very disturbing.

TABLE 14.2
Morbidity Risk Estimates for Parents and Siblings of Schizophrenic Index Cases

(*from Rosenthal, 1970*)

Study	Morbidity risk, %	
	Parents	Siblings
Brugger, 1928	4.3	10.3
Bleuler, 1930	2.0	4.9
Schulz, 1932	2.6	6.7
Luxenburger, 1936	11.7	7.6
Smith, 1936	1.2	3.3
Galatschjan, 1937	4.9	14.0
Strömgren, 1938	0.7	6.7
Kallmann, 1938	2.7	7.5
Bleuler, 1941	5.6	10.4
Kallmann, 1946	9.2	14.3
Böök, 1953	12.0	9.7
Slater, 1953	4.1	5.4
Hallgren-Sjögren, 1959	0.2	5.7
Garrone, 1962	7.0	8.6

The Twin Studies

A summary of the available twin studies appears in Table 14.3. The concordance rates reported in the several studies of monozygotic twins range with great variability from 0 to 86 percent. The rates of concordance for the dizygotic twins range from 2 to 14 percent. Concordance for the monozygotic twins is generally greater than that for the dizygotic twins, but it is always less than 100 percent. This is important, for if genetic transmission were the whole story of schizophrenia and one twin was schizophrenic, the other twin would be guaranteed a similar fate because monozygotic twins are genetically identical.

Gottesman and Shields (1972) recently studied all twins treated at the Maudsley and Bethlem hospitals in London, England, between

1948 and 1964. One of the problems of any genetic study of schizophrenia is the definition of concordance. Recognizing the potential problems and biases involved in making psychiatric diagnoses, often of people who were not hospitalized, Gottesman and Shields devised a three-grade system of concordance. All probands were of course hospitalized schizophrenics. The co-twins with the first grade of concordance were also hospitalized and diagnosed schizophrenic. Co-twins with the second grade of concordance were hospitalized but not diagnosed as schizophrenic; those with the third grade were abnormal but not hospitalized. Concordance rates for the monozygotic and dizygotic twins in the sample, figured cumulatively for the three grades, are shown in Table 14.4. As the definition of concordance is broadened, its rate increases in both monozygotic and dizygotic pairs, but concordance of the monozygotic pairs is always significantly higher than that of the dizygotic pairs.

Gottesman and Shields have also examined the relationship between severity of schizophrenia in the proband and the degree of concordance. Severity was defined in terms of the total length of hospitalization and the outcome, whether the patient recovered enough to leave the hospital and then engage in gainful employment. When one of a monozygotic pair was judged severely ill, concordance rates went up dramatically. For example, pairs of monozygotic twins were divided into two groups; in one group the probands had had less than two years of hospitalization, in the other more than two years of hospitalization. The

TABLE **14.3** *Concordance Rates in the Major Twin Studies of Schizophrenia* (*from Rosenthal, 1970*)

Study	Country	MZ twins		DZ twins	
		Number of pairs	Concordance, %	Number of pairs	Concordance, %
Luxenburger, 1928, 1934	Germany	17–27	33–76.5	48	2.1
Rosanoff et al., 1934–35	United States and Canada	41	61.0	101	10.0
Essen-Möller, 1941	Sweden	7–11	14–71	24	8.3–17
Kallmann, 1946	New York	174	69–86.2	517	10–14.5
Slater, 1953	England	37	65–74.7	115	11.3–14.4
Inouye, 1961	Japan	55	36–60	17	6–12
Tienari, 1963, 1968	Finland	16	0–6	21	4.8
Gottesman and Shields, 1966	England	24	41.7	33	9.1
Kringlen, 1967	Norway	55	25–38	172	8–10
Fischer, 1968	Denmark	16	19–56	34	6–15

TABLE **14.4** *Concordance in MZ and DZ Twins as Defined in Three Ways in the Gottesman and Shields Study.*

Definition of concordance	Concordance rates, %	
	MZ	DZ
1. Hospitalized and diagnosed schizophrenic	42	9
2. Hospitalized but not schizophrenic, plus those with first-grade concordance	54	18
3. Not hospitalized but abnormal, plus those with first- and second-grade concordance.	79	45

concordance rate for the first group was 27 percent, for the second 77 percent.

The definition of severity employed by Gottesman and Shields fits very well with the two types of premorbid adjustment distinguished in the preceding chapter. Patients who have been hospitalized for longer periods and whose prognoses are poor probably had poor premorbid adjustments. Thus genetic factors may have played a more important causative role in the disorder of these patients. This interpretation would also be consistent with the clinical picture of poor premorbids. After a gradual decline in functioning, they end up in a hospital, but their problems have not been precipitated by any severe environmental stress.

Questions of how data collected on twins should be interpreted may also be raised. Some have argued that the experience of being a monozygotic twin may itself predispose toward schizophrenia. Considering schizophrenia as an "identity problem," we might argue that being one member of an identical pair of twins could be particularly stressful. But schizophrenia occurs about as frequently in single births as in twin births. If the hypothesis were correct, simply being twins would have to in-

crease the likelihood of becoming schizophrenic—which it does not (Rosenthal, 1970).

The most critical problem of interpretation remains. Since the twins have been reared together, a common environment rather than common genetic factors could account for the concordance rates. The only conclusive data on this question would come from studies in which monozygotic twins have been reared apart from very early childhood, enabling the relative contributions of heredity and environment to be separately determined. The number of such pairs is small. Of the sixteen cases in the literature, ten were concordant and six discordant (Rosenthal, 1970). The concordance rate of this limited sample was therefore 62.5 percent, a finding that certainly supports the view that a predisposition for schizophrenia is genetically transmitted. Because of the small sample size, however, the data cannot be regarded as conclusive.

Adoptee Studies

Several studies have attempted to eliminate the possible effects of being reared in a deviant environment. Heston (1966) was able to follow up forty-seven people who had been born to schizophrenic mothers while they were in a state mental hospital. The infants were taken away from the mothers shortly after birth and given either to relatives or to foundling homes. The fifty control subjects were selected from among the residents of the same foundling homes that the children of the schizophrenic mothers had been sent to. The follow-up assessment consisted of an interview, MMPI questionnaire, IQ test, social class ratings, and the like. A dossier on each of these subjects was then rated independently by two psychiatrists, and a third evaluation was made by Heston. Ratings were made on a 0 to 100 scale of overall disability and, whenever possible, psychiatric diagnosis was offered. Ratings of disability proved to be quite reliable, and when the number of diagnostic categories was reduced to four—schizophrenia, mental deficiency, sociopathy, and neurosis—diagnostic agreement was also acceptable.

The control subjects were rated as less disabled than were the children of schizophrenic mothers. Similarly, thirty-one of the forty-seven children of schizophrenic mothers (67 percent) were given a psychiatric diagnosis, but only nine out of fifty control subjects (18 percent) were. None of the control subjects was diagnosed schizophrenic, but 16.6 percent of the offspring of schizophrenic mothers were so diagnosed.[3] In addition to this greater likelihood of being diagnosed schizophrenic, the children of schizophrenic mothers were more

likely to be diagnosed mentally defective, sociopathic, and neurotic (Table 14.5). They had spent more time in penal institutions, had been involved more frequently in criminal activity, and had more often been discharged from the armed services for psychiatric reasons. Heston's study clearly supports the importance of genetic factors in the development of schizophrenia. Children reared without contact with their so-called "pathogenic mothers" were still more likely to become schizophrenic than were the controls.

Another study, similar in intent to Heston's, has been carried out in Denmark (Kety, Rosenthal, Wender, and Schulsinger, 1968). The starting point for this investigation was a culling of the records of all children who had been adopted at an early age between the years 1924 and 1947. All adoptees who had later been admitted to a psychiatric facility and diagnosed schizophrenic were selected as the index cases (see page 132). From the remaining cases the investigators chose a control group who had no psychiatric history and who were matched to the index group on variables such as sex and age. Both the adoptive and the biological parents and the siblings and half-siblings of the two groups were then identified, and a search was made to determine who of them had a psychiatric history. As might be expected if genetic factors figure in schizophrenia, the biological relatives of the index cases were more often diagnosed schizophrenic than members of the general population. The adoptive relatives were not.

All the data collected so far indicate that genetic factors play an important role in the development of schizophrenia. Earlier twin and family studies deserved the criticism of environmentalists, who found them to be confounded by a confusion of genetics and envi-

---

[3] The 16.6 percent figure was *age-corrected.* This term refers to the correction of raw data to take into account the age of the subjects involved. If a subject in Heston's sample was only twenty-four at the time of the assessment, he might still have become schizophrenic at some later point in his life. The age correction procedure attempts to account for this possibility.

TABLE **14.5** *Heston's Study of Subjects Separated from Their Schizophrenic Mothers*

	Offspring of schizophrenic mother	Control offspring, mothers not schizophrenic
Number of subjects	47	50
Mean age at follow-up	35.8	36.3
Overall ratings of disability (low score indicates more pathology)	65.2	80.1
Number diagnosed schizophrenic	5	0
Number diagnosed mentally defective	4	0
Number diagnosed sociopathic	9	2
Number diagnosed neurotic	13	7

ronment. But later studies of children of schizophrenic mothers who were reared in foster homes and the follow-up of relatives of adopted schizophrenics indicate the importance of genetic transmission, for the potential biasing influence of the environment had been virtually removed. We cannot conclude, however, that schizophrenia is a disorder completely determined by genetic transmission. The less than 100 percent concordance rate of monozygotic twins would argue against this conclusion, and we must always keep in mind the distinction made between phenotype and genotype in Box 6.2. The diathesis-stress model, introduced in Chapter 6, seems appropriate for explaining schizophrenia. Genetic factors can only be predisposers for a disorder. Postnatal stress, either environmental or biological, is required to render this predisposition an observable pathology.

Biochemical Factors

Speculation concerning possible biochemical causes of schizophrenia began almost as soon as the syndrome was identified. Kraepelin, as already indicated, thought that poisons secreted from the sex glands affected the brain to produce the symptoms, and Carl Jung suggested the presence of "toxin X," which he thought would eventually be identified. The demonstrated role of genetic factors in schizophrenia also suggests that biochemicals should be investigated, for it is through the body chemistry that heredity may have an effect.

The extensive and continuing search for possible biochemical causes has a principal difficulty to overcome. If an abnormal biochemical is found in schizophrenics and not in control subjects, the difference in biochemical functioning may have been produced by a third variable rather than by the disorder. Most schizophrenic patients take tranquilizing medication. Although the effects of such drugs on behavior diminish quite rapidly once they are discontinued, traces of them may remain in the bloodstream for very long periods of time, making it difficult to attribute a biochemical difference between schizophrenic and control subjects to schizophrenia per se. The diets of patients and control groups may also be different. Institutionalized patients may smoke more, drink more coffee, and have a less nutritionally adequate diet than various control groups. They may also be relatively inactive. All these variables can conspire to produce biochemical differences in schizophrenic and control patients that confound attempts to seek deviant biochemicals in the schizophrenics. Nonetheless, the search for biochemical causes of schizophrenia goes on at a rapid rate. Two of the major areas of current investigation will be reviewed.

Taraxein

After a series of investigations performed in the late 1950s, Robert Heath of Tulane University announced that he had found a factor in the blood serum of schizophrenics and claimed that it was responsible for their psychotic condition. He called this factor taraxein and proposed that schizophrenia is a genetically determined disorder characterized by the presence of taraxein in the blood. Taraxein, a simple protein, was said to interact with other bodily substances to produce a toxic chemical. This poison in turn supposedly disturbed neural functioning, primarily in the septal region of the brain which controls pleasure and pain responses (Heath, 1960). Heath locates the biologic problem in this area because EEG

recordings from the septum of schizophrenics are abnormal. According to Heath, a deficit in pain-pleasure responses makes the patient aware that his affect is not the same as that of others, and he feels alienated from people.

In this early work Heath was able to isolate the blood fraction taraxin. Symptoms like those of schizophrenia were even induced in nonschizophrenic prison volunteers to whom this agent had been administered (Heath, Martens, Leach, Cohen, and Angel, 1957). Moreover, injections of taraxein altered the brain wave patterns recorded from the pleasure-pain septal area. Heath described the reactions of the volunteers.

There is marked blocking with disorganization and fragmentation of thought. There is impairment of concentration. Each subject has described this in his own words — some saying merely "I can't think"; "My thoughts break off"; others, "I have a thought but I lose it before I can tell you anything about it," etc. "My mind is a blank" is another common expression. It becomes impossible to express a complete thought. Often they will state only a part of a sentence. They appear generally dazed and out of contact with a rather blank look in their eyes. They become autistic, displaying a lessening of animation in facial expression. Subjective complaints of depersonalization are frequent. Attention span is markedly shortened with increase in reaction time. The symptoms often produce apprehension in the patients. The commonest verbalization of their concern is "I never felt like this in my life before." Virtually all have made this statement (p. 21).

One team of researchers, however, was unable to isolate taraxein in schizophrenic patients (Siegel, Niswander, Sachs, and Stavros,

1959). Others had difficulty replicating Heath's work even when supplied with extracts of taraxein prepared by Heath. But Heath continued his studies and later was able to refine his procedure for extracting taraxein from schizophrenic blood. He now claims that others failed to replicate his work because the taraxein he originally supplied to them was impure. Heath and Krupp (1967) later found taraxein in cells of the septal regions of the brains of schizophrenic patients who had died while displaying acute psychotic symptoms. This substance, now identified as a gamma globulin or antibodies, was present in amounts that correlated strongly with the severity of the disorder before death.

Heath theorizes that the septal area produces a substance alien to the body. Defenses are mobilized, and the antibody is formed. When taraxein reaches the septum, it interferes with neural functioning; this disruption in the passage of information from one neuron to another is manifested as the poor information processing of schizophrenia. Thus schizophrenia is, according to Heath, an autoimmune disease: the body manufactures antibodies that act against its own brain cells.

Neural Transmission Dysfunction

Another line of research has been directed toward a second possible malfunctioning of neural transmission in schizophrenics. The reasoning behind Friedhoff's work (1967) is as follows. Drugs that are known to reduce the symptoms of schizophrenia do *not* have a therapeutic effect unless they also have a potential for producing a muscle rigidity similar to that in Parkinson's disease (see page 421). Parkinsonism is associated with exceptionally low levels of dopamine, a precursor of the neurotransmitter norepinephrine, in an area of the

brain involved in muscle coordination. Therefore the antipsychotic drugs may also reduce dopamine levels. The drug mescaline is known to be structurally similar to dopamine; a defect in a normal metabolic process may produce a compound that is similar to dopamine and that is active in the same way mescaline is, disorganizing thought processes and inducing hallucinations.

Friedhoff has claimed to have found such a compound in the urine of schizophrenics. It is referred to as 3,4-dimethoxyphenylethylamine, or DMPEA. Other research confirms that DMPEA induces the symptoms of schizophrenia. It can be argued, for example, that if DMPEA is produced by an abnormal metabolic process, facilitating this process would exacerbate schizophrenic symptoms. The abnormal metabolic process by which DMPEA is produced is known. In two studies it has been facilitated, and the symptoms of the schizophrenic subjects worsened (Pollin, Cardon, and Kety, 1961; Brune and Himwich, 1963). The converse may also be true. If the abnormal metabolic process can be hindered, less DMPEA will be produced and symptomatology will be reduced. One study has attempted this and in fact reduced the symptoms of schizophrenia (Hoffer, Osmond, Callbeck, and Kahan, 1957).

Evaluation

Some evidence indicates that deviant biochemicals may be present in schizophrenics. The history of this area of research has been one of discovery followed by failures to replicate, however. Many methodological problems are associated with this research, and there are many confounds, unrelated to whether or not a subject is schizophrenic, that can produce biochemical differences. Thus for relatively new and promising biochemical studies such as those described, we must adopt a "wait and see" attitude. Even if supported by additional research, however, these studies indicate only that a particular biochemical is associated with schizophrenia. The deviant chemical could be produced after rather than before the onset of the disorder.

High-Risk Studies of Schizophrenia

Many studies are primarily concerned with fashioning a picture of how an individual develops schizophrenia. The earlier method of constructing developmental histories was to examine the childhood records of those who later became schizophrenics. This research has indeed shown that those who were to become schizophrenics were different from their contemporaries even before any serious problems were noted in their behavior. Albee and Lane and their colleagues have repeatedly found preschizophrenics to have a lower IQ than members of various control groups which usually consist of siblings and neighborhood peers (Albee, Lane, and Reuter, 1964; Lane and Albee, 1965). Investigations of the social behavior of preschizophrenics have yielded some interesting findings; schizophrenics have been described, for example, as disagreeable by their teachers (Watt, Stolorow, Lubensky, and McClelland, 1970) and as delinquent and withdrawn (Berry, 1967).

But these findings are gross and nonspecific; certainly the traits mentioned would also be found in children and adolescents who are not destined to become schizophrenic. The major limitation of this type of developmental research is that the data on which it relies were not originally collected with the intention of describing preschizophrenics or of predicting the development of schizophrenia from childhood behavior. More specific information is required if developmental histories are to be a source of new hypotheses.

Perhaps the most desirable way of collecting information about the development of schizophrenia would be to select a large sample of individuals and follow them for the twenty to forty-five years that are the period of risk for the onset of schizophrenia. But such a method would be prohibitively expensive, for only about one individual in a hundred eventually becomes schizophrenic. The yield of data from such a simple longitudinal study would be small indeed. The *high-risk method* overcomes this problem; only individuals whose risk of becoming schizophrenic in adulthood is greater than the average are selected for study. In most of the current research projects using this methodology, individuals who have a schizophrenic mother are selected as subjects.

The major advantages of this method are as follows.

1. Variables that have direct relevance to the development of schizophrenia can be chosen for study.
2. The data are collected before the individual becomes schizophrenic. Therefore, unlike studies of adult schizophrenics, these investigations will not be confounded by variables such as drugs, diet, and inactivity.
3. Finding variables that predict the occurrence of schizophrenia in adulthood may allow early intervention and the prevention of this serious disturbance.

In the early 1960s such a study was begun in Denmark by Sarnoff Mednick and Fini Schulsinger. Denmark was chosen because individuals can be followed up much more easily than is possible in America. In Denmark a lifelong and up-to-date listing of the address of every resident is kept, and a National Psychiatric Register maintains records on every psychiatric hospitalization in the country.

In Mednick and Schulsinger's study high-risk subjects were defined as those whose mothers were chronic poor premorbid schizophrenics. It was decided that the mother should be the parent suffering the disorder because paternity is not always easy to determine and because schizophrenic women have more children than do schizophrenic men. Low-risk subjects, individuals whose mothers were not schizophrenics, were matched to the high-risk subjects on variables such as sex, age, father's occupation, rural-urban residence, years of education, and institutional upbringing versus rearing by the family. A summary of the design

and expected results may be seen in Figure 14.3. When the study began, the mean age of both the high- and low-risk groups was about fifteen years. Each child in the study was given a battery of tests.

1. *Conditioning, stress, and generalization.* Psychophysiological measurements of heart rate, muscle potential, and GSR were recorded during a conditioning situation in which a neutral tone (CS) was paired with an irritating 96-decibel noise (UCS). After the children had been conditioned to react to the neutral tone, other similar tones but not of quite the same frequency as the CS were administered and the responses to each assessed.

2. *Continuous-association test.* The children

FIGURE **14.3**

Design and expected results of Mednick and Schulsinger's study (1968) of subjects with a high risk of developing schizophrenia.

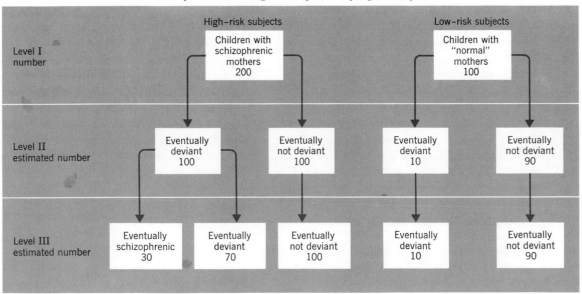

were given a single stimulus word and asked to associate to it for a period of one minute.

3. *School report.* The teachers of the subjects were questioned about the academic achievements of the children and about their social interaction.

4. *Midwife's report.* Births in Denmark are attended by a trained midwife rather than by a physician. Since some investigators have claimed that psychosis may be attributed to damage to the brain during pregnancy and delivery, reports on the circumstances of birth were collected from the midwives who had been in attendance.

During this initial phase of collecting data, an alarm network was set up to ensure that children who began to show psychiatric difficulties would be detected. In a 1968 report the histories of twenty children of the initial high-risk group who had by then required psychiatric care were reviewed. For comparison purposes each of these disturbed high-risk children was matched with one high-risk subject who had not broken down and with one low-risk subject. The matching variables were level of adjustment at the time of initial assessment, age, sex, and social class. The major findings of these comparisons were as follows.

1. Children in the disturbed high-risk group tended to lose their mothers to a mental hospital early and permanently. Their mothers were also rated as being more severely ill. These facts can be interpreted in two ways. Losing one's mother is stressful, or the severity of the mother's illness may mean that a stronger genetic predisposition is passed on.

2. Teachers reported that more members of the disturbed high-risk group, once they had become upset or excited, remained that way for a longer period of time than did members of the other two groups. More members of the disturbed high-risk group were also rated by the teachers as being aggressive, domineering, and disturbing to the class.

3. During the continuous-association test, members of the disturbed high-risk group had tended to drift away from the original stimulus word. Instead of continuing to give associations to the initial stimulus word, they began to respond to words that they themselves were using as responses, for example, "table-chair-high-low."

4. The disturbed high-risk group had given stronger GSRs to stressful stimuli. In addition, they had shown more evidence of conditioning to the neutral tone and more responsiveness to other similar tones than members of the other two groups. Their conditioned responses had become generalized. In this phase of the investigation another measurement was also taken, the degree of habituation to a stressful stimulus. Habituation was determined by the latency of the GSRs to repeated presentations of a stressful stimulus. If the subject becomes habituated to the stress, the GSRs occur only after a lengthening period of time. In comparison to the other two groups, subjects in the disturbed high-risk group showed no habituation, and in fact their GSRs occurred with increasing speed, suggesting increased responsiveness to the stimuli over time. In addition, the time it takes for the skin to return to base line conductance after the presentation of the stimulus was assessed. This measure was discovered to differentiate the groups better than any other obtained in the study. The rate at which the skin of the disturbed high-

risk group recovered after the GSR was found to be substantially faster than the recovery rate in the other two groups.

In interpreting all the information collected, Mednick focused on the psychophysiological responses. In an earlier paper (Mednick, 1958) he had postulated that schizophrenia is a learned thought disorder produced by autonomic hyperactivity. The tangential thinking of schizophrenics was suggested to be a set of conditioned avoidance responses that help the individual control his autonomic responsiveness. These avoidance responses—the irrelevant thoughts—are learned on those occasions when the preschizophrenic escapes from arousal by switching to a thought that interrupts the arousal stimulus. Because the irrelevant associations enable the individual to avoid a stressful stimulus, they are reinforced by less arousal and the probability is great that the preschizophrenic will engage in similar behavior in the future. The data from his present study led Mednick to modify one aspect of his earlier theory, for he had thought at that time that the schizophrenic is slow to recover from the momentary autonomic imbalance registered as the GSR.

According to the earlier version of the theory the preschizophrenic is especially prone to learn this avoidant pattern [in his thought processes] because of his extreme hyperresponsivity, excessive generalization and slow recovery from autonomic imbalance. However, the hypothesis of slow recovery has always caused critics to point out that this would cause the preschizophrenic to be reinforced more slowly and meagerly for avoidance than even the normal. The finding of an abnormally fast rate of recovery has forced us to alter the theory. It is now our hypothesis that one of the deter-

mining features of the preschizophrenic is his abnormally fast recovery; because of this fast rate of recovery he is more easily, quickly and thoroughly reinforced for avoidance than the normal. This taken together with the tendency to chronic hyperarousal will, in a harsh environment, inexorably push him to learn conditioned avoidant thought mechanisms (Mednick and Schulsinger, 1968, p. 289).

In a later report (Mednick, 1970) some more exciting data were presented. Earlier Mednick and Schulsinger had examined the frequency of individual birth complications in the various groups in their study. The many complications that might have been reported by the midwife—prematurity, anoxia or oxygen deprivation, prolonged labor, placental difficulty, umbilical cord complications, illness of mother during pregnancy, multiple births, and breech presentations (baby emerging feet first instead of head first)—were analyzed separately, but no conclusions could be drawn. One of Mednick's students, after grouping all the pregnancy and birth complications into a single category, made a startling finding. Seventy percent of the mothers of disturbed high-risk children had suffered one or more pregnancy or birth complication (PBC) while carrying or delivering the child as compared to 15 percent of the mothers of the nondisturbed but high-risk group and 33 percent of the mothers of the controls. Then in reexamining the psychophysiological differences previously discussed, Mednick determined that psychophysiological responses were deviant only in the subjects whose mothers had had one or more PBCs. Thus complications in the birth process may potentiate schizophrenia in a predisposed individual.

The high-risk method holds great promise of furthering our understanding of schizophrenia.

SUMMARY

Broad theoretical views such as those of Freud, Ullmann and Krasner, and Laing have not had great impact on research undertaken to determine the etiology of schizophrenia. Each of these workers placed undue and unsupported emphasis on particular causal factors. Freud thought that schizophrenia resulted from regression to the first psychosexual stage in which the ego is not differentiated from the id. Ullmann and Krasner postulate that schizophrenics do not attend to the social stimuli to which most people respond. They also regard schizophrenia as a social role maintained in large part by mental health professionals who reinforce "sick" behavior. For Laing schizophrenia is a label for the experience and behavior that constitute a person's attempts to cope with an impossible situation. Although popular and plausible, these theories lack empirical support.

Most research has tried to determine the etiological role of more specific variables such as social class, the family, and genetic and biochemical factors. The diagnosis of schizophrenia is most frequently applied to members of the lowest social class. Although some view the stresses of lower-class existence as a cause of schizophrenia, the available data are more consistent with the hypothesis that schizophrenics fail to achieve higher social status because of the disorder. Vague communications and conflicts are evident in the family life of schizophrenics, but it is unclear whether such factors contribute to schizophrenia or whether the presence of a schizophrenic family member disrupts the home.

The data on genetic transmission are impressive. The adoptee studies, which are relatively free from most criticisms that can be leveled at family or twin studies, show a strong relation between having a schizophrenic parent and the increased likelihood of developing the disorder. Perhaps the genetic predisposition has biochemical correlates, although research in this area permits only tentative conclusions. Much of the data we have reviewed are consistent with a diathesis-stress view of schizophrenia. Research on two potential stressors—being a member of the lower classes and of a troubled family—reveal that both may be operative, tipping the scale in a predisposed individual. Finally, results of Mednick's recent investigation suggest another potential stress, complications at birth.

CHAPTER 15

Child Psychoses

We have concentrated thus far on abnormal behavior in adulthood. Many psychogenic theorists, both of a psychodynamic and behavioral bent, regard childhood as a stage in life during which the seeds of later disorders are sown. But disordered behavior does not become evident only with physical maturity. Children—even those of preschool age—can suffer from debilitating psychological problems. In Chapter 17 we shall discuss mental retardation, an intellectual impairment. This chapter is devoted to a study of serious childhood psychopathology.

Profound disorders that have a resemblance to adult schizophrenia may make their appearance very early in life. The two major categories of these childhood psychoses are *childhood schizophrenia* and *early infantile autism*. The development of the concept of childhood schizophrenia and views about its etiology have been linked quite closely to descriptions of adult schizophrenia and theories advanced about its causes. Terms such as "dementia praecocissima" and childhood schizophrenia appeared shortly after Kraepelin coined his phrase dementia praecox and Bleuler his term schizophrenia. And as we shall see later in this chapter, theories of the etiology of both adult and childhood schizophrenia have many similarities. At the same time, however, because of the much earlier age of onset, there are clear-cut differences between the behavior manifested in adult schizophrenia and the disturbances that mark the behavior of children diagnosed as schizophrenic.

Early infantile autism is a newcomer to the literature on psychiatric classification and is not as yet included in DSM-II. The category, proposed by Leo Kanner in 1943, is a controversial one, for many question whether it should be considered an independent syndrome. We will first describe the clinical syndromes of the two categories and then the theories that try to explain them.

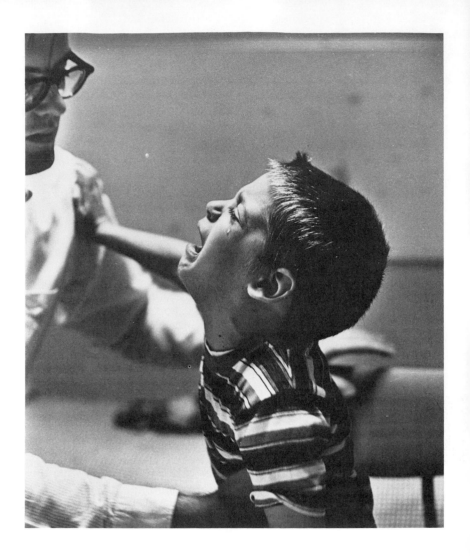

INFANTILE AUTISM

Some diagnosticians view autism as an earlier form of childhood schizophrenia and believe that the clinical pictures of the two disorders blend. Others consider autism a special form of mental retardation. The autistic child when first observed may seem to be normal and attractive, moving well and quickly with good coordination and appearing bright, although perhaps pensive or preoccupied. But he makes

FIGURE **15.1**

On the opposite page is a photograph of an autistic child who is obviously distressed at being touched by an adult. The child on the right has the aloof, detached look so common to the faces of autistic children.

his inaccessibility evident with his rejection of any social overture (Figure 15.1). For many diagnosticians this detachment and its apparent onset "from the moment of birth" make autism a very distinct and unique syndrome.

Descriptive Characteristics

As described by Kanner (1943) and Rimland (1964), autism consists of a specific constellation of behaviors.

Extreme Autistic Aloneness

An inability to relate to people or to any situation other than being alone in a crib is found from the very beginning of life. Autistic infants are often reported to be "good babies," apparently because they do not place many demands on their parents. They do not coo or fret or demand attention, nor do they reach out or smile or look at their mothers when being fed. When they are picked up or cuddled, they arch their bodies away from their caretakers rather than molding themselves against the adult as normal babies do. Autistic infants are content to sit quietly in their playpens for hours, never noticing the comings, goings, and doings of other people. After infancy they do not form attachments with people but instead may become extremely dependent on mechanical objects, such as refrigerators or vacuum cleaners. Because they avoid all social interaction, they fall rapidly behind their peers in development.

The autistic child's failure to relate to people and sometimes actively to avoid them was studied in a laboratory setting by Hutt and Ounsted (1966). Autistic and control children were led to a room that had five masks mounted on the walls. There were two human faces, one happy and one sad, a blank oval mask, and two animal masks, a monkey and a dog. The children were allowed to explore the room and spend as much time as they wanted viewing the various masks. They were observed through one-way mirrors, and the time spent viewing each face was recorded. Corroborating clinical impressions, the autistic children were found to spend significantly longer periods viewing the animal faces.

Speech Problems

Autistic children are commonly found to have certain difficulties with language. *Mutism,* complete absence of speech, is the most prevalent; about 50 percent of all autistic children never learn to speak (Rutter, 1966). Even when speech is present, many peculiarities are found, among them *echolalia.* The child echos, usually with remarkable fidelity, what he has heard another person say. In "delayed" echolalia he may not repeat the sentence or phrase until hours or weeks after hearing it. In one of our own cases, for example, speech was limited to the repetition of television commercials. Mute children who later do obtain some functional speech through training must usually first pass through a stage of echolalia before they can learn to respond meaningfully to questions or to use labels.

Another abnormality common in the speech of autistic children is *pronoun reversal.* The children refer to themselves as "he," or "you," or by their own proper names; the pronouns "I" or "me" are seldom used and then only when referring to others. Pronoun reversal is closely linked to echolalia. Since the child often uses echolalic speech, he will refer to himself as he had heard others speak of him, and pronouns are of course misapplied. For example,

PARENT: "What are you doing, Johnny?"
CHILD: "He's here."
PARENT: "Are you having a good time?"
CHILD: "He knows it."

As normal speech is built up, this pronoun reversal might be expected to disappear. It has been reported, however, to be highly resistant to change (Tramontana and Stimbert, 1970); some children have required very extensive training even after they have stopped parroting the phrases of other people.

Speech deficiencies are clearly one of the most serious problems of autistic children, for they may also leave a lasting mark of social retardation on the child. The link between social skills and language is made evident by the often spontaneous appearance of affectional and dependent behavior in these children after they have been trained to speak (Churchill, 1969; Hewett, 1965). Lack of language has been proposed as one of the reasons for the child's continuing isolation, but it does not explain the early signs of social disinterest.

An autistic child's ability or inability to speak is sometimes an effective means of predicting later adjustment. Rutter (1967) found that of thirty-two autistic children without useful speech at five years of age, only seven had acquired speech when followed up about nine years later. Eisenberg and Kanner (1956) had earlier followed up a sample of eighty autistic children classified according to whether or not they had learned to speak by age five. Fifty percent of the children who had been able to speak at this age were later rated as showing fair or good adjustment, but only 3 percent of the nonspeaking children were so rated. Most autistic children probably grow up to spend the greatest amount of their lives in mental institutions (Rimland, 1964).

Preservation of Sameness

The autistic child becomes extremely upset over changes in daily routine and his surroundings. An offer of milk in a different drinking cup or a rearrangement of furniture may make him cry or bring on a temper tantrum. Even common greetings must not vary.

. . . a beautiful girl of five, with autism, finally made contact with her teacher. Each morning she had to be greeted with the set phrase, "Good morning, Lily. I am very, very glad to see you." If even one of the very's was omitted or another added she would start to scream wildly (Diamond, Baldwin, and Diamond, 1963, p. 304).

Other Signs

In addition to the three major symptoms just described, autistic children have problems in eating, often refusing food or eating only one or a few kinds of food. They may also have difficulty walking but be quite proficient at twirling and spinning objects and in performing ritualistic hand movements. Other rhythmic movements, such as endless body rocking, please the autistic child. He may also become preoccupied with manipulating a mechanical object and be very upset when interrupted. Often the child has sensory problems. Some autistic children are first diagnosed as being deaf because they never respond to any noise; some appear even to be insensitive to noise or to light. Finally, the autistic child has been shown to be negativistic, turning his back on others, banging his head, and actively resisting whatever is expected of him (Cowan, Hoddinott, and Wright, 1965).

Case Example

Robbie was four years of age when his parents first sought behavior therapy for him. At that time he was virtually uncontrollable. He would do little that either of his parents told him to and, in fact, would often do the opposite of what they suggested. Although he "looked intelligent," he had never spoken. He seemed to be particularly fond of only one activity, unscrewing nuts and bolts wherever he could find them. Whenever left to himself, Robbie would begin, working with just his fingers, to try to undo any nuts he could find, often working for hours on a single one until it would begin to move. After unscrewing the nut and bolt, he would typically swallow them.

In interviews Robbie's parents described him as having been a "good baby," not crying very much and not placing very many demands on them. Apparently Robbie had been content, in fact had preferred, to be left alone in his crib at an early age. In thinking back to the time when they first noticed that something might be wrong, both parents agreed on one early phenomenon, which they had not considered particularly significant at the time. Robbie had actually seemed *not* to enjoy being held and cuddled by either of his parents. Often, when they tried to hold him and to look into his eyes, he would avoid their gaze and stiffen, seemingly becoming anxious and upset. As Robbie grew older, of course, the parents became worried about their lack of control over his behavior, his negativism, and his failure to talk. And as their concern deepened, they began to seek professional assistance. At various times Robbie had been diagnosed as retarded, as a childhood schizophrenic, as a symbiotic psychotic, as an anaclitic depressive,[1] and as autistic.

In the initial treatment sessions with Robbie several other aspects of his behavior were clearly exhibited. He apparently had the capacity to understand speech, even though he often appeared not to listen and did the opposite of what was requested. Four players, one of them being Robbie, gathered in a circle for a game of ball. Robbie was asked each time to throw the ball to a different person. In thirty trials not once did he throw the ball to the person whom he had been requested to throw it to. He always threw the ball to someone else. Even if he did not understand the requests, he would be expected to throw the ball to the correct person about one-third of the time simply by chance. The fact that he *never* made the correct response is evidence that he understood and chose deliberately not to comply with the request.

Robbie often gave the appearance of being tired, bored, and passive. When things became difficult during a language training session, for example, he might seem placid and calm and yawn a great deal. His outward appearance, however, was not an accurate reflection of

---

[1] Symbiotic psychosis, which is said to occur at about four years of age, is marked by an extreme reluctance to be separated from the mother (Mahler, 1952). Anaclitic depression is a term applied to the infant's profound sadness when separated from his mother for a prolonged period. Because there has been little systematic investigation of these syndromes, we mention them only in passing.

Robbie's internal state. In one instance Robbie, barefoot, got up and walked across the room and left glistening footprints on the tile floor. His feet were literally dripping with sweat.

CHILDHOOD SCHIZOPHRENIA

Descriptive Characteristics

The term childhood schizophrenia is generally applied to the psychotic behavior of a child over five years of age whose history indicates that he has regressed from an earlier higher level of adjustment, although some studies of child schizophrenics indicate that many have been profoundly backward in development from their earliest months. A group of British investigators have listed nine defining characteristics of childhood schizophrenia (Creak, 1963).

1. Gross and sustained impairment of emotional relationships.
2. A background of serious retardation in most skills, with normal intellectual functioning in particular areas.
3. No sense of personal identity, indicated by self-directed aggression and by a failure to use pronouns correctly.
4. Pathological preoccupation with and attachment to particular objects, without regard for their function.
5. Sustained resistance to any change in the environment and attempts to maintain sameness.
6. Abnormal perceptual experiences—exaggerated, diminished, or unpredictable responses to sensory stimuli.
7. Acute and illogical anxiety, sometimes manifested as terror of ordinary objects.
8. Inability to speak or underdeveloped and peculiar speech.
9. Distorted patterns of movements, such as explosive hyperactivity, arm flailing, and grotesque body contortions; and ritualistic movements such as body whirling and toe walking.

In the United States Lauretta Bender has been the most prominent worker in this field. She has focused on several physiological and motoric signs that she believes to be particularly important in the diagnosis of childhood schizophrenia (Bender, 1955). She finds that these children show an upset in physiological rhythms so that eating and sleeping are disordered. She also notes vasomotor disturbances: either the walls of the blood vessels do not constrict or expand as they should in response to heat and cold, or they overrespond as evidenced by excessive pallor and flushing. She also proposes that schizophrenic children are poorly coordinated and show a particular motoric response called "whirling." To test for this an examiner has the child close his eyes and stretch out both arms while he rotates the child's head. A schizophrenic child turns his body (whirls) to keep it in line with his moving head (Figure 15.2). Normal children over six years of age respond this way very rarely, trying instead to maintain their bodies in the same position.

Childhood schizophrenia, as the name suggests, is supposedly an early form of adult schizophrenia. There are indeed some similarities. Both have problems with interpersonal

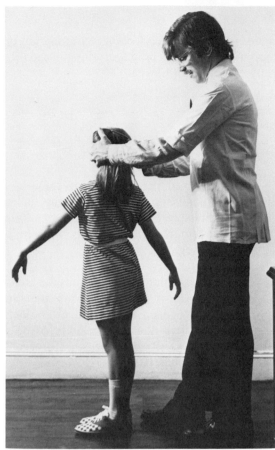

FIGURE **15.2**
Pictured here is an examiner testing for the presence of the whirling response, behavior which Bender considers an important diagnostic sign of childhood schizophrenia. When a schizophrenic child's head is turned, he tends to swing the rest of the body in the same direction.

Lotter (1966) has indicated the ratio as 2.5 to 1, but Rutter (1967) has placed it at 4.3 to 1. Moreover, unlike adult schizophrenia there is no preponderance of childhood schizophrenia among the lower classes. Finally, at least for adult schizophrenics who have had a good premorbid adjustment, prognosis is encouraging; but prognosis is uniformly poor for the schizophrenic child.

Bender (1970) has been able to follow the life course of a hundred childhood schizophrenics who were seen in Bellevue Hospital in New York City. At the time of follow-up they ranged in age from twenty-two to forty-six years. Two-thirds of these individuals were found in mental institutions. Of the remaining third, Bender noted

The thirty-seven individuals who are in community-living represent every level of adjustment; from one man who is now thirty-seven years old in a regressed dependent state, cared for by his dedicated mother since she removed him from Bellevue at eleven years because his father died in a mental hospital, to three college graduates, two of whom are successful professional men. . . . All are recognized or recognizable as schizophrenic, all are dependent in varying degrees on psychiatric guidance or treatment, agency support or unusual family or other social support. Twelve have been out since they left Bellevue in childhood. . . . Ten adolescent boys were able to leave institutions between fourteen and nineteen years . . . . About half were recognized as asocial, with court and training school records . . . (p. 170).

Thus, although there are differences between adult and childhood schizophrenia, one link is strong: schizophrenic children are very likely to be diagnosed as schizophrenic in adulthood.

relationships and show distorted patterns of behavior and affect. But there are several differences between the two categories. For example, delusions and hallucinations do not seem to be prevalent among schizophrenic children. Although the sex ratio is about equal among adult schizophrenics, childhood schizophrenia is more common among males.

Case Example

Kenny was five and a half when his parents sought professional help. His first five years were uneventful. He developed language normally, played often with several close friends, and got along well with his siblings. He then began kindergarten and the teacher soon complained that Kenny did not seem mature enough to attend school. She said that he refused to talk or to participate in games with other children. Often, when she tried to encourage him to join in certain activities, he would throw a tantrum.

At this time the parents did not notice anything unusual about Kenny's behavior at home, but as the year progressed he became more aloof and uncommunicative. At times he would appear panic-stricken for no apparent reason, running through the house crying in abject terror.

When the child was seen professionally, his poor coordination and clumsiness were evident. In addition, he exhibited the classic whirling response of schizophrenic children.

Childhood Schizophrenia and Infantile Autism: Different Syndromes?

A comparison of the kinds of behavior defining childhood schizophrenia and autism at first reveals few differences between them. Is there, then, any basis for making the differentiation? Bernard Rimland (1964) answers with a very definite yes.

. . . [there is] *sufficient information to demonstrate clearly that early infantile autism is not the same disease or cluster of diseases which has come to be called childhood schizophrenia, and that autism can and should be differentiated from it at all levels of discourse. Indeed, on reading many of the papers which describe schizophrenic children as autistic the writer is reminded of the story of the two men who were indistinguishable in appearance except that the tall thin one had red hair and only one leg* (p. 68).

Rimland contends that the label autistic is applied far too frequently, and that only about 10 percent of psychotic children should actually be so diagnosed. He has proposed several criteria by which autistic and schizophrenic children can be differentiated. It must be noted, however, that some of the differentiations he suggests are based on a definition of childhood schizophrenia which varies in a number of respects from the one we have just reviewed.

1. *Onset and course.* Autism is said to begin shortly after birth and is detectable at least by the time the child is two or three. In contrast, childhood schizophrenia is viewed as beginning later in life, after a period of seeming normality.
2. *Health and appearance.* Autistic children are usually described as especially healthy and good-looking (Kanner, 1949). Schizophrenic children, on the other hand, have many health problems and are not distinguished by any particular level of physical attractiveness (Bender, 1955).
3. *EEG findings.* The EEGs of schiz-

ophrenic children are frequently described as abnormal and immature (Bender, 1961), but such abnormalities are rarely reported for autistic children.

4. *Physical responsiveness.* Unlike autistic infants, those who are to become schizophrenic do mold to the bodies of their caretakers and are not reported as stiff and unresponsive (Bender, 1955).

5. *Autistic aloneness.* Disagreeing with Creak, Rimland argues that the schizophrenic child does not isolate himself.

6. *Need to preserve sameness.* Again, disagreeing with Creak, Rimland says that the childhood schizophrenic does not have the autistic child's need for a set routine and unchanged surroundings.

7. *Motor performance.* Autistic children are often described as graceful and dexterous in finger movements. Schizophrenic children are usually described as awkward and poorly coordinated.

8. *Language.* The specific language difficulties of autistic children, echolalia and pronoun reversal, are not found in schizophrenic children.

9. *Parents.* The parents of autistic children are often found to be well educated and to have high IQs. Moreover, there is a low incidence of familial mental disorders. In contrast, the parents of schizophrenic children do not have high IQs, and the incidence of mental disorders in their families is greater than that in the general population.

10. *Idiot savant performance.* As discussed in Box 17.1 (page 442), Rimland contends that many autistic children suffer from a particular kind of mental retardation which is characterized by extraordinary talents in isolated and limited areas. For example, he cites the case of an autistic child who, at seventeen months of age, could recite a complete aria from *Don Giovanni.* Such performances are not found in schizophrenic children.

Basing his work in part on the differences just listed, Rimland (1964) developed a checklist to help in differentiating autistic children from other children examined clinically. The instrument is filled out by the parents and covers aspects of behavior such as eating, cuddliness, and sensory responsiveness. In a recent report Rimland (1971) started with a sample of 2218 cases, about 10 percent of which were judged autistic on the basis of the rating scale. A comparison between autistic and nonautistic children on several of the key items appears in Table 15.1.

Rimland's report, coupled with the descriptive differences he has listed, gives some support to the notion that autistic children can be differentiated from the larger population of psychotic children. Nonetheless, diagnosing autism correctly may still present a serious problem. The usefulness of a test in diagnosis is affected by the base rate of the disorder in question, that is, the frequency of its occurrence in the general population. The base rate of childhood psychoses is generally reported to be about 4.5 cases per 10,000 in the general population (Lotter, 1966). According to Rimland, the base rate of autism among psychotic children is about one in ten. Thus the base rate for autism would be only 0.45 cases per 10,000 children in the general population, making its diagnosis extremely difficult.

To understand this point, consider what would happen if the diagnostician, wanting to make the maximum number of correct diagnoses of autism, decides to use no other information than the low base rate. By calling all the psychotic children he sees nonautistic, he would be correct 90 percent of the time! Of course in this extreme example he would also

THE SCHIZOPHRENIAS

misdiagnose all the autistic children. The point is that with such a low base rate, there are few diagnoses of autism to make, and therefore the diagnostic validity of the checklist is difficult to demonstrate. This point was well illustrated in a study which found that Rimland's checklist improved only slightly on base rate diagnoses (Masters and Miller, 1970).

ETIOLOGY OF CHILDHOOD PSYCHOSES

We turn now to an evaluation of the theory and research on childhood psychoses. A note of caution is in order. Some theorists attempt to account specifically for autism, but others deal more generally with childhood psychosis. Moreover, the diagnoses of the children referred to in many of the research reports are often questionable, with the diagnosis of autism perhaps being made too frequently.

Biological Bases of Childhood Psychoses

Several considerations make organic accounts of childhood psychoses plausible. First, the age of onset is often very early; autism is supposedly detectable in the first two years of life, and childhood schizophrenia also develops in early childhood. Were a psychological stress to precipitate such disorders, it would indeed have to be a particularly noxious event. Yet the available evidence does not indicate that psychotic children are reared in especially unpleasant environments or that they have suffered some severe trauma. Second, a syndrome quite similar to the symptoms of childhood psychoses may develop in the aftermath of brain diseases such as encephalitis. Third, mental subnormality is often associated with some kind of brain dysfunction, as will be seen in Chapter 17, and the majority of children with childhood psychoses are found to have low levels of intelligence (see Box 15.1).

Within the general framework of biological accounts of childhood psychoses, we can identify several particular topics of investigation: pregnancy and birth complications, abnormal EEGs and other neurological findings, and genetic factors.

Pregnancy and Birth Complications. Given that the onset of psychotic behavior in children is at a relatively young age, a likely candidate for early damage to the central nervous system might be brain insult during pregnancy or birth. Although pregnancy and birth complications (PBCs) are no more common in the gestation periods and deliveries of autistic children than in those of infants throughout the general population (Kanner, 1954; Kanner and Lesser, 1958), the majority of studies have indeed found a higher incidence of PBCs in the births of schizophrenic children (for example, Hinton, 1963; Gittelman and Birch, 1967). Other studies have failed to discover such a difference (Lotter, 1967). But even in the studies that have found *more* PBCs among schizophrenic children, the frequency has not been particularly high. For example, in the Gittelman and Birch study (1967) only 35 percent of the schizophrenic children's births were found to to have been difficult. We must therefore look further for a physiological cause of either autism or childhood schizophrenia.

Neurological Findings. If childhood psychoses are caused by abnormal brain functioning, this should be detectable in their EEGs or through a neurological examination, although such correlational evidence would not

TABLE **15.1** *Comparison of Autistic and Psychotic Children on Several Items from Rimland's Diagnostic Checklist* (*from Rimland, 1971*)

	Autistic, %		Nonautistic, %
Item	Speaking $n = 65$	Mute $n = 53$	$n = 230$
21. Did you ever suspect the child was very nearly deaf?			
—1 Yes	77	94	54
—2 No	23	6	46
	100	100	100
29. (Age 2-5) Is he cuddly?			
—1 Definitely, likes to cling to adults	2	2	20
—2 Above average (likes to be held)	8	8	18
—3 No, rather stiff and awkward to hold	90	88	56
—4 Don't know	0	2	6
	100	100	100
33. (Age 3-5) How skillful is the child in doing fine work with his fingers or playing with small objects?			
—1 Exceptionally skillful	71	75	33
—2 Average for age	6	9	23
—3 A little awkward, or very awkward	15	8	33
—4 Don't know	8	8	11
	100	100	100
40. (Age 3-5) How interested is the child in mechanical objects such as the stove or vacuum cleaner?			
—1 Little or no interest	19	9	23
—2 Average interest	4	0	21
—3 Fascinated by certain mechanical things	77	92	56
	100	100	100

TABLE **15.1** (*continued*)

Item	Autistic, %		Nonautistic, %
	Speaking $n = 65$	Mute $n = 53$	$n = 230$
45. (Age 3-5) Does child get very upset if certain things he is used to are changed (like furniture or toy arrangement, or certain doors which must be left open or shut)?			
__1 No	4	2	29
__2 Yes, definitely	87	86	41
__3 Slightly true	9	12	30
	100	100	100
71. (Age 3-5) Does the child typically say "Yes" by repeating the same question he has been asked? (Example: You ask "Shall we go for a walk, Honey?" and he indicates he does want to by saying "Shall we go for a walk, Honey?" or "Shall we go for a walk?")			
__1 Yes, definitely, does not say "yes" directly	94	12*	22
__2 No, would say "Yes" or "OK" or similar answer	0	3	8
__3 Not sure	4	6	8
__4 Too little speech to say	2	79	62
	100	100	100

* Speech item not applicable to the mute group.

Bender's theory integrates many of the data reviewed—genetic factors, PBCs, neurological impairments, and immature patterns of the EEGs. The last part of her theory, however, concerning the failure to form an adequate body image, is highly speculative. The data reviewed have little relation to concepts such as body image and ego boundary. Furthermore, this last part of her theory rests on the psychoanalytic assumption that psychotic behavior represents a failure of ego processes, a view which, as indicated in Chapter 14, has little data to support it.

Bernard Rimland

In an influential book Rimland (1964) proposed that the autistic child is genetically predisposed to superior development, but that this potential advantage also makes the child particularly vulnerable to damage from oxygen deprivation. Rimland suggests that anoxia affects the reticular formation, a primitive netlike area of nerve tissue in the central core of the brainstem. Damage to a certain area of the reticular formation is known to cause slow-wave activity in the cortex, which means that the brain is maintained in a state of underarousal. The end result, as Rimland sees it, is a cognitive impairment, an inability to relate new stimuli to remembered experience. Thus, through a biological route, Rimland derives a basic cognitive defect which he believes can account for the behavior of psychotic children.

What evidence is available to support this theory? Data that might indicate that autistic children may be predisposed toward higher intelligence are equivocal. Their parents have typically been found to be higher than average in educational achievement (Treffert, 1970) but, contrary to Rimland's claim, they have not always been found to have high IQs (Levine and Olson, 1968).

Rimland's supposition that the reticular formation in the brainstem is damaged is even more speculative. Most evidence does not indicate that the reticular formation is especially vulnerable to anoxia (Kessler and Neale, 1974). Furthermore, the notion that autistic children are characterized by a low level of arousal is supported only by the slow-wave activity found by Hermelin and O'Connor (1968).[2]

Finally, we should consider whether any evidence exists to support Rimland's claim that the primary defect leading to autism is an inability to relate new stimuli to remembered experience. Rimland believes that this inability to make new associations prevents the autistic child from deriving meaning from anything that happens to him. The child fails to develop an affectionate relationship with his family because he makes none of the normal associations between feeding and physical contact with the mother and derives none of the pleasure from this association that the normal child usually experiences. The autistic child's insistence that nothing in his surroundings or routine be altered is interpreted in a similar fashion. Environmental changes are considered by normal people to be minor or irrelevant because they are easily integrated with past experience. But because the autistic child can achieve no comprehensive ordering of the world, the strangeness of any slight change in surroundings looms in his perceptions and causes him emotional distress. In our opinion this part of the theory may be overstated, for autistic children *can* learn and thus are able to relate new stimuli to previous experience.

[2] It should be noted that Rimland does not commit himself to the reticular formation as the locus of damage. He focuses rather on the *psychological function* that is impaired and speculates that this malfunction *might be* controlled by the reticular formation.

Moore and Shiek

A theory similar to Rimland's has recently been proposed by Moore and Shiek (1971). They agree with Rimland that autistic children may be geniuses "gone awry," but they differ in the mechanism proposed for this arrested development. Their theory focuses on the possibility that the prepsychotic child may have been sensorially deprived while still in the womb. Moore and Shiek argue that because of accelerated development the psychotic child is "ready" to be born and ready to respond and socialize before the end of the usual pregnancy term. By not being born until the full nine months have passed, the child suffers from restricted sensory stimulation and a lack of social experience.

Given a fetus with a brain in an advanced state of developmental readiness for stimulation but residing within a restricted uterine environment, what would be the probable results? What are the effects of sensory restriction and failure to experience primary socialization when these two circumstances occur simultaneously (p. 454)?

Moore and Shiek note that the restriction of early environmental stimulation for animals dramatically affects their emotionality, learning ability, social behavior, and perception (Harlow and Harlow, 1966). And Rimland (1964) has remarked on the similarities between the behavior of autistic children and that of individuals who have experienced sensory deprivation. Subjects who are deprived of sensory stimuli for any length of time are "detached from the external environment" and "stare right at you but never see you" (p. 104).

Moore and Shiek also point out similarities between the behavior of autistic children and that of animals who have not been properly imprinted. Imprinting is a process whereby a neonate becomes attached to and learns from other members of its own species during a "critical period" of development. During this period the animal is inclined to follow a moving object in its vicinity, which is usually its mother. If by chance the object is other than a member of its own species and the animal follows and mimics it, the animal will thereafter lack interest in its own kind, much as the autistic child avoids human contact. Imprinting occurs only during one period of the neonate's development, usually just after birth. But if the psychotic child were to reach his critical period while still in the womb, he might imprint on this intrauterine environment. Moore and Shiek have wondered,

Does the autistic child's insistence on sameness in the environment, his repetitive and stereotyped behaviors, his hand regarding, and his failure to develop speech suggest that he was imprinted by an atypical environment at a critical period in his primary socialization? In this essentially unchanging environment, the fetus has only the heartbeats of himself and his mother, and perhaps the other rhythms of their bodies, to affect him. Is it possible that the autistic child is so imprinted with this relatively featureless, secluded, and limited world during critical developmental periods, when he should be vividly stimulated and experiencing primary socialization, that he in fact seems to be living "in his own world" after birth? Does it explain his apparent need to maintain environmental sameness? . . . Are autistic children, by their frequent obsessions with inanimate objects, demonstrating . . . that an individual at the proper time in life can become attached to both living and nonliving things in the surrounding environment (pp. 454–455)?

What kind of data could support this theory? First, like Rimland's theory, this account rests on the notion that autistic children are predisposed to precocious development and high intelligence. As we have just seen, the evidence on this point is equivocal. Second, the theory asserts that autistic children become accustomed to a low level of stimulation while in the womb. The autistic child should therefore be unable to accept "normal" levels of environmental stimulation and be overaroused by them. The data on EEG patterns are inconclusive on this point.

Moore and Shiek's hypothesis is fascinating and able to account for many facets of the behavior of autistic children. But it is, of course, a theory and there are no direct research data to support it as yet. Indeed, it is interesting to reflect on what kind of research *could* produce data that would support this highly speculative theory.

Psychological Theories of Childhood Psychoses

As might be expected, theorists of a psychogenic bent attribute childhood psychoses to early experiences, especially those between the mother and child. An inadequate diet of mothering, the nutrient which, in dynamic theories, is so essential for development, is considered to bring on childhood psychoses.

Bruno Bettelheim

Perhaps the best-known of the psychological theories was formulated by Bruno Bettelheim (1967). The basic supposition of Bettelheim's theory is that autism closely resembles the apathy and hopelessness found among inmates of German concentration camps during World War II (see pages 114–115). Bettelheim hypothesizes that the young infant is able to perceive the negative feelings of his parents who

reject him. He finds that his own actions have little impact on his unresponsive parents. The mother, on the one hand, may expect too much of the infant and be easily disappointed. Or the mother may expect too little, treating the child as a passive object. In either case the child comes to believe "that one's own efforts have no power to influence the world, because of the earlier conviction that the world is insensitive to one's reactions" (p. 46).

This experience of helplessness is viewed as extremely frustrating for the child. But he is unwilling to communicate his frustration because he feels that nothing good can come from it. He continues to withdraw from the world, his only activities—his ritualistic hand movements and echolalic speech—being more a means of shutting out the world than truly meeting it. An elaborate fantasy life is created, and insistence on sameness is the rule that brings permanence and order to his world. Safety resides only in seeing that everything about him stays exactly the same. Since the essential purpose of activity is to bring about change, the autistic child avoids any sort of action; he cannot move beyond a state in which the center of his universe must be a static environment.

Bettelheim's theory rests primarily on the notion that at early critical periods, when the effect on the child is profound, the parents mistreat him by not loving him. In his early papers Kanner described the parents of autistic children as cold, insensitive, meticulous, introverted, distant, and highly intellectual (Kanner and Eisenberg, 1955). He summed up his theory of how such traits affect the children by saying that they are reared in "emotional refrigeration." Others (for example, Singer and Wynne, 1963; Rimland, 1964) have also noted the detachment of parents of autistic children, although Rimland has used less pejorative adjectives. Singer and Wynne have described several means by which these parents "disaffiliate" themselves from their children. Some are cynical about all interpersonal relations and are emotionally cold; others are passive and apathetic; and still others maintain an obsessive, intellectual distance from people. But as Rutter (1968) has noted,

It is difficult to know how much weight to attach to these observations in that other workers have found a much greater variability in parental personality characteristics. . . . Perhaps many (but by no means all) of the parents are rather detached, organized, and meticulous people, although the adjective cold is probably inaccurate. But in this connection the high intellectual and social status of the parents needs to be kept in mind, and it is uncertain whether or not these characteristics are in excess in relation to the academic and professional circles from which the parents are drawn (p. 5).

The direction of a possible correlation between parental characteristics and autism is not easily determined. The deviant parental behavior that has been reported could be a reaction to the child's abnormality rather than the other way around. And if parental behavior causes childhood psychoses, why is the incidence of similar difficulties so low in siblings? Moreover, although the psychosis is a very severe one, the parental behavior that has been discussed does not appear likely to be more than mildly damaging. It would seem that only very gross mistreatment, such as keeping the child in a locked closet, could precipitate severe problems so early in life. Reports of exceedingly harsh treatment are generally lacking. The evidence for Bettelheim's theory is not compelling.

Social Learning Theory

Social learning theorists, like those who are psychoanalytically oriented, have postulated that certain childhood learning experiences cause psychotic childhood disorders. Ferster (1961), in an extremely influential article, suggested that the inattention of the parents, especially of the mother, prevents the associations that establish human beings as reinforcers from being made. And because the parents have not become reinforcers, they cannot control the child's behavior. Ferster's reasoning is as follows.

1. Behavior is primarily controlled by its consequences.
2. Initially, the young child responds only to primary reinforcers, such as food and milk.
3. As children grow older, their behavior comes more under the control of secondary and generalized reinforcers, such as praise and love, and these social rewards acquire their reinforcing properties through contiguous association with primary rewards.
4. The behavior of severely disturbed children is a consequence of inadequate secondary and generalized reinforcers.
5. The parents of disturbed children, especially those of autistic children, neglect the child, for example, by being involved in professional and other non-family-oriented activities.
6. Thus the child learns to function alone or autistically and never becomes responsive to human contact, having been deprived of it during the earlier stages of life.

An interesting consequence of Ferster's paper was a flurry of therapeutic work aimed at shaping the behavior of severely disturbed children (Davison, 1964; Wolf, Risley, and Mees, 1964; Lovaas, Freitag, Gold, and Kas-

Readers of this book have no doubt noticed that the authors are very critical of the various psychogenic theories, both psychoanalytic and learning. In addition to our aspirations to provide as scientifically accurate a textbook as possible, we are concerned about the impact that theories may have on people. Consider, for a moment, what your feelings might be if a psychiatrist or psychologist were to tell you that your unconscious hostility has caused your child to remain mute at the age of six. Or how would you feel if you were told that your commitment to professional activities has brought about the autistic behavior patterns of your child? The fact is, of course, that the truth of these allegations has yet to be demonstrated. But in the meantime a tremendous emotional burden is placed on parents who have, over the years, been told that they are at fault. But, you might say, have we not evidence that the families of disturbed children are "peculiar"? In Chapter 14 we have already shown how inconclusive such data are, and the strong possibility exists that any home problems are reactions to the behavior of the particular child rather than the cause of them, especially when there are normal siblings.

As Rimland has suggested, psychogenesis may be not only an inadequate hypothesis but also a pernicious one.

sorla, 1965). The investigators' successes in modifying behavior by applying primary and secondary reinforcers did not of course demonstrate that Ferster's etiological hypotheses were correct. As we have learned, the fact that therapy procedures are effective does not in any way prove what factors are causative. Indeed, Rimland may well insist that a biological dysfunction causes autism and yet, with perfect consistency, agree with Ferster's proposals about how best to handle these disturbed children.

If the effectiveness of the treatment recommended by Ferster must be disregarded, what is left to support his theory? Very little. Many of the comments made about Bettelheim's position are again applicable. Lack of parental attention seems an inadequate explanation for severe behavioral disturbances among children (see Box 15.2).

Information Processing: Perceptual Theories

Rutter (1968) views the basic defect that produces autism as a failure to comprehend sounds and language. The association of language difficulties with the syndrome and the prognostic significance of the autistic child's acquiring speech are the major pieces of evidence supporting his position.

Research has also been performed on other cognitive abilities of autistic children. In intelligence testing they do well on tasks involving immediate memory, for example, in digit span tests in which they must repeat a series of digits after hearing them. But they do very poorly on tests involving verbal concepts, abstraction, and symbolization (Rutter, 1968). Hermelin (1966) tested autistic children for their recall of eight-word messages which consisted either of two nonsense phrases—such as "half egg a pick"; "might got dress up"; or two meaningful sentences—"watch these green lights"; "eat bread and jam." The normal children in the control group recalled the meaningful sentences better than the nonsense phrases. In contrast, the autistic children typically recalled only the last part of a message, regardless of whether it was meaningful or not. Acquiring knowledge of the structure of language facilitates storage of word sequences. Without knowing this structure, sentences can be stored no more efficiently than can a string of unrelated words. The outcomes of both intelligence testing and experimental studies suggest, then, a basic impairment in language.

But are the language problems *primary*, or could they result from social withdrawal? Although some emotional disturbances might stem from the inability to comprehend, problems in social relationships are often noticeable even before language should be present. Moreover, so-called aphasic children, whose language disorders are caused by brain lesions, do not become psychotic because their ability to use words is impaired.

Another theory, proposed by Lovaas, attributes autism to a particular psychological deficit, stimulus overselectivity. In one study supporting this position, groups of autistic, retarded, and normal children were given a discrimination learning test (Lovaas, Schreibman, Koegal, and Rehm, 1971). In the training phase three different cues—a red floodlight, a noise, and the tactile sensations from the inflation of a blood pressure cuff—were all presented simultaneously. Each time a subject pressed a bar in response to this multidimensional cue, he was rewarded with candy. Once the response had been established, subjects moved to the testing phase; in addition to the complex combination of stimuli used in training, each stimulus was presented separately.

The most important part of the test was how the children responded when each of the three stimuli was presented by itself. Autistic children responded to only one of the three separately presented stimuli, retardates to two, and normal children to all three. Lovaas makes a plausible case in explaining how such overselectivity might account for the autistic child's failure to learn socially appropriate behavior. Taking an associationist view of learning, Lovaas notes that the stimuli which must be associated are often complex and several in number. Thus if the child attends to only one of them, he will naturally have problems in learning to associate stimuli.

In contrast to the single-process theories of Rutter and Lovaas, Wing and Wing (1970) have recently proposed that autism results from a multiplicity of impairments. In an earlier study (Wing, 1969) autistic children had been compared with groups of children with receptive aphasia—difficulties in comprehending speech—and with executive aphasia—difficulties in speaking; with children who were

TABLE **15.2** *Impairments of Function and Secondary Behavioral Problems in Autistic and Other Handicapped Children Two to Five Years of Age* (*from Wing, 1969*)

Diagnosis and number of children / Impairments and secondary behavior	Speaking autistic n = 20	Mute autistic n = 7	Receptive aphasic n = 11	Executive aphasic n = 10	Partially blind and deaf n = 15	Down's syndrome n = 15	Normal controls n = 25
Impairments in							
Response to sound	85	*86*	*100*	10	*93*	20	0
Comprehension of speech	100	*100*	*100*	20	*93*	(67)	4
Use of speech	100	NR	*82*	30	NR	40	32
Pronunciation	85	NR	*64*	*90*	NR	*73*	0
Right-left orientation and copying skilled movements	75	NR	18	*45*	NR	NR	40
Visual perception	95	*85*	18	0	*100*	27	0
Understanding and use of gestures	55	*85*	0	0	*60*	7	0
Abnormalities of behavior							
Preference for proximal senses	100	*85*	18	20	*87*	47	28
Stereotyped movements	95	*100*	18	30	*93*	20	4
Social withdrawal	95	*85*	(64)	20	(53)	13	0
Attachment to objects and routines	100	*100*	27	40	(60)	7	20
Irrational fears and lack of fear of real danger	100	*100*	18	20	*80*	40	20
Lack of play	95	*100*	(45)	20	*87*	27	0
Socially embarrassing behavior	90	*86*	45	40	*73*	27	28
Lack of nonverbal skills	0	43	*18*	*20*	93	73	*12*

Note. All values represent the percentage of children in each group with abnormal scores. Values in italics denote no significant differences from those for speaking autistic children. Values in parentheses denote significantly less abnormality than in autistic children but significantly more than in the control group. NR = not rated; some groups were not rated on certain items because they were too handicapped to show the necessary behavior.

both partially blind and deaf; with children who had been born with mongolism (Down's syndrome); and with normal children. All groups were given a number of tasks to perform and stimuli to respond to, and other aspects of behavior were observed. The results, summarized in Table 15.2, indicate that the performance and responses of normal children and those with Down's syndrome were alike and also different from those of the remaining groups. But the other groups also differed in their performances of particular tasks. For example, both autistic and aphasic children had difficulty with the tasks requiring speech. The aphasic children however, could use nonvocal communication to compensate whereas the autistic children did not. The autistic children also showed abnormalities in visual perception, tending to use peripheral rather than central vision, and were deficient in copying skilled movements and in right-left directional orientation. They were both insensitive and overly sensitive to certain sensory stimuli. Although *some* of these problems are found in *some* of the other groups studied, they were all *combined* only in the autistic children. The authors, Wing and Wing, conclude that

At the present stage, the most reasonable way of formulating the problem which takes [everything] into account is to say that autistic children appear to suffer from multiple impairments (which can vary in severity) affecting comprehension and use of speech, comprehension and use of gesture, auditory perception, visual perception, control of skilled movements, posture, autonomic function, and certain aspects of physical development. Each of these impairments can occur independently of the others in various chronic childhood conditions. When they occur together, the affected child will show the behavior pattern typical of early childhood autism . . . (p. 263).

The primary difficulty with such an explanation is the lack of supporting data. The Wing (1969) study shows only a *correlation* between certain cognitive impairments and the diagnosis of autism. Autistic behavior may plausibly follow from cognitive abnormalities, but the studies that might prove the impairments to be causative have not been done.

A Diathesis-Stress Hypothesis

We have seen that both biological and psychological theories about the causes of childhood psychoses have some credibility. Various neurological problems characterize *some* of these children and the parents of *some* are rather aloof and detached. Yet none of the theories by itself accounts for the syndrome; an interaction of several factors may offer a better explanation. Kanner himself (Kanner and Eisenberg, 1956), although stressing lack of affection by the parents, concluded that psychotic children have some inborn defect. A diathesis-stress model that includes both a physiological predisposition and psychological stresses may prove more satisfactory. We shall examine such a theory, proposed by Zaslow and Breger (1969), to illustrate in more detail the aspects of this approach.

Zaslow and Breger view autism as a failure to establish social relationships because the interactions between mother and child are from the very beginning unsatisfactory.[3] The early sensorimotor interactions—when the mother feeds the child and holds him if he is distressed—are considered formative. Mother, and by generalization other people, take on positive valence as they reduce stresses such as hunger and discomfort. This is the basis on which social attachment is built.

[3] Although Zaslow and Breger consider their theory to be an explanation of autism, they hold a broader definition of the disorder than workers such as Rimland.

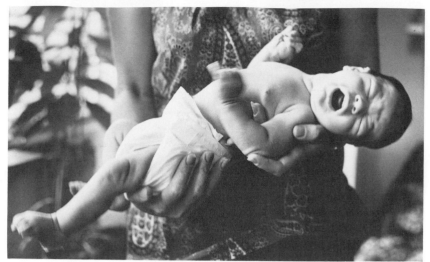

FIGURE **15.3**

The infant pictured here is arching its back and resisting close physical contact with its mother. The parents of autistic children frequently remember such reactions as the first indication of the later diagnosis.

In autism, a lack of satisfying sensorimotor interaction, in which the infant passes from a startle-like state of arousal and stress to a comfortable state of relaxation in human contact, may lead to a failure in adequate attachment. The autistic child then continues to show an aroused, startle-like reaction to people and holding (pp. 251–252).

Evidence indeed supports the notion that a child's response to being held may be inborn. Shaffer and Emerson (1964), for example, have indicated that infants may be classified as "cuddlers" and "noncuddlers," even before they have had much experience in being held (Figure 15.3). The noncuddlers resisted close physical contact with their mothers almost immediately and were found to be less intensely attached to them at the end of twelve months.

Zaslow and Breger point out that other factors may also decrease the amount of physical contact; the infant may be very active, or he may have physical ailments that make him cry and stiffen when held. Intellectual, aloof, and disaffiliating parents may be expected to pick up and play with their children less often. An inexperienced mother may find it difficult to cope with a child who seemingly rejects her

attempts to comfort it, which may explain why the rate of autism is higher among firstborn children (Rimland, 1964).

How do Zaslow and Breger account for the other aspects of the syndrome?

The autistic child's need for sameness in the environment, his tremendous sensitivity to small changes in the arrangement of objects in the immediate world, and his propensity for intense rage and upset over such changes all attest to his great reliance on place security over person security. Lacking the positive affective bond to mother which forms the secure base from which exploration and eventual mastery of the environment normally proceeds, the autistic child has become attached to his immediate and familiar environment and relies on this for security.[4]

The autistic child's attachment to objects such as mechanical appliances is part of the same process. . . . Most normal infants and children become attached to certain physical objects such as a blanket, a special doll or toy. . . . In autism we see an intensification

[4] Research with monkeys has indeed shown that they are more willing to explore a novel environment when their mothers are present.

of this process due to the lack of a satisfying human attachment . . . the attachment to . . . objects increases . . . as the positive attachment to mother decreases. (pp. 263–264).

Zaslow and Breger's diathesis-stress model is indeed a plausible account of much of the extant data, focusing on the child's aversion to being held as the diathesis and on parental detachment as the stress. Other possible predisposing factors, such as neurological impairments, are not dealt with in their theory but will probably be part of a more adequate account that is put together someday.

SUMMARY

In this chapter we have reviewed research and theory related to the severe disturbances of children. The information available suggests that two syndromes, childhood schizophrenia and infantile autism, can be identified. Both biological and psychological factors may be important in etiology. For childhood schizophrenia significant concordance among monozygotic twins, rather frequent PBCs, and EEG and neurological abnormalities suggest that biological factors may be causative. Evidence of brain dysfunction is less compelling for autism, and the information on genetic factors is less clear-cut. Some but not all autistic children appear to be born to highly intelligent parents who may not be physically comforting to them. The theoretical accounts of both childhood schizophrenia and autism must be regarded as highly speculative at this time.

CHAPTER 16

Brain Dysfunctions

In 1968, 25.9 percent of all first admissions to psychiatric hospitals were found to have an organic brain syndrome, and 34 percent of them were older than seventy-five. The statistics for patients who have been residents of psychiatric hospitals for some time are similar: 25.8 percent of them have organic impairments, and 31.8 percent of these patients are older than seventy-five (Rosen, Fox, and Gregory, 1972). The incidence of brain dysfunction, then, is high, especially among the aged.

An examination of the clinical syndromes that are attributable to brain pathologies may one day shed light on the so-called functional psychoses—those in which one or more of the normal activities of the individual are disturbed, but without known change in tissues or condition of the brain. The symptoms of brain pathologies frequently overlap those of other psychoses already discussed—the deep depressions and the schizophrenias. Some workers reason, therefore, that although no organic causes have been demonstrated for functional psychoses, eventually such causes may be found.

But the disordered behavior exhibited by a person with an organic impairment of the brain is not always simply a function of the brain area affected or of the extent of the damage. The behavior of two persons who have the same lesion in a particular area of the brain may vary widely. The preexisting personality of the individual interacts with the brain injury to produce the symptoms that are observed. Thus the manifestations of an organic brain disorder depend on other factors, even though the primary cause is an injury or pathological change in the brain. Moreover, as will become evident, there is considerable similarity in the symptoms shown by people with *different* brain dysfunctions.

CLINICAL FEATURES OF BRAIN DYSFUNCTION

According to DSM-II any of the following impairments can occur in an organic brain syndrome.

1. **Impairments of orientation.** The individual may not know who he is or where he is and loses all track of time, forgetting not only the day of the week but also the year.
2. **Impairment of memory.** Memory loss is especially great for recent events, less so for earlier life. The patient may resort to *confabulation,* making up stories to fill in the gaps in his memory.
3. **Impairment of intellectual function.** The individual may have difficulties in comprehension, learning, and making judgments. He is unable to formulate plans or reason effectively. The progressive deterioration of these intellectual functions is referred to as *dementia.*
4. **Emotional impairments.** Emotions may be labile or all affect may be blunted.

The preceding list indicates that most symptoms of brain disorders are cognitive and intellectual malfunctions. The primacy of cognitive deficits helps distinguish the organic syndromes from the neuroses and depressions, in which the stresses of experience and emotional problems are evident. Similarly, although schizophrenics show severe impairments in cognition and perception, they seldom show memory loss. The emotional impairments that a brain-damaged individual suffers may result directly from the brain injury, but they may also reflect the individual's *reaction to being cognitively impaired.* Kolb (1968) has described this perturbation.

Confronted with a problem he cannot solve, the brain-injured individual becomes suddenly anxious and agitated and may appear dazed. A change in his color may appear, he fumbles at the task, and he may present other evidence of autonomic disturbances, such as irregular pulse and changes in respiratory rate. If he was initially in good spirits, he now becomes evasive, sullen, irritable, and even aggressive (pp. 215–216).

Organic brain dysfunctions are diagnosed on the basis of a detailed history of the onset of cognitive and behavioral difficulties; a neurological examination of sensory and motor responses, especially of the reflexes, to determine whether there are localized impairments of the nervous system; EEGs and brain X-rays; an analysis of cerebrospinal fluids to determine whether infections, poisons, or blood are present; and psychological tests such as the Rorschach and the Reitan (see page 75) which assess the patient's perceptual, motor, and intellectual functions. When the brain pathology is serious, few diagnostic problems exist; injuries, alterations in structure, or other impairments are so severe that it does not take sophisticated procedures to determine that the patient has an organic dysfunction and to identify its nature. When the alterations are subtle, however, the sophisticated diagnostic tests developed for their detection are not always helpful. Nor is behavior a reliable key to the nature of the dysfunction. Patients who have *different* organic problems may show similar behavioral deficits and patients with the *same* organic impairment may behave quite differently. And, of course, the overriding difficulty in diagnosis is our woefully inadequate knowledge of the enormously complex brain (see Box 16.1 for a review of brain structure and function).

DSM-II classifies organic dysfunctions in two ways, by etiology and by particular clinical signs. In classifying by etiology the agent that produced the dysfunction is specified. The most important of these are infection, brain trauma, nutritional deficiencies, cerebrovascular accidents or strokes, tumors, degenera- tion, toxins, and metabolic and endocrine disturbances. Disorders such as epilepsy are classified by particular clinical signs, in this instance by seizures and the various forms that they take. All the organic syndromes described in this chapter are classified by etiology except for epilepsy.

ORGANIC BRAIN SYNDROMES CLASSIFIED BY ETIOLOGY

Brain Disorders Caused by Infection

Encephalitis

Encephalitis is a generic term that refers to an inflammation of brain tissue. The common form of encephalitis is *meningococcal meningitis,* a viral infection that inflames the meninges. In the acute phase of the disease the patient is delirious and disoriented. Later he may remain depressed, irritable, and experience difficulties in concentration and memory. Recovery is usually complete, but some patients may have permanent sensory and motor dysfunctions. If the disorder occurs in infants, they will often be mentally retarded (see Chapter 17).

Another form of encephalitis, *epidemic encephalitis,* is commonly referred to as sleeping sickness because the person with this viral infection is lethargic and sleeps for long periods of time, awaking only to take nourishment. After sleep the individual may be irritable and hyperactive. In delirium the patient may have convulsive seizures and hallucinations and be generally disoriented. Sleeping sickness, always a problem in certain parts of Africa and Asia because it is carried by the mosquito, is rare in the United States today, although there was an epidemic of this disease in the United States after World War I.

The aftereffects of this disorder appear to be especially severe among children. A previously well-behaved child, after recovering from epidemic encephalitis, may become hyperactive and aggressive and generally offensive in behavior. He may cheat, lie, strike and torment others, vandalize property, and run away from home. The disruption of the child's personality may persist into adulthood, when he may have to be hospitalized.

Neurosyphilis

In the past ten years the rate of reported cases of syphilis has doubled in the United States; because of the stigma associated with venereal disease, many more may go undetected and untreated. Several decades from now a large number of individuals may be hospitalized with neurosyphilis or general paresis. The spirochete *Treponema pallidum* (Figure 16.3, on color plate) invades the body through mucous membranes after being contracted during either intercourse or oral-genital contact. The disorder may also be transmitted from an af-

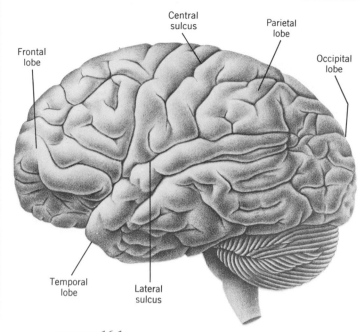

FIGURE **16.1**

Surface of one of the cerebral hemispheres, showing the principal areas of the cortex.

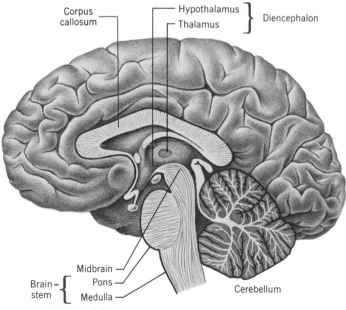

FIGURE **16.2**

Slice of brain through the medial plane, showing the internal structures.

BOX **16.1**

Structure and Function of the Human Brain

The brain is located within the protective covering of the skull and is enveloped with three layers of nonneural tissue, membranes referred to as *meninges*. Viewed from the top, the brain is divided by a midline fissure into two mirror-image cerebral hemispheres, which together in man constitute most of the *cerebrum*. The two hemispheres are connected by a band of nerve fibers called the *corpus callosum*. Figure 16.1 shows the surface of one of the *cerebral hemispheres*. The upper, side, and some of the lower surfaces of the hemispheres constitute the *cerebral cortex*. The cortex consists of six layers of tightly packed neuron cell bodies with many short, unsheathed interconnecting processes. These neurons, estimated to be 10 to 15 billion in number, make up a thin outer covering of the so-called gray matter of the brain. The cortex of man is vastly convoluted; the ridges are called *gyri* and the depressions between them *sulci* or fissures. Deep fissures divide the cerebral hemispheres into several distinct areas, called lobes. The *frontal lobe* lies in front of the central sulcus; the *parietal lobe* is behind it and above the lateral sulcus; the *temporal lobe* is located below the lateral sulcus; and the *occipital* lobe lies behind the parietal and temporal lobes. Different functions tend to be localized in particular areas of the lobes—vision in the occipital, discrimination of sounds in the temporal, reasoning and other higher mental processes plus the regulation of fine voluntary movements in the frontal, sensations from the musculature in a band in front of the central sulcus, sensations from the skin in a band behind this sulcus, and so on.

If the brain is sliced in half, separating the two cerebral hemispheres (Figure 16.2), additional important features can be seen. The gray matter of the cerebral cortex does not extend throughout the interior of the brain. Much of the interior is *white matter* and is made up of large tracts or bundles of myelinated (sheathed) fibers which connect cell bodies in the cortex with those in the spinal cord and in other centers lower in the brain. These centers are additional pockets of gray matter, referred to as *nuclei*. Some cortical cells project their long fibers or axons to motor neurons in the spinal cord, but others project them only as far as these clusters of connecting interneuron cell bodies. Four masses are deep within each hemisphere, called collectively the *basal ganglia*, and other important areas and structures of the brain also contain nuclei. The nuclei serve both as way stations, connecting tracts from the cortex with other ascending and descending tracts, and as integrating motor and sensory control centers.

In Figure 16.2 are shown four important functional areas or structures.

1. The *diencephalon*, connected in front with the hemispheres and behind with the midbrain, contains the *thalamus* and the *hypothalamus*. The thalamus is a relay station for all sensory pathways except the olfactory. Its nuclei receive nearly all impulses arriving from the different sensory areas of the body before passing them on to the cerebrum, where they are interpreted as conscious sensations. The hypothalamus is the highest center of integration for many visceral processes. Its nuclei regulate metabolism, temperature, water balance, sweating, blood pressure, sleeping, and appetite.

2. The *midbrain* is a mass of nerve fiber tracts connecting the cerebral cortex with the pons, the medulla oblongata, the cerebellum, and the spinal cord.

3. The *brainstem* is made up of the *pons* and *medulla oblongata* and functions primarily as a neural relay station. The pons contains tracts that connect the cerebellum with the spinal cord and the cerebellum with motor areas of the cerebrum. The medulla oblongata serves as the main line of traffic for the spinal cord tracts ascending to or descending from the higher centers of the brain. It also contains nuclei that maintain the regular life

rhythms of the heartbeat, of the diaphragm, and of the constricting and dilating blood vessels. In the core of the brainstem is the *reticular formation,* sometimes called the reticular activating system because of the important role that it plays in arousal and in the maintenance of alertness. The tracts of the pons and medulla send in fibers to connect with the profusely interconnected cells of the reticular formation, which in turn send fibers to the cortex, the basal ganglia, the hypothalamus, the septal area, and the cerebellum.

4. The *cerebellum,* like the cerebrum, is made up for the most part of two deeply convoluted hemispheres with an exterior cortex of gray matter and an interior of white tracts. The cerebellum receives sensory nerves from the vestibular apparatus of the ear and from muscles, tendons, and joints. The information received and integrated relates to balance and posture and to the smooth coordination of the body when in motion.

A fifth important part of the brain, not shown in Figure 16.2, is the limbic system, lower parts of the cerebrum that developed earlier than did the mammalian cerebral cortex. It is made up of cortex that is phylogenetically older than the so-called neocortex that covers most of the hemispheres. The *juxallocortex,* which consists of four or five layers of neurons, surrounds the corpus callosum and the thalamus. The *allocortex,* with only three layers of neurons, makes up the hippocampus, the cortex of the septum, and parts of the lower temporal lobes that surround the amygdaloid nucleus (one of the basal ganglia) in each of these lobes and the under portions of the hippocampus. The limbic system controls the visceral and physical expression of emotion—quickened heartbeat and respiration, trembling, sweating, and alterations in facial expressions—and the expression of appetitive and motivational drives—hunger, thirst, mating, defense, attack, and flight.

flicted mother to her fetus. The first indication of the disorder is a small sore on the lips, genitals, or anus which appears after ten to twenty days and then in a few weeks disappears. Before the sore disappears, a diffuse, copper-colored rash may cover the body. Fatigue, headache, and fever may accompany the rash.[1] Thereafter no overt difficulties are evident for many years, but during this period spirochetes may be invading the lymph glands, the bone marrow, and other tissues and organs of the body. Damage usually becomes observable when the individual is in his forties or fifties and the spirochetes have either invaded the walls of the heart, causing a heart attack, or penetrated neural tissue. The disorder is called general paresis when brain tissue is destroyed.

In the advanced stage of general paresis, the major symptoms are irritability, fatigue, depression, and some cognitive impairments. Later, deterioration becomes severe and diffuse; emotions are poorly controlled. Some patients have absurd and expansive delusions of grandeur.

Physical and neurological symptoms are variable. Headache, weight loss, and loss of tone in the facial muscles are frequent signs. Disturbances in the eyes are almost universal; in one such disturbance, the so-called Argyll-Robertson sign, the pupil responds normally to changes in distance, contracting properly for near vision, but does not contract for light. Loss of control of the voluntary musculature may be evidenced in tremors of the eyelids, lips, facial muscles, and fingers, mispronunciation and slurring of words, deterioration of handwriting, and a shuffling gait.

The two following cases illustrate the wide variety of symptoms.

[1] Unfortunately these early signs do not always occur, making detection of the disease difficult. For this reason blood tests are recommended if there is any suspicion of venereal disease.

A woman of twenty-six was brought to the hospital because she had become lost when she attempted to return home from a neighboring grocery store. About seven months before the patient's admission, her husband noticed that she was becoming careless of her personal appearance and neglectful of her household duties. She often forgot to prepare the family meals, or, in an apparent preoccupation, would burn the food. She seemed to have little appreciation of time and would not realize when to get up or go to bed. The patient would sit idly about the house, staring uncomprehendingly into space.

At the hospital the patient entered the admission office with an unsteady gait. There, by way of greeting, the physician inquired, "How are you today?" to which she replied in a monotonous, tremulous tone, "N-yes-s, I was-s op-er-a-ted on for pen-pendici-ci-tis." She never made any spontaneous remarks and when, a few days after her admission, she was asked if she were sad or happy, she stared vacantly at the physician, and, with a fatuous smile, answered, "Yeah." The patient sat about the ward for hours, taking no interest in its activities. Sometimes she would hold a book in her lap, aimlessly turning the pages, never reading but often pointing out pictures like a small child and showing satisfaction when she found a new one to demonstrate. Neurological examination showed dilated pupils that reacted but slightly to light on convergence. There was a tremor of lips and facial muscles on attempting to speak. The protruded tongue showed a coarse tremor.

*   *   *

M., aged forty-one, a roofing salesman, was transferred to a state hospital from the jail to which he had been sentenced for violation of the motor vehical laws. The [early] symptoms of the patient's oncoming disease were apparently slight. The informant, his sister, who had seen him but infrequently, stated that she had not noticed any change in him except that for a year he had seemed somewhat "worried." While driving his car, he disregarded the collector at a toll bridge and drove across the structure at high speed. When overtaken by a police officer, the patient was found to have no license to drive an automobile, the permit having been revoked several years previously. Three days later, while awaiting trial for this offense, he was again arrested for driving an automobile without a license. He was given a short sentence in jail, where a physician soon recognized the patient's disorder and had him committed to the hospital.

On arrival at the admission office of the hospital, he told the office attendant that he was going to give her a million dollars because she was "a nice lady." As he was being questioned for the usual admission data, he began to boast of his wealth, claiming that he had three automobiles, thousands of dollars in the bank, a "diamond watch," and much other valuable jewelry. His son, he said, was lieutenant governor of the state, was soon to be governor, and later would be president of the United States. After having expressed various absurdly grandiose plans, he added, "I have another plan, too. I'm going to the wardens of the prisons in this state and all the other states and I'm going to buy the prisoners. I'll have an agreement with the warden to take their prisoners and put them to work on farms, and I'll charge each prisoner $300 for doing it and for getting him out of jail. I made $105,000 with prisoners just last week, and when I get going, I'm going to make plenty of money" (Kolb, 1968, pp. 237–238).

Two types of neurosyphilis are often distinguished, meningoencephalitic syphilis, in which the primary damage is to the brain, and meningovascular, in which the primary damage is to the surrounding membrane and blood vessels of the brain rather than to the neural tissue itself. In meningoencephalitis two processes, inflammation and degeneration, begin in the frontal region and spread as the disease progresses. Because of general atrophy in the cerebral cortex, the sulci are widened and the brain actually shrinks in size. Scar cells multiply and blood vessels are kept from functioning. Even to the naked eye such a brain appears "moth-eaten" (Figure 16.4, on color plate). Meningovascular syphilis is usually categorized into additional types, depending on what location is primarily affected. Fortunately, neurosyphilis is not an inevitable result of exposure to *Treponema pallidum*. The disease develops in only about 5 percent of untreated syphilitics; in other cases the spirochetes are eliminated by an immune process not yet understood.

Brain Disorders Caused by Trauma

Traumatic brain injury may take one of three forms—concussions, contusions, and lacerations. There is some degree of hemorrhaging with almost any head injury, for ruptures occur in the tiny blood vessels in the area affected. In very severe injuries blood vessels may rupture throughout the brain.

Concussion. If the injury is a concussion, loss of consciousness is temporary, from several minutes to a few hours. A blow that forces the head to move abruptly, such as a knockout punch in boxing, jars the brain and disrupts circulatory and other functions momentarily. On regaining consciousness the individual is typically somewhat disoriented and may not remember events immediately preceding the insult. Some of the effects—nausea, dizziness, headache, confusion, and inability to concentrate—may persist for several weeks. There is, however, no permanent damage.

Contusion. Contusions are bruises of the neural tissue. The blow to the head is so severe that the brain, normally held in a fixed position, shifts and is compressed against the opposite side of the skull. The surface of the brain is actually bruised by being pushed against bone. The resulting coma may last several hours or even days, followed sometimes by a period of delirium. After consciousness is regained, behavior is generally similar to that after a concussion except that the disorientation is more severe. The injured person may be unable to speak or may go into convulsions. He is likely to suffer severe headaches and become irritable, being especially sensitive to noise and light. The contusion shown in Figure 16.5 (on color plate) is ample indication of how a series of severe blows to the head can eventually lead to a brain syndrome called "punch-drunkenness." Areas of brain tissue become permanently damaged by the accumulation of injuries; the individual cannot pay attention or concentrate, and memory as well as motor functions are disturbed. He speaks as though he were slightly drunk. Emotions are unstable and poorly controlled; intellectual impairment is sometimes profound.

Laceration. When an object actually enters the skull and pierces, ruptures, or tears brain tissue, the injury is called a laceration. The effect of the injury of course varies with the site of the brain tissue destroyed and the extent of the damage. The injured person is likely to lose consciousness immediately; sometimes coma and death follow. If the individual does survive, his intellect may be impaired and parts of his body may be paralyzed. The personality sometimes changes, and several years later he may develop epilepsy. But if the damage, although extensive, is not in a strategic location and if the patient's personality is well integrated, chances for recovery with adequate function are good.

A famous historical case, a remarkable survival after a brain laceration which must surely have destroyed thousands of neurons and which wreaked profound psychological changes, was reported by Dr. J. M. Harlow in 1968.

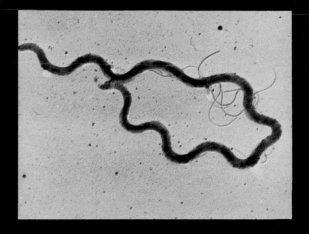

FIGURE **16.3**

The syphilitic spirochete, Treponema pallidum, *is transmitted from an already infected person by sexual intercourse or oral-genital contact.*

FIGURE **16.4**

The effects of neurosyphilis (general paresis) shown in horizontal section of the cerebrum. The diffuse atrophy of the convolutions of the cortex and of the associated white matter is evident, especially in the frontal lobes.

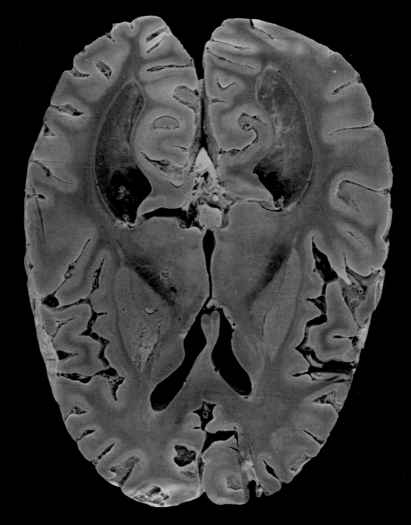

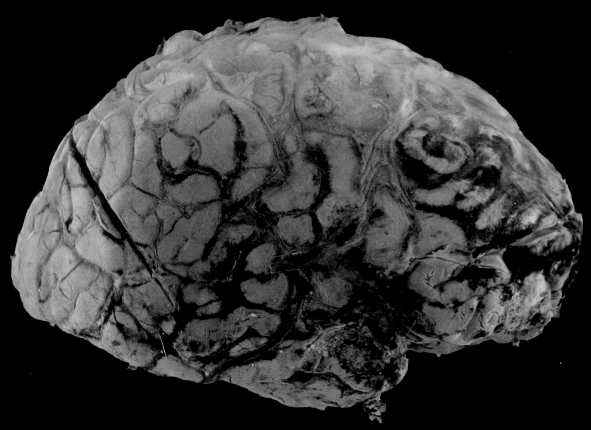

FIGURE 16.7
Surface of the right cerebral hemisphere showing multiple areas of hemorrhage after a skull fracture.

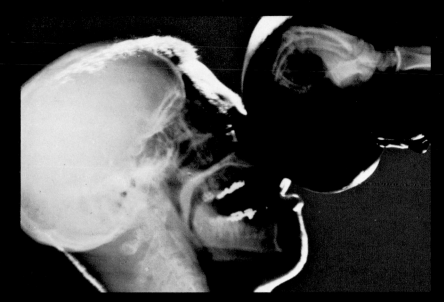

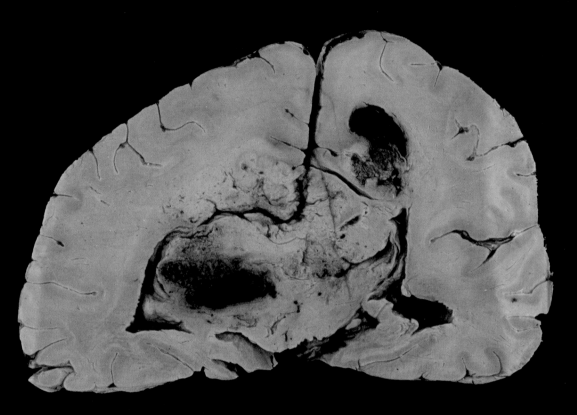

FIGURE **16.8**
Cross section of the cerebrum showing a malignant tumor extending from one hemisphere to the other through the corpus callosum. The gyri are noticeably flattened and the sulci narrowed.

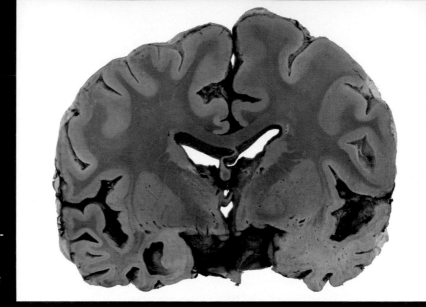

FIGURE **16.9**
The diffuse cortical atrophy associated with Alzheimer's disease, one of the presenile dementias, is shown in this cross section of the cerebrum.

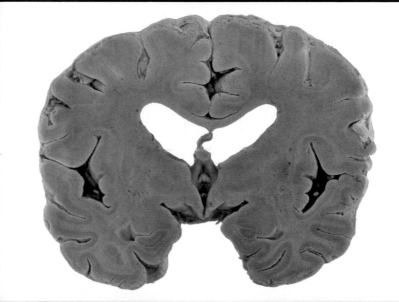

FIGURE **16.10**
In Huntington's chorea, a presenile dementia, the interior cavities (ventricles) are enlarged through atrophy of the brain, especially of the caudate nucleus, a basal ganglion forming part of the floor of the lateral ventricle in each hemisphere.

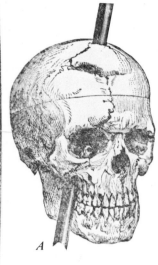

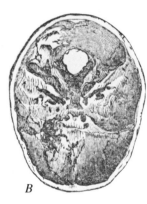

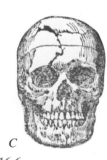

FIGURE 16.6

(A) A view of Gage's skull showing where the tamping iron entered; (B) an upward view from inside the skull, showing the size of the hole and some new bone partially covering it; and (C) comparative sizes of the tamping iron and Gage's cranium through which it passed.

The accident occurred in Cavendish, Vt., on the line of the Rutland and Burlington Railroad, at that time being built, on the 13th of September, 1848, and was occasioned by the premature explosion of a blast, when this iron, known to blasters as a tamping iron . . . was shot through the face and head.

The subject of it was Phineas P. Gage, a perfectly healthy, strong and active young man, twenty-five years of age . . . Gage was foreman of a gang of men employed in excavating rock, for the road way. . . .

The missile entered by its pointed end, the left side of the face, immediately anterior to [in front of] the angle of the lower jaw, and passing obliquely upwards, and obliquely backwards, emerged in the median line, at the back part of the frontal bone, near the coronal suture. . . . The iron which thus traversed the head, is round and rendered comparatively smooth by use, and is three feet seven inches in length, one and one fourth inches in its largest diameter, and weighs thirteen and one fourth pounds. . . .

The patient was thrown upon his back by the explosion, and gave a few convulsive motions of the extremities, but spoke in a few minutes. His men (with whom he was a great favorite) took him in their arms and carried him to the road, only a few rods distant, and put him into an ox cart, in which he rode, supported in a sitting posture, fully three quarters of a mile to his hotel. He got out of the cart himself, with little assistance from his men, and an hour afterwards (with what I could aid him by taking hold of his left arm) walked up a long flight of stairs, and got upon the bed in the room where he was dressed. He seemed perfectly conscious, but was becoming exhausted from the hemorrhage, which by this time, was quite profuse, the blood pouring from the lacerated sinus in the top of his head, and also finding its way into the stomach, which ejected it as often as every fifteen or twenty minutes. He bore his sufferings with firmness, and directed my attention to the hole in his cheek, saying, "The iron entered there and passed through my head" (pp. 330, 331, 332).

[Dr. Harlow illustrated his report with several drawings of how he imagined Gage's skull to be penetrated (Figure 16.6). He also described how the injury later affected Gage's behavior.] His physical health is good, and I am inclined to say that he has recovered. Has no pain in head, but says it has a queer feeling which he is not able to describe. Applied for his situation as foreman, but is undecided whether to work or travel. His contractors, who regarded him as the most efficient and capable foreman in their employ previous to his injury considered the change in his mind so marked that they could not give him his place again. The equilibrium or balance, so to speak, between his intellectual faculties and animal propensities, seems to have been destroyed. He is fitful, irreverent, indulging at times in the grossest profanity (which was not previously his custom), manifesting but little deference for his fellows, impatient of restraint or advice when it conflicts with his desires, at times pertinaciously obstinate, yet capricious and vascillating, devising many plans for future operations, which are no sooner arranged than they are abandoned in turn for others. . . . his mind is radically changed, so decidedly that his friends and acquaintances said he was "no longer Gage" (pp. 339–340).

Nutritional Deficiencies Producing Brain Dysfunction

Korsakoff's Psychosis

The primary symptoms of Korsakoff's psychosis are *anterograde* amnesia, a loss of memory for events that have just occurred, and *confabulation,* a filling in of these memory gaps with obviously false material. Shortly after dinner a patient with Korsakoff's psychosis may be asked what he had for the evening meal. Unable to recall the details, he quickly provides a description of an imaginary meal. It often happens, however, that such descriptions are patently false. A patient in a mental institution may state that he has just finished a meal of Beef Wellington with a delightful sauce containing truffles, apparently not recognizing the extreme improbability of being served such a meal in a mental hospital. Patients with Korsakoff's psychosis are usually lucid and friendly, yet they lack judgment, being unaware of the implausibility of the stories they tell and only poorly planning other aspects of their lives. They may become apathetic and sometimes grossly confused and severely disoriented.

Although tumors, trauma, and vascular changes have been noted as causes, the factor that most often brings on Korsakoff's psy-

chosis is a nutritional deficiency (Brion, 1969). Alcoholics who have not eaten properly for many years may develop the psychosis. Autopsy reveals lesions in the thalamus, the pons, the cerebellum, and in the mammillary bodies, small rounded structures which are located in the hypothalamus and which contain nuclei. The physiological damage produced by vitamin B deficiency and underlying Korsakoff's psychosis is referred to as Wernicke's disease (Adams, 1969). The psychosis is not inevitable with this pattern of brain damage, however, for the behavioral symptoms do not always appear.

Beriberi and Pellagra

A deficiency in thiamine, also known as vitamin B_1, damages the peripheral nerves and may change behavior. This deficiency, referred to as *beriberi,* used to plague the Far East, where polished rice was eaten. The patient with beriberi suffers from irritability, fatigue, and insomnia, weakened muscles, and extreme lassitude. *Pellagra,* a deficiency in niacin, is common where corn constitutes a large portion of the diet. At one time pellagra accounted for many admissions to mental hospitals in the southern United States, for pork and cornmeal were the mainstays of the day's principal meal. Now, with better nutrition, the syndrome has become rare. The physical symptoms are diarrhea and a reddening of the skin on the neck and the backs of the hands, the psychological symptoms depression, irritability, loss of recent memory, and difficulties in concentration. Untreated, the patient may become delirious and have hallucinations and other psychotic symptoms. Syndromes caused by vitamin deficiencies are treated with a protein- and vitamin-enriched diet. Except in severe and very advanced cases, good results can be expected.

Cerebrovascular Accidents and Brain Tumors

Cerebral Thrombosis and Hemorrhage

The blood vessels supplying the brain may be subject to malfunction. In *cerebral thrombosis* a blood clot forms and suddenly blocks circulation in the brain. Frequently arteriosclerosis (see page 423) has previously narrowed the space within cerebral blood vessels, making it impossible for the clot to pass. Carbon dioxide builds up and damages the neural tissues. The patient may die, suffer paralysis of half his body or of an arm or a leg, or lose other motor and sensory functions.

Another frequent impairment is *aphasia,* a disturbance of the ability to use words. The initiator of this damage may be a clot in the middle cerebral artery supplying the parieto-temporal region of the dominant cerebral hemisphere. A right-handed person depends on the parietotemporal region in his left hemisphere for his language skills, a left-handed person depends on this region in his right. Interestingly, damage to the right hemisphere in a right-handed person and to the left in a left-handed person will not disturb ability to use language.

Aphasia is generally divided into two types, receptive or sensory and motor. In sensory aphasias the individual has difficulty in understanding the meaning of words. He may have auditory aphasia and not understand the words spoken to him or visual aphasia and not understand the printed word. He will, however, be able to speak properly; and he may, for example, be able to read but not understand spoken speech, or he may understand spoken speech but not be able to read. With motor aphasia a person has problems in speaking words or sentences but suffers no deficit in comprehension.

In *cerebral hemorrhage* a blood vessel ruptures because of a weakness in its wall, damaging the brain tissue on which its blood spills. The psychological disturbance produced depends on the size of the vessel that has ruptured and on the extent and location of the damage. When a large vessel ruptures, the person suffers a major stroke. All functions of the brain are generally disturbed—speech, memory, reasoning, orientation, and balance. The person usually lapses into a coma and may die within two to fourteen days. If he survives he will probably have some paralysis and difficulties with speech and memory, although in some cases appropriate rehabilitation restores nearly normal functioning. Figure 16.7 (on color plate) shows the many areas of hemorrhaging on the surface of the right cerebral hemisphere after a skull fracture.

Brain Tumor

A *brain tumor* or neoplasm is an abnormal growth which can produce a wide variety of psychological symptoms as well as physical ones.

Tumors can be subclassified as either malignant or benign. Malignant growths interfere directly with neural functioning by destroying the original brain tissue from which they started to grow. Benign tumors do not destroy tissue but may as they grow increase intracranial pressure and thus disrupt the normal functioning of the brain. The clinical picture is highly variable, reflecting the size and location of the tumor, how fast it is growing, whether there is pressure, and whether brain tissue has been destroyed. Early physical symptoms are persistent headaches and vomiting. By looking into the eye through the pupil, a physician can detect a "choked disk" at the back of the retina. Intracranial pressure forces cerebrospinal fluid into the optic nerve. The area at the back of the retina where the nerve enters the eyeball, called the optic disk, becomes swollen and protrudes. The very first symptoms of a tumor that is located beneath the brainstem are sudden outbursts of emotion, inappropriate spells of laughing or crying which last for thirty to ninety seconds. Listlessness, depression, and a vague sense of anxiety may precede the physical symptoms of tumors located in other areas.

As the tumor continues to grow and intracranial pressure increases, vision may become double, reflexes may be impaired, and memory, attention, orientation for time and place, and reasoning are likely to be poor. Consciousness may seem to keep slipping away; there are often convulsive seizures and eventually stupor. The damage from a tumor in particular motor and sensory areas of the brain may produce localized disturbances of these functions. Coordination may be impaired, or the patient may have visual, olfactory, and auditory hallucinations. Tumors in the frontal, temporal, and parietal lobes may disturb the personality. The individual may be preoccupied and confused, depressed and irritable, and careless about dress, appearance, and work.

If either a benign or a malignant tumor continues to grow, the patient usually dies. Even if the tumor is removed, the functions that have been lost through the destruction of neural tissue do not return. A tumor extending from one hemisphere to the other through the corpus callosum is shown in Figure 16.8 (on color plate).

Degenerative Diseases

A large number of organic diseases appear to be correlated with advancing age. With the increased longevity of citizens in many modern societies, these problems of the later years are becoming much more prevalent than they once were.

Presenile Dementias

Rare forms of mental deterioration that begin when the individual is in his forties or fifties are referred to as presenile dementias. Alzheimer's disease, Pick's disease, Huntington's chorea, and Parkinson's disease are such disorders.

Alzheimer's Disease. Many of the characteristics of the presenile disorder Alzheimer's disease are illustrated in the following case history.

The first noticeable sign of difficulty was the fifty-one-year-old woman's jealousy toward her husband. Then a rapidly increasing loss of memory was observed. She could not find her way around her own apartment. Moreover, she sometimes thought that someone wanted to kill her and began shrieking loudly.

Her behavior in the institution reflected total perplexity, and she was disoriented in time and place. Periodically she was delirious— she dragged her bedding around, called her husband and her daughter, and seemed to have auditory hallucinations. She often shrieked for many hours.

Her ability to remember was severely disturbed. If one pointed to objects, she could name most of them correctly, but she forgot events immediately after they occurred. When reading she merged one line with another. When writing, she repeated some syllables and omitted others. When talking she used perplexing phrases and such . . . expressions as "milk-pourer" for "cup." She seemed no longer to understand the use of some objects. The generalized dementia continued. At the end, she was stuporous and laid in her bed with her legs drawn up under her.

Four and one-half years after the onset of the disease, the patient died (Wilkins and Brody, 1969, p. 110).

The brain tissue deteriorates rather rapidly in Alzheimer's disease, death usually occurring four or five years after the onset of symptoms. The disorder is three times more prevalent among women than among men. The disease was first described by the German neurologist Alois Alzheimer in 1860. It commences with difficulties in concentration; the individual appears absentminded and irritable, shortcomings which soon begin to interfere with the way he leads his life. He blames others for his own failings and has delusions that he is being persecuted. Memory continues to deteriorate, with the individual becoming increasingly disoriented and agitated.

The primary physiological changes in the brain, evident at autopsy, are senile plaques scattered throughout the cortex—small round areas in which tissue has degenerated into granular material and filaments—and tangled threadlike structures that have replaced normal nerve cells in the basal ganglia. Figure 16.9 (on color plate) shows the atrophy, or wasting away, in the convolutions of the cortex. The fissures widen and the ridges become narrower and flatter. Alzheimer's disease is probably *not* simply an early variant of senile dementia. It occurs much more abruptly and is distinguished by symptoms that are not notable in senile dementia, such as speech impairments, involuntary movements in the limbs, hyperactivity and agitation, and occasional convulsions, as well as by a much more rapid mental deterioration.

Pick's Disease. Another presenile disorder was first described by Arnold Pick, a Prague physician, in 1892. Pick's disease is a degenerative disorder of the central nervous system in which the frontal and temporal lobes atrophy. As the disease progresses, the deterioration becomes more and more pervasive. The total weight of the brain may be reduced to less than 1000 grams from the usual weight of about 1300 grams. As in Alzheimer's disease, the age of onset is generally in the forties and fifties, and the symptoms of the two disorders are also similar. The patient has difficulties with memory and in abstract thinking; he is confused and unable to concentrate and has transitory speech impairment; his affect may be blunted, and he is likely to be depressed and suspicious. The life expectancy after onset is usually four to seven years.

Huntington's Chorea. This degenerative disorder was first described by the American neurologist George Huntington in 1872, after his father and grandfather, both physicians, had observed the disease in several generations of a family. Symptoms usually begin when the individual is in his thirties and thereafter deterioration is progressive. The early behavioral signs are slovenliness, disregard for social convention, violent outbursts, depression, irritability, poor memory, euphoria, poor judgment, delusions, suicidal ideas and attempts, and hallucinations. The term chorea was applied to the disorder because of the patient's choreiform movements—involuntary, spasmodic jerking of the limbs, trunk, and head. These signs of neurological disturbance do not appear until after behavior has already started to deteriorate. Facial grimaces, a smacking of the lips and tongue, and explosive, often obscene speech are other symptoms. The afflicted individual is likely to have severe problems in speaking and walking. Eventually, there is a total loss of bodily control. Death is inevitable, but it may be delayed for ten to twenty years after the onset of the illness.

The following excerpts from the biography of the American folksinger Woody Guthrie illustrate the development of the disorder, some of the prominent clinical symptoms, and the personal tragedy of the illness.

[Describing the first signs, Woody's wife, Marjorie, commented] "What confused me, and Woody himself, in the early stage of the illness was that by nature he was a rather moody person. As early as 1948, we began to notice that he was more reflective, and often depressed by trivial things. . . . [Shortly thereafter] the symptoms of the disease had become more obvious. Woody developed a peculiar lopsided walk and his speech became explosive. He would take a deep sigh before breathing out the words. The moods and depressions became more exaggerated and more frequent. . . ." [In 1952 the first serious attack occurred. As his wife described it] "Woody had a violent outburst and foamed at the mouth." [He was hospitalized for three weeks and diagnosed as an alcoholic. After his release he had another violent seizure which, this time, led to a three-month hospitalization. Later] "the disease was making rapid progress. Woody found it increasingly difficult to control his movements, appearing to be drunk even when he wasn't drinking. Friends watched with apprehension as he dived into traffic, oblivious of danger, Chaplinlike, warding off each car as it sped toward him."

[Finally, in 1956, it was recognized that Guthrie had Huntington's chorea, and he spent his remaining years in hospitals. One incident related by his wife, which occurred shortly after his hospitalization, is especially poignant.] "In the early years of his stay in hospitals, Woody would leave every now and then on his own. One day he took the wrong bus and landed in some town in New Jersey. Noticing his disheveled appearance, his distraught air and halting gait, a policeman picked him up, took him to the local police station, and booked him on a vagrancy charge.

Woody told the police that he was not a homeless bum but a sick man. He explained that he was staying at a New York hospital and begged them to get him home. 'Well,' they said, 'if you're sick you can stay in our hospital.' Finally, they let him call me and I went tearing out to New Jersey.

When I arrived I was received by a staff doctor, a Viennese psychiatrist. 'Your husband is a very disturbed man,' he said imperiously, 'with many hallucinations. He says that he has written a thousand songs.'[2]

'It is true,' I said.

'He also says he has written a book.'

'That's also true.'

'He says that a record company has put out nine records of his songs!' The doctor's voice dripped disbelief.

'That is also the truth,' I said" (Yurchenco, 1970, pp. 139–148).

The disorder is a genetically determined one, passed on by a single dominant gene. The offspring of an individual with the disorder has a 50 percent chance of being afflicted. A postmortem examination of the brain of an individual with Huntington's chorea reveals widespread atrophy and scarring (Figure 16.10, on color plate). The major pathological change is a loss of neurons in one of the basal ganglia of each hemisphere. The cerebral cortex also atrophies, especially the frontal areas. Reduced levels of dopamine in the basal ganglia appear to be primarily responsible for the choreiform movements.

Parkinson's Disease. In 1817 James Parkinson described this disease which begins later in life, between the ages of fifty and seventy. The primary symptoms are severe muscular tremors, usually occurring at a rate of four to eight movements per second, which jerk the limbs, hands, neck, and face. Only muscles that are at rest are subject to tremors,

however, not those that are engaged in a coordinated movement. Other physiological effects include muscular rigidity, akinesia—an inability to initiate movements—and defects in balance. The face later becomes masklike and expressionless, the gait stiff and distinctive, with the upper part of the body moving forward ahead of the legs. The individual may have difficulty concentrating, become apathetic, and withdraw from social contact. About 90 percent of patients with Parkinson's disease are depressed, and in 30 percent intellectual deterioration is evident (DeJong and Sugar, 1971).

The etiology of the disorder varies. It is at times attributable to arteriosclerosis; other cases are the aftereffects of encephalitis. The basic brain pathology is a loss of the deeply pigmented nerve cells in the substantia nigra, a nucleus within the midbrain which is an important motor relay station. Figure 16.11 illustrates the difference between a normal and a Parkinsonian midbrain. The neurons in the substantia nigra that are destroyed are those that contain dopamine, the precursor of nor-

---

[2] In addition to misdiagnosing Mr. Guthrie, the physician had confused the concepts of delusion and hallucination.

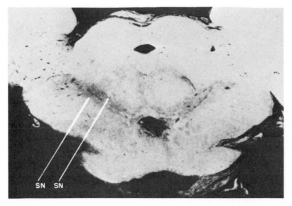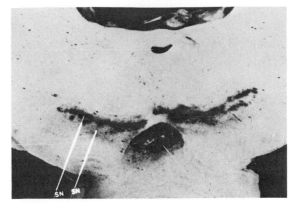

FIGURE **16.11**

Parkinson's disease, a presenile dementia marked by uncontrollable muscle tremors, is associated with a depigmentation of the substantia nigra, the major nucleus in the midbrain. The photograph on the left shows a normally pigmented substantia nigra, that on the right the same structure in the brain of a person with Parkinson's disease.

epinephrine, the neurotransmitter of the sympathetic nervous system. A reduced number of these cells means that the dopamine levels of the corpus striatum, a group of basal ganglia, are reduced. Norepinephrine cannot be formed, leaving unopposed the action of the cholinergic neurons of the nervous system, those that are activated by acetylcholine. With the cholinergic neurons unchecked by the presence of norepinephrine, too many of them fire, producing the uncontrollable muscular tremors. Parkinsonism can be treated either by the administration of anticholinergic drugs to reduce the action of the cholinergic neurons, or by giving the patient a precursor of dopamine, L-dopa.

Senile Dementia

In senile dementia there is a gradual deterioration in functioning. The individual may first be somewhat careless in personal hygiene and grooming and surprise those who know him with impulsive bursts of unexpected or unusual behavior. Gradually, memory impairment, especially for recent events, a lessening of alertness, incoherence, disorientation, and an intolerance for change mar the mind. The patient is increasingly out of contact with social reality; he reminisces and his interests narrow to himself and little else. He may be easily irritated and weep readily. Some patients become incontinent and are eventually grossly psychotic.

The patient had been widowed at the age of fifty and thereafter lived with one or another of her five children. She had always been easy going, happy, and contented. Although she liked things to be neat and tidy, she was not exceptionally meticulous or compulsive. All her life she had been physically active and had an excellent memory. The first indication of difficulty came in her late sixties when she lost some money that had been given to her. Soon thereafter she set out to visit one of her children but lost her way and needed police assistance. After this incident she was observed to lose her former

422   ORGANIC SYNDROMES

interest in reading, writing letters and knitting. During most of the year preceding hospitalization she was unable to recognize her children and frequently her conversation was unintelligible. She ate without assistance but had to be dressed, undressed, and taken to the toilet to avoid incontinence.

Consistent with her life-long personality traits, her manner in the hospital was pleasant and cooperative. However, her comprehension and social behavior were grossly impaired. She walked down the corridor with her arm around a physician's waist and tickled his ribs. She misinterpreted everyday situations: when given her first bath in the hospital she said, "I don't want to get in the boat—the current is too swift." Her stream of talk rambled. The following is a verbatim sample: "While it is not so bad in the morning—that girl was over and she was saying that there was nothing better than the bottom ones, and the cows and the calves were off and she was making out that . . . [unintelligible] . . . but I made out I never heard her. When they go out—you see—they don't bother taking the boxes. They just take everything with them." Her memory for both recent and remote events was close to zero. She was able to give her name correctly but when asked her age said, "I am twenty-one to twenty-two anyway, every minute." She could not give her birthday, year of her birth, or any information about her previous life. Six months after admission, she died of pneumonia, a frequent cause of death in senile patients (Rosen, Fox, and Gregory, p. 330).

Postmortem examinations reveal generalized brain atrophy, especially in the frontal lobes. The brain itself is smaller, having fewer cells; the cortical convolutions are narrower and the fissures between them wider. Senile plaques are scattered throughout the cortex. These changes may be the simple process of aging, whereby cells decay, or they may be the cumulative effects of the toxic processes—carbon monoxide, alcohol, minor strokes—to which a person is exposed in his life-span.

Of course, not all individuals who enjoy a long life become psychotic in their last years. Why is this so, for all brains are known to deteriorate to a certain extent in old age? Social isolation may be important. Williams and Jaco (1958), for example, found that a married person of age sixty is only a third as likely to develop a disorder of aging as are those whose spouses have died. Furthermore, more women than men develop these disorders, perhaps because women typically outlive their husbands by about five years and are socially isolated during this period of widowhood. A genetic factor may also be involved. Kallmann (1950) examined concordance rates for senile psychosis in monozygotic and dizygotic twins. The age-corrected concordance rate was found to be 43 percent among the monozygotic twins and only 7 percent among dizygotic twins.

Cerebral Arteriosclerosis

The onset of cerebral arteriosclerosis may be gradual or follow suddenly after a cerebrovascular accident such as a stroke. When the disease begins gradually, the first symptoms are often fatigue, headache, dizziness, and an inability to concentrate. Later memory deteriorates, affect becomes labile, and there is a decline in personal hygiene. With sudden onset an initial period of rather great confusion is typical. Individuals suffering from cerebral arteriosclerosis show less deterioration in functioning than individuals with senile psychosis and have more "up" periods during which their symptoms abate. Many of these aspects of the disorder are illustrated in the following case.

W. B., aged sixty-six, a bookkeeper by occupation, was admitted to the hospital when he suddenly suffered from an attack of vertigo and severe headache lasting for about twenty minutes. He then resumed his daily tasks although he felt weak and tired. On the following day, "for no reason that he can explain, as he claims he was not dizzy," his brother reported, "he just lost his balance and fell downstairs." He was then referred to the hospital for study and diagnosis.

The patient's brother added that eighteen months previous to this episode the patient first showed a change in behavior. He talked much less and "would often sit and look at absolutely nothing for long periods. For the past year he had been saying rather peculiar things. He became silly, flighty, and confused." While in the general hospital to which he had been admitted, he was constantly worrying over loss of his money, although there was no basis for such a belief. The brother described the patient's behavior in the general hospital as follows: "He was very confused. He would not remain in bed, and instead of getting out of the side of the bed, he would crawl over its foot and get out." . . . When asked the dates when he became ill, he maintained that he had not been ill. He gave his age, his birth year, and the current year correctly, but when asked the present date he replied, "The New York Giants won the first game, Brooklyn won the second game, and the third game was going home when I went." A month after admission he conversed freely and usually rationally with other patients and showed concern about the condition of the feeble ones. He continued, however, to manifest difficulty in concentration, in apperception, and in memory for recent events. He was then fully oriented as to time and place and recognized that his memory was impaired. He remarked to his physician, "I don't know. If I have to keep on this way, maybe the good Lord ought to take me." Four months after admission he was described as having periods of memory loss. Although the United States was then intently preoccupied with World War II, he took no interest in the world situation and important events. At times he showed difficulty in choosing the proper word and occasionally became quite irritated at himself for having this difficulty. Although he had completed three years of college, he was unable to answer simple mathematical questions and failed in an attempt to subtract from 100 by using 7 as the subtrahend and the successive differences as the minuend. Under the simple routine of hospital life and freedom from responsibility, the patient improved. Five and a half years after admission he was described as discussing his business affairs intelligently and as showing an interest in hospital activities and as being well informed on current events. Three years later there developed periods of twenty-four-hour duration during which he became excited, screamed at anyone who approached him, and often became quite threatening, although he never did violence to them. At such times he was somewhat confused (Kolb, 1968, pp. 246–247).

The symptoms are produced by a narrowing or obstruction of the blood vessels of the brain with fatty deposits, reducing or cutting off the supply of blood (Figure 16.12). In addition to the psychological effects already described, there may be blackouts, cardiac difficulties, kidney failure, and hypertension. Evidence indicates that genetic factors figure to some degree in cerebral arteriosclerosis (Kallmann and Jarvik, 1961).

Toxic Agents and Endocrine Dysfunctions

Toxic Substances

Brain dysfunctions can be produced by the ingestion of a variety of toxic substances such as drugs, gases, and heavy metals. Difficulties in concentration, disorientation, emotional instability, hyperactivity, and psychotic delusions and hallucinations are common symptoms. In Chapter 10 the effects of alcohol and other drugs on behavior were discussed; here it need be noted only that the affective, behavioral, and cognitive difficulties associated with drugs can be considered brain syndromes.

Other toxic agents such as lead, mercury, manganese, carbon monoxide, and carbon disulfide can seriously impair brain functioning. With excessive intake of lead, fluid accumulates in the brain, increasing intracranial pressure. Employees of manufacturing plants in which lead is used may suffer severe lead poisoning. They may hallucinate, become delirious, especially at night, and be subject to convulsions. Children who suffer from lead poisoning may become mentally retarded, a pressing problem in ghetto areas where young children are likely to eat the crumbling plaster and old paint that have fallen from the walls. Both are lead-based and can induce a toxic state. Children who chew on old toys and furniture painted with lead-based paints may also ingest too much of the poison.

Most mercury and manganese poisonings are the aftermath of accidents that occur in the industrial use of these metals. The first signs that too much mercury has been ingested are irritability, memory loss, and difficulties in concentration. Later the individual experiences impairments in hearing and speaking. Tunnel vision restricts his visual field to centrally located objects, and coordination becomes poor. In severe cases paralysis and death follow. Manganese poisoning impairs the brain and spinal cord. The gait and speech are affected, and the patient is restless and emotionally upset.

FIGURE **16.12**
(A) *A normal artery; (B) an artery whose inner space has been narrowed by a buildup of fatty deposits; and (C) a narrowed artery blocked by a blood clot.*

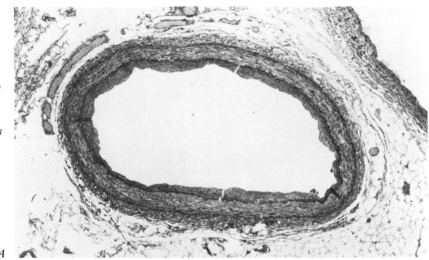

A

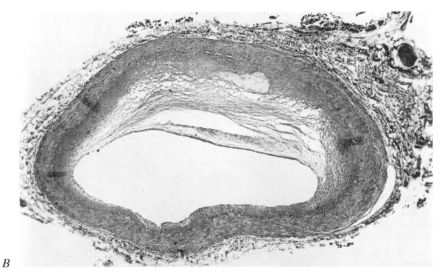

B

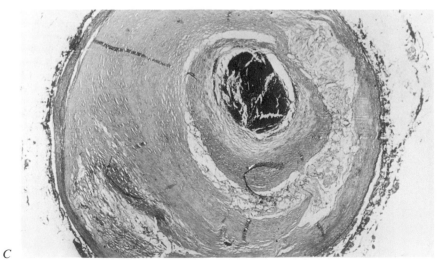

C

Endocrine Disturbances

Endocrine glands secrete their hormones directly into the bloodstream. Thus these powerful substances are delivered to nearly every cell in the body, including the neurons of the brain. Either oversecretions or undersecretions of the thyroid gland may bring on behavioral problems. In hyperthyroidism or *Graves' disease,* described by an Irish physician, Robert Graves, in the first part of the nineteenth century, an oversecretion of the hormone thyroxin speeds up metabolic processes, inducing a state of apprehension, restlessness, and irritability. Thinking proceeds at a rapid pace and may become confused in the process. About 20 percent of hyperthyroid patients may have transitory delusions and hallucinations. Hypothyroidism, which brings on a condition called *myxedema* in adults, is a deficiency in thyroid hormone. Metabolic processes are slowed down and so too are speech and thinking. The individual has poor emotional control and suffers from fatigue. He moves as little as possible and lacks interest in what is going on about him. As the disorder progresses, the skin becomes dry and brittle, and hair is lost from the eyebrows and the genital area. In severe cases depression may be deep enough to be considered psychotic. In children the disorder causes mental retardation (see Chapter 17). Fortunately, hypothyroidism is a very rare condition today, for the iodine of iodized salt prevents it.

The *adrenal cortex* is centrally involved in the activation of emergency biological responses and the energy needs of the human organism. Thus it is not surprising that a malfunction of the adrenals can cause an organic syndrome. A chronic insufficiency of cortisone secretion by the adrenal cortex produces *Addison's disease,* first described by the English physician Thomas Addison. The patient loses weight, suffers from low blood pressure, and is easily fatigued; his skin also darkens. He may be moderately depressed and become less sociable and ambitious. When abnormal growths on the cortices of the adrenal glands make them secrete too much cortisone, the condition produced is called *Cushing's syndrome.* Harvey Cushing, the American brain surgeon, described this disease. The afflicted individual has severe mood swings, none of them pleasant. He is most often depressed but may then become anxious, agitated, and irritable. Physical changes, some quite disfiguring ones—such as obesity, muscle wasting, changes in skin color and texture, and spinal deformity—can also occur.

EPILEPSY

We turn now to one of the brain syndromes defined by symptomatology rather than etiology. The incidence of epilepsy in the United States has been reported to be 29.8 cases per 100,000 people of the general population, with a slightly higher rate among males than females (Ervin, 1967). Epilepsy is not easily defined. One definition might state that epilepsy is a group of convulsive disorders brought on by pathology of the central nervous system. Certainly, the lay conception of epilepsy involves the notion of convulsion. In the neurology literature, however, forms of epilepsy in which no convulsion occurs are described. The definition must therefore refer to altered states of consciousness accompanied by sudden changes in the usual rhythmical electrical activity of the brain. In terms of neural functioning, epileptics are best regarded as representing one end of a continuum. They are individuals in whom a wide variety of circumstances can elicit a seizure or a sudden increase in brain activity. At the other end of the continuum are those in whom seizures or sudden discharging of neurons can be induced only by very unusual stimuli, such as the current used in electroconvulsive therapy.

For many years epileptics have carried the additional burden of being regarded as insane, mentally retarded, and, in general, emotionally unstable. These negative judgments are unsupported, except for some cases of psychomotor epilepsy (see page 430). The brains of epileptics do unquestionably function abnormally on occasion. Moreover, during a seizure the epileptic is obviously not behaving normally. Between seizures, and this fortunately accounts for most of the time, the psychological functioning of epileptics is usually fine.

A variety of conditions can precipitate an epileptic attack. First, a number of agents predispose a neuron to discharge, for example, strychnine poisoning and a low blood sugar level or hypoglycemia. Second, an attack may be triggered by external stimuli such as flashing lights or particular musical notes. Or brain diseases such as multiple sclerosis, tumors, and encephalitis may predispose neurons to discharge more readily. Finally, epileptic attacks can be brought on by stress and emotional difficulties (Smith, 1965).

Convulsions are generated by a massive discharge of groups of neurons. At first the discharge may be localized, but if it spreads the body is seized with the so-called grand mal convulsion. The areas involved in the spread of the discharge function as they would under normal conditions of stimulation: if the discharge spreads across visual areas, for example, the individual will have visual sensa-tions during his seizure. The following is a phenomenological description of a seizure, cast in an uncommonly favorable light.

The air was filled with a big noise and I thought it had engulfed me. I have really touched God. He came into me myself. Yes God exists, I cried, and I don't remember anything else. You all, healthy people, he said, can't imagine the happiness which we epileptics feel during the second before our fit. Mahomet, in his Koran, said he had seen paradise and had gone into it. All these stupid clever men are quite sure he was a liar and a charlatan. But no, he did not lie. He really had been in paradise during an attack of epilepsy; he was a victim of this disease like I was. I don't know if this felicity lasts for seconds, hours, or months, but believe me, for all the joys that life may bring, I would not exchange this one (Dostoyevsky, 1868).

Epilepsy is usually classified into four types.

1. **Grand mal** (great illness). The grand mal attack, the most severe form of seizure, is usually described as consisting of four phases. The *aura* is considered a signal or warning of the impending convulsion. It may take the form of dizziness, fear, or an unusual sensory experience such as ringing in the ears or a peculiar odor. The aura, the Latin word for breeze, usually precedes the "storm" of neuron discharge by a few moments, but the epileptic may have just enough time to sit or lie down. In the *tonic phase,* the beginning of the actual seizure, the muscles of the body suddenly become rigid. The patient loses consciousness and falls heavily to the ground if he has not been able to prepare for the attack. The trunk

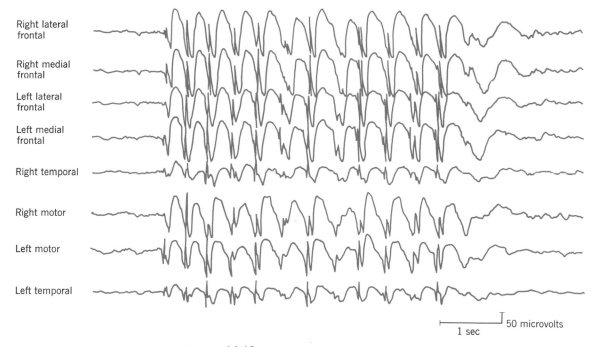

Right lateral
frontal

Right medial
frontal

Left lateral
frontal

Left medial
frontal

Right temporal

Right motor

Left motor

Left temporal

1 sec   50 microvolts

FIGURE **16.13**
Electroencephalograms taken during a short petit mal attack. Electrical
activity increases at all the recording sites.

and arms are extended, the legs out-
stretched; the eyes are open and pupils
dilated; corneal and light reflexes are absent. During this part of the convulsion
breathing is suspended and the face darkens. But then after nearly a minute the muscular tension gives way to the spasms of
the *clonic phase,* which lasts another one or
several minutes. Now the muscles contract
and relax, producing violent contortions and
jerking movements of the limbs. Breathing
resumes. The jaws also open and close, and
saliva collects on the lips. During this phase
the individual can bite his tongue and lose
sphincter control. Eventually, as the convulsive movements dissipate, the epileptic
seizure passes from the clonic phase into
coma. The individual remains unconscious
and the muscles relax. Upon awakening,

perhaps almost immediately or only after
several hours, the individual has no memory
of what happened after the beginning of the
tonic phase.

2. *Petit mal.* In a milder and briefer form of
epilepsy, the petit mal attack, there is
neither an aura nor a convulsion. Petit mal,
more frequent in children and rare after
twenty years of age, is only a momentary
disturbance or alteration of consciousness.
The person stops what he is doing and his
eyes roll up. There may be a few twitches
of the eye and face muscles, but in most instances such seizures are difficult to recognize. The person may be aware only that his
mind has gone blank for a few moments. An
EEG tracing taken during a short petit mal
attack is shown in Figure 16.13.

3. *Jacksonian or focal epilepsy.* The English

neurologist J. Hughlings Jackson first described epilepsy in which muscle spasms are limited to particular areas of the body. There are several variants, depending on the area of the brain in which the neurons discharge. A motor seizure may begin with discharge near the lateral sulcus and be manifested as twitches of the thumb and index finger. A discharge beginning in the visual cortex may produce hallucinations. Sometimes these seizures remain localized and there is no loss of consciousness. But they may also spread, perhaps beginning with the thumb and index finger and then extending to the hand, arm, and shoulder, and sometimes ultimately throughout the entire body. The attack is then much like that of grand mal epilepsy (Smith, 1965).

4. *Psychomotor epilepsy.* A psychomotor seizure begins with an aura and is followed by a complete loss of contact with the environment. But during the attack the epileptic appears conscious and engages in some sort of routine or organized activity. The act may be simple and repetitive, such as chewing or particular motions of the limbs, or the epileptic may engage in a complex and prolonged series of activities. Psychomotor seizures may last only a few seconds or minutes but occasionally much longer. After the attack the individual has no memory for his actions. The behavior of these people is often otherwise psychotic, even between seizures (Glaser, Newman, and Schafer, 1963).

F. F. Age 44. This woman has had a history of psychomotor seizures since the age of eighteen. During the seizure she would, in a stereotyped way, stroke or pat articles of furniture or curtains, salivate, groan, and clutch her mouth, as well as occasionally wander about in automatic fashion. She was frequently preoccupied with inadequate feelings concerning running her home, taking care of her family, and [her] social relationships. [She had] frequent episodes of paranoid psychosis . . . with delusions of reference and persecution, particularly concerning her neighbors (p. 351).

Psychomotor epilepsy is associated for the most part with abnormal electrical discharge from the temporal lobes. Although some reports indicate that antisocial and violent acts are committed during such seizures, a recent survey by Gunn and Fenton (1971) found that of 434 epileptics who had engaged in so-called automatisms, violence was extremely unusual. They found that the automatic behavior typically lasted only minutes, and that no attempt was made to conceal the acts undertaken during the seizure. They also surveyed epileptics in prisons and found that only 10 out of 150 cases reported a seizure within twelve hours before or after their last offense. There was little evidence that their criminal acts had been automatisms.

As previously mentioned, genetic factors appear to be of some importance in epilepsy, but that importance varies with the type of epilepsy. The evidence for a predisposition to develop petit mal epilepsy is strongest; one study found an 84 to 85 percent concordance rate in monozygotic twins. For psychomotor epilepsy the concordance rate in monozygotic twins was 75 percent (DeJong and Sugar, 1972). What may be inherited in epilepsy is an instability of nerve cells. As indicated earlier, seizures can be induced in anyone, but the kind of stimuli that can elicit them varies. Epilepsy can be treated with drugs such as Dilantin, but individuals vary in their response to it. When a tumor causes epilepsy, it is removed if at all possible.

SUMMARY

In this chapter we have reviewed the literature on organic brain syndromes, those classified by etiology and one, epilepsy, that is classified by symptomatology. The primary symptoms of these syndromes are cognitive dysfunctions—memory loss, disorientation, and dementia—although affective symptoms and psychotic delusions and hallucinations may also be evident. A wide variety of conditions can cause an organic syndrome. Among the most important are infection, trauma, nutritional deficiencies, cerebrovascular accidents, tumors, degenerative diseases, toxic agents, and malfunctions of the thyroid and adrenal glands. The symptoms of a particular brain injury or degeneration are quite variable, suggesting that the behavior exhibited by a brain-injured person is *not* simply related to his neurological pathology. Other as yet poorly understood factors seem to *interact* with brain injury in producing the symptoms that are observed.

Finally, epilepsy, a group of disorders characterized by abnormal brain activity and altered states of consciousness, was considered. The major types of epilepsy—grand mal, petit mal, Jacksonian, and psychomotor—can be precipitated by a variety of causes such as stress, particular sensory stimuli, and brain diseases. Available evidence also suggests the importance of genetic factors.

CHAPTER 17

Mental Retardation

According to the American Association on Mental Deficiency, an organization to which many professionals in the field belong, mental retardation " . . . refers to subaverage intellectual functioning which originates during the developmental period and is associated with impairment in adaptive behavior" (Heber, 1961, p. 3). In the view of these professionals a low IQ score does not by itself designate an individual as a mental retardate; he must also be unable to adapt to the natural and social demands of his environment. Moreover, the problems of the retardate manifest themselves early in life, before his sixteenth year, distinguishing him from those whose intelligence is impaired later in life, through a severe contusion for example. Thus three variables must be considered in deciding whether a person is mentally retarded: his measured IQ, his degree of social adaptation, and whether his difficulties were early in onset.

CLASSIFICATION AND DIAGNOSIS OF MENTAL RETARDATION

Levels of Retardation

The classification scheme of mental retardation adopted by the American Association on Mental Deficiency has now become part of DSM-II. Five levels are designated, each of them a specific subaverage range on the far left of the normal distribution curve of measured intelligence (see page 31). If all levels of retardation are included in prevalence figures, about one person in six must be considered retarded. Usually most of those in the borderline mental retardation group, people with IQs of from 68 to 83, are not included, however. With a cutoff point of IQ 67 the prevalence becomes about 3 percent of the population, which means that about 6,250,000 people in the United States are retarded. The following is a summary of how individuals at each level of mental retardation are described by Robinson and Robinson (1970).

Borderline Mental Retardation (Stanford-Binet IQ 68 to 83). With proper training most children falling within this IQ range are able to achieve social and vocational adequacy in adulthood. During school years they are often in classes for "slow learners." Although a large percentage fail to complete high school and can maintain only a low socioeconomic existence, most adults in this group blend in with the normal population. According to most legal and administrative guidelines, this group is usually not considered sufficiently retarded to be eligible for specialized services; they are admitted to no special classes or institutions. Only a small proportion of persons in this IQ range, those whose adaptive behavior is also deviant, are actually diagnosed as being mentally retarded.

Mild Mental Retardation (Stanford-Binet IQ 52 to 67). The mildly retarded comprise about 90 percent of all those who have IQs of less than 67. As children they are eligible for special classes for the educable mentally retarded. Adults are likely to be able to maintain themselves in unskilled jobs or in sheltered workshops, although they may need help with social and financial problems. Only about one percent are ever institutionalized, usually in adolescence for behavioral problems. Many of the mildly retarded show no signs of brain pathology and are members of families whose intelligence and socioeconomic levels are low.

Moderate Mental Retardation (Stanford-Binet IQ 36 to 51). About 6 percent of those with IQs of less than 67 are moderately retarded. Brain damage and other pathologies are frequent. During childhood these individuals are eligible for special classes for trainable retardates in which the development of self-care skills rather than academic achievement is emphasized. Many are institutionalized. Although most can do useful work, few hold jobs except in sheltered workshops or in family businesses. Most live dependently within the family. Few have friends of their own, but they may be left alone without supervision for several hours at a time. Their retardation is likely to be identified in infancy or early childhood, for their sensorimotor coordination remains poor, and they are slow to develop verbal and social skills.

Severe Mental Retardation (Stanford Binet IQ 20 to 35). About 3.5 percent of those with IQs of less than 67 are severely retarded. Most are institutionalized and require constant supervision. For children in this group to be able to speak and take care of their own basic needs requires prolonged training; the self-care training that is provided in the special classes within the school system is usually inadequate except for the upper portion of this group. As adults the severely retarded may be friendly but can usually communicate only briefly on a very concrete level. They engage in very little independent activity and are often lethargic, for the circumstances of their lives allow them little stimulation (Figure 17.1). Genetic disorders and environmental insults, such as anoxia at birth, account for most of this degree of retardation.

Profound Mental Retardation (Stanford-Binet IQ below 20). Only about 1.5 percent of the retarded are profoundly so, requiring total supervision and often nursing care all their lives.

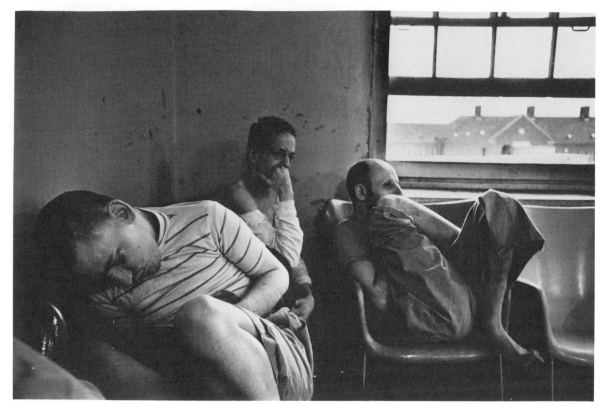

FIGURE **17.1**
All too often the mentally retarded who are hospitalized as children spend the rest of their lives in the hopeless, inhospitable environment of a state institution.

Very little training is usually given them because it is assumed that they can learn little except possibly to walk, utter a few phrases, feed themselves, and use the toilet. Many have severe physical deformities as well as neurological damage and cannot get around on their own. There is a very high mortality rate during childhood.

These categories are difficult to apply, partly because of the assessment devices that are used to measure intelligence and adaptive behavior. These issues will be discussed in the next section. But the social implications of labeling a child as mildly or moderately re-

tarded must also be considered. Ross (1974) points out that social agencies, such as schools, make inferences about the future development of children with low IQ scores, and that these expectations affect markedly the kind of educational settings in which such children are placed. A child labeled as moderately retarded, since he has an IQ score between 36 and 51, is generally judged to be "trainable." Those who are categorized as mildly retarded, with an IQ above 52 but below 67, are considered "educable." Educable children are expected to reach a sixth-grade level of academic achievement, but trainables are generally regarded as unable to learn any of the subject

ORGANIC SYNDROMES

matter usually taught in schools. So-called trainable children tend not to be given adequate opportunity to surpass the levels that are expected of them, which means, as Ross points out, that the prophecy of low achievement is self-fulfilling.

In the past virtually all retarded children have been considered unteachable or untrainable. They have been put in sheltered settings to try to keep them content, settings in which few demands are placed on them. Because the trainable-level retarded child has not been considered "bright" e_____ to be able to learn to read, few attem_____ made to teach him. The failu_____ tarded children to acquire var_____ and social skills may partly re_____ no technology adequate to_____ been developed. Recently, t_____ tion of operant teaching _____ tarded children have acquired s._____ were formerly thought incapable of lear___. such successes continue, the descriptions o____ each level of retardation may be inappropriate. In Chapter 19 this approach and its implications for teaching those previously thought to be unteachable will be described.

Intelligence Test Scores as a Criterion

Because the principal means of diagnosing mental retardation are the IQ tests that are currently available, the nature of these tests should be reexamined (see page 75). An intelligence quotient[1] is actually nothing more

[1] The actual number that stands for a person's IQ is arrived at by dividing his mental age, as determined through testing, by his chronological age, with chronological years above fourteen and sometimes sixteen disregarded; the quotient is then multiplied by 100 to eliminate the decimal. If a child's mental age is keeping up with his chronological years, his IQ will be 100, the average score.

than what an IQ test measures—even though the concept of intelligence has seemingly been reified by these tests, made into "a thing" that exists "out there."

When an individual takes an IQ test, he demonstrates how many problems of those that are being presented to him—whether they be to generate definitions of words or to manipulate small colored blocks to form a design—he can solve at that particular time and place. Scores on IQ tests do allow useful predictions to be made; Binet did succeed in predicting school performance on the basis of his test. Current IQ tests are similarly good at ___ting academic performance. And people _____rized by IQ scores so that other _____vior are anticipated. But _____ y of the intelligence test _____ o the fact that intelligence _____ an entity which is inferred _____ g and supposedly generating _____ omena, but which is not at _____ erhaps never will be, fully observ__.

Tradition__ IQ tests pose special problems when they are used to diagnose mental retardation.

1. Most IQ tests have not been standardized on nonwhite populations or institutionalized populations, groups that are heavily represented in the prevalence figures for mental retardation. Items that sample intelligent behavior of a white noninstitutionalized population may be very different from those that ought to be used to measure the intelligent behavior of a nonwhite institutionalized population.

2. Few of the intelligence tests have been validated for IQ scores of less than 70. Individuals of low intellectual functioning were not adequately represented in the groups

taking the tests when the scales were being compiled and standardized.

3. Many diagnoses of retardation are made when the child is quite young, less than five years of age. Measurements of the intelligence of very young children do not necessarily correlate highly with those obtained when the child is older.

4. The most reliable and frequently used tests for measuring the intelligence of children, the Stanford-Binet Intelligence Scale and the Wechsler Intelligence Scale for Children (WISC), were not devised to take into account other problems of the mentally retarded that may contribute to their poor performance on an IQ test. Children taking the Stanford-Binet test must repeat digits spoken to them by the tester, find objects in pictures, build simple structures with blocks to match those shown them, complete sentences, define simple words, detect fallacies in statements, supply rhyming words, and so on. The WISC consists of separate subtests, six of them verbal and testing the child's store of general information, his comprehension and abstract thinking, his vocabulary, and his abilities to repeat series of numbers and to solve problems in arithmetic. The other subtests evaluate nonverbal performances such as completing pictures or arranging them to depict a meaningful story, reproducing designs with blocks, assembling objects, and substituting a set of unfamiliar symbols for digits. The intelligence of blind, deaf, and nonverbal individuals is extremely difficult to assess by either of these instruments, for children who are handicapped in these ways are physically unable to complete all parts of the tests. Those with poor motor coordination may work out an intellectual solution to a problem but have trouble translating it into the verbal or motor behavior required by the test.

5. Before the IQ test is given, the tester must establish a degree of rapport with the child in order to obtain maximum performance. A poor black child may not readily be put at ease by a white middle-class psychologist. The testing situation itself may well be a traumatic one for the child, and for the parents as well, making a low score difficult to interpret.

6. Zigler, Butterfield, and Capobianco (1970) have shown that an institution can be a very socially depriving place for a child. When being tested the retarded child's atypical need for social reinforcement may make him attend too much to the adult and look to him for solutions to the test problems. The "outer-directedness" of the retarded child can keep him from concentrating on the tasks, resulting in a spuriously low IQ score.

The problems in testing the IQs of the retarded therefore justify a degree of caution in regarding their scores as unerringly valid indicators of their intelligence. At the same time, however, such tests have proved useful in providing information about retardates and in predicting their later intellectual and social achievements.

Adaptive Behavior as a Criterion

In addition to measured IQ, the American Association on Mental Deficiency's classification scheme emphasizes the importance of assessing adaptive behavior in determining the level of mental retardation. Two facets of adaptive behavior are described: "(1) the degree to which the individual is able to function and maintain himself independently, and (2) the degree to which he meets satisfactorily the culturally imposed demands of personal and social responsibility" (Heber, 1961, p. 61).

The standards of adaptive behavior vary with age. The individual must always be evaluated in terms of how he meets the standards of personal independence and social responsibility of his particular chronological age group. Unfortunately, the objective measures of adaptive behavior are few. The Vineland Social Maturity Scale (Doll, 1953) is the best measure currently available, although its norms are not as firmly established as those of the IQ tests. This scale is composed of 117 activities grouped into 8 categories of behavior. An interviewer asks a person well acquainted with the child, often a parent, to evaluate how well the child performs a variety of socially adaptive behaviors. Several sample items are shown in Table 17.1

Recently the American Association on Mental Deficiency has devised the Adaptive Behavior Scale, designed to provide information on the "way the individual maintains his personal independence in daily living [and] how he meets the social expectations of his environment" (Nihira, Foster, Shellhaas, and Leland, 1969, p. 5). As more research is generated to determine the usefulness, reliability, and validity of this scale, crucial information about the adaptive deficiencies of retarded persons may be provided.[2]

---

[2] Questions have been raised about the classification of intellectual and adaptive behavioral deficits that appear to be attributable to emotional disorders such as schizophrenia. A person who, for example, believes that he is Napoleon may do poorly on a standard IQ test and on an assessment of his social adjustment. The usefulness of labeling a person retarded as well as psychotic is unclear; the distinction between emotional and intellectual deficits is sometimes difficult to make, especially among children.

TABLE **17.1**

Sample Items from Vineland Social Maturity Scale with the Age at Which Performance Is Expected

(*from Doll, 1953*)

Age	Items
0–1	pulls self upright does not drool
1–2	pulls off socks eats with spoon
2–3	asks to go to toilet dries own hands
3–4	plays cooperatively at kindergarten level buttons coat or dress
4–5	uses pencil or crayon for drawing washes face unassisted
5–6	prints simple words is trusted with money
6–7	uses table knife for spreading goes to bed unassisted
7–8	tells time to quarter hour combs or brushes hair
8–9	uses tools or utensils reads on own initiative
9–10	makes minor purchases goes about town freely

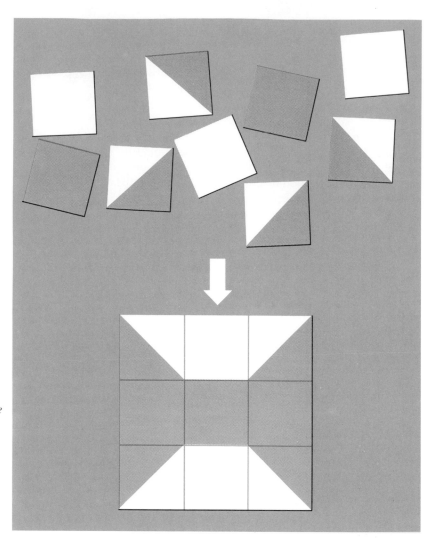

FIGURE **17.2**
In the WISC block design test, nine blocks and a series of printed designs like the one shown are presented to the examinee. He has to construct the design using the varicolored blocks. Each block has a white side, a colored side, and a side that is half and half, as well as sides with irrelevant colors.

EXPERIMENTAL STUDY OF SPECIFIC COGNITIVE FUNCTIONS

Intellectual functioning is for the most part judged on the basis of IQ scores, but a particular score provides only limited information on *how* a person thinks. The WISC may reveal that a child does very poorly on block design tasks (Figure 17.2), but why? What is there about the problem solving of this task that is particularly difficult for him and that psychologists might study? In the picture completion subtest of the WISC a series of pictures are presented to the child one at a time. He must identify the important part that is missing from each picture. This and other subtests have proved effective in picking out retardates. But what are the deficiencies in thinking that they test?

ORGANIC SYNDROMES

Laboratory Testing of the Retardate

Experimental psychologists have for years divided intelligence into functions such as perception, motor skills, short-term memory, long-term memory, speech, discrimination learning, and other phenomena and studied them in laboratories. But they have usually tested these functions in individuals whose IQ scores and social behavior are well within the normal range, if not above average; college students have frequently been the subjects in these experiments. Since the early 1960s, many workers have been studying experimentally the intellectual behavior of mental retardates in laboratory settings, giving careful consideration to the specific intellectual functions that are poorly developed in them. Approaching mental retardation in this fashion—making use of data and procedures rooted in the laboratory rather than relying on the more intuitive observations of clinicians whose judgments form the basis of the DSM-II scheme—would seem to have certain advantages. Experimentalists may one day be able to isolate variables that underlie the development and maintenance of subnormal functioning. Through comparison studies they may find out how the learning of retardates differs from that of normal children, and through special studies of retardates they may determine what factors help them to achieve certain patterns and levels of performance. Laboratory-based information on how to manipulate specific subnormal functionings may also help in formulating treatments.

The Developmental-Defect Controversy

Much of the experimental research in mental retardation has been devoted to determining whether the retarded person is *quantitatively* or *qualitatively* different from the normal person in his thinking and learning processes. The essential question is whether the retardate's cognitive development is the same as that of a normal person but proceeding at a slower rate—the developmental position—or whether he suffers from some cognitive deficit that makes his intellectual functioning different from that of normal persons—the defect position.

As already mentioned, an IQ score is arrived at by dividing the mental age (MA), the attained cognitive level that the individual reaches on the intelligence test, by the chronological age (CA) and multiplying by 100 to eliminate the decimal. For example,

$$\frac{MA\ (10\ years)}{CA\ (10\ years)} \times 100 = 100\ IQ$$

$$\frac{MA\ (10\ years)}{CA\ (8\ years)} \times 100 = 125\ IQ$$

$$\frac{MA\ (10\ years)}{CA\ (12\ years)} \times 100 = 83\ IQ$$

The developmental theorist who studies retardates sees IQ as measuring nothing more than how long it takes an individual to reach a certain cognitive level; he believes that the IQ reveals the rate of cognitive development. For example, an eight-year-old child with a mental age of eight would have an IQ of 100, the average. Developmentalists believe that his thinking is the same as that of a sixteen-year-old with an IQ of 50 who also has a mental age of eight. They propose that these individuals should perform equally on any new cognitive tasks devised to test them, regardless of the IQ. In their view it has merely taken the sixteen-year-old twice as long as the eight-year-old to reach the same state of development.

In contrast, the difference or defect theorist views the IQ as more than a rate of cognitive development. He assumes that IQ reflects certain features of an individual's cognitive or physiological functioning. People of the same MAs but with differing IQs are said to *think differently*. Difference theorists believe that even though the MAs are the same, the thinking processes by which they are attained vary.

The major developmental theorist is Zigler (1969). He is concerned with the cultural-familial retarded, those who have no demonstrated brain pathology, are mildly retarded, and have at least one parent or sibling who is also retarded. He believes that the cultural-familial retardate "is characterized by a slower progression through the same sequence of cognitive stages . . . and a more limited upper stage of cognition . . . than is characteristic of the individual of average intellect" (p. 537). Any differences found between retardates and MA-matched controls in performing cognitive tasks, will, according to Zigler, reflect noncognitive variables such as amount of education acquired, institutionalization, and anxiety. In his research he has attempted to prove that these variables do indeed interfere with learning. He has demonstrated that because of the deprived nature of his environment, the institutionalized individual responds to adult experimenters and testers in a way that interferes with optimal test results. He also proposes that "the retarded person, because of his high incidence of failure . . . , tends to distrust his own solutions to problems, and thus reacts quite differently [from the normal person] to external cues provided in the problem solving situation" (p. 412). Zigler's approach then is to determine the areas in which the familially retarded perform more poorly than MA-matched normal individuals to see whether poor performance may be attributed to environmental and social factors rather than to variables that stem from a low IQ.

Milgram (1971) is one of the major defect or difference theorists. He holds that retarded individuals are deficient in certain cognitive abilities, even when they are compared with normal persons of equal mental age. His research is directed toward isolating specific deficiencies of the retarded to which their low IQs can be attributed, with the hope that eventually deficiencies can be modified or retarded learning can at least be better understood.

The specific qualitative deficiency Milgram is concerned with is the retardate's failure to think of mediators to help him associate words. In a paired-associates learning task, for example, an individual is given several pairs of words to learn, cat-tree, spoon-table, knife-wall. Later he is given only the first item of each pair (cat, spoon, knife) and is required to recall the second item (tree, table, wall). Normal children commonly form verbal mediators to link the items of a pair—for example, the cat ran up the tree. Milgram has argued that because retarded children do not usually form mediators, they do poorly on this type of task. In support of his argument he administered a paired-associates test to retarded and normal children under two conditions. First the children were given only the paired words, but in the second round the children were provided a mediator for each pair. The retarded children performed more poorly than the nonretarded only when mediators were not provided, confirming the hypothesis that retarded children have trouble producing verbal mediators.

The short-term memory, selective attention, distractibility, and physiological arousal of the mentally retarded have also been studied in the attempt to discover particular deficiencies. But in comparing normal children and retardates on cognitive tasks, it is extremely difficult to control the motivational, environmental, and educational variables other than intelligence that might contribute to poor cognitive performance. It is still unclear how best to account for the consistently poor performance of retarded children on a variety of laboratory cognitive tasks.

TABLE 17.2 *Illustrative Organic Diseases Associated with Mental Retardation*

When disease develops	Types of disease		
	Systemic	Infectious	Traumatic
In utero (before birth)*	Down's syndrome Klinefelter's syndrome Cretinism Tay-Sachs disease Niemann-Pick disease Maple Syrup Urine disease Gargoylism	Rubella Syphilis Rh factor Toxoplasmosis Encephalitis	Cretinism Malnutrition Poisoning (lead, carbon monoxide, X-ray) Drugs
At or following birth		Encephalitis	All the above *plus* Anoxia Head injury Premature birth

* Several conditions in which the head size is grossly distorted have prenatal causes that have not been definitely established; examples are microcephaly or small head in which the development of the brain has been arrested; macrocephaly, large head with abnormal growth of supportive tissues; and hydrocephaly, large head with excessive cerebrospinal fluid.

ORGANIC CAUSES OF MENTAL RETARDATION

The several forms of mental retardation are likely to be caused by any number of factors or combinations thereof. Through the years the issue of whether mental retardation should be attributed primarily to organic factors or to the environment has aroused great controversy. But this debate has really focused on only one level of the disorder, the first, mild retardation. A distinction, most strongly suggested by Zigler (1968) and also by Robinson and Robinson (1965), is often made between mild retardation on the one hand and moderate, severe, and profound on the other. Cultural-familial or environmental factors are considered likely to be formative in mild retardation; and a single pathological organic factor, such as a defective gene or a brain trauma, is considered determinative in the more severe forms of the disorder.

Heber (1970) estimates that damage to the developing brain accounts for no more than 10 to 20 percent of the total population of the mentally retarded. These individuals generally have IQs of less than 55, falling into the moderate, severe, and profound retardation categories. They are fairly evenly distributed throughout all socioeconomic, ethnic, and racial groups. The greatest proportion of the mentally retarded—the so-called cultural-familial retardates—appear physically normal, giving no indication of brain pathology that can at present be detected. Most are mildly retarded with IQs above 55, and a great many of them are born and raised in deprived environments.

FIGURE **17.3**
A mongoloid child who has the slanted eyes, flat face and nose, and stubby fingers characteristic of the disorder.

to reproduce. Variations from the normal complement of forty-six chromosomes usually, but not always, cause very noticeable abnormalities in the developing child. The pairing of defective recessive genes means that they provide a faulty patterning for the production of an enzyme necessary for an important metabolic process.

Chromosomal Aberrations

Down's syndrome or *mongolism,* first described by Langdon Down in 1886, is the most prevalent single-factor cause of mental retardation, accounting for 10 to 20 percent of moderately to severely retarded children. Mongoloid children seldom have an IQ over 50. Their many physical abnormalities are rather apparent (Figure 17.3): eyes slanted upward and outward, a vestigial third eyelid in the inner corner of the eye, flat face and nose, overly large and often deeply fissured tongue, misshapen teeth, stubby fingers, fingerprints with L-shaped loops rather than whorls, protruding

belly, underdeveloped genitalia, and arms and legs that are smaller than normal.

Down's syndrome is caused by a chromosomal abnormality. The vast majority of mongoloid children have forty-seven chromosomes instead of forty-six. During the earliest stage of an egg's development the two chromosomes of pair 21 fail to separate, perhaps because they are so small. When the sperm and egg unite, chromosome pair 21 will thus have three chromosomes instead of the usual two. This is referred to as a trisomy of chromosome 21.

The risk of having a mongoloid child increases dramatically with the age of the mother: there is a one in 2000 chance of a mother in her twenties having such a child, and a one in 40 risk for a mother over forty. Fortunately, recently developed methods of testing the fluid in a pregnant woman's uterus can reveal whether the fetus is mongoloid. In a much rarer and inherited form of mongolism the extra chromosome 21 becomes attached to another chromosome. The risk of bearing a child with this type of mongolism does not increase with maternal age.

In *Klinefelter's syndrome* an extra X chromosome is usually at fault. This syndrome occurs only in males and accounts for about one percent of institutionalized male retardates. Only about 25 percent of males with this syndrome are retarded, and their retardation is likely to be mild or moderate rather than severe. The symptoms are usually noticed at puberty when the testes remain small and the boy develops feminine secondary sex characteristics such as enlarged hips.

Defective Genes

When a pair of defective recessive genes misdirect the formation of an enzyme, metabolic processes are disturbed. The problem may affect development of the embryo in the uterus or may not become important until much later in life.

In *phenylketonuria* (PKU) the infant, born normal, soon suffers from a deficiency of liver enzyme, phenylalanine hydroxylase, which is needed to convert phenylaline, an amino acid of protein foods, to tyrosine. Phenylaline and its derivative phenylpyruvic acid build up in the body fluids, ultimately wreaking irreversible brain damage. The frontal lobes are particularly affected. Inasmuch as these areas of the cortex are known to be crucial for normal thinking—although *how* is not known—it is not surprising that mental retardation is profound (Figure 17.4).

At about six months parents usually begin to notice a retardation in motor development and in general responsiveness. There may also be seizures and an unusual body odor from the presence of phenylpyruvic acid in the urine. Over 60 percent of children with PKU never learn to talk, and more than half of these individuals have IQs of less than 20.

Although a very rare disorder, with an incidence of about one in 20,000 births, it is estimated that one person in seventy is a carrier of the recessive gene. The disorder has the expected frequency of 25 percent among siblings. Fortunately, prevention of brain damage is facilitated by laboratory tests of the infant's blood for excessive phenylaline. Most states have laws requiring that this test be given four or five days after birth. If the test is positive, a diet low in phenylalanine is urged upon the parents as soon as possible. When the diet is restricted as early as the third month and until the age of six, when brain differentiation is relatively complete, cognitive development may be nearly normal.

Hundreds of recessive-gene disorders have been isolated, many of them causing mental retardation. Only a very minor percentage of the cases of mental retardation are accounted for by any single disorder, however. *Tay-Sachs* disease, a disorder of lipid metabolism transmitted by the pairing of single recessive genes, is found among Jews more often than any other ethnic group. It is characterized by increasing muscular weakness, visual deterioration, and convulsions. The child seldom lives beyond his third year (Kolb, 1968). *Niemann-Pick disease,* also a fatal inherited dysfunction in lipid metabolism, causes gastrointestinal disturbances, malnutrition, and progressive paralysis. *Maple Syrup Urine disease* is an inherited defect in amino acid metabolism and receives its name from the odor of the infant's urine. Deterioration of the muscles accompanies cerebral deterioration, and the child seldom survives its first year. A child afflicted with *gargoylism* has an enlarged head with protruding forehead, bushy eyebrows, thick lips, and deformed limbs. Many of these children survive into their teens.

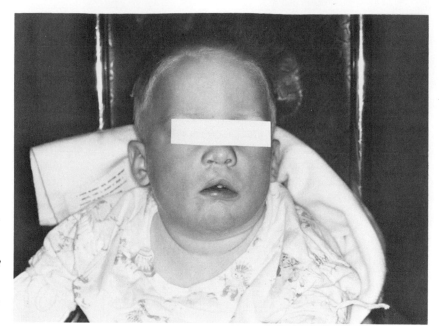

Infectious Diseases Causing Mental Retardation

Both before birth, through contagion of the mother, and after birth a child can be subjected to an infection which causes mental retardation.

If the mother is infected by *rubella* or German measles in the last six months of pregnancy, the fetus is not adversely affected. If, however, she contracts the disease during the first month of pregnancy, there is a 50 percent chance that her live-born child will suffer both mental abnormality and congenital physical defects, very often blindness. When the disease is contracted in the second month, the risk is reduced to 15 percent, in the third month to 10 percent (Kolb, 1968). Therapeutic abortions have been available for several years for pregnant mothers who have had German measles early in pregnancy.

Syphilis no longer causes as much mental retardation as it used to because in recent years pregnant women who are seen in prenatal clinics must have their blood tested. Many of the fetuses afflicted with congenital syphilis die before they are born. Others die during the first weeks of life. Congenital syphilis usually affects the child immediately if he lives, frequently causing mental retardation, blindness, and deafness. A rarer form of untreated syphilis is juvenile paresis. This disease begins to affect the central nervous system only after a number of symptom-free years, but thereafter intellectual deterioration is progressive (Robinson and Robinson, 1965).

Rh factors are substances that are present in the red blood cells of a large majority of human beings and of other higher animals. When they are introduced in the blood of a person whose own does not contain them, they act as antigens or foreign substances and stimulate the production of antibodies. If the blood of a fetus contains Rh factors but that of the mother is Rh negative, lacking in Rh factors, these substances will be introduced into the mother's blood for the first time by the fetus. The

ORGANIC SYNDROMES

mother produces antibodies which, when they in turn enter the bloodstream of the fetus, destroy red blood cells and cause oxygen deprivation. Since it takes time for the mother to produce the antibodies, firstborn children are less likely to be affected by Rh incompatibility than are subsequent children. The brain damage from oxygen deprivation in Rh incompatibility can be extensive if not treated. In recent years the newborn infant has been given a complete blood transfusion, and most children recover. Heber's (1970) summary of various studies indicates that the IQs of children who have suffered from Rh incompatibility and been treated are lower than those of control group children, but they are still within the average range.

Other very rare infectious diseases of the mother can affect the unborn child, among them toxoplasmosis (infection from a protozoan-like organism, *Toxoplasma*) and encephalitis. Heber (1970) concludes that "there is little broad-based data upon which to assess the role of maternal infections (other than rubella and syphilis) in the production of mentally retarded offspring" (p. 46).

After birth, infectious diseases can also affect a child's developing brain. Meningococcal meningitis may result in irreversible brain damage if contracted in infancy or early childhood. This infection in adulthood is usually far less serious, probably because the brain is largely developed by about the age of six (see Chapter 16).

There are several forms of childhood meningitis, a disease in which the protective membranes of the brain are acutely inflamed and fever is very high. Meningitis may cause severe mental retardation or death. Even if the child survives and is not severely retarded, he is likely to be moderately or mildly so. Other disabling aftereffects are deafness, paralysis, and epilepsy.

Traumas Causing Mental Retardation

Trauma of many kinds can cause mental retardation and other physical problems in the fetus either indirectly through the mother or directly to the infant after his birth. The specific forms and the severity of disorders are varied if they are caused by trauma; in fact, the diagnosis of "brain damage" through trauma is sometimes problematic, with the danger that reasoning can become circular and interfere both with scientific understanding of the disorder and treatment of it. Traumas that may damage the brain are lead poisoning, too frequent exposure to X-rays, carbon monoxide poisoning, poor diet, birth injury, head injury, and certain drugs.

Cretinism is caused by a severe deficiency in the output of the thyroid gland and is characterized by profound intellectual deficit as well as physical defects. The untreated child who has suffered this deficiency since birth has a short, dwarflike body, coarse features, a swollen abdomen, and short, stubby limbs (Figure 17.5). Although several factors may diminish the activity of the thyroid, historically the major cause has been lack of iodine in the diet of the pregnant mother, iodine being the major ingredient needed for the production of the hormone thyroxin. The infant is born with defective thyroid glands which remain underdeveloped or atrophy. The symptoms of cretinism become apparent during the early months, for development is very slow, and the baby is not responsive or alert. The incidence of cretinism is now very low because of the widespread use of iodized salt. An infant born with a thyroid deficiency can be given thyroid extracts, making a relatively normal development possible in many instances.

It has been estimated that throughout the world 300 million preschool children suffer mild to moderate *malnutrition* (Behar, 1968). A poor diet, and protein deficiencies in particu-

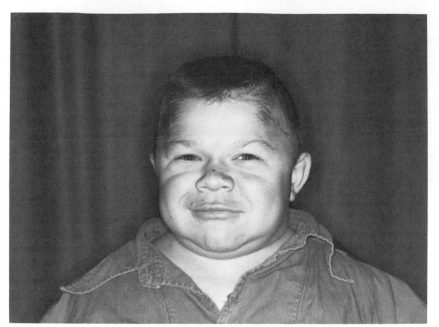

FIGURE **17.5**
Cretinism, caused by a deficiency in the output of the thyroid gland, is one of the severe forms of mental retardation. The features of this afflicted child are characteristically coarse.

lar, are believed to be especially harmful during the period of the brain's fastest growth, from five months before birth until ten months after. The effects of moderate and chronic malnutrition are not as well known. The effects of malnutrition have been studied in several ways, by manipulating the diets of animals, by observing those of human beings, and by examining the brains of children who have died of malnutrition. Animal research has convincingly demonstrated the ill effects of poor diet on brain development (Davison and Dobbing, 1966). The total number of brain cells is permanently reduced if the animal suffers from malnutrition during periods when they are dividing. But we cannot generalize across species, and it would be unethical to try to replicate these results with human infants. Some research, however, does reveal similar effects in human beings. In one study autopsies were performed on children who had died from malnutrition; all had a subnormal number of brain cells (Winick, Rosso, and Waterlow,

1970). In another study lower-class women were given multiple vitamins during pregnancy. They gave birth to children who, at age three, had higher IQs than those whose mothers had not had the special vitamin supplements (Harrell, Woodyard, and Gates, 1955). Thus there is some evidence that the pregnant woman's diet can influence the future IQ of the infant.

If the cells of the brain are completely deprived of oxygen for even a few short seconds during any period of the life cycle, they will die. *Anoxia,* which is usually only partial but still causes irreparable damage because the rate of metabolism in the brain is lowered, can occur before, during, or after birth. Research with animals has shown the harmful effects of oxygen deprivation, but generalization to humans may be unwarranted. Summarizing the results of research with human beings, Heber (1970) concludes that children who suffered oxygen deprivation at birth do not differ in intelligence from controls. He believes that

448

studies stressing the role of neonatal anoxia as an important cause of retardation are usually based on retrospective analysis of the histories of retarded persons and have failed to include appropriate nonretarded control groups.

When *prematurity* of birth is separated from the other variables that commonly accompany it—poor socioeconomic status, maternal age, health, medical care—there seems to be little relationship between it and neurological deficit or mental retardation. Robinson and Robinson (1965) conclude that prematurity per se is not usually dangerous to mental development, although the risk of retardation is quite high in children who are very small at birth.[3]

[3] Of course, prematurity tends to be associated with below-average size at birth. Thus an infant premature enough to be very small has a higher risk of being mentally retarded.

CULTURAL-FAMILIAL CAUSES OF MENTAL RETARDATION

As serious as the retardations attributed to various known and suspected single-factor organic causes may be, the majority of people considered retarded are only mildly so and do not have any identifiable physiological damage. The diagnosis of cultural-familial retardation is made on the basis of three criteria: mild retardation, no indication of brain pathology, and evidence of retardation in at least one of the parents or in one or more of the siblings. Very often mild retardation does not become evident until the child has trouble in school. If it is assumed that intelligence is normally distributed, there should be approximately the same number of people with IQs in the 55 to 70 range as there are in the 130 to 145 range. The lower range has twice as many people as the higher, however; cultural and social factors have been proposed as important variables.

Family Backgrounds of the Cultural-Familial Retarded

Robinson and Robinson (1965) report that a sizable proportion of the cultural-familial retarded come from stable lower-class families. There is steady employment, and the child's physical needs are met fairly adequately. But the intellectual and educational level in the home is low; few of the parents have IQs that exceed the borderline range (Heber, 1970). A large number of families live at this low socioeconomic level, making the incidence of cultural-familial retardation very great.

Children classified as cultural-familial retarded may also come from unstable, poverty-stricken families. In such homes shelter, food, clothing, and medical care are inadequate. The intelligence and intellectual achievement of the parents are very low. The family is often very disrupted and disintegrating, providing no social, emotional, or motivational support for the child.

Many research findings document the accuracy of these dismal characterizations of the homelife of the child with cultural-familial retardation. Benda, Squires, Ogonik, and Wise (1963) studied the families of 205 institutionalized mentally retarded children. The children had no obvious neurological symptoms, were four to fifteen years old, and had IQs above 50. Only 13 of the 205 children came from homes in which there was no apparent mental retardation in the immediate family. Only one-fourth of the families were both intact and able to provide even minimum food, shelter, clothing, and protection from danger. In most of the families certain members had

When surveying all the numerous potential dangers to the developing fetus in utero or to the growing child, we tend to forget that the overwhelming majority of births yield intact babies. But it is also clear that parents must bear considerable responsibility to make certain that their babies are born healthy. Sensible care during pregnancy is not too difficult, given a minimum economic level. A woman who even suspects that she is pregnant can make sure that her diet is adequate, avoid the excessive use of drugs, and decline medical X-rays, such as those that dentists take to detect cavities.

The controversial issue of eugenics must also be considered in any discussion of the control of childbearing and child rearing. It has been estimated that of the approximately 9000 mongoloid children born each year in the United States, two-thirds would not be conceived if women completed their childbearing by the age of forty (Sarason, 1972). We are now far afield of psychiatry and psychology per se, however, for what are the ethics of making a recommendation based on this estimate when thirty-nine out of forty births by mothers over forty do *not* yield mongoloid infants? And yet, as already noted, most states *require* testing a infant for PKU, and individual liberties do not appear thereby to have been infringed upon in any important way. But should society go so far as to advocate or require sterilization of those individuals who are likely to have deformed or severely retarded children? What about the mother who stands a one-in-ten chance of bearing a blind, retarded child because she has contracted rubella in her third month? Is our obligation to the unborn child better served by terminating a risky pregnancy or by taking the chance of allowing, or forcing, the birth of a child whose physical and mental handicaps may be devastating? Indeed, does the generally happy mongoloid child—especially if he is kept at home by courageous and loving parents—enjoy life any less than, for example, the harried suburban commuter who has a daily diet of 50 milligrams of Valium and 8 ounces of scotch, or the ghetto child whose opportunities may be compromised by the color of his skin?

violated societal norms severely enough that legal action had been taken against them. This study was somewhat biased, however, for a mildly retarded child is usually institutionalized only when the family unit cannot provide for his needs. The backgrounds of these institutionalized children were probably worse than are those of retarded children in general.

Not all children who are reared in deprived environments are retarded. Heber (1970) correlated the IQ scores of eighty-eight mothers in a city slum with their children's test scores and found that a minority of the mothers had given birth to a majority of the children whose IQs were in the mildly retarded range. For example, 17 percent of mothers with IQs of less than 68 had reared 54.5 percent of the children in that range and 32.9 percent of the children with IQs of 68 to 83.

Offspring of mothers whose IQs were less than 80, approximately half the sample, showed a decrement in measured intelligence with increasing age; the older children of these mothers had lower IQ scores than their younger siblings. Only 20 percent of the children less than six years of age had IQs lower than 80, but 50 percent of the children between seven and twelve years of age tested below 80, as did over 90 percent of those thirteen years of age. This tendency for scores to decrease as children grow older in deprived socioeconomic environments is often interpreted as evidence of the serious effects of such environments on intellectual development. The children of mothers who scored closer to the normal range, however, showed no decrease in intelligence as they grew older. Fewer than 20 percent of these children, regardless of their age, had IQs of less than 80. The deleterious effects of living in an impoverished environment are less if the mother's IQ is near average.

Problems of Interpretation

The effects of deprivation are very complex. Lower-class mothers tend to have poor diets, which can retard normal development of the fetus. As a growing child the ghetto youngster may eat chips of lead-based paint or plaster which fall from the walls and ceilings in old apartment buildings. The schools may not be as good and the parents may never read books or even newspapers or talk very much with their children. The family members may seldom venture from the few blocks of their neighborhood. But even knowing that a child is brought up in physical, cultural, and intellectual poverty does not always mean that environment is totally responsible for retardation. As Zigler (1968) has stated, "It is one thing to assert that the environment plays a role in determining the range of individual differences, and quite another to say that environmental events can cause the individual born with a normal intellect to be retarded, or that they can prevent retardation" (p. 528).

Some, however, feel that the relationship between poverty and mental retardation should no longer be regarded as correlational. Hurley (1969) feels that the evidence is sufficient to demonstrate that *poverty causes mental retardation*. The child reared in poverty is affected by innumerable intellectually stunting factors—both organic and environmental —ranging from the poor nutrition and the lack of prenatal care of his mother to his own malnutrition, his emotionally and intellectually depriving home and neighborhood, and the failure of his school system. These factors, either singly or in combination, may cause the kind of retardation that has been termed cultural-familial. The implication drawn by Hurley is that by eradicating poverty the majority of cases of mental retardation would be eliminated.

A Challenge to the Concept of Cultural-Familial Retardation

Family problems may lead to the inappropriate institutionalization of some children. In one part of a larger investigation, Braginsky and Braginsky (1971) interviewed cultural-familial

dures ranging from screaming and writhing nude on the floor to forced inactivity and sleep for several weeks. One could almost say, "You name it, someone thinks it's therapeutic." Although it might be entertaining to examine every school, we have opted for a selective review of the field, presenting sufficient detail about the more important approaches to give the reader a grasp of the basic issues as well as an overall perspective on the enterprise of changing behavior in a therapeutic context.

London (1964) categorizes psychotherapies into *insight* and *action* (behavioral) therapies. Behavior therapy is the subject of Chapter 19. Insight therapy, the topic in this chapter, assumes that behavior becomes disordered because the individual does not adequately understand what is motivating his actions, especially when different needs and drives conflict. Insight therapy tries to help people discover the true reasons they behave as they do. The assumption is that greater insight will yield greater control over behavior and subsequent improvement in it. The emphasis is less on changing behavior here and now than on uncovering its causes—both historical and current. To facilitate such insights, therapists of different theoretical persuasions have employed a variety of techniques, ranging from the free association of psychoanalysis to the reflective procedures of client-centered therapies.

THE PLACEBO EFFECT

For reasons that will become clear, it is appropriate to begin our discussion of psychotherapy with what has become known as the placebo effect. In an historical review, Shapiro (1971) suggests the following definitions.

A placebo *is defined as any therapy [psychological or otherwise] or that component of any therapy, that is deliberately used for its nonspecific, psychologic, or psychophysiologic effect [but] . . . is without specific activity for the condition being treated. . . .*

The placebo effect *is defined as the nonspecific, psychologic, or psychophysiologic effects produced by placebos (p. 440).*

The term placebo effect need not be restricted to therapy with an inert pill, as it sometimes is; it can also apply to therapeutic results, both psychological and physiological, brought about by any method that has no demonstrable specific action on the disorder being treated. In the field of drug therapy, for example, Shapiro (1960) concludes that until recently the history of medication has been largely a history of placebo effects, that is, benefits obtained from treatments which have value only to the extent that people *believe* they help. Frank (1961) relates placebo effects to faith healing in pre- or non-scientific societies. For centuries, suffering human beings have derived benefit from making pilgrimages to sanctified places such as Lourdes and from ingesting sometimes foul-smelling concoctions.

Many people tend to dismiss placebo reactions as "not real" or second-best. After all, if a person has a tension headache, what possible benefit can he hope to get from a pill that is totally devoid of chemical action or direct physiological effect? The fact is, however, that such benefits are often significant and even long-lasting. For example, Lasagna, Mosteller, Von Felsinger, and Beecher (1954) reported impressive relief from pain in surgical patients

BOX **18.1** *The Profession of Psychotherapy*

There are significant differences in the training of professionals who are regarded as legitimate purveyors of psychological services. A *psychiatrist* is a physician, holding an M.D. degree, who has taken postgraduate training, called a residency, wherein he receives supervision in psychotherapy, typically of a psychoanalytic kind. By virtue of the M.D. degree, the psychiatrist can also continue functioning as a physician — giving physical examinations, diagnosing medical problems, and the like. In actuality, however, the only aspect of medical practice which most psychiatrists engage in is prescribing *psychoactive drugs,* chemical compounds that exert changes on how people feel and think.

The term *psychoanalyst* is reserved for those individuals who have received specialized training at a psychoanalytic institute; the program usually involves several years of clinical training as well as an in-depth psychoanalysis of the trainee himself. Although Freud held that psychoanalysts do *not* require medical training (his daughter Anna, who does not have an M.D., is a so-called lay analyst), until recently most psychoanalytic institutes required an M.D. and a psychiatric residency. After the B.A., then, it can take up to ten years to become a psychoanalyst. Psychoanalysts are usually in private practice and their fees are extremely high.

To practice *clinical psychology* (the profession of the authors of this text) requires a Ph.D. degree, which usually entails four to five years of graduate study. Training in this field is much like that for other specialty areas of psychology (experimental, physiological, social, developmental, industrial) with a heavy emphasis on laboratory work, research design, statistics, and empirically based findings about human and animal behavior. In addition, however, a clinical psychologist learns how to deal with patients (or, as many term them, clients) in therapy settings, much as a psychiatrist in training does. He gets this training both in courses in which he masters specific techniques under close professional supervision, and, most intensively, in internship or postdoctoral training, during which the maturing clinician takes increasing responsibility for the care of clients.

There are other professions certified for psychotherapeutic practice. A *psychiatric social worker* obtains a Master of Social Work degree in a course of study that has traditionally been linked to psychiatric residency training. There are also master's and doctoral level programs in *counseling psychology,* somewhat similar to graduate training in clinical psychology but usually with less emphasis on research.

Recent years have seen a movement to "paraprofessional training," in which workers learn to conduct various forms of therapy under the close supervision of professionals. Behavior therapists have been particularly active in extending clinical responsibilities to assistants at the subdoctoral, submaster's, and even subbachelor's levels.

The actual therapy practiced by any of these individuals depends largely on factors such as the part of the country where the person happens to go to school. By and large, except for the use of drugs, specific therapy activities depend *very little* on academic degree.

The contemporary trend toward consumerism appears to be making some impact on the purchase of psychotherapeutic treatment. Until recently, the philosophy was *caveat emptor,* let the buyer beware. But how can most people make an informed decision on the credentials of someone offering treatment? Most states now have certification requirements. For example, in New York a person can present himself as a psychologist only if he has a Ph.D. and a year of supervised postdoctoral clinical experience. Yet there is still room for improvement. Currently, anyone in New York can call himself a psychotherapist and perform the same functions as a duly licensed person. Unfortunately, some unqualified people take advantage of this legal loophole, with the attendant dangers of "quackery" in their treatment of patients.

receiving saline injections. And Frank (1961) furnishes extensive evidence attesting to improvement in a variety of physical and mental problems after the ingestion of pills and exposure to other ministrations that, in themselves, could not possibly account for improvement.

A psychotherapist who places great stock in a particular theory may not like to think that his professional activities have no power other than to mobilize a person's expectancies for help. But psychotherapy research offers scant reassurance to the contrary (Bergin, 1971). Many researchers agree that, in psychotherapy as in much of medicine, *the most reliable effect is the placebo effect.* Even with the burgeoning experimental research in behavior therapy (to be described in Chapter 19), Frank (1972) claims that evidence for effects attributable to specific treatment rather than to the placebo phenomenon is exceedingly scarce, if indeed there is any at all.

The placebo effect has far-reaching implications for the nature of appropriate controls to apply when designing experiments. If every therapy procedure—however rationalized by its proponents—has placebo elements, it is essential to include a placebo control group in any experiment examining the efficacy of a technique. A good example of this practice is Paul's (1966) experiment on systematic desensitization discussed in the next chapter.

PSYCHOANALYTIC THERAPY

Despite the numerous critical attacks made both on psychoanalytic theory and on the effectiveness of psychoanalytic therapy, psychoanalysis remains the dominant force in American psychiatry and clinical psychology. In this section we will try to summarize the important features of classical—that is, traditional—psychoanalysis. Even though those following Freud have introduced various modifications in both theory and therapy, the core of psychoanalytically oriented therapy remains, in our opinion, the same (Figure 18.1).

Basic Techniques of Psychoanalysis

Classical psychoanalysis relates to Freud's second theory of anxiety, according to which neurotic anxiety is the reaction of the ego to the possible gratification of a previously punished and repressed id impulse (Freud, 1949). Tension or anxiety is created when a situation is encountered that reminds the unconscious part of the ego of a repressed conflict from childhood, usually relating to sexual impulses (see pages 108–109). Psychoanalytic therapy attempts to remove this repression and help the patient face the childhood conflict and resolve it in the light of adult reality. The repression, occurring so long ago, has prevented the ego from growing in an adult fashion, and the lifting of the repression is supposed to enable this relearning to take place. Treatment typically extends over several years, with as many as five sessions a week.

A number of techniques are used by psychoanalysts to facilitate this lifting of repression. Perhaps the best known and most important is *free association:* the patient, reclining on a couch, is encouraged to give free rein to his thoughts and feelings, and to verbalize whatever comes into his mind. The assumption is that with enough practice free association will facilitate the uncovering of unconscious mate-

This group portrait was taken at Clark University on Freud's only visit to the United States in 1909. Bottom, left to right: Freud; G. Stanley Hall, a pioneer in American academic psychology; and Carl Gustav Jung, one of Freud's followers. Top, left to right: Abraham A. Brill, an American psychiatrist; Ernest Jones, Freud's biographer; and Sandor Ferenczi, another early psychoanalyst.

rial. The analysand must follow the fundamental rule of reporting his thoughts and feelings as accurately as possible without screening out the elements he feels are unimportant or shameful. Freud assumed that thoughts and memories occurred in associative chains and that recent ones reported first would ultimately trace back to earlier crucial ones. In order to get to these earlier events, however, the therapist has to be very careful not to guide or direct the patient's thinking, and the patient himself must not monitor his thoughts. As Ford and Urban (1963) have paraphrased the analyst's directions for free association,

In ordinary conversation, you usually try to keep a connecting thread running through your remarks excluding any intrusive ideas or side issues so as not to wander too far from the point, and rightly so. But in this case you must talk differently. As you talk various thoughts will occur to you which you like to ignore because of certain criticisms and objections. You will be tempted to think, "that is irrelevant or unimportant, or nonsensical," and to avoid saying it. Do not give in to such criticism. Report such thoughts in spite of your wish not to do so. Later, the reason for this injunction, the only one you have to follow, will become clear. Report whatever goes through your mind. Pretend that you are a traveler, describing to someone beside you the changing views which you see outside the train window (p. 168).

But blocks do arise, virtually thrusting themselves across the thoughts supposedly given free rein. Such obstacles to free association were noted by Freud, who came to attach great importance to them, for they helped him formulate his concept of repression. He asserted that interference with free association is traceable to unconscious control over sensitive areas; it is precisely these areas that psychoanalytic therapists must probe most thoroughly.

Akin to free association is the *study of dreams,* for Freud assumed that during sleep the ego defenses are lowered, allowing repressed material to come forth. Truly important repressed material is, by definition, very threatening, and it would probably be defended against by censor functions of the ego. The dreams taken on a heavy symbolic content that helps disguise from the conscious ego the true significance of dream material. The content of dreams, then, is distorted by unconscious defensive structures that continue to fight to protect the ego from repressed impulses.

As presumably unconscious material begins to appear, another technique comes into play, *interpretation*. According to Freud, this stage helps bring about the desired corrective emotional experience. The analyst's goal is to help the person face the hitherto repressed and emotionally loaded conflict. At the "right time" the analyst begins to point out to the patient sources of resistance and the underlying meaning of dreams. Interpretation is the analyst's main weapon against the continued use of defenses. After noting the presence of defenses, as revealed by obstacles in free association, the analyst makes the patient more aware of them through interpretations. He points out how certain verbalizations of the patient relate to repressed unconscious material. He may also suggest what the manifest content of dreams *truly* means. If the interpretation is timed correctly, the patient can begin to examine the repressed impulse in the light of present-day reality. In other words, he can begin to realize that he no longer has to fear the expression of the impulse. This realization leads to further relaxation of defenses and still greater accessibility of repressed material.

In order to achieve the goal of making the unconscious conscious through appropriately timed interpretation, the therapist has to create certain conditions within the therapy hour. He must attempt at all times to be neutral and objective. He must not impose moral judgments on the person. He must at all costs not impose his own needs and desires on the patient's verbalizations and behavior. Feeling safe under these conditions, the patient presumably is enabled to uncover more and more repressed material. Interpretations are held to be particularly helpful in establishing the meaning of *resistances* that disturb the free association. The therapist points out avoidance by the patient, though it is common for the analysand to deny the interpretation. Interestingly, this denial is typically interpreted as a sign that the therapist's interpretation is correct rather than incorrect. The process of "working through" requires the patient to face up to the validity of the analyst's interpretations, often with great emotion. At the same time, however, the therapist must be careful not to force the interpretation on the patient.

Another facet of psychoanalytic therapy is the *transference neurosis*. It, too, facilitates the uncovering of unconscious infantile conflicts. Being a good observer, Freud noted that some of his patients acted toward him in an emotion-charged and unrealisitic way. For example, a patient much older than Freud would behave in a childish manner during a therapy session. Freud was aware that, although these reactions were often positive and loving, many times they were quite negative and hostile. Since these feelings seemed quite out of character with the ongoing therapy relationship, Freud assumed that they were relics, *transferred* to him from past attitudes toward important people in the patient's history, primarily parents. That is, he felt that patients responded to him *as if* he were one of the important people in their past. Freud utilized what he came to regard as an inevitable aspect of psychoanalysis by beginning to make clear to the patient the childhood origin of many of his concerns and fears. This revelation tended also to be an aid in lifting repressions and allowing

PATIENT (a fifty-year-old male business executive): I really don't feel like talking today.

ANALYST: (Remains silent for several minutes, then) Perhaps you'd like to talk about why you don't feel like talking.

PATIENT: There you go again, making demands on me, insisting I do what I just don't feel up to doing. (Pause) Do I always have to talk here, when I don't feel like it? (Voice becomes angry and petulant) Can't you just get off my back? You don't really give a damn how I feel, do you?

ANALYST: I wonder why you feel I don't care.

PATIENT: Because you're always pressuring me to do what I feel I can't do.

Comments. This excerpt must be viewed in context. The patient had been in therapy for about a year, complaining of depression and anxiety. Although extremely successful in the eyes of his family and associates, he himself felt weak and incompetent. Through many sessions of free association and dream analysis, the analyst had begun to suspect that the patient's feelings of failure stemmed from his childhood experiences with an extremely punitive and critical father, a man even more successful than the client, and a person who seemed never to be satisfied with his son's efforts. The exchange quoted was later interpreted by the analyst as an expression of resentment by the patient of his *father's* pressures on him and not of the analyst at all. The patient's tone of voice (petulant), as well as his overreaction to the analyst's gentle suggestion that he talk about his feelings of not wanting to talk, indicated that the patient was angry not at his analyst but at his father. The expression of such feelings to the analyst, transferred from the father to the analyst, was regarded as significant by the therapist and was used in subsequent sessions in helping the patient to reevaluate his childhood fears of expressing aggression toward his father.

the confrontation of hitherto buried impulses. This period in psychoanalytic treatment is commonly referred to as a transference neurosis, and in classical psychoanalysis it is regarded as essential to a complete cure. Indeed, it is precisely when the analyst notices transference developing that he begins to believe that the important neurotic conflict from childhood is being approached. An analyst encourages the development of transference, for he intentionally remains a shadowy figure, typically sitting behind the patient while the patient free-associates, so that the important person in the neurotic conflicts can be projected upon the relatively blank screen that the analyst provides. Precisely because the ther-

FIGURE **18.2**
*The photograph at the top
of this page shows the room
in which Freud saw many of
the patients written about in
his famous psychoanalytic
cases. Below, the ailing
Freud sits working at his
desk. On the opposite page
is a portrait of Freud at
twenty with his fiancée,
Martha Bernays.*

apy setting is so different from the childhood situation, transference neurosis is useful for interpretation purposes. The therapist can readily point out to the patient the irrational nature of his fears and concerns (Figure 18.2).

We turn now to some of the recent modifications of psychoanalytic theory and therapy.

Ego Analysis

The most important modifications in psychoanalytic theory come from a group generally referred to as ego analysts or neo-Freudians. The major figures in this loosely formed movement are Anna Freud (1946), Erik Erikson (1950), David Rapaport (1951), and Heinz Hartmann (1958). Basically, these writers regard Freud's model of man as being much too dependent on instinctual drives. Although Freud by no means ignored the interactions of the organism with the environment, his view was essentially a "push model" in which man is driven by intrapsychic urges. The ego analysts place greater emphasis on man's abil-

healthy fashion, man controls both it and the influence of situational events, selectively responding to consequences he has thoughtfully selected. . . . Man is not at the mercy of either [innate energies or situational events]. He can impose delay and thought between innate energies and action, thus postponing the reduction of such energies indefinitely. Learned responses, primarily thought, make this possible, and although originally they may be learned as a consequence of their energy-reducing function, later they may become relatively independent of such influences (drives) and control them. (Ford and Urban, 1963, pp. 187–188).

We have, then, a set of important *ego functions* that are primarily conscious, capable of controlling both id instincts and the external environment, and most significantly, not dependent on the id for their energy. Ego analysts assume that these functions and capabilities are present at birth and then developed through experience. These ego functions, which Freud underemphasized, have energies of their own and gratifications of their own, usually separate from the reduction of id impulses. And whereas society was, for Freud, essentially a negative inhibition against the unfettered gratification of libidinal impulses, the ego analysts hold that an individual's social interactions can provide their own special kind of gratification.

Since the ego analysts pay most attention to normal, adaptive behavior, their theoretical formulations of behavior disorder are relatively sparse. The principal idea, however, seems to be that behavior becomes pathological when ego control is endangered. Thus, when existing ego functions cannot control and direct libidinal energies or environmental demands, breakdown can occur. Therapy then should be a means by which ego control is reestablished,

ity to control his environment and to select the time and the means by which certain instinctual drives will be satisfied. The concept of *control,* already introduced in Chapter 5, is quite important to ego analysts. They tend also to focus on current living conditions rather than delving deeply into the historical causes of behavior.

The ego analysts do not view man as an automaton pushed hither and yon by imperative innate energies on the one hand and by situational events on the other, constantly seeking some compromise among these conflicting influences. When behavior develops in a although exactly what should be done and how have not been clearly spelled out.

The Ego Psychology of Harry Stack Sullivan

The views on the development of normal and abnormal behavior held by the American psychiatrist Sullivan (Figure 18.3) are generally considered to be a variation of ego psychology. His primary contributions derive from his emphasis on the interpersonal nature of emotional problems. The basic difficulty of patients, according to Sullivan, is so-called *parataxic distortions*, which are developed to protect the ego from some overwhelming anxiety. A parataxic distortion is essentially a misperception of reality stemming from some kind of childhood disorganization in interpersonal relationships. Parataxic distortions reflect attitudes toward people who were significant in the person's past, attitudes that are projected automatically, that is, unconsciously, into all interpersonal relationships, including that between patient and therapist (Wolberg, 1954). The principal goal of therapy is to bring these distortions to the patient's consciousness so that he can evaluate present reality and separate it from past conditioning and learning.

Sullivan was relatively vague, however, with respect to the means by which patients were actually to be changed. For example, it is not clear whether Sullivan assumes that the realization on the part of the patient of the role a given interpersonal relationship was playing in his discomfort would automatically lead to a reduction of anxiety feelings. Like the other ego analysts, Sullivan provides relatively sparse descriptions of specific therapeutic techniques (Ford and Urban, 1963).

Evaluation of Analytic Therapy

There are few issues in clinical and experimental circles more controversial than the

FIGURE **18.3**
Harry Stack Sullivan, the American ego analyst who emphasized interpersonal factors in the development and treatment of abnormal behavior.

question whether psychoanalysis and related therapies work. Some clinicians are uneasy with psychoanalytic concepts themselves, especially those that seem wedded to a notion of *an* unconscious. As one critic puts it, ". . . nothing can be said by the canons of modern philosophy of science, of the existence of the unconscious as a substantive entity: the assertion of its existence is in principle untestable and hence meaningless" (Levy, 1963, p. 22).

A close examination of Levy's harsh judgment makes clear one of the underlying themes of this textbook, namely the problem of paradigms. Those who think in psychoanalytic terms would probably take issue with "the canons of modern philosophy of science" themselves. This paradigm difference bears on an evaluation of the effectiveness of psychoanalysis (in all its various forms). What, for example, are the criteria for improvement? A principal criterion is the lifting of repressions, making the unconscious conscious. But how is that to be demonstrated? How does one determine whether a repression has been lifted? In practice, whatever attempts have been made to assess outcome have relied very heavily on projective tests like the Rorschach, which, in turn, rely heavily on the concept of unconscious. Clearly, if one rejects a priori that very concept, there is little common ground for discussion.

Furthermore, controversies surround the central concept of insight. Rather than accept the view that insight entails the recognition by the client of some important, externally valid historical connection or relationship, several writers (for example, Bandura, 1969; London 1964) propose that the development of insight is better understood as a *social conversion process,* according to which the patient accepts the belief system of his therapist. Marmor (1962) has suggested that insight means different things depending on the school of therapy; a patient treated by a proponent of any of the various schools gets insights along lines of the theoretical predilections of the particular therapy school. For example, Freudians tend to elicit insights regarding oedipal dilemmas, whereas Sullivanians produce insights regarding interpersonal relationships. Indeed, Levy (1963) goes so far as to say that the concept of the unconscious is actually nothing more than a disagreement between what a psychoanalytically oriented therapist and the analysand believe is the case.

One of the difficulties in evaluating criticisms like these stems from problems in evaluating the effectiveness of various kinds of therapies. The insight therapists argue that the worth or validity of a particular insight is to be gauged by its efficacy in producing a desired beneficial therapeutic change. But in the absence both of generally agreed upon criteria for therapeutic change and of well-controlled outcome data, reliance on efficacy for an evaluation of insight is very tenuous. Indeed, as London (1964) has pointed out, psychoanalysts typically classify an insight as merely intellectual if it is not followed by significant behavior change. Thus we have a circular argument: if the patient has an insight and improves, the insight was the "right" one; if improvement does not follow an insight, the insight was merely intellectual or feigned.

With all these cautions in mind, let us consider what efforts people have made to evaluate the power of psychoanalytic and ego-analytic therapy to effect desirable behavioral changes. The efforts have not been as great and sustained as we might hope. One reason may be the nonexperimental orientation of those involved in psychoanalytic practice. Although there are exceptions, those who work within a psychoanalytic framework tend to rely much less on scientific methods than those who, for example, work within a social-learning framework.

Like all therapy research, psychoanalytic research can be divided into studies concentrating on *outcome* or on *process*. Outcome studies address questions such as does the therapy work, and does it work better under one set of conditions than another. Process studies focus on what happens *during* therapy that can be related to the outcome. For example, does transference have to occur for beneficial change to take place?

The following generalizations about Freudian psychoanalysis were made by Luborsky and Spence (1971) on the basis of outcome research with some measure of controlled observation; no research on ego analysis will be reviewed because there is little if anything to report.

1. Patients with severe psychopathology (for example, schizophrenia) do not do as well as neurotics. This is understandable in view of Freud's admitted emphasis on neurosis rather than psychosis and in view of the heavy reliance psychoanalysis places on verbal abilities — a factor that is important in some of the following conclusions as well.
2. The more education a patient has the better he does in analysis, probably because of the heavy emphasis on verbal interactions.
3. There is only conflicting evidence about whether outcomes from psychoanalysis are better than would be achieved after the mere passage of time or by engaging other professional help, such as a family doctor (Bergin, 1971; Eysenck, 1952). This is *not* to say that psychoanalysis does no good, only that clear evidence is as yet lacking. The question being asked, however, is probably too complex to yield a single scientifically acceptable answer, since there is such great diversity in the characteristics of both patients and therapists, and in the severity of patients' problems.

It is even more difficult to draw general conclusions from process studies, primarily because the variables are so complex and, as already stated, inextricably bound up with concepts referring to unconscious processes. One of the variables, for example, is "associative freedom," or the extent to which the analysand can free-associate. If free association helps the analyst get to hitherto repressed material, presumably great facility in free-associating would predict a good outcome. Unfortunately, the relationship is much more complex, for the patient's free association interacts with the analyst's interpretations, and the effectiveness of these, in turn, depends on their timing — not to mention their accuracy. Because of these difficulties, coupled with the problems of defining outcome criteria and reliable measures, it is not surprising that there are no controlled data. Other process variables under study are productivity by patients during sessions and accuracy of interpretations; thus far the data are inconclusive (Luborsky and Spence, 1971).

Freud himself was not optimistic about studying psychoanalysis under scientific conditions; our evaluation of research to date confirms his gloomy prophecy. At this time evidence seems restricted to argumentation by analysts based on clinical case material. Such information, although not trivial, fails to meet many of the criteria for scientific evidence. As noted, the difficulty seems to lie mainly in the very nature of the concepts used. Controlled research on psychoanalysis may be a fruitless endeavor.

HUMANISTIC-EXISTENTIAL THERAPIES

Humanistic-existential therapies, like psychoanalytic therapies, are insight-oriented, being based on the assumption that disordered behavior can best be changed by increasing the individual's awareness of his motivations and needs (see London, 1964). But there is a useful contrast between psychoanalysis and its offshoots on the one hand and existential approaches on the other: the latter attribute considerable freedom of choice to the person.

Free will is regarded as man's most important characteristic. It is, however, a double-edged sword, for it not only offers fulfillment and pleasure but also threatens acute pain and suffering. Free will is an innately provided gift that *must* be used and that requires special courage to use. Not all of us can meet this challenge; those who cannot are said to be candidates for any of several variations of humanistic-existential therapies, among which are client-centered therapy, existential analysis, and Gestalt therapy.

Carl Rogers's Client-Centered Therapy

Carl Rogers (Figure 18.4) is an American psychologist whose theorizing about psychotherapy grew slowly out of years of intensive clinical experience. After teaching at the university level for many years, he helped organize the Center for Studies of the Person in La Jolla, California. Rogers makes several basic assumptions about the nature of man and the means by which one can try to understand him (Ford and Urban, 1963; Rogers, 1951, 1961).

1. One must adopt a phenomenological point of view (see page 4). Man can be understood only from the vantage point of his own perceptions and feelings. It is the way man construes events rather than the events themselves that the investigator must attend to.
2. The healthy person is aware of his behavior. In this sense, Rogers's system is similar to psychoanalysis and ego analysis in emphasizing the desirability of awareness of motives.
3. Man is innately good and effective; he becomes ineffective and disturbed only when faulty learning intervenes.
4. Behavior is purposive and goal-directed; people do not passively respond to the influence of their environment or to their inner drives. In this sense, Rogers is closer to ego analysts than to orthodox Freudian psychoanalysts.
5. The therapist should not attempt to manipulate events for the individual; rather he should create conditions that will facilitate independent decision making by the client.

Personality Development

Rogers postulates an innate tendency to *actualize*, this is, to realize one's potentialities. This idea is basic to his conception of man and therefore crucial to understanding his approach to therapy. In common with Freud and most of the social learning theorists discussed in the next chapter, Rogers holds that men try to reduce the biological tensions from hunger, thirst, and pain. But Rogers proposes that people, in addition and by their very nature, seek to learn new things and otherwise enhance their lives. In other words, people *seek out* pleasurable tension in addition to simply seeking to reduce unpleasurable tension. All behavior, for Rogers, originates in some way from this innate self-actualizing tendency, Furthermore, a person evaluates behavior for its contribution to personal growth or self. Thus behavior with positive consequences in relation to that goal tends to be repeated, but that with negative consequences tends not to be repeated.

Rogers assumes that the most effective learning takes place when a person does not have to struggle for and concern himself with approval from others. The most important evaluations come from the person himself, the self being oriented toward satisfying the innate self-actualizing tendency. Thus, when he receives *unconditional positive regard* from others, he is best able to evaluate how his own behavior can contribute to the enhancement of his own self (self-actualization). This is why, as

FIGURE **18.4**
Carl Rogers, the American humanistic psychologist who developed the client-centered approach to both individual and group psychotherapy.

we shall shortly see, the relearning that takes place in therapy is best done under conditions of unconditional positive regard rather than under judgmental scrutiny by a therapist. Rogers does not argue that ineffective or "bad" behavior should be ignored; rather, even when certain behaviors are discouraged by the environment, the person should still remain confident of being loved as a human being. Providing unconditional positive regard will not produce an antisocial individual because, as Rogers assumes, *people are innately good.*

The natural sequence of healthy development, however, can be interfered with by faulty learning. A person may accept evaluations by others as valid instead of paying heed to the internal evaluations provided by his own psyche and body. For example, someone may apply the denigrating evaluations of others to his own intrinsically good behavior and actually begin to believe them, as when a student regards himself as a worthless human being after being criticized by a teacher. The result is a conflict between self and experience.

This conflict, or incongruence, is an unpleasant state of affairs, creating anxiety. At some point the conflict begins to operate outside of the person's awareness. By the time he consults a therapist, an individual may not even know why he is unhappy.

Therapeutic Intervention

With this brief summary of Rogers's conception of man and the development of disordered behavior, we can now turn to an account of his client-centered psychotherapy. Consistent with the view that a mature and well-adjusted person makes his own judgments based on what is intrinsically satisfying and actualizing, Rogers prohibits the imposition of goals by the therapist upon the client. The therapist's job is to create suitable conditions so that the client can return once again to his basic nature and can himself judge which course of life is intrinsically gratifying to him. Again, because of Rogers's very positive view of man, he assumes that the decisions people make will not only make them happy with themselves but also turn them into good civilized people.

As for the techniques of therapy, Rogers's thinking has evolved from a clear specification of techniques (Rogers, 1942) to an emphasis on the attitude and emotional style of the therapist and a de-emphasis of specific procedures (Rogers, 1951). The main therapeutic task, as already indicated, is to create those conditions necessary for the client to change by himself. By conveying complete acceptance and unconditional positive regard, the therapist enables the client gradually to attend to conflicts between his ideal self (the one that he is capable of being) and the self he has become because of accepting the conflicting evaluations of others. The therapist encourages the client to talk about his most deeply felt emotions. The therapist must therefore have an empathic understanding of the client, so that he can perceive and fully comprehend the client's own feelings. While expressing understanding of the client's feelings, the therapist must be careful not to condemn them.

The basic therapeutic tool—namely the acceptance, recognition, and clarification of feelings—is used within the context of a warm therapeutic relationship. The therapist attempts to restate the emotional aspects, rather than the content, of what the client says.

This mirroring of feelings back to the client, it is assumed, gradually removes the emotional conflicts that are blocking self-actualization. For example, a man might report that he is having communication problems with his wife. Rather than inquire about the specifics of these problems, the client-centered therapist is more inclined to reflect back to the man his apparent concern about poor communication with someone he cares for. The therapist, it should be noted, is not being truly nondirective (a term often applied to Rogers), for he selectively attends to evaluative and feeling statements by the client, the assumption being that the client should be helped to examine these matters for himself (see Truax, 1966).

If these therapeutic conditions are met, the client begins to talk in a more honest way about himself. Rogers assumes that such talk in itself is largely responsible for changing behavior (see Box 18.3).

BOX **18.3**

Excerpt from a Client-Centered Therapy Session

CLIENT (an eighteen-year-old female college student): My parents really bug me. First it was Arthur they didn't like, now it's Peter. I'm just fed up with all their meddling.

THERAPIST: You really are angry at your folks.

CLIENT: Well, how do you expect me to feel? Here I am with a 3.5 GPA, and providing all sorts of other goodies, and they claim the right to pass on how appropriate my boyfriend is. (Begins to sob.)

THERAPIST: It strikes me that you're not just angry with them. (Pause) Maybe you're worried about disappointing them.

CLIENT: (Crying even more) I've tried all my life to please them. Sure their approval is important to me. They're really pleased when I get the A's, but why do they have to pass judgment on my social life as well?

Comments. Although the emotion expressed initially was one of anger, the therapist felt that the client was really fearful of criticism from her parents. Previous sessions had suggested that the client worked hard academically primarily to please her parents and to avoid their censure. She had always been able to win their approval by getting good grades, but more recently the critical eyes of her mother and father were being directed at the boys she was dating. The client was beginning to realize that she was having to arrange her social life to please her parents. Her neurotic fear of disapproval from her parents became the focus in therapy.

Evaluation

Largely because of Rogers's own insistence that the process and outcomes of therapy be carefully scrutinized and experimentally validated, numerous studies have attempted to evaluate client-centered therapy. Indeed, Rogers can be credited with stimulating the whole field of psychotherapy research. He and his students are mainly responsible for removing the mystique and unnecessary privacy of the consulting room by pioneering the use of tape recordings of therapy sessions for subsequent analysis by researchers of therapist-client interactions.

Probably the landmark in client-centered therapy research—and, indeed, in psychotherapy research overall—is the collection of studies reported by Rogers and Dymond (1954) from the University of Chicago Counseling Center. One of these can serve as an illustration of the kind of research Rogerians have done.

Butler and Haigh (1954) used the Q-sort technique to study changes in self-concept as a function of client-centered therapy. In the Q-sort technique a client categorizes a number of statements (for instance, "I am a hard worker," "I am likable") as they apply to him. The "him" can vary in a number of ways: for example, the client can be asked to sort according to how he sees himself now (real self), how he would like to be (ideal self), how his mother views him, and so forth. Since a principal goal of client-centered therapy is to reduce the distance between real self and ideal self (that is, to increase self-acceptance), Butler and Haigh had clients rate themselves before and after therapy. They also obtained ratings from "normal" controls (students who were not entering therapy) and from waiting-list controls (students who wanted therapy but were told they would have to wait two months). As Rogers would predict, the correlation between actual self and ideal self was very low for the student-clients before therapy

began but rather high for the normal controls: thus, people desiring therapy experience a discrepancy between actual self and ideal self whereas normals do not. The students who underwent client-centered therapy showed a significant increase in real-self–ideal-self correlation, but those on the waiting list did not change. The normals also did not change, remaining at their original high level. These results, and findings from studies reported elsewhere, suggest that client-centered therapy produces a desirable increase in congruence between how a person views himself and how he would like to be. It must be pointed out, however, that there was no control for the ever-present placebo effect in the Butler and Haigh study; virtually no psychotherapy research includes such controls.

In keeping with Rogers's phenomenological approach, the measures of results most frequently used are self-reports by clients, either in interviews or by various rating procedures like the Q-sort. Research on Rogerian therapy pays practically no attention to how patients actually *behave* following therapy. We have here a paradigm problem, inasmuch as Rogers's basic datum is the individual's own phenomenological evaluation and reaction to himself and events in his world; the overt behavior, it is held, follows from these perceptions and is not the proper object of study by the client-centered therapy researcher.

This neglect of behavior outside of the therapy session can create problems for clients who have never learned to behave in particular ways. A client whose feelings of inferiority are overcome during sessions might very well be at a loss to behave differently once he leaves the consulting room because he has never acquired an adequate repertoire of social skills. If he is truly to change his concept of himself, it would seem necessary to provide information to counteract a negative self-concept—in this case, interpersonal skills.

Rogers's emphasis on subjective experience also raises important epistemological problems, for the therapist must be able to make accurate and incisive inferences about what the client is feeling or thinking. Although the method seems to rely entirely on what the client says, Rogers asserts that clients can be unaware of their true feelings; indeed, it is this unawareness that brings most of them into therapy in the first place. As with psychoanalysis, one has to ask under what conditions may a therapist make an inference about internal processes of which a client is seemingly unaware, and then by what procedures can the usefulness or validity of that inference be evaluated.

Rogers may also be criticized for his assumption that there is a master motive of self-actualization. The problems of an innately given drive or motive are of course not limited to Roger's views. Difficulties crop up (see Chapter 4) whenever behavior is explained by inferring an internal concept for which there is little independent evidence. In other words, much of what Rogers talks about is readily explained by inferring the self-actualizing tendency. But is not such an "explanation" merely a redescription of the behavior that it is alleged to cause?

Then, of course, there is the question of the therapist's own influence on what happens in the therapy session. Rogers no longer refers to his therapy as nondirective, evidently an admission of the influence inherent in the therapeutic situation. That a client's verbal statements are shaped by Rogerians was shown by an analysis of one of Rogers's own therapy transcripts (see Truax, 1966).

Another point to consider is how faulty ideas are learned from the evaluation of others. Under what circumstances does such faulty learning occur? Why does the master motive not always predominate over the individual's learning? If the master motive is indeed always directing the person toward self-actualization, under what conditions does faulty learning take place, and what motives and needs are satisfied by such faulty learning?

Recall also that Rogers assumes that the psychologically healthy person is one who has made his own choices to satisfy his own self-actualizing tendencies. Rogers assumes that man by his very nature is good and that undesirable, self-defeating, or otherwise dangerous behavior is the result of learning that is not self-actualizing. But other social philosophers have taken a less optimistic view of men's nature. Thomas Hobbes, for example, stated that life is "nasty, brutish, and short." What do we do with a person who is behaving in a brutish fashion and yet asserts that this behavior is intrinsically gratifying and, indeed, self-actualizing?

It may be that the problem of extreme unreasonableness was not adequately handled by Rogers because he and his colleagues have concentrated on people who are only mildly disturbed rather than those with a psychotic disturbance. Rogerian therapy may not, in fact, be appropriate for severe psychological disturbance, as Rogers himself has warned. As a way to help many unhappy people understand themselves better (and *perhaps* even to help them behave differently), client-centered therapy may very well be appropriate and effective. As with most forms of therapy, however, the effectiveness of Rogerian procedures has not been well demonstrated, although this humanistic approach remains popular, especially in the encounter group movement (Chapter 20).

Existential Analysis

Those most commonly associated with existential analysis are the Danish philosopher Kierkegaard, the German philosophers Husserl and Heidegger, and the Swiss psychiatrists

FIGURE **18.5**
Two of the primary figures in the existential analysis movement: left, Rollo May: right, Abraham Maslow.

Binswanger and Boss. In this country the principal proponents have been Rollo May and the late Abraham Maslow (Figure 18.5). The following presentation of existential analysis is a distillation of the points of view of these men.

According to the existential position,

Man has the capacity for being aware of himself, of what he is doing, and what is happening to him. As a consequence, he is capable of making decisions about these things and of taking responsibility for himself. He can also become aware of a possibility of becoming completely isolated and alone, that is, nothing, symbolized by the ultimate nothingness of death. This is innately feared. He is not a static entity but in a constant state of transition. He does not exist; he is not a being; rather he is coming into being, emerging, becoming, evolving toward something. His ways of behaving toward himself and other events are changing constantly. His significance lies not in what he has been in the past, but in what he is now and the direction of his development, which is toward the fulfillment of his innate potentiality (Ford and Urban, 1963, p. 448).

We have already examined a similar point of view put forth by Carl Rogers. A further similarity between the two approaches is the method the existentialists propose for understanding man, the phenomenological research method. The existential therapist attempts to understand a person's problems through the subjective point of view of the client. In other words, the therapist tries to deal with reality not as he perceives it, but rather as it appears to the client. This approach, of course requires one human being to view things through the perspective of another. This is no easy task! Existentialists are aware of the difficulty, and they recommend that the therapist understand his own feelings and biases so that he can hold them in abeyance while he attempts to place himself within the phenomenological world of the client.

Another key feature of existential therapy is the importance of relating authentically to others. The assumption is that people define their identity and existence in terms of their interpersonal relationships. One way that a person can be threatened with an awareness of nonbeing—or alienation—is to be isolated from others. Even though he might be quite effective in dealing with people and his world as objects (see the discussion of Maddi's views in Chapter 6), anxiety can arise when he is deprived of open and frank relationships. Hence, even though the existential view is a highly subjective one, there is a strong emphasis on people *relating to others* in an open, honest, and loving fashion. The encounter group movement owes much to existential analysis (Chapter 20).

Like Rogers, the existentialists hold that behavior becomes disordered when man's natural tendency to fulfill his potential is interfered with. Events eliciting such anxiety that the person must expend his energies avoiding them are the usual happenstances by which the urge for self-fulfillment is blocked. Since in the existentialist view man creates his existence anew at each moment, the potential for disorder is ever-present. Everyone is subject to anxiety situations yet not everyone becomes neurotic or psychotic. Why, then, do some people break down and others do not? The response of the existentialists is that some people have developed a strong sense of their own identities and worth as human beings and are therefore less susceptible to existential breakdowns.

The goal of existential therapy is to make the patient more aware of his own potential for choice and growth. The person must be encouraged to accept responsibility for his own existence and to realize that, within certain limits, he can redefine himself at any moment and behave and feel differently within his own social environment. Since anxiety regarding authentic relating to others is assumed to interfere with becoming, presumably therapy somehow reduces this anxiety so that the person's natural tendency to lead a meaningful existence is able to assert itself. The existential writers, however, are very vague about how such relearning takes place and which techniques in therapy can achieve this goal. Clearly, the existential therapist must have the kind of attitude that Rogers advocates, namely suspending his own biases and perceptions so that he can better immerse himself in the patient's phenomenological world. The therapeutic relationship should become an authentic encounter between two human beings so that the patient can have some practice in relating to himself and to others in a straightforward fashion.[1]

Evaluation

Although existential therapists have published numerous case reports relating striking suc-

---

[1] It is interesting to note that this approach, which places so much emphasis on a person's perceptions, understanding, feelings, and other internal processes, is in a way very behavioristic in the overt sense of the word, for the person must at some point during therapy begin to behave differently both toward the therapist and toward the outside world so that his own existential condition can be changed.

cesses with a variety of clinical problems, there are no data that approach scientific rigor. What may be of more interest is a critical examination of their phenomenological approach to knowledge. Existentialism is entirely different from the paradigm emphasized in this book. Existentialists believe that efforts to approach human beings in scientific ways deny the unique humanness of human beings. But the alternative that they propose, although interesting and compelling, has its own problems. Since by definition a person's subjective experience is unique to himself, how can one know when a therapist is truly understanding a patient's world as it appears to him? The data that are available to a therapist are nothing more than the verbal and motor behaviors of the client; everything else necessarily remains an *inference* on the part of the therapist. To be sure, such inferences might seem very convincing to the therapist and even to the individual whose phenomenological world is being inferred; nonetheless, one must ask whether the patient *really* is perceiving things the way a therapist infers he is at any given time. As we suggested in Chapter 1, we are left with *constructs* formulated by observers in attempting to understand a particular part of the human world. This, of course, is not necessarily bad, for the attention that existentialists pay to subjective impressions and the emphasis that they place on a person's freedom to choose and ability to change at any time may, in fact, be important means of changing behavior. But without good outcome data, it is difficult to know for certain how helpful such attention is to the patient.

Gestalt Therapy

A school of psychotherapy that has developed over the past twenty years within the general framework of humanistic and existential

FIGURE **18.6**
Frederick (Fritz) Perls, colorful founder of Gestalt therapy.

therapies is Gestalt therapy; its most important proponent was the late Frederick S. Perls (Figure 18.6). After receiving medical training in Germany, Perls became a psychoanalyst but was rejected by European analysts because of his challenges to some of the basic precepts of psychoanalytic theory, particularly the important place accorded to the libido and its various transformations in the development of neurosis. He emigrated to South Africa to escape the Nazi persecutions in Germany and ultimately took up residence in the United States, where his ideas and techniques of therapy have undergone impressive growth (Perls, Hefferline, and Goodman, 1951; Perls, 1970).

Basic Concepts of Gestalt Therapy

Like Rogers, Perls holds that man has an innate goodness and that it is desirable to allow this basic nature to express itself. Psychological problems are seen as originating in frustrations and denials of man's innate goodness. Like other humanistic approaches, Gestalt therapy tends to emphasize the creative and expressive aspects of people, rather than the negative and distorted features which psychoanalytically oriented conceptualizations concentrate on.

Perls and his followers concentrate on the here and now, placing considerable importance on the individual as an actor, as a being who is responsible for his own behavior and who is capable of playing a central role in bringing about beneficial changes.

The patient who comes for help, seeking to relate more adequately with other people and to be able to express his feelings more directly is instructed to express what he is feeling at that moment to another person. The ways in which he stops, blocks, and frustrates himself quickly become apparent, and he can then be assisted in exploring and experiencing the blockings and encouraged to attempt other ways of expressing himself and of relating.

Thus, the general approach of Gestalt theory and therapy requires the patient to specify the changes in himself that he desires, assists him in increasing his awareness of how he defeats himself, and aids him in experimenting and changing. Blocks in awareness and behavior emerge in the same way that they manifest themselves in a person's life; his increased awareness of his avoidances and his relief as he becomes able to expand his experience and behavior are felt immediately in increases in capacity for living (*Fagan and Shepherd, 1970, p. 2*).

The foregoing description of Gestalt therapy makes it difficult to distinguish this approach from what Rogers prescribes. There is also said to be a relationship between Gestalt therapy and Gestalt psychology, a branch of psychology concerned primarily with perception. It may be that the closest similarity is found in Perls's emphasis on making a person *whole* once again, in touch with his feelings and thoughts, and allowing his behavior to be consonant with this unity.

The manner in which Gestalt therapy applies Gestalt psychology to personality development, and especially abnormal development, has been described by Wallen (1970). In the terminology of Gestalt psychology, the central aspects that we attend to as we view the world are referred to as *figure*. The remaining information is considered *ground*. To the Gestalt therapist, a human being must fulfill certain needs, and failure to do so causes him psychological suffering. As an example of how the two concepts are brought together, consider a person reading alone in a room. As he concentrates on the book, the book is the figure and everything else in the room is the ground. Suppose, however, that the person becomes thirsty and notices that his mouth is dry. The mouth now becomes the figure and the book becomes part of the ground. Awareness of the thirst, the current need, makes him do something about it, namely getting something to drink. The drink satisfies the thirst, relegating the sensations in the mouth to ground and allowing the person to return to his reading again, treating the book as a figure. Wallen uses this example to illustrate the importance of Gestalt formation and destruction. People have different needs at various times, and they must be satisfied. Some people, however, prevent a need from assuming the appropriate figure and thereby contribute to their own suffering, just as a thirsty person is likely to lose enjoyment in his reading if he does not get a drink of water. The healthy person, according to this formulation, is able to move flexibly from one figure to another, satisfying each particular need as it arises so that his behavior can be goal-directed and satisfying.

This kind of Gestalt formation and destruction is said to go on all the time; hence the Gestalt therapist can focus on what his client is doing right in the consulting room, here and now, without delving very much into the past. In the actual sessions, the therapist can see how the individual grapples with his emergent needs. Consider a patient who seems ready to cry and yet does not. The Gestalt therapist will notice wetness in the eyes and perhaps grimacing around the mouth; he will conclude that the figure of crying is emerging but is being prevented from becoming the dominant figure in the person's perceptual-emotional field. The therapist then can point out to the person what is happening and (presumably) encourage him to cry, that is, to focus on the figure, excluding everything else by relegating it to the ground. As the person becomes more and more practiced in focusing on emergent needs, he will learn a general skill of fulfilling needs as they arise.

Gestalt Therapy Techniques

A general rule is to emphasize the present. Perls feels very strongly that nothing exists but the now. The only things that can be coped with are faced in the present, though past and future experiences can also be brought into the present with the use of appropriate techniques.

The Gestalt therapist insists that the client talk in the present tense and direct his attention to current feelings and activities. Perls assumes further, as do other existentially oriented therapists, that people must bear continuing responsibility for what they are and what they are to become. One way this is achieved is by changing "it" language into "I" language.

THERAPIST: *What do you hear in your voice?*
PATIENT: *My voice sounds like it is crying.*
THERAPIST: *Can you take responsibility for that by saying, I am crying? (Levitsky and Perls, 1970, p. 142).*

This simple change in language, it is said, makes it easier for the patient to assume responsibility for particular feelings and behavior and reduces the sense of alienation between aspects of his very being. It helps the patient see himself as an active rather than a passive agent, as a responsible human being rather than as someone whose behavior is determined entirely by external events.

A convenient gambit for the Gestalt therapist is to have a client talk to a projection of a feeling, or to a person, object, or situation. Thus, seeing that a patient is crying, the Gestalt therapist might ask him to regard the tears as being in a chair opposite him and to speak to the tears. This tactic often seems to help people confront their feelings.

Another technique is to have the person behave opposite to the way he feels. Someone who is excessively timid might be asked in the therapy session to behave like an outgoing person. Perls assumes that the opposite side of the coin actually lies within the being of the person and that this confrontation allows the person to make contact with a part of himself that has been thus far submerged.

The interpretation of dreams is an important part of Gestalt therapy, although the Gestalt analysis of them is quite different from the psychoanalytic. Rather than the dream being considered a rich source of symbolism relating to unconscious processes,

Every image in the dream, whether human, animal, vegetable, or mineral is taken to represent an alienated portion of the self. By reexperiencing and retelling the dream over and over again in the present tense, from the standpoint of each image, the patient can begin to reclaim these alienated fragments, and accept them, live with them, and express them more appropriately (Enright, 1970, p. 121).

For example, a woman in Gestalt therapy dreamt of walking down a crooked path among tall straight trees. The therapist asked her to *become* one of the trees, and this made her feel serene and more deeply rooted. She then expressed her desire for such security. When asked to become the crooked path, she became tearful as she confronted the deviousness of the way she lived.

Once again, then, we see the attempt of the Gestalt therapist to externalize the feelings that a person has and that he has been customarily avoiding, so that he can more adequately confront them, become aware of them, and then presumably decide to change them.

The Gestalt Therapy Philosophy of Life

As Naranjo (1970) has pointed out, an important aspect of Gestalt therapy is a philosophy of life that the therapist (perhaps unwittingly) conveys to the patient. Although Perls repeatedly emphasized that the therapist should not "lay his own trip" on the patient, nonetheless a patient in Gestalt therapy seems to be provided with what the therapist regards as a desirable mode of living. That mode includes the following prescriptions.

1. One should be concerned much more with the present rather than with the past or the future.

2. One should deal more with what is here than with what is absent.
3. One should experience things rather than imagine them.
4. One should feel rather than think.
5. One should express one's feelings rather than justify or explain them, or judge those of others.
6. One should open one's awareness to pain as well as to pleasure.
7. One should not use the word should (except, perhaps, in this set of injunctions — authors' observation).
8. One should take responsibility for one's actions, feelings, and thoughts.
9. One should surrender to being the kind of person one is.

As Naranjo points out, all these prescriptions can be subsumed under the rubric of "living-in-the-moment," or as Perls puts it, *living in the now.*

Those who knew or met Fritz Perls are aware that he seemed to personify the ideals of his therapy. He was a very present-oriented, earthy, spontaneous individual, who placed great emphasis upon satisfying his own needs while at the same time respecting the needs of others. This philosophy can perhaps be summed up in the following poetic statement by Perls:

I do my thing and you do your thing. I am not in this world to live up to your expectations. And you are not in this world to live up to mine. You are you and I am I. And if by chance we find each other, it's beautiful. If not, then not.

Evaluation

As with nearly every school of therapy, our initial criticism concerns the lack of evidence supporting the efficacy of the therapy. Again, it is worth emphasizing that this comment does not mean that people who go through such therapy are necessarily wasting their time. On the contrary, many people are undoubtedly helped by therapists who follow Perls's thinking and use his therapeutic techniques. Rather, we wish to caution that at least a part of the therapeutic improvement might be attributable to the placebo effect or to any number of other factors.

A second critical point, already alluded to, is the gap between Perls's concepts and his techniques. This problem is common to all therapies, but there are special difficulties relating the theoretical concepts of Gestalt therapy to what is actually done with patients. Our own reading of the Gestalt therapy literature suggests that these therapists spend much or most of their time urging clients to be more expressive, more responsive to their own needs and to the feelings of others, and more spontaneous. Perls describes this activity as making the person more attentive to emerging gestalts, and he thereby aligns his psychotherapy with the experimental findings of Gestalt psychology. It is open to question, however, whether Perls's description is the most accurate or parsimonious way of talking about the techniques, and, most importantly, whether the use of such concepts helps clients the most and assists in the effective training of good Gestalt therapists.

A central part of Gestalt therapy is the forcefully conveyed existential message that a person is not a prisoner of his past, that he can make the existential choice at any time to be different, and that the therapist will not toler-ate stagnation. No doubt this optimistic view helps many people change. If the person does not know how to behave differently, however, considerable damage can be done to an already miserable individual.

A third difficulty we see with Gestalt therapy is similar to a complaint voiced about Rogers's client-centered therapy; indeed, it may be common to all humanistic-existential therapies. Suppose that a client feels the need to murder someone or to engage in behavior that, to outside observers, is surely undesirable. What is the therapist's responsibility? According to the theories of the existentialists, people are, by their very nature, good and beautiful. If the belief is valid, it would be reasonable to trust this intrinsic good nature and to encourage direct expression of needs. But are people always good? Sometimes clients—especially those who are psychologically troubled—feel they must do something that, in professional judgment, is not to their own best interests. At what point does the therapist intervene and impose his or her judgment? Our own reading of the Gestalt literature suggests that Gestalt therapists do *not* abdicate all decisions to their clients and that they do exert considerable influence on them, if only by virtue of the models they themselves provide (recall our earlier comments on Perls as a person). It is likely that most people adopt the values of their therapists (Rosenthal, 1955), and it seems preferable to us to admit this social influence so that it can be dealt with rather than to deny that such influence exists and perhaps allow for even greater "tyranny" of therapists over patients.

BOX **18.4** *Psychosynthesis and the Transpersonal Self*

The problem of paradigms, encountered so often in our review of abnormal psychology, is especially pertinent in connection with a development in personality theory and psychotherapy called psychosynthesis. Proposed originally in 1910 by an Italian psychiatrist, Roberto Assagioli, psychosynthesis holds that man has not only a biological and a psychological aspect to his personality but a spiritual one as well.

Assagioli assumes that, in addition to the self we usually experience, each of us also has access to a spirtual or "transpersonal" self, an awareness that transcends our usual experience and is similar to the reported experience of mystics and some people who have used psychedelic drugs. Whereas the usual conscious self tends to be defined in terms of symbols and roles—for example, the successful businessman whose sense of identity is in terms of his salary and professional achievements—the transpersonal self is asserted to be a deeper, more fundamental identity.

Psychosynthesis is said to allow the individual the opportunity to become aware of this expanded sense of self. The experience of this state of awareness is said to relieve many anxieties and doubts, enabling a person to participate more fully in everyday experience. There is less need to be guarded as an individual realizes that his identity is not limited to his roles, not limited to the sense of "I" that we usually experience. There is reported to be less concern with past failures and increased flexibility in coping with new situations.

Assagioli and others have devised many techniques to facilitate this expanded sense of transpersonal self. One is called "dis-identification," whereby a person is encouraged systematically (and briefly) to stop identifying with his own body, emotions, or intellect. It is suggested that he consider the implications of "having a body but not being only a body, having emotions but not being

the same as one's emotions, having an intellect which is a tool but not a total definition of one's self" (Fadiman, 1973). A variation of dis-identification is called astral projection, an imaginary trip in which the person is encouraged to view his everyday self leaving his body and flying upward to the stars to enjoy unity with nature and gain a perspective on his life which minimizes unnecessary cares. At the end of the mind-trip, the everyday self returns to the body, hopefully with a newly discovered sense that he is more than his body and normal consciousness. As these and other exercises are practiced, individuals report feeling detached from normal concerns; they realize that their behavior may have become dysfunctional because they have identified too strongly with one or another aspect of their lives.

Although Assagioli and his colleagues wrote before the widespread use of psychedelic drugs, psychosynthesis is especially appealing to those who have had positive experiences with chemicals like LSD and psilocybin. Anecdotal evidence suggests that many people are able—at least in the short run—to lose many of their needless worries by virtue of the enlarged perspective that often accompanies a "trip." It is possible that a drugless orientation such as psychosynthesis can convince some people that personal concerns need not be taken as seriously as seems inevitable in our everyday mode of existence.

We offer this brief description to illustrate an orientation to psychological suffering that is markedly different from anything thus far dealt with in this textbook. The evidence for this theory is still limited, but an increasing number of therapists using these techniques report success in dealing with a wide variety of conditions. As with psychoanalysis, however, it appears to be intrinsic to psychosynthesis that its basic assumptions cannot be scientifically proved or disproved.

SUMMARY

Insight therapies share the basic assumption that a person's behavior is disordered because he is not aware of what motivates his actions. Psychoanalysis and ego analysis tend to emphasize factors from the past, whereas most humanistic-existential approaches (like those of Rogers and Perls) appear to emphasize the current determinants of behavior.

Consistent with Freud's second theory of neurosis, psychoanalysis aims at uncovering childhood-based repressions so that infantile fears of libidinal expression can be examined by the adult ego in the light of present-day realities. Ego analysis puts more emphasis on the need of the patient to achieve greater control over the environment and over instinctual gratifications.

Rogers trusts the basic goodness of man's drive to actualize himself, and he proposes the creation of nonjudgmental conditions in therapy through unconditional positive regard to help clients view themselves more accurately and come to trust their own instincts for self-actualization. Existential therapists, influenced primarily by European existential philosophy, similarly regard man as having the innate ability to realize his potential, and they place heavy emphasis on the freedom of man's will to decide at any given moment to become different. Both Rogers and the existentialists assume that the only reality is the one that is perceived by the individual; thus the therapist must try at all times to view the world in the client's phenomenological frame of reference, rather than in his own.

The Gestalt therapy of Perls is usually regarded as humanistic-existential, yet it is different in important ways from the therapies of Rogers and other existentialists. Perls emphasizes living in the now, and the various techniques he and his followers have introduced are aimed at helping the client experience his current needs and to feel comfortable about satisfying them as they emerge. Thus the emphasis is on changing behavior, and yet the ultimate goal seems still to be increased awareness or insight into what is currently motivating the person.

In addition to some specific criticisms we have made on each of these insight therapies, there is a problem with all of them that impedes progress and refinement, namely an almost complete lack of scientific data to support the claims of efficacy and the assertions that changes do occur for the reasons expounded by the various theorists. Part of the difficulty may well be the ever-present paradigm problem, for some theorists — especially the existentialists — appear to dismiss a priori the need for and even the possibility of the kind of controlled research that most social scientists deem important. Perhaps the ultimate question (especially when great sums of money are involved in the fees people pay to therapists) is the very pragmatic one of whether people are helped by therapists. Even when patients do derive benefit, however, it is still possible that their improvement is attributable at least in part to the ubiquitous placebo effect.

CHAPTER 19

Behavior Modification

The various insight-oriented therapies share the assumption that dis- ordered behavior can be alleviated by enabling sufferers to know the reasons for their behavior. These therapies also share the hope that people in treatment will feel and behave better as a consequence of their increased awareness. And yet, behavior has sometimes been ig- nored in these systems, a neglect that opens them to criticism. An- other vulnerable aspect of insight therapies relates to their develop- ment and justification. The theorists described in the preceding chapter have operated almost entirely outside the mainstream of academic-experimental psychology. They were primarily practi- tioners, concerned with helping individuals who turned to them for as- sistance, and were seldom well grounded in the methodology and principles of experimental psychology.

Throughout this book we have stressed the utility of a scientific approach to the study of human behavior in general and abnormal behavior in particular. Over the past two decades an approach to psy- chotherapy has developed within a scientific framework; it is called *behavior therapy* or *behavior modification*. Initially the approach was restricted to therapy based on classical or operant conditioning, but today it is viewed more broadly as applied experimental psychology (see Bandura, 1969; Kanfer and Phillips, 1970).

Behavior modification, as now conceived, is an experimental ap- proach to the study of the alteration of deviant behavior, character- ized more by its epistemological stance — its search for rigorous stand- ards of proof — than by allegiance to any particular set of concepts(see Davison and Goldfried, 1973). In brief, behavior modification is an attempt to study and change abnormal behavior by drawing on the methods used by experimental psychologists in their study of normal behavior.

The beginning of behavior therapy is difficult to date specifically; some social scientists did not wake up one morning and say that today was the day that behavior therapy was to begin. Rather, over many years people in the clinical field began to develop a new set of assumptions about the best means of dealing with the problems that they encountered. There are four discernibly separate threads in the development of behavior therapy—counterconditioning, operant conditioning, modeling, and cognitive restructuring.

COUNTERCONDITIONING

In counterconditioning, illustrated in Figure 19.1, a response (R_1) to a given stimulus (S) is eliminated by eliciting a different behavior (R_2) in the presence of that stimulus. For example, if a child is afraid (R_1) of a harmless animal (S), one attempts to elicit a playful reaction (R_2) in the presence of the animal. Experimental evidence suggests that this counterconditioning, or response substitution, procedure can eliminate R_1. An early clinical demonstration of counterconditioning was a famous case reported by Mary Cover Jones (1924). She successfully eliminated a little boy's fear of rabbits by feeding him in the presence of a rabbit, beginning with the animal several feet away and gradually moving it closer on successive occasions. In this fashion the fear (R_1) produced by the rabbit (S) was "crowded out" by the stronger positive feelings associated with eating (R_2).

Systematic Desensitization

Thirty years later Joseph Wolpe (1958) employed similar techniques with fearful patients. He found that many of his clients, like the child treated by Jones, could be helped when they were encouraged to expose themselves gradually to the situation or object they feared while engaging in behavior that inhibited anxiety. Rather than have his patients eat, however, Wolpe taught them deep muscle relaxation, using training procedures adapted from earlier pioneering work by Jacobson (1929).

Jacobson had shown that strong emotional states like anxiety would be markedly inhibited if a person could learn to relax very deeply. In his many experiments various autonomic indices as well as self-reports reflected a marked reduction of anxiety in subjects who had been taught to let go of all their muscles.

Many of the fears felt by Wolpe's patients were so abstract—for example, fear of criticism or fear of failure—that it was impractical to present them *in vivo*, that is, in real life. Following earlier proposals by Salter (1949), Wolpe reasoned that he might have fearful patients *imagine* what they feared. Thus he formulated a new technique in therapy, which he called *systematic desensitization*, a term prob-

FIGURE **19.1**
Schematic diagram of counterconditioning, whereby an original response (R_1) to a given situation (S) is eliminated by evoking a new behavior (R_2) in the same situation.

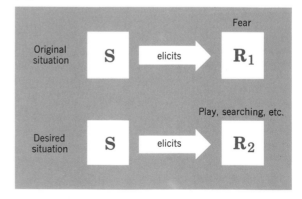

ably derived from the medical procedure of administering increasing doses of allergens to hay fever and asthma sufferers. In this procedure a deeply relaxed person is asked to imagine a graded series of anxiety-provoking situations; the relaxation tends to inhibit any anxiety that might otherwise be elicited by the imagined scenes. Over successive sessions a client is usually able to tolerate increasingly more difficult scenes as he climbs the hierarchy in his imagination. As has been documented by Wolpe as well as by many other clinicians (for example, Lazarus and Rachman, 1957), the ability to tolerate stressful imagery is generally followed by a reduction of anxiety in related *real-life* situations. The following case demonstrates how this clinical innovation has made it possible to treat a wider range of human neurotic fears and phobias than would have been feasible by dealing only with real-life stimuli.

A thirty-five-year-old substitute mail carrier consulted us after having dropped out of college sixteen years earlier because of crippling fears of being criticized. Earlier, his disability took the form of extreme tension related to tests and to speaking up in class. When we saw him, he was debilitated by fears of evaluations of his performance in sorting mail and by criticism in general. As a consequence, his everyday activities were severely constricted and, though highly intelligent, he apparently had to settle for an occupation that did not promise self-fulfillment.

After agreeing that a reduction in his unrealistic fears would be beneficial, the client was taught over several sessions to relax all the muscles of his body while in a reclining chair. A hierarchy of anxiety-provoking scenes was also drawn up in consultation with the client and he was later asked to imagine them in a relaxed state. For example:

You are saying "Good morning" to your boss.
You are standing in front of your sorting-bin in the post office, and your supervisor asks why you are so slow.
You are only halfway through your route, and it is already 2:00 p.m.
As you are delivering Mrs. MacKenzie's mail, she opens her screen door and complains about how late you are.
Your wife criticizes you for bringing home the wrong kind of bread.
The officer at the bridge toll gate appears impatient as you fumble in your pocket for the correct change.

These and other scenes were arranged in an anxiety hierarchy, from least to most fear-evoking, analogous to the gradual manner in which Jones brought the feared rabbit closer and closer to the little boy. Desensitization proper began when the client was instructed to imagine the easiest item, while at the same time relaxing as best he could. After ten sessions the man was able to imagine the most distressing scene in the hierarchy without feeling anxious, and gradually his tensions in real life became markedly less.

In clinical practice systematic desensitization has proved effective with a great variety of anxiety-related problems. Indeed, many of the complaints described in Part II of this book are amenable to the technique—phobias, obsessions and compulsions, fears of sexual intimacy, reactive depression, and psychosomatic disorders like ulcer, asthma, and hypertension (Wolpe and Lazarus, 1966). Getting the client to move from imagination to actuality is facilitated by homework assignments in which he places himself in progressively frightening situations between therapy sessions; such real-life exposures no doubt contribute to therapeutic gains (for example, Davison, 1968b; Sherman, 1972).

As with all the techniques described in this chapter, very rarely is only one procedure used exclusively. A person fearful of social interactions might well be given training in conversational and other social skills in addition to desensitization. Furthermore, the applicability of desensitization largely depends on the therapist's ingenuity in formulating a client's problems in terms of anxiety. For example, the problem of a client who is depressed and complains of feeling desperate and hopeless might well result from fears of sexual contact; the fear, then, would be the proper focus of desensitization. This issue is related to the question of "underlying causes," discussed at the end of this chapter (page 511).

Assertive Training

Another counterconditioning technique is Salter's (1949) *assertive training*. Many people are unable to express positive or negative feelings to others and are thus crippled in their social encounters. For example, an individual can suffer great inconvenience because he finds it difficult to ask for something that is his due. Salter assumes that the expression of resentment or appreciation can countercondition the anxiety associated with specific interpersonal situations. He therefore encourages socially inhibited people to express their feelings to others in a graded fashion, thereby making each new situation less and less aversive; the result is akin to what is supposed to happen during desensitization. Recent experimental work confirms the earlier clinical findings (see McFall and Marston, 1970).

Aversive Conditioning

Another related approach is *aversive conditioning,* which attempts to attach negative feelings to stimuli that are considered inappropriately attractive. For example, a boot fetishist (see Chapter 11) might desire to be less attracted to the sight or feel of boots. To reduce the attraction, a therapist could give the client repeated electric shocks when pictures of boots are presented. The method is similar to desensitization, but the goal is different, since the new response is an anxiety or aversive reaction that is to be substituted for a positive response. Other problems dealt with in this way include overeating, smoking, excessive drinking, exhibitionism, and transvestism.

Perhaps the most widespread use of aversive procedures—and certainly the most controversial—is with homosexuals who desire to change their sexual orientation. Many behavior therapists view homosexuality as a problem of inappropriate positive attraction to same-sexed stimuli; therefore their therapeutic approach is

"Do you have any idea when the meek shall inherit the earth?"

(DRAWING BY DANA FRADON; © 1972 THE NEW YORKER MAGAZINE, INC.)

to attempt to reduce this attraction. The literature on classical aversive conditioning (that is, pairing a neutral or positive stimulus with an unconditioned stimulus such as a shock) of animals suggests that negative reactions can be conditioned, so it is not surprising that various treatment programs have been formulated along these lines.

The most systematic research in this area has been done by Feldman and MacCulloch (1971). They have devised aversive techniques to discourage looking at homosexual stimuli. A homosexual man who desires to become less attracted to other men is asked to rate a series of pictures of males and females along a scale of increasing attractiveness. He is then

BOX 19.1 *Therapy for Sexual Dysfunctions by Masters and Johnson*

Masters and Johnson (1970) have not identified themselves as behavior therapists, but it seems appropriate for several reasons to include their work here. Many of their techniques have been used for some time by behavior therapists (for example, Wolpe, 1958). More importantly, their therapy procedures are based largely on their earlier laboratory work (Masters and Johnson, 1966), and they are strongly committed to evaluating their clinical outcomes in as controlled a fashion as possible.

In Chapter 11 we saw that Masters and Johnson view performance fears and the spectator role as the most important variables in maintaining sexual dysfunction. Numerous historical factors enter into the development of a variety of sexual dysfunctions, but all these etiologically relevant factors funnel into the common problems of fears about performance and assuming a spectator role (see Figure 11.8, page 290).

The basic assumption is that sexual enjoyment will naturally occur if fear does not interfere. The therapy proposed is aimed at reducing or eliminating fears of performance and taking the participants out of their maladaptive roles as spectators.

In the original program, couples participate in two weeks of intensive therapy. Each day the couple meets with a dual-sex therapy team, the assumption being that men understand men better than they understand women and vice versa. For the first several days the experiences of all couples are the same, regardless of their specific problem. During the first two days a complete social and sexual history is obtained and physical examinations are conducted so that any organic factors can either be excluded or be found and dealt with.

During the assessment interviews considerable attention is paid to the so-called "sexual value system," the ideas of each partner about what is acceptable and needed in a sexual relationship. Sometimes this sexual value system must be changed for one or both partners before sexual functioning can improve. For example, if one partner regards sexuality as ugly and unaccep-

table, it is doubtful that even the most powerful therapy can make that person and the partner enjoy sex. An important stipulation in these first few days of therapy is that any sexual activity between the two partners is expressly forbidden.

On the third day the therapists begin to offer interpretations about why problems have arisen and why they are continuing. In all cases the emphasis is placed upon problems in the relationship, not within either partner. The basic premise of their therapy is that ". . . there is no such thing as an uninvolved partner in any marriage in which there is some form of sexual inadequacy" (Masters and Johnson, 1970, p. 2). At this time the idea of the spectator role is introduced to the clients. For example, an impotent male usually worries about how well or poorly he is doing rather than participating freely. It is pointed out to the couple that this pattern of observation, while totally understandable in context, is blocking his natural responses and greatly interfering with sexual enjoyment.

At the end of the third day an all-important assignment is given to the couple, namely to engage in "sensate focus." The couple is instructed to choose a time based on "a natural sense of warmth, unit compatability, and/or even a shared sense of gamesmanship" (Masters and Johnson, 1970, p. 71) during which they are to undress and to give each other pleasure by touching each other's bodies. The co-therapists appoint one marital partner to do the first "pleasuring" or "giving"; the partner who is "getting" is simply to enjoy being touched. The one being touched, however, is *not* required to feel sexual and, moreover, takes responsibility for immediately telling the partner if something becomes distracting or uncomfortable. Then the roles are switched. Attempts at intercourse are forbidden. To Masters and Johnson this approach is a way of breaking up the frantic groping common among these couples. The "sensate focus" assignment may promote contact where none has existed for years; if so, it is the first step toward gradually reestablishing sexual intimacy.

This assignment may uncover deep animosities that have hitherto been hidden. Most of the time, however, partners begin to realize that there can be intimate encounters in bed that are not necessarily a prelude to sexual intercourse. On the second evening the partner being pleasured is instructed to give specific encouragement and direction by placing his or her hand on the hand of the giving partner in order to regulate pressure and rate of stroking. The touching of genitals and breasts is also now allowed, Still, however, there is no mention of an orgasm, and the prohibition on intercourse remains in effect. Diagrams are also presented if the partners are ignorant of basic female and male anatomy, as they often are. After this second day of sensate focusing, the treatment approaches branch out according to the specific problem or problems the couple has. As an illustration, we will outline the therapy for orgasmic dysfunction in the female.

After the sensate focus exercises have made the couple at least a little more comfortable with each other in bed, the wife's attention is directed to maximizing her own sexual stimulation without trying to have an orgasm. As a result her own sexual excitement generally builds. Data from the earlier controlled laboratory studies (Masters and Johnson, 1966) become useful now; the man is advised not to stimulate the clitoris directly, unless this is the stated wish of the partner, since women generally prefer stimulation around the clitoris and very light if any stimulation directly on it. The man is given very explicit instructions about generally effective means of manual manipulation of the female genital area, though of course the ultimate decisions must continually be made by the woman, who is encouraged to make her wishes perfectly clear to the man. As in the treatment of other dysfunctions, it is emphasized that having orgasms is not the focus of this interaction between partners.

After the woman has begun to enjoy being pleasured in this way, the next step is to transfer the source of sensate pleasure from the man's hand on her body to his penis inside her vagina. She is told to place herself on top of the man and gently to insert the penis; she is encouraged simply to tune in to the feelings that ensue. When she feels inclined, she can begin slowly to move her pelvis. She is encouraged to regard the penis as something for her to play with, and to provide pleasure for her. The male can also begin slowly to thrust. At all times, however, the wife must be able to decide when and what should happen next.

When the couple is able to maintain this containment for minutes at a time without the man's thrusting forcefully toward orgasm, a major change has usually taken place in their sexual interactions: for perhaps the first time the woman has been allowed to feel and think sexually and, indeed, selfishly about her own pleasure. In subsequent sessions most couples begin to have mutually satisfying intercourse.

Overall, the results have been extremely heartening: about 80 percent of the women who have undergone this therapy have been enabled to enjoy orgasms, sometimes for the first time in their lives.

Extreme clinical sensitivity is necessary in presenting these various treatment procedures to a couple who, after all, have often been having problems for many years. Sometimes, the mere discussion of sex occurs for the first time at the Masters and Johnson clinic. Surely the calm and open manner of the therapists must be extremely important in putting the couple at ease, encouraging the commitment to follow certain instructions, and changing their attitudes regarding sex and the activities that people may engage in together when making love. Although emphasis is placed on specific behavioral prescriptions, the therapist can never lose sight of the atmosphere that must be maintained in the consulting room and hopefully transferred over to the privacy of the bedroom where much of the *actual* therapy is taking place. Therefore, as in other areas of behavior therapy, there is a strong emphasis on technique, but also an appreciation of the interpersonal factors that are essential in setting the stage for behavior to change.

presented with the slide of the least attractive male for a period of eight seconds during which he can press a button to remove the male slide and thereby avoid a painful electric shock. Upon removal of the male slide, a "relief stimulus" is presented, a photo of a female he had previously rated as the most attractive. This procedure is followed over several sessions, until the patient reliably avoids staring at the most appealing male slides.

The results of their early work seem encouraging. Of their first forty-three male homosexual patients, more than half were judged to have become significantly more oriented toward heterosexual activities after an average of twenty aversive conditioning sessions. For example, thirteen were engaging in heterosexual intercourse whereas none was before therapy. Many others showed changes in sexual fantasy if not actual heterosexual behavior.

These findings are noteworthy in view of the admittedly limited nature of the therapy, for Feldman and MacCulloch intentionally excluded specific instruction in heterosexual behavior that would seem to be important in helping a homosexual change his conduct beyond merely reducing the sexual arousal experienced when looking at another man. It must be noted, however, that neither the Feldman-MacCulloch therapy nor any other has completely eliminated homosexual feelings or behavior.

In a manner similar to Wolpe's adaptation of Jones's *in vivo* treatment of the fearful child, behavior therapists have developed aversive therapy procedures to be practiced by clients through the exercise of their imaginations. Cautela (1966), adapting the procedures of Lazarus (1958), reported on the successful use of *covert sensitization*, as illustrated by the following excerpt from a treatment program with an alcoholic.

You are walking into a bar. You decide to have a glass of beer. You are now walking toward the bar. As you are approaching the bar you have a funny feeling in the pit of your stomach. Your stomach feels all queasy and nauseous. Some liquid comes up your throat and it is very sour. You try to swallow it back down, but as you do this, food particles start coming up your throat to your mouth. You are now reaching the bar and you order a beer. As the bartender is pouring the beer, puke comes up into your mouth. You try to keep your mouth closed and swallow it down. You reach for the glass of beer to wash it down. As soon as your hand touches the glass, you can't hold it down any longer. You have to open your mouth and you puke. It goes all over your hand, all over the glass and the beer. You can see it floating around in the beer. Snots and mucus come out of your nose. Your shirt and pants are full of vomit. The bartender has some on his shirt. You notice people looking at you. You get sick again and you vomit some more and more. You turn away from the beer and immediately you start to feel better. As you run out of the bar room, you start to feel better and better. When you get out into clean fresh air you feel wonderful. You go home and clean yourself up (Cautela, 1966, p. 37).

The client agrees to imagine such highly aversive situations over a number of sessions and at home as well, in the hope that his attraction to whatever causes him distress will be reduced by this admittedly unpalatable therapeutic procedure. Clinical evidence suggests that covert sensitization can be useful in helping clients to control habits such as overeating, drinking alcohol to excess, and smoking cigarettes.

Aversive conditioning is controversial for both ethical and scientific reasons. Ethically, a great outcry has been raised about inflicting pain and discomfort on people, even when they ask for it. Perhaps the greatest concern and anger have been voiced by the several gay liberation organizations; they hold that homosexuals who request painful treatment are actually seeking to punish themselves for behavior that a prejudiced society has convinced them is dirty. They accuse behavior therapists of impeding the acceptance of homosexuality as a legitimate life style when they accede to such requests for change (Silverstein, 1972). The issue is a difficult one to resolve.

From the scientific perspective, aversive procedures are subject to different conceptualizations; some view these techniques in counterconditioning terms, but others (like Feldman and MacCulloch, 1971) see them as a punishment (that is, an operant conditioning) technique in which a shock or a noxious image punishes a particular response. The issue is whether human beings can acquire stable conditioned aversive reactions by being shocked or nauseated. As pointed out in Chapter 5,

there is little evidence that a person will continue to react anxiously to an intrinsically harmless stimulus once he sees that he can no longer be shocked. Many behaviorists assert, therefore, that any beneficial outcomes from this kind of treatment cannot be attributed to conditioning.

Orgasmic Reorientation

A final procedure similar to systematic desensitization is designed to increase sexual arousal to stimuli with low arousal value for the client. In the aversive conditioning approach to homosexuality, the method was to reduce or eliminate the unwanted attraction to people of the same sex. Another tack is to work directly on increasing a desired attraction (Barlow, 1973; Wilson and Davison, 1973). The strategy here is to create a situation in which the person is confronted with a nonarousing stimulus and learns to respond to it with sexual feelings. The conceptual framework, again, is based on counterconditioning.

Davison (1968a) developed such a procedure for a young man complaining of complete reliance on sadistic fantasies for sexual arousal during masturbation. This twenty-one-year-old college student had become increasingly pessimistic about his future sociosexual development, fearing that he might one day act out his fantasies and hurt a woman. After determining that the client's core problem was, indeed, these fantasies, the behavior therapist instructed him to masturbate at home in the following fashion.

When assured of privacy in his dormitory room (primarily on the weekend), he was first to obtain an erection by whatever means possible—undoubtedly with a sadistic fantasy, as he indicated. He was then to begin to masturbate while looking at a picture of a sexy, nude woman (the "target" sexual stimulus); *Playboy* magazine was suggested to him as a good source. If he began losing the erection, he was to switch back to his sadistic fantasy until he could begin masturbating effectively again. Concentrating again on the *Playboy* picture, he was to continue masturbating, using the fantasy only to regain erection. As orgasm was approaching, he was at all costs to focus on the *Playboy* picture, even if sadistic fantasies began to intrude. It was impressed on him that gains would ensue only when sexual arousal was associated with the picture, and that he need not worry about indulging in sadistic fantasies at this point. . . . (Davison, 1968a, p. 84).

After successfully performing this task, the client was instructed to change his masturbation practice by using less openly provocative pictures and bringing them into the masturbation sequence earlier. This therapy, used along with several other techniques, proved to be beneficial in relieving the client of his exclusive reliance on sadistic fantasies.

Before we leave these "counterconditioning procedures," a caveat is in order. We have discussed these techniques as "counterconditioning" only because most workers favor a response substitution paradigm for explaining them. A given technique, however, may achieve its effects for reasons quite different from those that are proposed by a particular theorist. Behavior therapists have been attentive to this important question, as we shall see later in this chapter when we review the process research that has been done on systematic desensitization.

OPERANT CONDITIONING (SHAPING)

In the 1950s a number of investigators, primarily in the United States, suggested that therapists should focus on overt behavior shaped by rewards and punishments (Skinner, 1953). In the belief that the complex, puzzling, often bizarre behavior of psychiatric patients could be approached in this way, many experimentally minded psychologists tried to bring conceptual and practical order into the chaos of institutions for the severely disturbed. The following studies will give some of the flavor of this kind of work.

The Token Economy

Perhaps the most extensive and best-known work in behavior modification within the operant tradition was reported by Ayllon and his colleagues (Ayllon and Azrin, 1968). The program was called the token economy (Figure 19.2). On the basis of earlier work by Staats and Staats (1963) with children, they set aside an entire ward of a mental hospital for a series of experiments in which rewards were provided for activities such as making beds and combing hair. Patients were systematically

FIGURE **19.2**
(A) The patient is receiving tokens or coupons in payment for her completion of several jobs at a community mental health day center. The bulletin board at the upper left specifies the number of tokens to be earned by carrying out particular work assignments. (B) Two of the coupons dispensed at this center.
[PICTURE COURTESY OF THE OXNARD (CALIFORNIA) MENTAL HEALTH CENTER AND DR. ROBERT P. LIEBERMAN.]

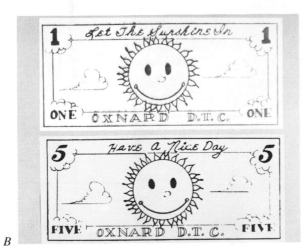

B

reinforced with plastic tokens that could later be exchanged for special privileges such as a private room or extra visits to the canteen. The entire life of each patient was as far as possible controlled by this regime. Table 19.1 shows some of the tasks and the rewards that could be earned performing them.

These studies demonstrated how even markedly regressed adult hospital patients could be significantly affected by systematically manipulating reinforcement contingencies, that is, rewarding some behavior to increase its frequency, or ignoring or punishing it to reduce its frequency.

In order to show that a stimulus following a behavior actually reinforces the behavior, an experiment has to demonstrate not only that the behavior increases when the reinforcement follows, but also that the behavior declines when the reinforcement is withdrawn. (Recall from Chapter 4 that the ABAB design is most frequently employed.) Ayllon and his associates demonstrated this effect for several behaviors; Figure 19.3 shows the typical curve indicating how conduct such as brushing teeth and making beds markedly decreased when rewards were withdrawn, returning to a higher frequency when rewards were reinstated.

Since Ayllon's original hospital work, numerous similar programs have been instituted throughout the country. The evidence seems clear that at least short-term changes in numerous overt behaviors can be effected by manipulating the reinforcement contingencies

TABLE **19.1** *Sample of Ward Behaviors Required To Earn Tokens* (*from Ayllon and Azrin, 1965*)

Type of job	Duration	Tokens paid
1. Kitchen Chores Patient assembles necessary supplies on table. Puts one pat of butter between two slices of bread for all patients. Squeezes juice from fruit left over from meals. Puts supplies away. Cleans table used.	10 min	1
2. Coffee Urn Patient assembles cleaning compound and implements. Washes five-gallon coffee urn using brush and cleaning compound. Rinses inside, washes and dries outside. Puts implements away.	10 min	2
3. Ice Carrier Patient goes with attendant to area adjacent to ward where ice machine is located, taking along ten-gallon ice container. Scoops flaked ice from machine into container and carries it to the kitchen.	10 min	2
4. Shakers Patient assembles salt, sugar, and empty shakers on table, fills shakers, and puts supplies away.	10 min	2
5. Pots and Pans Patient runs water into sink, adds soap, washes and rinses all pans used for each meal. Stacks pans and leaves them to be put through automatic dishwasher.	10 min	6
6. Steam Table Patient assembles cleaning supplies. Washes and dries all compartments used for food. Cleans and dries outside of table. Places all pans in proper place on steam table.	10 min	5

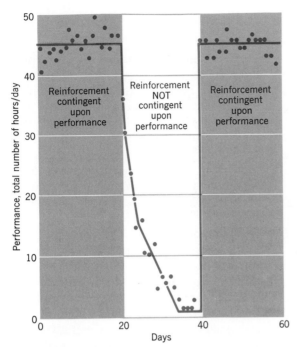

FIGURE **19.3**

Frequency of behavior as a function of reinforcement contingencies in the token economy. Adapted from Ayllon and Azrin, 1964.

of patients within the protected hospital setting. Whether the many characteristics of adult mental patients, as detailed in Chapter 13, can be changed by such procedures, however, is very much an open question.

Operant Work with Children

Some of the best operant conditioning behavior therapy has been done with children, perhaps because the kinds of problems most often encountered with youngsters "fit" especially well with an approach that emphasizes control through contingencies in the environment. Children, after all, tend more than adults to be under continual supervision and (potential) control by others. At school their behavior is scrutinized by teachers, and when they come home parents frequently supervise their play and other social activities.

The range of childhood problems dealt with through operant conditioning is very broad indeed, including bed-wetting, thumbsucking, tantrums, asthmatic attacks, and poor school performance. In this section we will discuss operant programs with aggressive and retarded children.

Operant Work with Aggressive Children

For many years Patterson (1971) and his colleagues and students at the Oregon Research Institute have systematically attempted to influence the behavior of children in their own homes and in schools. Their principal focus has been highly aggressive boys. Instead of having a child visit a consulting room for one or more hours per week for therapy, they have tried (1) to change the manner in which parents and teachers reinforce a child so as (2) ultimately to change the child's behavior.

This tack might appear obvious. It is not. For years child therapy took place in one-to-one situations; the parent(s) would bring a child to a psychotherapist and then wait outside the consulting room while the therapist attempted to probe the psyche of the child, often by means of so-called play therapy, so as to effect desired change. Dissatisfaction with this ineffective treatment strategy (for example, Levitt, 1971) has been an impetus to deal more directly with the actual problematic behavior of the child, particularly in an operant fashion. As with other kinds of behavior modification, the therapist has moved out of the office into those natural settings where the child-client does most of his behaving.

In the initial phase of Patterson's program, the parent learns to *observe* and *record* both the child's problematic behavior and his or her own behavior in interaction with the child. It is not unusual, for instance, to find that a parent who complains of a child's constant interruptions actually attends more to that behavior than to more desirable behaviors — attention, even if in the form of scolding, can increase the frequency of behavior. Sometimes an extensive period of observation in a clinic or laboratory is required in order to show both the investigators and the parent what the reinforcement contingencies are (assuming that the natural setting can be reproduced adequately in the clinic). Patterson and his group have often made use of a manual (Patterson and Gullion, 1968) in helping parents learn to observe and record their own behavior and that of their children.

In the second phase of training, reinforcement contingencies are changed. Once the parent has learned how to observe and to record various behaviors, he or she must be taught to apply specific reinforcement contingencies to particular patterns of child behavior. For example, having determined that yelling at the dinner table usually leads to attention, the parent might decide to ignore yelling (that is, to extinguish it) and observe the subsequent change. Parents can be trained to reinforce appropriately either individually or in groups. Sometimes it is necessary for investigators to visit a home as well or to make telephone contacts to insure that reinforcement procedures are being properly followed.[1]

The results of this program have been very encouraging. After three months of at-home reinforcement for nonaggressive behavior, parents of highly aggressive boys were able to reduce the frequency of deviant behavior by an average of 60 percent (Patterson, 1973). Other studies have replicated these strong effects

[1] Operant behavior therapists must of course determine that the behavior being shaped or extinguished is in fact operant behavior. A child who is crying because of physical pain should be attended to if his behavior is to be changed.

even when those receiving therapy were compared to appropriate control groups. Evidence indicates that improvements often endure for several months after the period of intensive parental training and home observations. It does appear, however, that most families require periodic "retraining," and Patterson soberly suggests that long-term reduction in aggressive behavior may require regular retraining indefinitely. Even so, however, the approach is preferable to institutionalization.

The Oregon group has also worked in classrooms. A teacher's attention is often attracted by behavior *not* related to studying. Furthermore, the rewards for nonacademic behavior are ample; a child who clowns around and does not do his work generally gets attention from his peers as well as from the teacher. Numerous behavior modification programs in schools have attempted to reduce antisocial or deviant behavior and to increase social reinforcement for adaptive behavior. Reinforcement can take various forms, both "natural" reinforcements such as smiles or praise and artificial rewards like tokens that are exchangeable for, say, candy (backup reinforcers). Many studies have demonstrated the power of such programs in reducing aggressive behavior and increasing task attention in children (O'Leary and O'Leary, 1972).

Operant Work with Retarded Children

Very encouraging results have also been achieved by applying operant techniques to retarded children. As we pointed out in Chapter 17, the labeling of certain children as "trainable" on the basis of an IQ score may discourage attempts to teach certain skills such as reading and writing. Many operant conditioners have challenged assumptions about trainability, much to the benefit of many families. Among the other problems dealt with have been poor toilet habits (Minge and Ball, 1967) and hyperactive behavior (Doubros, 1966).

Perhaps the most significant and heartening changes have been in the area of intellectual development. One example among many is a study by Ayllon and Kelly (1972). First they showed that measured IQ could be significantly raised in "trainable" retarded children (IQ below 55) simply by providing tokens as reinforcers following acceptable performances in the various subtests; the average gain was approximately 10 percent of the total possible score. Even more striking were the results from a six-week program at a school for retarded children. Two groups of children were carefully matched on IQ. One group was assigned to an experimental program while the control subjects merely continued in the ongoing academic program of the school. In the innovative program, which used specially designed academic materials in arithmetic, spelling, copying, and reading, children were reinforced with tokens depending on their achievements. The children were able to exchange their tokens for a variety of desirable things (soft drinks, candy, and extra privileges such as playing records and watching television).

Testing at the end of the six-week program showed that the IQ of the experimental subjects increased by an average of almost four points, whereas that of the control children actually decreased by nearly three points. Since the two samples had been carefully matched before the operant training program began, we can conclude that the program was responsible for the improvement.

Although programs such as these may offer hope to those responsible for the well-being of retarded children, their effects must not be overestimated. The changes shown in the Ayllon and Kelly study were statistically significant, but the children still remained retarded, that is, their posttreatment scores were still very far below average. On the other hand, such programs—and scores of others throughout the country—do carry an important message, namely that one should not despair of making a beneficial impact on problems simply because currently available procedures have been unsuccessful.

Generalization of Treatment Effects

A problem common to all therapies is generalizing to real life whatever gains have been achieved in therapy. Insight therapists assume that the transfer of therapeutic effects is achieved through a restructuring of the underlying personality. An environmentalist, such as a behavior therapist, must explain how changes brought about by his manipulations can persist once a client returns to his everyday situation—which often is assumed to have produced the problem in the first place!

Behavior therapists have tried to meet this challenge in several ways. Because laboratory findings indicate that intermittent reinforcement—rewarding behavior only a small portion of the time it appears—makes a new behavior more enduring, many operant programs take care to move away from continuous schedules of reinforcement once a given behavior is occurring with satisfactory regularity. For example, if a teacher has succeeded in helping a disruptive child spend more time in his seat by praising him generously for each arithmetic problem that he finishes while sitting in his chair, she will gradually reward him for every other problem, and ultimately only infrequently. The hope is that the satisfactions of being a good pupil will make the child less dependent on the teacher's approval. Another strategy is to move from artificial

BOX **19.2** *Self-Control*

One of the most exciting areas in behavior modification is self-control (Goldfried and Merbaum, 1973; Mahoney, 1972). Much of the research and theory reviewed in this chapter seems to assume that the human being is a relatively passive recipient of stimulation from the environment. Given this apparent dependence on the external world, how can we account for behavior that appears to be autonomous, willed, and often contrary to what might be expected in a particular situation? How, for example, do we account for a person on a diet refraining from eating a luscious piece of chocolate cake when hungry?

Psychoanalytic writers, including the ego analysts, handle the issue by positing within the organism some kind of internal agent. Thus many ego analysts assert that the ego can operate on its own power, making deliberate decisions for the entire psychic system—including decisions that go against the wishes of the id. Behaviorists, especially Skinner (1953), have objected to this kind of "explanation," regarding it as simply a relabeling of the phenomenon.

Perhaps the most widely accepted behavioral view of self-control is Skinner's: an organism engages in self-control when it arranges the environment so that only certain controlling stimuli are present. A person wishing to lose weight rids his home of fattening foods and avoids passing restaurants when hungry. Behavior remains a function of the environment, but the environment itself is seen as manipulatable by the organism.

A related conception of self-control among behavior therapists is Bandura's (1969) explanation of aversive conditioning: rather than being passively conditioned to feel distaste for stimuli that have been paired with

reinforcers to those that naturally occur in the social environment. An example would be maintaining a token program only for as long as necessary to encourage certain desired behavior and then "weaning" the person from these artificial rewards to natural reinforcers such as praise from peers.

Another way in which generalization can be effected involves the client's taking a more active role. As an example, consider some recent work of Drabman, Spitalnik, and O'Leary (1973). In a three-month after-school program for disruptive young boys, the investigators rewarded nondisruptive classroom behavior, appropriate reading behavior, *and* self-ratings shock, a person learns a skill of aversive self-stimulation that can be deliberately used in real life. According to this view a person resists a temptation by deliberately recalling his prior aversive experience when being shocked or nauseated during therapy.

In our opinion, self-control places a strain on the behavioristic paradigm. In each of the last two paragraphs, a person is described as deciding something, arranging things, stimulating himself, and so forth. Each of these statements presupposes a conception of the person as an *initiator* of action, as the place where self-control *begins*.

Consider a cigarette box devised by Azrin and Powell (1968). This device allowed a smoker to obtain a cigarette only after a given period of time had passed, perhaps one hour. Many smokers were able to cut down on their cigarette use as the waiting period was gradually extended. But any smoker could at any time have broken the contract and sought cigarettes from other sources. This self-control device, then, could have an effect on a person only if he were committed to using it, and the behavior change procedure could be regarded as relying on self-control only if the person were *not* restrained by others to stay with the regime. For if we could construe the taking of cigarettes only from the special box as being under environmental control—the therapist's insistence that the smoker not seek another source—the control would be external, not self-exercised.

What is only beginning to attract the attention of behaviorists is the *commitment* to change that a client must have (see Kanfer and Karoly, 1972). Even the most powerful change procedure will have limited effect on a person who is not resolved to use it.

that agreed with ratings by a specially trained teacher. That is, the pupils were taught that they could earn special privileges not only if they met the criteria set by the teacher but also if they honestly evaluated their own behavior as the teacher would. The findings replicated many other studies by showing that during token reinforcement imposed by the teacher, disruptive behavior decreased and academic behavior improved. *In addition,* and most importantly, this improvement generalized to periods of each class during which the child *himself judged* how well he was doing and *reinforced himself* accordingly; as a result improved performance transferred to periods of

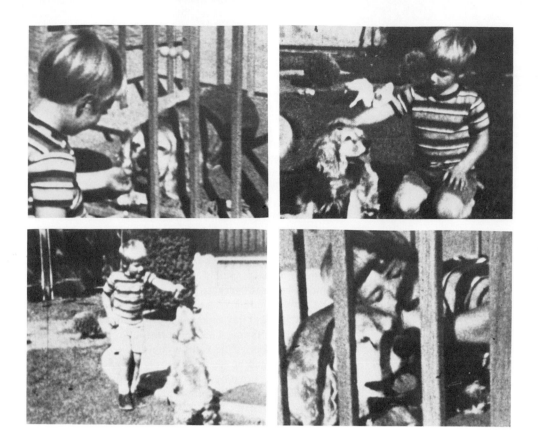

time when the pupil was not under direct external environment control (see Box 19.2).

The implications are clear: at least with disruptive children, providing reinforcements for self-evaluation might be one effective way to transfer behavior changes to situations in which the original controlling agent (the behavior modifier) is absent.

MODELING

Modeling is the third thread in the development of behavior modification. As we noted in Chapter 2, social learning approaches generally take into account not only classical and operant conditioning but also the effects of modeling. The importance of modeling and imitation in behavior is self-evident, for children as well as adults are able to acquire complex responses merely by observing models performing them. The research program of Bandura and his associates (Bandura, 1969) has shown the power of this kind of learning in helping people acquire novel responses in a relatively short time.

The effectiveness of modeling in clinical work was shown in a study by Bandura, Blanchard, and Ritter (1969). These investigators examined the possibility that various modeled

FIGURE **19.4**
Pictures from Bandura's research showing the successful outcome of modeling treatment for dog phobia. After watching models interact fearlessly with dogs, phobic children were able to approach the animals and even sleep with them.

FIGURE **19.5**
Arnold A. Lazarus, one of the principal figures in contemporary behavior therapy.

situations could help people with snake phobia markedly reduce their fear. The researchers exposed fearful adults to both live and filmed displays of people with snakes, gradually increasing the models' closeness to the animals. Results indicated decided reduction of fear. Other research has shown that children's fear of dogs (Hill, Liebert, and Mott, 1968) and of dentists (Adelson, Liebert, Poulos, and Herskovitz, 1972) can be reduced through modeling (Figure 19.4).

Some of the clinical work of Lazarus (Figure 19.5), one of the leading behavior therapists, may also be regarded as an example of modeling. In a procedure called *behavior rehearsal*, Lazarus (1971) demonstrates for a client how to handle a difficult interpersonal problem in a better way. The client observes the therapist's exemplary performance and then attempts to imitate it during the therapy session. By continual practice and observation, the client can frequently acquire entire repertoires of more effective and more satisfying behavior. Often videotape equipment can be creatively used to facilitate such modeling and imitation. Experimental validation of such procedures is beginning to appear in the literature (for example, O'Connor, 1969).

COGNITIVE RESTRUCTURING IN BEHAVIOR MODIFICATION

The emphasis in the therapies discussed thus far has been on the direct manipulation of overt behavior and occasionally covert behavior. Relatively little attention has been paid to direct manipulation of the thinking and reasoning processes of the client. Perhaps as a reaction to insight therapy, behavior therapists initially discounted the importance of using cognitive concepts, regarding an appeal to thinking and believing as a return to the "mentalism" that Watson vigorously objected to in the early part of the twentieth century (see Chapter 2). If behavior modification is to be taken seriously as applied experimental psychology, however, it is entirely consistent to incorporate theory and research in cognitive processes. Indeed, in recent years behavior therapists have been making explicit use of cognitive concepts in attempting to understand and modify overt and covert behavior in clinical settings. The following case illustrates the beneficial effects of such cognitive restructuring.

A man had been diagnosed as paranoid schizophrenic, primarily because of his complaints of "pressure points" on his forehead and other parts of his body (Davison, 1966). He believed that these pressure points were signals from outside forces helping him make decisions. These paranoid delusions had been resistant to drug treatment and other psychotherapeutic approaches. The behavior therapist, in examining the man's case history, hypothesized that the patient became very anxious and tense when he had to make a decision, that his anxiety took the form of muscular tension in certain bodily parts, and that he misconstrued the tension as "pressure points" from helpful spirits. Both patient and therapist agreed to explore the possibility that the pressure points were in fact part of a tension reaction to specific situations. For this purpose, the therapist decided to teach the man deep muscle relaxation, with the hope that relaxation would enable the man to control his tensions (including the "pressure points") and thereby permit him to reconstrue these sensations in a naturalistic rather than a paranoid way.

But it was important first to interest the man in attending sessions with a therapist who was raising questions about an important part of his delusional system. So in the first session the therapist asked the patient to extend his right arm, clench his fist, and bend his wrist downward so as to bring the fist toward the inside of the forearm. The intent was to produce a feeling of tension in his forearm; this was precisely what happened, and the man noted that the feeling was quite similar to his pressure points.

Extensive relaxation training enabled the man to begin to control his anxiety in various situations within the hospital and at the same time to reduce the intensity of the "pressure points." As he gained control over these feelings, he referred more and more to these "pressure points" as "sensations," and his conversation in general began to lose its earlier paranoid flavor.

Davison suggested that the relaxation training had been a means of enabling the patient to test a nonparanoid hypothesis, to see it confirmed, and thereby to shake off a belief about these sensations that had contributed to a diagnosis of paranoia.

Rational-Emotive Therapy

For many years the clinical work of a New York psychotherapist, Albert Ellis, has existed outside the mainstream of behavior modification, but it has begun to engage the interest of behavior therapists. The principal thesis of what he calls rational-emotive therapy is that sustained emotional reactions are attributable to internal sentences that people say to themselves. For example, a depressed person may say to himself, several times a day, "What a worthless person I am." (see the earlier discussion of Beck, pages 183–185). Ellis proposes that people cognitively interpret what is happening around them, that sometimes these interpretations can cause emotional turmoil, and that a therapist's attention should be focused on these internal sentences and not so much on historical causes or, indeed, on overt behavior (Ellis, 1962).

Ellis lists a number of assumptions people can make that may lead to distress (see Box 19.3). One such notion is that it is necessary to be thoroughly competent in everything one does. Ellis suggests that many people actually believe this untenable assumption, and that they evaluate every event within this context.

Thus, if a person makes an error, it becomes a catastrophe since it violates his deeply held conviction that he must be perfect. It sometimes comes as a shock to clients to realize that they actually believe such strictures and are as a result running their lives in such a way as to make it virtually impossible to live comfortably.

In a sense, Ellis seems to be preaching an ethical system. He is suggesting that a great deal of emotional suffering is engendered by unrealistic goals, that these goals are subject to modification, and that modifying them can enable a person to reduce his subjective discomfort. Indeed, the reduction of stress can often increase adaptive performance so that, ironically, a goal is more closely approached in this fashion than if it is viewed as a "must" or a "should." Like Wolpe's systematic desensitization technique, Ellis's rational-emotive therapy is beginning to attract the attention of a number of experimentally minded investigators (for instance, Goldfried, Decenteceo, and Weinberg, in press; Meichenbaum, 1972). This work appears at present to be one of the most promising and interesting areas in behavior therapy.

BOX **19.3** *Ellis's Basic Irrational Assumptions*

Irrational Idea No. 1: The idea that it is a dire necessity for an adult human being to be loved or approved by virtually every significant other person in his community. . . .

Irrational Idea No. 2: The idea that one should be thoroughly competent, adequate, and achieving in all possible respects if one is to consider oneself worthwhile. . . .

Irrational Idea No. 3: The idea that certain people are bad, wicked, or villainous and that they should be severely blamed and punished for their villainy. . . .

Irrational Idea No. 4: The idea that it is awful and catastrophic when things are not the way one would very much like them to be. . . .

Irrational Idea No. 5: The idea that human unhappiness is externally caused and that people have little or no ability to control their sorrows and disturbances. . . .

Irrational Idea No. 6: The idea that if something is or may be dangerous or fearsome one should be terribly concerned about it and should keep dwelling on the possibility of its occurring. . . .

Irrational Idea No. 7: The idea that it is easier to avoid than to face certain life difficulties and self-responsibilities. . . .

Irrational Idea No. 8: The idea that one should be dependent on others and needs someone stronger than oneself on whom to rely. . . .

Irrational Idea No. 9: The idea that one's past history is an all-important determiner of one's present behavior and that because something once strongly affected one's life, it should indefinitely have a similar effect. . . .

Irrational Idea No. 10: The idea that one should become quite upset over other people's problems and disturbances. . . .

(Italics removed, Ellis, 1962, pp. 61–85)

RESEARCH IN SYSTEMATIC DESENSITIZATION

By now you should have some grasp of the scope of behavior modification and its historical development. Perhaps the most important characteristic of this field is its devotion to experimental investigation. The long-term goal in all the approaches discussed is to build a scientifically based technology of behavior change.[2]

Research in behavior modification has become voluminous in recent years. Several journals are devoted entirely to this field and many others frequently publish articles on behavior therapy. There are also several professional associations in the United States and abroad devoted to furthering interest in this approach to clinical work. In this section research in one subarea, desensitization, will serve to illustrate the interplay of clinical and experimental work in behavior therapy.

Outcome Research in Desensitization

Laboratory workers became interested in finding out why desensitization works because of clinical reports indicating that the technique is indeed effective in reducing, if not eliminating, neurotic fears. The early work of Wolpe and Lazarus (for example, Wolpe, 1958; Lazarus, 1963) is therefore rightfully accorded a respected and enduring place in the regard of psychologists and other mental health workers.

Initial steps in the experimental investigation of the procedure were taken by Lazovik and Lang (1960) and Lang and Lazovik (1963). These two experiments were concerned primarily with assessing the procedure under relatively controlled laboratory conditions. In the

[2] That science will lead to the most effective clinical procedures is an *assumption*. There is nothing inherent in science that guarantees victories for those studying human behavior. Simply because we have reached the moon by playing the science game does not necessarily mean that the same set of rules applies to human behavior. The existentialists, whose paradigm emphasizes free will, assume that the nature of man cannot be meaningfully probed by following the kinds of rules emphasized in this textbook. While the authors are placing their bets on the kind of work described in this chapter, it nonetheless remains an article of faith that advances in therapy will most likely come from behavior modification.

earlier clinical reports, judgments of improvement had been made by the clinicians involved in the treatment, and other therapeutic procedures were usually employed along with desensitization. For greater control Lang and Lazovik decided to desensitize a simple phobia (fear of snakes) under conditions in which measurements of the subjects' pretreatment and posttreatment approaches to the snakes could be made by testers who were not involved in the desensitization. These experiments showed that, indeed, desensitization can lead to measurable and significant reductions in the avoidance of a phobic object.

One of the most widely known and highly regarded experiments in systematic desensitization and in psychotherapy research as a whole was conducted by Paul (1966), who compared the effectiveness of systematic desensitization with a placebo and insight therapy. He recruited students suffering from fear of speaking in front of groups ("interpersonal performance anxiety") for an experiment investigating diverse methods for reducing unrealistic fears. Before treatment all students had to deliver a speech in front of an audience, and numerous measures of their anxiety were taken (physiological measures, self-report measures, and behavioral observations; see Chapter 5). Students were then assigned to one of three different treatments. The first was systematic desensitization. The second was an "attention-placebo" treatment. Subjects in this group were led to believe that a pill would reduce their overall sensitivity to stress; to convince them, Paul had them listen to a tape described as one used to train astronauts to function under stress. They listened to this "stress tape" for several sessions after ingesting the "tranquilizer." In reality, the pill was a placebo, and the tape contained sounds that had been shown in other research to be quite boring. In this way Paul raised subjects' expectations that they would be helped with their social anxieties. The third treatment was insight therapy. Subjects met with skilled insight-oriented therapists to talk over their anxieties; the therapists were free to structure the sessions in any way they saw fit. All treatments were limited to five sessions, a number settled on by the insight therapists when they were asked how many sessions they would need to make a measurable impact on this kind of problem. An important feature of Paul's experimental design was that insight therapists were trained to do systematic desensitization and thereby participated in each of the treatments administered. In this way Paul anticipated the criticism that any superiority of systematic desensitization could be attributed to the greater enthusiasm shown by the therapists.

The results of this important study revealed that subjects who had received systematic desensitization improved more than the attention-placebo and insight subjects, who reacted about the same to their forms of therapy. Students receiving these two treatments did, however, show significant improvement. The results, then, indicate that systematic desensitization is superior to both insight therapy and to a placebo for the treatment of speech anxiety. These results persisted in a two-year follow-up study (Paul, 1967).

Process Research in Desensitization

These initial experiments did not consider the question of what made the procedure work. Subsequent experimenters, confident that the procedure was effective both in the clinic and under controlled laboratory conditions, conducted studies to try to discover the mechanisms that could account for the efficacy of the procedure. We shall describe one of them in some detail.

In Wolpe's original formulation of the desensitization procedure, he asserted that it is necessary to expose fearful people in a graded fashion to situations that they fear while at the same time associating each exposure with a nonanxiety state (deep muscle relaxation). In an experiment designed to evaluate this hypothesis, Davison (1968b) dismantled the desensitization procedure in the following way: if muscle relaxation is indeed important in reducing fear through desensitization, then exposing subjects in a graded fashion to anxiety-eliciting stimuli *without* accompanying relaxation should not be as effective as the normal procedure. Therefore, one group of snake phobics, the exposure group, imagined a series of anxiety-evoking stimuli in the graded fashion typical in desensitization but without any muscle relaxation.

Another control condition was necessary to test the counterconditioning notions of Wolpe. Recall that the desensitization technique is applied within a clinical context in which clients expect to improve. To control for these extraneous effects a pseudodesensitization group was formed. These subjects received as much relaxation training as desensitization subjects, but the relaxation was not associated with anxiety-provoking stimuli. The situations that these pseudodesensitization subjects imagined had nothing to do with their anxieties. Again, if the association of relaxation with situations *relevant* to the target behavior is important, this pseudodesensitization procedure would not be expected to have as much beneficial effect as the actual desensitization condition.

The third treatment in Davison's experiment was desensitization. Subjects in this group imagined a graded series of anxiety-evoking stimuli at the same time that their muscles were relaxed. This group was expected to show more improvement than all the others if

TABLE 19.2 *Summary of Experimental Design Used To Determine the Role of Counter-conditioning in Systematic Desensitization*

(from Davison, 1968b)

Group	Pretreatment assessment (E_1)	Treatment procedure (E_2)	Posttreatment assessment (E_1)
Desensitization	Avoidance test with anxiety self-reports	Relaxation paired with graded imagined aversive stimuli	Avoidance test with anxiety self-reports
Pseudodesensitization	Same	Relaxation paired with imagined snake-irrelevant stimuli	Same
Exposure	Same	Imagined graded aversive stimuli without relaxation	Same
No treatment	Same	No treatment	Same

Wolpe's insistence on this contiguous pairing was indeed important. Finally, there was a fourth, no-treatment group, to control for the effects of having fear assessed before and following treatment. It was possible that subjects who are afraid of snakes will reduce their fear to a measurable degree merely by having that fear measured twice.

There is another feature of the experimental design that is important. In order to control for sheer amount of exposure to imagined stimuli, subjects in the exposure and the pseudodesensitization control groups were *yoked* to subjects in the desensitization group. That is, each desensitization subject, unbeknownst to her, had a "partner" in each of the other control groups whose number of scenes imagined was determined in advance by her progress up the anxiety hierarchy. In this fashion, any differences among the groups could not be attributed to the number of stimuli imagined. The design of this experiment is summarized in Table 19.2.

The results (Figure 19.6) revealed that de-

sensitization subjects improved significantly more than all other groups; only when aversive stimuli were paired with relaxation was there any reduction in fear. These findings lend strong support to the idea that desensitization

FIGURE 19.6

Results of Davison's (1968b) experiment showing the greater improvement of desensitization subjects compared to that of other groups.

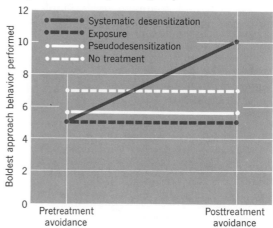

is effective because it involves counterconditioning, that is, because subjects imagine anxiety-evoking stimuli while their bodies are responding in quite another way.

No single experiment ever settles an issue completely, however, and many other researchers have investigated this fascinating procedure. There is still lively controversy about the best way to conceptualize the processes responsible for the behavioral changes (see the reviews by Wilson and Davison, 1971, and Davison and Wilson, 1973).

SOME SPECIAL ISSUES IN BEHAVIOR MODIFICATION

We have reviewed the development of theory and research in behavior therapy, paying special attention to the manner in which researchers have tried to validate procedures and isolate the significant variables. The field is expanding each year, and while this expansion occurs everyone concerned with therapy should remain aware of the problems and issues that transcend particular experimental findings. We think the following considerations need to be kept clearly in mind.

The Behavioral Focus on Current Maintaining Variables

An important defining characteristic of behavior therapy is its focus on current maintaining variables rather than historical etiological ones. Masters and Johnson, for example, feel that performance fears and the spectator role are responsible for the maintenance of most human sexual dysfunctions regardless of etiology. Religious orthodoxy and psychosexual trauma might well be important historical factors, but they are significant in the present only because they make people fearful of their sexual performance and prone to watch their sexual activities from a distance instead of losing themselves in the excitement of arousal. Behavior therapists tend to concentrate their efforts on just such maintaining variables — regardless of what factors have brought them into being.

Internal Behavior

In Chapter 4 we demonstrated the use that can be made of intervening processes and explanatory fictions to relate data meaningfully and to generate fruitful hypotheses. We should examine this issue again in connection with behavior modification. The field is often mistakenly equated with the radical behavioristic positions of Watson and Skinner — that it is not useful or legitimate to make inferences about internal processes in the organism. Our intent is to present a mediational point of view as persuasively as we can, although not all contemporary behavior therapists (for example, Ullmann and Krasner, 1969; Bijou and Baer, 1961) are in agreement with our view. They have every right to define the field in any way they consider useful.

The position we share with others (see Bandura, 1969; Kanfer and Phillips, 1970; Meyer and Chesser, 1970) is that behavior modification, as applied experimental psychology, is legitimately concerned with internal as well as external events, provided the internal mediators are securely anchored to observable stimuli or responses. Behaviorists do not have to ignore the internal life of human beings; but they do differ from psychologists with other views in the rigor of their inferences to internal processes and in the care they take to ensure that inferences are parsimonious as well as productive of good explanations and future testable hypotheses.

Underlying Causes

This issue of internal mediators bears on the misconception that behavior therapy deals with symptoms while other therapies, particularly psychoanalytically oriented ones, are concerned with "root" or "underlying" causes. To many people a determinant of behavior that is assumed to lie in the unconscious is somehow more "underlying" or "basic" than a determinant that is anchored in the environment. This conception fails to consider that science searches for the most significant causes of behavior. If "underlying" is defined as "not immediately obvious," behavior therapists indeed search for underlying causes. If such causes are taken to be the strongest and most significant ones, that is, the controlling variables, the task of behavior therapists is the same as for all other therapists—to find those strongest causes (Bandura, 1969).

Symptomatic Treatment

The matter of underlying causes is relevant to another frequent misunderstanding about behavior therapy—the allegation that only symptoms are dealt with, not causes. Our review of the field has necessarily been fragmented because we have dealt with separate techniques one at a time. In clinical practice, however, most behavior therapists employ several procedures at once or sequentially in an attempt to deal with all the important controlling variables; this approach is generally referred to as *broad-spectrum behavior therapy* (Lazarus, 1971). For example, a woman fearful of leaving her home might well be desensitized to images of walking out of her door and successive activities. Over the years, however, she may also have built up a dependent relationship with her husband. As she becomes bolder in venturing forth, the change might disrupt the equilibrium that she and her husband have, in a nonverbalized fashion, worked out. To attend only to her fear of leaving home would be incomplete behavior therapy (Lazarus, 1965) and might even lead to the replacement of the agoraphobia with another difficulty that would serve to keep the woman at home—a problem frequently called "symptom substitution."

In a related vein, it is often said that behavior therapists invariably focus only on a patient's complaint as stated during the first interview. The facts are otherwise. A clinical graduate student was desensitizing an undergraduate for test anxiety. The client made good progress up the hierarchy of imagined situations, but was not improving at all in the real world of test taking. The supervisor of the graduate student suggested that the therapist find out whether the client was studying for his tests. It turned out that he was not; worry about the health of his mother was markedly interfering with his study habits. Thus the goal of making the client nonchalant about taking tests was perhaps unrealizable, for he was approaching the tests themselves without adequate preparation. On the basis of additional assessment, the therapy shifted away from desensitization to a discussion of how the client could deal with his realistic fears about his mother's possible death.

Behavioral approaches to homosexuality also highlight the necessity of determining the principal controlling variables. As we suggested in Chapter 12, there is more to homosexuality than sexual attraction to the same sex, which has been treated largely through aversive conditioning. Many female homosexuals, for example, speak of their lesbian relationships in nonsexual terms, emphasizing emotional closeness and mutual interdependence. A therapist consulted by such an individual who clearly wished to change her homosexual orientation would be unwise to choose aversive conditioning as the principal therapeutic procedure.

Relationship Factors

Because of the scientific language typically employed in the literature on behavior therapy, the mistaken impression is often conveyed that behavior therapists are little if at all concerned with the therapist-client relationship: whether, for example, the client trusts the therapist, believes he can be of assistance, and the like. Although behaviorists have, indeed, tried to emphasize the learning mechanisms that operate in the various techniques, they have never discounted the importance of the client's feelings about the therapist. Arnold Lazarus has been particularly outspoken in this respect for many years, indeed, ever since he introduced the term "behavior therapy" into the literature in 1958. Research in behavior therapy has, in fact, already documented the importance of sometimes vaguely defined relationship factors. In the Paul (1966) study (pages 507–508), for example, considerable and long-lasting improvement was observed in subjects who were given the attention-placebo treatment. Thus, while desensitization subjects improved more than the others, the significant improvement in the placebo group demonstrates the substantial contribution of the warm, trusting relationship that is part of this specific behavioral technique.

Flesh on the Theoretical Skeleton

The issue of determining the most important controlling variables is related to another overlooked aspect of behavior therapy—indeed, of any therapy—namely moving from a general principle to a concrete clinical intervention.

To illustrate, let us consider a study in which undergraduates were trained to analyze the behavior of severely disturbed children in operant conditioning terms (Davison, 1964). The students were encouraged to *assume* that the important determinants of these children's deviant behavior were the consequences of that behavior. Armed with M & M candies as reinforcers, these student-therapists attempted to bring the behavior of the severely disturbed children under their control. This abstract orientation, however, had to be translated into actual operations. The choices of reinforcers and of behaviors to reinforce had to be made by the therapist on the scene—not an easy task by any means. An example of the resourcefulness and ingenuity required is found in the decision of a student who noticed that one child appeared to be losing interest in earning the candies. Working within a framework that required an effective reinforcer, the therapist looked around in his environment for another possible incentive. Luckily, he noticed that each time the child passed a window, she would pause for a moment to look at her reflection. The therapist obtained a mirror and was subsequently able to make "peeking into the mirror" the reinforcer for obeying his instructions. The opportunity to look into a mirror was made contingent on certain behaviors; the peeks into the mirror were used in the same *functional* way as the M & M candies. Thus, *guided by a general principle, the therapist had to rely on improvisation and inventiveness as demanded by the clinical situation.*

A newcomer to this field can get the impression that doing therapy along behavioral lines is easy and straightforward, that the application of a general principle to a particular case is a simple matter. Those who have worked as behavioral clinicians, however, believe otherwise. Although a given theoretical framework guides the clinician's thinking and therapeutic behaviors, it is by no means sufficient.

. . . *the theoretical notions to which a clinician subscribes seem to bear importantly on the specific decisions he makes in a particular case. The clinician in fact approaches his work with a given set, a framework for ordering the complex data that are his domain. But frameworks are insufficient. The clinician, like any other applied scientist, must fill out the theoretical skeleton. Individual cases present problems that always call for knowledge beyond basic psychological principles (Lazarus and Davison, 1971, p. 203).*

The need to translate principles into actions does not, however, place behavior therapy outside of experimental psychology, to which it looks for philosophical and empirical justification. Anyone who has conducted a psychological experiment knows full well the ingenuity necessary to translate an abstractly phrased hypothesis into operational terms so that it can be tested. The preceding quotation from two behavior therapists is very similar to the following one from an article written by two hard-nosed experimental social psychologists.

In any experiment, the investigator chooses a procedure which he intuitively feels is an empirical realization of his conceptual variable. All experimental procedures are "contrived" in the sense that they are invented. Indeed, it can be said that the art of experimentation rests primarily on the skill of the investigator to judge the procedure which is the most accurate realization of his conceptual variable and has the greatest impact and the most credibility for the subject (Aronson and Carlsmith, 1968, p. 25).

Thus behavior therapists are faced with the same kinds of decision-making challenges that their experimental colleagues face. Although we recognize that there are no easy solutions in dealing with human problems, we believe that the behavior therapy approach holds considerable promise for devising effective means of modifying abnormal behavior.

SUMMARY

In this chapter we have reviewed theory and research in behavior modification, a branch of clinical psychology which attempts to apply the methodologies and principles of experimental psychology to the therapeutic modification of human behavior. Several subareas of this burgeoning field were surveyed: counterconditioning—eliciting an antagonistic response in the presence of a stimulus which evokes an undesired response; operant conditioning—teaching desired responses and discouraging undesired ones by applying contingencies such as reward and punishment; modeling—helping the client to acquire new responses and unlearn old ones by observing models; and cognitive restructuring—encouraging behavior change by direct alteration of mediating thoughts. Experimental work in systematic desensitization—a widely used technique for reducing unrealistic fears—was reviewed as a case study in behavior therapy research. The Masters and Johnson work on treating human sexual inadequacies was summarized to show the subtle interactions between clinical sensitivities to human needs and specific behavioral techniques. Finally, several important issues in behavior therapy, such as the role of underlying causes and relationship factors, were discussed in the hope of providing the reader with a better and more sophisticated grasp of a field that is both promising and controversial.

CHAPTER 20

Group Therapy, Community Psychology, and Biological Treatment

A serious crisis in the alleviation of human psychological suffering is the ever-worsening manpower shortage (see, for instance, Albee, 1969; Arnhoff, Rubinstein, and Speisman, 1969). Even overlooking the difficulties in defining mental disorder and in determining how many people need professional assistance, most writers agree that in the foreseeable future America's mental health needs are unlikely to be met, given present estimates of the incidence of disorder and of the numbers of professionals being trained.

What form can viable solutions take? Behavior therapy has been touted for its potential impact on manpower shortages by virtue of its efficiency. A single traditional clinician who averages 200 sessions per client—hardly an exaggerated figure, in fact, probably a gross underestimate—could see in individual psychotherapy about 40 clients every five years, assuming an average workweek of 40 hours. Compare this with a behavior therapist who may average 40 sessions per client; he could treat five times the number seen by the traditional clinician. If there is no loss in effectiveness, there could be a dramatic reduction in the manpower shortage.

Even assuming this analysis, however, shortages will continue to exist, if for no other reason than that supply tends to create demand! Increased availability of professional assistance for psychological suffering tends to encourage more people to seek out help, particularly if the stigma associated with seeing a "shrink" disappears, as seems to be happening.

In this chapter we review three broad areas of therapeutic intervention. Although different from one another in many important ways, they nonetheless share this characteristic: they make far more efficient use of professional time than the one-to-one therapies reviewed in the preceding two chapters. In group therapy a professional treats a number of patients simultaneously; community psychology is oriented toward prevention and treating the problems of patients in their natural surroundings; and biological treatment involves dispensing somatic treatments—drugs, electroconvulsive therapy, and surgery—which are clearly less time-consuming than one-to-one treatment. All three, then, are more economical than individual therapy. As we will soon see, however, economy is not the primary reason that any of the three is used. Rather, each developed from a particular rationale for effective treatment.

INSIGHT-ORIENTED GROUP THERAPY

Economy is an obvious advantage of therapy in groups: a single therapist can treat more people and charge them lower fees than he would if he were seeing them individually. It would be a mistake, however, to regard the possible value of groups only in economic terms. Most group therapy proponents regard groups as *uniquely* appropriate for accomplishing certain goals. Aronson (1972), for example, notes that group members can learn vicariously (see Chapter 2) when attention is focused on another participant. Social pressures, too, can be surprisingly strong in groups. For example, if a therapist tells an individual client that his behavior seems hostile even when hostility is not intended, the message may be rejected; however, if three or four other people agree with the interpretation, the person concerned may find it much more difficult to reject the observation. In addition, many people derive comfort and support solely from the knowledge that others have problems similar to theirs.

As we saw in the two preceding chapters, the literature on one-to-one psychotherapy is confusing and extensive: so too is the information available on group therapy. Virtually every technique or theory employed in individual therapy has been (or can be) used for treating people in groups. Thus there are psychoanalytic groups (Slavson, 1950; Wolf, 1949), Gestalt groups (Perls, 1969), client-centered groups (Rogers, 1970), behavior therapy

groups (Lazarus, 1968a; Paul and Shannon, 1966), and countless other kinds. We shall examine just a few group psychotherapies in hopes of imparting some idea of the range of theories and procedures prevalent.

Moreno's Psychodrama

J. L. Moreno, a Viennese psychiatrist, is said to have coined the term "group psychotherapy" in 1931. He is unquestionably one of the most influential and colorful figures in the field. The essence of the form of group therapy he introduced—psychodrama—is to have participants act out their feelings as if in a play. A patient might be asked to converse with another group member playing the role of his father. By this means, the patient is apparently helped to express his feelings and perceptions about his father more effectively than by verbalizing his feelings. "We must stimulate the patients to be concrete, and bring forth their feelings and thoughts in a structured form" (Moreno and Kipper, 1968, p. 56). Like other forms of group therapy, psychodrama makes unique use of the group as a vehicle for changing people, rather than merely as a more efficient way of treating greater numbers of people at a single time. In psychodrama a number of people are essential so that a host of potential actors are available to stage dramatic presentations that presumably reveal people's true feelings and conflicts (Figure 20.1).

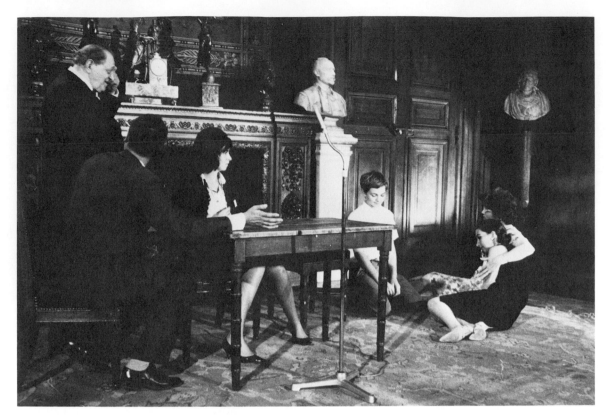

FIGURE **20.1**

J. L. Moreno, standing on the left, conducts a psychodrama session. The participants are acting out a contrived scene in order to explore some emotional problem.

To facilitate therapeutic role taking, Moreno uses an actual stage so that the members of the group can be encouraged to view the proceedings as a kind of drama; the presence of an audience also contributes to the theatrical atmosphere. Moreno has suggested many kinds of role taking to promote the expression and confrontation of true feelings. For example, the *mirroring technique* is designed for patients who have difficulty expressing themselves in action or in words: another person, an "auxiliary ego," portrays the patient as best he can, thereby furnishing him concrete information on how others view him. At all times the emphasis is on expressing in dramatic form true feelings about certain situations. The ther-

apist is an important participant in these activities, sometimes actively directing the "play" so that maximum therapeutic gain can be achieved.

Should this be classified as insight or action-oriented therapy? Clearly, the therapist assumes responsibility for what happens during the session; furthermore, he goads the patients into specific behaviors during treatment. On the other hand, the ultimate goal of the treatment is seen by Moreno as insight into one's actual motivations. In this sense psychodrama is an insight therapy that goes beyond reliance on verbal interpretive methods (as in psychoanalysis) but that still emphasizes the importance of helping the patient achieve an under-

TREATMENT

standing of his actual motivations and needs.

Unfortunately there is no body of research on psychodrama, so it is difficult to assess the efficacy of Moreno's ideas.

Sensitivity Training and Encounter Groups

Without question, one of the most exciting developments in clinical psychology and psychiatry in recent years is the sensitivity training group, or T-group, movement. Aronson (1972) differentiates the T-group from the more radical "encounter group," which grew in popularity primarily on the West Coast at such places as the Esalen Institute. T-groups, he contends, tend to rely more on verbal procedures and to avoid the physical contact employed by many encounter groups. Aronson's distinction is not accepted by all workers, however. Rogers (1970) traces the development of encounter groups to his training of counselors at the University of Chicago in 1946, in which he emphasized personal growth and improved interpersonal communication. We would agree with his judgment that T-groups and encounter groups are usually impossible to distinguish nowadays.

The T-group was originally conceived in 1947 at the National Training Laboratories in Bethel, Maine. The impetus came from colleagues of Kurt Lewin, a famous social psychologist at MIT. The initial groups were made up of people in industry, and the goal was to increase efficiency in business practices at the highest levels of management by making executives more aware of their impact on other people and of their own feelings about others. Over the past twenty years, many other kinds of people have participated in such groups, including no doubt many readers of this book.

The T-group is best viewed as educational. Generally speaking, the content of the learning in a T-group is information about one's self and one's relationships with others. Individuals are often drawn to T-groups because, even when apparently functioning quite well and without marked unhappiness, they have the feeling that they are missing something in life, or perhaps they are concerned with interpersonal problems. Aronson lists some general goals of T-groups.

1. To develop a willingness to examine one's behavior and to experiment with new ways of behaving.
2. To learn more about people in general.
3. To become more authentic and honest in interpersonal relations.
4. To become better able to work cooperatively with people other than in an authoritative or submissive manner.
5. To develop the ability to resolve conflicts through logical and rational problem solving rather than through coercion or manipulation.

In the most general terms T-groups and encounter groups provide a setting where people are encouraged to behave in an unguarded fashion and then are helped to see how they come across to others, how they affect others, and how they feel about what they are doing. Aronson provides the following description of how a group session may get started.

. . . *he* [*the leader*] . . . *falls into silence. Minutes pass. They seem like hours. The group members may look at each other or out the window. Typically, participants may look at the trainer for guidance or direction. None is forthcoming. After several minutes, someone might express his discomfort. This may or may not be responded to. Eventually, in a typical group, someone will express annoyance at the leader: "I'm getting sick of this. This is a waste of time. How come you're not doing your job? What the hell are we paying you for? Why don't you tell us what we're supposed to do?" There may be a ripple of applause in the background. But someone else might jump in and ask the first person why he is so bothered by a lack of direction—does he need someone to tell him what to do? And the T-group is off and running (Aronson, 1972, p. 241).*

Levels of Communication

Figure 20.2 is Aronson's schematic representation of a dyadic or two-person interaction. In our everyday lives, each of us often operates at level P_3, namely behaving in some verbal or nonverbal way toward another person. Frequently, the recipient of our behavior looks at P_3 and responds at R_4, evaluation. There are obviously many points at which misjudgments can occur. For example, the recipient at R_3 may misinterpret P's intention because of any number of factors. Even though the person may feel warmly toward the recipient (P_1), he may have difficulty expressing warmth and therefore display sarcasm at P_3. The recipient may then interpret P's intention (R_3) as a wish to hurt him, rather than as a desire to express warm feelings toward him. Without the open discussion of feelings that is encouraged in a T-group, the recipient can reject the person (R_4) as a nasty individual and never come to understand that the person really feels warmly (P_1) but has not learned to express his feelings (P_3) appropriately. Or the following might occur. A person may be expressing warm feelings in a totally open way at P_3 but the recipient, for reasons of his own, may be so suspicious of any expression of warmth that he misinterprets the person's intentions (R_3) and rejects him instead of acknowledging and enjoying the expression of warmth. A properly run T-group encourages the participants to break down their interpersonal communications and reactions into all the various components so that they can examine their true feelings toward another person and their perceptions of what they are receiving from that person.

The T-group provides a setting where people are given the opportunity to talk frankly and to listen to one another. Usually, the material on which the group works is provided by the ongoing interaction, rather than from an examination of past histories, as might be the case in a psychoanalytically oriented group. The emphasis on openness is not necessarily a violation of a person's right to privacy, though there is little question that sometimes people feel pressured to reveal more about themselves in certain groups than they might wish. Naturally, the experienced and competent group leader watches for undue coercion and directs the stream of conversation away from an individual when he senses excessive probing into the person's private feelings.

One of the principal tools for achieving the kind of learning desired in a T-group is undisguised feedback from fellow group members, including the trainer. Thus A may be continually interrupting B and yet be unaware of his true feeling of dislike for B. Other group members, or the leader, might interject a comment to A that he is apparently having difficulty expressing certain feelings to B and perhaps would like to do so more directly than by interrupting. Furthermore, A might be made aware of the negative impact that his constant interruption has on B, perhaps even more negative than an honest expression of dislike.

Role of T-group Leader

Let us now summarize and extend what Aronson sees as the role and the function of the group leader in the T-group.

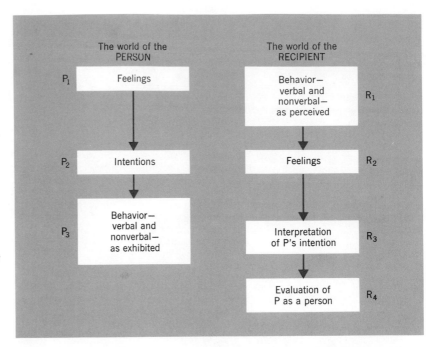

FIGURE **20.2**
Schematic representation of a two-person interaction. The diagram illustrates the different levels of communication possible. After Aronson, 1972.

1. The leader or trainer is a full member of the group. His own feelings, reactions, and effects on others are as legitimate a part of the subject matter as those of any other group member. Unlike the usual therapeutic role, the T-group leader does not hold himself aloof from his clients.

2. Being a professional, however, the leader is busy doing other things as well. He may occasionally comment on what is going on in the group, or he may step in to help people with difficult encounters or help participants discuss their feelings about others rather than their judgments of them.

3. On the assumption that discoveries by one's self are more meaningful and longer-lasting than insights and observations doled out by experts, the group leader tries whenever possible not to intervene. At times, for example, the best tack is to remain silent.

4. A competent trainer will make every effort not to impose his will and ideas on the other participants, but he is of course aware of the very powerful position that he occupies

in the group and of his impact on group members. It seems likely that some of the unfortunate abuses of encounter groups and T-groups can be attributed to the all-too-human tendency of some trainers to wield this power.

Transfer of Learning

The criticism has been made that those who participate in T-groups learn only how to participate in T-groups. They are not able to transfer to real-life situations those insights and other skills that have been acquired in a group (Houts and Serber, 1972). Transfer of learning is a difficult problem for, whether we like it or not, the real world is not set up like a T-group to encourage openness and frankness. A person may offend others by expressing feelings openly and honestly to those who are not operating by the rules of a T-group. Indeed, as Aronson reminds us, if someone insists that others be totally open when they do not want to be, he is being insensitive to their feelings and

FIGURE **20.3**
Participants in sensitivity or encounter groups are often instructed to engage in activities involving close physical contact, in the hopes of removing inhibitions.

so has *not* learned from what otherwise might have been a good T-group experience. Is this to say that T-group experiences can never transfer to the real world? Not necessarily, for a knowledge of how one feels about others and how one comes across to them may be extremely useful in everyday activities even if the overt behavior encouraged in a T-group is not continued.

It is especially important for professional therapists to be aware of their own feelings about others and how they come across to them; we have already discussed the insistence of analytically oriented therapists that each would-be psychotherapist undergo a psychoanalysis of his own precisely so that he can become aware of his own biases and not allow them to interfere with his own work. Perhaps T-group experiences could serve a similar function for therapists of many persuasions.

Variations

There are numerous variations on the sensitivity or encounter group theme. Rogers's (1970) encounter groups tend to follow the outlines of his individual client-centered therapy as summarized in Chapter 18; he frequently clarifies feelings, assuming that growth can occur as people confront their emotions with honesty. The group leader—or "facilitator"—tends to be less active than in the T-groups Aronson describes. Some groups may meet for hours at a time, perhaps over a weekend, with little if any sleep allowed. Such *marathons* (Bach, 1966; Mintz, 1967; Stoller, 1968) are based on the assumption that fatigue and extended exposure to a particular set of social-influence conditions will weaken "defenses" and help the participants become more open. Many group enthusiasts, especially those of an encounter persuasion (Figure 20.3), use exercises to break the ice (Schutz, 1967). For example, one person may be instructed to close his eyes and allow himself to be carried around by the group members, to foster trust in them. In another exercise two people stare into each other's eyes without speaking. These maneuvers, and many others, seem to share the subgoal of loosening people up, making clear to them that this social setting operates by rules which hold that it is acceptable to express one's feelings openly without censorship or fear of punishment. Drug addict "Synanon" groups, however, tend to be brutal in the directness of their confrontations (Yablonsky, 1962). More recently, Bindrim (1968) has introduced nudity as an aid to lowering defenses.

Evaluation

We turn now to the important issue of research with T-groups. Do they really work? Like other therapies, the T-group and encounter movement has its share of glowing testimonials.

I have known individuals for whom the encounter experience has meant almost miraculous change in the depth of their communication with spouse and children. Sometimes for the first time real feelings are shared. . . . I have seen teachers who have transformed their classroom . . . into a personal, caring, trusting, learning group, where students participate fully and openly in forming the curriculum and all the other aspects of their education. Tough business executives who described a particular business relationship as hopeless have gone home and changed it into a constructive one (Rogers, 1970, p. 71).

Such observations, especially by a highly skilled and innovative clinician, contribute to the growing faith many people have in encounter groups. As we have already seen from Chapter 4, however, such data do not satisfy most scientists of human behavior.

It is extraordinarily difficult to do good research with T-groups because the independent variables are so complex and difficult to control. Nonetheless, Aronson (1972) points to a number of studies supporting the contention that properly run training groups do bring about measurable and significant changes in behavior outside the group setting. In one study (Miles, 1965) colleagues of people who had been in a group indicated whether they had noticed any changes in the behavior of the participants once they returned to the large industrial organization for which the study was run. They also evaluated a control group composed of managers who had not gone through the T-group experience. Generally, the participating managers were viewed by their associates as having become more interpersonally sensitive, as having increased in communication and leadership skills, and as being more relaxed and more considerate of others. Unfortunately, as Aronson notes, the colleagues making these ratings may well have been aware of which people had been in the T-group, thus possibly introducing observer bias. Gibb (1971) also reviews scores of studies—some of good quality—and suggests that beneficial changes do occur in many group members.

A sobering finding is recent evidence on "casualties" from T-groups (for example, Yalom and Lieberman, 1971). As Serber (1972) has pointed out, a person may be confronted with a serious deficiency in his interpersonal functioning, such as a degree of shyness that impedes satisfying interpersonal relationships. If, as often seems to happen, the leader allows discussion to shift away from that person on the assumption that confrontation with the difficulty is sufficient in itself, that individual may very well leave the group feeling *worse* about himself. It appears that, like other interventions, psychotherapy can hurt as well as help (Bergin, 1966). T-group and encounter group experiences may exert powerful effects on people, but these events will not always work to the benefit of all participants.

No extensive research has been done on the effects of encounter and T-groups. But experimentally oriented psychologists, aware of the need for controlled evaluation, have begun to study this important development in psychology.

BEHAVIOR THERAPY GROUPS

Arnold Lazarus (1968a), a pioneer in group behavior therapy, has pointed out that a behavior therapist may, primarily for reasons of efficiency, choose to deal with several people suffering from the same kind of problem by seeing them in a group rather than seeing them individually. The emphasis, as in one-to-one therapy, remains on interactions between the therapist and each individual patient or client.

Individualized Behavior Therapy in Groups

Good examples of this individualized approach can be seen in the numerous studies of group desensitization (for example, Lazarus, 1961; Paul and Shannon, 1966). In a group context a single therapist can teach deep muscle relaxation and present items from a common anxiety hierarchy to each member of the group simultaneously, thus saving therapist time (Figure 20.4).

Another example of individualized behavior therapy in groups is given in a report by Lazarus (1968a) of the treatment of several impotent men in a group and of several frigid women in another group. Treatment in each group involved didactic discussion of sexual functioning, including noncoital methods of providing sexual pleasure to a partner, as well as group desensitization of related sexual fears. Therapeutic messages and procedures emanate from a single therapist to each of a number of people at the same time (Figure 20.5A).

But members of groups are also likely to interact with one another. Lazarus points out that behavior therapy may also be employed in a group setting where the group itself is an important vehicle of change; in other words, the group can be not only an efficient way of doing therapy but also a uniquely appropriate setting in which to bring about desirable behavioral changes. As illustrated in Figure 20.5B, the lines of communication in such a group are among all participants, not just between therapist and participants. As an example of this second type of behavior therapy group, we turn to Lazarus's account of assertive training groups.

Assertive Training Groups

The assumption of assertive training is that many human problems can be alleviated by encouraging people to express more openly their feelings of resentment as well as of warmth and cordiality. Behavior therapy for nonassertive individuals allows them to reduce their anxiety about expressing their inter-

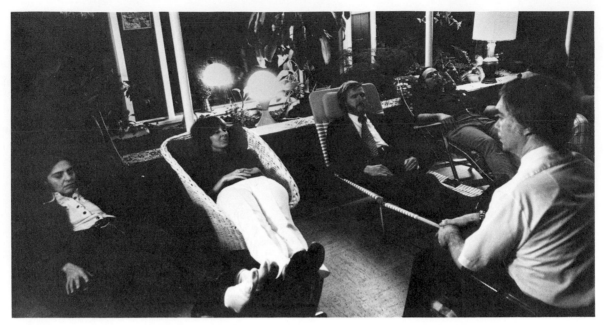

FIGURE **20.4**
Systematic desensitization conducted for a group by Arnold A. Lazarus,
who has led the extension of behavior modification to group settings.

personal feelings and to acquire new habits of assertion within the educative atmosphere of a group.

Lazarus suggests that an assertive training group be composed of about ten people of the same sex. At the first meeting the behavior therapist describes the general goals of the therapy group, commenting particularly on the problems that nonassertiveness can create for individuals in our society. He also suggests that the therapy group can provide a good setting for cooperative problem solving. Like Rogers, he emphasizes honesty and acceptance within the group, rather than the kind of

FIGURE **20.5**
Distinction between (A) individualized group therapy and (B) group therapy in which interactions among all the members are regarded as important. Arrows refer to lines of communication and influence; T stands for therapist, P for patient.

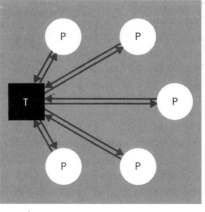

A

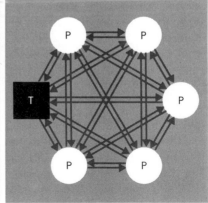

B

TREATMENT

showmanship and falseness that often characterizes ordinary social groups. The therapist also stresses constructive criticism and diligent practice of new skills. Then each group member introduces himself briefly, and the other members are encouraged to comment on such things as the manner in which the person presented himself, especially if he did so in an apologetic way.

Of particular importance are *assignments* carried out by the members *between consecutive group sessions:* attention is paid to behavior not just in the group but in real life as well. People are encouraged to describe both successful and unsuccessful attempts at assertive behavior on the outside, and sometimes role playing is employed within the group to enable a person to improve upon past or anticipated performances. The emphasis at all times is on the benefits to be derived from appropriate and effective expression of both positive and negative feelings. If the therapist is sensitive and skillful, he is able to create an atmosphere in which group members begin to trust themselves in expressing criticism without fearing that they are hurting other people's feelings.

Although there are some similarities between Lazarus's assertive training groups and the sensitivity training groups described earlier, the important difference is the attention Laz-

arus pays to between-session activities; the group is oriented to helping people make specific changes outside the group therapy setting. Although T-groups are similarly concerned with helping people change outside of the therapy setting, as yet much less systematic attention has been paid to what clients do between group sessions (see Box 20.1).

Overall Evaluation of Group Therapy

The variety of therapy in groups is staggering, as should be obvious even from our selective review. What seems to be common to all therapy groups is the assumption that behavior can be changed in settings larger than the traditional one-to-one situation. Whether the focus is on increasing insight into one's motivations or behavior within the group or on encouraging people to behave differently outside of the group seems to depend on each therapist's model. Moreover, recent trends suggest a blurring of the distinction between insight and behavioral groups—something we saw already at the end of the preceding chapter. Controlled research on the effectiveness of groups and the processes underlying their efficacy is just beginning, so it seems premature to draw general conclusions.

COMMUNITY PSYCHOLOGY

Perhaps the best way to characterize community psychology or psychiatry is to say that they represent a set of attitudes rather than a body of theory and therapeutic techniques (Rappaport and Chinsky, 1974). The approach is one of *seeking* rather than waiting. Waiting is the mode of nearly all therapies reviewed thus far. A professional person with an advanced

degree is available to provide assistance in his office or in a hospital to individuals who, usually out of extreme suffering, initiate the contact themselves or are referred by the courts. The seeking mode, in contrast, provides mental health services outside of professional settings, often in a person's own community; troubles are actually sought out by

Behavior therapists have begun to consider the use of encounter group
procedures for producing specified behavioral changes. Liberman (1972)
has recently proposed a schema linking various exercises with behavioral
goals, as illustrated in Table 20.1.

TABLE **20.1**

*The Use of Structured Exercises To
Promote Behavioral Change in Groups*

(*from Liberman, 1972, pp. 101–102*)

Exercise	Behavioral goal
One member breaks into circle of members with arms interlocked	To enable a new group member or an alienated member to feel part of the group (initiation)
Sensory awareness exercises	To teach individuals who are overly intellectual and verbal to integrate their sensory inputs
Making noises, playing tag, simulating children in a playground	To reduce anxiety and diffidence in a beginning group; to warm up the group; to foster regression which helps members at least temporarily to suspend defensive behavior
Simulated karate, arm wrestling, other "combat" games	To dessipate hostile tensions between members, and to teach aggressive responses
Member is instructed to relate feelings directly to each other member	To teach emotional assertiveness; to desensitize anxiety attached to assertiveness

TREATMENT

TABLE **20.1** (*continued*)

Exercise	Behavioral goal
Tug of war	To teach teamwork and organizational effort; to teach reciprocity in responding to the other team
Part of a whole, group pretzel	To promote cohesion and involvement
Fantasy games and Gestalt exercises	To arouse affect and to give members the opportunity to work through a problem relationship emotionally—a corrective emotional experience
Members are instructed to express positive feelings to each other nonverbally	To teach individuals how to give and accept affection
Mirror game	To teach how to follow another person's lead and how to move so that the other can follow easily
In pairs, one member sums up and paraphrases partner's statement before going on to make his own statement	To teach each partner to listen carefully and empathize with his partner.

these workers, some of whom are subdoctoral paraprofessionals supervised by psychologists or psychiatrists; the emphasis is on early prevention of difficulties rather than the "repair work" commonly performed in the waiting mode.

Community Mental Health Centers

Why this shift to an activist community orientation? For many years objections were raised about how few people could avail themselves of psychotherapeutic services, which are typically very expensive, in very short supply, and apparently appropriate only to so-called YAVIS clients—individuals who are young, attractive, verbal, intelligent, and successful. There was also the growing belief that emotional difficulties could be better dealt with in their earliest stages of development, rather than after crises or complete deterioration. Indeed, "primary prevention" seeks to forestall problems altogether by changing the conditions that are assumed to cause them. Perhaps the greatest single impetus to this movement was a practical one: in 1963 President John F. Kennedy proposed a "bold new approach" to dealing with problems of mental illness, and Congress passed the Community Mental Health Centers Act funding hundreds of community-based centers across the country.

The main objective of a community mental health center is to provide mental health care in a person's own community, thereby reducing the necessity to institutionalize a seriously disturbed individual in a large state hospital, usually far from his home. A related purpose is to provide outpatient services that would not otherwise be available because of high cost. Finally, the center is supposed to provide consultation services to the local community.

How, specifically, are these goals approached? The centers themselves are staffed by psychiatrists, psychologists, social workers, nurses, and a host of paraprofessionals who are indigenous to the community and can help bridge the gap between the middle- and upper-middle-class professional on the one hand, and on the other a community with groups of people for whom psychotherapy is an alien concept. Typically there are facilities for short-term inpatient care, thereby providing an alternative to hospitalization. There is generally a 24-hour walk-in crisis service as well, offering "rap sessions" for younger members of the community.

A wide range of services is included under the rubric of "consultation" and "education." Consider an effort made by the Westside Community Mental Health Center in 1971 during enforced school busing in San Francisco.

We designed a program in which we placed a professional staff person on a school bus to ride to and from school with grade school children; in addition this staff person had streetcorner meetings with the parents about their busing concerns, and acted also as their advocate to the schools. Knowing the children would be experiencing separation anxiety in this . . .[situation], we had our Hospital Art Department design coloring books with maps of the territory they would cover on the bus route; we attempted to introduce play materials and games that would be helpful to the children, would encourage the children to carry "transitional objects" from home on the bus such as dolls, teddy bears, special favorite toys. Our staff member met with the children before they boarded the bus, talked to them on the bus, again in their new schoolyard and on the way back home again (Heiman, 1973, p. 60).

Activities emanating from these centers can also take the form of calling a rent strike, should staff members decide that better housing conditions could alleviate emotional suffering. Or suggestions might be made by a center's staff to change physical arrangements in a local factory in order to reduce the boredom or tension in a given job; a possible data base for this kind of intervention can be seen in Box 20.2. Moreover, activities such as these need not emanate solely from community mental health centers; mental health workers can readily operate from university departments, social welfare agencies, and even private offices.

Seeking Mode versus Waiting Mode

Contrasting their seeking and waiting modes is a useful way of distinguishing community psychology and psychiatry from the traditional model of private practitioner and mental hospital. But what does the action-oriented seeking attitude of community psychology mean in terms of what is offered to people in their communities? In other words, does community psychology represent a new conceptual mode as well? Do these workers have models of human behavior that are different from the older ones, so that a seeking mode makes especially good sense? Are the techniques employed by community psychologists different from those one finds in private practice? The answer is complex.

Rappaport and Chinsky (1974) propose a scheme to clarify a too often confused area. They suggest that every type of mental health care has two components: the style of delivery component and the conceptual component. The delivery component relates to the difference between seeking and waiting, to an *attitude* about making services available. Community psychology, as we have seen, has a seeking orientation. The conceptual component, on the other hand, relates to the theoretical and data-based underpinnings of the services. Two examples are disease and learning approaches. Table 20.2 illustrates how these two conceptual modes combine with either style of delivery. For example, a 24-hour-a-day "hotline" in a suicide prevention center would be in the community psychology seeking mode. But what specifically the people manning the phones say and do when a call comes in relates to the conceptual mode. One worker might be psychoanalytic in his approach, another might construe suicide threats in learning terms. Clearly, the phone calls would differ greatly—but the community psychology flavor would be there in both. The conceptual components section of Table 20.2 is, of course, expandable almost infinitely. Whether a particular conceptual orientation is more or less suited to one of the two delivery modes is a separate—and crucial—question that creates ongoing controversy among community psychologists and psychiatrists.

Paraprofessionals in Community Psychology

One feature of community programs is the use of paraprofessionals. The first program was probably that at Harvard University (Umbarger, Dalsimer, Morrison, and Breggin, 1962), in which students spent several hours per week as companions to patients in mental hospitals (see Guerney, 1969, for numerous examples of other programs). The argument can be made that hiring local nonprofessionals is particularly valuable because of their similarity to those being treated. Acceptance by the community would seem to be a vital factor in the success of community-based programs. An upper-middle-class psychiatrist whose residence is in the suburbs might well have difficulty establishing rapport with a lower-class ghetto resident. Yet it is open to question whether a nonprofessional has all the qualities and talents necessary to make effective therapeutic interventions. Surely much depends on

BOX **20.2** *Environmental Psychology*

One of the most recent developments in psychology as related to community mental health is the study of the ways in which the arrangement of the physical environment affects behavior (see Sommer, 1969; Proshansky, Ittelson, and Rivlin, 1972). A fascinating example of such research is some work by Baum and Valins (1973). The guiding assumption is a proposal by Calhoun (1970) that within a given physical space, there is a limit to the amount of social interaction that animals can tolerate before stress is created. Baum and Valins term as "unwanted social interaction" any degree of social contact among people that exceeds some optimal level; any environment that provides unwanted social interaction is regarded as crowded (Figure 20.6).

In an initial field study, they found that students living in older dormitories on a university campus complained of more overcrowding than those living in newer ones. Furthermore, when confronted with miniature bedroom and lounge areas and asked to place miniature figures in them until "you would feel crowded," the residents of the older dormitories placed far fewer figures than did those from the newer dormitories, indicating that they could feel crowded with fewer people than those in the newer dormitories did. The subjects in this research study were freshmen who had been *assigned* to their dormitories, thus controlling for self-selection factors that might render the analysis of the data more ambiguous.

In a subsequent study, a subject coming from either the older dorms or from the newer residences was told to wait in a room in the laboratory with another subject. In reality the other student was a "stooge," an accomplice of the experimenter. The hypothesis was that the students from the older accommodations, being more sensitive to crowding, would sit farther away from the stooge than those coming from newer dorms. This prediction was confirmed. Moreover, hidden observers counted the number of seconds within a five-minute period that each subject glanced over in the direction of the stooge. Again significant differences emerged: "older-dorm" students looked at the stooge significantly less often than did "newer-dorm" students, and moreover, reported being more uncomfortable after the enforced waiting period.

These data have led Valins and Baum to question why students would feel more crowded in the older dormitories. The first obvious question was whether, in fact, older dormitories were more crowded in absolute terms than the newer dormitories. This seemed not to be the case with respect to numbers of people per square foot of living area. What differentiated the two sets of dormitories, however, was the *configuration* of the space. The older dormitories were constructed along traditional hall lines; a typical floor contained a number of bedrooms, with two students to a bedroom, each of which opened out directly onto the hall. All three dozen students on a given floor shared one large bathroom and lounge. By contrast, the newer dormitories, with a comparable number of students per floor, were arranged in individual suites with separate living areas and bathrooms to accommodate small groups of four to six students, again two to a bedroom. Thus the residents of the older dormitories apparently had to interact daily with more people than did the residents of newer ones. Privacy was simply more difficult to obtain, and Baum and Valins assumed that such forced interaction with larger numbers of students would create more unwanted social contacts among students in the older dorms. It did not seem surprising that the students in the older dorms felt more crowded.

The thrust of this research is clear. Although provided with comparable amounts of physical living space, students living in older dormitories, where there would seem to be a far greater incidence of unwanted social interaction, are more sensitive to crowding. The implications of such research are important. Among other things, it suggests that architects interested in designing living environments for people should take care to minimize unwanted social interaction by providing certain degrees of privacy. Such work may well cast light on the alarmingly high incidence of violence and emotional turmoil that has come to characterize urban living.

FIGURE **20.6**
The new field of environmental psychology is concerned, among other things, with the stresses of overcrowded urban life.

TABLE 20.2 *Some Possible Models for Mental Health Service*

(adapted from Rappaport and Chinsky, 1974)

		Style of delivery component	
		Waiting mode	Seeking mode
Conceptual component*	Disease conception	Mental illness and disease explanations of abnormal behavior. Therapist waits for patient to contact him and then uses insight therapy.	Mental illness and disease explanations of abnormal behavior. Prevention of illness is emphasized through public education and extension of traditional treatments into community settings.
	Behavioral conception	Learning theory interpretation of emotional dysfunction. Therapist waits for client to contact him and then uses techniques such as systematic desensitization.	Learning theory interpretation of emotional dysfunction. Professional extends services into the community through public education; training of various nonprofessionals in behavior modification techniques and social learning principles.

* Listed here as examples are only two of a large number of possible conceptual components.

what the paraprofessional is supposed to do. The data on this question are far from adequate.

With these general considerations in mind, we turn now to a review of several programs that are part of community psychology. The heterogeneous nature of the field will soon become apparent.

Prevention in Community Psychology

Zax and Cowen (1972) have reviewed an important aspect of community psychology, prevention. The basic assumption of prevention programs is that some psychopathology might very well have its genesis, at least in part, in social institutions that shape behavior. Since powerful determinants of behavior are to be found in community situations such as schools, the attention of psychologists and other mental health workers should be focused on how social environments foster or inhibit adaptive behavior. The unit of analysis therefore becomes a social institution such as a school rather than an individual. A further working assumption is that it is easier to prevent the development of a psychological problem than to handle it once it has developed. This is as yet an untested assumption, but as we shall see it is likely to be a very useful one.

Examples of preventive community psychology are the various "enrichment" programs that have been devised to remedy maladaptive psychological problems that seem attributable to poor social conditions. For instance, project Head Start was initiated by the federal government to enhance the psychological and educational development of disadvantaged children, primarily those from lower-income areas. As yet there are few firm data about the effectiveness of such programs in achieving their stated goals, though this lack by no means suggests that the efforts should cease. The rationale for the programs is that certain human problems are a function of the failure to develop the social and intellectual skills that the larger society values and indeed demands. This model of psychopathology is quite different from one that concentrates on intrapsychic determinants of behavior that are only moderately affected by social conditions in, say, the schools.

Residential Noninstitutional Programs

Residential centers for disadvantaged youth have concentrated on teaching vocational and educational skills, even to those who would be diagnosed, psychiatrically, as showing antisocial reaction or perhaps even schizophrenic reaction. Again, the assumption is that personality maladjustment is a function of intellectual and vocational deprivation resulting from adverse social conditions. Some residential units have been located within a community itself (for example, Goldenberg, 1969) in the belief that training is most effective within a familiar urban setting. Other apparently effective work, however, has been done in state schools located quite a distance from the homes of the youths involved (for example, Cohen and Filipczak, 1971).

Most projects tend to be nonspecific in the actual techniques used. In contrast, one notable program, Cohen's National Training School project, is organized exclusively on operant conditioning lines: residents earn increased privileges within the institution for performing various criterion behaviors, such as studying a certain number of hours.

Another excellent example of a residential program carefully conceived along operant conditioning lines is the work of Montrose Wolf of the University of Kansas (Phillips, Phillips, Fixsen, and Wolf, 1972). "Achievement Place," located in a middle-class community, is run by a young couple who act as surrogate parents for about a dozen boys referred from the courts for delinquent behavior (Figure 20.7). As with Cohen's work, specific prosocial behaviors earn specific amounts of reinforcement. The program has had encouraging results in helping boys return to their communities without the stigma and deterioration that all too often follow institutionalization in jails or state hospitals. The actual cost to county or state authorities for financing such decentralized, nonprison, noninstitutional facilities is far less than that for traditional hospitals or prisons.

Suicide Prevention Centers and Telephone Crisis Services

An increasingly widespread community agency is the suicide prevention center, modeled after the Los Angeles Suicide Prevention Center, founded in 1958 by Farberow and Shneidman. Staffed largely by nonprofessionals under the supervision of psychologists or psychiatrists, these centers attempt to provide 24-hour consultation to people in suicidal crises. Usually the initial contact is made by telephone. The worker tries to assess the likelihood that the caller will actually make a serious suicide

FIGURE **20.7**

At Achievement Place, a foster home for delinquent boys, operant conditioning principles are effectively used to extinguish aggressive behavior and teach social skills. This photograph shows the youths voting on an issue at a family conference. The professional teaching parents and the youths hold a family conference each day to establish and modify rules of conduct, to decide consequences for one another's violations of the rules, to make constructive criticisms about any aspect of the treatment program, and to elect and evaluate a peer manager who oversees many of the youths' daily activities (PHOTOGRAPH COURTESY OF ELERY PHILLIPS, ELAINE PHILLIPS, DEAN FIXEN, AND MONTROSE WOLF.)

attempt and, most importantly, tries to establish personal contact that may dissuade the caller from suicide Figure 20.8 consists of a summary sheet used by telephone workers at the Suicide Prevention Center in Buffalo, New York.

Specialists hold that phone attendants in these centers should work toward the following goals (Speer, 1972).

1. "Tuning in," communicating empathy to the caller.
2. Conveying understanding of the problem.

3. Providing information regarding sources of help, for example, mental health clinics, psychologists, psychiatrists.
4. Obtaining an agreement from the caller to take some specific steps away from suicide, for example, making an appointment to come to the center itself.
5. Providing some degree of hope to the caller that the crisis will end and that life will not always appear so hopeless.

The potential value of such community facilities is made evident by data showing that most suicides give warnings—"cries for help"—before taking their lives (see Chapter 8). Most often their pleas are directed first to relatives and friends, but there are many potential suicides who are isolated from these sources of emotional support; for such individuals the knowledge of a hotline phone number may save their lives.

It is exceedingly difficult to do controlled research on suicide. An evaluation of the effectiveness of suicide prevention centers is similarly problematic, for a large proportion of those who call are not heard from again. For example, Speer (1971) found that more than 95 percent of callers did not use the service repeatedly. Does this mean that the phone contact helped so much that no further consultation was needed? Perhaps so, but it is also possible that many callers killed themselves after the phone call. One study (Weiner, 1969) found no differences in the suicide rates of cities with hotline services and those without. Although numerous factors might have masked real differences, we cannot conclude from these data that the centers *have* demonstrated their effectiveness.

Speer (1972) attempted to evaluate one crisis phone service. From callers who ultimately visited the center he got ratings of their reactions to the worker on the phone. The ratings were related to the specific goals mentioned, such as "tuning in." The study is worth examining more closely, for it sheds light on the kind of research people in the field are doing and on the difficulties such research poses. The subjects were thirty-four callers to a suicide prevention center who subsequently appeared for individual counseling. Some were asked to rate their reactions to the phone call that had led them to the center; others were asked to rate their reactions to the preceding plea for help, the last one made to a personal acquaintance, friend, or relative before calling

the center. In this way Speer hoped to learn whether, on the average, potential suicides derive more comfort and benefit from a service or from a friend or relative (who is presumably not trained in taking crisis calls.)

The results are sobering: of the seven scales used, only one showed that calls to the center were significantly more helpful than calls to a friend. Speer concludes that, in this instance, there was no evidence of superiority of a hotline service in achieving the goals specified for it.

Is there anything else that we can say about this study? What we find striking is the failure of the author to consider a possible confound in the design. When a person calls a crisis service, he may be decidedly more desperate than when he phones a friend or relative. Those who rated the phone calls to the service may therefore have been recording their reactions in far more unhappy and more suicidal moods than the individuals asked to remember and rate calls to friends. If so, there might very well be a significant difference in the efficacy of the two kinds of calls, a difference that would provide much-needed justification for the continuation or even the expansion of such centers.

Once again, we are left with little if any convincing data. Human lives are precious, however, and since many people who contact prevention centers weather a suicidal crisis successfully, there is no reason to discontinue these efforts until unequivocal data are available.

Synanon: Institutional and Group Therapy for Drug Addiction

In 1959 Charles E. Dederich, a former business executive who had overcome severe alcoholic problems, set up a house in Santa Monica, California, for about fifty drug addicts.

SPCS, INC., BUFFALO, NEW YORK

INITIAL CONTACT SHEET (Telephone)

I. <u>Identifying Information</u>: (1-6) ☐☐☐☐☐☐   Case No._____
    1 2 3

(7)   Line: S T P   (8-9) ☐ Counselor_____
       Mo. Date Yr.   hr. min.
(10-14) Date: ☐☐☐   (15) ☐ Day:___ (16-19) Call Began ☐☐☐ A/P ☐
                                                          min.
                              (20-22) Call Duration ☐☐☐

        1
(24) ☐ <u>Caller</u>: (for self   other)   <u>Other</u>: Subject of Call_____
     Name:_____   2
                                               Name:_____

     Address:_____   Address:_____

     Phone:_____   Phone:_____

(25) ☐ Catchment Area: Relationship to Caller_____

(72-73) ☐☐☐☐ Census Tract

        <u>Caller (or Subject of Call)</u>
                               1 2   1 2 3 4 5
(26-27) Age: ☐☐   (28) ☐ Sex: M F   (29) ☐ Marital Status: U M S D W
(30) ☐ Occupation:_____   (32) ☐ Living Situation:___Alone
                                                           With:_____
(31) ☐ Education:_____
Affect and Behavior During Call: (33) ☐ Crying____   (34) ☐ Agitated____
        (35) ☐ Hostile____   (36) ☐ Difficulty talking/unresponsive____
        (37) ☐ Normal____   (38) ☐ Depressed____   (39) ☐ Intoxicated____
        (40) ☐ Tripping____   (41) ☐ Other____

II. <u>Identification of Problem</u> (Check all Appropriate; double check primary problem):
    (42-43) ☐☐

    1 Alcoholism ____   13 Legal   ____   Sexual:
    2 Anxiety   ____   14 Lonely   ____   24   Heterosexual____
    3 Confusion ____   15 Medical   ____   25   Homosexual ____
    4 Depression ____   Problems ____   26   Other   ____
    5 Drugs: 16 Pregnancy ____   27   Social Withdrawal____
         Type   ____   17 Reality   28   Suicidal   ____
         Amount ____   Distortion ____   29   Other   ____
    6 Employment ____   Relationship:
    7 Financial ____   18   Marital ____
    8 Homeless/Stranded____ 19   Parental ____
    9 Homicidal ____   20   Dating   ____
       Illegal Activities: 21   Family   ____
    10   Theft   ____   22   Other   ____
    11   Assault ____   23 School   ____
    12   Other   ____

III. <u>Assessment of Lethality</u>:
    A. Suicidal Behavior:
    (44) ☐ Current Ideation: 0 1 2 3 4 5   None _____
    (45) ☐ Current Suicidal Attempt (describe):_____ None _____
    (46) ☐ Other Suicidal Behavior (describe):_____   None _____
    (47) ☐ History of Attempts: Date _____ Method_____
                                   Outcome_____

B. Suicidal Plan:
(48) ☐ Specificity: 1.Vague_____ 2.Explicit_____
(49) ☐ Method: 1.Hi-Lethal_____ 2.Lo-Lethal_____ What:_____
(50) ☐ Availability of Means: 1.Yes____ 2.No_____ 3.Obtainable_____

C. Resources:
(51) ☐ Internal (e.g. coping ability)_____
(52) ☐ External (e.g. significant other)_____

D. (53) ☐ Communication: 1.Significant Other _____ 2.SPCS _____
                            3.Therapist elsewhere _____ 4.Other_____

E. (54) ☐ Age: 1.Below 40_____ 2.Above 40_____
F. (55) ☐ Sex: 1.M____ 2.F____
G. (56) ☐ Marital Status: 1.U 2.M 3.S 4.D 5.W
H. (57) ☐ Physical Illness: 1.Yes___ 2.No___ What?_____
I. (58) ☐ Drinking: 1.Yes___ 2.No___
J. (59) ☐ Recent Loss or Threat of Loss: 1.Yes___ 2.No___ What?_____
K. (60) ☐ Unexplained Change in Behavior: 1.Yes___ 2.No___
L. (61) ☐ Isolation: 1.Yes___ 2.No___
M. (62) ☐ Depression:
            1.Trouble Sleeping___4.Hopelessness: Severe_____ Moderate_____
            2.Loss of Appetite___ 5.Crying: Frequent_____
            3.Loss of Weight___ 6.Crying: Uncontrollable_____
     (63) ☐ Estimated Suicidal Risk: 1.Low___ 2.Mod.___ 3.High___ 4.Undet.___

IV. Disposition:
Resources Mobilized (check where appropriate)
(64) ☐ Traced____ (65) ☐ Rescue Squad____ (66) ☐ Police____ (67) ☐ Home Visit_____
(68) ☐ Significant Other____ Who?_____
(69) ☐ Appointment Made____ When?_____
(70) ☐ Other:_____

NARRATIVE SUMMARY (including Outcome and Recommendations):

(71) ☐ Follow-Up Requested: 1.Yes___ 2.No___

     Outcome of Follow-Up: (3/1/72)

FIGURE 20.8   *Initial contact sheet used by a telephone attendant at the Buffalo Suicide
Prevention Center. The form is organized to speed the recording of crucial
bits of information.*

Surviving largely by donations from neighboring communities, this small social unit gradually developed into a remarkable treatment setting for narcotics addicts. Although Synanon does not entirely fit the seeking mode of community psychology, we include it here because it is far removed from individual, medically oriented, office-based treatment.

The program at Synanon demands of an addict complete honesty about himself and provides the opportunity, usually for the first time, to achieve self-esteem without drugs. Synanon is a social system isolated from the larger society. Basic to this social system is the requirement to remain clean of drugs and to assume responsibility for one's own behavior. Yablonsky (1962, 1965) finds several important forces operating at Synanon.

1. *Involvement.* Since Synanon is a residence for ex-addicts, a new arrival finds himself in a familiar social setting composed of people with whom he has a great deal in common; in contrast, in traditional treatment settings an addict is confronted with a professional with whom he has difficulty identifying and whom he may not even understand or respect.

2. *An achievable status system.* An addict is presented with some realistic possibilities to achieve prestige through legitimate means. He is regarded as one of the staff, rather than as an inmate or patient in a one-down position.

3. *New social role.* Residents acquire a social role entirely different from their typically criminal role in the outside society. Indeed, many ex-addicts at Synanon have remained in the organization as it has expanded across the country.

4. *Social growth.* Living in this community and participating in its life, the ex-addict develops new abilities to communicate and work with others, and comes also to realize that honesty and industriousness can be legitimate and desirable behavior patterns.

5. *Social control.* Synanon has very strict social norms, which the addict is generally motivated to abide by. The threat of ostracism becomes very meaningful to the resident and serves to control any temptations to return to drugs. Among the specific forms of control are "haircuts," which are brutal verbal attacks from other members when someone misbehaves. Such haircuts are given at "synanon" sessions, group discussions usually considered to be a variation of an encounter group. The residents are held strictly accountable for their behavior by fellow residents who understand all too well the kind of lying and manipulativeness that the drug addict typically lives by on the outside (Figure 20.9).

6. *Empathy and self-identity.* What seem to develop over a period of time are a higher level of understanding of others' feelings and a firmer sense of who the person is.

Much of what goes on at Synanon seems readily translatable into social learning terms. Because the residents are all former addicts, the newcomer might be expected to acquire new patterns of behavior by observing models with whom he can readily identify. Furthermore, there are very strict and explicit contingencies, both positive and negative. For example, should a resident use drugs, he is severely punished in a group therapy session. Yet he is able to recover status and other social rewards by engaging in noncriminal, nonaddict behavior within the community, for example by cleaning a toilet. Within this isolated social setting the Synanon resident is given the opportunity not to rely on drugs, to develop as a person, and to acquire the skills that are necessary for social and vocational adjustment. It is also interesting to note that getting off the drugs, that is, overcoming actual physiological addiction, seems to be much less of a problem than is sometimes assumed. It is noteworthy that Synanon emphasizes the social factors in drug addiction, relatively little attention being paid to any physical addiction. Numerous other facilities similar to Synanon have developed, for example, Daytop Village.

Whether Synanon and related programs are the best approach to eliminating addiction is as yet unclear. For one thing, a large proportion of addicts who enter Synanon drop out. Perhaps the approach is appropriate for only a certain segment of the drug addict population. Even so, there is great promise in an attack on drug addiction that looks beyond the chemical factors to the social variables that expose people to drugs and that maintain a setting in which drug-related behaviors are the only available options.

Overall Evaluation of Community Psychology Work

The results of community mental health programs are hard to evaluate primarily because the research designs employed are either inadequate or, more likely, because the questions being asked are extremely complicated. Moreover, when large populations rather than single individuals are treated, outcomes of particular therapies are difficult to rate, especially in view of the lack of agreement on indices of improvement. This problem applies particularly to programs that take as a unit an entire community or subcommunity.

Although many workers regard community psychology as unique in its emphasis on the sociocultural milieu in determining behavior (both breakdown and improvement), there are as yet no data reflecting on the actual processes that might be responsible for any improvements observed. For example, Hobbs (1966), reporting on the effects of "Project Re-Ed," states as the basic theoretical assumption of the program that the "child is an inseparable part of a small social system, of an ecological unit made up of the child, his family, his school, his neighborhood, and community" (p. 1108). Aside from saying that a human being must be understood in the context of his social milieu, it is difficult to see what further information is contained in this very general statement. And yet this judgment may be too harsh, for we might well recall the pioneering work in France of Pinel (Chapter 1), whose "moral therapy," with its emphasis on creating normalized sociocultural environments, brought about considerable improvement in severely disturbed patients; it may be that certain aspects of the community mental health movement represent a welcome return to earlier "nonscientific" methods of helping mentally troubled individuals.

An apparently integral feature of much community psychology work is a renunciation of political and moral neutrality (Kelly, 1970; Denner and Price, 1973). When a community-oriented worker assumes that social conditions of one kind or another are creating problems and when he does not focus on helping the client (which may be an entire neighborhood) *adjust to* the stress, he necessarily becomes a social activist to some degree. His clinical work can sometimes take the form of challenging a school board or city hall.

Moreover, the danger must be faced that well-meaning professionals may *impose* values and goals on their clients. In a sense, John Kennedy's launching of the community mental health movement proclaimed that the federal government is rightfully concerned about improving the mental health of Americans. But what is mental health? Who is to decide? To what extent do the people being served by community psychologists have a say in how they are to be helped?

Perhaps the most salient feature of community psychology is the array of community mental health centers funded through the federal government since 1963. The problems of these centers have been highlighted in a rather controversial critique by Ralph Nader's group (see Holden, 1972). The crux of this report is that the centers were based on a good and commendable set of ideas but that the implementation has been poor. Often the problem is one of old wine in new bottles. Nader's group points out that the centers are usually controlled by psychiatrists whose training and outlook are tied to one-to-one therapy along medical model (typically psychoanalytic) lines; the "fit" between this model and the problems of the groups of lower-income people who are the centers' primary constituencies is often loose.

Further, Nader alleges, centers are inaccessible to many of the people they are supposed to serve—inaccessible not only geographically but also with regard to the policy making of each center. Several examples are cited in the Nader report. The center in Bakersfield, California, is supposed to serve an area heavily populated by Mexican-American and black farm workers, but in 1970 only 14 of 284 new patients were nonwhite. Another center, located in Pontiac, Michigan, was said by Nader's group to be oblivious to racial tensions and drug abuse. And in centers that have tried more diligently to become involved in the real social problems of their communities, there has often been strife and controversy.[1]

Enthusiasm for community psychology must unfortunately be tempered with awareness of social reality—the conditions of deprivation

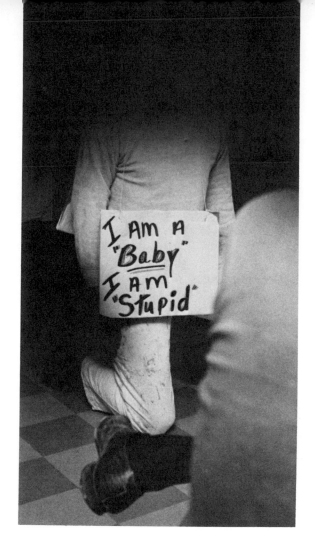

that community psychologists assume produce and maintain disordered behavior. To train a black youngster for a specific vocational slot can have a beneficial long-term outcome for the individual only to the extent that society at large provides the appropriate opportunity to use these skills. Those who work in the community mental health movement are of course aware that racial and social prejudices play a central role in limiting the access of many minority groups to the rewards of the culture at large. Although the kind of efforts just described must of course continue if our so-

[1] Devastating cutbacks in federal funding for community mental health centers threaten to make this promising movement a short-lived one.

The Synanon Philosophy

The Synanon Philosophy is based on the belief that there comes a time in everyone's life when he arrives at the conviction that envy is ignorance; that imitation is suicide; that he must accept himself for better or for worse as is his portion; that though the wide universe is full of good, no kernel of nourishing corn can come to him but through his toil bestowed on that plot of ground which is given to him to till. The power which resides in him is new in nature, and none but he knows what it is that he can do, nor does he know until he has tried. Bravely let him speak the utmost syllable of his conviction. God will not have his work made manifest by cowards.

A man is relieved and gay when he has put his heart into his work and done his best; but what he has said or done otherwise shall give him no peace. As long as he willingly accepts himself, he will continue to grow and develop his potentialities. As long as he does not accept himself, much of his energies will be used to defend rather than to explore and actualize himself.

No one can force a person towards permanent and creative learning. He will learn only if he wills to. Any other type of learning is temporary and inconsistent with the self and will disappear as soon as the threat is removed. Learning is possible in an environment that provides information, the setting, materials, resources, and by his being there. God helps those who help themselves.

—MKK

FIGURE **20.9**
At Synanon breaking the rules is punished by public humiliation. On the right is the philosophy that Synanon members strive to live by.

ciety has any commitment to fostering social and mental well-being, we must not lose sight of the real limitations of such training programs. Furthermore, it is possible that many programs may backfire by raising expectations that are dashed once again by the realities of the larger culture. Dealing with this quandary is central to the mental health professional's job once he ventures forth from the consulting room into the community.

BIOLOGICAL TREATMENT

All the therapeutic procedures considered thus far are psychological in nature; changes are sought by providing new learning experiences, by raising expectations for help, or by providing insight. Clearly, however, behavior can be affected by direct manipulations of the body. We saw a good illustration of the intimate relationships between mind and body in Chapter 7 on psychosomatic disorders. If psyche and soma are only two ways of talking about the same thing, it is reasonable to expect behavioral changes to follow certain kinds of biological interventions.

There are three major types of biological treatment for abnormal behavior—drugs, convulsive therapies, and surgical procedures. There is evidence that *some* methods are effective in treating *some* behavioral problems. But, as we have cautioned many times before, this evidence does not provide support for a biological theory of the etiology of any of these disorders. This point is especially significant since biological therapies have *not* usually been discovered through speculation on the biological etiology of a particular behavior disorder. Rather, the majority of the currently used treatments were found by accident.

Drug Therapies

Three major categories of drugs have been used for some time in the amelioration of psychological disorders: minor tranquilizers, major tranquilizers, and antidepressants. More recently a number of other drugs have been used for particular behavior disorders: lithium carbonate for manic-depressive psychosis, Antabuse for alcoholism, and methadone for heroin addiction. Table 20.3 summarizes several widely used drugs, giving both their generic and brand names. The classification presented in the table is based on behavioral effects; it should be noted that drugs producing similar effects can be very dissimilar chemically.

Although we have reserved our discussion of therapeutic drugs for this chapter, the sad truth is that many of them could well have been mentioned in Chapter 10 on drug addic-tion and drug dependence. Methadone is a good example, for this drug is emerging as a possible alternative to heroin in the illicit drug trade. Even the minor tranquilizers can be abused, and some of them, like Miltown, are physically addictive over long periods of regular use. Both because of our psychological needs and because of the physiological realities of our bodies, human beings are all too prone to use psychoactive chemicals in self-defeating ways.

Minor Tranquilizers

As the name suggests, minor tranquilizers are used to reduce anxiety that is not of major proportions. Typically, they are prescribed for outpatients who suffer neurotic (unrealistic) anxiety, psychosomatic disorders involving tension, or perhaps neurotic depression. The first class of drugs in this category to gain widespread acceptance was the barbiturates, which have been used to relieve anxiety since the turn of the twentieth century. But because of hazards such as addiction and undesirable side effects (see Chapter 10), they were supplanted in the 1950s by a host of newly developed minor tranquilizers. The first of these was patented in 1952 by Berger and called meprobamate. The tranquilizer business subsequently boomed, with numerous entries finding their way into the marketplace. Tranquilizers quickly became an accepted part of American culture, anxious businessmen and housewives being commonly depicted as popping "happy" pills to get through their trying days.

Even though there has been little controlled research on the effectiveness of minor tranquilizers (Millon, 1969), they are widely used and accepted as valuable therapeutic agents. General practitioners usually prescribe these drugs for outpatients, making controlled research

TABLE **20.3** *Several Psychoactive Drugs Categorized by Their Effects on Behavior*

		Generic	Trade
Minor tranquilizers		meprobamate	Miltown Equanil
		chlordiazepoxide diazepam	Librium Valium
Major tranquilizers (antipsychotics)		chlorpromazine triflupromazine thioridazine	Thorazine Stelazine Mellaril
Antidepressants	Tricyclics	imipramine amitriptyline doxepin	Tofranil Elavil Sinequan
	Monoamine oxidase inhibitors	phenelzine tranylcypromine	Nardil Parnate

very difficult. What clinical evidence is available, however, does suggest that such drugs do indeed calm many patients. But even though they may be of some value in seeing a person through a time of stress, the drugs merely make the life of the chronically tense person more tolerable without changing his basic problems.

Major Tranquilizers

In 1950 chlorpromazine, which is now sold under the trade name Thorazine, was synthesized in France for use as an antihistamine. In early tests it was observed that the drug had additional effects such as decreasing the person's interest in what was going on in his environment. This observation led to tests on clinical populations.

Chlorpromazine, which is in a class of drugs known as phenothiazines, was first used therapeutically in the United States in 1954 and rapidly became the preferred treatment for schizophrenics. By 1970 over 85 percent of all patients in state mental hospitals were receiving chlorpromazine or one of the other phenothiazines.

There is little doubt that the phenothiazines are useful in managing schizophrenic patients, and for this reason they are often referred to as antipsychotic drugs. In one study, conducted by the National Institute of Mental Health, newly admitted patients in nine different hospitals were randomly assigned to one of four treatments on a double-blind basis (Cole, 1964a). Three of the treatments were different types of phenothiazine and the fourth was a placebo. The physicians in charge were allowed to use a flexible dosage schedule so that they could adjust drug level to meet each patient's needs. After six weeks of treatment, three different measures were made of each patient: a global rating by physician and nurse of severity of mental illness and improvement, a one-hour diagnostic interview, and daily observations by ward personnel.

For the global ratings of improvement the data were as follows: none of the patients on any of the phenothiazines was rated as worse, 5 percent were rated as having shown no change, and 95 percent were rated as improved (75 percent of these as much or very much improved). For the patients on placebo 15 percent were rated as worse, 25 percent as having shown no change, and 60 percent as having improved (but only 10 percent of these were in the "very much" category). From the psychiatric interview and the behavior ratings, twenty-one measures were derived on variables such as social participation, confusion, and self-care. As can be seen in Table 20.4, the drug patients were better than those on the placebo on thirteen of the twenty-one measures.

Such evidence is impressive. But is phenothiazine medication the preferred treatment when it is compared with other potential treatments a hospitalized schizophrenic patient might receive? In an attempt to answer this question, May (1968) assigned first-admission schizophrenic patients in a psychiatric hospital to one of five treatment groups:

1. Individual psychotherapy conducted by psychiatric residents.
2. Phenothiazine drugs.
3. Individual psychotherapy plus phenothiazine medication.
4. Electroconvulsive therapy (to be discussed later in this section).
5. Milieu therapy, in which the hospital administration tries to make the total living experience of the patient therapeutic.

Two classes of dependent variables were analyzed: clinical ratings by nurses and therapists concerning the patient's progress, and data on release rate and length of time spent in the hospital. Drugs alone and the psychotherapy-plus-drugs combination were the two best treatments according to all the clinical measures. These two treatments were also superior in terms of both length of stay and the number of releases, indicating again the superiority of phenothiazine treatment. Moreover, phenothiazines alone were found to be as effective as phenothiazines plus an extensive course of psychotherapy. At least when done by psychiatric residents, psychotherapy may well be superfluous for hospitalized schizophrenics.

Although phenothiazines reduce symptomatology so that the patient can be released from the hospital, they should not be viewed as cure-alls. What, for example, happens to a patient when he is discharged? Typically, patients are kept on so-called *maintenance doses* of the drug; they continue to take their medication and return to the hospital on occasion for adjustment of the dose level. But it turns out that released patients being maintained on phenothiazine medication make only marginal adjustments to the community. The phenothiazines do not turn a socially incompetent poor premorbid schizophrenic into a "pillar of the community." Furthermore, readmissions are frequent. The advent of the "phenothiazine era" probably had a great impact on reducing the frequency of long-term institutionalization. But in its place has come the "revolving door," the pattern of admission, discharge, and readmission so prevalent at this time.

Finally, the potentially serious side effects of phenothiazines must be noted. Patients generally report that taking the drugs is unpleasant, causing fatigue, dryness of the mouth, and blurred vision. Perhaps this subjective unpleasantness is one of the reasons why maintenance programs have proved so difficult, for patients simply discontinue taking the drugs. Another important side effect of the phenothiazines is motor disturbances involving the nonvoluntary musculature, producing symptoms resembling Parkinson's disease (see Chapter 16). This side

TABLE 20.4 *Differences in Behavior of Phenothiazine and Placebo Patients in the NIMH Study of the Clinical Effectiveness of Phenothiazines. The Higher the Score, the Greater the Improvement* (*from Cole, 1964a*)

Symptom or behavior	Placebo	Drug	Difference
Social participation	0.49	1.51	1.02
Confusion	0.33	1.11	0.78
Self-care	0.13	0.88	0.75
Hebephrenic symptoms	−0.13	0.58	0.71
Agitation and tension	0.27	0.95	0.68
Slowed speed	−0.07	0.57	0.64
Incoherent speech	−0.17	0.43	0.60
Irritability	−0.20	0.40	0.60
Indifference to environment	−0.05	0.45	0.50
Hostility	0.09	0.54	0.45
Auditory hallucinations	0.18	0.62	0.44
Ideas of persecution	0.36	0.78	0.42
Disorientation	0.16	0.37	0.21

effect, however, can be controlled by additional drugs to suppress these symptoms. Among the other side effects are low blood pressure and jaundice. In spite of these difficulties phenothiazines will undoubtedly continue to be the primary treatment for schizophrenics until something better is discovered. They are surely preferable to the straightjackets formerly used to restrain patients.

Antidepressants

The *tricyclics* and the *monoamine oxidase* (MAO) *inhibitors* are two subcategories of antidepressants. Both classes of drugs were discovered for the "wrong reasons." Imipramine, a tricyclic, is structurally similar to the phenothiazines; hence it was hoped that it might also be an effective treatment for schizophrenics. Early clinical work with the drug showed that it was of little value with schiz-

ophrenics, but it did produce an unexpected elevation in mood; this discovery led to its subsequent use as an antidepressant. The MAO inhibitor iproniazid was originally used in the treatment of tuberculosis. The observation that this drug elevated the mood of tubercular patients led to its subsequent use as an antidepressant.

The available data suggest that the tricyclics are effective drugs for depression (Davis, Klerman, and Schildkraut, 1967). But it is also clear that tricyclics do not benefit *all* depressives. Thus research directed at determining which depressed patients are most likely to benefit from the drug is important. Such research has been carried out using the endogenous-exogenous depression dichotomy discussed in Chapter 8 (page 177–181). The tricyclic drugs are effective primarily with endogenous depressives (Lapolla and Jones, 1970; Raskin, Schulterbrandt, Boothe,

Reatig, and McKeon, 1970). Like the phenothiazines, the tricyclics also produce some undesirable side effects. Subjectively, these include dry mouth, constipation, dizziness, palpitations, and blurred vision. Moreover, drug therapy with depressives who are outpatients runs the risk that they will take suicidal overdoses.

In contrast to the tricyclics, the therapeutic effectiveness of the MAO inhibitors has not been well substantiated (Goodman and Gilman, 1970). For example, in a review from 1958 to mid-1967, comparing a MAO inhibitor to a placebo, fifteen studies demonstrated a statistically significant superiority of an MAO inhibitor over placebo, but thirteen studies failed to demonstrate such superiority (Davis, Klerman, and Schildkraut, 1967).

Interest in MAO inhibitors appears to have declined in recent years both because of the failure to demonstrate their effectiveness and because of their severe side effects. MAO inhibitors have greater toxic effects than any other drug used for the treatment of behavior disorders; these harmful effects involve the liver, brain, and cardiovascular system. Moreover, these drugs have even been found to interact with other drugs or foods to cause death. Patients taking MAO inhibitors should avoid foods and beverages high in tyramine, a fermentation by-product: cheeses like Camembert and cheddar, wines like Chianti, and fish such as pickled herring and lox (Honigfeld and Howard, 1973).

Lithium Carbonate

Recently there has been great interest in the possibility of using lithium carbonate in the treatment of mania. The drug was discovered by Cade in 1949, who noted its sedative effect on guinea pigs. It was not used widely in the United States until very recently, however,

for it had been judged dangerous after causing a few deaths. In these instances it had been ingested unrestrictedly as a salt substitute.

Although there is some evidence for the effectiveness of lithium carbonate as a treatment for mania, whether it is the best biological treatment available is unclear. For example, in a double-blind experiment in which lithium was compared with chlorpromazine, 78 percent of the manics were helped by lithium but only 36 percent were helped by chlorpromazine (Johnson, Gershon, and Hekimian, 1968). But another study, also employing a double-blind methodology and also comparing lithium with chlorpromazine, did not find it to be more effective (Spring, Schweid, Gray, Steinberg, and Horwitz, 1970).

In addition to the claim that lithium is an effective treatment for mania, it has also been proposed that the drug can lift depression and, when given during a manic period, can prevent subsequent depression. Few controlled investigations of these alleged effects have been conducted, and the results of the poorly executed studies that have been reported show no consistent pattern (Davis and Fann, 1971).

Antabuse (disulfiram)

Antabuse is frequently used in the treatment of alcoholism. Patients are instructed to take a daily dose of the substance, which alters the way alcohol is metabolized by the liver. Because of this change in metabolism a toxic by-product is produced that leads to very aversive physiological effects if the patient drinks alcohol. The first reactions are likely to be flushing, heart palpitations, and a drop in blood pressure. These are followed by nausea, vomiting, and difficulty in breathing, conditions that can last for several hours. In fact, should a goodly amount of alcohol be consumed, the effects can even culminate in death. Antabuse, then, does not "cure" alcoholism; rather it

The use of Antabuse to treat excessive drinking by making the ingestion of alcohol extremely unpleasant, if not dangerous, highlights a general problem in chemotherapy. Often the availability of apparently effective chemical agents blinds practitioners and researchers to the fact that patients may not want to take the medication. We have already seen some of the side effects of Thorazine (such as Parkinsonian-like symptoms), and, indeed, it is fair to say that there is no drug currently available that does not exact some kind of cost which can discourage prescribed use. An individual on Thorazine, for example, may have to be warned about driving a car since the depressant (that is, tranquilizing) effects of this powerful drug increase reaction time and perhaps impair judgment as well. By the same token, a mood elevator like Elavil may handicap the user in normal day-to-day activities. Antabuse seems to present a peculiar set of problems in that a heavy drinker must continue the drug regularly with full knowledge that imbibing his favorite beverage will most surely lead to acute discomfort. The question then becomes how can the clinician motivate the drinker to begin using the drug and remain with it. As we pointed out in our discussion of alcoholism (Chapter 10), people drink excessively for many reasons. A nonaddicted individual who seeks the numbing effects of alcohol may be unable to face life's problems. Perhaps his marital relationship is difficult, or perhaps his anxieties about dealing with authority figures are so great that, without his daily ration of martinis, he suffers psychological distress of enormous proportions. If he is denied his crutch, what is he left with? For these and other reasons, to use Antabuse without taking care to help the person deal with the stresses that trigger drinking may be unwise and even antitherapeutic.

creates a situation in which continued drinking is almost suicidal (see Box 20.3).

There are data demonstrating the effectiveness of the treatment (for example, Bourne, Alfred, and Bowcock, 1966). In one study that compared Antabuse with other treatments including aversive conditioning, hypnotherapy, and milieu therapy (Wallerstein, 1957), Antabuse was found to be the most effective. A critical problem, however, lies in *motivating patients to stay on the drug*. Patients do not frequently volunteer for such treatment and those who do often fail to take the Antabuse

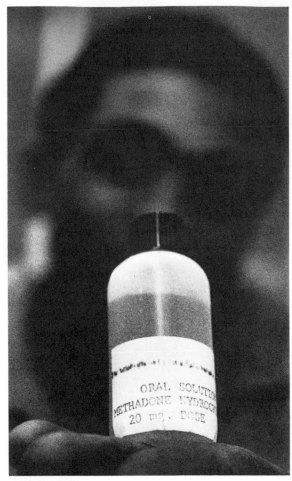

FIGURE **20.10**
At a Veterans Administration hospital a heroin addict holds his morning dose of methadone, an addictive drug prescribed to counteract the physical craving for heroin.

regularly. Thus, even though effective, Antabuse has been of only limited use in dealing with alcoholism.

Methadone

Recent years have seen great interest in the use of methadone, a synthetic narcotic, for the treatment of heroin addiction. The primary action of methadone is one of substitution, elimi-

nating the craving for heroin and setting up a blockade to its effects so that "highs" are not experienced should heroin be taken. It is not designed to produce a nonaddict, since methadone itself is addicting. Rather, the drug appears to be useful for hard-core, high-dosage, and recidivistic addicts in facilitating rehabilitation (Figure 20.10).

The first major methadone program was established by Dole and Nyswander in 1964. Within five years, they claimed to have successfully treated over a thousand heroin addicts (Dole, Nyswander, and Warner, 1968). People are admitted into their program only if they are over eighteen years of age, have at least three years of addiction history, are not addicted to barbiturates or alcohol, and have no psychiatric or epileptic complications. The treatment is divided into several phases during which the addict moves from inpatient to outpatient status and finally back into the community. Methadone does, indeed, appear to hold some promise as a treatment for some heroin addicts. It seems to be relatively safe (its primary side effects being constipation and weight gain), and it is cheap, costing only about three cents per day to administer. Clearly, putting a heroin addict onto a maintenance methadone program should reduce his involvement in criminal activity. As we noted previously (Chapter 10), the high cost of maintaining a heroin habit leads many addicts into a life of crime. Methadone replacement therapy can reduce the likelihood of this effect by supplying a substitute narcotic administered legally. Additionally, methadone may not produce the same kind of euphoric effects that are present when heroin is taken.[2] As a result addicts may have better occupational adjustment.

[2] The initial claim was that methadone did *not* produce a high. The recent development of a black market for it in New York City, however, suggests that this may not be the case.

Dole and Nyswander selected 12 heroin addicts from a group of 150 prisoners with the worst criminal records in the Rikers Island Prison in New York. After a seven-month follow-up, seven of the twelve were employed, five had some drug or law problem, and three were back in jail but not re-addicted. *All had discontinued using heroin.* In this case, methadone was not a complete success, but given the usually much higher rate of re-addiction and involvement with the law, it appears to have had a beneficial effect.

Methadone, however, is not a universally applicable treatment. Luria (1970), for example, estimates that it is successful in only between 10 to 20 percent of the addict population. Large numbers of addicts who go on methadone drop out of the program. Another negative view has been offered by Dobbs (1971), who has recently reported on a methadone program in Washington, D.C. Urine samples were routinely collected from these patients and analyzed for the presence of heroin so that the number of patients in the program still continuing to use heroin could be determined. The majority of the 100 patients in his sample had at least one or more positive urine specimens, indicating continued use of heroin even while on methadone. These findings suggest that methadone may not exert as strong a blockage or cross-tolerance effect as had been previously supposed. Finally, methadone treatment has been attacked for merely changing a heroin addict into a methadone addict—both drugs are narcotics. There is the risk that, with the option of having the addict switch from heroin to methadone, the development of programs that try to prevent or eliminate addiction to *any* kind of narcotic will be discouraged. This last criticism is a substantial one, but it should not obscure the usefulness of methadone maintenance treatment for hard-core, criminal addicts.

Psychosurgery

Burkhardt, in 1890, performed brain surgery on a psychotic to excise those parts of the cortex that he thought harbored hallucinations and delusions. Public outcries against this procedure led to its abandonment until Moniz and Lima, in 1936, performed an operation called a *prefrontal leucotomy.* Their purpose was to sever the connection between the thought center (the frontal lobes) and the emotion center (the thalamus). Shortly thereafter, Freeman and Watts (1942) reported success in the United States with a similar operation which was called a *prefrontal lobotomy.* Their idea was that the frontal lobes of disturbed patients exaggerate the emotions produced in the thalamic region. With the paths between these two areas cut, the patient should worry much less about trivial matters.

Since the advent of psychosurgical procedures (reminiscent of the prehistoric practice of trephining, see Chapter 1), the most commonly performed operation is termed *thalamofrontal sectioning,* which includes prefrontal leucotomy, prefrontal lobotomy, and transorbital lobotomy. Each of these procedures is illustrated in Figure 20.11. In the prefrontal lobotomy and leucotomy, small holes are drilled on the side or on the top of the skull. A sharp instrument is then inserted and rotated in an arc anterior to (that is, in front of) the frontal lobes so that the nerve paths linking the frontal area of the brain to the thalamus are severed. In the transorbital technique, the instrument is inserted through the thin structure separating the eye and the brain.

As with most of the treatments we have discussed, there was an initial flurry of interest in psychosurgical procedures coupled with enthusiastic claims for their effectiveness. While the techniques were in relatively widespread use, they were applied to schizophrenics, depres-

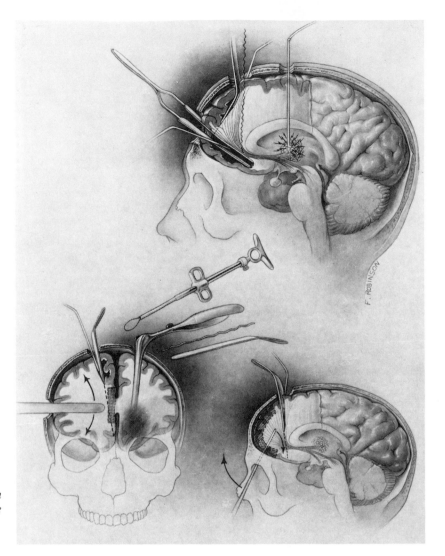

FIGURE **20.11**
Psychosurgeons attempt to eliminate especially troublesome behavior, such as uncontrollable seizures, by cutting the connections between various brain structures. The three sketches show several psychosurgical techniques.

sives, and less frequently to persons with personality disorders and to neurotics (especially obsessives). The results of studies attempting to assess the efficacy of the treatment were largely equivocal. For example, Robbin (1958, 1959) compared changes in lobotomy patients and controls. Lobotomy was found to produce a slightly greater discharge rate, but more of these patients were subsequently readmitted. Similarly, Barahal (1958) did a five-to-ten-year follow-up on 1000 lobotomy cases: the results led him to emphasize the high rate of undesirable side effects, such as seizures, ex-

treme listlessness, and even stupor. In sum, surgical procedures have little to recommend them; they lack demonstrated effectiveness and can have serious, *irreversible* consequences. With the advent of phenothiazines in the mid-1950s, the popularity of surgical techniques dropped off dramatically.

Convulsive Therapy

Interest in the therapeutic induction of convulsions began in the 1930s. Sakel, in 1933, produced comas in patients with large doses of insulin. He theorized that psychoses result from too much adrenaline, which can be neutralized by insulin. Similarly, Meduna, in 1935, induced convulsions with the drug metrazol because he thought that convulsions were antagonistic to schizophrenia. In 1937 Cerletti and Bini used electricity as a more effective means of inducing a convulsion. Their idea was that the convulsion brings the patient close to death, thus mobilizing his biological defenses and starting a process leading to recovery.

The electric means of inducing a convulsion, electroconvulsive therapy, or ECT, became the preferred method and has remained essentially unchanged since its introduction by Cerletti and Bini. Electrodes are placed on each side of the patient's forehead, and a current of approximately 150 volts is allowed to pass between them for a period of about two seconds, inducing a grand mal seizure (see Chapter 16). A period of electrical silence in the patient's brain follows; then there is a gradual resumption of the preconvulsive pattern. Patients nowadays are typically given a muscle relaxant beforehand to reduce the incidence of bone fractures and bruises occasionally suffered during ECT. A usual ECT regime entails about twenty treatments given at a rate of about three per week (Figure 20.12).

Following ECT the patient is often very confused and shows loss of memory for both material before the treatment and new material presented within one hour of the treatment. Typically, the confusion and loss of memory disappear within a month.

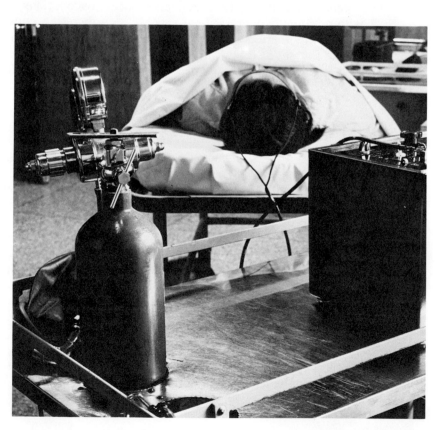

FIGURE **20.12**
A mental patient about to receive an electroconvulsive shock treatment. The machine at the right delivers 150 volts across electrodes attached to both sides of the patient's head.

Electroconvulsive therapy, although originally applied to both schizophrenics and depressed patients, is now primarily used for profoundly depressed people. As we saw previously when we reviewed the May (1968) study, phenothiazine medication is more effective for schizophrenics than is ECT. For severe depressives, though, ECT seems to be the most effective biological treatment currently available. In one study depressed patients were randomly assigned to ECT, to one of three drug therapies, or to a placebo drug.

At the end of the treatment period, 76 percent of the patients in the ECT group were rated as improved, as were 44 percent of those in the drug groups and 42 percent of those in the placebo group (Greenblatt, Grosser, and Wechsler, 1964). The findings of many other studies generally confirm the effectiveness of ECT with profoundly depressed patients.

In spite of the promise of carefully administered ECT for severely depressed patients, many professionals object to its use. For one thing, it is possible that damage to brain tissue may occur (see Maher, 1966); since nervous tissue does not regenerate, adverse and irreversible damage may be a high cost of the treatment. Another problem is the fear that many patients have of ECT treatment. In spite of amnesia for the episode, and regardless of the use of muscle relaxants to prevent bone fractures, patients and their families are often reluctant to undergo or to sanction such treatments (at least without considerable urging from medical staff). Another source of the "bad press" of ECT among both professionals and lay people is the violent nature of the procedure, although the amount of writhing and groaning has diminished greatly with the use of relaxants. ECT does entail the deliberate induction of a seizure and subsequent unconsciousness, if not pain, and many people therefore consider the "cure" worse than the "disease." On the other hand, it is difficult to dismiss ECT entirely since the data support its effectiveness in the treatment of depression.

SUMMARY

Group therapy and community psychology share the important assumption that disordered (and normal) behavior is largely shaped by, or can at least be changed by, social variables such as group pressure. There is a great variety of both theory and method in group therapy and community psychology. Some group therapists aim at increased insight and heightened awareness (for example, psychodrama and encounter groups) while others focus on the group as a useful vehicle to promote specific behavior changes (such as behavior therapy groups). The work in the vague field known as community psychology is also characterized by numerous conceptual models and clinical procedures; what they seem to share is a seeking orientation—an attitude of venturing forth from the professional office and dealing with human problems in a real-life setting. For some of the biological therapies, such as tranquilizers and ECT, there is evidence to support their effectiveness, but for others, for instance, psychosurgery, there are no data to commend them. Even when judged successful, however, the changes effected by biological treatment should not be considered as "complete cures," and undesirable side effects are frequently present. As with most contemporary professional activities in practically every other area of abnormal psychology dealt with in this book, scientifically acceptable supporting evidence is just beginning to appear.

References

Abse, D. W. *Hysteria and related mental disorders.* Baltimore: Williams and Wilkins, 1966.

Adams, R. D. The anatomy of memory mechanisms in the human brain. In G. A. Talland & N. C. Waugh (Eds.), *The pathology of memory.* New York: Academic Press, 1969.

Adelson, R., Liebert, R. M., Poulos, R. W., & Herskovitz, A. A modelling film to reduce children's fear of dental treatment. *International Association of Dental Research Abstracts,* March 1972, 114.

Agras, S., Sylvester, D., & Oliveau, D. The epidemiology of common fears and phobias. Unpublished manuscript, 1969.

Albee, G. W. We have been warned. In W. Ryan (Ed.), *Distress in the city.* Cleveland, Ohio: The Press of Case Western Reserve University, 1969.

Albee, G. W., Lane, E. A., & Reuter, J. M. Childhood intelligence of future schizophrenics and neighborhood peers. *Journal of Psychology,* 1964, **58**, 141-144.

Alexander, F. *Psychosomatic medicine.* New York: Norton, 1950.

Alexander, R., & Staub, H. *The criminal, the judge, and the public: A psychological analysis.* Glencoe, Ill.: The Free Press, 1929.

Alvarez, R. R. A comparison of the preferences of schizophrenics and normal subjects for rewarded and punished stimuli. Unpublished doctoral dissertation, Duke University, 1957.

American Law Institute. *Model penal code: Proposed official draft.* Philadelphia: The American Law Institute, 1962.

American Psychiatric Association. *Diagnostic and statistical manual of mental disorders.* (2nd ed.) Washington, D.C.: American Psychiatric Association, 1968.

Arieti, S. *Interpretation of schizophrenia.* New York: Basic Books, 1955.

Arnhoff, F. N., Rubinstein, E. A., & Speisman, J. E. (Eds.) *Mental health manpower.* Chicago: Aldine, 1969.

Aronson, E. *The social animal.* San Francisco: Freeman, 1972.

Aronson, E., & Carlsmith, J. R. Experimentation in social psychology. In G. Lindzey and E. Aronson (Eds.), *The handbook of social psychology.* Vol. 2. *Research methods.* Menlo Park, Calif.: Addison-Wesley, 1968.

Assagioli, R. *Psychosynthesis: A manual of principles and techniques.* New York: Hobbs, Dorman and Co., 1965.

Ausubel, D. P. Causes and types of narcotic addictions: A psychosocial view. *Psychiatric Quarterly,* 1961, **35**, 523-531. (a)

Ausubel, D. P. Personality disorder is disease. *American Psychologist.* 1961, **16**, 69-74. (b)

Ax, A. F. The physiological differentiation between fear and anger in humans. *Psychosomatic Medicine,* 1953, **15**, 433-442.

Ayllon, T., & Azrin, N. H. The measurement and reinforcement of behavior of psychotics. *Journal of the Experimental Analysis of Behavior,* 1965, **8**, 357-383.

Ayllon, T., & Azrin, N. *The token economy: A motivational system for therapy and rehabilitation.* New York: Appleton-Century-Crofts, 1968.

Ayllon, T., Haughton, E., & Hughes, H. B. Interpretation of symptoms: Fact or fiction? *Behaviour Research and Therapy,* 1965, **3**, 1-8.

Ayllon, T., & Kelly, K. Effects of reinforcement on standardized test performance. *Journal of Applied Behavior Analysis,* 1972, **4**, 477-484.

Azrin, N. H., & Powell, J. R. Behavioral engineering: The reduction of smoking behavior by conditioning apparatus and procedure. *Journal of Applied Behavior Analysis,* 1968, **1**, 193-200.

Bach, G. R. The marathon group: Intensive practice of intimate interactions. *Psychological Reports,* 1966, **181**, 995-1002.

Bagby, E. The etiology of phobias. *Journal of Abnormal Psychology,* 1922, **17**, 16-18.

Bailey, D. S. *Homosexuality and the Western Christian tradition.* London: Longmans, Green, 1955.

Bancroft, J. H., Jones, G. H., & Pullan, B. R. A simple transducer for measuring penile erections, with comments on its use in the treatment of sexual disorders. *Behaviour Research and Therapy,* 1966, **4**, 239-241.

Bandura, A. *Principles of behavior modification.* New York: Holt, Rinehart and Winston, 1969.

Bandura, A., Blanchard, E. B., & Ritter, B. Relative efficacy of desensitization and modelling approaches for inducing behavioral, affective, and attitudinal changes. *Journal of Personality and Social Psychology,* 1969, **13**, 173-199.

Bandura, A., & Menlove, F. L. Factors determining vicarious extinction of avoidance behavior through symbolic modeling. *Journal of Personality and Social Psychology,* 1968, **8**, 99-108.

Bandura, A., & Rosenthal, T. L. Vicarious classical conditioning as a function of arousal level. *Journal of Personality and Social Psychology,* 1966, **3**, 54-62.

Barahal, H. S. 1000 prefrontal lobotomies: Five-to-ten-year follow-up study. *Psychiatric Quarterly,* 1958, **32**, 653-678.

Barber, T. X. *Hypnosis: A scientific approach.* New York: Van Nostrand Reinhold, 1969.

Barber, T. X. *LSD, marihuana, yoga and hypnosis.* Chicago: Aldine, 1970.

Barber, T. X., & Calverley, D. S. Experimental studies in "hypnotic" behavior: Suggested deafness evaluated by delayed auditory feedback. *British Journal of Psychology,* 1964, **55**, 439-446. (a)

Barber, T. X., & Calverley, D. S. An experimental study of "hypnotic" (auditory and visual) hallucinations. *Journal of Abnormal and Social Psychology,* 1964, **63**, 13-20. (b)

Barber, T. X., & Silver, M. J. Fact, fiction, and the experimenter bias effect. *Psychological Bulletin Monograph Supplement,* 1968, **70**, 1-29.

Barlow, D. H. Increasing heterosexual responsiveness in the treatment of sexual deviation: A review of the clinical and experimental evidence. *Behavior Therapy,* 1973, in press.

Basedow, H. *The Australian aboriginal.* London: Adelaide, 1925.

Bateson, G., Jackson, D. D., Haley, J., & Weakland, J. Toward a theory of schizophrenia. *Behavioral Science,* 1956, **1**, 251-264.

Baum, A., & Valins, S. Residential environments, group size and crowding, *Proceedings of the 81st Annual Convention of the American Psychological Association.* Washington, D.C.: American Psychological Association, 1973.

Beck, A. T. *Depression: Clinical, experimental and theoretical aspects.* New York: Harper and Row, 1967.

Beck, A. T., Ward, C. H., Mendelson, M., Mock, J. E., & Erbaugh, J. K. Reliability of psychiatric diagnosis 2: A study of consistency of clinical judgments and ratings. *American Journal of Psychiatry,* 1962, **119**, 351-357.

Becker, H. S. *Outsiders: Studies in the sociology of deviance.* New York: The Free Press, 1963.

Behar, M. Prevalence of malnutrition among preschool children of developing countries. In N. W. Scrimshaw & J. E. Gordon (Eds.), *Malnutrition, learning and behavior.* Cambridge, Mass.: M.I.T. Press, 1968.

Belliveau, F., & Richter, L. *Understanding "Human Sexual Inadequacy."* New York: Bantam Books, 1970.

Benda, C. E., Squires, N. D., Ogonik, M. J., & Wise, R. Personality factors in mild mental retardation: Part I. Family background and sociocultural patterns. *American Journal of Mental Deficiency,* 1963, **68**, 24-40.

Bender, L. Twenty years of research on schizophrenic children with special reference to those under twenty years of age. In G. Kaplan (Ed.), *Emotional problems of early childhood.* New York: Basic Books, 1955.

Bender, L. Brain and child behavior. *Archives of General Psychiatry,* 1961, **4**, 531-547.

Bender, L. The life course of schizophrenic children. *Biological Psychiatry,* 1970, **2**, 165-172.

Benjamin, H. Transvestism and trans-sexualism. *International Journal of Sexology,* 1953, **7**, 12-14.

Bentler, P. M., & Prince, C. Personality characteristics of male transvestites: III. *Journal of Abnormal Psychology,* 1969, **74**, 140-143.

Bentler, P. M., & Prince, C. Psychiatric symptomatology in male transvestites. *Journal of Clinical Psychology,* 1970, **26**, 434-435.

Bentler, P. M., Shearman, R. W., & Prince, C. Personality characteristics of male transvestites. *Journal of Clinical Psychology,* 1970, **26**, 287-291.

Bergin, A. E. Some implications of psychotherapy research for therapeutic practice. *Journal of Abnormal Psychology,* 1966, **71**, 235-246.

Bergin, A. E. The evaluation of therapeutic outcomes. In A. E. Bergin & S. L. Garfield (Eds.), *Handbook of psychotherapy and behavior change: An empirical analysis.* New York: Wiley, 1971.

Bergler, E. Personality traits of alcohol addicts. *Quarterly Journal of Studies on Alcohol,* 1946, **7**, 356-361.

Bergler, E. *Homosexuality: Disease or way of life.* New York: Hill and Wang, 1957.

Bernstein, D. A. The modification of smoking behavior: A review. *Psychological Bulletin,* 1969, **71**, 418-440.

Berry, J. C. Antecedents of schizophrenia, impulsive character and alcoholism in males. Paper presented at the American Psychological Association convention, Washington, D.C., 1967.

Bettelheim, B. *The informed heart.* New York: The Free Press, 1960.

Bettelheim, B. *The empty fortress.* New York: The Free Press, 1967.

Bieber, I., Dain, H. J., Dince, P. R., Drellich, M. G., Grand, H. C., Gundlach, R. H., Kremer, M. W., Rifkin, A. H., Wilbur, C. B., & Bieber, T. B. *Homosexuality: A psychoanalytical study.* New York: Random House, 1962.

Bijou, S. W., & Baer, D. M. *Child development.* Vol. 1. *A systematic and empirical theory.* New York: Appleton-Century-Crofts, 1961.

Bindrim, P. A report on a nude marathon: The effect of physical nudity upon the practice interaction in the marathon group. *Psychotherapy: Theory, Research and Practice,* 1968, **5**, 180-188.

Bleke, R. R. Reward and punishment as determiners of reminiscence effects in schizophrenic and normal subjects. Unpublished doctoral dissertation, Duke University, 1953.

Bleuler, E. *Dementia praecox, or the group of schizophrenias,* 1911. English translation by J. Zinkin. New York: International Universities Press, 1950.

Bockhoven, J. *Moral treatment in American psychiatry.* New York: Springer, 1963.

Bolles, R. C. Species-specific defense reactions and avoidance learning. *Psychological Review,* 1970, **77**, 32-48.

Bosch, G. *Infantile autism.* New York: Springer-Verlag, 1970.

Bourne, P. G., Alford, J. A., & Bowcock, J. Z. Treatment of skid row alcoholics with disulfiram. *Quarterly Journal of Studies on Alcohol,* 1966, **27**, 42-48.

Brady, J. P., & Lind, D. L. Experimental analysis

of hysterical blindness. *Archives of General Psychiatry,* 1961, **4**, 331-359.

Braginsky, B. M., Grosse, M., & Ring, K. Controlling outcomes through impression management: An experimental study of the manipulative tactics of mental patients. *Journal of Consulting Psychology,* 1966, **30**, 295-300.

Braginsky, D. D., & Braginsky, B. M. *Hansels and Gretels: Studies of children in institutions for the mentally retarded.* New York: Holt, Rinehart and Winston, 1971.

Brecher, E. M., & the Editors of *Consumer Reports. Licit and Illicit Drugs.* Mount Vernon, N. Y.: Consumers Union, 1972.

Bridger, W. H., & Mandel, I. J. Abolition of the PRE by instructions in GSR conditioning. *Journal of Experimental Psychology,* 1965, **69**, 476-482.

Brion, S. Korsakoff's syndrome: Clinco-anatomical and physiopathological considerations. In G. A. Talland & N. C. Waugh (Eds.), *The pathology of memory.* New York: Academic Press, 1969.

Broen, W. E., & Storms, L. H. Lawful disorganization: The process underlying a schizophrenic syndrome. *Psychological Review,* 1966, **73**, 265-279.

Brown, G. W. Length of hospital stay and schizophrenia: A review of statistical studies. *Acta Psychiatry et Neurology Scandanavia,* 1960, **35**, 414-430.

Brown, W. F. Heredity in the psychoneuroses. *Proceedings of the Royal Society of Medicine,* 1942, **35**, 785-790.

Brune, G. G., & Himwich, H. E. Biogenic amines and behavior in schizophrenic patients. In *Recent Advances in Biological Psychiatry.* Vol. 5. New York: Plenum, 1963.

Burton, R. *The anatomy of melancholy,* 1621. (13th ed.) London: Thomas Davison, White Friars, 1827.

Buss, A. H. *Psychopathology.* New York: Wiley, 1966.

Buss, A. H., & Lang, P. J. Psychological deficit in schizophrenia: I. Affect, reinforcement, and concept attainment. *Journal of Abnormal Psychology,* 1965, **70**, 2-24.

Butler, J. M., & Haigh, G. V. Changes in the relation between self-concepts and ideal concepts consequent upon client-centered counseling. In C. R. Rogers & R. F. Dymond (Eds.), *Psychotherapy and personality change.* Chicago: University of Chicago Press, 1954.

Calhoun, J. B. Space and the strategy of life. *Ekistics,* 1970, **29**, 425-437.

Cameron, N. *Personality development and psychopathology: A dynamic approach.* Boston: Houghton Mifflin, 1963.

Campbell, D., Sanderson, R. E., & Laverty, S. G. Characteristics of a conditioned response in human subjects during extinction trials following a single traumatic conditioning trial. *Journal of Abnormal and Social Psychology,* 1964, **68**, 627-639.

Cannon, W. B. "Voodoo" death. *American Anthropologist,* 1942, **44**, 169-182.

Cash, T., Neale, J. M., & Cromwell, R. L. Span of apprehension in schizophrenia: Full-report technique. *Journal of Abnormal Psychology,* 1972, **79**, 322-327.

Cashman, J. A. *The LSD story.* Greenwich, Conn.: Fawcett Publications, 1966.

Castiglioni, A. *Adventures of the mind.* New York: Knopf, 1946.

Cautela, J. R. Treatment of compulsive behavior by covert sensitization. *Psychological Record,* 1966, **16**, 33-41.

Cavanaugh, D. K., Cohen, W., & Lang, P. J. The effect of "social censure" and "social approval" on the psychomotor performance of schizophrenics. *Journal of Abnormal and Social Psychology,* 1960, **60**, 213-218.

Chafetz, M. E. Addiction. II. Alcoholism. In A. M. Freedman & H. I. Kaplan (Eds.), *Comprehensive textbook of psychiatry.* Baltimore: Williams and Wilkins, 1967.

Chapman, L. J. Intrusion of associative responses into schizophrenic conceptual performance. *Journal of Abnormal and Social Psychology,* 1958, **56**, 374-379.

Chapman, L. J. The problem of selecting drug-free schizophrenics for research. *Journal of Consulting Psychology,* 1963, **27**, 540-542.

Chapman, L. J., & Chapman, J. P. Illusory correlation as an obstacle to the use of valid psychodiagnostic signs. *Journal of Abnormal Psychology*, 1969, **74**, 271-287.

Chapman, L. J., & Chapman, J. P. *Disordered thought in schizophrenia*. New York: Appleton-Century-Crofts, in press.

Chapman, L. J., Chapman, J. P., & Miller, G. A. A theory of verbal behavior in schizophrenia. In B. A. Maher (Ed.), *Progress in experimental personality research*. Vol. 1, New York: Academic Press, 1964.

Chappell, D., Geis, G., Schafer, S., & Siegel, L. Forcible rape: A comparative study of offenses known to the police in Boston and Los Angeles. In J. M. Henslin (Ed.), *Studies in the sociology of sex*. New York: Appleton-Century-Crofts, 1971, 169-192.

Chein, I., Gerard, D. L., Lee R. S., & Rosenfeld, E. *The road to H: Narcotics, delinquency, and social policy*. New York: Basic Books, 1964.

Churchill, D. W. Psychotic children and behavior modification. *American Journal of Psychiatry*, 1969, **125**, 1585-1590.

Churchill, W. *Homosexual behavior among males: A cross-cultural and cross-species investigation*. Englewood Cliffs, N.J.: Prentice-Hall, 1967.

Cleckley, H. *The mask of sanity*. (4th ed.) St. Louis, Mo.: Mosby, 1964.

Clausen, J. A., & Kohn, M. L. Relation of schizophrenia to the social structure of a small city. In B. Pasamanick (Ed.), *Epidemiology of mental disorder*. Washington, D.C.: American Association for the Advancement of Science, 1959.

Cochrane, R. High blood pressure as a psychosomatic disorder: A selective review. *British Journal of Social and Clinical Psychology*, 1971, **10**, 61-72.

Cohen, B. D., & Camhi, J. Schizophrenic performance in a word communication task. *Journal of Abnormal Psychology*, 1967, **72**, 240-246.

Cohen, H. L., & Filipczak, J. *A new learning environment*. San Francisco: Jossey-Bass, 1971.

Cole, J. O. Phenothiazine treatment in acute schizophrenia: Effectiveness. *Archives of General Psychiatry*, 1964, **10**, 246-261. (a)

Cole, J. O. Therapeutic efficacy of antidepressant drugs. *Journal of the American Medical Association*. 1964, **190**, 445-455. (b)

Coleman, J. C. *Abnormal psychology and modern life*. (4th ed.) Chicago: Scott, Foresman, 1972.

Conger, J. J. The effects of alcohol on conflict behavior in the albino rat. *Quarterly Journal of Studies on Alcohol*, 1951, **12**, 1-29.

Conger, J. J., Sawrey, W. L., & Turrell, E. S. The role of social experience in the production of gastric ulcers in hooded rats in a conflict situation. *Journal of Abnormal and Social Psychology*, 1958, **57**, 214-220.

Conn, J. H., & Conn, R. N. Discussion of T. Barber's "Hypnosis as a causal variable in present-day psychology: A critical analysis." *Journal of Clinical and Experimental Hypnosis*, 1967, **15**, 106-110.

Coppen, A. The biochemistry of affective disorders. *British Journal of Psychiatry*, 1967, **113**, 1237-1264.

Costello, C. G. Dissimilarities between conditioned avoidance responses and phobias. *Psychological Review*, 1970, **77**, 250-254.

Cowan, P. A., Hoddinott, B. A., & Wright, B. A. Compliance and resistance in the conditioning of autistic children: An exploratory study. *Child Development*, 1965, **36**, 913-923.

Creak, M. Childhood psychoses: A review of 100 cases. *British Journal of Psychiatry*, 1963, **109**, 84.

Creak, M., & Ini, S. Families of psychotic children. *Journal of Child Psychology and Psychiatry*, 1960, **1**, 157-175.

Davis, J. M. Efficacy of tranquilizing and antidepressant drugs. *Archives of General Psychiatry*, 1965, **13**, 552-572.

Davis, J. M., & Fann, W. E. Lithium. In *Annual review of pharmacology*, Palo Alto, Calif.: Annual Reviews, 1971, 285-302.

Davis, J. M., Klerman, G., & Schildkraut, J. Drugs used in the treatment of depression. In L. Efron, J. O. Cole, D. Levine, & J. R. Wittenborn, *Psychopharmacology, A review of prog-*

ress. Washington, D.C.: U.S. Clearinghouse of Mental Health Information, 1967.

Davison, A. N., & Dobbing, J. Myelination as a vulnerable period in brain development. *British Medical Bulletin,* 1966, **22,** 40-44.

Davison, G. C. A social learning therapy programme with an autistic child. *Behaviour Research and Therapy,* 1964, **2,** 149-159.

Davison, G. C. Differential relaxation and cognitive restructuring in therapy with a "paranoid schizophrenic" or "paranoid state." *Proceedings of the 74th Annual Convention of the American Psychological Association.* Washington, D.C.: American Psychological Association, 1966.

Davison, G. C. Elimination of a sadistic fantasy by a client-controlled counterconditioning technique. *Journal of Abnormal Psychology,* 1968, **73,** 84-90. (a)

Davison, G. C. Systematic desensitization as a counterconditioning process. *Journal of Abnormal Psychology,* 1968, **73,** 91-99. (b)

Davison, G. C. Appraisal of behavior modification techniques with adults in institutional settings. In C. M. Franks (Ed.), *Behavior therapy: Appraisal and status.* New York: McGraw-Hill, 1969.

Davison, G. C., & Goldfried, M. R. Postdoctoral training in clinical behavior therapy. *Menninger Clinic Bulletin Number 17,* 1973.

Davison, G. C., & Wilson, G. T. Processes of fear reduction in systematic desensitization: Cognitive and social reinforcement factors in humans. *Behavior Therapy,* 1973, **4,** 1-21.

DeJong, R. N., & Sugar, O. *The yearbook of neurology and neurosurgery.* Chicago: Year Book Medical Publishers, 1971.

Dejong, R. N., & Sugar, O. *The yearbook of neurology and neurosurgery.* Chicago: Year Book Medical Publishers, 1972.

Dekker, E., & Groen, J. Reproducible psychogenic attacks of asthma. *Journal of Psychosomatic Research,* 1956, **1,** 58-67.

Dekker, E., Pelse, H. E., & Groen, J. Conditioning as a cause of asthmatic attacks. *Journal of Psychosomatic Research,* 1957, **2,** 97-108.

de Lint, J., & Schmidt, W. The epidemiology of

alcoholism. In Y. Israel & J. Mardones (Eds.), *Biological basis of alcoholism.* New York: Wiley, 1971.

Denner, B., & Price, R. H. (Eds.) *Community mental health: Social action and reaction.* New York: Holt, Rinehart and Winston, 1973.

Diamond, S., Baldwin, R., & Diamond, R. *Inhibition and choice.* New York: Harper and Row, 1963.

Dobbs, W. H. Methadone treatment of heroin addicts. *Journal of the American Medical Association,* 1971, **218,** 1536-1541.

Dokeki, P. R., Polidoro, L. G., & Cromwell, R. L. Commonality and stability of word association responses in good and poor premorbid schizophrenics. *Journal of Abnormal Psychology,* 1965, **70,** 312-316.

Dole, V. P., Nyswander, M. E., & Warner, A. Successful treatment of 750 criminal addicts. *Journal of the American Medical Association,* 1968, **206,** 2708-2711.

Doll, E. A. *Measurement of social competence: A manual for the Vineland Social Maturity Scale.* Circle Pines, Minn.: American Guidance Service, Inc., 1953.

Dollard, J., & Miller, N. E. *Personality and psychotherapy.* New York: McGraw-Hill, 1950.

Dostoyevsky, F. *The idiot,* 1868. New York: Random House, 1935.

Doubros, S. G. Behavior therapy with high level, institutionalized, retarded adolescents. *Exceptional Children,* 1966, **33,** 229-233.

Douglas, J. D. *The social meanings of suicide.* Princeton, N.J.: Princeton University Press, 1967.

Drabman, R. S., Spitalnik, R., & O'Leary, K. D. Teaching self-control to disruptive children. *Journal of Abnormal Psychology,* 1973, **82,** 10-16.

Dunham, H. W. *Community and schizophrenia: An epidemiological analysis.* Detroit: Wayne State University Press, 1965.

Durkheim, E. *Suicide,* 1897. (2nd ed., 1930, in French.) English translation by J. A. Spaulding and G. Simpson. New York: The Free Press, 1951.

Edwards, A. L. *The social desirability variable in*

personality research. New York: Dryden Press, 1957.

Eisenberg, L., & Kanner, L. Early infantile autism. *American Journal of Orthopsychiatry,* 1956, **26,** 556-566.

Ellenberger, H. F. The story of "Anna O": A critical review with new data. *Journal of the History of the Behavior Sciences.* 1972, **8,** 267-279.

Ellingson, R. J. Incidence of EEG abnormality among patients with mental disorders of apparently nonorganic origin: A criminal review. *American Journal of Psychiatry,* 1954, **111,** 263-275.

Ellis, A. *The folklore of sex.* New York: Grove Press, 1961.

Ellis, A. *Reason and emotion in psychotherapy.* New York: Lyle Stuart, 1962.

Endler, N. S., Hunt, J. McV., & Rosenstein, A. J. An S-R inventory of anxiousness. *Psychological Monographs,* 1962, **76,** No. 536.

Engel, B. T., & Bickford, A. F. Response specificity: Stimulus response and individual response specificity in essential hypertension. *Archives of General Psychiatry,* 1961, **5,** 478-489.

English, H. B. Three cases of the "conditioned fear response." *Journal of Abnormal and Social Psychology,* 1929, **34,** 221-225.

Enright, J. B. An introduction to Gestalt techniques. In J. Fagan & I. L. Shepherd (Eds.), *Gestalt therapy now: Theory, techniques, applications.* Palo Alto, Calif.: Science and Behavior Books, 1970.

Erikson, E. H. *Childhood and society.* New York: Norton, 1950.

Ervin, F. R. Brain disorders. IV: Associated with convulsions. In A. M. Freedman & H. I. Kaplan (Eds.), *Comprehensive textbook of psychiatry.* Baltimore: Williams and Wilkins, 1967.

Evans, R. B. Childhood parental relationships of homosexual men. *Journal of Consulting and Clinical Psychology,* 1969, **33,** 129-135.

Eysenck, H. J. The effects of psychotherapy: An evaluation. *Journal of Consulting Psychology,* 1952, **16,** 319-324.

Eysenck, H. J. *Dynamics of anxiety and hysteria.* London: Routledge and Kegan Paul, 1957.

Eysenck, H. J. Classification and the problem of diagnosis. In H. J. Eysenck (Ed.), *Handbook of abnormal psychology.* London: Pitman, 1960.

Eysenck, H. J. *Fact and fiction in psychology.* Baltimore: Penguin Books, 1965.

Fadiman, J. Personal communication, 1973.

Fagan, J., & Shepherd, I. L. (Eds.) *Gestalt therapy now: Theory, techniques, applications.* Palo Alto, Calif.: Science and Behavior Books, 1970.

Feldman, M. P., & MacCulloch, M. J. *Homosexual behavior: Therapy and assessment.* Oxford, England: Pergamon Press, 1971.

Fenichel, O. *The psychoanalytic theory of neurosis.* New York: Norton, 1945.

Ferster, C. B. Positive reinforcement and behavioral deficits of autistic children. *Child Development,* 1961, **32,** 437-456.

Ferster, C. B. Classification of behavioral pathology. In L. Krasner & L. P. Ullmann (Eds.), *Research in behavior modification.* New York: Holt, Rinehart and Winston, 1965.

Ford, C. S., & Beach, F. A. *Patterns of sexual behavior.* New York: Harper, 1951.

Ford, D. H., & Urban, H. B. *Systems of psychotherapy: A comparative study.* New York: Wiley, 1963.

Forsyth, R. P. Blood pressure responses to long-term avoidance schedules in the restrained rhesus monkey. *Psychosomatic Medicine,* 1969, **31,** 300-309.

Fontana, A. Familial etiology of schizophrenia: Is a scientific methodology possible? *Psychological Bulletin,* 1966, **66,** 214-228.

Frank, G. A. The role of the family in the development of psychopathology. *Psychological Bulletin,* 1965, **64,** 191-208.

Frank, J. D. *Persuasion and healing.* New York: Schocken Books, 1961.

Frank, J. D. The bewildering world of psychotherapy. Paper presented at the 80th Annual Convention of the American Psychological Association, Honolulu, Hawaii, 1972.

Freed, E. X. Anxiety and conflict: Role of drug-dependent learning in the rat. *Quarterly Journal of Studies on Alcohol,* 1971, **32,** 13-29.

Freeman, W., & Watts, J. *Psychosurgery.* Springfield, Ill.: Charles C Thomas, 1942.

Freud, Anna. *The ego and mechanisms of defense.* New York: International Universities Press, 1946.

Freud, S. Three contributions to the theory of sex, 1905. In A. A. Brill (Ed.), *The basic writings of Sigmund Freud.* New York: Modern Library, 1938.

Freud, S. Analysis of a phobia in a five-year-old boy, 1909. In *Collected works of Sigmund Freud.* Vol. 10. London: Hogarth Press, 1955.

Freud, S. A case of paranoia running counter to the psychoanalytical theory of the disease, 1915. In *Collected papers.* Vol. 2. London: Hogarth Press, 1956.

Freud, S. Mourning and melancholia, 1917. In *Collected papers.* Vol. 4. London: Hogarth Press and the Institute of Psychoanalysis, 1950.

Freud, S. *The problem of anxiety,* 1926. New York: Norton, 1936.

Freud, S. *An outline of psychoanalysis,* 1940. Standard ed. Vol. 24. London: Hogarth Press, 1964. (a)

Freud, S. *An outline of psychoanalysis,* 1940. Translated and newly edited by James Strachey. New York: Norton, 1959. (b)

Freud, S. *A general introduction to psychoanalysis.* New York: Garden City Publishing Company, 1949.

Freund, K. A laboratory method for diagnosing predominance of homo- and hetero-erotic interest in the male. *Behaviour Research and Therapy,* 1963, **1**, 85-93.

Friedhoff, A. J. Metabolism of dimethoxyphenylethylamine and its possible relationship to schizophrenia. In J. Romano (Ed.), *The origins of schizophrenia.* New York: Excerpta Medica, 1967.

Gagnon, J. H. Sexual conduct and crime. In D. Glazer (Ed.), *The handbook of criminology.* Chicago: Rand McNally, in press.

Gagnon, J. H., & Simon, W. *Sexual conduct: The social origins of human sexuality.* Chicago: Aldine, 1973.

Garcia, J., McGowan, B. K., & Green, K. F. Biological constraints on conditioning. In A. H. Black

& W. F. Prokasy (Eds.), *Classical conditioning II: Current research and theory.* New York: Appleton-Century-Crofts, 1972.

Garmezy, N. Approach and avoidance behavior of schizophrenic and normal subjects as a function of reward and punishment. *American Psychologist,* 1952, **7**, 334.

Garmezy, N. The prediction of performance in schizophrenia. In P. Hoch and J. Zubin (Eds.), *Psychopathology of schizophrenia.* New York: Grune and Stratton, 1966.

Garmezy, N. Vulnerability research and the issue of primary prevention. *American Journal of Orthopsychiatry,* 1971, **41**, 101-116.

Garrone, G. Étude statistique et genetique de la schizophrenie à Geneve de 1901 à 1950. *Journal de Genetique Humaine,* 1962, **11**, 89-219.

Gebhard, P. H. Incidence of overt homosexuality in the United States and western Europe. In J. M. Livingood (Ed.), *National Institute of Mental Health Task Force on Homosexuality: Final report and background papers.* Rockville, Md.: National Institute of Mental Health, 1972.

Gebhard, P. H., Gagnon, J. H., Pomeroy, W. B., & Christenson, C. V. *Sex offenders.* New York: Harper and Row, 1965.

Geer, J. H., Davison, G. C., & Gatchel, R. I. Reduction of stress in humans through nonveridical perceived control of aversive stimulation. *Journal of Personality and Social Psychology,* 1970, **16**, 731-738.

Gibb, J. R. The effects of human relations training. In A. E. Bergin & S. L. Garfield (Eds.), *Handbook of psychotherapy and behavior change: An empirical analysis.* New York: Wiley, 1971.

Gibbs, J. (Ed.) *Suicide.* New York: Harper and Row, 1968.

Gittleman, M., & Birch, H. G. Childhood schizophrenia: Intellect, neurologic status, perinatal risk, prognosis, and family pathology. *Archives of General Psychiatry,* 1967, **17**, 16-25.

Glaser, G. H., Newman, R. J., & Schafer, R. Interictal psychosis in psychomotor-temporal lobe epilepsy: An EEG psychological study. In G. H. Glaser (Ed.), *EEG and behavior.* New York: Basic Books, 1963.

Glover, E. *On the early development of mind.* New York: International Universities Press, 1956.

Goffman, E. *Asylums.* Garden City, N.Y.: Doubleday, 1961.

Goldberg, E. M., & Morrison, S. L. Schizophrenia and social class. *British Journal of Psychiatry,* 1963, **109**, 785-802.

Goldenberg, I. I. *Prospectus and guidelines for residential youth centers.* Washington, D.C.: U.S. Department of Labor, Office of Special Manpower Programs, 1969.

Goldfarb, W. *Childhood schizophrenia.* Cambridge, Mass.: Harvard University Press, 1961.

Goldfried, M. R., Decenteceo, E. T., & Weinberg, L. Systematic rational restructuring as a self-control technique. *Behavior Therapy,* in press.

Goldfried, M. R., & Merbaum, M. (Eds.) *Behavior change through self-control.* New York: Holt, Rinehart, and Winston, 1973.

Goldfried, M. R., Stricker, G., & Weiner, I. B. *Rorschach handbook of clinical and research applications.* Englewood Cliffs, N.J.: Prentice-Hall, 1971.

Goldstein, A. S. *The insanity defense.* New Haven, Conn.: Yale University Press, 1967.

Goldstein, M. J., Held, J. M., & Cromwell, R. L. Premorbid adjustment and paranoid-nonparanoid status in schizophrenia. *Psychological Bulletin,* 1968, **70**, 382-386.

Goodman, L., & Gilman, A. *The pharmacological basis of therapeutics.* New York: Crowell, Collier and Macmillan, 1970.

Goodwin, D. W., Crane, J. B., & Guze, S. B. Alcoholic "blackouts": A review and clinical study of 100 alcoholics. *American Journal of Psychiatry,* 1969, **126**, 191-198.

Gottesman, I. Differential inheritance of the psychoneuroses. *Eugenics Quarterly,* 1962, **9**, 223-227.

Gottesman, I., & Shields, J. *Schizophrenia and genetics.* New York: Academic Press, 1972.

Grace, W. J., & Graham, D. T. Relationship of specific attitudes and emotions to certain bodily diseases. *Psychosomatic Medicine,* 1952, **14**, 243-251.

Graham, D. T. Health, disease and the mind-body problem: Linguistic parallelism. *Psychosomatic Medicine,* 1967, **29**, 52-71.

Graham, D. T., Kabler, J. D., & Graham, F. K. Physiological responses to the suggestion of attitudes: Specificity of attitude hypothesis in psychosomatic disease. *Psychosomatic Medicine,* 1962, **24**, 159-169.

Graham, D. T., Stern, J. A., & Winokur, G. Experimental investigation of the specificity of attitude hypothesis in psychosomatic disease. *Psychosomatic Medicine,* 1958, **20**, 446-457.

Graham, P. J., Rutter, M. L., Yule, W., & Pless, I. B. Childhood asthma: A psychosomatic disorder? Some epidemiological considerations. *British Journal of Preventive Medicine,* 1967, **21**, 78-85.

Granick, S. Comparative analysis of psychotic depressives with matched normals on some untimed verbal intelligence tests. *Journal of Consulting Psychology,* 1963, **27**, 439-443.

Gray, J. *The psychology of fear and stress.* New York: McGraw-Hill, 1971.

Greenblatt, M., Grosser, G. H., & Wechsler, H. Differential responses of hospitalized depressed patients to somatic therapy. *American Journal of Psychiatry,* 1964, **120**, 935-943.

Greer, S. Study of parental loss in neurotics and sociopaths. *Archives of General Psychiatry,* 1964, **11**, 177-180.

Grinker, R. R., & Spiegel, J. P. *Men under stress.* Philadelphia: Blakiston, 1945.

Gubbay, S., Lobascher, M., & Kingerlee, P. A neurological appraisal of autistic children: Results of a Western Australia survey. *Developmental Medicine and Child Neurology,* 1970, **12**, 422-429.

Guerney, B. G. (Ed.) *Psychotherapeutic agents: New roles for nonprofessionals, parents and teachers.* New York: Holt, Rinehart and Winston, 1969.

Gunn, J., & Fenton, G. *Lancet,* June 5, 1971, 1173-1176.

Guze, S. B., & Perley, M. J. Observations on the natural history of hysteria. *Journal of Psychiatry,* 1963, **119**, 960-965.

Haggard, E. Some conditions determining adjustment during and readjustment following experimentally induced stress. In S. Tomkins (Ed.), *Contemporary psychopathology*. Cambridge, Mass.: Harvard University Press, 1943.

Hall, C. S. *A primer of Freudian psychology*. New York: New American Library, 1964.

Hare, R. D. *Psychopathy: Theory and research*. New York: Wiley, 1970.

Harlow, H. F., & Harlow, M. K. Learning to love. *American Scientist*, 1966, **54**, 244-272.

Harlow, J. M. Recovery from the passage of an iron bar through the head. *Publication of the Massachusetts Medical Society*, 1868, **2**, 327 ff.

Harrel, R. F., Woodyard, E., & Gates, A. D. *The effects of mothers' diets on the intelligence of offspring*. New York: Teachers College Press, Columbia University, 1955.

Hartmann, H. *Ego psychology and the problem of adaptation*. New York: International Universities Press, 1958.

Heath, R. G. A biochemical hypothesis on the etiology of schizophrenia. In D. D. Jackson (Ed.), *The etiology of schizophrenia*. New York: Basic Books, 1960.

Heath, R. G., & Krupp, I. M. Schizophrenia as an immunologic disorder. *Archives of General Psychiatry*, 1967, **16**, 1-33.

Heath, R. G., Martens, S., Leach, B. E., Cohen, M., & Angel, C. Effect on behavior in humans with the administration of taraxein. *American Journal of Psychiatry*, 1957, **114**, 14-24.

Heber, R. (Ed.) A manual on terminology and classification in mental retardation. (2nd ed.) *American Journal of Mental Deficiency, Monograph Supplement*, 1961.

Heber, R. *Epidemiology of mental retardation*. Springfield, Ill.: Charles C Thomas, 1970.

Hedblom, J. H. The female homosexual: Social and attitudinal dimensions. In J. A. McCaffrey (Ed.), *The homosexual dialectic*. Englewood Cliffs, N.J.: Prentice-Hall, 1972.

Heiman, N. M. Postdoctoral training in community mental health. *Menninger Clinic Bulletin Number 17*, 1973.

Henry, J. P., Stephens, P. M., Axelrod, J., & Miller, R. A. Effect of psychosocial stimulation on the enzymes involved in the biosynthesis and me-

tabolism of noradrenaline and adrenaline. *Psychosomatic Medicine*, 1971, **23**, 227-237.

Herbert, J. Personality factors and bronchial asthma: A study of South African Indian children. *Journal of Psychosomatic Research*, 1965, **8**, 353-364.

Hernández-Peón, R., Chávez-Ibarra, G., & Aguilar-Figueroa, E. Somatic evoked potentials in one case of hysterical anesthesia. *EEG and Clinical Neurophysiology*, 1963, **15**, 889-892.

Hermelin, B. *Recent psychological research*. In J. K. Wing (Ed.), *Early childhood autism: Clinical, educational, and social aspects*. Elmsford, N.Y.: Pergamon Press, 1966.

Hermelin, B., & O'Connor, N. Measures of occipital alpha rhythm in normal, subnormal, and autistic children. *British Journal of Psychiatry*, 1968, **114**, 603-610.

Heston, L. L. Psychiatric disorders in foster home reared children of schizophrenic mothers. *British Journal of Psychiatry*, 1966, **112**, 819-825.

Hewett, F. M. Teaching speech to an autistic child through operant conditioning. *American Journal of Orthopsychiatry*, 1965, **33**, 927-936.

Hilgard, E. R. *Hypnotic susceptibility*. New York: Harcourt Brace Jovanovich, 1965.

Hill, D. EEG in episodic psychotic and psychopathic behavior: A classification of data. *EEG and Clinical Neurophysiology*, 1952, **4**, 419-442.

Hill, J. H., Liebert, R. M., & Mott, D. E. W. Vicarious extinction of avoidance behavior through films: An initial test. *Psychological Reports*, 1968, **12**, 192.

Hinton, G. G. Childhood psychosis or mental retardation: A diagnostic dilemma II. Pediatric and neurological aspects. *Canadian Medical Association Journal*, 1963, **89**, 1020-1024.

Hobbs, N. Helping disturbed children: Psychological and ecological strategies. *American Psychologist*, 1966, **21**, 1105-1115.

Hoffer, A., Osmond, H., Callbeck, M. J., & Kahan, I. Treatment of schizophrenia with nicotinic acid and nicitinamide. *American Journal of Psychiatry*, 1957, **144**, 917.

Hoffman, M. *The gay world*. New York: Basic Books, 1968.

Hokanson, J. E., & Burgess, M. The effects of three types of aggression on vascular processes. *Journal of Abnormal and Social Psychology,* 1962, **65**, 446-449.

Hokanson, J. E., Burgess, M., & Cohen, M. F. Effects of displaced aggression on systolic blood pressure. *Journal of Abnormal and Social Psychology,* 1963, **67**, 214-218.

Hokanson, J. E., DeGood, D. E., Forrest, M. S., & Brittain, T. M. Availability of avoidance behaviors for modulating vascular-stress responses. *Journal of Personality and Social Psychology,* 1971, **19**, 60-68.

Hokanson, J. E., Willers, K. R., & Koropsak, E. Modification of autonomic responses during aggressive interchange. *Journal of Personality,* 1968, **36**, 386-404.

Holden, C. Nader on mental health centers: A movement that got bogged down. *Science,* 1972, **177**, 413-415.

Hollingshead, A. B., & Redlich, F. C. *Social class and mental illness: A community study.* New York: Wiley, 1958.

Honigfeld, G., & Howard, A. *Psychiatric drugs: A desk reference.* New York: Academic Press, 1973.

Hooker, E. Homosexuality. In D. L. Sills (Ed.), *International encyclopedia of the social sciences.* Vol. 14. New York: Crowell Collier and Macmillan, 1968.

Houts, P. S., & Serber, M. (Eds.) *After the turn-on, what? Learning perspectives on humanistic groups.* Champaign, Ill.: Research Press, 1972.

Humphreys, L. *Tearoom trade: Impersonal sex in public places.* Chicago: Aldine, 1970.

Hurley, R. L. *Poverty and mental retardation: A causal relationship.* New York: Random House, 1970.

Hutt, C., Hutt, S. J., Lee, D., & Ounsted, C. Arousal and childhood autism, *Nature,* 1964, **204**, 908-909.

Hutt, C., & Ounsted, C. The biological significance of gaze aversion with particular reference to the syndrome of infantile autism. *Behavioral Science,* 1966, **11**, 346-356.

Ikard, F. F., Green, D. E., & Horn, D. The development of a scale to differentiate between types of smoking as related to the management of affect. Paper presented at the annual meeting of the Eastern Psychological Association, Washington, D.C., 1968.

Ingram, I. M. The obsessional personality and obsessional illness. *American Journal of Psychiatry,* 1961, **117**, 1016-1019.

Innes, G., Millar, W. M., & Valentine, M. Emotion and blood pressure. *Journal of Mental Science,* 1959, **105**, 840-851.

Jacobson, E. *Progressive relaxation.* Chicago: University of Chicago Press, 1929.

Jarvik, M. E. The role of nicotine in the smoking habit. In W. A. Hunt (Ed.), *Learning mechanisms in smoking.* Chicago: Aldine, 1970.

Jellinek, E. M. Phases of alcohol addiction. *Quarterly Journal of Studies on Alcohol,* 1952, **13**, 673-684.

Jersild, A. T., & Holmes, F. B. *Children's fears.* New York: Teachers College Press, Columbia University, 1935.

Jersild, A. T., Markey, F. V., & Jersild, C. L. Children's fears, dreams, wishes, daydreams, likes, dislikes, pleasant and unpleasant memories, In A. T. Jersild (Ed.), *Child psychology.* Englewood Cliffs, N.J.: Prentice-Hall, 1960.

Johnson, A. M., Falstein, E. I., Szurek, S. A., & Svendson, M. School phobia, *American Journal of Orthopsychiatry,* 1941, **11**, 701-702.

Johnson, G., Gershon, S., & Hekimian, L. Controlled evaluation of lithium and chlorpromazine in treatment of manic states. *Comprehensive Psychiatry,* 1968, **9**, 563-573.

Jones, E. *The life and work of Sigmund Freud.* Vol. 2. New York: Basic Books, 1955.

Jones, M. C. A laboratory study of fear: The case of Peter. *Pedagogical Seminary,* 1924, **31**, 308-315.

Jones, M. C. Personality correlates and antecedents of drinking patterns in males. *Journal of Consulting and Clinical Psychology,* 1968, **32**, 2-12.

Jones, M. C. Personality antecedents and correlates of drinking patterns in women. *Journal of Consulting and Clinical Psychology,* 1971, **36**, 61-70.

Kallmann, F. J. The genetics of psychosis. *American Journal of Human Genetics,* 1950, **2**, 385.

Kallmann, F. J. Twin and sibship study of overt male homosexuality. *American Journal of Human Genetics,* 1952, **4**, 136-146. (a)

Kallmann, F. J. Comparative twin study in the genetic aspects of male homosexuality. *Journal of Nervous and Mental Disease,* 1952, 115, 283-298. (b)

Kallmann, F. J., & Jarvik, L. F. Individual differences in constitution and genetic background. In J. E. Birren (Ed.), *Handbook of aging and the individual.* Chicago: University of Chicago Press, 1961.

Kallmann, F. J., & Roth, B. Genetic aspects of preadolescent schizophrenia. *American Journal of Psychiatry,* 1956, **112**, 599-606.

Kameny, F. E. Gay liberation and psychiatry. *Psychiatric Opinion,* 1971, **8**, 18-27.

Kanfer, F. H., & Karoly, P. Self-control. A behavioristic excursion into the lion's den. *Behavior Therapy,* 1972, **3**, 398-416.

Kanfer, F. H., & Phillips, J. S. *Learning foundations of behavior therapy.* New York: Wiley, 1970.

Kanner, L. Autistic disturbances of affective contact. *Nervous Child,* 1943, **2**, 217-250.

Kanner, L. Problems of nosology and psychodynamics of early infantile autism. *American Journal of Orthopsychiatry,* 1949, **19**, 416-426.

Kanner, L. To what extent is early infantile autism determined by constitutional inadequacies? *Association for Research in Nervous and Mental Disease,* 1954, **33**, 378-385.

Kanner, L., & Eisenberg, L. Notes on the follow-up studies of autistic children. In P. Hoch and J. Zubin (Eds.), *Psychopathology of childhood.* New York: Grune and Stratton, 1955.

Kanner, L., & Lesser, L. Early infantile autism. *Pediatric Clinic of North America,* 1958, **5**, 711-730.

Kasl, S. V., & Cobb, S. Blood pressure changes in men undergoing job loss: A preliminary report. *Psychosomatic Medicine,* 1970, **6**, 95-106.

Katchadourian, H. A., & Lunde, D. T. *Fundamentals of human sexuality.* New York: Holt, Rinehart and Winston, 1972.

Kelly, E., & Zeller, B. Asthma and the psychiatrist. *Journal of Psychosomatic Research,* 1969, **13**, 377-395.

Kelly, J. G. Antidotes for arrogance: Training for community psychology. *American Psychologist,* 1970, **25**, 524-531.

Kennedy, W. A. School phobia: Rapid treatment of 50 cases. *Journal of Abnormal Psychology,* 1965, **70**, 285-289.

Kessel, N., & Walton, A. *Alcoholism.* Baltimore: Penguin Books, 1965.

Kessler, P., & Neale, J. M. Hippocampal damage and Mednick's theory: A critique. *Journal of Abnormal Psychology,* 1974, in press.

Kety, S. S., Rosenthal, D., Wender, P. H., & Schulsinger, F. The types and prevalence of mental illness in the biological and adoptive families of adopted schizophrenics. In D. Rosenthal & S. S. Kety (Eds.), *The transmission of schizophrenia.* Elmsford, N.Y.: Pergamon Press, 1968.

Kimble, G. *Hilgard and Marquis' Conditioning and learning.* New York: Appleton-Century-Crofts, 1961.

Kinsey, A. C., Pomeroy, W. B., & Martin, C. E. *Sexual behavior in the human male.* Philadelphia: Saunders, 1948.

Kinsey, A. C., Pomeroy, W. B., Martin, C. E., & Gebhard, P. H. *Sexual behavior in the human female.* Philadelphia: Saunders, 1953.

Klee, G. D., Bertino, J., Weintraub, W., & Callaway, E. The influence of varying dosage on the effects of lysergic acid diethylamide (LSD-25). *Journal of Nervous and Mental Disease,* 1961, **132**, 404-409.

Klee, G. D., & Weintraub, W. Paranoid reactions following lysergic acid diethylamide (LSD-25). In P. B. Bradley, P. Demicker, & C. Radonco-Thomas (Eds.), *Neuro-psychopharmacology.* Amsterdam, Netherlands: Elsevier, 1959.

Kleeman, S. T. Psychiatric contributions in the treatment of asthma. *Annals of Allergy,* 1967, **25**, 611-619.

Klein, M., Heimann, P., Isaacs, S., & Riviere, J. *Developments in psychoanalysis.* London: Hogarth Press, 1952.

Kleinmuntz, B. *Personality measurement: An introduction.* Homewood, Ill.: Dorsey Press, 1967.

Kluger, J. M. Childhood asthma and the social milieu. *American Academy of Child Psychiatry,* 1969, **8**, 353-366.

Knapp, P. H. The asthmatic and his environment. *Journal of Nervous and Mental Disease,* 1969, **149**, 133-151.

Knight, R. P. The dynamics of chronic alcoholism. *Journal of Nervous and Mental Disease.* 1937, **86**, 538-548.

Kohn, M. L. Social class and schizophrenia: A critical review. In D. Rosenthal & S. S. Kety (Eds.), *The transmission of schizophrenia.* Elmsford, N.Y.: Pergamon Press, 1968.

Kolb, L. C. *Noyes' modern clinical psychiatry.* (7th ed.) Philadelphia: Saunders, 1968.

Kolodny, R. C., Masters, W. H., Hendryx, J., & Toro, G. Plasma testosterone and the semen analysis in male homosexuals. *New England Journal of Medicine,* 1971, **285**, 1170-1174.

Kopfstein, J. M., & Neale, J. M. A multivariate study of attention dysfunction in schizophrenia. *Journal of Abnormal Psychology,* 1972, **80**, 294-299.

Kraepelin, E. *Lehrbuch der Psychiatrie.* (5th ed.) Leipzig: Barth, 1896.

Kraepelin, E. *Lectures on clinical psychiatry,* 1904. New York: Hafner, 1968.

Kranz, H. *Lebenschicksale krimineller Zwillinge.* Berlin: Springer-Verlag, 1936.

Kreitman, N., Sainsbury, P., Morrissey, J., Towers, J., & Scrivner, J. The reliability of psychiatric assessment: An analysis. *Journal of Mental Science,* 1961, **107**, 887-908.

Kuhn, T. S. *The Copernican revolution.* New York: Random House, 1959.

Kuhn, T. S. *The structure of scientific revolutions.* Chicago: University of Chicago Press, 1962.

Kutchinsky, B. *Studies on pornography and sex crimes in Denmark.* Copenhagen: New Social Science Monographs, 1970.

Lacey, J. I. Somatic response patterning and stress: Some revisions of activation theory. In M. H. Appley & R. Trumbull (Eds.), *Psychological stress.* New York: McGraw-Hill, 1967.

Lachman, S. J. *Psychosomatic disorders: A behavioristic interpretation.* New York: Wiley, 1972.

Laing, R. D. Is schizophrenia a disease? *International Journal of Social Psychiatry,* 1964, **10**, 184-193.

Landis, C., & Mettler, F. A. *Varieties of psychopathological experience.* New York: Holt, Rinehart and Winston, 1964.

Lane, E. A., & Albee, G. W. Childhood intellectual differences between schizophrenic adults and their siblings. *American Journal of Orthopsychiatry,* 1965, **35**, 747-753.

Lang, P. J. The mechanics of desensitization and the laboratory study of fear. In C. M. Franks (Ed.), *Behavior therapy: Appraisal and status.* New York: McGraw-Hill, 1969.

Lang, P. J., & Lazovik, A. D. Experimental desensitization of a phobia. *Journal of Abnormal and Social Psychology,* 1963, **66**, 519-525.

Lange, J. *Verbrechen als Schicksal.* Leipzig: Georg Thieme Verlag, 1929.

Lapolla, A., & Jones, H. Placebo-control evaluation of desipramine in depression. *American Journal of Psychiatry,* 1970, **127**, 335-338.

Lasagna, L., Mosteller, F., Von Felsinger, J. M., & Beecher, H. K. A study of the placebo response. *American Journal of Medicine,* 1954, **16**, 770-779.

Lazarus, A. A. New methods of psychotherapy: A case study. *South African Medical Journal,* 1958, **33**, 660.

Lazarus, A. A. Group therapy of phobic disorders by systematic desensitization. *Journal of Abnormal and Social Psychology,* 1961, **63**, 504-510.

Lazarus, A. A. The results of behavior therapy in 126 cases of severe neurosis. *Behaviour Research and Therapy,* 1963, **1**, 69-79.

Lazarus, A. A. Behavior therapy, incomplete treatment, and symptom substitution. *Journal of Nervous and Mental Disease,* 1965, **140**, 80-86.

Lazarus, A. A. Behavior therapy in groups. In G. M. Gazda (Ed.), *Basic approaches to group psychotherapy and counseling.* Springfield, Ill.: Charles C Thomas, 1968. (a)

Lazarus, A. A. Learning theory and the treatment of depression. *Behaviour Research and Therapy,* 1968, **6**, 83-89. (b)

Lazarus, A. A. *Behavior therapy and beyond.* New York: McGraw-Hill, 1971.

Lazarus, A. A., & Davison, G. C. Clinical innovation in research and practice. In A. E. Bergin & S. L. Garfield (Eds.), *Handbook of psychotherapy and behavior change: An empirical analysis.* New York: Wiley, 1971.

Lazarus, A. A., Davison, G. C., & Polefka, D. Classical and operant factors in the treatment of a school phobia. *Journal of Abnormal Psychology,* 1965, **70,** 225-229.

Lazarus, A. A., & Rachman, S. The use of systematic desensitization in psychotherapy. *South African Medical Journal,* 1957, **31,** 934-937.

Lazovik, A. D., & Lang, P. J. A laboratory demonstration of systematic desensitization psychotherapy. *Journal of Psychological Studies,* 1960, **11,** 238-247.

Leahy, M. R., & Martin, I. C. A. Successful hypnotic abreaction after twenty years. *British Journal of Psychiatry,* 1967, **113,** 383-385.

Lester, D. Attempts to predict suicidal risk using psychological tests. *Psychological Bulletin,* 1970, **74,** 1-17.

Lester, D., & Greenberg, L. Nutrition and the etiology of alcoholism. *Quarterly Journal of Studies on Alcohol,* 1952, **13,** 320-330.

Levine, M., & Olson, R. P. Intelligence of parents of autistic children. *Journal of Abnormal Psychology,* 1968, **73,** 215-217.

Levitsky, A., & Perls, F. S. The rules and games of Gestalt therapy. In J. Fagan & I. L. Shepherd (Eds.), *Gestalt therapy now.* Palo Alto, Calif.: Science and Behavior Books, 1970.

Levitt, E. E. Research on psychotherapy with children. In A. E. Bergin & S. L. Garfield (Eds.), *Handbook of psychotherapy and behavior change: An empirical analysis.* New York: Wiley, 1971.

Levy, L. H. *Psychological interpretation.* New York: Holt, Rinehart and Winston, 1963.

Lewinsohn, P. H. A behavioral approach to depression. In R. J. Friedman & M. M. Katz (Eds.), *The psychology of depression: Contemporary theory and research.* Washington, D.C.: Winston-Wiley, in press.

Lewinsohn, P. H., & Libet, J. M. Pleasant events, activity schedules and depressions. *Journal of Abnormal Psychology,* 1972, **79,** 291-295.

Liberman, R. P. Learning interpersonal skills in groups: Harnessing the behavioristic horse to the humanistic wagon. In P. S. Houts & M. Serber (Eds.), *After the turn-on, what? Learning perspectives on humanistic groups.* Champaign, Ill.: Research Press, 1972.

Libet, J. M., & Lewinsohn, P. H. The concept of social skill with special reference to the behavior of depressed persons. *Journal of Consulting and Clinical Psychology,* 1973, **40,** 304-312.

Liddell, H. S. *Emotional hazards in animals and man.* Springfield, Ill.: Charles C Thomas, 1956.

Liebert, R. M., & Baron, R. A. Short-term effects of televised aggression on children's aggressive behavior. In J. P. Murray, E. A. Rubinstein, & G. A. Comstock (Eds.), *Television and social behavior.* Vol. 2. Washington, D.C.: U.S. Government Printing Office, 1972.

Linton, H. B., & Langs, R. J. Empirical dimensions of LSD-25 reactions. *Archives of General Psychiatry,* 1964, **10,** 469-485.

Lisman, S. A., & Cohen, B. D. Self-editing deficits in schizophrenia: A word-association analogue. *Journal of Abnormal Psychology,* 1972, **79,** 181-188.

Livingood, J. M. (Ed.) *National Institute of Mental Health Tcck Force on Homosexuality: Final report and background papers.* Rockville, Md.: National Institute of Mental Health, 1972.

Loeb, A., Beck, A. T., Diggory, J. C., & Tuthill, R. The effects of success and failure on mood, motivation and performance as a function of predetermined level of depression. Unpublished study, University of Pennsylvania, 1966.

London, P. *The modes and morals of psychotherapy.* New York: Holt, Rinehart and Winston, 1964.

Loraine, J. A., Adamopoulos, D. A., Kirkham, E. E., Ismail, A. A. A., & Dove, G. A. Patterns of hormone excretion in male and female homosexuals. *Nature,* 1971, **234,** 552-555.

Lotter, V. Epidemiology of autistic conditions in young children I. Prevalence. *Social Psychiatry,* 1966, **1,** 124-137.

Lotter, V. Epidemiology of autistic conditions in young children II. Some characteristics of parents and children. *Social Psychiatry*, 1967, **1**, 163-173.

Lovaas, O. I., Freitag, G., Gold, V. J., & Kassorla, I. C. Experimental studies in childhood schizophrenia: Analysis of self-destructive behavior. *Journal of Experimental Child Psychology*, 1965, **2**, 67-84.

Lovaas, O. I., Schreibman, L., Koegel, R., & Rehm, R. Selective responding by autistic children to multiple sensory input. *Journal of Abnormal Psychology*, 1971, **77**, 211-222.

Luborsky, L., & Spence, D. P. Quantitative research on psychoanalytic therapy. In A. E. Bergin & S. L. Garfield (Eds.), *Handbook of psychotherapy and behavior change: An empirical analysis.* New York: Wiley, 1971.

Lucchesi, B. R., Schuster, C. R., & Emley, G. S. The role of nicotine as a determinant of cigarette smoking frequency in man with observations of certain cardiovascular effects associated with the tobacco alkaloid. *Clinical Pharmacology and Therapeutics*, 1967, **8**, 789-796.

Luparello, T. J., McFadden, E. R., Lyons, H. A., & Bleecker, E. R. Psychologic factors and bronchial asthma. *New York State Journal of Medicine*, 1971, **71**, 2161-2165.

Luria, D. B. *Overcoming drugs: Program of action.* New York: McGraw-Hill, 1970.

Lyght, C. E. (Ed.) *The Merck manual of diagnosis and therapy.* (11th ed.) Rahway, N.J.: Merck Sharp and Dohm Research Laboratories, 1966.

Lykken, D. T. A study of anxiety in the sociopathic personality. *Journal of Abnormal and Social Psychology*, 1957, **55**, 6-10.

Lystad, M. M. Social mobility among selected groups of schizophrenics. *American Sociological Review*, 1957, **22**, 288-292.

Maddi, S. R. The existential neurosis. *Journal of Abnormal Psychology*, 1967, **72**, 311-325.

Maher, B. A. *Principles of psychopathology: An experimental approach.* New York: McGraw-Hill, 1966.

Mahler, M. S. On child psychosis and schizophrenia: Autistic and symbiotic infantile psychoses. In *Psychoanalytic Study of the Child.* Vol. 7. New York: International Universities Press, 1952.

Mahoney, M. J. Research issues in self-management. *Behavior Therapy*, 1972, **3**, 45-63.

Maier, N. R. F. *Frustration: The study of behavior without a goal.* New York: McGraw-Hill, 1949.

Main, T. F. Perception and ego-function. *British Journal of Medical Psychology*, 1958, **31**, 1-7.

Mandler, G. Anxiety. In D. L. Sills (Ed.), *International encyclopedia of the social sciences.* New York: Crowell Collier and Macmillan, 1966.

Mandler, G., & Sarason, S. B. A study of anxiety and learning. *Journal of Abnormal and Social Psychology*, 1952, **47**, 561-565.

Marin, P., & Cohen, A. Y. *Understanding drug use: An adult's guide to drugs and the young.* New York: Harper and Row, 1971.

Markham, J. M. What's all this talk of heroin maintenance? *New York Times Magazine*, July 2, 1972.

Marks, I. M. *Fears and phobias.* New York: Academic Press, 1969.

Marks, I. M., & Gelder, M. G. Different onset ages in varieties of phobia. *American Journal of psychiatry*, 1966, **123**, 218, 221.

Marlatt, G. A., Demming, B., & Reid, J. B. Loss of control drinking in alcoholics: An experimental analogue. *Journal of Abnormal Psychology*, 1973, **81**, 233-241.

Marmor, J. Psychoanalytic therapy as an educational process: Common denominators in the therapeutic approaches of different psychoanalytic schools. In J. H. Masserman (Ed.), *Science and psychoanalysis.* Vol. 5. *Psychoanalytic education.* New York: Grune and Stratton, 1962.

Martin, B. The assessment of anxiety by physiological behavioral measures. *Psychological Bulletin*, 1961, **58**, 234-255.

Martin, D., & Lyon, P. *Lesbian/woman.* New York: Bantam Books, 1972.

Masters, J. C., & Miller, D. E. Early infantile autism: A methodological critique. *Journal of Abnormal Psychology*, 1970, **75**, 342-343.

Masters, W. H., & Johnson, V. E. *Human sexual response.* Boston: Little, Brown, 1966.

Masters, W. H., & Johnson, V. E. *Human sexual inadequacy.* Boston: Little, Brown, 1970.

May, P. R. A. *Treatment of schizophrenia: A comparative study of five treatment methods.* New York: Science House, 1968.

McCary, J. L. *Human sexuality.* New York: Van Nostrand Reinhold, 1967.

McClelland, D. C., Davis, W. N., Kalin, R., & Wanner, E. *The drinking man.* New York: The Free Press, 1972.

McCord, W., & McCord, J. *The psychopath: An essay on the criminal mind.* New York: Van Nostrand Reinhold, 1964.

McCord, W., McCord, J., & Gudeman, J. Some current theories of alcoholism. *Quarterly Journal of Studies on Alcohol*, 1959, **20**, 727-749.

McCord, W., McCord, J., & Gudeman, J. *Origins of alcoholism.* Stanford, Calif.: Stanford University Press, 1960.

McFall, R. M., & Marston, A. R. An experimental investigation of behavior rehearsal in assertive training. *Journal of Abnormal Psychology*, 1970, **76**, 285-303.

McGhie, A., & Chapman, J. S. Disorders of attention and perception in early schizophrenia. *British Journal of Medical Psychology*, 1961, **34**, 103-116.

McGuigan, F. J. Covert oral behavior and auditory hallucinations. *Psychophysiology*, 1966, **3**, 421-428.

McGuire, R. J., Carlisle, J. M., & Young, B. G. Sexual deviations as conditioned behaviour: A hypothesis. *Behaviour Research and Therapy*, 1965, **2**, 185-190.

McNeil, E. *The quiet furies.* Englewood Cliffs, N.J.: Prentice-Hall, 1967.

Mednick, S. A. A learning theory approach to research in schizophrenia. *Psychological Bulletin*, 1958, **55**, 316-327.

Mednick, S. A. Breakdown in individuals at high-risk for schizophrenia: Possible predispositional perinatal factors. *Mental Hygiene*, 1970, **54**, 50-63.

Mednick, S. A., & Schulsinger, F. Some premorbid characteristics related to breakdown in children with schizophrenic mothers. In. D. Rosenthal and S. S. Kety (Eds.), *The transmission of schizophrenia.* Elmsford, N.Y.: Pergamon Press, 1968.

Medvedev, Z. *A question of madness.* New York: Knopf, 1972.

Meehl, P. E. Schizotaxia, schizotypy, schizophrenia. *American Psychologist*, 1962, **17**, 827-838.

Meichenbaum, D. Ways of modifying what clients say to themselves. *Rational Living*, 1972, **7**, 23-27.

Mello, N. K., & Mendelson, J. H. Experimentally induced intoxication in alcoholics: A comparison between programmed and spontaneous drinking. *Journal of Pharmacology and Experimental Therapy*, 1970, **173**, 101.

Mendels, J. *Concepts of depression.* New York: Wiley, 1970.

Mendels, J., & Cochrane, C. The nosology of depression: The endogenous-reactive concept. *American Journal of Psychiatry*, 1968, **124**, 1-11.

Mendelson, J. H. Experimentally induced chronic intoxication and withdrawal in alcoholics. *Quarterly Journal of Studies on Alcohol*, 1964, Supplement 2.

Metzner, R., Litwin, G., & Weil, G. M. The relation of expectation and mood to psilocybin reactions. *Psychedelic Review*, 1965, **5**, 3-39.

Meyer, V., & Chesser, E. S. *Behavior therapy in clinical psychiatry.* Baltimore: Penguin Books, 1970.

Mézey, A. G., & Cohen, S. I. The effect of depressive illness on time judgment and time experience. *Journal of Neurological and Neurosurgical Psychiatry*, 1961, **24**, 269-270.

Miles, M. Changes during and following laboratory training: A clinical experimental study. *Journal of Applied Behavioral Science*, 1965, **1**, 215-242.

Milgram, N. A. Cognition and language in mental retardation: A reply to Balla and Zigler. *American Journal of Mental Deficiency*, 1971, **76**, 33-41.

Miller, N. E. *The influence of past experience upon the transfer of subsequent training.* Unpublished doctoral dissertation, Yale University, 1935.

Miller, N. E. Studies of fear as an acquirable drive. I. Fear as motivation and fear-reduction as reinforcement in the learning of new responses.

Journal of Experimental Psychology, 1948, **38,** 89-101.

Miller, N. E. Liberalization of basic S-R concepts: Extensions to conflict behavior, motivation, and social learning. In S. Koch (Ed.), *Psychology: A study of a science.* Vol. 2. New York: McGraw-Hill, 1959.

Miller, W. R., & Seligman, M. E. P. Depression and the perception of reinforcement. *Journal of Abnormal Psychology,* 1973, **82,** 62-73.

Millon, T. *Modern psychopathology.* Philadelphia: Saunders, 1969.

Milton, O., & Wahler, R. G. (Eds.) *Behavior disorders: Perspectives and trends.* (2nd ed.) Philadelphia: Lippincott, 1969.

Minge, M. R., & Ball, T. S. Teaching of self-help skills to profoundly retarded patients. *American Journal of Mental Deficiency,* 1957, **71,** 864-868.

Mintz, E. Time-extended marathon groups. *Psychotherapy,* 1967, **4,** 65-70.

Mintz, R. S. Psychotherapy of the suicidal patient. In H. L. P. Resnik (Ed.), *Suicidal behaviors.* Boston: Little, Brown, 1968.

Mintz, S., & Alpert, M. Imagery vividness, reality testing, and schizophrenic hallucinations. *Journal of Abnormal Psychology,* 1972, **79,** 310-316.

Mirsky, I. A. Physiologic, psychologic, and social determinants in the etiology of duodenal ulcer. *American Journal of Digestive Diseases,* 1958, **3,** 285-314.

Mischel, W. *Personality and assessment.* New York: Wiley, 1968.

Mishler, E., & Waxler, N. *Interaction in families: An experimental study of family processes and schizophrenia.* New York: Wiley, 1968.

Mittleman, B., & Wolff, H. G. Emotions and gastroduodenal function. *Psychosomatic Medicine,* 1942, **4,** 5-61.

Mohr, J. W., Turner, R. E., & Jerry, M. B. *Pedophilia and exhibitionism.* Toronto: University of Toronto Press, 1964.

Money, J. Components of eroticism in man. I: The hormones in relation to sexual morphology and sexual desire. *Journal of Nervous and Mental Disease,* 1961, **132,** 239-248.

Money, J. *Sex errors of the body.* Baltimore: The Johns Hopkins Press, 1968.

Money, J. Sexual dimorphism and homosexual gender identity. *Psychological Bulletin,* 1970, **74,** 425-440.

Moore, C., & Shiek, D. Toward a theory of early infantile autism. *Psychological Review,* 1971, **78,** 451-456.

Moreno, J. L., & Kipper, D. A. Group psychodrama and community-centered counseling. In G. M. Gazda (Ed.), *Basic approaches to group psychotherapy and group counseling.* Springfield, Ill.: Charles C Thomas, 1968.

Morris, A. A. Criminal insanity. *Washington Review,* 1968, **43,** 583-622.

Mowrer, O. H. A stimulus-response analysis of anxiety and its role as a reinforcing agent. *Psychological Review,* 1939, **46,** 553-565.

Mowrer, O. H. On the dual nature of learning—a reinterpretation of "conditioning" and "problem-solving." *Harvard Educational Review,* 1947, **17,** 102-148.

Mowrer, O. H., & Viek, P. An experimental analogue of fear from a sense of helplessness. *Journal of Abnormal and Social Psychology,* 1948, **43,** 193-200.

Naranjo, C. Present-centeredness: Technique, prescription, and ideal. In J. Fagan & I. L. Shepherd (Eds.), *Gestalt therapy now: Theory, techniques, applications.* Palo Alto, Calif.: Science and Behavior Books, 1970.

Nathan, P. E., Titler, N. A., Lowenstein, L. M., Solomon, P., & Rossi, A. M. Behavioral analysis of chronic alcoholism. *Archives of General Psychiatry,* 1970, **22,** 419-430.

National Commission on Marihuana and Drug Abuse. *Marihuana: A signal of misunderstanding.* New York: The New American Library, 1972.

Neale, J. M., & Cromwell, R. L. Attention and schizophrenia. In B. A. Maher (Ed.), *Progress in experimental personality research.* Vol. 5. New York: Academic Press, 1970.

Neale, J. M., & Katahn, M. Anxiety, choice and stimulus uncertainty. *Journal of Personality,* 1968, **36,** 238-245.

Neale, J. M., Kopfstein, J. H., & Levine, A. Premorbid adjustment and paranoid status in schizophrenia: Varying assessment techniques and the influence of chronicity. Paper presented at the 80th Annual Convention of the American Psychological Association, Honolulu, Hawaii, 1972.

Neale, J. M., & Liebert, R. M. Reinforcement therapy using aides and patients as behavioral technicians: A case report of a mute psychotic. *Perceptual and Motor Skills,* 1969, **28**, 835-839

Neale, J. M., & Liebert, R. M. *Science and behavior: An introduction to methods of research.* Englewood Cliffs, N.J.: Prentice-Hall, 1973.

Neale, J. M., McIntyre, C. W., Fox, R., & Cromwell, R. L. Span of apprehension in acute schizophrenics. *Journal of Abnormal Psychology,* 1969, **74**, 593-596.

Nesbitt, P. D. Smoking, physiological arousal, and emotional response. *Journal of Personality and Social Psychology,* 1973, **25**, 137-144.

Neuhaus, E. C. A personality study of asthmatic and cardiac children. *Psychosomatic Medicine,* 1958, **20**, 181-186.

Nihira, K., Foster, R., Shellhaas, M., & Leland, H. *Adaptive Behavior Scales.* Washington, D.C.: American Association on Mental Deficiency, 1969.

Nunnally, J. C. *Psychometric theory.* New York: McGraw-Hill, 1967.

O'Connor, R. D. Modification of social withdrawal through symbolic modeling. *Journal of Applied Behavior Analysis,* 1969, **2**, 15-22.

O'Leary, K. D., & Becker, W. C. Behavior modification of an adjustment class: A token reinforcement program. *Exceptional Children,* 1967, **33**, 637-642.

O'Leary, K. D., & O'Leary, S. G. (Eds.) *Classroom management.* Elmsford, N.Y.: Pergamon Press, 1972.

Orne, M. T. The nature of hypnosis: Artifact and essence. *Journal of Abnormal and Social Psychology,* 1959, **58**, 277-299.

Orris, J. B. Visual monitoring performance in three subgroups of male delinquents. Unpublished M.A. thesis, University of Illinois, 1967.

Pahnke, W. N. *Drugs and mysticism.* Unpublished doctoral dissertation, Harvard University, 1963.

Parker, N. Twins: A psychiatric study of a neurotic group. *Medical Journal of Australia,* 1964, **2**, 735-741.

Patterson, G. R. Behavioral intervention procedures in the classroom and in the home. In A. E. Bergin & S. L. Garfield (Eds.), *Handbook of psychotherapy and behavior change: An empirical analysis.* New York: Wiley, 1971.

Patterson, G. R. Follow-up evaluation of a program for parents' retraining of their aggressive boys. In F. Lowey (Ed.), Symposium on the seriously disturbed pre-school child. *Canadian Psychiatric Association Journal,* 1973, in press.

Patterson, G. R., & Gullion, M. E. *Living with children: New methods for parents and teachers.* Champaign, Ill.: Research Press, 1968.

Paul, G. L. *Insight vs. desensitization in psychotherapy.* Stanford, Calif.: Stanford University Press, 1966.

Paul, G. L. Insight versus desensitization in psychotherapy two years after termination. *Journal of Consulting Psychology,* 1967, **31**, 333-348.

Paul, G. L., & Shannon, D. T. Treatment of anxiety through systematic desensitization in therapy groups. *Journal of Abnormal Psychology,* 1966, **71**, 124-135.

Paulson, G. W., & Gottlieb, G. A. Longitudinal study of the electroencephalographic arousal response in depressed patients. *Journal of Nervous and Mental Disease,* 1961, **133**, 524-528.

Pavlov, I. P. *Lectures on conditioned reflexes.* New York: International Publishers, 1928.

Perls, F. S. *Gestalt therapy verbatim.* Moab, Utah: Real People Press, 1969.

Perls, F. S. Four lectures. In J. Fagan & I. L. Shepherd (Eds.), *Gestalt therapy now: Therapy, techniques, applications.* Palo Alto, Calif.: Science and Behavior Books, 1970.

Perls, F. S., Hefferline, R. F., & Goodman, P. *Gestalt therapy: Excitement and growth in the human personality.* New York: Julian Press, 1951.

Pervin, L. A. The need to predict and control under conditions of threat. *Journal of Personality,* 1963, **31**, 570-585.

Peters, J. E., & Stern, R. M. Specificity of attitude hypothesis in psychosomatic medicine: A re-examination. *Journal of Psychosomatic Research,* 1971, **15**, 129-135.

Pfeiffer, E., Eisenstein, R. B., & Dabbs, G. E. Mental competency evaluation for the federal courts: I. Methods and results. *Journal of Nervous and Mental Disease,* 1967, **144**, 320-328.

Phillips, E. L., Phillips, E. A., Fixsen, D. L., & Wolf, M. M. *The teaching-family handbook.* Lawrence, Kans.: Kansas Printing Service, 1972.

Phillips, L. Case history data and prognosis in schizophrenia. *Journal of Nervous and Mental Disease,* 1953, **117**, 515-525.

Pokorny, A. D. Myths about suicide. In H. L. P. Resnik (Ed.), *Suicidal behaviors.* Boston: Little, Brown, 1968.

Pollin, W., Cardon, P. V., & Kety, S. S. Effects of amino acid feedings in schizophrenic patients treated with iproniazid. *Science,* 1961. **133**, 104.

Popham, R. E., & Schmidt, W. *Statistics of alcohol use and alcoholism in Canada, 1871-1956.* Toronto, Canada: University of Toronto Press, 1958.

Price, R. H. *Abnormal behavior. Perspectives in conflict.* New York: Holt, Rinehart and Winston, 1972. (a)

Price, R. H. Psychological deficit versus impression management in schizophrenic word association performance. *Journal of Abnormal Psychology,* 1972, **79**, 132-137. (b)

Proctor, J. T. Hysteria in childhood. *American Journal of Orthopsychiatry,* 1956, **28**, 394-407.

Proshansky, H. M., Ittelson, W. M., & Rivlin, L. (Eds.) *Theory and research in environmental psychology.* New York: Holt, Rinehart and Winston, 1972.

Purcell, K., Brady, K., Chai, H., Muser, J., Molk, L., Gordon, N., & Means, J. The effect on asthma in children of experimental separation from the family. *Psychosomatic Medicine,* 1969, **31**, 144-164.

Purcell, K., & Weiss, J. H. Asthma. In C. G. Costello (Ed.), *Symptoms of psychopathology: A handbook.* New York: Wiley, 1970.

Quay, H. C. Psychopathic personality as pathological stimulus seeking. *American Journal of Psychiatry,* 1965, **122**, 180-183.

Rachman, S. Sexual fetishism: An experimental analogue. *Psychological Record,* 1966, **16**, 293-296.

Rado, S. An adaptational view of sexual behavior. In P. Hoch & J. Zubin (Eds.), *Psychosexual development in health and disease.* New York: Grune and Stratton, 1949.

Rapaport, D. *The organization and pathology of thought.* New York: Columbia University Press, 1951.

Rappaport, J., & Chinsky, J. M. Models for delivery of service: An historical and conceptual perspective. *Professional Psychology,* 1974, in press.

Rappaport, M. Competing voice mesages: Effects of message load and drugs on the ability of acute schizophrenics to attend. *Archives of General Psychiatry,* 1967, **17**, 97-103.

Raskin, A., Schulterbrandt, J., Boothe, J., Reatig, N., & McKeon, J. Treatment, social and psychiatric variables related to symptom reduction in hospitalized depressives. In J. R. Wittenborn, S. Goldberg, & P. May (Eds.), *Psychopharmacology and the individual patient.* New York: Raven Press, 1970.

Rees, L. The significance of parental attitudes in childhood asthma. *Journal of Psychosomatic Research,* 1963, **7**, 181-190.

Rees, L. The significance of parental attitudes in childhood asthma. *Journal of Psychosomatic Research,* 1964, **7**, 253-262.

Reid, E. C. Autopsychology of the manic-depressive. *Journal of Nervous and Mental Disease,* 1910, **37**, 606-620.

Reiss, A. J., Jr. The social integration of queers and peers. *Social Problems,* 1961, **9**, 102-120.

Reitan, R. M. Psychological deficits resulting from cerebral lesions in man. In J. M. Warren & K. Akert (Eds.), *The frontal granular cortex and behavior.* New York: McGraw-Hill, 1964.

Rescorla, R. A., & Solomon, R. L. Two-process learning theory: Relationships between Pavlovian conditioning and instrumental learning. *Psychological Review,* 1967, **74**, 151-182.

Resnik, H. L. P. (Ed.) *Suicidal behaviors.* Boston: Little, Brown, 1968.

Richards, L. G., & Carroll, E. E. Illicit drug use and addiction in the United States: Review of available statistics. *Public Health Reports,* 1970, **85**, 1035-1041.

Richter, C. P. On the phenomenon of sudden death in animals and man. *Psychosomatic Medicine,* 1957, **19**, 191-198.

Ridgeway, J. R. Who's fit to be free? *The New Republic,* 1967, **156**, 24-26.

Rimland, B. *Infantile autism.* New York: Appleton-Century-Crofts, 1964.

Rimland, B. Psychogenesis versus biogenesis: The issues and the evidence. In S. C. Plog & R. B. Edgerton (Eds.), *Changing perspectives in mental illness.* New York: Holt, Rinehart and Winston, 1969.

Rimland, B. The differentiation of childhood psychoses: An analysis of checklists for 2,218 psychotic children. *Journal of Autism and Childhood Schizophrenia,* 1971, **1**, 161-174.

Ringuette, E. L., & Kennedy, T. An experimental study of the double-bind hypothesis. *Journal of Abnormal Psychology,* 1966, **71**, 136-142.

Robbin, A. A. A controlled study of the effects of leucotomy. *Journal of Neurology, Neurosurgery, and Psychiatry,* 1958, **21**, 262-269.

Robbin, A. A. The value of leucotomy in relation to diagnosis. *Journal of Neurology, Neurosurgery, and Psychiatry,* 1959, **22**, 132-136.

Robbins, L. N. *Deviant children grown up.* Baltimore, Md.: Williams and Wilkins, 1966.

Robey, A. Criteria for competency to stand trial: A checklist for psychiatrists. *American Journal of Psychiatry,* 1965, **122**, 616-622.

Robinson, H. B., & Robinson, N. M. *The mentally retarded child: A psychological approach.* New York: McGraw-Hill, 1965.

Robinson, H. B., & Robinson, N. M. Mental retardation. In P. H. Mussen (Ed.), *Carmichael's manual of child psychology.* Vol. 2. (3rd ed.) New York: Wiley, 1970.

Rodnick, E. H., & Garmezy, N. An experimental approach to the study of motivation in schizophrenia. In M. R. Jones (Ed.), *Nebraska symposium on motivation.* Vol. 5. Lincoln: University of Nebraska Press, 1957.

Roe, A., Burks, B., & Mittelman, B. Adult adjustment of foster home children of alcoholic and psychotic parentage and the influence of the foster home. *Memoirs of the Section on Alcohol,* Yale University, 1945.

Rogers, C. R. *Counseling and psychotherapy: New concepts in practice.* Boston: Houghton Mifflin, 1942.

Rogers, C. R. *Client-centered therapy.* Boston: Houghton Mifflin, 1951.

Rogers, C. R. *On becoming a person: A therapist's view of psychotherapy.* Boston: Houghton Mifflin, 1961.

Rogers, C. R. *Carl Rogers on encounter groups.* New York: Harper and Row, 1970.

Rogers, C. R., & Dymond, R. F. (Eds.) *Psychotherapy and personality change.* Chicago: University of Chicago Press, 1954.

Rokeach, M. *The three Christs of Ypsilanti.* New York: Knopf, 1964.

Rosen, A., Hales, W.M., & Simon, W. Classification of suicidal patients. *Journal of Consulting Psychology,* 1954, **18**, 359-362.

Rosen, E., Fox, R., & Gregory, I. *Abnormal psychology.* (2nd ed.) Philadelphia: Saunders, 1972.

Rosenhan, D. L. On being sane in insane places. *Science,* 1973, **179**, 250-258.

Rosenthal, D. Changes in some moral values following psychotherapy. *Journal of Consulting Psychology,* 1955, **19**, 431-436.

Rosenthal, D. *Genetic theory and abnormal behavior.* New York: McGraw-Hill, 1970.

Rosenthal, R. *Experimenter bias in behavioral research.* New York: Appleton-Century-Crofts, 1966.

Ross, A. O. *Psychological disorders of children: A behavioral approach to theory, research and therapy.* New York: McGraw-Hill, 1974.

Ross, H. L. Modes of adjustment of married homosexuals. *Social Problems,* 1971, **18**, 385-393.

Roueche, B. *Alcohol: Its history, folklore, effects on the human body.* New York: Grove Press, 1962.

Rubin, R. T., Gunderson, E. K. E., & Doll, R. E. Life stress and illness patterns in the U.S. Navy. *Archives of Environmental Health,* 1969, **19**, 753-757.

Ruskin, A., Board, O. W., & Schaffer, R. L. Blast hypertension: Elevated arterial pressure in victims of the Texas City disaster. *American Journal of Medicine,* 1948, **4**, 228-236.

Rutter, M. The influence of organic and emotional factors on the origins, nature and outcome of childhood psychosis. *Developmental Medicine and Child Neurology,* 1965, **7**, 518-528.

Rutter, M. Prognosis: Psychotic children in adolescence and early adult life. In J. K. Wing (Ed.), *Childhood autism: Clinical, educational, and social aspects.* Elmsford, N.Y.: Pergamon Press, 1966.

Rutter, M. Psychotic disorders in early childhood. In A. J. Cooper (Ed.), Recent developments in schizophrenia. *British Journal of Psychiatry,* 1967, special publication.

Rutter, M. Concepts of autism: A review of research. *Journal of Child Psychology and Psychiatry,* 1968, **9**, 1-25.

Rutter, M., & Lockyear, L. A five to fifteen year follow-up of infantile psychosis I. Description of sample. *British Journal of Psychiatry,* 1967, **113**, 1169-1182.

Ryan, D. V., & Neale, J. M. Test taking sets and the performance of schizophrenics on laboratory tasks. *Journal of Abnormal Psychology,* 1973, in press.

Saghir, M. T., & Robins, E. Homosexuality: I. Sexual behavior of the female homosexual. *Archives of General Psychiatry,* 1969, **20**, 192-201.

Saghir, M. T., Robins, E., & Walbran, B. Homosexuality: II. Sexual behavior of the male homosexual. *Archives of General Psychiatry,* 1969, **21**, 219-229.

Salter, A. *Conditioned reflex therapy.* New York: Farrar, Straus, 1949.

Sandifer, M. G., Pettus, C., & Quade, D. A study of psychiatric diagnosis. *Journal of Nervous and Mental Disease,* 1964, **139**, 350-356.

Sarason, I. G. *Abnormal psychology: The problem of maladaptive behavior.* New York: Appleton-Century-Crofts, 1972.

Sarbin, T. R. Contributions to role-taking theory: I. Hypnotic behavior. *Psychological Review,* 1950, **57**, 255-270.

Sawrey, W. L., & Weisz, J. D. An experimental method of producing gastric ulcers: Role of psychological factors in the production of gastric ulcers in the rat. *Journal of Comparative and Physiological Psychology,* 1956, **49**, 457-461.

Schachter, S., & Latané, B. Crime, cognition, and the autonomic nervous system. In D. Levine (Ed.), *Nebraska symposium on motivation.* Vol. 12. Lincoln: University of Nebraska Press, 1964.

Scheerer, M., Rothman, E., & Goldstein, K. A case of "idiot savant": An experimental study of personality organization. *Psychological Monographs,* 1945, **58** (Whole No. 269).

Schmauk, F. J. Punishment, arousal, and avoidance learning in sociopaths. *Journal of Abnormal Psychology,* 1970, **76**, 443-453.

Schultes, R. E. Hallucinogens of plant origin. *Science,* 1969, **163**, 250.

Schur, E. M. Drug addiction in England and America. In D. Wakefield (Ed.), *The Addict.* Greenwich, Conn.: Fawcett Publications, 1965.

Schutz, W. C. *Joy.* New York: Grove Press, 1967.

Schwartz, M. S. The economic and spatial mobility of paranoid schizophrenics. Unpublished M.A. thesis, University of Chicago, 1946.

Sears, R. R., Maccoby, E. E., & Levin, H. *Patterns of child rearing.* Evanston, Ill.: Row, Peterson, 1957.

Seligman, M. E. P. Depression and learned helplessness. In R. J. Friedman & M. M. Katz (Eds.), *The psychology of depression: Contemporary theory and research.* Washington, D.C.: Winston-Wiley, in press.

Seligman, M. E. P. Phobias and preparedness. *Behavior Therapy,* 1971, **2**, 307-320.

Selling, L. S. *Men against madness.* New York: Greenberg, Publisher, 1940.

Selye, H. *The stress of life.* New York: McGraw-Hill, 1956.

Serber, M. The experiential group as entertainment. In P. S. Houts & M. Serber (Eds.), *After the turn-on, what? Learning perspectives on hu-*

manistic groups. Champaign, Ill.: Research Press, 1972.

Shaffer, H. R., & Emerson, P. E. Patterns of response to physical contact in early human development. *Journal of Child Psychology and Psychiatry,* 1964, **5**, 1-13.

Shagass, C., & Schwartz, M. Cerebral cortical reactivity in psychotic depressives. *Archives of General Psychiatry,* 1962, **6**, 235-242.

Shakow, D. Psychological deficit in schizophrenia. *Behavior Science,* 1963, **8**, 275-305.

Shapiro, A. K. A contribution to a history of the placebo effect. *Behavioral Science,* 1960, **5**, 109-135.

Shapiro, A. K. Placebo effects in medicine, psychotherapy, and psychoanalysis. In A. E. Bergin & S. L. Garfield (Eds.), *Handbook of psychotherapy and behavior change: An empirical analysis.* New York: Wiley, 1971.

Shapiro, A. P. An experimental study of comparative responses of blood pressure to different noxious stimuli. *Journal of Chronic Diseases,* 1961, **13**, 293-311.

Shaw, D. M. Mineral metabolism, mania, and melancholia. *British Medical Journal,* 1966, **2**, 262-267.

Sherman, A. R. Real-life exposure as a primary therapeutic factor in the desensitization treatment of fear. *Journal of Abnormal Psychology,* 1972, **79**, 19-28.

Shneidman, E. S. Suicide. In *Encyclopedia Britannica.* Chicago: Encyclopedia Britannica, 1973.

Shneidman, E. S., & Farberow, N. L. A psychological approach to the study of suicide notes. In E. S. Shneidman, N. L. Farberow, & R. E. Litman (Eds.), *The psychology of suicide.* New York: Jason Aronson, 1970.

Shneidman, E. S., Farberow, N. L., & Litman, R. E. (Eds.) *The psychology of suicide.* New York: Jason Aronson, 1970.

Siegel, M., Niswander, G. D., Sachs, E., & Stravros, D. Taraxein: Fact or artifact? *American Journal of Psychiatry,* 1959, **115**, 819-820.

Silverstein, C. Behavior modification and the gay community. Paper presented at the annual convention of the Association for Advancement of Behavior Therapy, New York City, 1972.

Simeons, A. T. W. *Man's presumptuous brain: An evolutionary interpretation of psychosomatic disease.* New York: Dutton, 1961.

Simon, W., & Gagnon, J. H. The lesbians: A preliminary overview. In J. H. Gagnon & W. Simon (Eds.), *Sexual deviance.* New York: Harper and Row, 1967.

Simon, W., & Gagnon, J. H. Psychosexual development. In J. H. Gagnon & W. Simon (Eds.), *The sexual scene.* Chicago: Aldine, 1970.

Simon, W., & Gilberstadt, H. Analysis of the personality structure of 26 actual suicides. *Journal of Nervous and Mental Disease,* 1958, **127**, 555-557.

Singer, M., & Wynne, L. C. Differentiating characteristics of the parents of childhood schizophrenics, childhood neurotics, and young adult schizophrenics. *American Journal of Psychiatry,* 1963, **120**, 234-243.

Skinner, B. F. *Science and human behavior.* New York: Macmillan, 1953.

Skinner, B. F. "Superstition" in the pigeon. *Journal of Experimental Psychology,* 1948, **38**, 168-172.

Skrzypek, G. J. The effects of perceptual isolation and arousal on anxiety, complexity preference and novelty preference in psychopathic and neurotic delinquents. *Journal of Abnormal Psychology,* 1969, **74**, 321-329.

Slater, E. The thirty-fifth Maudsley lecture: Hysteria 311. *Journal of Mental Science,* 1961, **107**, 358-381.

Slater, E., & Glithero, E. A follow-up of patients diagnosed as suffering from hysteria. *Journal of Psychosomatic Research,* 1965, **9**, 9-13.

Slater, E., & Shields, J. Genetic aspects of anxiety. In M. H. Lader (Ed.), *Studies of anxiety.* Ashford, England: Headley Brothers, 1969.

Slavson, S. R. *Analytic group psychotherapy with children, adolescents and adults.* New York: Columbia University Press, 1950.

Smith, B. H. *Principles of clinical neurology.* Chicago: Year Book Medical Publishers, 1965.

Solomon, R. L., Kamin, L. J., & Wynne, L. C. Traumatic avoidance learning: The outcomes of several extinction procedures with dogs. *Journal of Abnormal and Social Psychology,* 1953, **48**, 291-302.

Sommer, R. *Personal space: The behavioral basis of design.* Englewood Cliffs, N.J.: Prentice-Hall, 1969.

Spanos, N. P. Barber's reconceptualization of hypnosis: An evaluation of criticisms. *Journal of Experimental Research in Personality*, 1970, **4**, 241-258.

Speer, D. C. Rate of caller re-use of a telephone crisis service. *Crisis Intervention*, 1971, **3**, 83-86.

Speer, D. C. An evaluation of a telephone crisis service. Paper presented at Midwestern Psychological Association meeting, Cleveland, Ohio, 1972.

Spitzer, R., & Endicott, J. Diagno II: Further developments in a computer program for psychiatric diagnosis. *American Journal of Psychiatry*, 1969, **125**, 12-21.

Spring, G., Schweid, D., Gray, G., Steinberg, J., & Horwitz, M. A double-blind comparison of lithium and chlorpromazine in the treatment of manic states. *American Journal of Psychiatry*, 1970, **126**, 1306-1309.

Srole, L., Langner, T. S., Michael, S. T., Opler, M. K., & Rennie, T. A. C. *Mental health in the metropolis: The midtown Manhattan study.* New York: McGraw-Hill, 1962.

Staats, A. W., & Staats, C. K. *Complex human behavior.* New York: Holt, Rinehart and Winston, 1963.

Stearns, J. *The sixth man.* New York: Macfadden-Bartell, 1961.

Stephens, J. H., & Kamp, M. On some aspects of hysteria: A clinical study. *Journal of Nervous and Mental Disease*, 1962, **134**, 305-315.

Sternbach, R. A. *Principles of psychophysiology.* New York: Academic Press, 1966.

Stoller, F. H. Accelerated interaction: A time-limited approach based on the brief intensive group. *International Journal of Group Psychotherapy*, 1968, **18**, 220-235.

Stone, L. J., & Hokanson, J. E. Arousal reduction via self-punitive behavior. *Journal of Personality and Social Psychology*, 1969, **12**, 72-79.

Szasz, T. S. The myth of mental illness. *American Psychologist*, 1960, **15**, 113-118.

Szasz, T. S. *Law, liberty, and psychiatry.* New York: Macmillan, 1963.

Szasz, T. S. *The manufacture of madness.* New York: Harper and Row, 1970.

Tate, B. G., & Baroff, G. S. Aversive control of self-injurious behavior in a psychotic boy. *Behaviour Research and Therapy*, 1966, **4**, 281-287.

Taterks, S., & Kety, S. S. Study of correlation between electroencephalogram and psychological patterns in emotionally disturbed children. *Psychosomatic Medicine*, 1955, **17**, 62-72.

Taylor, J. A. A personality scale of manifest anxiety. *Journal of Abnormal and Social Psychology*, 1953, **48**, 285-290.

Terman, L. M. Kinsey's *Sexual Behavior in the Human Male:* Some comments and criticisms. *Psychological Bulletin*, 1948, **45**, 443-459.

Thigpen, C. H., & Cleckley, H. *The three faces of Eve.* Kingsport, Tenn.: Kingsport Press, 1954.

Thorndike, E. L. *The psychology of wants, interests and attitudes.* New York: Appleton, Century, 1935.

Tramontana, J., & Stimbert, V. Some techniques of behavior modification with an autistic child. *Psychological Reports*, 1970, **27**, 498.

Treese, R. L. Homosexuality: A contemporary view of the biblical perspective. Paper prepared for the Consultation on Theology and the Homosexual, Glide Urban Center and the Council on Religion and the Homosexual, San Francisco, August 22-24, 1966.

Treffert, D. A. The epidemiology of infantile autism. *Archives of General Psychiatry*, 1970, **22**, 431-438.

Truax, C. B. Reinforcement and nonreinforcement in Rogerian psychotherapy. *Journal of Abnormal Psychology*, 1966, **71**, 1-9.

Tuckman, J., Kleiner, R. J., & Lavell, M. Emotional content of suicide notes. *American Journal of Psychiatry*, 1959, **116**, 59-63.

Turner, R. J., & Wagonfeld, M. O. Occupational mobility and schizophrenia. *American Sociological Review*, 1967, **32**, 104-113.

Ullmann, L. P., & Krasner, L. *A psychological approach to abnormal behavior.* Englewood Cliffs, N.J.: Prentice-Hall, 1969.

Umbarger, C. C., Dalsimer, J. S., Morrison, A. P., & Breggin, P. R. *College students in a mental hospital.* New York: Grune and Stratton, 1962.

United States Department of Health, Education and Welfare. *Smoking and health,* Public Health Service Publication No. 1103. Washington, D.C.: U.S. Government Printing Office, 1964.

Von Felsinger, J. M., Lasagna, L., & Beecher, H. K. The response of normal men to lysergic acid derivatives. *Journal of Clinical and Experimental Psychopathology,* 1956, **17**, 414-428.

Von Wright, J. M., Pekanmaki, L., & Malin, S. Effects of conflict and stress on alcohol intake in rats. *Quarterly Journal of Studies on Alcohol,* 1971, **32**, 420-441.

Waldfogel, S. Emotional crisis in a child. In A. Burton (Ed.), *Case studies in counseling and psychotherapy,* Englewood Cliffs. N.J.: Prentice-Hall, 1959.

Wallen, R. Gestalt therapy and Gestalt psychology. In J. Fagan & I. L. Shepherd (Eds.), *Gestalt therapy now: Theory, techniques, applications.* Palo Alto, Calif.: Science and Behavior Books, 1970.

Wallerstein, R. S. et al. *Hospital treatment of alcoholism: A comparative, experimental study.* New York: Basic Books, 1957.

Walters, C., Shurley, J. T., & Parsons, O. A. Difference in male and female responses to underwater sensory deprivation: An exploratory study. *Journal of Nervous and Mental Disease,* 1962, **135**, 302-310.

Ward, C. H., Beck, A. T., Mendelson, M., Mock, J. E., & Erbaugh, J. K. The psychiatric nomenclature: Reasons for diagnostic disagreement. *Archives of General Psychiatry,* 1962, **7**, 198-205.

Watson, J. B. Psychology as the behaviorist views it. *Psychological Review,* 1913, **20**, 158-177.

Watson, J. B., & Rayner, R. Conditioned emotional reactions. *Journal of Experimental Psychology,* 1920, **3**, 1-14.

Watt, N. F., Stolorow, R. D., Lubensky, A. W., & McClelland, D. C. School adjustment and behavior of children hospitalized for schizophrenia as adults. *American Journal of Orthopsychiatry,* 1970, **40**, 637-657.

Webb, W. W. Conceptual ability of schizophrenics as a function of threat of failure. *Journal of Abnormal and Social Psychology,* 1955, **50**, 221-224.

Weinberg, G. *Society and the healthy homosexual.* New York: St. Martin's Press, 1972.

Weinberg, M. S. The male homosexual: Age-related variations in social and psychological characteristics. *Social Problems,* 1970, **17**, 527-537.

Weiner, H., Thaler, M., Reiser, M. F., & Mirsky, I. A. Etiology of duodenal ulcer: I. Relation of specific psychological characteristics to rate of gastric secretion. *Psychosomatic Medicine,* 1957, **19**, 1-10.

Weiner, J. W. The effectiveness of a suicide prevention program. *Mental Hygiene,* 1969, **53**, 357-363.

Weitzenhoffer, A. M., & Hilgard, E. R. *Stanford hypnotic susceptibility scale, Forms A and B.* Palo Alto, Calif.: Consulting Psychologists Press, 1959.

West, D. J. *Homosexuality.* Chicago: Aldine, 1967.

White, W. A. *Outlines of psychiatry.* (13 ed.) New York: Nervous and Mental Disease Publishing Company, 1932.

Whitlock, F. A. The aetiology of hysteria. *Acta Psychiatrica Scandinavica,* 1967, **43**, 144-162.

Wickens, D. D., Allen, C. K., & Hill, F. A. Effects of instruction on extinction of the conditioned GSR. *Journal of Experimental Psychology,* 1963, **66**, 235-240.

Wiggins, J. Inconsistent socialization. *Psychological Reports,* 1968, **23**, 303-336.

Wilkins, R. H., & Brody, I. A. Alzheimer's disease. *Archives of Neurology,* 1969, **21**, 109-110.

Williams, H., & McNicol, K. N. Prevalence, natural history and relationship of wheezy bronchitis and asthma in children: An epidemiological study. *British Medical Journal,* 1969, **4**, 321-325.

Williams, R. J. Biochemical individuality and cellular nutrition. Prime factors in alcoholism. *Quarterly Journal of Studies on Alcohol,* 1959, **20**, 452-463.

Williams, W. S., & Jaco, E. G. An evaluation of functional psychosis in old age. *American Journal of Psychiatry,* 1958, **110**, 910-916.

Wilson, G. T., & Davison, G. C. Aversion techniques in behavior therapy: Some theoretical and metatheoretical considerations. *Journal of Consulting and Clinical Psychology,* 1969, **33,** 327-329.

Wilson, G. T., & Davison, G. C. Processes of fear reduction in systematic desensitization: Animal studies. *Psychological Bulletin,* 1971, **76,** 1-14.

Wilson, G. T., & Davison, G. C. Behavior therapy and homosexuality: A critical perspective. *Behavior Therapy,* 1973, in press.

Wing, L. The handicaps of autistic children: A comparative study. *Journal of Child Psychology and Psychiatry,* 1969, **10,** 1-40.

Wing, L. The syndrome of early childhood autism. *British Journal of Hospital Medicine,* Sept. 1970, 381-392.

Winick, M., Rosso, P., & Waterlow, J. Cellular growth of cerebrum, cerebellum, and brain stem in normal and marasmic children. *Experimental Neurology,* 1970, **26,** 393-400.

Wittman, C. Refugees from Amerika: A gay manifesto. *San Francisco Free Press,* January 7, 1970.

Wolberg, L. R. *The technique of psychotherapy.* New York: Grune and Stratton, 1954.

Wolf, A. The psychoanalysis of group. *American Journal of Psychotherapy,* 1949, **3,** 16-50.

Wolf, M., Risley, T., & Mees, H. Application of operant conditioning procedures to the behavior problems of an autistic child. *Behavior Research and Therapy,* 1964, **1,** 305-312.

Wolf, S., & Goodell, H. *Harold G. Wolff's stress and disease.* (2nd ed.) Springfield, Ill.: Charles C Thomas, 1968.

Wolpe, J. *Psychotherapy by reciprocal inhibition.* Stanford, Calif.: Stanford University Press, 1958.

Wolpe, J. *The practice of behavior therapy.* Elmsford, N.Y.: Pergamon Press, 1969.

Wolpe, J., & Lazarus, A. A. *Behavior therapy techniques: A guide to the treatment of neuroses.* Elmsford, N.Y.: Pergamon Press, 1966.

Wolpe, J., & Rachman, S. Psychoanalytic "evidence," a critique based on Freud's case of Little Hans. *Journal of Nervous and Mental Disease,* 1960, **131,** 135-147.

World Health Organization. *World Health Statistics Annual, 1969.* Geneva, Switzerland: 1972.

Yablonsky, L. The anti-criminal society: Synanon. *Federal Probation,* 1962, **26,** 50-57.

Yablonsky, L. *Synanon: The tunnel back.* Baltimore: Penguin Books, 1967.

Yalom, I. D., & Lieberman, M. A. A study of encounter group casualties. *Archives of General Psychiatry,* 1971, **25,** 16-30.

Yurchenco, H. *A mighty hard road: The Woody Guthrie Story.* New York: McGraw-Hill, 1970.

Zaslow, R. W., & Breger, L. A theory and treatment of autism. In L. Breger (Ed.), *Clinical cognitive psychology.* Englewood Cliffs, N.J.: Prentice-Hall, 1969.

Zax, M., & Cowen, E. L. *Abnormal psychology: Changing conceptions.* New York: Holt, Rinehart and Winston, 1972.

Zeigler, F. J., Imboden, J. B., & Meyer, E. Contemporary conversion reactions: A clinical study. *American Journal of Psychiatry,* 1960, **116,** 901-910.

Zigler, E. Mental retardation. In P. London & D. Rosenhan (Eds.), *Foundations of abnormal psychology.* New York: Holt, Rinehart and Winston, 1968.

Zigler, E. Development versus difference theories of mental retardation and the problem of motivation. *American Journal of Mental Deficiency,* 1969, **73,** 536-556.

Zigler, E., Butterfield, E. C., & Capobianco, F. Institutionalization and the effectiveness of social reinforcement: A five- and eight-year follow-up study. *Developmental Psychology,* 1970, **3,** 255-263.

Zigler, E., & Phillips, L. Psychiatric diagnosis and symptomatology. *Journal of Abnormal and Social Psychology,* 1961, **63,** 69-75.

Zilboorg, G., & Henry, G. W. *A history of medical psychology.* New York: Norton, 1941.

Glossary

Acute schizophrenic. Patient who has shown a rapid onset of schizophrenic behavior and has had little hospitalization.

Addiction. See *drug addiction*.

Addison's disease. An endocrine disorder produced by *cortisone*[1] insufficiency and marked by weight loss, fatigue, and a darkening of the skin.

Adrenal glands. Two small areas of tissue, located just above the kidneys; the inner core of each gland, the medulla, secretes *epinephrine* and *norepinephrine*, the outer cortex, *cortisone* and other steroid hormones.

Adrenaline. A hormone which is secreted by the *adrenal glands*; also called *epinephrine*.

Affect. A subjective feeling or emotional tone often accompanied by bodily expressions noticeable to others.

Affective disorder. A *psychosis* characterized by disabling mood disturbances.

Affirming the consequent. An error in logic by which, if A causes B on one occasion, it is assumed that A is the cause when B is observed on any other occasion.

Agoraphobia. A cluster of fears centering around being in open spaces and leaving the home.

Alcoholism. A behavioral disorder marked by continuous and excessive consumption of alcoholic beverages; a physiological dependence on alcohol. See *drug addiction*.

Alkaloid. Organic base found in seed plants, usually in mixture with a number of similar alkaloids; alkaloids are the active chemicals giving many drugs their medicinal properties and other powerful physiological effects.

Alpha rhythm. The dominant pattern (8 to 13 cps) of the *brain waves* of a resting but awake adult.

Altruistic suicide. As defined by Durkheim, self-annihilation that the person feels will serve a social purpose, such as the self-immolations practiced by Buddhist monks during the Vietnam war.

Alzheimer's disease. A *presenile dementia* involving a progressive atrophy of cortical tissue and marked by speech impairment, involuntary movements of limbs, occasional *convulsions*, intellectual deterioration, and psychotic behavior.

Ambivalence. The simultaneous holding of strong positive and negative emotional attitudes toward the same situation or person.

American Law Institute Guidelines. Rules proposing insanity to be a legitimate defense plea if during criminal conduct individual could not judge right from wrong or control his behavior as required by law. Repetitive criminal acts are disavowed as a sole criterion. Compare *McNaghten rule* and *irresistible impulse*.

[1] Italicized words or variants of these terms are themselves defined elsewhere in the glossary.

Amino acid. One of a large class of organic compounds, important as the building blocks of proteins.

Amnesia. Total or partial loss of memory which can be associated with *hysteria,* an *organic brain syndrome,* or *hypnosis.*

Amphetamines. A group of stimulating drugs which produce heightened levels of energy and, in large doses, nervousness, sleeplessness, and paranoid *delusions.*

Anaclitic depression. Profound sadness of an infant when separated from its mother for a prolonged period.

Anal stage. In psychoanalytic theory, the second *psychosexual stage,* occurring during the second year of life, during which the anus is considered to be the principal *erogenous zone.*

Analgesia. Insensitivity to pain without loss of consciousness; sometimes found in *hysterical conversion reaction.*

Analogue experiment. Experimental study of a phenomenon different from but related to the actual interests of the investigator.

Analysand. A person being psychoanalyzed.

Analyst. See *psychoanalyst.*

Anesthesia. Impairment or loss of sensation, usually of touch but sometimes of the other senses; often part of *hysterical conversion reaction.*

Animal phobias. Fear and avoidance of small animals.

Anomic suicide. As defined by Durkheim, self-annihilation triggered by the person's inability to cope with sudden and unfavorable change in his social situation.

Anorexia. A *psychophysiological disorder* characterized by the inability to eat or to retain any food or by a prolonged and severe diminution of appetite.

Anoxia. Deficiency in oxygen reaching the tissues severe enough to damage the brain permanently.

Antabuse (disulfiram). A drug which makes the drinking of alcohol produce nausea and other unpleasant effects.

Antidepressant. A drug which alleviates *depression,* usually by energizing the patient and thus elevating mood.

Antisocial personality. A diagnosis applied to individuals who have repeated conflicts with society, are selfish, do not experience guilt, and are incapable of loyalty to others. The term is synonymous with sociopath and psychopath.

Anxiety. An unpleasant feeling of generalized fear and apprehension accompanied by increased physiological arousal. In learning theory considered a drive which mediates between a threatening situation and avoidance behavior. Anxiety can be assessed by self-report, by measuring physiological arousal, and by observing overt behavior.

Anxiety neurosis. Disorder in which anxiety is felt in so many situations that it appears to have no specific cause; in addition to diffuse anxiety, the patient may suffer acute attacks. Often referred to as *free-floating anxiety.*

Aphasia. Loss or impairment of the ability to use language because of lesions in the brain. **Executive,** difficulties in speaking or writing the words intended. **Receptive,** difficulties in understanding written or spoken language.

Arousal. A state of activation, either behavioral or physiological.

Ascriptive responsibility. The social judgment that someone who has committed an illegal act should be punished for it; contrast with *descriptive responsibility.*

Assertive training. *Behavior therapy* procedures which attempt to help a person express more easily his legitimate feelings of resentment or approval.

Asthma. A *psychophysiological disorder* characterized by narrowing of the airways and increased secretion of mucus, which often cause breathing to be extremely labored and wheezy.

Attention. Maintenance of a readiness to respond; or focusing on relevant information.

Aura. Signal or warning of an impending epileptic *convulsion,* taking the form of dizziness or an unusual sensory experience.

Autism. Absorption in self or fantasy as a means of avoiding communication or escaping objective reality. See also *infantile autism.*

Autonomic nervous system. Division of the nervous system which regulates involuntary functions; innervates *endocrine glands, smooth muscle,* and heart muscle; initiates the physiological changes that are part of expression of emotion.

Aversive conditioning. A *behavior therapy* procedure which pairs a noxious stimulus, such as a shock, with situations that are undesirably attractive.

Aversive stimulus. A stimulus that elicits pain, fear, or avoidance.

Avoidance learning. An experimental procedure in which a neutral stimulus is paired with a noxious one so that the organism learns to avoid the previously neutral stimulus.

Barbiturate. A class of synthetic *sedative* drugs which are addictive and in large doses can cause death because the diaphragm relaxes almost completely.

Basal ganglia. Clusters of nerve cell bodies (*nuclei*) deep within the *cerebral hemispheres*.

Behavior assessment. Sampling of ongoing conditions, feelings, and overt behavior in their situational context, to be contrasted with the *projective test* and *personality inventory*.

Behavior genetics. The study of individual differences in behavior that are attributable in part to differences in genetic makeup.

Behavior modification, behavior therapy. A branch of psychotherapy narrowly conceived as the application of *classical* and *operant conditioning* to the alteration of clinical problems, but more broadly conceived as applied experimental psychology.

Behavior rehearsal. A *behavior therapy* technique in which a client practices a new behavior in the consulting room, often aided by demonstrations of the therapist.

Behaviorism. School of psychology associated with John B. Watson, who proposed that observable behavior, not consciousness, is the proper subject matter of psychology. Currently, some who consider themselves behaviorists do use *mediational* concepts, provided they are firmly anchored to observables.

Beriberi. A disease attributed to lack of *thiamine* and marked by irritability, fatigue, insomnia, and weakened muscles.

Beta rhythm. The dominant pattern (14 to 25 cps) of *brain waves* found in an alert adult responding to a stimulus. See also *alpha rhythm*.

Biophysical system. As applied by Masters and Johnson, the part of the sexual response system that includes the genitalia and *hormones*.

Bisexual. One who engages in both *heterosexual* and *homosexual* relations.

Borderline mental retardation. A limitation in mental development measured on IQ tests at between 68 and 83; people in this IQ range are usually not included in statistics on retardation and are able to achieve vocational and social competence.

Brain wave. Rhythmic fluctuations in voltage between parts of the brain produced by the spontaneous firings of its *neurons*; recorded by the *electroencephalograph*.

Brainstem. The part of the brain connecting the spinal cord with the *cerebrum*; contains the *pons* and *medulla oblongata* and functions as a neural relay station.

Butch (dyke). Slang terms for a *lesbian* whose dress and appearance are not feminine and who has assumed some aspects of the male role.

Case study. The collection of historical or biographical information on a single individual, often including his experiences in therapy.

Castration. Technically, surgical removal of the *testes* or ovaries, but in the vernacular may refer to removal of the *penis*.

Castration anxiety. Fear of having the genitals removed or injured.

Catatonic immobility (catatonia). Fixity of posture, sometimes grostesque, maintained for long periods with accompanying muscular rigidity, trancelike state of consciousness, and *waxy flexibility*.

Catatonic schizophrenic. Psychotic patient whose primary symptoms alternate between stuporous immobility and excited agitation.

Cathartic method. Therapeutic procedure introduced by Breuer in late nineteenth century whereby a patient relives an earlier emotional catastrophe and reexperiences the tension and unhappiness.

Central nervous system. The part of the nervous system which in vertebrates consists of the brain and spinal cord and to which all sensory impulses are transmitted and from which motor impulses pass out; also supervises and coordinates the activities of the entire nervous system.

Central sulcus. A major fissure transversing the middle of the top and lateral surfaces of each *cerebral hemisphere,* dividing the *frontal lobe* from the *parietal.*

Cerebellum. An area of the hindbrain concerned with balance, posture, and motor coordination.

Cerebral arteriosclerosis. A chronic disease impairing intellectual and emotional life and caused by a reduction in the brain's blood supply through a buildup of fatty deposits in the arteries.

Cerebral cortex. Thin outer covering of each of the *cerebral hemispheres,* highly convoluted, and made up of nerve cell bodies, which constitute the *gray matter* of the brain.

Cerebral hemisphere. Either of the two halves which make up the *cerebrum.*

Cerebral hemorrhage. Bleeding onto brain tissue from ruptured blood vessel.

Cerebral thrombosis. Formation of blood clot in cerebral artery, blocking circulation in that area of brain tissue and producing paralysis, loss of sensory functions, and even death.

Cerebrovascular accident (stroke). Internal injury to brain tissue through rupture or blocking of a large blood vessel in the *cerebrum,* impairing mental functioning.

Cerebrum. Two-lobed structure extending from the *brainstem* and constituting anterior part of brain. Largest and most recently developed portion of brain in man; coordinates sensory and motor activities as well as being seat of higher cognitive processes.

Childhood schizophrenia. A disorder usually distinguished from *infantile autism* and characterized by onset after age five, gross emotional impairment, perceptual distortions, and peculiar body movements.

Chlorpromazine. Generic term for one of the most widely used *major tranquilizers,* sold under the name *Thorazine.*

Choreiform. Pertaining to the involuntary, spasmodic, jerking movements of the limbs and

head found in *Huntington's chorea* and other nervous disorders.

Chromosomes. Threadlike bodies within the nucleus of the cell, DNA being the principal constituent: regarded as carrying the *genes.*

Chronic. Of lengthy duration or recurring frequently, often with progressing seriousness.

Chronic schizophrenic. Psychotic patient who had deteriorated over a long period of time before diagnosis and who has usually been hospitalized for more than two years.

Chronic undifferentiated schizophrenia. A diagnosis frequently applied to patients who do not fit neatly into one of the other *schizophrenic* subcategories.

Civil commitment. Procedure whereby a person can be legally certified as mentally ill and hospitalized, even against his will.

Clang association. A stringing together of words because they are similar in sound, with no attention paid to their meaning, for example, "How are you Don, pawn, gone?"

Classical conditioning. A basic form of learning whereby a neutral stimulus is repeatedly paired with another stimulus (called the *unconditioned stimulus,* UCS) that naturally elicits a certain desired response (UCR). After repeated trials the neutral stimulus becomes a *conditioned stimulus* (CS) and evokes the same or similar response, called now the *conditioned response* (CR).

Client-centered therapy. A *humanistic-existential insight therapy,* developed by Carl Rogers, which emphasizes the importance of the therapist's understanding the client's subjective experiences and assisting him to increase his awareness of the current motivations for his behavior; the goal is not only to reduce anxieties but also to foster actualization of the client's potential.

Climacteric. The period of life in late middle age when the female's menstruation ceases and the sexual activity and competence of the male may be reduced.

Clinical psychologist. An individual who has usually earned a Ph.D. degree in psychology and whose training includes an internship in a mental hospital or clinic.

Clitoris. Small heavily innervated erectile structure located above the vaginal opening; primary site of female responsiveness to sexual stimulation.

Clonic phase. Stage of violent contortions and jerking of limbs in a *grand mal epileptic* attack.

Cocaine. A pain-reducing and stimulating *alkaloid* obtained from coca leaves; increases mental powers, produces euphoria, and heightens sexual desire.

Cognitive restructuring. A *behavior therapy* procedure which attempts to alter the manner in which the client thinks about his life so that he changes his overt behavior.

Coitus. Sexual intercourse.

Colic. A condition sometimes found in infants in which gas collects in the stomach and produces distress.

Community mental health, community psychology. An approach to therapy which emphasizes prevention and the seeking out of potential difficulties rather than waiting for troubled individuals to initiate consultation. The location for professional activities tends to be in the persons' natural environment rather than in the therapist's office.

Competency to stand trial. Legal decision whether a person can participate meaningfully in his own defense.

Compulsion. Irresistible impulse to repeat an irrational act over and over again.

Concordance. As applied in *behavior genetics*, the similarity in psychiatric diagnosis or in other traits in a pair of twins.

Concrete reasoning. A pattern of thinking in which abstractions and generalizations cannot be made and terms and details of conversation are interpreted literally.

Concussion. A jarring injury to the brain produced by a blow to the head; usually involves a momentary loss of consciousness followed by transient disorientation and memory loss.

Conditioned response (CR). Response elicited by a given neutral stimulus (CS), after it has be-

come conditioned by repeated contingent pairings with another stimulus (UCS) that naturally elicits this same or similar response.

Conditioned stimulus (CS). A neutral stimulus which, after repeated contingent pairings with another stimulus (UCS) that naturally elicits a certain response (UCR), comes to elicit the same or a similar response, called the *conditioned response* (CR).

Confabulation. Filling in gaps in memory caused by brain dysfunction with made-up and often improbable stories which the subject accepts as true.

Confounds. Variables whose effects are so intermixed that they cannot be measured separately, making the design of the *experiment* internally invalid and its results impossible to interpret.

Congenital. Existing at or before birth but not acquired through heredity.

Construct. An entity inferred by a scientist to explain observed phenomena. See also *mediator*.

Contingency. A close relationship, especially of a causal nature, between two events, one of which regularly follows the other.

Control group. Subjects in an *experiment* for whom the *independent variable* is not manipulated, thus forming a base line against which the effects of the manipulation can be evaluated.

Contusion, cerebral. A bruising of neural tissue marked by swelling and hemorrhage and resulting in coma; may permanently impair intellectual functioning.

Convulsion. Violent and extensive twitching of the body caused by involuntary pathological muscle contractions.

Convulsive therapy. A biological therapy which induces *convulsions* by drugs or electric shock in hopes of effecting beneficial behavior change. See *electroconvulsive therapy*.

Coprophilia. Marked interest in excrement and in handling feces for sexual gratification.

Corpus callosum. Large band of nerve fibers connecting the two *cerebral hemispheres*.

Correlational method. Research strategy used to establish whether two or more variables are related. Such relationships may be positive—

as values for one variable increase, those for the other do also—or negative—as values for one variable increase, those for the other decrease.

Cortisone. A hormone secreted by the adrenal cortices.

Co-twin. In a *behavior genetic* study using the *twin method*, the member of the pair who is tested later to determine whether he has the same diagnosis or trait discovered earlier in his birth partner, the *index case*.

Counterconditioning. Relearning achieved by eliciting a new response in the presence of a particular stimulus.

Covert sensitization. A form of aversive therapy in which the subject is told to imagine the undesirably attractive situations and activities at the same time that unpleasant feelings are induced by imagery.

Cretinism. Condition beginning in prenatal or early life characterized by *mental retardation* and physical deformities; caused by severe deficiency in the output of the *thyroid gland*.

Critical period. Stage of early development in which organism needs certain inputs and during which important irreversible patterns of behavior are acquired. See *imprinting*.

Cultural-familial retardation. Mild backwardness in mental development with no indication of brain pathology but evidence of similar limitation in at least one of the parents or siblings.

Cunnilingus. Oral stimulation of female genitalia.

Cushing's syndrome. An endocrine disorder produced by oversecretion of *cortisone* and marked by mood swings, irritability, and agitation.

Defect theorist. In the study of *mental retardation*, a person who believes that the cognitive processes of retardates are qualitatively different from those of normal individuals; contrast with *developmental theorist*.

Defense mechanism. In psychoanalytic theory, a reality-distorting strategy unconsciously adopted to protect the *ego* from anxiety.

Delirium. A state of great mental confusion marked by disorientation, clouding of consciousness,

disordered speech, excitement, restlessness, and often *delusions* and *hallucinations*.

Delirium tremens (DTs). One of the *withdrawal symptoms* when a period of heavy alcohol consumption is terminated; marked by fever, sweating, trembling, cognitive impairment, and *hallucinations*.

Delusion. A belief contrary to reality, firmly held in spite of evidence to the contrary; common in paranoid disorders. **Of control,** belief that one is being manipulated by some external force such as radar, TV, or a creature from outer space. **Of grandeur,** belief that one is an especially important or powerful person. **Of persecution,** belief that one is being plotted against or oppressed by others.

Dementia. Progressive and marked deterioration of mental functioning.

Dementia praecox. An older term for *schizophrenia*, chosen to describe what was believed to be an incurable deterioration of mental functioning beginning in adolescence.

Demographic variable. Varying characteristic which is a vital or social statistic of an individual, sample group, or population, for example, age, sex, *socioeconomic status*, racial origin, education and the like.

Demonology. The doctrine that a person's abnormal behavior is caused by an autonomous evil spirit dwelling within him.

Dependent variable. In a psychological *experiment*, the behavior that is measured and is expected to change with manipulation of the *independent variable*.

Depersonalization neurosis. Disorder marked by feelings of unreality and estrangement from the self and the environment; patient may feel that he is someone else or is watching himself.

Depression. Emotional state marked by great sadness and apprehension, feelings of worthlessness and guilt, withdrawal from others, loss of sleep, appetite, and sexual desire, and either lethargy or agitation.

Depressive neurosis. Reaction marked by excessive sadness that had its beginnings in a specific environmental event.

Descriptive responsibility. In legal proceedings, the judgment that the accused has performed an illegal act; contrast with *ascriptive responsibility*.

Developmental theorist. In the study of *mental retardation*, a person who believes that the cognitive development of retardates has simply been slower than that of normal individuals, not qualitatively different; contrast with *defect theorist*.

Diathesis. Constitutional *predisposition* toward a disease or abnormality.

Diathesis-stress theory. A model which, as applied in psychopathology, assumes that individuals predisposed toward a particular mental disorder will be profoundly affected by stress and will then manifest abnormal behavior.

Diencephalon. Lower area of the forebrain containing the *thalamus* and *hypothalamus*.

Directionality problem. A difficulty in *correlational* research whereby it is known that two variables are related but it is unclear which is causing the other.

Disease. The medical concept that distinguishes an impairment of the normal state of the organism by its particular group of *symptoms* and its specific cause.

Disorientation. A state of mental confusion with respect to time, place, or identity of self, other persons, and objects.

Displacement. A *defense mechanism* whereby an emotional response is unconsciously redirected from a perhaps dangerous object or concept to a substitute less threatening to the *ego*.

Dissociation. A process whereby a group of mental processes is split off from the mainstream of consciousness, or behavior loses its relationship with the rest of the personality.

Dizygotic (fraternal) twins. Birth partners who have developed from separate fertilized eggs and who are only 50 percent alike genetically, no more so than siblings born from different pregnancies.

DMPEA (3,4-dimethoxyphenylethylamine). A compound asserted to be produced in schizophrenics and to cause their cognitive disorganization.

Dominant gene. One of a pair of *genes* which is stronger than the other and determines that

the *trait* it fosters will prevail in the *phenotype*.

Dopamine. A precursor of the *neurotransmitter* *norepinephrine*.

Double bind. An interpersonal situation in which an individual is confronted, over long periods of time, by mutually inconsistent messages to which he must respond. Believed by some theorists to cause *schizophrenia*.

Double-blind procedure. A method for reducing the biasing effects of the expectations of subject and experimenter; neither is allowed to know whether the *independent variable* of the *experiment* is being applied to the particular subject.

Down's syndrome (mongolism). A form of *mental retardation* caused by an extra *chromosome*. The child's IQ is usually less than 50, his physical characteristics distinctive, the one most often noted being slanted eyes.

Dream interpretation. A key psychoanalytic technique in which the unconscious meanings of dream material are uncovered.

Drive. A *construct* explaining the motivation of behavior; or an internal physiological tension impelling an organism to activity.

Drug addiction. Physiological reliance on a drug developed through continual use; characterized by *tolerance* and *withdrawal*.

Drug dependence. Habitual use of a drug out of psychological but not physiological need; contrast with *drug addiction*.

DSM-II. The current diagnostic and statistical manual of the American Psychiatric Association.

Dualism. Philosophical doctrine that man is both a mental and a physical being and that these two aspects are separate but interacting; advanced in its most definitive statement by Descartes. Contrast with *monism*.

Durham decision. A 1954 American court ruling that an accused person is not *ascriptively responsible* if his crime is judged attributable to mental disease or defect.

Dysfunction. Impairment or disturbance in the functioning of an organ or organ system.

Dyspareunia. Painful or difficult sexual intercourse, the pain or difficulty usually caused by infection or a physical injury such as torn ligaments in the pelvic region.

Echolalia. The immediate and sometimes pathological repetition of the words of others; a speech problem often found in autistic children. In **delayed echolalia** this inappropriate echoing takes place hours or weeks later.

Ego. In psychoanalytic theory, the predominantly conscious part of the personality, responsible for decision making and for dealing with reality.

Ego analysis. An important set of modifications of classical *psychoanalysis,* based on a conception of the human being as having a stronger, more autonomous *ego* with gratifications independent of *id* satisfactions. Sometimes called ego psychology.

Egoistic suicide. As defined by Durkheim, self-annihilation committed because the individual feels extreme alienation from others and from society.

Ejaculate. To expel semen, typically during male orgasm.

Ejaculatory incompetence. Inability to *ejaculate.*

Electra complex. See *Oedipus complex.*

Electrocardiograph. Device for recording the electrical activity that occurs during the heartbeat.

Electroconvulsive therapy (ECT). Treatment which produces a *convulsion* by passing electrical current through the brain; useful in alleviating profound *depression*, although typically an unpleasant and occasionally dangerous procedure.

Electroencephalogram (EEG). A graphic recording of electrical activity of the brain, usually that of the *cerebral cortex*, but sometimes the electrical activity of lower areas.

Electrolyte. Compound which dissolves and dissociates into electrically charged particles that move and thus permit the passage of electric current. The electrolytes *sodium* and *potassium chloride* play an important role in the transmission of nerve impulses.

Empathy. Awareness and understanding of another's feelings and thoughts.

Encephalitis. Inflammation of brain tissue caused by a virus.

Encounter group. See *sensitivity group.*

Endocrine gland. Any of a number of ductless glands which release *hormones* directly into the blood or lymph. The secretions of some endocrine glands increase during emotional arousal.

Endogenous. Attributable to internal causes.

Endogenous depression. Profound sadness assumed to be caused by a biochemical malfunction in contrast to an environmental event; more recently regarded simply as having a more severe set of *symptoms* than *exogenous* or *neurotic depression.*

Enticement. Legal means of securing arrest whereby a police officer sets up a situation in which an illegal act can be committed but intent is in the mind of the person committing the crime.

Entrapment. Illegal means of arrest whereby the police officer sets up a situation that induces another person to perform an illegal act that he might not otherwise engage in.

Environmental psychology. A recent community-oriented psychology which assumes that people's feelings and behavior are importantly a function of their physical setting.

Enzyme. A complex protein produced by the cells to act as a catalyst in regulating metabolic activities.

Epidemic encephalitis. Form of *encephalitis* characterized by lethargy and prolonged periods of sleeping. Also known as sleeping sickness.

Epilepsy. An altered state of consciousness accompanied by sudden changes in the usual rhythmical electrical activity of the brain. See also *grand mal, petit mal, Jacksonian,* and *psychomotor epilepsy.*

Epinephrine. Hormone secreted by the medulla of of the *adrenal gland;* its effects are similar, but not identical, to those of stimulating the sympathetic nerves; causes an increase in blood pressure, inhibits peristaltic movements, and liberates glucose from the liver. Also called *adrenaline.*

Erogenous. Capable of giving sexual pleasure when stimulated.

Eros (libido). Freud's term for the life-integrating instinct or force of the *id*, sometimes equated with sexual drive; compare *Thanatos.*

586 ABNORMAL PSYCHOLOGY

Essential hypertension. A *psychophysiological disorder* characterized by high blood pressure that cannot be traced to an organic cause; causes enlargement and degeneration of small arteries, enlargement of the heart, and kidney damage.

Estrogen. Female sex hormone produced especially in the ovaries; stimulates the development of and maintains the secondary sex characteristics, such as breast enlargement.

Etiology. The factors that contribute to the development of a disorder.

Eugenics. Science concerned with improving the hereditary qualities of the human race through social control of mating and reproduction.

Ex post facto analysis. In a psychological experiment, an attempt to reduce the *third-variable problem* by picking subjects who are matched on characteristics that may be *confounds*.

Excitement phase. As applied by Masters and Johnson, the first stage of sexual arousal which is initiated by any appropriate stimulus.

Exhibitionism. Marked preference for obtaining sexual gratification by exposing one's genitals to an unwilling observer.

Existential analysis. See *humanistic-existential therapy*.

Existential neurosis. Disorder in which patient feels alienation, considers life meaningless and no activity worth selecting and pursuing. See also *premorbid personality*.

Exogenous. Attributable to external causes.

Exogenous depression. Profound sadness assumed to be caused by an environmental event.

Exorcism. Casting out of evil spirits by ritualistic chanting or torture.

Experiment. The most powerful research technique for determining causal relationships, requiring the manipulation of an *independent variable* the measurement of a *dependent variable*, and the *random assignment* of subjects to the several different conditions being investigated.

Experimental neurosis. Unrealistic anxiety induced in laboratory animals and viewed as analogous to human neurosis.

Extinction. Elimination of a classically *conditioned response* by the omission of the *unconditioned stimulus*. In *operant conditioning* the elimination of the *conditioned response* by the omission of *reinforcement*.

Family interaction method. A procedure for studying family behavior by observing their interaction in a structured laboratory situation.

Family method. Research strategy in *behavior genetics* in which the frequency of a *trait* or of abnormal behavior is determined among relatives who have varying percentages of shared genetic background.

Fear-drive. In the Mowrer-Miller theory, an unpleasant internal state which impels avoidance. The necessity to reduce a fear-drive can form the basis for new learning.

Fear-response. In the Mowrer-Miller theory, a response to a threatening or noxious situation which is covert and unobservable but which is assumed to function as a stimulus to produce measurable physiological changes in the body and observable overt behavior.

Fellatio. Oral stimulation of the *penis*.

Fetishism. Reliance on an inanimate object or a part of the body for sexual arousal.

Fixation. In psychoanalytic theory, the arrest of *psychosexual* development at a particular stage through too much or too little gratification at that stage.

Flat affect. A deviation in emotional response wherein virtually no emotion is expressed whatever the stimuli, or emotional expressiveness is blunted; or a lack of expression and muscle tone in the face.

Flight of ideas. Rapid shift from one subject to another in conversation, with only superficial associative connections; a symptom of the manic phase of *manic-depressive psychosis*.

Follow-up study. A research procedure whereby individuals observed in an earlier investigation are contacted at a later time.

Forced-choice selection. Format of a *personality inventory* in which the response alternatives for each item are equated for social desirability.

Forensic psychiatry. The branch of psychiatry that deals with the legal questions raised by disordered behavior.

Free association. A key psychoanalytic procedure, in which the *analysand* is encouraged to give free rein to his thoughts and feelings, verbalizing whatever comes into his mind without monitoring its content; the assumption is that, over time, hitherto repressed material will come forth for examination by the analysand and his *analyst*.

Free-floating anxiety. Continual anxiety not attributable to any specific situation or reasonable danger.

Frontal lobe. The forward or upper half of each *cerebral hemisphere*, in front of the *central sulcus*; active in reasoning and other higher mental processes.

Frottage. Preference for obtaining sexual satisfaction by rubbing or pressing against another person without sexual intercourse.

Fugue. A *hysterical dissociative reaction* in which the individual flees to a new locality, sets up a totally new life, and is amnesic for his previous life, although he retains his faculties and appears normal to others.

Functional psychosis. A condition in which thought, behavior, and emotion are disturbed without known pathological changes in tissues or the conditions of the brain.

Galvanic skin response (GSR). Change in electrical conductivity of the skin caused by in-increase in activity of sweat glands when the *sympathetic nervous system* is active, in particular when the organism is anxious.

Gay. A colloquial term for a *homosexual*; now often adopted by homosexuals who have openly announced their sexual orientation.

Gay liberation. The often militant movement seeking to achieve civil rights for homosexuals and recognition of the normality of *homosexuality*.

Gender identity. The individual's sense of being a man or a woman.

Gene. An ultramicroscopic area of the *chromosome*; the smallest physical unit of the DNA molecule that carries a piece of the information of heredity.

General paresis. See *neurosyphilis*.

Genital stage. In psychoanalytic theory, the final *psychosexual stage* reached in adulthood, in which heterosexual interests predominate.

Genotype. An individual's unobservable, physiological genetic constitution; the totality of *genes* possessed by an individual. Compare *phenotype*.

Gerontosexuality. Preference for older people as sexual partners.

Gestalt therapy. A *humanistic-existential insight therapy*, developed by Fritz Perls, which attempts to encourage clients to satisfy their emerging needs so that their innate goodness can be expressed.

Gestation period. The length of time, normally nine months in humans, during which a fertilized egg develops into an infant ready to be born.

Glans. The heavily innervated tip of the *penis*.

Glove anesthesia. An hysterical lack of sensation in the part of the hand that would usually be covered by a glove.

Going in drag. Dressing in female attire, usually with extensive makeup, by a male *homosexual*.

Grand mal epilepsy. The most severe form of *epilepsy*, involving loss of consciousness and violent *convulsions*.

Graves' disease. An endocrine disorder resulting from oversecretion of hormone *thyroxin*; metabolic processes are speeded up, producing apprehension, restlessness, and irritability.

Gray matter. Neural tissue made up largely of nerve cell bodies; constitutes the cortex covering the *cerebral hemispheres,* the *nuclei* in lower brain areas, columns of the spinal cord, and the ganglia of the *autonomic nervous system*.

Grimace. Distorted facial expression, often a *symptom* of *schizophrenia*.

Group therapy. Method of treating psychological disorders whereby several persons are seen simultaneously by a single therapist.

Gyrus. A ridge or convolution of the *cerebral cortex*.

Habituation. In physiology, a process whereby

an organism's response to the same stimulus temporarily lessens with repeated presentations.

Hallucination. A perception in any sensory modality without relevant and adequate external stimuli.

Hallucinogen. A drug or chemical whose effects include *hallucinations*. Hallucinogenic drugs such as *LSD*, *psilocybin*, and *mescaline* are often called *psychedelic*.

Hashish. The dried resin of the *Cannabis* plant, stronger in its effects than the dried leaves and stems which constitute *marihuana*.

Hebephrenic schizophrenic. Psychotic patient whose behavior is marked by silliness, incoherent speech, *hallucinations*, *delusions*, and considerable deterioration.

Hermaphrodite. A person with parts of both male and female genitalia.

Heroin. An extremely addictive *narcotic* drug derived from *morphine*.

Heterophobia. Fear of the opposite sex, considered by psychoanalysts and some learning theorists to be an explanation of *homosexuality*.

Heterosexual. One who engages in sexual relations with members of the opposite sex.

High-risk method. A research technique, used especially in the study of *schizophrenia*, involving the intensive examination of people who have a high probability of later becoming abnormal.

Hives. A transient skin condition characterized by slightly raised, itching patches; often considered a *psychophysiological disorder*.

Homophobia. Fear of *homosexuality*.

Homosexuality. Sexual desire or activity directed toward a member of one's own sex.

Hormone. A chemical substance produced by an *endocrine gland* and released into the blood or lymph for the purpose of controlling the function of a distant organ or organ system. *Metabolism*, growth, and development of secondary sexual characteristics are among the functions so controlled.

Humanistic-existential therapy. An *insight* psychotherapy which emphasizes the individual's subjective experiences, free will, and ever-present ability to decide on a new life course.

Huntington's chorea. A fatal *presenile dementia*, passed on by a single *dominant gene*. The *symptoms* include spasmodic jerking of the limbs, psychotic behavior, and mental deterioration.

Hypertension. Abnormally high arterial blood pressure, with or without known organic causes. See *essential hypertension*.

Hyperventilation. Very rapid and deep breathing associated with high levels of anxiety; causes level of carbon dioxide in blood to be lowered, with possible loss of consciousness.

Hypnosis. A trancelike state or behavior resembling sleep, characterized primarily by increased suggestibility and induced by suggestion.

Hypochondriacal neurosis. A condition in which patient is preoccupied with bodily functions and imagined illnesses.

Hypothalamus. A collection of nuclei and fibers in the lower part of the *diencephalon*; concerned with the regulation of many visceral processes, such as *metabolism*, temperature, water balance, and so on.

Hysteria (hysterical state). Physical incapacity that makes no anatomical sense, for example, *glove anesthesia*. An older term for *hysterical conversion reaction*.

Hysterical neurosis. Disorder taking a variety of forms which can be grouped together as two types. **Conversion reaction**, paralysis, lack of sensation, sensory disturbances, and insensitivity to pain without organic *pathology*. **Dissociative reaction**, alteration in consciousness manifested as *amnesia, fugue, multiple personality*, and *somnambulism*.

Id. In psychoanalytic theory, that part of the personality present at birth, composed of all the energy of the *psyche* and expressed as biological urges which strive continually for gratification.

Ideas of reference. *Delusional* thinking which reads personal significance into seemingly trivial remarks and activities of others and completely unrelated events.

Idiot savant. An individual with a rare form of *mental retardation*, being extraordinarily talented in one or a few limited areas of intellectual achievement.

Imipramine. An *antidepressant* drug, one of the *tricyclic* group, effective primarily in alleviating *endogenous depression.*

Impotence—primary. The physical or psychological condition of a male who has never had an erection sufficient for either heterosexual or homosexual intercourse. **Secondary,** inability of the male to have an erection sufficient for intercourse, although he has a history of at least one successful *intromission.*

Imprinting. The irreversible acquisition of behavior by a neonate of a social species during a *critical period* of development. The neonate is attracted to and mimics the first moving object seen, thereby acquiring specific patterns of behavior.

In absentia. Literally, "in one's absence." Courts are concerned that a person be able to participate personally and meaningfully in his own trial and not be tried *in absentia* because of a distracting mental disorder.

In vivo. As applied in psychology, taking place in a real-life situation.

Inappropriate affect. Emotional responses which are out of context, such as laughter when hearing sad news.

Incest. Sexual relations between close relatives for whom marriage is forbidden, most often between daughter and father or between brother and sister.

Incidence. The rate at which new cases of a particular disorder occur in a given place at a given time; compare with *prevalence.*

Incoherence. In *schizophrenia,* a *thought disorder* wherein verbal expression is marked by disconnectedness, fragmented thoughts, jumbled phrases, and *neologisms.*

Independent variable. In a psychological *experiment,* the factor, experience, or treatment which is under the control of the experimenter and which is expected to have an effect on the subjects as assessed by changes in the *dependent variable.*

Index case. The person who in a genetic investigation bears the diagnosis or *trait* that the investigator is interested in. Same as *proband.*

Infantile autism. A childhood disorder usually differentiated from *childhood schizophrenia* and characterized by very early onset, extreme aloneness, *mutism* or *echolalic* speech, and intolerance of change in routine.

Infectious disease. Illness caused when a microorganism, such as a germ or a virus, invades the body, multiplies, and attacks a specific organ or organ system; pneumonia is an example.

Insanity defense. Legal argument that a defendant should not be held *ascriptively responsible* for an illegal act if his conduct is attributable to mental illness.

Insight therapy. A psychotherapy which attempts to impart to a patient greater awareness of what motivates his behavior, the assumption being that disordered behavior is caused by *repression* or other unconscious conflicts.

Instrumental learning. See *operant conditioning.*

Intelligence quotient (IQ). A common measure of intelligence arrived at by dividing the *mental age* achieved on a test by chronological age and multiplying the result by 100.

Intelligence test. Standardized means of assessing a person's current mental abilities, for example, the Stanford-Binet test and the Wechsler Adult Intelligence Scale.

Interpretation. In *psychoanalysis,* a key procedure in which the *analyst* points out to the *analysand* where *resistances* exist and what certain dreams and verbalizations reveal about impulses repressed in the *unconscious.*

Introjection. In psychoanalytic theory, the unconscious incorporation of the values. attitudes, and qualities of another person into the individual's own ego structure.

Intromission. Insertion of *penis* into *vagina* or anus.

Introspective method. A procedure whereby trained subjects are asked to report on their conscious experiences; the principal method of study in early twentieth-century psychology.

Introversion-extroversion. In Eysenck's theory of personality, a dimension referring for the most part to conditionability. Extroverts are said to acquire *conditioned responses* slowly and lose them rapidly: the reverse is true of introverts.

Involutional melancholia. An *affective disorder* characterized by profound sadness and occurring at a person's *climacteric* in late middle age.

Irresistible impulse. The term used in an 1834 Ohio court ruling on criminal responsibility in which it was decided that an *insanity defense* can be established by proving that the accused had an uncontrollable urge to perform the act.

Jacksonian epilepsy. A form of *epilepsy* in which muscle spasms are limited to a particular part of the body

Juvenile paresis. A form of syphilis which is congenital and is similar to the adult disorder; the onset of deterioration is at twelve to fourteen years, after a symptom-free childhood.

Klinefelter's syndrome. A disorder of males in which an extra X *chromosome* usually keeps the testes small at puberty, may produce *mental retardation,* and may cause secondary female sex characteristics to develop.

Korsakoff's psychosis. A chronic brain disorder produced by vitamin B deficiency and marked by loss of memory and associated *confabulation*; chronic alcoholics are especially susceptible.

La belle indifférence. The blasé attitude *hysterics* often have toward their *symptoms.*

Labile. Easily moved or changed; quickly shifting from one emotion to another or easily aroused.

Laceration. Tearing of brain tissue by an object entering the skull, often causing paralysis, intellectual impairment, or even death.

Latent stage. In psychoanalytic theory, the fourth *psychosexual stage,* from ages six to twelve, during which id impulses play a minor role in motivation.

Lateral sulcus. A major horizontal fissure along the side of each *cerebral hemisphere,* separating the *frontal* and *parietal lobes* from the *temporal lobe.*

Learned helplessness. In learning experiments on *depression,* a concept referring to an animal's passive acceptance of discomfort after he has found that his responses do not provide a means of escape.

Learning model. As applied in abnormal psychology, a set of assumptions that abnormal behavior is learned in the same way as other human behavior.

Lesbian. Female *homosexual.*

Lesion. Any localized abnormal structural change in organ or tissue caused by disease or injury.

Leucotomy. Psychosurgical procedure similar to *lobotomy.*

Libido. See *Eros.*

Limbic system. Lower parts of the *cerebrum* made up of primitive cortex; controls visceral and bodily changes associated with emotion and regulates drive-motivated behavior.

Lithium carbonate. A drug believed to be of some use in treating *manic-depressive psychosis*; alters *metabolism* of *norepinephrine* in the brain.

Lobotomy. A brain operation in which the nerve pathways between the *frontal lobes* of the brain and the *thalamus* are cut in hopes of effecting beneficial behavioral change.

Loose association. In *schizophrenia,* an aspect of *thought disorder* wherein the patient has difficulty sticking to one topic and drifts off on a train of associations evoked by an idea from the past.

LSD (*d*-lysergic acid diethylamide). A drug synthesized in 1938 and discovered to be a *hallucinogen* in 1943; derived from lysergic acid, the principal constituent of the *alkaloids* of ergot, a grain fungus which in earlier centuries brought on epidemics of spasmodic ergotism, a nervous disorder sometimes marked by psychotic symptoms.

Major tranquilizer. A drug which strongly suppresses arousal and is used primarily to calm psychotic patients; also referred to as antipsychotic.

Malingering. Faking an incapacity in order to avoid work, often difficult to distinguish from a *hysterical conversion reaction.*

Malleus Maleficarum (The Witches' Hammer). A manual written by two Dominican monks in the fifteenth century to provide rules for identifying and trying witches.

Mammillary body. Either of two small rounded structures located in the *hypothalamus* and consisting of *nuclei.*

Manic-depressive illness, manic-depressive psychosis. Originally described by Kraepelin, an *affective disorder* characterized by alternating moods of euphoria and profound sadness or by one of these moods.

Maple Syrup Urine disease. An inherited defect in *amino acid metabolism* causing *mental retardation* and death usually within first year.

Marathon group. A group session run continuously for a day or even longer, typically for *sensitivity training,* the assumption being that defenses can be worn down by the physical and psychological fatigue generated by intensive and continuous group interaction.

Marihuana. A nonaddictive *psychedelic* drug derived from the dried and ground leaves and stems of the female hemp plant, *Cannabis sativa.*

Masochism. Marked preference for obtaining or increasing sexual gratification through subjection to pain.

Masturbation. Self-stimulation of the genitals, typically to *orgasm.*

Mate-swapping. Exchanging marital partners for sexual relations.

McNaghten rule. A British court decision of 1843 which stated that an *insanity defense* can be established by proving that the defendant did not know what he was doing or did not realize that it was wrong.

Mediator. In psychology, an inferred state intervening between the observable stimulus and response, being activated by the stimulus and in turn initiating the response; in more general terms, a thought, drive, emotion, or belief. Also called a *construct.*

Mediation theory. In psychology, the view that certain stimuli do not directly initiate an overt response but activate an intervening process, which in turn initiates the response; an explanation of thinking, drives, emotions, and beliefs in terms of stimulus and response.

Medical model (disease model). As applied in abnormal psychology, a set of assumptions that conceptualizes abnormal behavior as being similar to physical diseases.

Medulla oblongata. An area in the *brainstem* through which nerve fiber tracts ascend to or descend from higher brain centers.

Megalomania. Paranoid *delusion of grandeur* in which an individual believes himself to be an important person or to be carrying out great plans.

Menage a trois. A domestic arrangement whereby a married couple and a lover of one of the pair form a single household with the approval of the other married partner; also used in referring to sexual relations among three people.

Meninges. The three layers of nonneural tissue that envelop the brain and spinal cord.

Meningococcal meningitis. A form of *encephalitis* which inflames the *meninges,* producing acute *delirium* and *disorientation.*

Mental age. The numerical index of an individual's cognitive development determined by standardized *intelligence tests.*

Mental retardation. Subnormal intellectual functioning associated with impairment in social adjustment and beginning in childhood.

Meprobamate. Generic term for *Miltown,* a *minor tranquilizer,* the first introduced and one of the most widely used.

Mescaline. An *hallucinogen* and *alkaloid* which is the active ingredient of *peyote.*

Metabolism. The sum of the intracellular processes by which large molecules are broken down into smaller ones, releasing energy and wastes, and by which small molecules are built up into new living matter, consuming energy.

Methadone. A synthetic addictive *narcotic* increasingly used with *heroin* addicts, acting as a substitute for heroin by eliminating its effects and the craving for it.

Methedrine. A very strong *amphetamine,* sometimes shot directly into the veins.

Midbrain. The middle part of the brain which consists of a mass of nerve fiber tracts connecting the spinal cord and *pons, medulla,* and *cerebellum* to the *cerebral cortex.*

Mild mental retardation. A limitation in mental development measured on IQ tests at between 52 and 67; children with such a limitation are considered the educable mentally retarded and are placed in special classes.

Milieu therapy. Behavior change procedure which attempts to make the total environment conducive to psychological improvement.

Miltown. Trade name for *meprobamate,* one of the principal *minor tranquilizers.*

Minnesota Multiphasic Personality Inventory (MMPI.) A lengthy *personality inventory* by which an individual is diagnosed through his true-false replies to groups of statements indicating *anxiety, depression,* masculinity-femininity, and paranoia.

Minor tranquilizer. A drug which reduces moderate to low levels of *anxiety;* most often used with neurotic disorders.

Mirroring. A *psychodrama* technique in which an individual sees himself portrayed by another person, thereby acquiring a better idea of how he is viewed by others.

Misdemeanor. Illegal conduct which is not a gross violation of law; distinguished from a felony, which is punishable by a term in a state or federal prison. Vagrancy and "lewd and lascivious behavior" are examples.

Mixed design. A research strategy in which both *correlational* and *experimental* variables are used; assigning subjects from discrete populations to two experimental conditions is an example.

Model. A set of concepts from one domain applied to another by analogy. For example, in trying to understand the brain we may assume that it functions like a computer.

Modeling. Learning by observing and imitating the behavior of others.

Moderate mental retardation. A limitation in mental development measured on IQ tests at between 36 and 51; children with this degree of retardation are often institutionalized and their training is focused on self-care rather than development of intellectual skills.

Mongolism. See *Down's syndrome.*

Monism. Philosophical doctrine that ultimate reality is a unitary organic whole and that therefore mental and physical are one and the same. Contrast with *dualism.*

Monoamine oxidase (MAO) **inhibitors.** A group of *antidepressant* drugs which inhibit the action of the enzyme monoamine oxidase, which in turn inactivates *norepinephrine.* More norepinephrine becomes available in the *sympathetic nervous system* and mood is elevated. Can have serious, even fatal, side effects.

Monozygotic twins. Genetically identical siblings who have developed from a single fertilized egg.

Moral anxiety. In psychoanalytic theory, the *ego's* fear of punishment for failure to adhere to the *superego's* standards of proper conduct.

Moral treatment. A therapeutic regimen, introduced by Philippe Pinel during the French Revolution, whereby mental patients were released from their restraints and were treated with compassion and dignity rather than with contempt and denigration.

Morbidity risk. The probability that an individual will develop a particular disorder.

Morphine. An addictive narcotic *alkaloid* extracted from *opium;* used primarily as an analgesic and *sedative.*

Mourning work. In Freud's theory of *depression,* the recall by a depressed person of memories associated with a lost one, serving to separate the individual from the deceased.

Multiple-base-line design. An experimental design in which two behaviors of a single subject are selected for study and a treatment is applied to one of them; the behavior that is not treated serves as a base line against which the effects of the treatment can be determined. Common design in operant research.

Multiple personality. A *hysterical dissociative reaction* in which an individual has distinctly different personalities at various times.

Mutism. The inability or refusal to speak.

Myxedema. An endocrine disorder of adults produced by thyroid deficiency; metabolic processes are slowed, and the patient becomes lethargic, slow-thinking, and depressed.

Narcotic. One of the addictive *sedative* drugs, for example, *morphine* and *heroin;* in moderate doses relieves pain and induces sleep.

Necrophilia. Erotic attraction toward and stimulation by dead bodies which may be expressed overtly in copulation with a corpse.

Negativism. A tendency to behave in a manner opposite to the desires of others or to what is expected or requested.

Neo-Freudian. A person who has contributed to the modification and extension of Freudian theory.

Neologism. A word made up by the speaker that is usually meaningless to a listener.

Neoplasm. See *tumor*.

Neurasthenic neurosis. Disorder in which patient complains of chronic fatigue and weakness not attributable to illness or excessive physical activity; the simplest activities require great effort.

Neurodermatitis. Chronic disorder in which patches of the skin become inflamed; a *psychophysiological disorder.*

Neurology. The scientific study of the nervous system and especially its structure, functions, and abnormalities.

Neuron. A single nerve cell.

Neurosis. One of a large group of nonpsychotic disorders characterized by unrealistic *anxiety,* and other associated problems, for example, phobic avoidances, *obsessions,* and *compulsions.*

Neurosyphilis (general paresis). Infection of the *central nervous system* by the spirochete *Treponema pallidum,* which destroys brain tissue; marked by eye disturbances, tremors, and disordered speech as well as severe intellectual deterioration and psychotic symptoms.

Neurotic anxiety. In psychoanalytic theory, fear of the consequences of expressing previously punished id impulses; more generally, unrealistic fear.

Neurotic depression. Excessive sadness which had its beginnings in a specific environmental event.

Neuroticism. In Eysenck's theory of personality, a dimension referring to the ease with which people can become autonomically aroused.

Neurotransmitter. Chemical substance important in transferring a nerve impulse from one cell to another.

Niacin. One of the complex of B vitamins.

Nicotine. The principal *alkaloid* of tobacco.

Niemann-Pick disease. An inherited disorder of lipid (fat) *metabolism* producing *mental re-*tardation and paralysis and causing early death.

Norepinephrine. A hormone liberated with *epinephrine* in the adrenal medulla and similar to it in action; and a *neurotransmitter* secreted at the nerve endings of the *sympathetic nervous system*; a strong vasoconstrictor.

Normal curve. As applied in psychology, the bell-shaped distribution of a measurable *trait* depicting most people in the middle and few at the extremes.

Nosology. A systematic classification of diseases.

Nucleus. In anatomy, a mass of nerve cell bodies (*gray matter*) within the brain or spinal cord by which descending nerve fibers connect with ascending fibers.

Object choice. In the psychology of sex, the type of person or thing selected as a focus for sexual activity.

Objective anxiety. In psychoanalytic theory, the *ego's* reaction to danger in the external world; same as realistic fear.

Obsession. Intrusive and recurring thought which seems irrational and uncontrollable to the person experiencing it.

Obsessive-compulsive neurosis. Disorder in which mind is flooded with persistent and uncontrolable thoughts or the individual is compelled to repeat certain acts again and again.

Occipital lobe. The posterior area of each *cerebral hemisphere,* situated behind the *parietal* and above the *temporal lobes*; responsible for reception and analysis of visual information and for some visual memory.

Oedipus complex. In Freudian theory, the desire and conflict of the four-year-old male child who wants to possess his mother sexually and to eliminate the father rival. The threat of punishment from the father makes the boy *repress* these id impulses. Girls have a similar sexual desire for the father, which is repressed in analogous fashion and is called the Electra complex.

Operant behavior. A response which is supposedly voluntary and operates on the environment, modifying it so that a reward or goal is attained.

ABNORMAL PSYCHOLOGY

Operant conditioning. The acquisition or elimination of a response as a function of the environmental contingencies of *reward* and *punishment*.

Operational definition. A definition of a theoretical concept which equates it with a set of observable operations that can be measured.

Opium. The dried milky juice obtained from the immature fruit of the opium poppy. This addictive *narcotic* produces euphoria and drowsiness and reduces pain.

Oral stage. In psychoanalytic theory, the first *psychosexual stage* which extends into the second year, during which the mouth is the principal *erogenous* zone.

Organic brain syndrome. A mental disorder in which intellectual or emotional functioning or both are impaired through a pathology or dysfunction of the brain.

Orgasm (climax). The involuntary, intensely pleasurable, climactic phase in sexual arousal, lasting a number of seconds and usually involving muscular contractions and *ejaculation* in the male and similar contractions in the genitalia of the female.

Orgasmic reorientation. A *behavior therapy* procedure in which a client learns to respond sexually to a previously neutral or aversive stimulus via a graduated program of masturbation while looking at photographs of this stimulus.

Outcome research. Research on the effectiveness of psychotherapy. Contrast with *process research*.

Panic reaction. In psychoanalytic theory, a sudden and inexplicable outburst of fear which is acute and overwhelming and may have disordering effects on the personality.

Paradigm. A set of basic assumptions that outline the universe of scientific inquiry, specifying both the concepts regarded as legitimate and the methods to be used in collecting and interpreting data.

Paradigm clash. The conflict created when a basically different set of assumptions threatens to replace a prevailing *paradigm,* for example, Copernicus' proposal that the sun—not the earth—is the center of the solar system.

Paranoid schizophrenic. Psychotic patient who has numerous systematized *delusions* as well as *hallucinations* and *ideas of reference.*

Paranoid state. A transitory *psychosis* characterized principally by *delusions of persecution* or *grandeur;* contact with reality is impaired but the patient's behavior is essentially normal except for the delusions.

Paraprofessional. In clinical psychology, an individual lacking a doctoral degree but trained to perform certain functions usually reserved for clinicians, for example, a college student trained and supervised by a behavioral therapist to shape the behavior of autistic children through contingent reinforcers.

Parasympathetic nervous system. The division of the *autonomic nervous system* which is involved with maintenance; it controls many of the internal organs and is active primarily when the organism is not aroused.

Parataxic distortion. According to the ego analyst Harry Stack Sullivan, an unconscious misperception of reality stemming from a childhood disorganization in interpersonal relationships and extended to all later relationships.

Parietal lobe. The middle division of each *cerebral hemisphere,* situated behind the *central sulcus* and above the *lateral sulcus;* receiving center for sensations of the skin and of bodily positions.

Parkinson's disease. A *presenile dementia* characterized by uncontrollable and severe muscle tremors, a stiff gait, a masklike, expressionless face, and withdrawal.

Pathology. The anatomical, physiological, and psychological deviations of a disease or disorder; and the study of these abnormalities.

Pearson product moment correlation coefficient (*r*). A statistic, ranging in value from -1.00 to $+1.00$; the most common means of denoting a correlational relationship. The sign indicates whether the relationship is positive or negative; the magnitude indicates the strength of the relationship.

Pedophilia. Preference for obtaining sexual gratification through contact with youngsters defined legally as underage.

Pellagra. A deficiency disease produced by lack of *niacin*; marked by reddening of the skin on neck and hands and by *depression,* memory loss, and difficulty in concentration.

Penile plethysmograph. Device for recording changes in penile size and thus for detecting erection.

Penis. The male organ of copulation.

Peptic ulcer. A lesion in the lining of the stomach or duodenum caused by excessive secretion of hydrochloric acid or susceptibility of the mucous membrane to its digestive action; generally regarded as a *psychophysiological disorder.*

Personality disorder. A heterogeneous diagnostic category, considered neither neurotic nor psychotic; one of a group of maladaptive patterns of behavior such as *alcoholism* and unconventional sexual practices.

Personality inventory. Self-report questionnaire by which examinee indicates whether statements assessing habitual behavioral tendencies apply to him.

Petit mal epilepsy. A form of *epilepsy* involving a momentary alteration in consciousness, more frequent in children than adults.

Peyote. A *hallucinogen* obtained from the root of the peyote cactus, the active ingredient being the *alkaloid mescaline.*

Phallic stage. In psychoanalytic theory, the third *pschosexual stage,* extending from ages three to six, during which maximal gratification is obtained from genital stimulation.

Phenomenology. As applied in psychology, the view that the phenomena of subjective experience should be studied because behavior is considered to be determined by how the subject perceives himself and the world rather than by objectively described reality.

Phenothiazine. Class name for a group of non-addictive drugs which relieve psychotic symptoms and which are considered *major tranquilizers*; their molecular structure, like that of the *tricyclic drugs,* consists of three fused rings.

Phenotype. The totality of observable characteristics of a person; compare with *genotype.*

Phenylketonuria (PKU). A genetic disorder which, through a deficiency in a liver enzyme, phenylalanine hydroxylase, causes severe *mental retardation* unless phenylalanine can be largely restricted from diet until the age of six.

Phillips Scale. Series of questions which is filled out by the researcher from the case history of a schizophrenic and used to assess his *premorbid adjustment.*

Phobia. Intense irrational fear and avoidance of specific objects and situations.

Physiology. Study of the functions and activities of living cells, tissues, and organs and of the physical and chemical phenomena involved.

Pick's disease. A *presenile dementia* involving diffuse atrophy of *frontal* and *temporal lobes,* impairing memory, concentration, and ability to think abstractly; eventually results in psychosis and death.

Placebo. Any therapy or inactive chemical agent, or any attribute or component of such a therapy or chemical, which affects a person's behavior for reasons having to do with his expectation of change.

Placebo effect. The action of a drug or psychological treatment that is not attributable to any specific operations of the agent. For example, a tranquilizer can reduce anxiety both because of its special biochemical action and because the recipient expects relief.

Plateau phase. In sexual arousal, the second stage during which excitement and tension have reached a stable high level before *orgasm.*

Pleasure principle. In psychoanalytic theory, the demanding manner by which the *id* operates, seeking immediate gratification of its needs.

Pons. An area in the *brainstem* containing nerve fiber tracts connecting the *cerebellum* with the spinal cord and with motor areas of the *cerebrum.*

Positive spikes. An EEG pattern recorded from the *temporal lobe* of the brain, with frequencies of 6 to 8 cps and 14 to 16 cps; often found in impulsive and aggressive people.

Potassium chloride. An electrolyte which, along with *sodium chloride,* is involved in transmission of the nerve impulse within the neuron.

Predisposition. An inclination or tendency to respond in a certain way, either inborn or acquired; in abnormal psychology, a factor which lowers the ability to withstand stress and inclines some part of the individual's constitution toward pathology.

Premature ejaculation. Inability of the male to inhibit his *orgasm* long enough for mutually satisfying sexual relations.

Premorbid adjustment. In research on *schizophrenia,* the social and sexual adjustment of the individual before the onset or diagnosis of his *symptoms*; patients with good premorbid adjustment are those found to have been relatively normal earlier, but those with poor premorbid adjustment had inadequate interpersonal and sexual relations.

Premorbid personality. Maddi's term for a person who plays social roles well and satisfies his biological needs and yet has a feeling of emptiness and lack of fulfillment; he is regarded as a candidate for *existential neurosis.*

Preparatory interval. In a *reaction time test,* length of time between a warning signal and the actual stimulus for the response.

Preparedness. In *classical conditioning* theory, a biological *predisposition* to be especially sensitive to particular stimuli and to associate them readily with the *unconditioned stimulus.*

Presenile dementia. A degeneration of brain tissue occurring when the individual is in his forties or fifties and causing progressive mental deterioration.

Prevalence. The percent of a population being studied that has a particular disorder at a given time; compare with *incidence.*

Primary impotence. See *impotence.*

Primary narcissism. In psychoanalytic theory, the part of the *oral stage* of *psychosexual* development during which the *ego* has not yet differentiated from the *id.*

Primary orgasmic dysfunction. Inability of a woman ever to have had an *orgasm* from either masturbation or intercourse.

Primary process. In psychoanalytic theory, one of the *id's* means of reducing tension, by imagining what it desires.

Proband. The person who in a genetic investigation bears the diagnosis or *trait* that the investigator is interested in. Same as *index case.*

Process research. Research on the psychological mechanisms responsible for the outcomes of therapy. Compare with *outcome research.*

Profound mental retardation. A limitation in mental development measured on IQ tests at less than 20; children with this degree of retardation require total supervision of all their activities.

Prognosis. A prediction of the likely course and outcome of an illness.

Projection. A *defense mechanism* whereby characteristics or desires unacceptable to the *ego* are attributed to someone else.

Projective test. A psychological assessment device employing a set of standard but vague stimuli, on the assumption that unstructured material will allow unconscious motivations and fears to be uncovered. The Rorschach series of inkblots is an example.

Pronoun reversal. A speech problem in which the child refers to himself as "he" or "you" and uses "I" or "me" in referring to others; often found in the speech of autistic children.

Psilocybin. A *psychedelic* drug extracted from the mushroom *Psilocybe mexicana.*

Psyche. The soul, spirit, or mind as distinguished from the body; in psychoanalytic theory, the totality of the *id, ego,* and *superego* including both conscious and unconscious components.

Psychedelic. A drug which expands consciousness; see also *hallucinogen.*

Psychiatrist. A physician (M.D. degree) who has taken specialized postdoctoral training, called a residency, in the diagnosis, treatment, and prevention of mental and emotional disorders.

Psychoactive drug. A chemical compound having a psychological effect, altering mood or thought processes; a *tranquilizer* is an example.

Psychoanalysis. A term referring primarily to the therapy procedures pioneered by Freud, entailing *free association, dream interpretation,* and working through of the *transference neurosis.* More recently the term has come to encompass the numerous variations on basic Freudian therapy.

Psychoanalyst (analyst). A therapist who has taken specialized postdoctoral training in psychoanalysis, after earning either an M.D. or a Ph.D.

Psychodrama. A kind of group psychotherapy, introduced by Moreno, in which patients play out, in theatrical settings, their feelings toward important figures and situations in their lives.

Psychogenesis. Development from psychological origins as distinguished from somatic origins; contrast with *somatogenesis.*

Psychological autopsy. Analysis of an individual's suicide through the examination of his letters and through interviews with friends and relatives in the hope of discovering why he took his life.

Psychological deficit. Term used to indicate that performance of a pertinent psychological process is below that expected of the normal person.

Psychological test. Standardized procedure designed to measure subject's performance of a particular task or to assess his personality.

Psychomotor epilepsy. Form of epileptic seizure in which the individual loses contact with the environment but appears conscious and performs some routine, repetitive act or engages in more complex activity.

Psychopath. See *antisocial personality.*

Psychophysiological disorder. A disorder characterized by physical *symptoms,* which may involve actual tissue damage, usually in one organ system, produced in part by continued mobilization of the *autonomic nervous system* under stress. *Hives* and *ulcers* are examples.

Psychosexual stages. In psychoanalytic theory, critical developmental phases which the individual passes through, each stage characterized by the body area providing maximal erotic gratification. The adult personality is formed by the pattern and intensity of instinctual gratification at each stage.

Psychosexual trauma. As applied by Masters and Johnson, earlier frightening or degrading sexual experience which is related to present human sexual inadequacy.

Psychosis. A severe mental disorder in which thinking and emotion are so impaired that the individual is seriously out of contact with reality.

Psychosocial system. As applied by Masters and Johnson, the social, psychological, and cultural attitudes toward sexual responding.

Psychosomatic disorder. See *psychophysiological disorder.*

Psychosurgery. Any surgical technique in which neural pathways in the brain are cut in order to change behavior. See *lobotomy.*

Psychosynthesis. An orientation to therapy, introduced by Roberto Assagioli in 1910, which assumes that man can have a spiritual, transpersonal existence that transcends his everyday mental and physical experiences, thereby relieving himself of neurotic cares and behavioral deficits. See also *transpersonal.*

Psychotic depression. Profound sadness marked by *delusions* and unjustified feelings of unworthiness.

Psychoticism. In Eysenck's theory of personality, a dimension referring to degree of contact with reality.

Punishment. In psychological experiments, any noxious stimulus imposed on the animal to reduce the probability that it will behave in the way deemed by the experimenter to be incorrect.

Q-sort. A personality test in which the respondent sorts a number of descriptive statements into categories ranging from "very characteristic" to "very uncharacteristic," depending on how they apply to him. Often used in research on *client-centered therapy.*

Random assignment. A method of assigning subjects to groups in an *experiment* that gives each subject an equal chance of being in each group. The procedure helps to ensure that groups are comparable before the experimental manipulation begins.

Rape. To force sexual intercourse on another person.

Rational-emotive therapy. A *cognitive restructuring behavior therapy,* introduced by Albert Ellis and based on the assumption that much disordered behavior is a function of what people tell themselves, The therapy aims directly to alter the goals individuals set for themselves, particularly those that are unrealistic such as "I must be universally loved."

Raynaud's disease. A *psychophysiological disorder* in which capillaries, especially of the fingers and toes, are subject to spasm; characterized by cold, moist hands, commonly accompanied by pain, may progress to local gangrene.

Reaction formation. A *defense mechanism* whereby an unconscious and unacceptable impulse or feeling which would cause anxiety is converted into its opposite so that it can become conscious and be expressed.

Reaction time test. A procedure for determining the interval between the application of a stimulus and the beginning of the subject's response.

Recessive gene. A *gene* which must paired with one identical to it in order to determine a *trait* in the *phenotype.*

Refractory phase. Brief period after stimulation of a nerve, muscle, or other irritable element during which it is unresponsive to a second stimulus; or period after intercourse during which the male cannot have another *orgasm.*

Regression. A *defense mechanism* in which anxiety is avoided by retreating to the behavior patterns of an earlier *psychosexual stage.*

Reinforcement. In *operant conditioning,* increasing the probability that a response will recur either by presenting a contingent positive event or by removing a negative one; or any satisfying event or stimulus, which, by being contingent with a response, rewards and strengthens this response which precedes it and increases the probability that the subject will so respond again.

Reliability. The extent to which a test, measurement, or classification system produces the same scientific observation each time it is applied.

Repression. A *defense mechanism* whereby impulses and thoughts unacceptable to the *ego* are pushed into the *unconscious.*

Resistance. During *psychoanalysis,* the defensive tendency of the unconscious part of the *ego* to ward off from consciousness particularly threatening repressed material.

Resistance to extinction. The tendency of a *conditioned response* to persist in the absence of any *reinforcement.*

Resolution phase. In the sexual arousal cycle, the last stage during which sexual tensions abate.

Response acquiescence. A "yea"-saying *response set,* or agreeing with a question regardless of its content.

Response deviation. A tendency to answer questionnaire items in an uncommon way regardless of their content.

Response hierarchy. The ordering of a series of responses according to the likelihood of their being elicited by a particular stimulus.

Response set. The tendency of an individual to respond in a particular way to questions or statements on a test—for example, with a "False"—regardless of the content of each query or statement.

Reticular formation. Network of *nuclei* and fibers in the central core of the *brainstem*; important in arousing the cortex and maintaining alertness, in the processing of incoming sensory stimulation, and in adjusting spinal reflexes.

Retrograde amnesia. The forgetting of recent events.

Retrospective report. A recollection by an individual of a past event.

Revealed-differences technique. A procedure for studying family behavior by observing its members in a laboratory as they try to agree on an answer to a particular question.

Reversal design (ABAB design). An experimental design in which behavior is measured during a base line period (A), during a period when a treatment is introduced (B), during the reinstatement of the conditions that prevailed in the base line period (A), and finally during a reintroduction of the treatment (B). Common in operant research.

Reward. In psychological experiments, any satisfying event or stimulus which, by being contingent with a response, reinforces this response which it follows and increases the probability that the subject will so respond again.

Rh factors. Substances present in the red blood cells of most people. If Rh factors are present in the blood of a fetus but not in that of the mother, her system produces antibodies which may enter the bloodstream of the fetus and indirectly damage the brain.

Rorschach test. A *projective test* in which the examinee is instructed to interpret a series of ten inkblots reproduced on cards.

Rubella (German measles). An infectious disease which if contracted by the mother during the first three months of pregnancy has a high risk of causing *mental retardation* and physical deformity in the child.

Sadism. Marked preference for obtaining or increasing sexual gratification by inflicting pain on another person.

Saliromania. Obtaining sexual gratification by soiling or mutilating female clothing or bodies.

Schizophrenia. A group of psychotic disorders characterized by major disturbances in thought, emotion, and behavior—disordered thinking in which ideas are not logically related, perception and attention are faulty; bizarre disturbances in motor activity; impairment in the connection between perception and emotion, making emotionality flat, inappropriate, ambivalent, or labile; reduced tolerance for stress of interpersonal relations, causing patient to withdraw from people and reality, often into a fantasy life of *delusions* and *hallucinations*.

Schizophrenogenic. Causing or contributing to the development of *schizophrenia*; often applied to the cold, conflict-inducing mother who is alleged to make her children schizophrenic.

School phobia. An acute, irrational dread of attending school, usually accompanied by somatic complaints; the most common *phobia* of childhood.

Secondary impotence. See *impotence.*

Secondary process. The reality-based decision-making and problem-solving activities of the *ego*; compare with *primary process.*

Sedative. A drug which slows bodily activities, especially those of *central nervous system;* used to reduce pain and tension and to induce relaxation and sleep.

Senile dementia. A form of *psychosis* brought on by progressive deterioration of the brain caused in part by aging; marked by carelessness in personal hygiene, memory impairment, and gross disorientation.

Senile plaques. Small areas of tissue degeneration in the brain, made up of granular material and filaments.

Sensate focus. Term applied to exercises prescribed at the beginning of the Masters and Johnson sex therapy program; partners are instructed to fondle each other to give pleasure but to refrain from intercourse, thus reducing anxiety about sexual performance.

Sensitivity (encounter) group. A small group of people who spend a period of time together both for therapy and for educational purposes; participants are encouraged or forced to examine their interpersonal functioning and their often-overlooked feelings about themselves and others.

Separation anxiety. A fear experienced when a person is away from someone on whom he is very dependent; said to be important in *school phobia.*

Severe mental retardation. A limitation in mental development measured on IQ tests at between 20 and 35; individuals so afflicted often cannot care for themselves, communicate only briefly, and are listless and inactive.

Sex-change surgery. Operation removing existing genitalia of a *transsexual* and providing an artificial substitute for the genitals of the opposite sex.

Sexual analism. Exclusive reliance on the anus for penile insertion.

Sexual oralism. Exclusive reliance on oral-genital contact for sexual gratification.

Sexual value system. As applied by Masters and Johnson, the activities that an individual holds to be acceptable and necessary in a sexual relationship.

Shaping. In *operant conditioning,* reinforcing responses that are successively closer approximations of the desired behavior.

Shell shock. A confused, disorientated state appearing in soldiers exposed to the strains of modern warfare.

Sibling. One of two or more persons having the same parents.

Simple schizophrenic. A person whose problems begin at an early age with withdrawal and apathy, and who becomes progressively more inaccessible and demented; *delusions* and *hallucinations* are infrequent.

Single-subject experimental designs. Designs for experiments conducted with a single subject; procedures include the *reversal* and *multiple-base-line* designs in operant research.

Situational orgasmic dysfunction. Inability of a woman to have an *orgasm* in particular situations.

Skeletal (voluntary) muscle. One of the muscles which clothe the skeleton of the vertebrate, being attached to bone, and which are under voluntary control.

Skinner box. A laboratory apparatus in which an animal is placed for an *operant conditioning* experiment; contains a lever or other device which the animal must manipulate to obtain a reward or avoid punishment.

Sleeping sickness. See *epidemic encephalitis.*

Slow brain waves. The theta rhythm (4 to 7 cps) usually recorded by EEG from subcortical parts of the brain and the delta rhythm (less than 4 cps) normally recorded during deep sleep; sometimes recorded in awake sociopaths.

Smooth (involuntary) muscle. Thin sheets of muscle cells associated with *viscera* and walls of blood vessels; performs functions not under direct voluntary control.

Social phobia. Collection of fears linked to the presence of other people.

Socioeconomic status. Relative position in the community as determined by occupation, income, and amount of education.

Sociopath. See *antisocial personality.*

Sodium chloride. One of the *electrolytes* which, along with *potassium chloride,* is involved in transmission of the nerve impulse within the neuron.

Sodomy. Originally, penetration of the male organ into the anus of another male; broadened in English law to include heterosexual anal intercourse and by some state statutes to cover all oral-genital contacts.

Soma. The totality of an organism's physical make-up.

Somatic weakness. Vulnerability of a particular organ or organ system to psychological stress and thereby to a particular *psychophysiological disorder.*

Somatogenesis. Development from bodily origins as distinguished from psychological origins; compare with *psychogenesis.*

Somnambulism. Sleepwalking; often identified as a *hysterical dissociative reaction.*

Specific-attitudes theory. Hypothesis that certain attitudes are associated with certain *psychophysiological disorders,* for example, that a person who feels mistreated may develop *hives.*

Specific-reaction theory. Hypothesis that an individual develops a given *psychophysiological disorder* because of the innate tendency of his autonomic system to respond in a particular way to stress, for example, by increasing heart rate or developing tension in the forehead.

Spectator role. As applied by Masters and Johnson, a pattern of behavior in which the individual's focus on and concern for sexual performance impedes his natural sexual responses.

Stability-lability. A dimension of classifying the responsiveness of the *autonomic nervous system.* Labile individuals are those in whom a wide range of stimuli can elicit autonomic *arousal.* Stable individuals are not so easily aroused.

Statistical model. As applied in abnormal psychology, a set of assumptions by which a substantial deviation from the average is considered to be abnormal.

Statistical significance. A magnitude of difference that has a low probability of occurring by chance alone and is by convention regarded as important.

Statutory rape. Sexual intercourse, whether forced or not, with a female who is below an age fixed by local statute as that of consent.

Stimulant. A drug which increases alertness and motor activity and at the same time reduces fatigue, allowing an individual to remain awake for an extended period of time.

Stress. A stimulus which strains the physiological or psychological capacities of an organism.

Sulcus (fissure). A shallow furrow in the *cerebral cortex* separating adjacent convolutions or *gyri*.

Superego. In psychoanalytic theory, the part of the personality that acts as the conscience and reflects society's moral standards as they have been learned from parents and teachers.

Symbiotic psychosis. Disorder of childhood marked by extreme reluctance of the child to be separated from his mother.

Sympathetic nervous system. The division of the *autonomic nervous system* which acts on bodily systems—for example, speeding up the contractions of the blood vessels, slowing those of the intestines, and increasing the heartbeat—to prepare the organism for exertion, emotional stress, and extreme cold.

Symptom. An observable physiological or psychological manifestation of a *disease*.

Synanon. A residential mutual-help community, primarily for drug addicts, in which participants are held responsible for their behavior and encouraged, through harsh and direct feedback, to change their behavior.

Synapse. A small gap between two *neurons* where the nerve impulse passes from the axon of the first to the dendrites of the second.

Syndrome. A group or pattern of *symptoms* which tend to occur together in a particular *disease*.

Systematic desensitization. A major *behavior therapy* procedure which requires a fearful person, while deeply relaxed, to imagine a series of progressively more fearsome situations. The two responses of relaxation and fear are incompatible and fear is dispelled. Useful for treating psychological problems in which *neurotic anxiety* is the principal difficulty.

Systematized delusion. A highly organized set of mistaken beliefs which has become the dominant focus of the paranoid patient's life.

Systemic disease. Malfunction of an organ or organ system, not produced by infection or trauma, and often attributable to an inherited defect; diabetes is an example.

Tachycardia. Racing of the heart, often associated with high levels of anxiety.

Tarantism. Wild dancing mania, prevalent in the thirteenth century in western Europe; supposedly incited by the bite of a tarantula.

Taraxein. A protein (a gamma globulin) in the blood serum of schizophrenics, asserted by Heath to be responsible for their psychosis.

Tay-Sachs disease. A disorder of lipid (fat) *metabolism* causing severe *mental retardation,* muscular weakness, eventual blindness, and death in about the third year.

Taylor Manifest Anxiety Scale. Fifty items drawn from the MMPI as a self-report questionnaire to assess anxiety.

Tearoom. Homosexual term for a public toilet used for impersonal sexual encounters.

Temporal lobe. A large area of each *cerebral hemisphere* situated below the *lateral sulcus* and in front of the *occipital lobe;* contains primary auditory projection and association areas and general association areas.

Testability. The extent to which a scientific assertion is amenable to systematic testing.

Testes. Male reproductive glands or gonads; the site where sperm develop and are stored.

Testosterone. Male sex hormone secreted by the *testes*; responsible for the development of sex characteristics such as enlargement of the testes and growth of facial hair.

Tetrahydrocannabinol (THC). The major active chemical in *marihuana* and *hashish*.

Thalamus. A major brain relay station consisting of two egg-shaped lobes located in the *dien-*

cephalon; receives impulses from all sensory areas except for the olfactory and transmits them to the cerebrum.

Thanatos. In psychoanalytic theory, the death instinct, which is the second of the two basic instincts within the *id,* the other being *Eros.*

Thematic Apperception Test (TAT). A *projective test* consisting of a set of black and white pictures reproduced on cards, each depicting a potentially emotion-laden situation. The examinee, presented with the cards one at a time, is instructed to make up a story about each situation.

Thiamine. One of the complex of B vitamins.

Third-variable problem. The difficulty in *correlational research* on two variables whereby their relationship may be attributable to a third variable.

Thorazine. Trade name for *chlorpromazine,* one of the *major tranquilizers* and a member of the *phenothiazine* group of drugs.

Thought disorder. The critical aspect to be looked for in diagnosing *schizophrenia;* evidenced by problems such as *incoherence, loose associations,* and *concrete reasoning* and speech marked by *neologisms* and *clang associations.*

Thyroid gland. Endocrine structure whose two lobes are located on either side of the windpipe; secretes *thyroxin.*

Thyroxin. Iodine-containing hormone secreted by the *thyroid gland;* participates in regulation of carbohydrate *metabolism,* thus determining the level of activity and in infants growth, development, and intelligence.

Token economy. A *behavior modification* procedure, based on *operant conditioning* principles, in which institutionalized patients are given artificial rewards such as poker chips for socially constructive behavior. The tokens themselves can be exchanged for desirable items and activities such as cigarettes and extra time away from the ward.

Tolerance. A physiological condition in which greater and greater amounts of an addictive drug are required to produce the same effect. See *drug addiction.*

Tonic phase. State of rigid muscular tension and suspended breathing in a *grand mal epileptic* attack.

Trait. A somatic characteristic or an enduring *predisposition* to respond in a particular way, distinguishing one individual from another.

Tranquilizer. A drug which reduces anxiety and agitation.

Transference. The venting of the *analysand's* emotions, either positive or negative, by his treating the *analyst* as the symbolic representative of someone important in his past. An example is the analysand's becoming angry with the analyst to release emotions actually felt toward his father.

Transference neurosis. A crucial and neurotic phase of *psychoanalysis* during which *analysand* reacts emotionally toward the *analyst,* treating him as a parent and reliving childhood experiences in his presence; enables both analyst and analysand to examine hitherto repressed conflicts in the light of present-day reality.

Transpersonal self. In *psychosynthesis,* a term for a spiritual awareness that is said to transcend usual experience and to be similar to a *psychedelic* state of consciousness.

Transsexual. A person who believes that he is opposite in sex to his biological endowment.

Transvestism. The practice of dressing in the clothing of the opposite sex, usually for the purpose of sexual arousal.

Trauma. A severe physical injury or wound to the body caused by an external force; or a psychological shock having a lasting effect on mental life.

Traumatic disease. Illness produced by external assault such as poison, a blow, or stress, for example, a broken leg.

Tremor. An involuntary quivering of voluntary muscle, usually limited to small musculature of particular areas.

Trephining. A crude surgical practice of the Stone Age, whereby a hole was chipped in the skull of a person who was behaving peculiarly, presumably to allow the escape of evil spirits.

Tricyclic drug. One of a group of *antidepressants* so-called because the molecular structure of each is characterized by three fused rings; effective primarily in alleviating *endogenous depression.*

Trisomy. A condition wherein there are three rather than the usual pair of *chromosomes* within the cell nucleus.

Troilism. Preference for performing sexually in front of others.

Tumor (neoplasm). Abnormal growth which when located in the brain can be either malignant and directly destroy brain tissue, or benign and disrupt functioning by increasing intracranial pressure.

Twin method. Research strategy in *behavior genetics* in which *concordance* rates of *monozygotic* and *dizygotic* twins are compared.

Two-factor theory. Mowrer's theory of avoidance learning according to which (1) fear is attached to a neutral stimulus by pairing it with a noxious *unconditioned stimulus*, and (2) a person learns to escape the fear elicited by the *conditioned stimulus*, thereby avoiding the UCS. See *fear-drive*.

Ulcer. A break in skin or mucous membrane accompanied by tissue disintegration; in the stomach or duodenum, a lesion in the lining caused by excessive secretion of hydrochloric acid; generally regarded as a *psychophysiological disorder*.

Unconditional positive regard. According to Rogers, a critical attitude for the client-centered therapist to adopt toward the client, who needs to feel accepted totally as a person in order to evaluate the extent to which his current behavior contributes to his self-actualization.

Unconditioned stimulus (UCS). A stimulus which elicits an instinctual, *unconditional response*; meat powder producing salivation is an example.

Unconscious. A state of unawareness without sensation or thought; in psychoanalytic theory, the part of the personality, in particular the *id* impulses, or id energy of which the *ego* is unaware.

Vagina. The sheathlike female genital organ which leads from the uterus to the external opening.

Vaginal barrel. The passageway of the vaginal canal leading from the external opening to the uterus.

Vaginal orgasm. Sexual climax experienced through stimulation of the *vagina*.

Vaginismus. Painful, spasmodic contractions of the outer third of the *vaginal barrel*, making insertion of the *penis* impossible or extremely difficult.

Validity—internal. The extent to which experimental results can be confidently attributed to the manipulation of the *independent variable*. **External,** the extent to which research results may be generalized to other populations and settings. As applied to psychiatric diagnoses, **concurrent,** the extent to which previously undiscovered features are found among patients with the same diagnosis; **predictive,** the extent to which predictions can be made about the future behavior of patients with the same diagnosis; **etiological,** the extent to which a disorder in a number of patients is found to have the same cause or causes.

Variable. A characteristic or aspect on which people, objects, events, or conditions vary.

Vicarious conditioning. Learning by observing the reactions of others to stimuli or through listening to what they say.

Vineland Social Maturity Scale. An instrument for assessing how many age-appropriate, socially adaptive behaviors a child engages in.

Viscera. The internal organs of the body located in the great cavity of the trunk proper.

Vitamin. Any of various organic substances which are as far as is known essential to the nutrition of many animals, acting usually in minute quantities to regulate various metabolic processes.

Voodoo death. The demise of a member of a primitive culture after breaking a tribal law or being cursed by the witch doctor.

Voyeurism (peeping). Marked preference for obtaining sexual gratification by watching others in a state of undress or having sexual relations.

Waxy flexibility. An aspect of *catatonia* in which the patient's limbs can be moved into a variety of positions, thereafter maintained for unusually long periods of time.

Wernicke's disease. The physiological damage to the *thalamus, pons, cerebellum,* and *mammillary bodies* associated with *Korsakoff's psychosis*.

Whirling response. The tendency of the *child schizophrenic* to turn his entire body if his head is rotated by an examiner.

White matter. Neural tissue, particularly of the brain and spinal cord, consisting of tracts or bundles of myelinated (sheathed) nerve fibers.

Withdrawal symptoms. Negative physiological and psychological reactions evidenced when a person suddenly stops taking an addictive drug; cramps, restlessness, and even death are examples. See *drug addiction*.

Word association test. Experimental procedure in which a list of words is read to the subject who has been instructed to respond to each with the first word that comes to mind.

Working through. In *psychoanalysis*, the arduous, time-consuming process through which the *analysand* faces up to the validity of the *analyst's interpretations* and confronts hitherto repressed material until his problems are satisfactorily solved.

Zoophilia (bestiality). Erotic fixation on animals which may be expressed overtly, either in intercourse or masturbation.

Zygote. The fertilized egg cell formed when the male sperm and female ovum unite.

FIGURE **13.5** Van Bucher/Photo Researchers.

FIGURE **14.1** James Gelruin/ Black Star.

FIGURE **14.2** Ken Heyman.

FIGURE **15.1** Alan Grant.

FIGURE **15.2** Marlis Müller.

FIGURE **15.3** Marlis Müller.

FIGURE **16.6** New York Academy of Medicine.

FIGURE **16.11** Courtesy Department of Neuropathology, New York State Psychiatric Institute, State of New York Department of Mental Hygiene.

FIGURE **16.12** Courtesy American Heart Association.

FIGURE **17.1** Bill Stanton/Magnum.

FIGURE **17.3** Bruce Roberts/ Rapho Guillumette.

FIGURE **17.4** Armed Forces Institute of Pathology.

FIGURE **17.5** Armed Forces Institute of Pathology.

FIGURE **18.1** Culver Pictures.

FIGURE **18.2** Page 466, Edmund Engelman; Page 467, Culver Pictures.

FIGURE **18.3** Wide World Photos.

FIGURE **18.4** The Bettmann Archive.

FIGURE **18.5** (Left) Courtesy **Dr. Rollo May,** (right) Courtesy Brandeis University.

FIGURE **18.6** Real People Press.

FIGURE **19.4** Courtesy Professor Albert Bandura, Stanford University. From A. Bandura and F. L. Menlove, "Factors determining vicarious extinction of avoidance behavior through symbolic modeling," *Journal of Personality and Social Psychology,* 1968, **8,** 99-108.

FIGURE **19.5** Van Bucher/Photo Researchers.

FIGURE **20.1** Courtesy Dr. J. L. Moreno.

FIGURE **20.3** Ken Heyman.

FIGURE **20.4** Van Bucher/Photo Researchers.

FIGURE **20.6** (Top) Rogers/ Monkmeyer, (bottom) Constantine Manos/Magnum.

FIGURE **20.9** Page 540, Ken Heyman.

FIGURE **20.10** Wide World Photos.

FIGURE **20.11** Courtesy Dr. William Beecher Scoville. From his article "Recent trends in lobotomy," *Acta Neurologia Latinoamericana,* 1955, **1,** 353.

FIGURE **20.12** St. Louis Post Dispatch/Black Star.

COLOR PLATE CREDITS

Drugs of Abuse   Courtesy National Audiovisual Center.

Figure 16.3   Courtesy Dr. Julia Levy, The University of British Columbia.

Figures 16.4, 16.7, 16.8, 16.9 and 16.10   Courtesy of Neuropathology, New York State Psychiatric Institute, State of New York Department of Mental Hygiene.

Figure 16.5   Howard Sochurek.

Name Index

Eysenck, H. J., 31, 32, 33, 118, 131, 470

F

Fadiman, J., 483
Fagan, J., 479
Falstein, E. I., 136
Fann, W. E., 546
Farberow, N. L., 198, 533
Feldman, M. P., 305, 306, 307, 489, 492, 493
Fenichel, O., 183, 243
Fenton, G., 430
Ferenczi, S., 463
Ferster, C. B., 185, 191, 397
Filipczak, J., 533
Fixsen, D., 533
Fontana, A., 362
Ford, C. S., 294
Ford, D. H., 463, 467, 468, 471, 476
Forrest, M. S., 112
Forsyth, R. P., 164
Foster, R., 437
Fox, R., 237, 256, 348, 349, 407, 423
Frank, G. A., 113
Frank, J. D., 460, 462
Freed, E. X., 245
Freeman, W., 549
Freitag, G., 397
Freud, A., 466
Freud, S., 22, 35, 36, 37, 38, 39, 108, 109, 110, 113, 120, 123, 130, 141, 144, 145, 182, 183, 185, 194, 256, 259, 287, 307, 354, 356, 357, 359, 378, 462, 463, 464, 466, 467, 470, 471, 484
Freund, K., 286
Friedhoff, A. J., 373

G

Gage, P. P., 415
Gagnon, J. H., 277, 281, 309, 310, 312, 313
Galen, 8
Garcia, J., 130

Garmezy, N., 209, 346
Garrone, G., 367
Gatchel, R. I., 118, 185
Gates, A. D., 448
Gebhard, P. H., 277, 278, 293, 296, 297
Geer, J. H., 118, 185
Geis, G., 281
Gelder, M. G., 134
Gerard, D. L., 258
Gershon, S., 546
Gibbs, J., 193, 522
Gilberstadt, H., 195
Gilman, A., 546
Gittelman, M., 391
Glaser, G. H., 430
Glithero, E., 143
Glover, E., 123
Goffman, E., 228, 338
Gold, V. J., 397
Goldberg, E. M., 360
Goldenberg, I. I., 533
Goldfarb, W., 393
Goldfried, M. R., 66, 485, 500, 505
Goldstein, A. S., 222
Goldstein, K., 442
Goldstein, M. J., 339
Goodell, H., 155
Goodman, L., 546
Goodman, P., 478
Goodwin, D. W., 240
Gottesman, I., 146, 367, 368, 369
Gottlieb, G. A., 192
Grace, W. J., 156
Graham, D. T., 152, 156, 157
Graham, F. K., 156
Graham, F. P., 231
Graham, P. J., 166
Granick, S., 181
Graves, R., 427
Gray, G., 546
Gray, J., 137
Green, D. E., 260
Green, K. F., 130
Greenberg, L., 249
Greenblatt, M., 552
Greer, S., 208
Gregory, I., 237, 256, 407, 423

Griesinger, W., 17
Grinker, R. R., 113
Groen, J., 168, 169
Grosse, M., 355
Grosser, G. H., 552
Gubbay, S., 393
Gudeman, J., 247
Guerney, B. C., 529
Gullion, M. E., 498
Gunderson, E. K. E., 152
Gunn, J., 430
Guthrie, W., 420, 421
Guze, S. B., 143, 240

H

Haggard, E., 115
Haigh, G. V., 474
Hales, W. M., 195
Haley, J., 363
Hall, C. S., 109
Hall, G. S., 463
Hare, R. D., 211, 213, 217
Harlow, H. F., 395
Harlow, J. M., 415, 416
Harlow, M. K., 395
Harrell, R. F., 448
Hartmann, H., 466
Haughton, E., 28
Heath, R. G., 372, 373
Heber, R., 432, 437, 441, 447, 448, 449, 450, 451
Hedblom, J. H., 314
Hefferline, R. F., 478
Heidegger, M., 475
Heiman, N. M., 528
Heimann, P., 302
Hekimian, L., 546
Held, J. M., 339
Hendryx, J., 308
Henry VIII, 14, 316
Henry, G. W., 6
Henry, J. P., 164
Herbert, J., 171
Hermelin, B., 392, 394, 399
Hernández-Peón, R., 146
Herskovitz, A., 503
Heston, L. L., 370, 371
Hewett, F. M., 383
Hilgard, E., 20, 21

Lazarus, A. A., 96, 137, 185, 282, 330, 487, 488, 492, 503, 507, 511, 512, 513, 515, 523, 524, 525
Lazovik, A. D., 507
Leach, B. E., 372
Leahy, M. R., 141
Leary, T., 5, 267
Lee, D., 392
Lee, R. S., 258
Leland, H., 437
Lesser, L., 391, 393
Lester, D., 195, 249
Levin, H., 110
Levine, M., 394
Levitsky, A., 480
Levitt, E., 497
Levy, L. H., 468, 469
Lewin, K., 517
Lewinsohn, P. H., 185, 186, 191
Liberman, R. P., 522, 526
Libet, J. M., 186
Liddell, H. S., 115
Liebert, R. M., 83, 84, 86, 90, 95, 503
Lind, D. L., 145
Livingood, J. M., 322
Linton, H. B., 269
Lisman, S. A., 352
Litman, R. E., 198
Litwin, G., 268
Lobascher, M., 393
Lockyear, L., 392
Loeb, A., 181
London, P., 460, 469, 470
Loraine, J. A., 308
Lot, 315–316
Lotter, V., 386, 388
Lovaas, O. I., 397, 399
Lowenstein, L. M., 246
Lubensky, A. W., 374
Luborsky, L., 469, 470
Lucchesi, B. R., 259
Lunde, D. T., 278, 280
Luparello, T. J., 168
Luria, D. B., 549
Luther, M., 10
Lyght, C. E., 161
Lykken, D. T., 214, 215
Lyon, P., 307, 312, 318

Lyons, H. A., 168
Lystad, M. M., 360

M

Maccoby, E. E., 110
MacCulloch, M. J., 305, 306, 307, 489, 492, 493
Maddi, S. R., 148–150, 477
Maher, B. A., 28, 30, 32, 59, 103, 105, 163, 334, 552
Mahler, M. S., 384
Mahoney, M. J., 500
Maier, N. R. F., 115
Main, T. F., 38
Malin, S., 245
Mandel, I. J., 113
Mandler, G., 114, 116
Marin, P., 266
Markey, F. V., 136
Markham, J. M., 255
Marks, I. M., 130, 134
Marlatt, G. A., 241
Marmor, J., 469
Marston, A. R., 488
Martens, S., 372
Martin, B., 105
Martin, C. E., 296, 297, 298
Martin, D., 307, 312, 318
Martin, I. C. A., 141
Maslow, A., 476
Masters, J. C., 389
Masters, W. H., 271, 281, 283, 284, 285, 287, 288, 289, 290, 291, 292, 308, 490, 491, 510, 513
May, P. R. A., 544, 552
May, R., 476
McCary, J. L., 272
McClelland, D. C., 244, 374
McCord, J., 208, 247
McCord, W., 208, 247
McFadden, E. R., 168
McFall, R. M., 488
McGhie, A., 330, 331
McGowan, B. K., 130
McGuigan, F. J., 350
McGuire, R. J., 280
McIntyre, C. W., 348, 349
McKeon, J., 546

McNaghten, D., 219, 226
McNeil, E., 204
McNicol, K. N., 166
Mednick, S. A., 374, 375, 376, 377
Meduna, L. J., 551
Medvedev, Z., 226
Meehl, P., 366
Mees, H., 397
Meichenbaum, D. H., 505
Mello, N. K., 240
Mendels, J., 55, 180, 183
Mendelson, J. H., 240, 246
Mendelson, M., 58, 59
Menlove, F., 45
Merbaum, M., 500
Mesmer, A., 18, 19, 21
Metesky, G., 224
Mettler, F. A., 104
Metzner, R., 268
Meyer, E., 143
Meyer, V., 148, 151, 510
Mézey, A. G., 181
Michael, S. T., 360, 361
Miles, M., 522
Milgram, N. A., 440
Millar, W. M., 161
Miller, D E., 389
Miller, G. A., 352, 353
Miller, N. E., 82, 110, 111, 112, 113, 127, 245
Miller, W. R., 187, 190
Millon, T., 542
Milton, O., 206
Mintz, E., 522
Mintz, S., 194, 349
Mirsky, I. A., 160
Mischel, W., 66, 70, 116
Mishler, E., 364, 365
Mittelman, B., 159, 160, 249
Mock, J. E., 58, 59
Mohr, J. W., 277, 280
Money, J., 274, 314
Moore, C., 395, 396
Moreno, J. L., 515
Morris, A. A., 218
Morrison, A. P., 529
Morrison, S. L., 360
Mosteller, F., 460
Mott, D. E. W., 503

Rosso, P., 448
Roth, B., 393
Rothman, E., 442
Roueche, B., 247
Rouse, C., 222, 223, 224, 227
Rubin, R. T., 152
Rubinstein, E. A., 514
Ruskin, A., 101
Rutter, M., 382, 383, 386, 392, 393, 397, 399
Ryan, D. V., 358

S

Sachs, E., 372
Saghir, M. T., 301, 302, 306
Sakel, M., 550
Salter, A., 486, 488
Sanderson, R. E., 113
Sarason, I. G., 453
Sarbin, T., 20
Sawrey, W. L., 159, 160
Schachter, S., 215, 216, 217
Schafer, S., 281
Schafer, R., 430
Schaffer, R. L., 161
Scheerer, M., 442, 443
Schildkraut, J., 545, 546
Schmauk, F. J., 216
Schreibman, L., 399
Schulsinger, F., 370, 374, 375
Schulterbrandt, J., 545
Schunk, J., 163
Schur, E. M., 253
Schuster, C. R., 259
Schutz, W. C., 521
Schwartz, M., 192
Schwartz, M. S., 360
Schweid, D., 546
Sears, R. R., 110
Seligman, M. E. P., 130, 187, 188, 190
Selye, H., 153
Serber, M., 519, 522
Shaffer, H., 402
Shagass, C., 192
Shakow, D., 349
Shannon, D. T., 515, 523
Shapiro, A. K., 460
Shapiro, A. P., 164

Shaw, D. M., 192
Shearman, R. W., 276
Shellhaas, M., 437
Shepherd, I. L., 479
Sherman, A. R., 488
Shiek, D., 395, 396
Shields, J., 139, 367, 368, 369
Shneidman, E. S., 193, 196, 198, 533
Siegel, L., 281
Siegel, M., 372
Silver, M. J., 85
Silverstein, C., 307, 319, 493
Simeons, A. T. W., 155
Simon, W., 195, 309, 310, 312, 313
Singer, M., 396, 397
Skinner, B. F., 44, 45, 148, 494, 500, 510
Skryzpek, G. J., 218
Slater, E., 139, 143, 146
Slavson, S. R., 515
Smith, B. H., 428, 430
Solomon, P., 246
Solomon, R. L., 108, 129
Sommer, R., 530
Spanos, N. P., 26
Speer, D. C., 534, 535
Speisman, J. E., 514
Spence, D. P., 469, 470
Spiegel, J. P., 113
Spinoza, B., 80
Spitalnik, R., 500
Spitzer, R., 64, 65
Spring, G., 546
Squires, N. D., 449
Srole, L., 360, 361
Staats, A. K., 494
Staats, C. K., 494
Staub, H., 226, 227
Stavros, D., 372
Stearns, J., 311
Steinberg, J., 546
Stephens, J. H., 145
Stephens, P. M., 164
Stern, J. A., 157
Stern, R. M., 157
Sternbach, R. A., 152
Stimbert, V., 382
Stoller, F. H., 521

Stolorow, R. D., 374
Stone, L. J., 161, 162
Storms, L. H., 351
Stricker, G., 66
Sugar, O., 421, 430
Sullivan, H. S., 468
Svendson, M., 136
Sylvester, D., 123
Szasz, T. S., 40, 225, 226, 227, 228, 229, 232, 317, 320
Szurek, S. A., 136

T

Tate, B. G., 96, 97
Taterks, S., 392
Taylor, J. A., 104, 116
Terman, L. M., 298, 299
Thaler, M., 160
Thigpen, C. H., 94
Thorndike, E., 43, 127
Titler, N. A., 246
Toro, G., 308
Tramontana, J., 382
Treese, R. L., 315
Treffert, D. A., 394
Truax, C. B., 38, 473, 475
Tuckman, J., 194
Turner, R. E., 277, 280
Turner, R. J., 360
Turrell, E. S., 159

U

Ullmann, L. P., 45, 145, 146, 185, 355, 358, 378, 510
Umbarger, C. C., 529
Urban, H. B., 463, 467, 468, 471, 476

V

Valentine, M., 161
Valins, S., 530
Viek, P., 115
Von Felsinger, J. M., 270, 460
Von Wright, J. M., 245

W

Wagonfeld, M. O., 360

Wahler, R. G., 40, 206
Walbran, B., 301, 302, 306
Waldfogel, S., 136
Wallen, R., 479
Wallerstein, R. S., 547
Walton, A., 235
Wanner, E., 244
Ward, C. H., 58, 59, 63
Ward, W. S., 20
Warner, A., 548
Waterlow, J., 448
Watson, J. B., 34, 41, 42, 43, 47, 113, 127, 510
Watt, N. F., 371
Watts, J., 549
Waxler, N., 364, 365
Weakland, J., 363
Webb, W. W., 346
Wechsler, D., 75
Wechsler, H., 552
Weil, G. M., 268
Weinberg, G., 295
Weinberg, L., 505
Weinberg, M., 311, 312
Weiner, H., 160
Weiner, I. B., 66
Weiner, J. W., 535

Weintraub, W., 267, 270
Weiss, J. H., 164, 169
Weisz, J. D., 159
Weitzenhoffer, A. M., 21
Wender, P. H., 370
West, D. J., 293
Weyer, J., 11, 25
White, W. A., 329
Whitlock, F. A., 143
Wickens, D. D., 113
Wiggins, J., 210
Wilkins, R. H., 418
Willers, K. R., 161
Williams, H., 166
Williams, R. J., 247, 249
Williams, W. S., 423
Wilson, G. T., 132, 493, 510
Wilson, R., 206
Wing, L., 399, 400
Winick, M., 448
Winokur, G., 157
Wise, R., 449
Wittman, C., 318
Wolberg, L., 468
Wolf, A., 515
Wolf, M., 397
Wolf, M. M., 533

Wolf, S., 155
Wolfenden, Sir John, 319
Wolff, H. G., 159, 160
Wolpe, J., 34, 121, 126, 139, 486, 488, 490, 505, 507, 508, 509
Woodyard, E., 448
Wright, B. A., 383, 392
Wynne, L. C., 129, 396, 397

Y

Yablonsky, L., 257, 522, 538
Yalom, I. D., 522
Young, B. J., 280
Yule, W., 166
Yurchenco, H., 421

Z

Zaslow, R. W., 401, 402, 403
Zax, M., 532
Zeller, B., 172
Ziegler, F. J., 143
Zigler, E., 56, 57, 58, 436, 440, 441, 450, 451
Zilboorg, G., 6

Subject Index

American Psychological Association, 232, 319
Amnesia, 52, 122, 140–142
  and alcoholism, 239, 416
  and brain disorders, 408, 417, 424
  and electroconvulsive therapy, 551
Amphetamines, 233, 256, 263
  see also color plates on drugs
Anaclitic depression, 384 n
Anal personality, 36, 147–148
Anal stage, 36
Analgesia, 142, 143, 145, 146
Analogue experiment, 86–87, 128
Anatomy of Melancholy, 11
Anesthesia, 18, 20, 140, 142
"Animal magnetism," 18
Animal phobias, 132–133, 134, 138
  treatment of, 503
Anna O., case of, 19, 22, 22–23 n
Anomic suicide, 194–195
Anorexia, 187, 188
Anoxia, and infantile autism, 394; mental retardation, 448–449, schizophrenia, 327
Antabuse, 546–547
Anterograde amnesia, 416
Anticholinergic drugs, 422
Antidepressants, 545–546
Antipsychotic drugs, 543
Antisocial personality, 32 n, 33, 203–218
  and alcoholism, 237; drug abuse, 258
  and avoidance learning, 211, 214–216
  central nervous system activity, 211
  descriptions, 203–208
  DSM-II description, 203, 208
  genetic correlates, 210–211
  role of the family, 208–210
  underarousal, 215, 217–218, 258
Anxiety, assessment of, 103, 104
  with brain tumor, 418
  as a construct, 104–105, 108
  and control, 114–115, 118–119
  and depression, 174
  in exhibitionism, 280
  low levels in sociopaths, 214–216
  with LSD, 268–269; marihuana, 265
  in neuroses, 120, 129, 134, 136, 138–139, 143, 146
  psychoanalytic theory, 108–110, 124, 462
  as stress in psychophysiological disorders, 151, 153; asthma, 167, 171; essential hypertension, 161
  stimulus-response analysis, 110–114
  in theories of alcoholism, 246; drug abuse, 258

trait and situation anxiety, 116–117
  treatment of, by insight therapy, 459–484; by systematic desensitization, 486–488, 506–510
Anxiety neurosis, description, 52, 109, 122, 138
  genetic factors, 131, 139–140
  learning theories, 139; and lack of control, 139
  psychoanalytic theory, 139
Aphasia, 399, 400, 401, 417
Argyll-Robertson pupil, 412
Arousal, and the autonomic nervous system, 104, 106–107, 114, 131, 151, 155
  in depressives, 192
  and lack of control, 114–115, 118–119
  in phobics, 131, 134, 138
  in psychophysiological disorders, 151; asthma, 164–165, 168; essential hypertension, 161–162; ulcer, 158
  in schizophrenics, 376–377
  sexual, 105, 273, 274, 278, 280, 282–283, 284, 286–287, 301, 312–313, 314
  and smoking, 260–261
  underarousal in sociopaths, 215, 217–218, 258
  see also Electrocardiograms, Electroencephalograms, Galvanic skin response
Ascriptive responsibility, 225–226
Assertive training, 488, 523–524
Assessment techniques, 62–78
Asthma, description and incidence, 52, 164–167
  effects of age of onset, 166, 168
  etiological factors and theories: biological predisposition, 171; classical conditioning, 169; diathesis-stress, 171; family role, 169–171; Graham's specific-attitudes theory, 156; personality traits, 171; psychological, allergic, and and infective factors, 167–168, 169
Asylums, conditions in modern institutions, 219, 220–221, 229, 341, 434
  development of, 11–17
Attention, in schizophrenia, 331, 347–349
Aura, 428
Autism, as symptom of schizophrenia, 332–333
  see also Infantile autism
Autoimmune reaction theory of schizophrenia, 373
Automobile accidents, and alcoholism, 234, 236, 240; marihuana, 264; phobias, 128
Autonomic lability, 131
  see also Arousal
Autonomic nervous system, 34, 104, 106–107, 114, 131, 151, 155, 217
Aversive conditioning, 488–489, 492–493
Avoidance learning, 110

in schizophrenics, 376–377
in sociopaths, 211, 214–216

B

Baquet, 18, 19
Barbiturates, 193, 233, 255–256, 263
  see also color plates on drugs
Basal ganglia, 411
  in Alzheimer's disease, 419; Huntington's chorea, 421, Figure 16.10 (color plate); Parkinson's disease, 422
Beck Depression Inventory, 187–188, 189
Bedlam, 14
Behavior genetics, 131, 132–133
Behavior modification, 485–513
  with an autistic child, 383–384
  clinical ingenuity, 512–513
  cognitive restructuring, 504–506
  counterconditioning, 486–494; by assertive training, 488; by aversive conditioning, 488–489, 492–493; by orgasmic reorientation, 493–494; by systematic desensitization, 486–488, 506–510
  definitions of, 485, 510
  mediators, 510–511
  modeling, 502–504
  operant conditioning, 494–502; of aggressive children, 497–498; generalizations of effect, 499–502; of retarded children, 434, 498–499; the token economy, 494–495
  relationship factors, 512
  and self-control, 500–501
  of sexual dysfunction, 490–491
  special issues, 510–513
  symptom substitution, 511
Behavior therapy, *see* Behavior modification
Behavior therapy groups, assertive training, 523–524
  individualized, 523
Behaviorism, 41–45
Benzedrine, 256
Beriberi, 416
Bestiality, 273
Beta rhythm, 212
Biochemical factors in Parkinson's disease, 421–422
  in theories of depression, 191–193; homosexuality, 305–308; schizophrenia, 371–374
Birth complications, *see* Pregnancy and birth complications
Birth weight, and mental retardation, 449 n

Bisexuality, 293–294, 295
Blackouts, in alcoholism, 239, 240; cerebral arteriosclerosis, 425; epilepsy, 428, 429, 430
Borderline mental retardation, 433
Brain, structure and function, 410–411
Brain pathology, *see* Organic brain syndromes
Brain surgery, 549–552
Brain tumors, 417–418, Figure 16.8 (color plate)
Brain waves, 211, 212–213
"Butch," 307, 313

C

California Psychological Inventory, 265
Cannabis sativa, 233, 261, 262
Cardiovascular reactions, in Addison's disease, 427; cerebral arteriosclerosis, 425
  to alcohol, 236, 240; amphetamines, 256
  in DSM-II, 52, 152
  in essential hypertension, 161, 163, 164
  as heroin withdrawal symptoms, 251
  as side effects of MAO inhibitors, 546
Case study method, 94–96
Castration anxiety, and homosexuality, 303
Catatonia, 332
Catatonic schizophrenia, 332, 333, 334–335
Cathartic method, 22, 141 n
Cerebellum, 411
  lesions in Korsakoff's psychosis, 416
Cerebral arteriosclerosis, 423–425
  cause of Parkinson's disease, 421
  and cerebrovascular accident, 423
Cerebral cortex, 410–411
  cortical responses in an analgesia, 146; to cocaine, 257
  lesions in Alzheimer's disease, 419; neurosyphilis, 413, Figure 16.4 (color plate); senile dementia, 423
  sensory stimuli of psychotic depressives, 192
Cerebral hemorrhage, 414, 417, Figure 16.7 (color plate)
Cerebral thrombosis, 417
  and arteriosclerosis, 417, 423
Cerebrovascular accidents, 417, 423
Child-rearing practices, *see* Family role
Childhood phobias, 136–137, 138
Childhood schizophrenia, Bender's descriptions and theory, 385, 386, 393–394
  classification, 379
  compared to infantile autism, 387–389, 390–391
  descriptive characteristics, 379, 385–387

Criminal behavior, of the alcoholic, 234–235, 237; children of schizophrenic mothers, 370; the drug addict, 251–254, 258
  and marihuana, 262, 263
  see also Antisocial personality
Criminal responsibility, 218–219, 222–229
  defendant's right not to be examined by psychiatrist, 230–231
  Szasz's views on, 225–229
Critical periods, in brain development, 445, 448
  in Moore and Shiek theory of infantile autism, 395
Cultural-familial retardation, 441–442, 449–453
  challenge to the concept, 451–453
  family backgrounds, 449–451
Current and Past Psychopathology Scales, 64–65
Cushing's syndrome, 427

D

Dan, case of, 204–206
Daytop Village, 539
Defense mechanisms, 36, 109–110, 147–148, 243
Delayed auditory feedback, 27
Delirium, in alcoholism, 239, 240, 242
  in encephalitis, 409; pellagra, 417
  with lead poisoning, 425
Delirium tremens (DTs), 240, 242
Delta rhythm, 212
Delusions, absent in childhood schizophrenia, 386; simple schizophrenia, 334
  of control, 330, 335, 336
  of grandeur, in schizophrenia, 330, 335; in neurosyphilis, 17, 41, 412, 413
  in Huntington's chorea, 420, 421
  paranoid, 335, 339, 356–357
  persecutory, in Alzheimer's disease, 419; with amphetamines, 256; in schizophrenia, 330, 335, 336
  prevalence in schizophrenia, 337
  of psychotic depressives, 176, 181
  in schizophrenic with good premorbid adjustment, 339
  systematized, 330–331, 335
Dementia, 408
  in brain disorders, 412, 414, 416, 417, 418–419, 420, 421, 422–423, 424–425
Dementia praecox, 17, 327
Demographic variables, 197–198
Demonology, 7, 9, 10
Dependent variable, 84, 99

Depersonalization neurosis, 121 n, 122, 134, 148
Depressants, 236, 251, 255
  see also color plates on drugs
Depression, with agoraphobia, 134; asthma 167; existential neurosis, 148
  with alcohol, 240, 246; psychedelic drugs, 269
  anaclitic, 384 n
  antidepressant drugs, 187, 192–193, 542, 545–546
  with brain disorders, 41, 409, 412, 417, 418, 420, 421
  depressive neurosis, 52, 122, 176–181, 185–190
  description, 17, 173–182
  DSM-II classification, 51, 175
  endogenous versus exogenous, 177–181
  involutional melancholia, 175–176
  manic-depression, 17, 175, 191
  psychotic depression, 175–182, 192
  theories of, 182–193
Depressive neurosis, 52, 122, 176–181, 185–190, 542
Descriptive responsibility, 225–226
Desensitization, 486–488, 506–510
Diathesis-stress theory, of childhood psychoses, 401–403
  definition of, 131
  of depression, 193
  in neuroses, 131, 150
  in psychophysiological disorders, 157–158, 160, 164, 171
  in schizophrenia, 371, 376–377
Dilantin, 430
3,4-Dimethoxyphenylethylamine (DMPEA), 373
Direct observation of behavior, 76–78, 104, 173
Directionality in correlational research, 90
Disease model, *see* Medical model
Disorientation, 408
  in alcoholism, 240
  in Alzheimer's disease, 419; senile dementia, 422
  with brain tumor, 418; concussion and contusion 414; toxic agents, 425
Displacement, 110
Dissociative reaction, description and incidence, 122, 140, 141, 142
  learning avoidance theory, 141
  psychoanalytic repression theory, 140
Disulfiram, 546–547
Dizygotic twins, definition of, 133
Doors of Perception, 5
Dopamine, 373, 421–422
Double-bind theory of schizophrenia, 363–366
Double-blind technique, 85

Down's syndrome (mongolism), 401, 444–445
Downward drift theory of schizophrenia, 360
Dreams, in Gestalt therapy, 480–481; psychoanalysis, 463–464
Drug abuse, hard drugs, 249–258
  LSD and other hallucinogenics, 266–270
  marihuana, 261–266
  nicotine, 258–261
  in suicide, 193, 255, 546
  in therapy, 542, 546, 549
  see also Alcoholism
Drug culture, 5–6, 258, 263, 264, 265–266, 267
Drug therapies, Antabuse for alcoholism, 546–548
  antidepressants: tricycles for endogenous depression, 545; MAO inhibitors, 192, 545, 546
  Dilantin for epilepsy, 430
  L-dopa, anticholinergic drugs for Parkinson's disease, 422
  lithium carbonate for mania and depression, 546
  major tranquilizers for schizophrenia, 543–544
  methadone for heroin addiction, 548–549
  minor tranquilizers for neurotic anxiety, tension, and neurotic depression, 542–543
DSM-II, on alcoholism, 233–234
  description, 50–52
  on depression, 51, 175
  on drug dependence, 233–234
  on mental retardation, 432–434
  on neuroses, 120–121
  new listing for homosexuality, 319
  on organic brain syndromes, 408, 409
  problems with, 55–62
  on psychophysiological disorders, 151–152
  on schizophrenia, 333, 337
  on sexual behavior, 271–272
  on sociopathy, 203
Durham test, 219, 222, 224, 227
"Dyke," 307
Dyspareunia, 152, 272, 289, 291

E

Early infantile autism, *see* Infantile autism
Echolalia, 382, 388
Ego, 35–39
Ego analysis, 37, 466–468
Ego functions, 467
Egoistic suicide, 194
Ejaculatory incompetence, 289
Electra complex, 37, 144

Electrocardiograph, 106, 217, 260
Electroconvulsive therapy, 550–552
Electroencephalograms (EEGs), 212–213
  of autistic children, 392, 394, 396
  of depressives, 192
  for diagnosis of organic brain syndromes, 408
  after electroconvulsive shock, 551
  of a petit mal attack, 429
  of psychomotor epilepsy, 430
  of schizophrenic children, 387–388, 392
  of schizophrenics, 348, 372
  of sociopaths, 211
Electroencephalograph (EEG), 75, 212–213
Electrolyte metabolism in depressives, 191–192
Encephalitis: epidemic, 409; meningococcal, 409, 447
Encounter groups, 517–523
  casualties of, 522–523
  communication in, 518–519
  description, 517–518
  evaluation of, 522–523
  goals of, 517
  role of leader, 518–519
  transfer of learning, 519–521
  variations of, 521–522
Endocrine disturbances, 152, 427, 447
  in homosexuality, 308
Endogenous depression, 177–181, 545
Environmental psychology, 530–531
Epilepsy, genetic factors in, 430
  grand mal, 428–429
  incidence and definition, 7–8, 427–428
  Jacksonian, 429–430
  petit mal, 429
  psychomotor, 430
Epinephrine, 104
Eros, 35
Essential hypertension, description, 52, 161
  etiological factors and theories: inability to control stress, 161–163; inhibited aggression, 161–162; repeated or prolonged stress, 163–164; stressful conditions, 161
Estrogen, 308
Eugenics, 450
Evolution theory of psychophysiological disorders, 154–155
Ex post facto analysis, 92
Exhibitionism, 280–281
Existential neurosis, 122, 148–150
Existential therapies, *see* Humanistic therapies

Grief, normal, 177, 179
  psychoanalytic theory of abnormal grief, 182–183
Group therapy, 515–525
  behaviorally oriented: assertive training, 523–525; encounter, 526–527; individualized, 523
  evaluation of, 525
  insight-oriented: through psychodrama, 515–517; through sensitivity training and encounter, 517–523

H

Hallucinations, absent in childhood schizophrenia, 386; simple schizophrenia, 334
  with brain tumor, 418; Graves' disease, 427; Huntington's chorea, 420; Jacksonian epilepsy, 430; lead poisoning, 425; pellagra, 417; toxic agents, 425
  from cocaine, 257; hallucinogenic drugs, 266–267, 270; marihuana, 265
  in delirium tremens, 239, 240, 242
  in schizophrenia, 331–332, 335, 336, 349–350
  in withdrawal from barbiturates, 255–256
Hallucinogenic drugs, 5–6, 266–270
Harrison Narcotics Act, 249
Hashish, 233, 261–262, 263, 264
  see also color plates on drugs
Head Start program, 533
Hebephrenic schizophrenia, 333, 336, 340
Helplessness, and anxiety, 114, 115, 118, 139, 185, 186
  learned helplessness and depression, 186–191
Heroin, 233, 251, 252, 253, 254, 255, 263
  methadone treatment, 548–549
  overdose mystery, 254
  see also color plates on drugs, Synanon
Heterogeneity of symptoms, in diagnostic classes, 55–57
Historical analysis, 5–6
History of psychopathology, 5–22
Hives, 52
  in Graham's specific-attitudes theory, 156, 157
Homicide: and alcoholism, 235; rape, 281
Homosexuality, behavior therapy and, 488, 489–493
  biological bases, 305–306, 307–308
  cross-cultural data on, 294, 314–316
  description, 272, 293–294
  and DSM-II, 272, 319
  female, 297–298, 301–302, 312–314
  gay liberation, 318–319, 320–321

gender identity and, 306, 307
  heterophobia and, 302–306
  homophobia and, 295
  Kinsey reports, 295–301
  laws against, 316–318, 319, 322
  male, 296–297, 301–302, 309–312; aging in male homosexuals, 311–312; male in heterosexual marriages, 311; male life styles, 309–311; male prostitution, 310; sperm abnormalities, 308
  in other mammals, 294
  religion and, 315
  sociological views on, 308–314
  statistics, 293, 297, 298, 301
  theories of, 39, 243, 300–301, 302–308, 356–357
Hospitalization, of autistic children, 383
  in brain disorders, 407, 420, 423, 424–425
  involuntary, 228–229, 230, 232
  in mental retardation, 341, 433–434, 451–453
  of schizophrenic children, 386
  of schizophrenics, 327, 333, 337–338, 340–341, 355, 358, 368–369, 543–544
  see also Commitment
Human sexual inadequacy, bad counsel, 271, 291
  in DSM-II, 52, 271–272
  etiology, 289–292
  research, 283–288
  therapy, 490–491
  types, 288–289
Humanistic therapies, 470–482
  client-centered therapy, 471–475
  existential analysis, 475–478
  Gestalt therapy, 478–482
  psychosynthesis, 483
Huntington's chorea, 420–421, Figure 16.10 (color plate)
Hydrocephaly, 441 n
Hypertension, in alcoholism, 240; cerebral arteriosclerosis, 424
  see also Essential hypertension
Hyperthyroidism, 427
Hypnosis, as an anesthetic, 20–21
  controversy over as a state, 26–27
  early developments, 18–22
  Freud's study, 22, 36, 120
Hypochondriacal neurosis, 121 n, 122
Hypothalamus, 411
Hypothyroidism, 427
Hysteria, description and incidence, 18, 52, 140, 142–143, 144–145, 151
  early studies, 18, 22, 36, 120, 142

genetic and biological factors, 146
psychological versus organic cause, 143
theories of, 144–146
Hysterical neuroses, *see* Hysteria
Hysterical states, *see* Hysteria

I

Id, definition of, 35, 39
Ideas of reference, 335
Idiot savant, 390, 442–443
Illusory correlation, 69–70
Imipramine, 454
Imitation, *see* Modeling
Impotence, 271, 291
    primary, 288; secondary, 288
Imprinting, 395
Incest, 277
Incidence, definition, 361
Independent variable, 84, 99
Index case, 132
Infantile autism, Bettleheim's theory, 396–397
    as category, 379, 380
    compared to childhood schizophrenia, 387–389, 390–391
    descriptive characteristics, 379, 380, 381–384
    diathesis-stress theory, 401–403
    Ferster's theory, 397–399
    genetic factors, 393
    information-processing–perceptual theories, 399–401
    Moore and Shiek's theory, 395–396
    neurological findings, 389, 392; IQ, 392
    and pregnancy and birth complications, 391
    Rimland's theory, 394; and the idiot savant, 443
Infection as cause of brain disorders: encephalitis, 409; neurosyphilis, 409, 412–414
Infection as cause of mental retardation: childhood meningitis, 447; encephalitis, 409, 447; neurosyphilis, 446; Rh factors, 446–447; rubella, 446; toxoplasmosis, 447
Inferences in science, 81–82, 98
Inquisition, 10–11
Insight therapy, 459–484
    humanistic-existential therapies, 470–482; existential analysis, 475–478; Gestalt therapy, 478–482; psychosynthesis, 483; Roger's client-centered therapy, 471–475
    placebo effect, 460, 461
    psychoanalytic therapy, 460–470; ego analysis,

466–468; evaluation of, 468–470; psychoanalysis, 462–466; Sullivan's ego psychology, 468
    psychotherapy profession, 461
Instrumental learning, *see* Operant conditioning
Insulin shock therapy, 550
Intellectual impairment, with barbiturates, 255–256; LSD, 267; marihuana, 264–265
    in schizophrenia, 329–332, 347–353
    see also Dementia, Mental retardation
Intelligence quotient, 435, 439
Intelligence tests, 75–76, 435, 437–438
Intercourse: during menstruation, 288; pregnancy, 288
Interpretation, 464
Interviews, 63–65
Introjection, 182–183, 194
Introspective method, 41
Introversion-extroversion, 31–32, 33
Involutional melancholia, 175–176
Irresistible-impulse concept, 219, 222

J

Jacksonian epilepsy, 429–430
Jim, case of, 206–207
Judgment, lack of, *see* Dementia
Juvenile delinquency, and adult sociopathy, 206, 209
    after encephalitis, 409
    treatment, 533
Juvenile paresis, 446

K

Kinsey reports, description, 295–296
    homosexual-heterosexual rating scale, 297
    on men, 296–297
    problems and implications, 298–301, 317
    on women, 297–298
Klinefelter's syndrome, 445
Korsakoff's psychosis, 416

L

La belle indifférence, 143
La Bicêtre, 15–16
Laceration, 414–415
Language disturbances, *see* Speech impairment
Latency stage, 36
Law of effect, 43–44

L-dopa, 422
Lead poisoning, 425, 447
Learning, types studied by psychologists: classical conditioning, 42–43; instrumental learning, 43–45; modeling, 45
Learning curve, 43–44, 46
Learning model of psychopathology, 45–47, 48
Learning views, of alcoholism, 244–246
    of childhood psychoses, 397–398
    of depression, 185–191
    of exhibitionism 280–281; fetishism, 274; sadism and masochism, 283; transvestism and transsexualism, 274
    of homosexuality, 300–301, 305–306
    of neuroses, 121, 150; anxiety neuroses, 139; conversion reaction, 145–146; dissociative reaction, 141; existential neurosis, 150; obsessions and compulsions, 148; phobias, 34, 43, 113, 127–130
    of psychophysiological disorders, 157; asthma, 169
    sociopathy and avoidance learning, 211, 214–217
    of schizophrenia, 355, 358
Legal insanity, *see* Criminal responsibility
Lesbianism, 297–298, 301–302, 307, 312–314, 320
Leucotomy, 549, 550
Libido, definition of, 35, 36
Librium, 543
Limbic system, 411
    of sociopaths, 211
Lithium carbonate, 546
Little Albert, case of, 34, 43, 47, 113, 127
Little Hans, case of, 123–126, 130, 134, 150
Lobotomy, 549–550
Loose associations, 329–330, 350–352
LSD, 233, 263, 266–270
    variables affecting reactions to, 267–270
    see also color plates on drugs
Lunatics Tower, 15
d-Lysergic acid diethylamide, *see* LSD

M

Macrocephaly, 441 n
Malingering, 143
Malleus Maleficarum, 11
Malnutrition, with alcoholism, 239, 240; amphetamines, 256; narcotics addiction, 251
    cause of mental retardation, 447–448
Mammillary bodies, in Korsakoff's psychosis, 416
Manganese poisoning, 425

Mania, 7, 8, 9, 17, 175, 191
    treated with lithium carbonate, 546
Manic-depressive psychosis, 17, 175, 191
Manie sans delire, 204
Maple Syrup Urine disease, 445
Marathon group session, 521
Marihuana, 233, 261–266
    effects, 263–265
    National Commission on Marihuana and Drug Abuse, 1972 report, 263–264, 265, 266
    steppingstone theory, 263
    use, legal penalties, 266; reasons for, 265–266
    see also color plates on drugs
Masochism, 282–283
Masturbation, 271, 273, 274, 279, 280, 287, 301, 312, 493–494
Mattachine societies, 318
McNaghten rule, 219, 222, 224, 226
Mediators, 45, 81–82, 510–511
Medical model, 32–41, 47–48
    infectious, 33, 34, 48
    psychogenic disease model, 35–37, 38–39
    systemic, 33, 34, 47, 48
    traumatic, 33, 34, 43, 48
Medulla oblongata, 411
Melancholia, 7–8, 13, 14
Memory impairment, in brain disorders, 408, 416, 417, 418, 419, 420, 422–423, 424–425
    with dissociative reactions, 140–142
    after electroconvulsive therapy, 551
    with psychedelic drugs, 268
Meningitis, 409
    as a cause of mental retardation, 447
Menopause, 176
Mental age, 435 n, 439
Mental retardation, behavior therapy for, 498–499
    categories and DSM-II description, 51, 432–435
    criteria for diagnosing, 432, 435–437
    cultural-familial causes, 449–451
    developmental-defect controversy, 439–440
    experimental studies, 438–440
    organic causes, 441–449
    and paired-associates learning, 440
Meprobamate, 542
Mercury poisoning, 425
Mescaline, 263, 267, 373
    see also color plates on drugs
Mesmerism, *see* Hypnosis
Methadone, 548–549
Methaqualone, 255 n
Methedrine, 256

description, 52, 122, 146–147
as learned behavior reinforced by consequences, 147
Occipital lobe, 410
Oedipal conflict, 36, 37, 125–126, 140, 144, 277, 302–303
One Flew Over the Cuckoo's Nest, 228
Operant conditioning, 43, 44, 127, 129
in behavior therapy, 494–502
in theories of alcoholism, 245; anxiety, 111; asthma, 157; depression, 185–186; neuroses, 127; 129, 141, 148, 150; sociopathy, 211, 212–217
Operationism, 82
Opium, 233, 250, 251
see also color plates on drugs
Oral stage, 36, 182, 185, 243
Organic brain syndromes, DSM-II classification, 51, 407–409
caused by cerebrovascular accidents, 417; degeneration, 418–425; endocrine disturbances, 427; infection, 409, 412–414; nutritional deficiencies, 416–417; toxic agents, 425; trauma, 414–416; tumor, 417; epilepsy, 427–430
Organic psychosis, 407
Orgasm: clitoral versus vaginal, 287; simultaneous, 287–288
Orgasmic dysfunction, 289, 291
primary, 289; situational, 289
treatment for, 490–491
Orgasmic reorientation, 493–494

P

Panic reaction, 109
in agoraphobia, 134
Paradigm, clash, 26–27; examples in abnormal psychology, 25, 28–29, 46–47, 478, 484, 501
definition of, 23–25, 30
Ptolemaic versus Copernican, 24–25
Paranoid schizophrenia, 335–336, 356
Paranoid state, 7–8, 51–52, 356–357
Paraprofessionals, 461, 528–529, 532
Parataxic distortion, 468
Parental child abuse, and alcoholism, 255
Parietal lobe, 410
Parkinson's disease, 421–422
Pate v. *Robinson,* 230
Pedophilia, 277–278
Pellagra, 416–417
Penile plethysmograph, 286
Penis, size and sexual enjoyment, 288

Pepsinogen levels, 160
Peptic ulcer, *see* Ulcer
Perception, altered perceptions with psychedelic drugs, 267, 268–269
in schizophrenia, 331–332, 347–350
Persecutory delusions, in Alzheimer's disease, 419; with amphetamines, 256
in schizophrenia, 330, 335, 336
Personal Preferences Schedule, 74
Personality disorders, 52
see also Addiction, Alcoholism, Antisocial personality, Sexual deviations
Personality inventories, 69–75, 195, 197
Personality traits, in studies of asthma, 171; LSD use, 268–270; marihuana use, 265; suicide, 195–197; transvestism, 276
in theories of alcoholism, 246–247; drug abuse, 258
Petit mal epilepsy, 429
Peyote, 267
see also color plates on drugs
Phallic stage, 36
Phenomenological approach, 4, 104
descriptions of anxiety, 103; depression, 173; epileptic seizure, 428
in existential analysis, 476–477
in Rogers's client-centered therapy, 471, 474, 475
Phenothiazines, 543–545
Phenotype, definition of, 132
Phenylketonuria (PKU), 445
Phillips Scale of Premorbid Status of Schizophrenia, 338, 340–341
Phobias, biological factors, 129, 131
description and incidence, 52, 122, 123
subclassification, 131–138
theories, 123–129, 130
therapy for, 486–488, 506–510
Physiological factors, in assessment of anxiety, 103, 104, 106–107
in studies of asthma, 167, 171; childhood psychoses, 393; conversion reaction, 146; homosexuality, 308; infantile autism, 399–401; neurotic anxiety, 131; phobias, 134, 138; sexual dysfunction, 291–292; sociopathy, 211, 217–218; ulcer, 160
in theories of addiction to hard drugs, 257; alcoholism, 247, 249; depression, 191–193; essential hypertension, 161; homosexuality, 305–308; infantile autism, 394; psychophysiological disorders, 153; schizophrenia, 371–374
Pick's disease, 419–420

ABNORMAL PSYCHOLOGY

Pineal gland, 154
Placebo, 145
Placebo effect, 460, 462
Pleasure principle, 35
Pons, 411
  lesions in Korsakoff's psychosis, 416
Positive spikes, 212
Poverty, and mental retardation, 449–450
  and schizophrenia, 90, 360–361
Pregnancy and birth complications (PBCs), and
    childhood schizophrenia, 389
  and infantile autism, 389
  and mental retardation, 448–449
  in schizophrenia, 377
Premature ejaculation, 288–289
Prematurity, and mental retardation, 449
Premorbid adjustment, in schizophrenia, 338–339,
    369
Premorbid personality, 149, 150
Preparedness, in classical conditioning theory of
    phobias, 130
Primal scene, 37
Primary process, 35
Proband, 132
Profound mental retardation, 433–434
Projection, 110, 356–357
Projective tests, 65–70
Pronoun reversal, 382, 388
Prostitution, and male homosexuality, 310
Psilocybin, 6, 263, 267, 270
  see also color plates on drugs
Psychedelic drugs, 5–6, 233, 266–270
Psychiatric social worker, 461
Psychoanalysis, basic techniques, 462–466
  evaluation of, 468–470
Psychoanalyst, 461
Psychoanalytic model, 35–37
  evaluation of, 37, 38–39
  psychosexual stages, 36–37
  topography of the mind, 35–36
Psychoanalytic views, of alcoholism, 243–244
  of anxiety, 108
  of depression, 182–183, 194
  of homosexuality, 39, 243, 302–303, 356–357
  of neuroses, 120; anxiety neurosis, 139; conver-
    sion reaction, 144; dissociative reaction, 140;
    obsessions and compulsions, 147–148; phobias,
    123–126, 134
  of psychophysiological disorders, 155
  of schizophrenia, 345–355
  of sexual deviations, 273; exhibitionism, 273;

fetishisms, 274; incest, 277; sadism-masochism,
    282–283; transvestism and transsexualism, 274
  of suicide, 194
Psychodrama, 515–517
Psychogenesis, 18–22, 34, 48, 120, 398
Psychological deficit, 345
Psychological tests, 65–76
Psychomotor epilepsy, 430
Psychopathy, see Antisocial personality
Psychophysiological disorders, description, 151,
    152–153
  in DSM-II, 52, 152
  specific disorders: asthma, 164–171; essential hy-
    pertension, 161–164; ulcer, 158–160
  theories of, 153–157
Psychosexual stages, 36–37
Psychosomatic disorders, see Psychophysiological
    disorders
Psychosurgery, 549–550
Psychosynthesis, 483
Psychotherapy, profession of, 461
  see also Insight therapy
Psychotic depression, 175–182, 192
Psychoticism, 32, 33
Punishment, effects on schizophrenics, 346–347

Q

Q-sort, 474
Question of Madness, 226

R

Random assignment, 85, 99
Rape, 281–282
Rational-emotive therapy, 505–506
Raynaud's disease, in Graham's specific-attitudes
    theory, 156–157
Reaction formation, 110, 147
Reaction time tests: to study arousal, 118, 119;
    attention of schizophrenics, 88, 347, 348
Reality principle, 35
"Refugees from Amerika: A Gay Manifesto," 318
Regression, 110
Reitan tests, 75, 408
Reliability, 81, 98
  of DSM diagnosis, 58–62
Repression, 109–110, 140, 463–464
Resistance, in psychoanalysis, 464
Response sets, 71–74

ABNORMAL PSYCHOLOGY